Selected Plays of David Davis

Selected Plays of David Davis

*For Gene McKinney, who got this all started,
and Kathy and Elizabeth, who help it keep going.*

Copyright © 2024 by David Davis

All rights reserved. No part of this book may be reproduced or transmitted in any form or by any means, electronic or mechanical, including photocopying, recording, or any information storage and retrieval system, without permission in writing from the author.

ISBN: 978-1-6653-0756-7 - Paperback
ISBN: 978-1-6653-0757-4 - Hardcover
eISBN: 978-1-6653-0758-1 - eBook

These ISBNs are the property of BookLogix for the express purpose of sales and distribution of this title. The content of this book is the property of the copyright holder only. BookLogix does not hold any ownership of the content of this book and is not liable in any way for the materials contained within. The views and opinions expressed in this book are the property of the Author/Copyright holder, and do not necessarily reflect those of BookLogix.

Library of Congress Control Number: 2024909597

∞ This paper meets the requirements of ANSI/NISO Z39.48-1992 (Permanence of Paper)

052024

Contents

Introduction	vii
Night of the Hawk	1
Five Exits	39
Divergent Illusions	79
Figures	131
Soon	177
Café	219
The Hermit	261
Naked Theatre	291
Angel	333
In Silence and the Dust	379
Sex and Violence for Women	429
One-Act Plays	477
She Was a Singer	479
The Computer	523
Fowl Time	543
May	559
Short Plays	577
Me, My Coke, and You	579
These Days	587
Kneeling	593
A Play to be Titled Later	599
The Interview	603
Modern Life	611
Monologue	617
No	621
Pre-need	625
Sports	631
The Meeting	637
The Room	641
Waiting	645

Introduction

These are not all the plays I wrote over my career. I left out some for various reasons. A few of those omitted were based on other people's writings (a Reader's Theatre version of Edgar Allan Poe's works, an updating of a Restoration Comedy, etc.) I have also not included some that I simply was never happy with and don't want to be remembered for. There are also a couple from early in my life that I simply can't find a copy of any more. There might be some of those hidden in my files, but they are probably not worth digging out for this volume.

The scripts are not in chronological order. Many went through multiple versions and overlap in time. Nor are they in order of production, since some of my early work is not my best work and often years passed between even the final draft and the eventual production. Plus, a few of these have not been given full productions, only workshops, staged reading, or just public readings. Rather I have arranged them into three categories, full lengths, one-acts, and shorts. The shorts are not all 10-minute plays, which is the fashion of the moment, but are all too short to be considered one-acts. Within each grouping, they are basically in the order in which they were most successful, in one sense or another.

The shows never became Broadway hits and only a few won any kind of prizes or public acclaim, but I am think at least some of them are good plays. I like to believe that, while they may not be great plays, they are good plays that never succeed because of my lack of sales ability or lack of the type of personally needed to achieve much in a very collaborative art. But I hope they are worth preserving, at least a little bit.

Night of the Hawk

I guess this would be considered my most "successful" play in that it was produced twice in New York City. The first production was by American Theatre of Actors in 1987. They did it for two weeks in their off-off-Broadway theatre, then moved it up to their off-Broadway space for a week. Kathy and I went up to see the last rehearsal and the first couple of nights and had a succession of unique experiences. We stayed for a couple of nights at the Coast Guard base on Governor's Island in New York Harbor; Kathy was an officer in the Public Health Service and eligible to stay in visiting officers' quarters. That led to my unexpected experience of having to give directions around Manhattan to a New York cab driver, who had no idea where the Governor's Island Ferry port was.

The stage manager for the production was also on the staff of the "Kate and Allie" show, a very popular sit-com at the time. She got us onto the list of people admitted to the taping of the show one afternoon while we were there. This made it seem like we were really dealing with big-time theatre people, which may have helped when my new in-laws came down from Poughkeepsie to see the show. I'm not sure what they thought of the script, but since I was scrounging for a job in those days it probably didn't hurt to give the impression that I was more than just an unemployed college professor.

Another production came along in 1994 when Generic Theatre, a regional theatre in Norfolk, VA, did a production on their second stage. We didn't get to see that one, but it was still nice to get a production.

The third production came in 2003 when the Legacy of Southern Theatre, a very small off-off-Broadway organization, produced the show in New York. Kathy, Elizabeth, and I went up to see it. This time it was Kathy's brother and his wife and daughter who ventured into the city to see what Kathy's crazy husband had done this time. Both the little girls were far too young to be paying attention to this type of performance, but they managed to sit through it without causing any disturbance. Walking the streets of Manhattan after the show looking for ice cream at almost midnight was indeed an experience to remember.

NIGHT OF THE HAWK

A Drama By David Davis

Member
All rights & privileges.

David Davis
100 Hunters Ridge Court
Roswell, GA 30076
daviddaviswriter@gmail.com

Copyright 1987 David Davis

CAST OF CHARACTERS

JOEY...A Young Man

ANN..A Young Woman

REV. MISS MISSY JONES..Pastor of a Small Church

SETTING

The time is the 1980s. The location is a small church outside a little town. The church is plain, with no icons, statues, etc. The windows, which may be suggested by lighting, are colored glass but without a pattern or picture. The only ornament is a bare cross hanging upstage center. There should be no definite indication of the denomination of the church. It is any small, poor church with well-worn furnishings. In the center is a communion table. There may be one or two pulpits on the podium. A cabinet for the communion bread and wine is on one side. There are at least two entrances, one on the upstage side and the other through what would be the congregation's pews. Despite its bareness and lack of decoration, the church is still sturdily pleasing in its simplicity. In addition, at the moment there are the remnants of decorations for a wedding, mostly in the form of large candle holders with partly burned candles, still arranged about the church. It is night, and a thunderstorm is approaching. The play is presented in one continuous scene.

> AT RISE it is dark. The stage is empty. There is a flash of lightning, then thunder. A door creaks, then is quietly shut. JOEY, an unkempt, unshaven young man, the kind usually seen hitch-hiking, enters, followed by ANN, also unkempt and the type of young woman often seen along the side of the road. Both carry backpacks with sleeping bags tied on. Both are slightly wet from the rain that can be heard beginning to fall. The sound of rain with occasional thunder and lightning will be in evidence through most of the play. JOEY and ANN begin to quietly move to center stage.

JOEY: Damn.

ANN: What?

JOEY: Nothing. Just bad memories.

ANN: Don't tell me you were an alter boy.

JOEY: I served my time, though not quite that way.

ANN: When was this?

JOEY: Long, long ago. A previous life probably. You ever go to church?

ANN: My father sent me to Sunday School for a while when I was a kid. Always hated it, having to dress up and act nice. Made me nervous.

JOEY: Not your style, all right.

ANN: Shit.

JOEY: Nervous now?

ANN: Not enough to go back out in the rain.

JOEY: Don't you think God will get you for sneaking in, or for wearing pants in church?

ANN: More likely for running around with a bastard like you.

JOEY: Well, don't worry; God doesn't hang around churches much anymore.

ANN: How would you know?

JOEY: Take my word for it. It's not God you have to worry about, it's the people in churches who will kill you.

ANN: You think anybody's here?

JOEY: Let's find out. HELLO. ANYBODY HERE? HELLO. (pause.) Guess not.

> They lay their backpacks down and remove their wet coats.

ANN: What kind of church is this?

JOEY: What difference does it make? It's shelter from the storm, and that's what churches should be, believe it or not.

ANN: You think it's going to get any worse?

JOEY: Oh, it's going to be one tree-splitter of a storm, that's for sure.

ANN: I bet we tracked all kinds of mud in here. Somebody is going to be awful mad tomorrow.

JOEY: Yes, heaven knows you should never allow dirt in church.

> JOEY begins exploring around in the dark.

ANN: What are you doing?
JOEY: Just looking around.
ANN: Be careful, it's dark.
JOEY: I can see that. I do not plan to impale myself on a crucifix.
ANN: What?
JOEY: Never mind.

> ANN begins to follow JOEY around the stage.

ANN: What do you reckon these candles are for?
JOEY: They probably torture an atheist every Friday night.
ANN: Shit.
JOEY: Churches have been known to do worse.
ANN: I bet it's pretty, with all the candles lit.
JOEY: The smoke ascending to heaven like a prayer.
ANN: Shut your face.
JOEY: You really nervous, being in a church?
ANN: It's just a little weird, dark and all.
JOEY: Not your usual hangout.
ANN: That's for sure.
JOEY: You know, this place is strange.
ANN: You gettin' nervous now?
JOEY: No, it's just that this is pretty plain for a church, no statues or icons.
ANN: I what?
JOEY: Icons, you cons, deacons.
ANN: Shit.

> JOEY crosses to pulpit.

JOEY: Shall I give my famous sermon on the evils of moderation and virginity?
ANN: No.
JOEY: My fellow heretics, I stand before you today with a hard-on. I stand before you with horniness in my heart. God's eye is on the sparrow, and my eye is on your tits. Repent, repent, I say; lay your body on the alter of God, and spread your legs.

ANN: Stop it.

JOEY: Agape, philos, eros; there are three kinds of love. What the world needs now is more eros. And the greatest of these is eros. Give your soul to God, give your heart to a friend, but give your pussy to me.

ANN: Stop it!

JOEY: I am the shepherd, you are the sheep, let me fuck your ass.

ANN: Damnit! Stop!

> Pause.

JOEY: OK, OK, don't bust a gut.

> JOEY comes down from the pulpit and crosses to ANN. He starts to caress her breasts.

ANN: Cut it out.

> She pushes him away.

JOEY: What's the matter?

ANN: Not here.

JOEY: Why not? We're alone.

ANN: It's a church, for Christsake.

JOEY: So?

ANN: Didn't your mother ever tell you not to screw around in church?

JOEY: No.

ANN: Good God.

JOEY: God knows when you fuck, whether you're in church or out. He's seen your naked ass humping away in the bushes. Being in church isn't going to make it any more right or wrong. Besides, doesn't it sound exciting, fucking on the alter?

ANN: Go to hell.

> JOEY grabs ANN from behind, his hands on her breasts, kissing her neck.

JOEY: Hey, come on, it won't be so bad. Warm us both up.

> Suddenly the lights come on as MISSY enters upstage and flicks the switch. ANN and JOEY are frozen for a second, hands still on breasts, then ANN tries to pull away. JOEY slowly releases her.

JOEY: Hello.

MISSY: Uh, hello.

JOEY: We just dropped in to get out of the rain. We didn't mean to disturb you.

ANN: We didn't think anybody was here.

MISSY: Oh.

JOEY: We were thumbing out on the highway. We yelled when we came in.

MISSY: I had fallen asleep, back in my office.

JOEY: You work here?

MISSY: I'm the pastor.

JOEY: No shit?

ANN: Joey!

MISSY: God sent out a call, and got a wrong number.

JOEY: Well how do you like that.

MISSY: I'm Melissa Jones. Missy to my friends. Even they have trouble calling me Rev. Jones.

JOEY: Well, Rev. Jones. I guess we'll be moving along now.

ANN: What?

MISSY: I thought you wanted to get out of the rain?

JOEY: We didn't think anybody was here.

MISSY: It's still raining, and getting worse.

JOEY: We don't want to trouble you.

ANN: Speak for yourself.

MISSY: It's no trouble. Churches should be shelters.

ANN: Thank you.

JOEY: Get your stuff. We're leaving.

ANN: What's with you?

MISSY: I didn't know my presence was so fearsome.

ANN: It's not to me.

JOEY: Let's just say your profession arouses unpleasant associations.

MISSY: They must be pretty bad memories to drive you back out into a storm like this.

ANN: He's been weird ever since we came in.

JOEY: I've been rained on before; I've been preached at before. I prefer being rained on.

MISSY: I wasn't planning on conducting a service.

JOEY: Well, Praise the Lord.

MISSY: My father could preach a sermon at the drop of a hat, but it takes me hours just to get up my courage, not to mention prepare something to say. I'd say you're pretty safe from me.

JOEY: Your father was a preacher?

MISSY: One of the best.

JOEY: And you still did this?

MISSY: What do you mean?

JOEY: What kind of preacher was he, hellfire and damnation, "Sinners in the hands of an angry God?"

MISSY: When the occasion demanded.

JOEY: I don't doubt it.

MISSY: That's not my style though.

JOEY: Doesn't hell seem real coming from a woman's lips?

MISSY: Let's just say I prefer a more positive approach.

JOEY: God is love, that sort of thing.

MISSY: Something like that. So, will you be staying until the storm is past?

ANN: All hell is going to break loose out there.

JOEY: There could be more fire and brimstone in here. Look at her. I know her, all flint and kindling just waiting for a stone.

ANN: What are you talking about?

MISSY: It seems unfair to force someone else into the cold and wet just because you might want to run from God.

ANN: Yeah.

JOEY: I'm no Jonah.

ANN: What?

JOEY: Not what, who.

MISSY: So, what's to run from?

JOEY: My image. My mirror image, reversed left to right, right to whatever. Maybe I don't like what I see.

MISSY: Me? I'm your opposite?

JOEY: Opposite? Complement? Do you like what you see in your mirror?

MISSY: I'm not sure I'm following this.

ANN: Well, I know I'm not going to follow anybody out into that storm. Listen to that thunder. You want to get hit by lightning or catch your death, go ahead. I'll meet you somewhere.

MISSY: Maybe it won't last long. When it lets up, I'll drive you both into town.

ANN: Sounds good to me.

MISSY: I think you're out voted.

JOEY: Charity sometimes backfires. Blows up right in your face.

MISSY: I'll take my chances.

JOEY: Yes, do your job, Preacher. Care for the less fortunate. "What you do for the least of these, you do also unto me." Just be careful that when you look through a glass darkly, you don't see yourself face to face.

    JOEY sits down.

ANN: Are you staying?

JOEY: What does it look like?

ANN: Well, good.

JOEY: Just don't say I didn't warn you.

MISSY: This will be more pleasant if we have names.

ANN: I'm Ann. This is Joey.

MISSY: Nice to meet you.

ANN: Are you really a preacher?

MISSY: Honest to God.

JOEY: Women's lib strikes again.

MISSY: Well, let's just say God is an equal opportunity employer.

ANN: I never met a woman preacher before.

MISSY: Is it really that amazing?

ANN: I don't know, I just never heard of one. I thought there was some kind of rule.

JOEY: Usually there is, unless you're Joan of Arc or some other kind of saint.

MISSY: Sorry, no vision of the Deity here. Just an ordinary woman.

JOEY: Oh, I don't know about ordinary. No ordinary person becomes a preacher, so a woman preacher must be extraordinary in some way. Somebody God really had it in for. Confess, Preacher, what was your great sin that the sadistic God above decided to punish by consigning you to a life of everlasting piety?

MISSY: Being a minister is not exactly what I would call torture. It has its rewards.

JOEY: Don't give me that. The hours are lousy, the pay stinks, everybody dumps on you, and you have to smile and be perfect when you really want to scream and kick. It's a major league punishment reserved as a purgatory for big time sinners. You probably seduced your grandfather and murdered your grandmother. You stabbed your lovers to death at the moment of orgasm, all 233 of them. You had oral sex with your mother-in-law during your wedding reception! That kind of thing.

ANN: Joey!

MISSY: I once stole a piece of bubble gum from a store, does that qualify me?

JOEY: No, all that gets you is a week at church camp.

MISSY: Well, I don't think I've done anything big league, as you call it. I guess I don't know why God decided that I should be a preacher, but He did, so here I am. Actually, I guess my father had a lot to do with it. He died while I was still in high school, but I can still remember him standing in the pulpit. He was a good man.

JOEY: How did you find a church that would take you? Or were you assigned by some bishop?

MISSY: Does it matter?

JOEY: Just trying to figure out how holy you really are.

MISSY: I'm a minister, not a saint.

JOEY: The churches I know, a woman would have to be a saint before she was allowed to be a minister, and maybe not even then.

There is a bright flash of lightning and a loud crack of thunder.

ANN: Damn. Oh, sorry.

JOEY: And the answer comes from on high.

ANN: Not funny.

JOEY: You're not married, are you? Let me see your hands.

MISSY: There's no wedding ring, if that's what you're looking for.

JOEY: I thought as much. Well, that eliminates muff-diving your in-laws.

ANN: Joey! Damnit, this is a church!

JOEY: Ann, believe me, God already knows about oral sex. Maybe even more than you do.

MISSY: Still, uh, Joey, this is mixed company, as they say.

JOEY: Preacher, the dirtiest jokes I ever heard, and the foulest language ever used in my presence, both came from the mouths of women. I certainly don't see how I can offend Ann by mentioning something she likes very much for me to do to her. And I would hope the God would be more concerned about real sins, but if we must discuss verbal offenses to the High and Holy, certainly He is more concerned about profane uses of His Holy Name than about coarse references to a harmless form of sexual activity. So, the only one left to be offended is you, and I suspect that an unmarried, female minister, who one must assume has had very limited sexual experience due to the nature of her calling, and the effect that calling would have on men who might consider making advances, might pretend offense but secretly be excited by exposure to such erotic and forbidden language.

MISSY: Well, you're wrong.

JOEY: About which?

ANN: What are you talking about?

JOEY: Explain it to her. She's a little slow at times.

ANN: I am not. You just use such damn big words.

MISSY: Basically he said that since I'm an unmarried minister that I must not have much sexual experience, so I really enjoy hearing him talk dirty, though I won't admit it.

ANN: Oh.

JOEY: After all, who the hell would seduce a preacher?

MISSY: The amount of my sexual experience has nothing to do with my reaction to sexually explicit language. I know many older couples who have had more sex than you ever dreamed of who cringe at the sound of four letter words.

JOEY: We are not talking about our parents. They are not here. We are talking about you, about us, the Last Generation, we who grew up with the Pill in one hand and the Bomb in the other. What makes you cringe, Preacher, me saying fuck, or dozens of two-bit despots slaughtering people by the thousands with guns they got from us? Does it hurt more if I say cunt, or if factories pump enough smoke into the sky to poison every lake and stream in the country? Where is your God damned holy church now, with people sleeping in the streets and the Defense Department drawing up new ways to die? Are you really more worried about what man is screwing what woman than you are over which greedy idiots are screwing the entire world?

MISSY: One thing being wrong does not make something else right.

JOEY: Touche. I see I have a worthy adversary.

MISSY: I am not here to argue with you.

JOEY: No. You are a preacher. You are here to save my soul. I'll make a deal with you, Preacher. You try to save my soul, and I'll try to ravish your body.

ANN: Joey!

JOEY: So, we'll make it a threesome. I always did enjoy a little group sex. That would certainly be a new experience for you, wouldn't it, Preacher?

ANN: Don't take him seriously. He likes to kid around, try to shock people. Don't let him worry you.

JOEY: Maybe the thing that's really worrying her is that maybe I'm not serious.

MISSY: Maybe I better give you and your wife a ride into town now.

JOEY: What wife?

MISSY: Oh. I see.

JOEY: We screw around a little, but it's not legal.

ANN: You had to tell, didn't you? You just had to tell, big man. You got your own little whore, is that it? You think that's going to turn her on?

JOEY: Never can tell.

ANN: Why are you doing this? Why?

JOEY: I'm not sure. Maybe it's a challenge. Maybe I feel sorry for her. Maybe I just like her tits. You do have nice tits, Preacher.

MISSY: I will try to take that as a complement.

JOEY: I'd like to see them naked sometime.

MISSY: Don't hold your breath.

JOEY: Not much for the direct approach, eh?

MISSY: While I might admire your honesty, your morality leaves something to be desired.

JOEY: Well, one out of two ain't bad.

MISSY: Two out of two would be better.

JOEY: Are we now to hear your famous sermon on sexual purity and the body being the temple of God?

MISSY: Only on request.

JOEY: Save it for when I'm eighty and can't get it up anymore.

MISSY: Then either I drive you into the motel now, or you go back out into the rain from whence you came.

> There is another bolt of lightning, and the sound of a tree falling.

ANN: What was that?

JOEY: Maybe you better go and see, Preacher. God may have other plans for this evening.

MISSY: Wait here. I'll be right back.

JOEY: Oh, I'm not planning on going anywhere.

MISSY exits.

ANN: Damn you, Joey. Leave her alone.
JOEY: Jealous?
ANN: No. It just ain't right.
JOEY: Suddenly you know right from wrong?
ANN: Damn it, I ain't as stupid as you treat me. That lady ain't done nothing to us; why are you trying to scare her? She must be half convinced you're going to rape her, and no matter what you think she wouldn't enjoy it.
JOEY: No?
ANN: No. Now let's just take the free ride into town and find some other place to wait out the storm, OK?
JOEY: Maybe. If we get a choice.
ANN: What do you mean?
JOEY: Just wait.
ANN: Fuck.
JOEY: I'd be glad to.
ANN: Oh, shit.
JOEY: Not right now, thank you.
ANN: You bastard, quit playing with me.
JOEY: You won't even let me touch you in here.
ANN: You know what I mean.
JOEY: Unfortunately, I do.
ANN: Why the hell do I put up with you?
JOEY: Because it's a lonesome world. Because I'm great in bed. Because I put up with you.
ANN: One day you'll push me too far.
JOEY: Could be. You ever been in a threesome?
ANN: No, and I'm not going to be. I take my men one at a time.
JOEY: One right after the other, like potato chips.

ANN tries to slap JOEY, but he grabs her and pulls her to him.

ANN: Damnit, let go!

MISSY enters. Again, everybody freezes for an instant in surprise, then ANN tries to pull away but is only slowly released.

MISSY: I must say that you two make coming into church an interesting experience.
JOEY: We were just having a mild disagreement on the definition of group sex.
ANN: Liar.
MISSY: Well, if you two will control yourselves for a while, we have a more pressing problem

to deal with. A tree has fallen on the parking lot, blocking my car. I don't think the car is damaged beyond a few scratches, but it won't be going anywhere until the tree is moved.

JOEY: How big a tree?

MISSY: Too big for us to move alone. It's going to take a crane or a power saw.

ANN: Can you call somebody?

MISSY: That is part two of our problem. The phones are out.

JOEY: The tree must have knocked down the line.

MISSY: Or the storm has taken the entire phone system out.

ANN: You mean we're stuck here?

MISSY: It looks that way. At least until the storm is over.

JOEY: Well, isn't life full of little surprises. You know, Preacher, it wasn't too smart telling us the phones are out. No telling what a sex maniac might do if he knew you couldn't call for help.

MISSY: And what should I have done?

JOEY: Oh, said that you had called for help, but that there had been several other calls for assistance, and the police didn't know how long it would be before they could get here. That would explain a long delay, but still keep any intruder on the defensive.

MISSY: Well, I did call a friend of mine earlier in the evening, and he expects me home just any time now. I'm sure he will start checking on me soon.

JOEY: Good, nice recovery. You stay cool and learn fast. I like that.

MISSY: I'm glad you approve.

JOEY: Of course, you said we were stuck here until the storm was over, so the new story doesn't wash anymore.

MISSY: I guess I never developed any skill at dissembling.

JOEY: Oh, I doubt that.

ANN: Well, are we stuck here or aren't we?

JOEY: Oh, yes.

ANN: Oh. Well, don't worry, Missy. He talks big, but he won't really hurt you.

MISSY: No, I don't think he would.

JOEY makes an over-elaborate bow. MISSY curtsies in return.

ANN: If you two start dancing, I think I'll puke.

JOEY: What, dance in church? How scandalous!

ANN: Well, what about eating, is that allowed?

JOEY: Only if you have food.

ANN: Don't you have some left?

JOEY: That was breakfast.

ANN: Nothing?

JOEY: Not a crumb.

MISSY: You haven't eaten since breakfast?

ANN: No.

JOEY: The wild, romantic life of adventure does not always come with three meals a day.

MISSY: I wonder...

ANN: You got something?

> MISSY crosses to the communion cabinet.

MISSY: I thought there was most of a loaf left. It's a little stale.

JOEY: We're used to leftovers.

MISSY: Might as well finish up the wine too, I guess.

> MISSY carries the bread and wine to the table.

JOEY: Any glasses?

MISSY: In the cabinet.

JOEY: A loaf of bread, a jug of wine, and thou.

MISSY: No, none for me.

> JOEY gets three goblets and takes them to the table where MISSY is dividing the bread into two hunks. JOEY pours the wine into the glasses.

JOEY: But we insist. After all, you are the host. You must join us. Take some bread too.

MISSY: Well, just a little. You two need it more than I do.

> JOEY tears a piece of bread off his half and gives it to MISSY.

JOEY: But man does not live without at least a little bread.

> All three are now standing around the communion table. JOEY hands out the rest of the bread and wine.

ANN: Is it OK to eat this stuff? I mean, it isn't holy or anything, is it?

JOEY: For Christsake, eat the bread.

MISSY: It's OK.

JOEY: If there is anything holy here, it's us, not the bread.

> A flash of lightning, then a loud thunderclap is heard.

JOEY: Ah, the Voice of God.

ANN: What?

MISSY: In the Bible, thunder is often referred to as the voice of God, or vice versa.

ANN: Oh.

MISSY: The problem is trying to figure out what He's saying.

JOEY: Probably that he's sorry he promised Noah no more floods.

MISSY: Could be.

JOEY: You want some more bread?

MISSY: No, thank you. I'm on a diet.

JOEY: You would ration the Body of God?

MISSY: I limit my eating of breads to keep my waist from getting bigger than my hips.

JOEY: Yes, you must keep a sexy figure, just in case.

MISSY: I need to stay in shape to remain healthy.

JOEY: To preserve the beauty of the Temple of Christ.

MISSY: To keep it a fit dwelling place for the Lord.

JOEY: But never to reveal its glory to man, or share its delights with others.

ANN: What the hell are you two talking about now?

JOEY: Dieting.

ANN: Sure. And I'm the President of the United States.

MISSY: You know, Joey, you interest me.

JOEY: I'm happy to hear that.

MISSY: Not that way. I mean you're curious, not what I expected. Sometimes you're as coarse as a stevedore, then as subtle as a Yale lawyer. You certainly know more about the Bible than most people.

JOEY: I read it once upon a time. I liked the "eat, drink and be merry" part.

ANN: Is that in the Bible?

JOEY: Believe it or not.

ANN: Is it?

MISSY: Yes. But it's usually taken out of context.

JOEY: "So I hated life, because what is done under the sun was grievous to me; for all is vanity and chasing the wind. Then I commanded mirth, because a man has no better thing under the sun, than to eat, drink, and be merry; for that shall abide with him of his labor the days of his life which God gives him under the sun."

MISSY: I'm impressed.

ANN: That's the Bible?

JOEY: How should we live, Preacher? Tomorrow we die, and the Lord comes like a thief in the night. Is not The Preacher right? Eat, drink, and be merry.

MISSY: You are not at all what you seem.

JOEY: Maybe I'm the Devil.

MISSY: Maybe you are.

JOEY: Or perhaps an angel. They come in guises too.

MISSY: Sent with what message?

JOEY: Who knows? Not loving is a greater sin than loving wrong, a pop-up behind third is the shortstop's play, God is a lesbian, who knows?

MISSY: And maybe you're just a cocky ex-seminarian who fell from grace.

ANN: He ain't no angel, I can tell you that.

JOEY: What, isn't screwing me pure heaven?

ANN: You're good, but you ain't that good.

JOEY: Well, maybe it takes two to tango.

ANN: Don't push it, boy.

MISSY: Enough! I don't wish to hear about your sexual athletics.

ANN: Sorry.

MISSY: What I want to know is who you are and why you're here.

JOEY: We told you, we came in to get out of the rain.

MISSY: But where are you from, where are you going?

JOEY: Ask me no questions, I'll tell you no lies.

ANN: How original.

JOEY: Shut your face.

MISSY: Are you two in some kind of trouble? Are you running from something?

JOEY: Like from jail maybe?

MISSY: Or angry husbands, or abusive parents.

JOEY: I'm afraid it isn't that simple.

ANN: I ain't no criminal. I can't say for him, I ain't known him that long.

MISSY: Well?

JOEY: You are in no danger of being arrested for harboring a criminal.

MISSY: That doesn't answer the question.

JOEY: She is from one place, I am from another, we are going anywhere to get away from everywhere for no reason at all and the only person chasing us is ourselves, at least as far as I know. And that is all the answer you are going to get.

MISSY: That isn't good enough.

JOEY: What are you going to do, Preacher, pull a gun and shoot us if we don't tell you our life stories? Will you torture me until I talk? Am I to be cast out into the rain by your strong right hand unless I satisfy your every whim? Now look at me and tell me why I'm laughing.

MISSY: So, it's Joey and Ann, the mysterious strangers.

JOEY: Those may be our real names.

MISSY: And we are to sit here in uneasy silence, as mis-trustful strangers, until the storm passes.

JOEY: Oh, hell no, Preacher. We're going to play cards.

    JOEY goes to his pack and gets a deck of cards.

ANN: Joey, it's a church.

JOEY: OK, OK, so we won't bet real money. What's your game, Preacher. Five Card Stud, Blackjack, Spades, Old Maids? How about a few quick rounds of Strip Poker, just to break the ice and get all friendly?

ANN: Joey!

JOEY: Well?

MISSY: I don't think Strip Poker would be appropriate.

JOEY: It was worth a shot. So, what's it going to be?

MISSY: I think I remember how to play War.

JOEY: Violence instead of sex. OK, Preacher, it's your church.

MISSY: It's only a game, Joey.

JOEY: Isn't everything?

ANN: Where do we play?

JOEY: Right here. Circle up, ladies.

> JOEY sits center stage.

ANN: Is it OK?

MISSY: Well, it isn't traditional, but I guess there's nothing inherently wrong.

JOEY: That means it's OK.

> The women sit down, one on each side of JOEY.

JOEY: OK, everybody lays down one card at a time from their stack, without looking. High card wins and takes the other cards. A tie is a "war" and each side puts down three cards face down, then the forth card face up. High card takes the whole pile.

MISSY: I remember.

> JOEY deals the cards.

JOEY: When did you play cards, Preacher?

MISSY: A few times in high school.

JOEY: Ever play for money?

MISSY: Once. I lost. Never again.

JOEY: What would your congregation say if they found out you had actually gambled for money?

MISSY: Oh, a few might be surprised, but it might make me seem a little more human.

JOEY: So I guess it wouldn't do any good to try to blackmail you.

MISSY: Not with that little indiscretion.

JOEY: So, what have you done that you would pay blackmail to keep quiet?

MISSY: If there was anything, do you think I would confess it to you?

JOEY: Your trick, Ann.

ANN: Oh, sorry.

JOEY: I thought confession was good for the soul.

MISSY: Confession to God or the person sinned against.

JOEY: Nobody ever confesses to you, as God's representative on Earth, let's say?

MISSY: I do a certain amount of counseling, and in that context people sometimes tell me things they would not want known by the public. Sometimes just talking something over helps a lot.

JOEY: So who do you talk to? Who helps you ease your conscience?

MISSY: Have you ever heard of prayer?

JOEY: War.

MISSY: What? Oh.

JOEY: Three face down, one face up.

MISSY: I know.

JOEY: Preacher's luck.

MISSY: It never lasts.

JOEY: God might be nice to talk to, but it's not the same as a shoulder to cry on. Preacher's aren't allowed to be human, they can never blow up, never have a weak moment of yielding to temptation.

ANN: The King is high.

MISSY: Thanks. I do admit there are certain expectations that can be unrealistic.

JOEY: So the congregation plays Christian on Sunday, then twists the scripture to fit their lifestyles, while you have to jerk off in a single bed, curse only silently, and cry alone, just to preserve their "expectations."

    Pause.

MISSY: Is that what happened to you?

JOEY: Am I right?

MISSY: One becomes a minister for reasons other than comfort or pleasure.

JOEY: To get to heaven? To earn the blessing of a long dead father? Pie in the sky is a fast way to starve on earth.

MISSY: One becomes a minister to serve others; that is its own reward.

JOEY: Serve others. How many churches would not have you be a minister under any circumstances? How fast would this church dump you for a man if it could? How many polite smiles hiding hate has your "service" prompted. How many people consider you a radical weirdo that they want nothing to do with? God in Heaven, you must be the loneliest woman on earth.

    Lightning flash, thunderclap, then darkness as the lights go out.

JOEY: Humm, maybe God doesn't like cards in church after all.

ANN: That's not funny.

JOEY: I have the feeling they are not going to come back on right away.

MISSY: It's beginning to look like you're right. You two just sit still, I'll light some of the candles.

> MISSY goes to the pulpit for some matches, then goes around the room lighting candles.

ANN: Ooo, that's pretty.

MISSY: There was a wedding this afternoon. I hadn't gotten around to taking them down yet, thank goodness. The bride and groom were high school sweethearts. The girl belonged to the church. They're off to Florida by now.

ANN: It sounds very nice.

JOEY: Just lovely. And now we have a candlelight service.

MISSY: The groom is going to be starting the pre-dental program at the university in the Fall. His father is the local dentist. It was really a very nice ceremony.

JOEY: Nothing like marrying money.

MISSY: I think they loved each other, though they are a little young.

JOEY: Yeah, he loved her bod, she loved his money, and they were too Christian to just screw around. Now she'll put him through dental school, then he'll divorce her for some dental hygienist with big tits because he never got to fuck around in college and feels trapped and cheated.

MISSY: You are the eternal optimist, aren't you.

JOEY: Why don't you do that, Ann, marry some rich kid?

ANN: Introduce me to one.

JOEY: You're not going to meet any hanging around me.

ANN: Maybe one day I'll start looking somewhere else.

JOEY: Who'll keep you warm at night then?

ANN: I'll find somebody. Always have.

JOEY: For how long?

ANN: Longer than you can hold on to 'em.

JOEY: Use them up and throw them away.

MISSY: Is that all life is, sex?

JOEY: We wouldn't be alive without it.

MISSY: Some of us survive. Oh, you mean our parents.

JOEY: Either way.

ANN: Don't you get crazy after a few weeks, you know?

JOEY: With her it's a permanent condition.

MISSY: How long has this been going on?

JOEY: Since the dawn of man.

MISSY: I mean you two.

ANN: Two, three months.

JOEY: Winter's coming, have to keep warm some way.

MISSY: That's all she is to you, a hunk of flesh to keep you warm at night?

JOEY: Yes. And that's all I am to her.

ANN: Well...

JOEY: Did you ever kiss an electric blanket?

MISSY: No.

JOEY: Jerking off is like kissing your blanket. It's warm and soft, but that's not quite enough. Even Linus grows up eventually.

MISSY: That's disgusting.

JOEY: But truthful, isn't it?

MISSY: I wouldn't know.

JOEY: Don't try to tell me you've never let your fingers do the walking. There are other clefts than the one in the rock, and that sweet vertical smile between your legs spreads into such a wide grin at your golden touch.

> MISSY turns away.

JOEY: There's no shame in a little autoerotism, Missy. But you have to admit it isn't the real thing. Nothing like a little sharing and Christian fellowship with a hard cock to make you worship God's creation, right?

> Pause.

JOEY: Don't tell me you're another Saint Joan, with body aflame but hymen intact. Oh God, you are. All you've ever had is that Goddamn blanket.

MISSY: My personal life is none of your business.

JOEY: How cruel can God get?

MISSY: I don't need your pity, Mister Big Hunk of Flesh. I feel sorry for anyone who considers copulation and electric blankets as similar.

JOEY: Well, you certainly have no basis for comparison. Don't condemn what you don't know.

MISSY: I know there's a difference between an orgasm and an electric shock.

JOEY: So, you have indulged in the solitary pleasures. Maybe even with some help from something else electric, the big ten incher no doubt, carefully hidden under the mattress when not in use, on the side of the bed no one ever uses. This is the holy Saint Missy of the size D batteries, welcoming none to her chaste inner chamber. Well, won't that get you to heaven in robes of white.

MISSY: Are you finished yet?

JOEY: Maybe, maybe not.

MISSY: Either way, I think it's time for you to leave.

ANN: Oh God, what did he say now?

MISSY: Just quietly get your packs and leave. You are trespassing on private property, and if you don't leave, I will have you arrested.

ANN: What the hell was all that gobbledygook?

JOEY: Preacher.

MISSY: Yes.

JOEY: Go to hell.

ANN: Joey! Missy, please, I don't know what he said wrong this time, but I apologize for him. He's just an asshole, but he really won't hurt you, and it's still raining cats and dogs outside. Trees are falling, the power is out, and there may be live power lines laying in the road. Don't kick us out. It would be like walking through a swamp in the dark out there, never knowing what you're going to step on.

JOEY: If she wants us to go, let's go. Shit.

ANN: Missy, please.

JOEY: Come on, let's leave the little cherry in her place. Let her face another dark night alone.

> JOEY starts to pull ANN away.

MISSY: Wait.

JOEY: Yes?

MISSY: It's so dark and....What will you do to me?

JOEY: Nothing you don't want done.

ANN: He won't hurt you, Missy. I promise. Just let us stay.

MISSY: I want you to leave as soon as the storm stops.

ANN: Oh, thank you.

JOEY: I don't want to stay where I'm not wanted.

ANN: Sit down and shut up, damnit. You want to get soaked to the bone?

JOEY: I don't want anybody to think they are being forced to accept me.

MISSY: Forget it. Just sit down and play your hand.

JOEY: You want to? You want to play it out?

MISSY: I want you to sit down, shut up, and play cards. OK?

JOEY: Your wish is my command.

> All sit again.

ANN: You can be a royal pain in the ass, you know that?

MISSY: Could we just play cards?

ANN: Sorry. But you see what I have to put up with.

JOEY: You can leave anytime you fucking well please.

MISSY: Damn it, be quiet! Both of you.

JOEY: Well, cussing like a preacher. I'm proud of you.

MISSY: Please be quiet and play.

JOEY: Sure. Fine. I've got the king of hearts.

MISSY: Then it's your trick.

> There is a pause to play a hand, then JOEY speaks.

JOEY: Tell me something about this church, Preacher.

MISSY: What?

JOEY: It seems pretty plain, not much decoration except for the candles, and they were for a wedding. No statues, no pattern to the stained glass, just that empty cross.

MISSY: Cheaper.

JOEY: Oh.

MISSY: This is a pretty poor church, when you get right down to it.

JOEY: So, no worshiping a stained glass Jesus.

MISSY: No, thank God.

JOEY: After all, Jesus was just a stinking Jew who liked to go fishing, drink a little wine, and hang around prostitutes and whores.

MISSY: If you are trying to shock me again, I think I am beyond that now.

JOEY: But am I right?

ANN: Shut up, Joey.

JOEY: Fuck off. Am I right?

MISSY: That stinking Jew is all that stands between you and hell.

JOEY: Agreed, Sister. But am I right?

ANN: Joey.

JOEY: Damnit, shut up.

MISSY: Considering the hygiene of the time, he probably had a body odor that we would consider unpleasant. He is known to have gone fishing on several occasions, certainly drank wine, and associated with some women of loose morals. These are not the parts of his life that are significant to us today.

JOEY: The man without sin, let him cast the first stone.

> Pause.

ANN: I thought we were going to play cards.

JOEY: I thought you were going to shut up.

> ANN throws her cards at JOEY, gets up and crosses to her pack, and sits.

ANN: Fucking asshole!

JOEY: My, my, such language, and in church too.

ANN: Eat shit.

JOEY: Well, heaven knows I've taken enough of yours.

MISSY: That's enough.

ANN: He treats me like a goddamned child, like I haven't got two cents worth of brains.

MISSY: Frankly, I don't see why the two of you stay together.

JOEY: Such is love.

ANN: Shit.

MISSY: I don't think either of you have the slightest idea what love is, and I feel very sorry for you.

JOEY: Do you?

MISSY: Listen, I may be a virgin, but that doesn't mean I never loved anybody.

JOEY: No?

ANN: You're a virgin? Good God, but you must be over thirty.

JOEY: Ann lost hers as soon as she found out what it was.

ANN: I lost mine when some sixteen year old asshole like you raped me in the back seat of his father's car.

JOEY: I was never sixteen.

ANN: When my father found out, he almost beat me to death.

MISSY: My God.

ANN: I was fourteen fucking years old, and everybody's been fucking me around ever since.

MISSY: God.

JOEY: You appear to have grown to like it.

ANN: I like sex, I ain't so fond of getting screwed.

MISSY: How could you like it after all that?

ANN: Damnit, woman, it feels good, like you're worth something to somebody, like somebody loves you at least for a few minutes, even if they don't. You must be one cold fish.

MISSY: But it isn't love. Not real, true, lasting love.

ANN: No, but it's better than nothing.

JOEY: You said you loved somebody once. Who?

MISSY: Oh. Well, my parents.

JOEY: Them, or what they did for you? Did you love them or owe them?

MISSY: Both.

JOEY: Yeah, sure. If your parents had beat you, if your friends had picked on you, if your great God had not been good to you and given you food and other luxuries, would you still have loved them?

MISSY: Yes. (Pause.) Differently maybe. I don't know.

JOEY: Morality can be just another way of hiding our loneliness, Missy.

MISSY: So what do you live by, whatever feels good? That won't build many bridges.

JOEY: No. But obeying the letter of the law and forgetting the spirit seems to be building on sand as well.

MISSY: So what do you do? What are the rules?

JOEY: It's like Zen Chess, there are no rules. At least none that can't change.

MISSY: Tennis with no net?

JOEY: It's a lot harder than it sounds.

MISSY: I think I prefer the net. At least I have something to aim for.

JOEY: Each to their own.

    Pause.

JOEY: You got a john around here?

MISSY: Down at the end of the hall, on the right.

JOEY: I shall return.

MISSY: Better take a candle.

JOEY: Oh yes, a lamp unto my feet and a light unto my path to the toilet.

    JOEY takes a candle and exits upstage.

ANN: Weird son of a bitch, ain't he?

MISSY: I still don't know why you stay with him.

ANN: And I don't know why you're still cherry.

MISSY: I guess each has a cross to bear. When did you meet him?

ANN: Two, three months ago. He just appeared in town one day.

MISSY: Where's home?

ANN: Little town in Virginia. He was working as a busboy at the diner. I used to just hang out there a lot. We had a few laughs, and one thing just sort of lead to another. When he said he was moving on, it just seemed sort of right to go along. My father was coming down pretty hard on me for not getting a job right out of high school, among other things, and I was getting tired of being black and blue. I guess it just got to the point that leaving was easier than staying, and Joey was my ticket out.

MISSY: I see.

ANN: We stop places. He's taught me the ropes, how to take care of myself. There are places in most towns, street corners or something. Go there in the morning and you can pick up a job of some kind for a day, loading or cleaning or something. And maid services usually need people, and I can waitress when I get a chance. Joey will bus tables or wash dishes, pick fruit, whatever. It's honest, and I haven't had to hook or anything. Anyway, we'll get a few bucks, then hitch a couple hundred miles and stop again when the money runs low. He's kept me out of trouble. We don't always eat regular, but, like I said, it beats being black and blue. He's a bastard sometimes, but, well...

MISSY: It's better than being beaten by your father.

ANN: Yeah.

MISSY: I never have been able to understand child abuse. My father was very strict, held me to the highest standards, but he never touched me in anger, never laid a hand on me. Just his look was enough to make me cry. I never wanted to disappoint him.

ANN: Yeah, well, my Dad wasn't like that.

MISSY: I guess I can see how Joey might be a preferred alternative.

ANN: He's OK.

MISSY: Where are you headed?

ANN: Nowhere that I know of. Mostly south, but that may be just for the winter. If he's headed any place particular, he ain't told me about it.

MISSY: What else do you know about him?

ANN: Not much. Hell, I ain't even sure that's his real name. He doesn't talk much about himself.

MISSY: You don't even know where he's from?

ANN: No. He just popped out of the air one day. Say, are you afraid he's an escaped killer or something?

MISSY: No, I don't think he's a criminal. Mental patient maybe.

ANN: Nah. He's too smart to be crazy.

MISSY: I'm not sure it works that way. I just wish I knew what he was after.

ANN: You mean besides sex?

MISSY: Nobody wants just sex. Besides, he's getting that from you.

ANN: I guess.

MISSY: Do you love him?

ANN: You are old fashioned, ain't you?

MISSY: Do you?

ANN: I don't know. Sometimes I hate his guts, like when he treats me like an idiot. He is hell on wheels in bed though.

MISSY: A hunk of flesh?

ANN: You wouldn't understand.

MISSY: Try me.

ANN: Just the way he holds me, sort of wrapping me up in his arms. It's warm. I can forget for a while. That's worth a whole lot.

MISSY: I see.

ANN: Say, do you want to fuck him? Is he getting you turned on?

MISSY: I'm just curious.

ANN: My God, he is.

MISSY: I just wonder how he got to know so much about religion. He's obviously not your ordinary bum off the street.

ANN: But I am?

MISSY: I didn't mean that.

ANN: It don't take three hands to play strip poker, Missy. You want to screw him, go ahead. We ain't married; he don't need my damned permission.

MISSY: I am not trying to steal your man. I'm just curious.

ANN: Shit, what does that mean, that you want to sit and watch? Or that I get to chain him down so you don't run off with him?

>JOEY enters unnoticed.

ANN: My God, you are a fool. A fool and a virgin, a total waste. You need your cunt fucked, and you think I care? I should feel sorry for you and lend you my man? Just what the hell do you think I am, just a third hand for strip poker, a hunk of flesh, slightly used?

JOEY: I think I missed something.

ANN: She's a God damned fool.

JOEY: Call no man fool, for as ye judge, so also shall ye be judged.

ANN: I ain't no useless innocent, don't know tit from twat.

JOEY: Yes, walking into this church is certainly interesting.

MISSY: Ann and I don't seem to be communicating very well.

JOEY: A tit is a breast or nipple, a twat...

MISSY: I know my tit from my twat.

ANN: I wouldn't bet on it.

MISSY: That is not the source of the misunderstanding. You have conned her into thinking that I actually want to have sex with you.

JOEY: Don't you?

MISSY: No.

JOEY: Does she?

ANN: Hell yes. I bet her panties are already wet.

JOEY: There does seem to be a disagreement here.

MISSY: It's just because neither of you can conceive of someone not basing their actions on base instincts.

JOEY: So, shall we get down to basics.

MISSY: Not funny.

JOEY: Sorry. So, on what criteria do you base your actions?

MISSY: Reason, logic, ethics.

JOEY: I see, therefore I am. And which of those lofty considerations is dear, uncomprehending Ann mistaking for passion and lust?

MISSY: My curiosity has logically been aroused by the conflict between your appearance and your obvious intelligence and education, especially in theology.

JOEY: And since, like a true Christian, you judge people by their appearance, it upsets you when you judge so wrongly.

MISSY: That is not what I meant.

JOEY: But it is what you said.

MISSY: You compound the paradox deliberately by refusing to divulge your name, address, or anything else, and by continual use of vulgar and suggestive language, yet you also quote the Bible word for word. You look like trash, you talk like trash, you act like trash, then you turn around and hand me a pearl, and I want to know just who in hell you are.

JOEY: Were I in hell, I suppose I would be a devil. And as tempted as I am at times to believe that Christ came the second time a few weeks after Pentecost, and that this is hell and I am in it, I suppose you would not agree. So, in truth, what you want to know is who on earth I am.

ANN: Bullshit.

MISSY: My sentiments exactly.

JOEY: Well, I shall follow Pharisaic tradition and answer a question with a question. What difference does it make to you who I am? I came from the night, and to the night I shall return, all in the passing of a few hours. During that time we will talk, play cards, you and I may or may not make love, Ann may or may not leave me, the roof may or may not leak, and you will never see me again either way. So I ask, what difference does it make to you who on earth I am?

ANN: You screw her, and you can kiss me good-bye, and that's a promise.

JOEY: Ah, serial monogamy, a woman's most cherished illusion.

ANN: The only illusion around here is you dreaming you've got me in your back pocket, you asshole.

JOEY: I like to keep you next to my heart.

ANN: Fuck.

MISSY: Shut up! This is a church, God damnit! Oh my God, what am I saying?

JOEY: You just asked God to damn this church. I doubt your congregation would approve.

MISSY: You shut up too! Every time I think we're getting anywhere, that I'm finally going to learn something about you, it all goes haywire. Pow! Down the chute.

JOEY: Ann, it seems our dear Pastor would like to have an intellectually probing conversation devoid of all interruptions and references to biology or bodily functions or other basic aspects of human personality. In other words, she wants you to shut up and quit cussing.

ANN: Well, she can take a flying leap for all I care, I ain't letting either one of you push me around anymore.

JOEY: Admirable independence. A fine example of American spirit.

MISSY: Oh, stuff it.

JOEY: You didn't like my cussing, now you don't like my proper English. Are you sure you want me to talk at all?

MISSY: No, I want you to shut up

JOEY: Then how can I answer your many questions.

MISSY: You didn't answer any while you were talking, so I don't see as it makes any difference.

JOEY: But you have yet to answer my question.

MISSY: What difference does it make?

JOEY: Yes, that one.

MISSY: No, what difference would it make if I did answer? You'd just weasel out some other way.

JOEY: You might be surprised. I like little head games like this. I so rarely get to play an equal.

ANN: You ain't getting any tonight, I guarantee you that, not from me.

JOEY: You're not in this game.

ANN: No, and I may not be in this church much longer either.

JOEY: Oh, and when did you develop a liking for walking through swamps in the dark?

ANN: It'll stop sooner or later.

JOEY: Yes, there's always a rainbow.

MISSY: That's what I mean.

JOEY: What?

MISSY: We know it will stop because of Noah's rainbow. You keep coming up with these allusions.

ANN: Shit. You're both crazy. Talk, talk for all I care. Just leave me out of it.

    ANN crosses and sits by her pack.

JOEY: So, Preacher, shall we begin our little intercourse?

ANN: Hey, I thought you were just going to talk.

JOEY: I thought you were going to shut up.

ANN: Asshole.

MISSY: Please! We are just going to talk, nothing else. OK?

ANN: OK, OK! Shit.

JOEY: Well?

MISSY: Well what?

JOEY: What difference does it make to you who I am?

MISSY: Oh. (Pause.) I'm not sure. Maybe it just disturbs me that someone so intelligent and knowledgeable about religion should be wandering around like a bum.

JOEY: You mean it bothers you that someone so like you could end up walking the streets.

MISSY: Something like that.

JOEY: That somebody so like you could give in to carnal lusts and engage in a life of sin.

MISSY: Maybe.

JOEY: And you're afraid that if you gave in to the same lusts that you too would end up wandering in the darkness, searching for your lost soul. So, what you want is another reason for my fall, some other cause to which you would be immune, so you would feel free to indulge in the pleasures of the flesh. That is why it matters.

MISSY: No.

JOEY: Is lying a sin?

MISSY: Of course.

JOEY: Then why do you keep lying to yourself? Isn't that just as bad? You know you want to get laid.

MISSY: I am not lying to myself.

JOEY: Missy, sin is in the heart, not in the hand. No act, even killing, is wrong if the reasons are right. God ordered the Israelites to commit genocide when they invaded the Promised

Land; we don't put that in the same category as the Nazi Holocaust. There is sin in tearing yourself apart trying to suppress natural, God-given desires.

MISSY: I am not tearing myself apart!

JOEY: Damn it, God gave you that body. He intended for you to get horny. There's nothing wrong with that. Why do you think it's so evil?

MISSY: It's not evil, it's just...temptation...temptation to do evil.

JOEY: Temptation to love is evil?

MISSY: No...yes... it's sex that's evil, not love. I mean sex without marriage, without love.

JOEY: Which is it, marriage or love? They're not the same. You can have one without the other.

MISSY: You can't have a real marriage without love.

JOEY: Then there are one hell of a lot of fornicators out there wearing wedding rings. And what about love without marriage, is that evil? Can kindness and compassion really be evil, even if they lead to unmarried sex?

MISSY: Yes.

JOEY: Why?

MISSY: Because God said so.

JOEY: But why did he say so?

MISSY: I don't know!

JOEY: But a true Christian is supposed to follow the spirit of the Law, not just the letter. I want to be a true Christian, so I have to know the why behind the rule. Rules change. Rules need breaking sometimes. Christ had a big reputation as a rule breaker, because He was trying to teach that the reasons for the rules were more important than the rules themselves. So, I want to know why is sex so fucking wrong?!

MISSY: I don't know!

JOEY: You don't know?! What the hell kind of preacher are you? You're supposed to have answers, a scripture for every occasion.

MISSY: It isn't that easy.

JOEY: Didn't they teach ethics in that seminary you went to? Or did you just memorize rules? You're supposed to have answers for us poor, misguided sinners. That's your job, to reveal the Truth. But no, one hard question and you don't know.

MISSY: All right!

JOEY: Not even a pat answer from the official party line?

MISSY: No! I've spent too much time giving pat answers to questions. Suddenly one day I was the one asking the questions, and the answers weren't so pat anymore. It wasn't such a problem when I was in school. I went to a college run by the church, then straight into the seminary. If you didn't believe the party line you wouldn't have been there in the first place. I was busy, there were lots of things to do, lots of people around who all believed the same things. We all had the same morals, so there was a lot of reinforcement. Be good, go to church, dress right, that was what got approval. We were all playing the same game by the same rules, and I was very good at it. Very good. Even in the seminary there were lots of other women like me, my friends. We were all in the same boat. But the other women had other majors, religious education, church music, something. So they married preachers. None of the men, even the music directors, wanted to be the "preacher's husband." So, eventually I ended up here. The Real World. Half my congregation is sleeping around. The kids in the youth group have more experience than I do. I don't fit in anywhere anymore. I'm the third wheel, the odd chair. I can only be invited to the polite parties, the church socials, where I sit with the old women. And suddenly I don't have the answers anymore. Everybody I went to seminary with is married. Most have kids. There's somebody for them to come home to. I go to the hospital to visit the sick and envy them for the company they get. I was asleep in my office tonight because I couldn't stand the thought of going home. So, there it is. You win. I have no answers. I am horny, and I am lonely, and it is tearing me apart to be so lonely, but nobody wants to marry a female preacher, and I don't know what to do about it. But I am damn sure that having sex with you, and taking a chance on getting knocked up by some educated bum is not going to help.

JOEY: Ah, yes, birth control. Sex without it would be a sin. And I imagine you'd have to drive at least fifty miles to find a drug store where nobody knew you.

MISSY: At least.

JOEY: Which makes getting the Pill a little difficult.

MISSY: No kidding. And what kind of looks do you think I'd get if I walked into the local drug store and bought a package of contraceptive sponges? Half the employees go to this church.

JOEY: Oh, the horror! The gossip! (chanting) "The Preacher's getting laid, the Preacher's getting laid."

MISSY: Oh, that would be a scene, wouldn't it. Well, my fine theologian, there we stand. I may not be so absolutely confident of right and wrong anymore, but I am very sure that illegitimate pregnancies are wrong. I am also sure that whatever you think of it, and whatever problems it has, that I value my career, and that this church would not tolerate an unmarried minister on birth control. No church is that liberal. So you can taunt my virginity all you want, but you're not going to do anything about it.

JOEY: Missy, I've had a vasectomy.

MISSY: I don't believe you.

JOEY: Want to see my scar?

MISSY: I'll take your word for it.

ANN: Hey, you never told me.

JOEY: You never needed to know.

ANN: Shit.

JOEY: No one would ever know. Perfectly safe.

MISSY: That's not the point.

JOEY: What is the point?

MISSY: It would still be wrong.

JOEY: Why?

MISSY: It's not just sex I need, it's love. We're not in love, not to mention married. I don't love you. I don't even know you, and that would make it wrong.

JOEY: Love comes in all sizes. Maybe I love you a little bit. Why pass up the little loves?

MISSY: Because they might destroy the big one.

JOEY: Does it really make sense that someone who loves you would want you to have suffered being alone?

MISSY: I don't know. (Pause.) You're still evading the question, you know that.

JOEY: You mean, who I am?

MISSY: Yes.

JOEY: Well, well, just who am I? Why do I know so God damned much about religion yet play the cynic? Why do I seem to know so much about how you feel, and even more surprising, care about it? Why am I such a Godforsaken bastard? Because I'm a P.K. too. Does that explain it?

MISSY: You're a preacher's kid?

JOEY: My father was God's own man, and I grew up in the church, literally. I was the perfect child, raised to follow the Lord in all my ways, like Samuel in the temple, told to listen to the Spirit of Christ. And, God damn it, I did. But being the preacher's kid is like watching a magic show from backstage, you see the tricks. First you get to drink the grape juice left in the unused glasses after the Lord's Supper. Takes some of the magic out of it, you know. Then it was overhearing the deacons making plans for keeping the blacks out if any dared try to worship God with us. Then it was listening to my own father, who was never on time for anything in his life, preach a sermon about the virtue of punctuality. Eventually you realize that there are damned few Christians in churches; that it's mostly modern day Pharisees. They don't care about you, they care about the rules. Though they have long since forgotten the reason for the rules. They're their rules, and you damn well better not break them. Do they care how lonely you are? Hell no! But there's a rule saying unmarried people don't fuck, and you damned well better not break it. Even if the reason for the rule died when the Pill was born. It's the rules that matter, the old fashioned family values, the WASP culture and morality. Well, Jesus was a Jew, and he said the Pharisees were worse than the heathen. They should have known better. Is it wrong to heal on the Sabbath? Is it wrong to eat the Show Bread? Is it wrong to love for a night?

MISSY: So, you have a past after all. A preacher's kid.

JOEY: Another preacher's kid. Isn't it amazing how many people churches destroy?

MISSY: Are you referring to you or me?

JOEY: I'd say it's a little too early to tell.

MISSY: So a little hypocrisy caused you to throw the baby out with the bathwater, to forget all the good the Church as done and could do, to chuck it all and go wandering around the country seducing women.

JOEY: Christianity has destroyed more cultures, killed more people, and caused more wars than any political movement in history. The Inquisition, the Crusades, the missionaries...

MISSY: So it's powerful, good or bad. It's still real. Or don't you believe in anything at all.

JOEY: Oh, I believe. I just reach very different conclusions about the details.

MISSY: And you may be more right about some things than I am, I don't know. I know I'm certainly not as sure about certain things as I used to be. Being a minister does that to you, it seems. But is all this any reason for you to throw your life away?

JOEY: Who says I'm throwing it away?

MISSY: Well, you certainly don't seem to be doing any good for anybody. Show me your faith by your works.

JOEY: Oh, I help out a little bit here and there. I've certainly made Ann's nights a little more enjoyable lately. And nobody's beat her up in three months. She even gives every indication that she's able to take care of herself now.

ANN: You bet your boots.

JOEY: So, maybe I can help you with your little problem before I move on.

MISSY: Don't give me that. You're no knight in shining armor riding around the country saving damsels in distress. You're a two-bit stud with no thoughts beyond your next conquest. Is that your grand quest in life, how many virgins you can "save "?

JOEY: No. You're a detour on my quest, as you call it. What my quest is is none of your business. Better you don't know. All you need to know, Missy, is that I am a man with very few illusions left. A man who once was very much like you. What I am is here and willing to be used for a night. The rest is up to you.

Pause. The rain begins to slow, and then stops.

ANN: Are you two finished?

JOEY: I think we're through talking.

ANN: Good, because the rain is stopping.

JOEY: So?

ANN: So I want to go.

MISSY: Isn't it still too dark outside? To muddy or something?

JOEY: Yeah, what's your hurry?

ANN: It's time to go. We've caused enough trouble as it is.

JOEY: You getting jealous? Afraid you might have to sit and watch?

ANN: I'm afraid that swelled head of yours is about to bust. Now let's go.

JOEY: Go ahead if you're so anxious.

ANN: Listen close, asshole. Either we go now, or you never see me again.

JOEY: If that's the way you want it.

ANN: Nothing is going to happen here.

JOEY: Maybe, maybe not.

ANN: Shit. That's it?

JOEY: Looks that way.

ANN: Just like that?

JOEY: Just like that.

ANN: You're dumping me for a cherry.

JOEY: If that's how it works out.

ANN: So I am just a hunk of flesh to you, a god damned blanket.

JOEY: My electric whore.

ANN: Well, God damn you, good riddance. I'd had about as much of you as I could stand anyway. And you know something, Mr. High and Holy, I may be just a fucking cunt and an easy lay, but I'm better than both of you. Standing around arguing over who's the most holy. Shit. Ain't neither one of you worth piss.

JOEY: Now I know you're jealous.

ANN: Jealous? Of what? You, Mr. High and Holy Know It All, the best lay in fifty states? You ain't so perfect. The fucking may be right or wrong, I don't know and I don't care, but your treating me like dirt, like something to scrape off your boots, like something beneath you, to be used and thrown away, that ain't right. I'm as much a person as you are, even if I ain't as smart. I cared about you. I'm a human being, and I deserve better.

MISSY: Ann...

ANN: And you, Miss Holy Virgin, who cares so much for humanity that she has sacrificed her personal pleasure and happiness to serve mankind, you think you're so fucking good? You care about people so much, how come you never got close to one? We're all so wonderful, until we get close enough to smell? Then you cross your legs and hide in the pulpit. So, you're a female preacher. Big shit. We got female jockeys, female wrestlers, female senators, female anything. But we're still women, and like it or not, one of the things God made women to do is love some poor, dumb man. One at a time, up close and personal, not just in theory. You know, you ain't no more human than he is, cause neither one of you feels a damn thing about anybody but yourselves. Two sides of the same stinking coin.

MISSY: Maybe we love something more important than any single individual.

ANN: Maybe there ain't nothing more important than a single individual. From what little I know, that's what Jesus seemed to think. He junked all the rules and religions and just cared about the people. So, you both blew it. Now, I, for one, am blowing this joint. You can stand there and argue with her, or fuck her, or hang yourself on the cross for all I care, but if you ever want to see my cute little pussy again, you'll walk out of here right now.

   Pause.

MISSY: You better go.

JOEY: No.

ANN: You ain't gonna get nothing off'a her.

JOEY: Maybe not. But I care enough to try.

ANN: You was warned.

JOEY: Just shut the fuck up and get out. I'm tired of your yapping.

ANN: Silence is awful lonesome.

JOEY: Get the hell out!

ANN: You had your chance, Mister.

   ANN grabs her pack and exits.

JOEY: (quietly) Be careful. (to MISSY) Well, she certainly told us off, didn't she?

MISSY: I wouldn't say she was totally wrong.

JOEY: Maybe.

MISSY: If you hurry, you can catch her.

JOEY: She'll be all right, she can take care of herself now. Maybe she's better off without me, if what she said was so true.

MISSY: You can't stay here, you know that.

JOEY: I'll be gone before daylight.

MISSY: I'm trying to say that you should go, now.

JOEY: Then what would you do?

MISSY: Does it matter?

JOEY: Yes. To me.

MISSY: What if nothing happens?

JOEY: Then I passed up one good woman to take a chance on a better one.

MISSY: Better?

JOEY: More like me.

MISSY: Yes. High and holy and living on dreams that never turn out to be what we expected.

JOEY: Nothing ever does.

MISSY: Including love?

JOEY: It's never what you expect. Neither is sex.

MISSY: Then maybe you better just leave me with my illusions.

JOEY: It's not better or worse, just different.

MISSY: I don't think I want any more surprises.

JOEY: Missy.

> JOEY crosses to MISSY and with one finger lightly begins to draw a circle around her nipple. MISSY stares at the finger, but does not move.

MISSY: Why are you doing this?

JOEY: Because if somebody had made me feel a little more normal a few years ago, maybe I wouldn't have done quite so much rebelling. Because I enjoy it.

MISSY: Stop.

JOEY: Why?

> MISSY finally pulls away.

MISSY: Because.

JOEY: Just because?

MISSY: Because...because there's got to be something wrong with this. I can't just have sex with the first guy that walks in out of the rain, no matter who he is. What do I know about you? You're no immaculate angel, that's for sure.

> JOEY crosses to his pack and gets something from it. Crossing back to MISSY he rolls up his sleeves.

JOEY: Maybe I'm not an immaculate angel. Fine, I never claimed to be. But there aren't any needle marks on me, and I think Ann was evidence enough that I prefer women. It's always wise to be safe though, I can understand that. Here.

> He tosses a strip of three wrapped condoms to her.

MISSY: You think you have the answer for everything, don't you? Well, you're wrong. It's not enough just to make it clean and safe. It's not enough just to be honest and take our little loves. All that does is make it not wrong. And being not wrong isn't good enough. It has to be right. And there is a difference.

JOEY: Boy, did I underestimate you. I didn't think there was anybody like you left. It's a good surprise.

MISSY: This isn't sanctified sex we're talking about here. You're no holy messenger sent by God to "comfort" me. This is human sex and human need, so morality still matters. And just being not wrong is not a high enough standard.

JOEY: You're right. Absolutely right. I'm proud of you.

MISSY: So, Hot Shot, what's your answer now?

JOEY: "Love one another, even as I have loved you."

MISSY: I've heard the verse. He wasn't talking about sex.

JOEY: Neither am I, really. You're hurting; I can help. Sex just happens to be the way. Missy, where it's not wrong to love, isn't it wrong not to love? Isn't that what it's all about? That makes it right for me.

MISSY: Your Christian duty?

JOEY: Call it what you will.

MISSY: That is a twist. Jesus commands you to seduce that virgin.

JOEY: You can build a life of "thou shall nots," and never get to the "thou shalls."

MISSY: OK, OK, it would be your good deed for the day. But what about me? What makes it more than just lust for me? What makes it right for me?

>   Pause.

JOEY: Maybe it would help heal an old wound.

MISSY: What wound?

JOEY: Churches burn people in lots of ways besides at the stake. I got burned when some deacons called a special business meeting while my father was on vacation. With no notice they fired him for not being "fundamentalist" enough. Didn't even give him time to find another church. He ended up selling insurance. Broke his heart. Burned me bitter and angry and not very trusting, and that makes it pretty tough to get along out there. The scars show. The nerves are still exposed. You end up walking in the rain. Tonight you've shown me that maybe there is one really moral person left. That helps. But what I haven't seen is the passion, the compassion, that keeps your morality from just becoming a new set of rules. Sooner or later tonight I'm going back out into that dark. I'd like to take a little hope with me, a little balm of Gilliad to cool my fevered brow. It might make a difference.

MISSY: I see.

>   Pause.

JOEY: The rain has stopped.

MISSY: Yes.

JOEY: I guess that must be the moon shining on the windows.

MISSY: I guess.

JOEY: Sure makes for some weird colored light.

MISSY: Yes.

> JOEY reaches for her. At first she comes to him, then pulls away.

MISSY: I'm afraid.

JOEY: Of what?

MISSY: The unknown. Myself. That I'll like it too much.

JOEY: That you will become a raging nymphomaniac and screw every man in town, then start on the women, and end up molesting little boys?

MISSY: Something like that.

JOEY: Won't happen.

MISSY: What will?

JOEY: We'll make love two or three times, you'll fall asleep, and when you wake up, I'll be gone. But there will be a change. You'll feel a little more human, a little more normal. You won't ever tell a soul, and nobody will ever know, but people will notice a difference. And sooner or later a man will show an interest in you, and you won't be quite so scared, and you won't shut him off so automatically. And maybe he'll be somebody who can stay a little longer.

> JOEY puts his arms around her from behind.

MISSY: How do we get this lonely?

JOEY: Just let me hold you for a while. There's no sin in that, is there?

MISSY: Just temptation. (Pause.) What would you do if after all this I decided not to?

JOEY: Leave you in the hand of God, and lift you up in prayer.

MISSY: "Dear God, help the virgin preacher get laid."

JOEY: Something like that.

MISSY: How ironic, you praying for me. I think I like that.

JOEY: I can pray for you either way.

MISSY: Will you kiss me goodbye?

JOEY: You mean now? Or later?

> MISSY turns. They kiss. Lights aimed at the audience fade up, preventing them from seeing the stage. When the lights fade down, the stage is empty.

CURTAIN

Five Exits

Five Exits is a bill of five one-acts about death. There is a progression in the order. In the first, the only two people attending a high school class reunion contemplate how they want to live their last days. In the second, one of the characters is about to die. In the third, a man reacts to a death. In the fourth, someone dies. And in the last play, the characters are already dead.

This bill was the winner of the 1997 Getchell New Play Award from the Southeast Theatre Conference (SETC), a national contest. My family and I got to attend the SETC conference where the play was given a staged reading, and I had to give an acceptance speech at the awards dinner. I was followed to the podium by Alan Menkin, the composer of so many songs for Broadway musicals and Disney movies. After the speeches, my daughter, Elizabeth, who liked the songs from "The Little Mermaid" and "Pocahontas", got to meet him. My script was also published in the SETC "Southern Theatre" magazine, which I hoped might result in some university productions. It did not, as it had not for my friend from Southern Illinois University grad school, Ken Robbins, who had won the award the year before.

However, in 1999, First Stages Productions, a community theatre in Dayton, OH, which did sometimes get scripts from SETC, produced the play. The three of us went up for opening night. We flew in, and despite some problems at the airport, managed to have time in the afternoon to see the National Museum of the Air Force in Dayton in the afternoon. Elizabeth, then just 8 years old, stood in the reception line with me after the show and shook hands with people just like it was something she did all the time.

FIVE EXITS

A Bill of Five Scenes By David Davis

Member
All rights & privileges.

David Davis
100 Hunters Ridge Court
Roswell, GA 30076
daviddaviswriter@gmail.com

Copyright 1995 David Davis

ACT I

SCENE ONE—REUNION

AT RISE: The private dining room of a small restaurant in eastern North Carolina, 1990. There is a large table with 12 place settings, a banner saying "Class of 1940 Reunion," and a small table off to one side with a couple of enlarged (maybe 10x12) old black and white photos, a photo album, and an old notebook or two. "When I'm Sixty-Four" by the Beatles is heard in the background. WAYNE, 65, dignified, dressed well in suit and tie, sits alone at the table. He gets up and looks at the photographs. There is a long pause. The music ends. Suddenly, SARA, 68, hale and hardy, enters, seemingly in a rush. She carries a basket or vase and some flowers which, during the course of the scene, she will arrange into a centerpiece for the table. She stops just inside the entrance, takes in the scene, stares at the man a minute. WAYNE looks back at her.

SARA: Wayne Davis, is that you? These glasses are half covered with flour, but I don't think I'm seeing a ghost.

WAYNE: Sara? Sara Butts?

SARA: Wayne, it is you. Lands, I ain't seen you in...in...a coon's age.

WAYNE: (Pointing at banner.) It has been a long time. You're still beautiful, Sara.

SARA: And you're still a handsome man, you old devil. But, my, my, I didn't expect to see you here.

WAYNE: I was beginning to wonder if anybody was going to show up.

SARA: Oh, lands, are you the only one here?

WAYNE: Except for you, now.

SARA: Oh, I'm sorry I'm late. Becky Ballinger's husband called just as I was walking out the door. They had to put her back in the hospital, her kidneys you know.

> SARA takes off her coat and puts it on the back of one of the chairs.

WAYNE: No, I didn't know.

SARA: Oh, no, you wouldn't. She's already been on dialysis twice. She's too old to get a transplant. I don't think she's going to make it this time.

WAYNE: I'm very sorry to hear that. I guess I've lost touch more than I thought.

SARA: Lost touch? Lands, you ain't even been in hollering distance for years. I don't even know how you found out about this reunion.

WAYNE: I started subscribing to the Mount Olive paper about a year ago. Some things were happening, and I started wondering about some of the people I had left behind, people like you. Maybe especially you. Paper takes about a week to get to me, so I miss all the church socials. Saw the notice about the reunion in time though. I just didn't think I'd be the only one who showed up.

SARA: Well, there weren't but fifteen of us to start with. Not even enough to kill a hog for.

WAYNE: Even so...

SARA: (Indicating place settings on table.) We didn't even plan for but 12, and that counted the spouses. We're dropping like flies.

WAYNE: We can't all be dead.

SARA: Near about. I had to get a third black dress just to give the funerals some variety.

WAYNE: (Crossing to photos.) I know Kent and Brownie died in the war, and Buddy in a car wreck in 55. And Rachel died in childbirth, oh, about 1950. I knew that.

SARA: Cecil had a heart attack a little over a year ago. Died on the operating table. Douglas is in a nursing home up by Goldsboro. Stroke left him little more than a vegetable. Peter Ruffin lives over in Rose Hill, but he has Parkinson's pretty bad and hardly leaves the house.

WAYNE: We men don't seem to be doing too well.

SARA: If it wasn't for the husbands, this would be a hen party all right.

WAYNE: I read about your husband's death in the Mount Olive paper a year ago. I'm sorry, really sorry.

SARA: I was just relieved when his pain finally stopped.

WAYNE: Yes.

    Pause. SARA sits.

SARA: Hazel married Leslie Ballinger, Becky's older brother.

WAYNE: I remember Leslie. He had this coal black hair that he wore in a pompadour and had to keep combing all the time.

SARA: Lands, he's bald as a turtle now. They live out in San Francisco. Both fine and dandy far as I know. I was expecting Betty Creech to show up. I don't know why she's not here, unless she just couldn't move her three hundred pounds out of the chair.

WAYNE: Three hundred...? Little Betty?

SARA: Near about. About as wide as she is tall now, poor thing. Carolyn Wilson was to be here, but her husband is sick up in Chapel Hill. Florine Falk lives down in Carolina Beach; she's a widow but I thought she'd be here. It's not that long a drive. Betty Kay well, you remember Betty Kay.

WAYNE: Oh yes. Nobody could forget Betty Kay.

SARA: Nobody will say it out loud, but she got AIDS, supposedly from a blood transfusion, but, well, you remember Betty Kay. I thought she might show up tonight, but it looks like not.

WAYNE: AIDS. Good Grief. (He sits.)

SARA: Seems like a lot to bear for just 15 people, doesn't it. Like when they passed out the grief we stood in line twice. A lot's happened in the past 50 years. Most of it not what we expected.

WAYNE: Well, at least not what we expected fifty years ago. (Pause.) You remember the night before I left?

SARA: How could I forget? We had a class picnic in the park. It was real dark, and we slipped away from the old folks. You had a fever blister, and the next day I had one too. Lands, if anybody had seen us! I gave you my class ring to take with you to Texas.

WAYNE: I still have it.

SARA: And every time I get a fever blister, I think of you. Oh, that was a long time ago.

WAYNE: Kent was the only one who had a car, so we rode four to a seat into Mount Olive on Saturday nights.

SARA: Me in your lap, you with your arms around. Holding hands walking down the street. Getting orange juice from that booth on Main Street. I remember that. I dreamed about those days for a long time. Even when I thought I'd gotten over you, you'd come to me in dreams. Why did you leave me, Wayne? I'd have loved you.

WAYNE: You know, I've been asking myself the same question lately. (Gets up and moves away from her.) Back then, I just had to get away from this town, all the people who thought the world ended at the edge of the tobacco field. But, well, we were just kids. Just dreaming some crazy dreams.

SARA: But we made so many plans. You going off to college and become a preacher. Then we would get married and you'd get a church someplace around here, maybe down by White Lake where we could go swimming. It was a beautiful dream.

WAYNE: Well, yes, it was. But it was mostly your dream. I did become a preacher, though. And you did get married.

SARA: But not to you. You married that girl in the Seminary. And you ain't lived within five hundred miles of here since you left home. We graduate one day and the next day you're on a train to Texas. I wrote you, and you wrote back a few love letters, but after a while you stopped. That hurt, Wayne. Your Mama would hear from you, and I'd find out bits and pieces of news, but after she passed on while everybody was away during the war, nobody hardly knew where you were.

WAYNE: The West is a big place. It's easy to get lost out there.

SARA: Is your wife with you? I'd kind of like to meet her.

WAYNE: I buried her in Tucson five years ago.

SARA: I'm sorry.

WAYNE: It seems a long time ago.

    SARA stands and moves away a little.

SARA: You seem changed, Wayne.

WAYNE: Heck, it was 50 years ago.

SARA: Not just the years; sadder.

WAYNE: I was 15 years old when I graduated. School only went to the 11th grade. I was a kid. Life hadn't had a chance to chew me up and spit me out. What did I know then?

SARA: You were the smartest in the class. The only one who went off to college.

WAYNE: You were going to go too. After you saved some money.

SARA: Then the war came along. I ended up building cargo ships down in Wilmington. Rosie the Riveter, that's me. You believe that? Then the war ended and the men came home. Not only did I lose my job, the colleges were so flooded with GI Bill I couldn't even get in until 1950. By then had a husband, two kids, and a full-time job at the pickle factory. Took me 12 years to get through, taking a course here and there, stopping all together when I had a babe in arms. I made it though. B.A. in Home Economics. Ended up a manager at the pickle factory before I retired. Some dreams are hard to stop.

WAYNE: You always were quite a woman. Two kids, eh?

SARA: Three afore it was over with. All grown and gone now. Raleigh, Atlanta, even up in Boston for the girl. Hard to believe my daughter would marry a yankee, but she did. Yeah, two boys and a girl. You?

WAYNE: Boy and a girl. Grown and moved out long ago.

SARA: (She sits again.) Why'd you never come home, Wayne? There were churches here that wanted pastors.

WAYNE: I never fit in here, you know that. Kept getting above my raising. Even in school I wasn't like the rest of you. Why do you think I left?

SARA: You were younger and smarter, that's all. I was the odd one out.

WAYNE: You?

SARA: A year older than anybody else cause I had to repeat the year my mama was sick. When you started stealing kisses, I got ribbed about robbing the cradle even though we were in the same grade, you being a year younger and me a year older than the others. I loved you, but sometimes I wondered even then if you went with me just because everybody else was already paired off.

WAYNE: Now, you know that's not...

SARA: Don't sweet talk me, Wayne Davis. I not only went through it myself, I pulled three kids from gangly teens to wedded and bedded, I know how the mating game works. I was tall, old, and had a turkey neck even at 18.

WAYNE: Damn it, I was fifteen, what did I know?

SARA: What are you now, Wayne Davis? Why are you here and why didn't you pay any of us any mind all this time. I thought we were friends if nothing else. What happened in those long years? You didn't kill nobody, did you?

WAYNE: No, I haven't been locked up in the Texas pen.

SARA: We're getting old, Wayne. This may be a little farm town in East Carolina, but you're going to have a hard time shocking me. I been to too many unexpected funerals and weddings to be surprised by much any more.

WAYNE: Oh, it's nothing like that. It's just a long story.

SARA: Nobody waiting at home for me. You got to be more entertaining than television.

WAYNE: Well, I guess you deserve the truth. (Stands.) I owe you that much. I think I loved you, but I was so anxious to get out of here. Nobody here seemed to care for anything except the tobacco crop. And you were just like the others, never looking past this little town.

SARA: This is where...

WAYNE: I know, I know. When I finally got out, I hit Texas like a house afire. I was a thousand miles away from home, going to college full time and holding down a couple of part-time jobs. It was like if I could learn enough, I'd never have to go back. Got through college in three years. I turned 18 and graduated in 1943. I had left the tobacco dust far behind. Then I went to Seminary. In 1943, going to seminary was a suspect thing to do. Two of our friends were already dead by then, and no end in sight. But I had "the Call." At least I believed it back then.

SARA: We all knew you did. Nobody here said anything against you.

WAYNE: No, nobody would say anything. Oh, but that's only the beginning. I zipped through the seminary in Fort Worth, finishing just as the war was ending. And getting married even before I finished. You, Mama, this whole town were far away then. I was called to a church up in Oklahoma. A brown land, everything was brown, the land, the houses, the people. I turned 21 about as far from home as you can get, and glad to be there.

SARA: Oh, Wayne.

WAYNE: I'm sorry. But in 1945 it was the truth. (Pause.) You want to know a secret, Sara? You can't make a living being a preacher. It looks good compared to farming tobacco, but when you got a wife and kids and you're trying to live off what a little Baptist church pays, you soon learn that prayer won't pay the phone company. You also learn that not all deacons are Christians. I went through half a dozen little country churches, scattered all over the West, in about 15 years and finally realized that I was disgusted with churches, broke, and my kids were living on beans and cornbread.

SARA: Oh my.

WAYNE: I started teaching religion at a little college. I enjoyed that, but then one of my kids got arthritis that made the hospitals rich and me even poorer and forced us to move to Arizona. I couldn't get another college job out there. I ended up teaching in high school, then junior high, then selling tile floors, then finally walking around an empty building at night with nothing but a walkie-talkie and a key to the guard boxes. Just a grumpy old man trying to make it to Social Security.

SARA: Wayne...

WAYNE: (He sits.) After Lillie died I ended up with little but memories. Last year I retired from whatever was left and moved to a little town called Carefree, Arizona. It's just a wide spot in the road, not even as big as here, but it's quiet and people don't ask too many questions. My only occupation is finding a reason to get up in the morning. And that is what happened to the Valedictorian of Duplin High, Class of 1940.

SARA: Oh, Wayne.

WAYNE: Not what you come home to brag about.

SARA: We're neither one what we thought we'd be, Wayne. Building ships in Wilmington was my big adventure.

WAYNE: You got what you wanted. Husband, kids, college, good job. You lived here the way you always said you wanted to. I'm the one who didn't live up to my promise.

SARA: Now-a-days seems like all I do is sit around here and watch people die. I've cooked too much potato salad in my life.

WAYNE: You've got something to hold on to here. Something that will hold on to you.

SARA: I've only had one man in my life, and he's gone. The kids are far away. As you pointed out, my friends seem to be either dead or with one foot in the grave. Except for you, and I'm not even sure you're the man I used to know.

WAYNE: I'm not.

SARA: You need to move back home, Wayne.

WAYNE: My home is in Arizona.

SARA: You're alone there.

WAYNE: I'm alone anywhere. I'll tell you one more thing, Sara. A year ago, I was laid up in the hospital. Wasn't sure I was ever going to get out. Started wondering what had happened to all those I had left behind. Especially you. I was wondering what if..., well, I'm not real pleased how my life turned out. That's a sad thing to say, but it's the truth. I just started thinking if I had done this or that different...If maybe I had come home...to you.

SARA: Oh, Wayne.

WAYNE: I guess I got lucky. The tumor was next to, but not in my brain. I should be fine, at least until something else comes up. But being that close, well, you start to worry about different things, what you're missing, what you missed. Who you missed. You want to see the country, Sara? I'll turn in my return ticket, we'll rent a car, and I'll drive you clear across the country. There's sights out there take your breath away.

SARA: Lands! Wouldn't that be a kick in the pants.

WAYNE: Get the blood moving. Like we were 18 and starting out again.

SARA: Don't tease me like this.

WAYNE: I'm serious.

SARA: Wayne, don't talk this way. You know I can't do that.

WAYNE: Why not?

SARA: Why not?....Because I don't need to go to Timbuktu. I need to be home.

WAYNE: Sounds like home is mighty lonely. How attached can you be to a graveyard?

SARA: Better than no roots at all. I'm settled here. I can look out my window and remember my husband walking up the path, the sun setting behind him. I can hold my family bible and remember him reading it to the kids every night. I can look at the bedrooms and remember the goodnight kisses. I can look at the flowers I planted years ago that come back every Spring. I can put those flowers on the graves of my parents, my husband, my sister, Buddy and Kent and Brownie and Rachel and Cecil...

>Pause.

WAYNE: Sara, we took different roads. I wandered around, saw how mean people can be as only a preacher can, learned how few people want to learn anything as only a teacher can, and learned to be alone as only a night watchman can. You kept the home fires burning and stood by your family. But we ended up in the same place. We are both getting old, we are both alone, and we are both watching our friends die around us. We've got another ten years maybe, before we get too old to enjoy riding this merry-go-round. Are you going to sit by the fireside even after the fire has gone out. Won't you get cold?

SARA: Have you even got a fireside to sit by?

WAYNE: Tell you what, you come out to Carefree and see. Lots of people come to Arizona for the winter. Let the sun warm your bones a little. See someplace different.

SARA: I don't want to see someplace different.

WAYNE: Why not?

SARA: I'm not like you, I need to be home. I belong here. My memories are here. I can see my old doll chest, or a picnic table in the park, and I'm a child again. These memories are mine, you can't take them away. They're the air I breathe, the sunshine as night closes in. I have to be here.

WAYNE: (Crossing to table to look at pictures) You know, I used to hate this town, but there were some good memories. So, I drove around the old place before I came here tonight. The lake where I used to fish is now a turkey processing plant dumping pond. We used to grow tobacco and corn, now it's turkeys and hogs and the place stinks to high heaven. The pickle plant was the only industry around, now there are three turkey plants, a lumberyard, and a furniture factory. The general store is closed and boarded up, but there's a Walmart and a Bi-Lo at the exit to an interstate that wasn't even planned 50 years ago. I couldn't even find the old school.

SARA: They moved the road.

WAYNE: What?

SARA: They tore down the school and moved the road to connect up better with the new main road. There's nothing there but an empty field. Built a separate elementary and high school upwind of the turkey plant over by where the lake used to be.

WAYNE: Well, I'm sure that's good. But it isn't home. Not to me. I tried to watch the sunset, and the trees got in the way. I've been out west too long, gotten used to the dust and the open spaces. Sunsets like fires in the sky. Some places there are sand dunes any beach would give its eye teeth for, and not a drop of water in sight. It's another world, Sara. You ought to see it.

SARA: With you?

WAYNE: Well, the thought had crossed my mind. That's why I came back. Maybe three years out of 65 isn't such a big deal as three years out of 15.

SARA: But maybe 50 years is.

WAYNE: Maybe. Maybe not. Isn't it worth taking a chance? I'm not asking you to sell your house. Just give me some time. Come explore my world. A month, a couple of weeks. Let's find out how much difference 50 years makes.

SARA: And maybe in 50 years this old town has gotten bigger and a little bit better. Maybe it's a new town that needs exploring. (Pause.) I could put you up for a while.

WAYNE: Well, now, that would give the church folks some gossip.

SARA: These folks know me, they won't say much. Not that it seems to matter anymore. Seems like only yesterday you would have done darn near anything for a kiss from me, and here I am offering to let you stay in my house.

Pause.

WAYNE: Now that is a tempting offer. You always were a tempting woman, Sara.

SARA: Well, I don't know how much temptation is left in these old bones, but there's still swings in the park and orange juice on Main Street.

WAYNE: Oh lord, Sara. I can almost taste it.

SARA: So you'll stay?

WAYNE: Well...

SARA: Come on, call back a little of the daring young man I used to know and give me and this town another try. I think we might be worth it.

> Pause. He moves away from her.

WAYNE: Oh, lands, Sara, you do make it hard on a man. You hold yourself out like an angel holding out her arms, but your feet are glued to the kitchen floor. If we could fly away, I'd grab on in an instant. But you tie yourself down to this town like tobacco leaves tied to a curing stick. I'm very flattered, Sara, really. Fifty years ago I would have been excited by the thought of just sleeping under the same roof with you. But that was 50 years ago. I ran from this town once, I don't intend to come back. Much as you make me want to. Guess I shouldn't have come this time. I was just too curious. I hoped you and I..., well, I just wondered if there were any loose ends I needed to tie up.

SARA: Just me, looks like.

WAYNE: Not much of a reunion.

> He takes a flower out of the centerpiece and gives it to SARA.

SARA: Not what I expected anyway.

WAYNE: Sorry to disappoint you.

SARA: No, not disappointed. Surprised. Taken aback. Life was not kind to the class of 1940. I guess I just never thought you and I would be the survivors, or that we would be so far apart.

WAYNE: I loved you, you know. But you were always stuck to this town.

SARA: I loved you, but you were always headed off somewhere I didn't want to go.

WAYNE: How things change.

SARA: Yes.

> The lights fade.

SCENE TWO—GOD

> AT RISE we see a desk, chair, telephone on desk, etc. "Take Care of Business, Mr. Businessman" by Ray Stevens is heard in the background. In the chair sits MAC, older businessman type, talking on the phone. The music ends.

MAC: Yeah, yeah. No, that's not acceptable; Thirty percent or it's no deal. OK, OK, I can handle that. You just handle your end. OK, OK, give me the specs.

> GOD enters from the opposite side that MAC is looking. She is a very sexy woman in a very sexy dress, etc. MAC does not notice her at first.

MAC: OK, got it. Let's cut that a sixteenth. Have you filed the notice yet? Good, wait until the last minute, just before the office closes. (Sensing something, he looks around.) What the hell? How did you get... Uh, I'll call you back, Harry. Somebody just came in the office. Yeah, soon as I can. (Hangs up.) Can I help you?

GOD: I need to talk to you.

MAC: Well, I usually enjoy talking to a beautiful woman, but I'm right in the middle of some important business. Could you check with Mabel, my secretary, and see when I've got some time? I guess she just stepped away from her desk for a minute.

GOD: No, she's there.

MAC: Then how did you get in? I mean, she usually would buzz me and let me know someone was waiting.

GOD: I didn't exactly come through the door.

MAC: What? I mean, who are you? What do you want? We haven't met; I'd remember you, that's for sure.

GOD: Why thank you. You might have heard of me. I'm God, and I need to talk to you.

MAC: Excuse me, you're who?

GOD: God. Yahweh, Allah, The Supreme Deity.

MAC: Yeah, right. Let's just step out into the outer office and Mabel will take care of you.

GOD: I don't expect you to believe me.

MAC: Well, let's just say you don't exactly look like any god I ever heard off.

GOD: I was feeling a little feminine today. Tomorrow I may look like Arnold Schwarzenegger. On Saturdays I look like George Burns. That's usually good for a laugh.

MAC: Lady, you look more like God's wet dream than anything else.

GOD: Well, you know what I always say, if you've got it, flaunt it. And I'm God; if I want it, I've got it.

MAC: No kidding.

GOD: I'm God, OK? I can look like anything I want. You think I would choose to look like, maybe, Mother Teresa?

MAC: Uh, Right. Uh, just let me give Mabel a little call, tell her to hold my calls so we can talk.

GOD: Not necessary.

MAC: Huh?

GOD: Your phone isn't going to ring. We won't be disturbed. And even if you yell, Mabel won't hear you. I'm not crazy, Mac. I'm God.

MAC: Sure. I believe you. No problem. You're God. So, uh, what's up, God?

GOD: You're going to take some persuading. OK, I expected that. OK, OK, uh, you're thinking it's a pity such a hot pair of hooters are hooked to a brain whose wiring shorted out.

MAC: Well, you don't exactly have to be omniscient to figure that out.

GOD: You have a mole right at the base of your penis. Usually it's no problem, but you've had two other moles turn into carcinomas, so every year your doctor has to check it during your physical and it embarrasses you when he asks you to move your penis so he can get a good look at the mole.

MAC: OK, so you've seen my medical records. That's illegal but not divine.

GOD: You had sex with Mary Jo Anderson May 18, 1938. She was only 17. You got her pregnant, she went for an abortion and died on the operating table of an illegal abortion mill.

MAC: Hey, now wait a minute!

GOD: Don't try to deny it.

MAC: Now look here. I was not the only guy to have sex with Mary Jo. And I didn't know she was going to get an abortion. She did that on her own.

GOD: But you were the father.

MAC: You don't know that. I certainly don't. Nobody knew who the father was.

GOD: Oh yes, I do.

MAC: Well, I had no way of knowing. There were at least two other...

GOD: In 1957, you "persuaded" a banker, one of your old army buddies, in a very private conversation, to deny a loan to Herbert J. Ross, who owned a used car lot that was in direct competition with you. Within three months Mr. Ross was bankrupt. The day after he filed the bankruptcy papers, he put a 35 automatic in his mouth and tried to see how many times he could pull the trigger. Actually managed to pull the trigger twice. You bought out his inventory at ten cents on the dollar, used the profit to open a new car dealership, and just kept branching out from there. Stocks, bonds, real estate, insurance, light manufacturing. All that from cutting somebody else out.

MAC: It was all legal. And I never told him to kill himself. That was his idea. This is business. You fail, you just learn your lessons, get a new business, and start all over, not try to eat bullets. People tried to pull the same stuff on me.

GOD: But you were too smart.

MAC: Obviously not as smart as the detective you've got working for you.

GOD: Ah, yes. Last night you dreamed about having anal sex with Mabel, though I assure you, she does not like anal sex. When you were nine, you stole some bubble gum from Hansen's Grocery on the corner and got away with it because you put it in your brother's bookbag and he was the one who got caught. Would you like me to go on? (Pause. He does not answer.) You don't have any superstitions except walking under ladders, that you won't do. You haven't told anybody yet, but you are thinking about trading your BMW for a Volvo because you've noticed that your driving isn't a good as it used to be and you want a heavier, safer car, even if it isn't as powerful. When your mother died, you slipped your old Eagle Scout badge into her hand just before they closed the casket because it was the thing that had made her most proud of you. Still want more? When you were …

MAC: Stop. (Pause.) I still don't know who you are, but no detective is that good.

GOD: Well, that's progress.

MAC: OK, somehow you've got me pegged. That doesn't prove you're God. You want me to believe you're God, do a miracle or something.

GOD: Oh, I don't do miracles anymore. They never convince anybody over the long haul. Never really did any good at all. Most I ever got from doing miracles was six weeks in Vegas subbing for Sigfred and Roy. Give me a break here, I read your mind, I tell you your dreams, I tell you secrets only you know; what do you want? I'm not going to drop a magnitude 8 earthquake on downtown just to make you feel better.

MAC: OK, OK, let's just say you're God, or an angel, or the devil. The devil I might believe. You look more like something the devil would cook up, that's for sure.

GOD: Am I that tempting?

MAC: I'm not Faustus, lady. You're hot, but you're not that hot.

GOD: Well, some self-control, how encouraging. If somewhat disappointing.

MAC: I don't think God would be so into sex. You must be the devil.

GOD: Hey, I made sex. It was my idea, remember? It was Paul and Augustine that got it all screwed up. Man, were they in therapy like forever when I got hold of them.

MAC: Look, I'm not a bible-thumper, I'm a businessman. You want to argue theology, call the Pope.

GOD: Believe me, I tried. Man wouldn't listen. Just kept saying all those Hail Mary's. I think I scared him. I finally figured out I needed a business person, somebody who knows how to get things done. So, I start looking around and you seem to fit the bill. A borderline case. A couple of major black marks, but no real evil, some good things, but not anywhere near a saint. Someone who's older, who's getting close to, well, let's just say a man who might be interested in negotiating something, given the circumstances.

MAC: Oh really? So, get to the point; what do you want with me? I got a big deal about to go through.

GOD: Oh yes, the almighty bottom line. I keep my books a little differently.

MAC: So?

GOD: Take care of business, Mr. Businessman, while you can.

MAC: What's that supposed to mean?

GOD: I'm giving you a chance to balance out your account in my ledger book. To date you owe a modicum of faith and a measure of works. Consider this a margin call before the exchange closes.

MAC: Are you saying I'm going to die?

GOD: Of course you are. Everybody dies. That's part of the deal.

MAC: I mean soon.

GOD: Define soon. I always have trouble with time. That's what I get for being eternal.

MAC: Say, this year.

GOD: What's a year? Once around the sun? Who says the planet will make it round again. Tomorrow and tomorrow and tomorrow, who knows? Your heart will beat until it stops. Why worry over details? Look at the big picture, isn't that what you say? Some days the market is up, some days it's down. Isn't it better to invest for the long term?

MAC: Invest in what?

GOD: You believe in God?

MAC: I guess there is one. You, the jury is still out.

GOD: You used to believe. That time in France...

MAC: There are no atheists in foxholes.

GOD: Or charging machine gun nests?

MAC: Dumbest thing I ever did.

GOD: You saved your buddies.

MAC: Most of them died anyway. There were a lot more machine guns in France. I got a Silver Star, a Purple Heart, a ticket home, and a leg that hurts to this day.

GOD: But I was real to you then.

MAC: I believed in some old man with a white beard who kick-started the universe and saved the good guys in the end. Not Miss Universe with half her boobs hanging out.

GOD: Hey, I'm flexible. Now you're not even into old men.

MAC: Herbert Ross was a good guy. The good guys lost. You didn't keep your end of the bargain.

GOD: That's what you thought the deal was. That wasn't the deal.

MAC: So what is the deal?

GOD: Change your will.

MAC: What?

GOD: Your wife is dead, your kids have got more than enough as it is. You don't even like your son, he's too much like you. You can leave them some, but I need some for other things.

MAC: Such as?

GOD: There's a hospice down on 5th Street. The food bank, a shelter for homeless kids. Don't break up the businesses, just leave them shares, in trust, an endowment they can keep getting income from. I don't like asking this, you know. But things have changed. The little people can't do it all anymore. I have to go where the money is.

MAC: So what's in it for me?

GOD: What do you care, you'd be dead. You really can't take it with you, you know.

MAC: You said this was a deal, balancing accounts.

GOD: Let's just say it might cover some debts owed to Mary Jo and Herbert and a couple of others I could name.

MAC: Don't put those on my head. I had nothing to do with...

GOD: It was just business.

MAC: Herbert, yes. Mary Jo, well, she was that kind of girl.

GOD: Oh. You mean a loose woman? The kind that lets just anybody love her? Gives herself up for other people? Maybe even dies to save your hide? A woman like me?

MAC: No, that's not what I mean!

GOD: So what do you mean?

MAC: Look, I'm sorry she died. I liked her. I didn't want her to die, I didn't want her to have an abortion, I didn't even know she was pregnant till after she died, and I certainly didn't force her to have sex. I've never raped anybody, I've never murdered anybody, I've never even tried to hurt anybody since the war ended. I took advantage of some loopholes and some contacts, but I never, ever did anything illegal, so don't you or anybody else try to pin anything on me. I already give the maximum deduction to charity. There's no guilt trip here, lady. I'm an Eagle Scout, a war hero, a respected businessman, and I've done my civic duty. I was president of the chamber of commerce, and this community has more businesses and employment because of me, so don't run that routine. I'm not Simon Legree. I just live in the real world, not some fantasy land.

GOD: Maybe that's the problem.

MAC: What do you want? Money? You got a tax number? Where's my upside?

Pause.

GOD: OK. Let's deal. I want 80% of gross assets, in trusts. I'll give you a list of who gets what. Taxes split proportional to shares. Any challengers to will forfeit their share if, or should I say when, they lose. My lawyer goes over the will. I need it signed, sealed, and delivered by close of business Friday. That's what I want. Now what do you want? What is your price?

MAC: What have you got?

GOD: I'm God, I've got it all. Anything you want.

MAC: Why by Friday?

GOD: Maybe there's a deadline.

MAC: I don't like the sound of that.

GOD: So maybe you think I am God?

MAC: Maybe I think you know things. Somehow. But I don't believe you can offer me anything I want. There are some things even God wouldn't sell. Not at any price.

GOD: Such as?

MAC: A first class ticket straight to heaven. Somebody else's soul. Herself.

GOD: Really? What an interesting theology. What if you're wrong? Which would you choose? Take your best shot, we'll negotiate from there.

MAC: What makes me think you can deliver?

GOD: Oh, I always keep my promises. After all, if you can't trust God,...

MAC: Yeah, sure.

GOD: You see, Mac, that's part of the deal. You have to have a little faith, you know.

MAC: Eighty percent of gross against the word of some broad who doesn't do miracles.

GOD: Call it an oral contract. And I am a miracle. We're all miracles. (Pause.) It's all on the line, Mac. It's put up or shut up time.

MAC: Is my mother in heaven?

GOD: That's confidential information. Why do you want to know?

MAC: I think she is. But if not, maybe part of the deal...

GOD: Oh, good. That's smooth. Grab the sympathy points. Noble, self-sacrificing. If she is God, this should really tug her heartstrings. Good tactic. I like it.

MAC: Now who's the cynic.

GOD: Hey, you know everything, you get disappointed a lot. No, mothers and other kin are off the table. It's you and me, buddy boy.

MAC: Well, I guess all the money in the world won't do me any good if I'm going to die on Friday.

GOD: Too much money isn't good for you anyway, rots your teeth.

MAC: How about eternal life?

GOD: Hey, you get that anyway. Only question is where.

MAC: On earth. In an eternally young body.

GOD: Oh, good. You did read your mythology.

MAC: Living forever wouldn't be much fun if I just kept getting older, now would it? I've already got enough aches and pains and parts that don't work.

GOD: I can see how that could be a problem. However, much as I would like, that isn't possible. Oh, I could do it. But, it isn't kosher. Even Elijah had to take a ride to the great white way; he just got a limo.

MAC: So I'm supposed to trade 80% of gross for a ticket straight to heaven?

GOD: Hey, tickets to heaven are free. You just have to ask for one and take it when it comes. But, well, let's just say the money would be earnest money, a sign of your good faith. Showing your faith by your works, so to speak.

MAC: I see.

GOD: So, have we got a deal?

MAC: No.

GOD: No?

MAC: Not yet. For 80% I want the ticket, and you.

GOD: Me?

MAC: Let's just say I want to love my God with all my heart and all my soul and all my body.

GOD: Now this is getting interesting. Anybody ever tell you you are a dirty old man?

MAC: All the time. It's like business, all they can do is turn you down. But if you don't ask...

GOD: Ask and you shall receive, seek and you shall find. That's what the Bible says anyway. And the Gates of Heaven shall be open to you...

MAC: Whoa. I want it in advance. A down payment, while I'm still alive to enjoy it. I'm not sure what the rules are up there. Maybe sex isn't the same.

GOD: Maybe it's better.

MAC: Maybe I want to hedge my investments.

GOD: 70% of gross and just the ticket.

MAC: All or nothing.

GOD: Didn't I write somewhere that you shouldn't tempt the Lord, your God?

MAC: Maybe you should go talk to Ted Turner or Bill Gates. They've got more than I do.

GOD: Oh, they're on the list, when their time comes. I just wanted to start small and work my way up.

MAC: You know where the door is, if you need it.

GOD: No, I don't need it. And no, I don't sell myself. Love is a gift, not a prize. You have to give yourself to me, and I give myself to you. It's a relationship, not a deal. No codicils allowed. So, I guess we don't have a deal after all.

MAC: I guess not.

GOD: Well, see you around.

MAC: That's it? No counter-offers?

GOD: Somehow I don't think I'm cut out for business. I'm going to have to go reassess my position. This free enterprise may not be all the Republicans claim. I did like meeting you though. Sometimes being leered at a little does my old heart good. See you around.

MAC: Wait. You mentioned something about a free ticket.

GOD: Federal Express. Special Saturday delivery, right to your home. All you have to do is open the envelop.

MAC: And that's it?

GOD: That's it.

MAC: I see. (Pause.) You know, I'm seeing my lawyer later this afternoon anyway. Maybe I might like to make a few adjustments, a little more here, a little less there. No need to concern yourself with the details. Just an aroused concern for my fellow man, shall we say.

GOD: We are always grateful for any good will.

MAC: Perhaps you can join me for dinner tonight. Purely social, of course. Talk of business forbidden.

GOD: That might be interesting.

MAC: Shall we say seven? Shall I pick you up?

GOD: Oh, that won't be necessary. I'll just drop in, so to speak.

MAC: So to speak.

>   The phone rings.

GOD: That would be for you. Nobody knows I'm here. You better get it, you don't have much time. You do make being God interesting. See you at seven.

>   GOD exits. The phone keeps ringing. The lights fade.

SCENE THREE—OLD FRIENDS

    AT RISE we see a park bench in the center of an empty stage. "Old Friends," by Paul Simon, is heard in the background. A wind seems to blow across the stage. An OLD MAN enters, walks around the stage as if waiting for someone, then finally sits on the bench as the song ends. There is a long pause. The music ends.

OLD MAN: (Sings) In 18 and 14 we took a little trip, along with Col. Jackson down the mighty Mississip, we took a little bacon and we took a little beans...Green grow the lilacs and so does the rue... (Speaks) Bill?... (Sings) Sometimes I feel like a motherless child, sometimes I feel like a motherless...Oh, the great speckled bird of the bible...(Speaks) Down by the stream, Bill and I... (Sings) Amazing Grace, how sweet.... (Speaks) In 1943, August 7, 1943, it was so hot...that was the summer...and her breasts, I mean, her breasts...I mean.... (Sings) How much is that doggie in the window, the one with the waggly tail?.... (Speaks) Then the kids...Jim, then Tami, then Fred, poor Fred.... Bill and I, I mean, Bill and I went.... Ann, oh Ann. Bill? He's not coming, you fool.

    He stands and paces in front of the bench.

Damn blood pressure. Can't sit and think at the same time. One hundred and seventy three funerals. I can't believe it. One hundred and seventy three funerals. One hundred seventy three damn little cards. I put them in order, then I counted them. One hundred seventy three. Ann was number seventy-nine. Fred was number one hundred twenty three. I counted. If I had twenty dollars for each one, I could pay for my own funeral. Bill?

    He sits again.

Whew. Not as young as I used to be. As I was saying just yesterday, I'm not as young...Isn't it strange to be.... You know, Bill, sometimes I wish medicine tasted like candy. Chocolate candy, with the cream centers. Or chocolate covered cherries. Would it kill us? A little chocolate. Anne used to like chocolates. I brought her some our first date. Just a little box, it was the war. Maybe four pieces. Hard to get in those days. But it got her attention. (Sings) Candy kisses, wrapped in paper. (Speaks) Old songs. I like the old songs. I liked rock and roll too, at least the old rock and roll. Drove the kids up a wall. And the country music. Ann said I had no taste. I didn't like the hard rock though, all those amps in overdrive. Johnny Rivers, Paul Simon. Kids ended up liking jazz just to be different from me. But the old songs, I like those, Bill. The hymns, the real folk music...(Sings) Alas my love, you do me wrong...(Speaks) That's the real music of the people. Last night, for instance, the Lawrence Welk rerun, they played Silent Night, it was a Christmas show, now that's a folk song even though we know who wrote it. It's part of us now, it's not going to fade away just because somebody grows up or a generation dies out like we're doing. (Sings) There's be blue birds over the white cliffs of Dover. (Speaks) I tell you, Bill, some things will outlive even us. Bill? Bill, where'd you go? You're not taking a leak behind a tree again are you? Bill? This is a park, for god's sake. Bill?

He gets up and starts looking for Bill.

Bill? Oh, yeah. He hasn't come yet. Getting a little fuzzy around the edges sometime. Some days I'm fine. Most days, actually. Then something will happen, and I'm off on a tangent for a while. Like counting all those funeral cards, why in the world would I do that? Stupid thing to do. Like when Fred died. I was fine when Ann died. All broke up of course, but the mind was clear as a bell. But when Fred died, that seemed to take something. Losing a son... I just couldn't seem to go in a straight line after that. I'd be talking about one thing and suddenly be off hiking down some railroad track in France like the war was yesterday. Bill noticed it. Said it scared him about me, like I was getting Alzheimer's or something. But I still remember yesterday, so it's not Alzheimer's. Just yesterday, or was it the day before, I was sitting here on this bench telling Bill about the time Tami fell in the poison ivy and we had to practically bathe her in calamine lotion for a week. We were right here, it was a little cloudy and the sunset got as red as an apple, hanging there with the trees like skeletons sticking up in front of it and Bill saying ain't that something, and that was just yesterday so it ain't Alzheimer's or even senility because I know my address and phone number, I know my name and my age and where I was born and what unit I was in the army and every little village we fought in and the name of every guy who bought the farm while in my squad and all my kids' birthdays and even Ann's birthday and I don't even need to remember that anymore so I'm not senile, I just get a little fuzzy around the edges when something happens like today, but I can't remember what happened today to make me where I can't remember. Damn it, where is Bill? He could tell me. He's always here by now.

Pause. He sits on the bench again.

(Sings) It's a long way to Tipperary, it's a long way to go...When Johnny comes marching home again, hurrah, hurrah...My wild Irish Rose, the sweetest flower that grows...Yesterday, all my troubles seemed so far away, now it looks....I can't be contented with yesterday's glory, I can't live on promises winter to spring, today is my moment and now is my story, I'll laugh and I'll cry and I'll sing. Today while the blossoms still cling to the vine, I'll...(speaks) Bill?...(Sings) A million tomorrows shall all pass away, ere I forget...(Speaks) Bill? Bill? Bill?

The lights fade. End of ACT I.

ACT II

SCENE ONE—ONE MORE SPARROW

AT RISE we see a cemetery, one fresh grave with flowers, no headstone. Other graves with headstones, a few vacant spaces. "Will The Circle Be Unbroken" is heard in the background. It is early afternoon, the present. TOM, 40's, chubby, stands by the new grave. He wears a suit and tie, having been to the funeral that morning. After a moment, ELLEN, mid-20's, beautiful, enters, carrying a thermos bottle. She is dressed in jeans and a sweatshirt but is still beautiful. She wanders among the graves, reading the headstones as if looking for one in particular. She finds the spot she is looking for, one of the vacant spaces, and stands looking at it for a long moment. She notices TOM, and crosses to the new grave. She stands silent for another moment. The music ends.

ELLEN: Is this Mr. Wayne?

TOM: Yes.

ELLEN: I heard he died.

TOM: Yes.

ELLEN: You must be his son.

TOM: Yes.

ELLEN: I'm sorry.

TOM: I've often regretted being his son myself.

ELLEN: No, I meant I'm sorry he died.

TOM: You didn't know my father, did you?

ELLEN: No. I mean, I knew who he was. I saw him in church sometimes. Before he got so sick. He seemed like a nice old man.

TOM: He was seventy. Which seems old only to those under forty.

ELLEN: Oh. (Pause.) I take it you two did not get along.

TOM: He was not an easy man to get along with, but, I guess that doesn't matter now.

ELLEN: No, I guess not.

TOM: He just never quite understood that somebody could think differently than he did and not be wrong.

ELLEN: I can see how that might be a problem.

TOM: It wasn't a problem to him, of course, but it drove everybody else up a wall.

ELLEN: I guess.

TOM: If you finally understand everything when you get to heaven, he must be having the shock of his life.

ELLEN: A real eye-opener, eh?

TOM: You might say that. Death as an eye-opening experience.

ELLEN: We can only hope.

    Pause.

TOM: Can I help you?

ELLEN: What?

TOM: If you didn't know my father, is there some other way I can help you?

ELLEN: Oh. (Pause.) Maybe. I'm not sure.

TOM: Yes?

ELLEN: I came here to look at my grave.

    TOM looks at her.

ELLEN: There. Next row, two down. The family plot. Which my doctor says I will soon be inhabiting. No, wrong word. You don't inhabit a grave. That's like saying you live in a grave. What's the right term?

TOM: You lie in a grave. You are laid to rest, so you lie in a grave. All laid out.

ELLEN: Well, that gives getting laid a whole new meaning, doesn't it.

TOM: Not really. In Elizabethan England sexual intercourse was called the "little death." They thought having an orgasm shortened your life by one day. Not very scientific, but very poetic. The idea entered the language by way of Shakespeare and the other Elizabethan poets.

ELLEN: Is that where "dying in your arms" comes from?

TOM: Possibly.

ELLEN: Death, the ultimate orgasm. Well, that's a new point of view. I kind of like that concept. Gives me something to look forward to. And I just wanted to see what kind of flowers I'd be fertilizing.

TOM: None. The caskets are watertight. It's the law. Have to keep your germs out of the water supply.

ELLEN: So I'll be no help to the worms either.

TOM: No. (Pause.) If you're looking to help something, you could donate your body to science.

ELLEN: Oh, you think some medical student would love to see this body stretched out naked on an autopsy table.

TOM: If it was a guy, he wouldn't have the heart to cut you open. Some female would have to do it. You could donate your organs. Help somebody else live.

ELLEN: By the time what I got is through with my organs, nobody is going to want them. All they're going to be able to do with me is shut me in a box and drop me in the cold, cold ground.

TOM: AIDS?

ELLEN: I wish. Then I might at least have a few years left. No, I'm dying the old fashioned way, cancer of just about everything. (Pause.) The funeral was this morning?

TOM: Yes.

ELLEN: Why are you here? Shouldn't you be at home eating potato salad and thanking the mourners?

TOM: Yes. I came back...I came back because...because I don't know when I'll be back. It feels funny to have mixed feelings at a funeral.

ELLEN: How was the funeral?

TOM: Well, nobody fainted, a few people cried, and the pallbearers didn't drop the casket, so I guess it was an artistic success.

ELLEN: Did Rev. James officiate?

TOM: Yes.

ELLEN: How did he do? Would I want him to say mine?

TOM: He did OK, I guess. My father had picked out all the songs and ceremonies before he died. Even which scriptures to read. Didn't leave much room for a preacher to maneuver. Not that he could do much improvising anyway, he's too new to have known my father very well. (Pause.) Nobody knew my father very well.

ELLEN: Well, he doesn't know me very well either. (Pause.) Did he suffer much? Your father, not Rev. James.

TOM: He died as he lived, slowly, methodically, taking much longer to do it than anybody imagined was possible, making everybody else wait until he had done it perfectly, a death with no loose ends or shortcuts. He always sweated the small stuff and ignored the big stuff. He kept a record of the pennies he put in gumball machines, but was once five years late filing his tax return. He died a penny at a time, and was very late to his own funeral. It cost him a lot of pain and everybody else a lot of grief.

ELLEN: Oh.

TOM: And a bad time was had by all.

ELLEN: I'll try to keep that in mind. You seem to have leapfrogged through the grieving process.

TOM: Life will simpler without him. I feel sorry for him, for the way he lived, not that he died. I worry about my mother being alone. Death only solves problems for the dead.

ELLEN: We hope it does anyway.

TOM: Yes. Having much pain? The last few months were pretty rough for Dad.

ELLEN: Oh, I got along OK for a couple of months after the diagnosis. Then I took a turn for the worse, as the saying goes. Then the cure got worse than the disease. I stopped the medication, except for a few painkillers, a couple of months ago, took off for New York for a week. Saw the Statue of Liberty, World Trade Center, all the museums, three Broadway shows, two off-Broadway. Got as much entertainment and beauty as I could handle. Last night I was there I entered an amateur contest at a strip bar. Got disqualified for going too far.

TOM: I didn't think there was such a thing as too far in New York.

ELLEN: I didn't either. I had my picture taken at one of those glamour photo studios where they do your hair and makeup for you. Had the pictures framed for my parents. I looked pretty good.

TOM: I'm sure you did.

ELLEN: I made a videotape for them. A last goodbye they will get after I'm gone. Then I read War and Peace. I can't do much but sit around and read now. Read the Diary of Anne Frank, lot of other stuff I should have read years ago. About a week ago I stopped reading and started watching Marx Brothers movies over and over. Harpo makes me cry every time he plays the harp. (Pause.) I made a will. A Living Will too. No resuscitation or artificial life support. My father had a yelling, screaming fit when he found out about that. It took him hours to understand that he couldn't ground me or take away my car keys and force me to tear it up.

TOM: So, all the loose ends are tied up. Nice neat little package all ready to go in the mail.

ELLEN: Federal Express, overnight delivery. I bought a book about poisons. I am not overly fond of pain. Thought I'd explore my options, as they say. Know any good ways to die?

TOM: Not personally.

ELLEN: No, I mean...

TOM: No. A well-placed bullet in the brain should be a quick way to die. Carbon-monoxide is supposedly a painless way to die. Fighting for a good cause is a noble way to die. Dying in your sleep is a quiet way to die. Having a massive heart attack while having sex with three other people on your hundredth birthday is probably the best way to die. But there is no good way to die.

ELLEN: Carbon-monoxide, that's what that doctor in Michigan with the death machine uses, isn't it?

TOM: Which are you afraid of, dying or death?

ELLEN: What?

TOM: "To sleep, perchance to dream. Aye, there's the rub. Who knows what dreams may come when we have shuffled off this mortal coil."

ELLEN: Hamlet, right?

TOM: Yes.

ELLEN: You an English professor?

TOM: Guilty as charged. Elizabethan English, to be precise. The worst kind of English professor known to man.

ELLEN: Don't you believe in heaven?

TOM: I'm not dying.

ELLEN: Yes you are. We're all dying, Mister. Some of us just know when. But we all end up here.

TOM: Touche'.

> She lies down on one of the old graves, crossing her arms over her chest.

ELLEN: Try one on for size. One size fits all.

TOM: They don't cross your arms like that anymore. Down by your side, or one hand on top of the other on your stomach.

ELLEN: Like this?

TOM: Something like that. Depends on the embalmer.

> She tries various positions, then finally sits up, unsatisfied.

ELLEN: I never could get comfortable that way. Not that it makes any difference.

TOM: You can specify your position if you leave it in writing.

ELLEN: What about one hand on my crotch and the other on my breast.

TOM: Only if your next of kin has a great sense of humor. And the casket is kept closed. No funeral director is going to let the dead jerk off in their viewing room. Not to mention what Rev. James would say.

> She stands up.

ELLEN: Takes all the fun out of dying, doesn't it?

TOM: No fun at all.

ELLEN: How fast does a body decay?

TOM: It depends on how tight the casket is sealed. If it's air-tight, it takes years. Bones and hair could last for centuries. Let bugs and water get in, few years all you have is a grease spot.

ELLEN: That's what I like, a straight answer. Thank you. Ellen, in a few years you will be a grease spot. Greasy kid stuff.

TOM: Looking for sympathy?

ELLEN: Lord, no. I'm sick of sympathy. Makes me barf. After the drugs I'm all barfed out. Besides, I'm beginning to like it out here. It's usually quiet, the grass is soft. Lots of stars at night. Not all that bad. I just might go ahead and move in.

TOM: That's not funny.

> Pause.

ELLEN: It's the pain that scares me. Losing control of my body. Shitting and not even knowing it. I don't want that. I don't want to lie in some bed, too weak to move, needles in both arms, tubes sticking into my nose and bladder, wearing a diaper, staring at the ceiling, praying for another shot of painkiller that never does the whole job. I don't want that.

TOM: I don't blame you.

ELLEN: I been around long enough to know heaven isn't angels and harps, and hell isn't fire and brimstone, but I figure there is something else, beyond. I don't have much control over that though. I've done what I've done; I believe what I believe. It's the ferry ride to the other side that scares me. (Pause.) It was cancer?

TOM: Dad? Yes. Metastasized renal cell carcinoma, to be precise. Kidney, pleura, liver, then lungs. It was probably in his little toe before it was over with.

ELLEN: You were there at the end?

TOM: Yes. Mom and I. He just stopped breathing. He had barely done that the past couple of weeks.

ELLEN: No last words?

TOM: He never had much to say to us.

ELLEN: You really didn't get along, did you?

TOM: I loved my father. I did not like him. As far as I know, nobody liked my father. Even my mother didn't like my father, and she married him. I guess she must have liked him once, but that must have been long before I was born. You could love him, sometimes even understand him, but not like him. He was not a man who could be liked.

ELLEN: So, why are you here? He's in the ground; you've done your duty. Why stay?

TOM: I don't know. (Pause.) He lived seventy years, but as far as I know, he never enjoyed any of it. I felt sorry for him. I am trying to find a way never to be like him. But when I speak, I hear his voice in my mouth. I hear his silences between my words. Nobody came to his funeral except Mom's relatives and friends. His relatives are old and far away, and there were no friends. I look at him, and I see myself, and I hate it. (Pause.) In the movie "All That Jazz" death was a beautiful, bare-breasted woman dressed in white, a wonderful new lover full of promise. I hope that's what death looked like to my father. He needed something like that.

ELLEN: A bare-breasted woman in white, eh?

TOM: According to Bob Fosse, the director.

ELLEN: Well, that's OK for your father and you, but it doesn't do much for me.

TOM: What would you like, a knight in shining armor on a big white horse?

ELLEN: No, just a man, a strong man with nice firm muscles to pick me up in his arms like a baby and carry me through the long, white tunnel to a soft, warm place where we sit and wait for my grandparents to die. Then Gramps can hold me, and we can stay together until the others join us. A soft, warm place.

TOM: Sounds like I want a naked whore and you want a Sealy Posturpedic with an electric blanket.

ELLEN: And a teddy bear. I want my teddy bear. A strong man, Gramps, my teddy bear, and an electric blanket.

TOM: I hope you get it.

>   Pause.

ELLEN: You know, one of the weird things about dying young is that nobody you know is going to be on the other side waiting for you.

TOM: A opportunity to make new friends.

ELLEN: Expand my horizons.

TOM: New experiences.

ELLEN: New sights, new sounds, new tastes, new smells. Do you eat in heaven? Can you eat all you want and not get fat?

TOM: Jesus ate some honey after he was resurrected. Other than that, the theological record is rather silent on the culinary delights of the departed.

ELLEN: Bible says you're not married in heaven either. Wonder if that means you can screw around.

TOM: Probably wrong question to ask. It's probably so different we don't even know which questions to ask.

    Pause.

ELLEN: A bare-breasted woman in white.

TOM: According to Bob Fosse. Probably different for everybody.

ELLEN: Do you mind talking about all this?

TOM: Because I just buried my father? Maybe talking helps.

ELLEN: People die every day, by the thousands. Sometimes it's us. Just routine.

TOM: Part of life. Always seems to come as a surprise though. I don't understand why. We're all born and we all die. One of the few things we all actually have in common. Mohammed died, Buddha died, even Jesus died, at least temporarily. But it's still a surprise when it's us.

ELLEN: It's getting cold.

TOM: The sun is starting to go down.

ELLEN: The sunset of our lives. How cliché.

TOM: Would you like my coat?

ELLEN: What, so that I don't catch my death? No, I'm OK. At least as OK as I get. Not that it matters. Maybe I should get used to being cold.

TOM: Do not go gentle into that good night. Rage, rage against the dying of the light.

ELLEN: Dylan Thomas.

TOM: Very good.

ELLEN: I only know the famous ones. (Pause.) What if I didn't want to rage. What if I wanted to go gently?

TOM: What do you mean?

ELLEN: Take some pills or something. I could start to lose it anytime. A few more weeks at most. I don't want to wait too long. I just want somebody to hold my hand. Somebody that's not freaking out. My mother is a basket case as it is. She would have a fit if she knew where I was. My father is in deep denial; keeps saying "don't worry, they'll find a cure soon." He would drag this out as long as possible, praying for a miracle while I lie there out of my head with pain. I don't want to go that way.

TOM: No husband, I take it.

ELLEN: Personally, I was a slut. Men don't marry sluts.

TOM: Oh.

ELLEN: I always thought the best way to get to know an interesting man was to screw him. I got to know a lot of interesting men. Never found one so interesting that I wanted to keep screwing him.

TOM: I see. You regret it now?

ELLEN: No. I had a lot of fun. And I've got a lot of very good friends. At least I had a lot of friends. Now it seems nobody wants to get in touching distance, not to mention in bed. Anticipatory necrophilia, I guess. No, that would mean they want to screw me.

TOM: Anticipatory necrophilia aversion.

ELLEN: I guess. Anyway, I'm too alive for the ones that like 'em dead, and too dead for the ones that like 'em alive. And nobody wants to walk death to the grave.

TOM: In the Medieval morality play, "Everyman," only "Good Works" goes with Everyman to the grave. Very Catholic. Protestant version would have "Faith" walk the final mile. I guess both are pretty cold comfort compared to a pair of warm arms. But, you're really always alone anyway. From the moment they cut the cord, you're alone. Life, death, you're alone.

ELLEN: Boy, cheer me up, why don't you.

TOM: Wouldn't want you to bust a gut laughing.

ELLEN: Now wouldn't that do me in.

TOM: I'd have to carry you away.

ELLEN: I'm dying up here and can't get a laugh if my life depended on it.

TOM: Maybe it does. At least for a while.

>   Pause.

ELLEN: What's your name?

TOM: Tom.

ELLEN: Ellen. You're an unusual man, Tom.

TOM: There's no need to be polite about it.

ELLEN: You're a weird man, Tom.

TOM: Thank you. Probably just my reaction to a weird day.

ELLEN: Nothing throws you though, cool as a cucumber, no matter what.

TOM: Mr. Spock, that's me. Or so I'm told.

ELLEN: Spock?

TOM: From Star Trek, the half-human, half-Vulcan with no emotions, just logic. It's not a new accusation. I don't seem to react at others do. I don't know why. I just seem to see everything from a distance. My father died. Well, he was supposed to. He was old and had cancer; what else should happen? It's not like death is bad. What if nobody died? We would have overpopulated this planet long before now. More likely we'd still be in the trees. Death is how we change, evolve; the weak, unsuitable, or just unlucky, dying sooner, making way for those more adapted to the environment. Death is necessary. Death is good. Who wants to live forever? How much life can one person take? Even if you didn't just keep getting older and older, sooner or later you would have done everything there was to do, felt every emotion there was to feel, and you'd end up callous and cold, an unfeeling heart of ice like me.

ELLEN: I didn't mean that. I just...

TOM: Forget it. I need to face a few ghosts today.

ELLEN: It's just that most people freak out when I talk about dying.

TOM: You break a taboo. Speak of the devil and up he pops. You're supposed to see the true value of life, live one day at a time, savor each instant, embrace life, and leave us words of deep wisdom about how to live a life of meaning and joy, not talk about poisons or the flowers you might fertilize. You remind us of our own mortality, and we don't like it.

ELLEN: Except you.

TOM: I am sated with thoughts of my own mortality. You can add no more, the bucket is full. We're staring death in the eye, and we can see the patterns on the retinas. We're so close we're getting cross-eyed, and that makes everything else look akilter.

ELLEN: You write poetry too, don't you?

TOM: It is required of English professors, part of the tenure evaluation. Fortunately, they only count the publications, not read the poems themselves. Mine are all bad. I'm sorry I let my iambic pentameter peak out.

ELLEN: That's OK. I kind of like the sound of looking "akilter." Maybe I've been akilter all my life.

TOM: It means slanted, out of line, not in proper order.

ELLEN: That's me OK. And coming to the end of the line, slanted or not. It would be nice to end my sentence with an exclamation point, not dribble off in ellipsis points. I'm just not sure I can face an exclamation point alone.

> Pause.

TOM: You know, in surfing you get points not only for how close to the break you ride, but also for how long you ride the wave.

ELLEN: Like your father.

TOM: My father tried to ride the sand dunes.

ELLEN: I've already got sand between my toes.

TOM: No man is an island, complete unto himself. Every man's death diminishes me.

ELLEN: Send not to ask for whom the bell tolls, it tolls for thee. I told you I'd been reading.

TOM: Very good.

ELLEN: Are you less of a person because you father died?

TOM: I am a different person because my father died.

ELLEN: Better or worse, all things considered?

TOM: All things considered,...maybe a little better. But my father was one of the negatives of life. He held it back, made it poorer. I bet you make life better.

ELLEN: I never quite seemed to find a reason to be here. I would like a chance to play the game a little more, but I don't have one. All I can do is improve my life by ending it. While it is still my life. While the memories I still have are mostly happy. While I still have memories. While the only tears are for what never was.

TOM: If you're asking my approval, you don't have it.

ELLEN: Last time I read the rules, I don't need your approval.

TOM: So what do you need?

ELLEN: I need someone to hold me. To be there when the lights go out.

TOM: That's your parents job.

ELLEN: Would you have wanted your father to hold you?

TOM: (Pause.) No. Not him.

ELLEN: Who?

TOM: My wife. My daughter.

ELLEN: You're a lucky man, Tom. I never got that far. I was a spring fling, a grope in the dark. There's nobody here but you.

TOM: You don't even know me.

ELLEN: You can be who I dream you to be. Nobody else can do that.

TOM: I'm not your knight on a white horse.

ELLEN: I can skip the horse. God knows I can skip the armor. I need a man whose heart is pure.

TOM: The Holy Grail is lost again, Ellen. And I'm not the man to find it. This is not my cup to drink.

ELLEN: You'll die too, one day, you know that.

TOM: I am beginning to understand that.

ELLEN: You'll want somebody to hold you then. Maybe you'll be lucky and your wife or daughter will be there. I hope so. Or maybe it will have to be a stranger, somebody who understands that even if we all face death alone we can still hold each other as we cross the river. Somebody who will stay with us till we reach the other shore. Because they know that they too someday will cross over. I think you might be that kind of man.

> ELLEN opens her thermos bottle and crosses to her gravesite,
> pours contents into a cup, and drinks some.

ELLEN: Now I lay me down to sleep. I pray the lord my soul to keep. When I die before I wake, I pray the lord my soul to take.

> TOM looks at her. She takes another drink.

ELLEN: Excuse me for not offering you some. I'm usually not that rude, but I doubt you would care for this. (She takes another drink.) Homemade poison. Surprisingly easy to find the ingredients, once you know what to look for. Supposedly painless, but not real fast acting. (Drains cup with one last swallow.) Tastes really lousy though. (Pause.) You know, I would really appreciate a hug right now.

> He comes to her and hugs her, then holds her in his arms as
> she weakens.

ELLEN: I think I need to lie down.

> They collapse to the ground slowly, with TOM holding ELLEN
> like a baby in his arms.

ELLEN: A beautiful, bare-breasted woman in white, eh?

TOM: For you, a strong young man with dark eyes who will pick you up in his arms and carry you to a bed with silk sheets where he will love you forever.

ELLEN: My luck, I'll get Woody Allen in a Motel 6.

TOM: Not you, first class all the way, Tom Cruise in a Hilton.

ELLEN: Sorry to put this on you. I just didn't want to be alone, you know?

TOM: Yes.

ELLEN: Thank you.

TOM: Thank you.

>He holds her gently as she slowly dies. When he is sure she is dead, he lays her gently on top of her grave, placing her hands by her side, straightening her legs. He stands and looks at her for a moment.

TOM: Oh hell.

>He puts one of her hands on her breasts, the other on her crotch.

TOM: They'll change it, of course, but you can have one last laugh. (Pause.) Goodby, Ellen. Good journey, and warm winds blow thee to thy rest. I'll look you up when I get to the other side. Take care.

>He stands silent for a moment, then exits. The lights slowly fade.

SCENE TWO—AFTER

> AT RISE we see an empty room, no decorations, no windows, no nothing except a few plain, wooden, straight-back chairs scattered randomly around the room. "When The Roll Is Called Up Yonder" is heard in the background. ALF sits in one of the chairs. He is an old man, dressed in a nice suit. He may have a cane. He sits unmoving for a long time. Finally, the one door opens and KIP enters. He is also an old man dressed in a suit, but he looks very different from ALF. He takes a step or two into the room and the door swings shut behind him. He looks around, looks at ALF, finally picks a chair and sits. Nobody moves for a long time. The music ends.

KIP: So.... Been dead before?

> ALF looks at KIP. Long pause.

ALF: Not that I know of.

KIP: I just wondered. I wasn't sure if that reincarnation thing, you know,...I'm new here.

ALF: You think I'm not? Do I look so much deader than you?

KIP: No, no. I was just hopping you might know...you know...

ALF: No, I don't know.

KIP: Not even where...?

ALF: No.

KIP: I mean, it doesn't look like..., or, you know, the other place.

ALF: It looks like a cheap set for "No Exit."

KIP: What?

ALF: "No Exit." The play. Three people trapped together in a room for eternity. Their hell.

KIP: I didn't get to the theatre much. I ran a little grocery. Open every night until nine. Mom and Pop store. Decent living, but no way to get rich. I enjoyed it though. Kept me busy, got to meet all kinds of people. Had the kids help out in the store when they got big enough. It kept them out of trouble and let me watch them grow up. That was good. You?

ALF: I was a college professor. What you would probably refer to as an egghead or some appellation like that. I spent most of my time reading old books and trying to enlighten students who considered Charles Schultz a theologian.

KIP: Oh. So you think this is....? I wasn't expecting...

ALF: I don't know what it is.

KIP: I wasn't a real religious person, you know, I tried to keep an open mind. But I tried to be honest and do right. I believed, in my own little way. I never thought I'd end up in..., you know.

ALF: I don't know what it is. I don't know where we are. I remember a severe chest pain, then a white light, then this room. I draw no conclusions.

KIP: Oh. Well, I'm pretty sure I'm dead. A semi full of watermelons losing its brakes and pinning you against a wall doesn't take many prisoners. No, I'm pretty sure I'm dead. I just can't figure out...here.

ALF: We have established that it does not conform to any of the popular conceptions of the afterlife.

KIP: Blast, man, this place would freak Billy Graham out.

ALF: Nevertheless, we appear to be here.

KIP: Have you tried to get out?

ALF: You try.

> KIP goes to the door and tries to open it but cannot. He knocks on it.

KIP: (Yelling) Anybody out there?

ALF: I never received any reply.

KIP: Damn. So, what do we do now?

ALF: Do?

KIP: Yes, do. I mean we have to do something, don't we?

ALF: It would appear obvious to me that "something" is exactly what we cannot do.

KIP: What?

ALF: We are dead. We are in a locked room with no windows. There is nothing in the room but a few chairs. I would suggest that our choices of action are standing, sitting, and lying on the floor.

KIP: Oh. I've never been much good at waiting. One reason I liked running a store, there was always something that needed doing. Doing nothing for eternity; I guess that could be hell. I'm not sure I could take that.

ALF: What are your options, committing suicide?

KIP: Huh? Oh, when I'm already.... Well, might be worth a shot, if things get bad enough. Couldn't hurt, as the saying goes.

ALF: Are you sure?

KIP: Well...

ALF: What if this is purgatory? What if this waiting is purging our souls. Killing yourself, or the equivalent thereof, might just move you down to a real hell.

KIP: You Catholic?

ALF: No. I'm just, as you say, keeping an open mind.

KIP: So, you're saying we should just wait and try to think good thoughts?

ALF: As far as I know, we should assume the lotus position and contemplate our navels while praying toward Mecca by shouting praise Jesus in Hebrew.

KIP: No need to get sarcastic.

ALF: No? Well, when the occasion does arise, don't hesitate to inform me.

KIP: I'll do that.

> KIP takes a chair and sits as far away from ALF as he can. There is a long pause.

KIP: The name is Kip, by the way. Walter Kipling, but everybody called me Kip......Just in case you ever need to know, you know.

> Pause.

ALF: Alfred Hill.

> Pause.

KIP: Well, Alf, uh, what did you teach in college?

ALF: Comparative religions.

KIP: Religion? Well now, you must feel like a fool.

ALF: Thank you for reminding me of my fallibility. It is comforting to me to know I face the prospect of enduring eternity with a gentleman of such empathy. I am attempting to console myself with the thought that everybody from Abraham to Buddha was just as mistaken.

KIP: So, nobody in all them religions said...this...

ALF: Hardly.

KIP: Well, what do you know. But you do think we're dead.

ALF: I think that would be a reasonable working hypothesis. Beyond that, I confess I am somewhat at a loss.

KIP: But if you had to guess...?

ALF: I once heard a physics professor discuss the end of the universe. He speculated that intelligence would spread throughout the universe in such a way that previously existing intelligences, namely human beings, would be recreated in order to help direct the collapse of the universe in such a way that intelligence itself would survive. In effect, we would become god and bring ourselves back to life. My point is that there are more ways of looking at the afterlife than contained in the religions traditions and more things in heaven and earth than the mind of man can comprehend.

KIP: Any chance you could put any of that in plain English?

ALF: Kip, old boy, I don't know beans. Until somebody else walks in that door, or the walls fly away, or fifty million angels appear dancing on the chairs, I am very humbled and very confused.

KIP: You think somebody else might come in?

ALF: Well, there are more chairs, but I wouldn't take that as conclusive.

KIP: Still....

> Pause. KIP circles the room as if looking for a secret door or a peephole or something, fails to find anything, then begins to pace.

ALF: If you get physically tired, please let me know.

KIP: Huh?

ALF: I was just wondering if you would get tired. Will we get tired, physically, if we exert ourselves? Will we get sleepy, or will the consolation of sleep be denied us?

KIP: You mean, you think we might not...be normal anymore?

ALF: Well, the lack of any sanitary facilities makes me hope that in at least one respect we won't be.

KIP: What...oh, no john.

ALF: Precisely. Though, I confess I have not yet felt the need. Nor hunger or thirst. That at least is biblical.

KIP: Yeah. You know, I think I might miss eating. I liked a good pizza...with anchovies. I liked pizza with anchovies. And ice cream. But not on pizza, I mean, you know... I could eat a quart at a sitting. Chocolate ripple.

ALF: I fear those pleasures of the flesh may be denied us. No desires, no pleasures, we may be as detached from the physical world as the Buddha himself. Nirvana as an empty room.

KIP: What about sex? I mean, will we get horny?

ALF: If you and I are to be the only two occupants, I confess I sincerely hope not.

KIP: Well, yeah, I mean, I was real straight myself, but, you know, I mean, this is just so different than what I expected, I don't know what to expect. It was just a question, you know, not a...

ALF: Yes.

KIP: You know, I really think we ought to try to get out of here. Nothing personal, but eternity in here just doesn't appeal to me. I can live without the angels and harps and streets of gold stuff, but I need something, you know,...something.

ALF: Very well, let us assume, for purposes of discussion, that we do want to leave this room. How?

KIP: How?....Well, we could break down the door.

ALF: Go ahead.

KIP: OK, OK.

>   KIP crosses to door, examines it carefully, pushes it a couple of times, kicks it twice, then bumps it with his shoulder halfheartedly.

KIP: Ow! Doesn't even budge.

ALF: And I take it we can forget about there being no pain in this heaven.

KIP: Yeah, you can forget about that one. We can get hurt, but not eat or have sex. So maybe this is hell. Damn. I thought I tried...I mean, I really thought...

ALF: Perhaps hell is a possibility we should more seriously consider.

KIP: You're saying we deserve to be in hell?.

ALF: Do you?

KIP: I didn't think so. Do you?

ALF: How does one decide who goes to hell? Shall we balance my good deeds against my bad? And what about my deeds done with good intentions that had undesired results? And what is good or bad, and who am I to say? Did Hitler think himself evil when he ordered the Holocaust? Or did he, in his own mind, think he was purifying the world of a great evil? And what makes me think I can discern the difference between good and evil more accurately? But perhaps it is faith that is the determining factor. In which case, how does one measure faith? And what is enough? Perhaps we are so different from God that we have no possibility of being able to determine how such a decision is made. Perhaps God is so different that every statement about God is both true and false....

KIP: Stop! Enough! Damned egghead. Did you ever kill anybody?

ALF: No. Not personally, anyway. Perhaps some corporate guilt associated with supporting the war in Vietnam. Maybe some guilt from not giving enough to charity...

KIP: OK, OK. Did you ever, personally, rape anybody?

ALF: No.

KIP: Molest any kids? Get anybody pregnant you weren't married to? Commit armed robbery? Beat anybody up after you got out of the sixth grade?

ALF: No. I suspect my most serious personal crime was boring my students to death.

KIP: That I believe.

ALF: Other than that, I led what most people would consider a very boring life. I was a faithful husband, a reasonable father, and an uninspired academic. I suspect that on whatever basis the assignment to eternal accommodations is made that I would fall clearly near the borderline. So if you expect to decide whether we are in heaven or hell based on my past life, I fear the evidence is inconclusive.

KIP: Great, just great. You're boring and I'm small potatoes.

ALF: I at least used to think that salvation did not correlate with socio-economic status.

KIP: What? Speak English.

ALF: I don't think being small potatoes gets you sent to hell.

KIP: Yeah, I guess not. Well, hell, I wasn't no saint either, but I don't think I did anything really bad. I tried not to anyway. I ran an honest store, no short-weighting, none of that stuff. Penny-ante poker, maybe a whore at the lodge conventions, and church only on the holidays. Not real bad, not real good. I sent my kids to church every Sunday, though. Raised them right. I don't know, I guess I just figured God would cut me a little slack. I was just, you know, a regular guy.

ALF: In plain words.

KIP: A whore's not really cheating, is it? I mean, I used condoms. It was only at conventions, you know, once a year, out of town. That's not too bad, is it? It was just, you know, a guy thing. I loved my wife, tried to do right by her. That's OK, isn't it?

ALF: I don't think I'm in a position to say.

KIP: I mean, I tried, I really tried. It's just, you know, you got to live too, be human once in awhile. Even you understand that don't you?

ALF: What do you mean, even me?

KIP: Well, being religious and all, studying all the time. You still had to, you know, let loose somehow, however people like you do it.

ALF: However people like me...?

KIP: You know, that think all the time and don't feel, don't...

ALF: I see. Well, unlike you, I was never of the opinion...I didn't believe God would ever cut me a little slack. I had to get it right. I started out as a Christian theologian, but studying the Old Testament led me to look at Judaism too, then the history of Christianity and its conflicts with Islam lead me to study Islam, and from there it was off to Hinduism, and Buddhism, and Taoism, and Confucianism, Shintoism, Bahai, Zoroastrianism and on and on. I wanted to know everything anybody had ever thought abut God. What did they all agree on? Anything? If they did, wouldn't that be sure to be right? I thought it was important to know. Perhaps I left humanity behind long before I got close to heaven. Perhaps that is my sin, that my belief was just an idea without a man behind it. Maybe that is worthy of hell.

KIP: You know, even when you make sense, I don't understand you.

ALF: I guess I tried to know God without ever looking inside myself. Maybe I cared more about doctrine than about the people who touched me every day.

KIP: Well, maybe. Still don't seem like a hanging offense though. I don't know, we still just seem like regular joes. Seem like to me that if we are in hell, so is almost everybody else.

> Pause. KIP walks around a little, sits, stands, sits again.

KIP: So what do we do?

ALF: Do? DO? We don't do anything! We're dead, we can't DO anything.

> Pause.

KIP: I can't accept that.

ALF: You can't accept it? You can't accept it? Well then, what in heaven or hell are you going to do about it?

KIP: I'm not sure yet. But you know the old saying, where there's life there's... (Long pause.) No. You don't have to have life to have hope. I don't care if this is heaven or hell or whatever. If there is anything here, and there is, then there has to be a god. And if there's a god, I got a shot. Somewhere there's a god, and this ain't all. I got to believe that. I got to.

ALF: God may not be as humane as you think. Nothing here seems to be what we think.

KIP: Look, you think what you want, and I'll think what I want. OK? I don't need any stuffed shirt telling me the facts of life, or death, or whatever, OK? If I want to believe, just let me believe!

ALF: Fine. Just don't expect me to agree with you.

KIP: Fine. Deal.

> The door opens. An Angel, very "gay," enters carrying a clipboard.

ANGEL: Oh, here we are. Sorry to have kept you gentlemen waiting so long, but there was a massacre in Africa and we got way behind. Now, let's see, which of you is Walter Kipling?

KIP: Uh, me. Kip Kipling.

ANGEL: Oh, isn't that cute. Let's see, you are assigned to Sector 409, Level Gamma, Grid coordinates 243 by 817. That's a little corner grocery and topless donut shop. You'll be the manager. You'll have an apartment over the store. Your wife will join you in, let's see, three years, two months, and twenty-seven days. She'll work in the store with you.

KIP: A topless donut shop?

ANGEL: You know, women, boobs, no shirt, no bra, they're the waitresses. Coffee, donuts, maybe some bagels. Use your initiative.

KIP: I'm going to run a topless donut shop? I must be in heaven.

ANGEL: Well, not really. Those topless waitress can be real bitchy, take it from me. They think just because they show their boobs, they're too good to wipe the counter. Well, let me tell you…Oh, you'll find out, it's all pretty much the same here. OK, take this paper, turn right, go down the hall to the end, and ask for Ralph. He'll give you your ID, credit card, keys to the store, and put you in a cab. You'll find an orientation book by the cash register. Read it, and then if you have any questions there's a hotline number to call. OK?

KIP: Uh, sure. Uh, nice meeting you, Alf. Maybe I'll see you around.

ALF: Somehow I doubt that.

KIP: Well, whatever. (To Angel) Uh, thanks.

ANGEL: Just doing my job. Good luck.

    KIP exits.

ANGEL: So, you must be Alfred Hill.

ALF: Yes. A topless donut shop?

ANGEL: Hey, each to their own, that's what I always say.

ALF: Yes, I expect you would say something like that.

ANGEL: Now, now, let's not be rude.

ALF: Young man, I have suffered too many surprises today to deal with much more. The very concept of the afterlife including a topless donut shop is simply the straw breaking the camel's back. Just tell me where to go, and I will go quietly, never daring to assert ever again that I know anything about religion.

ANGEL: Well, Mr. Hill, I'm sorry, but it isn't that simple.

ALF: Oh, no, not…

ANGEL: No, I don't mean that. You're going back.

ALF: Back?

ANGEL: Another life.

ALF: Oh, God, no.

ANGEL: 'fraid so.

ALF: Am I to be a cow? A dog? Some starving child?

ANGEL: Oh no, nothing like that. You're moving up. You'll be a bodhisattva.

ALF: A bodhisattva?

ANGEL: You know, somebody who puts off nirvana to go back and help others get to…

ALF: I know what a bodhisattva is. But I'm not Buddhist.

ANGEL: So, call it a saint.

ALF: Oh, please God, no, not a saint. Anything but that.

ANGEL: Sorry. God likes a little irony sometimes. Besides, it's a complement. Only the best get to go back, the ones that can be improved.

ALF: Oh God, no. It's not supposed to be this way. Nothing is what it's supposed to be.

ANGEL: It never is. Let's just say that this is your penance. A chance to help some people out. You had the head part pretty good, you just, you know, need a little more soul. Here, take this paper, go down the hall to the left until you have to turn again, take the left fork and go to the desk at the end of the hall. And, hey, enjoy it. You get to be a kid again.

ALF: I never liked being a kid. I hated it. Why do you think I read so much and turned into such a snob?

ANGEL: Well, this time I think you may find it fun. After all, third time's a charm.

ALF: Third time?

ANGEL: See, you learn something every day. OK, left, then left again. Don't want you to get lost in here. I've got to run; there's a war starting in Asia. Hey, it's a life. Get some good out of it.

>ANGEL hustles ALF out the door. The lights fade.

CURTAIN

Divergent Illusions

This is a full-length bill of absurd comic sketches about the differences in men's and women's illusions about sex and love. Some scenes are actually one-acts, while others are very brief and some have no words. It was produced by Koality Presentations in Atlanta in 2000, so not only my family but some of my friends from work or church actually came to see it. It had previously been done in a shortened form by Artists Repertory Theatre for the Orlando Fringe Festival in 1999. Several of the longer scenes have also been done at various theatres as one-act plays. For example, "DramaPlay" was done at the Neighborhood Playhouse in Atlanta in 1995 and at STAGE Theatre in Dallas in 1993. "Bed" was done by the Apprentice Company of the Alliance Theatre, under the direction of Brenda Bynum, as one of a bill of one-acts.

DIVERGENT ILLUSIONS

By David Davis

Member
All rights & privileges.

David Davis
100 Hunters Ridge Court
Roswell, GA 30076
daviddaviswriter@gmail.com

Copyright 1992 David Davis

CAST OF CHARACTERS

SIX ACTORS (MINIMUM) .... 2 Females, 4 Males

STAGE MANAGER .... Female

LIGHT OPERATOR .... Male

SETTINGS

The settings for the various scenes are described at the beginning of each scene. These are usually very simple and quickly changeable, so that changing the set is not a factor in setting the tempo of the show.

START

>AT RISE: A bare stage. Houselights are still up, the stage dark. The houselights fade, the stagelights come up. Nothing happens. The stage fades out, the house fades up. Pause. The houselights fade out, the stagelights fade up. Nothing happens. The stage fades out, the house fades up. Pause. A WOMAN (Stage Manager) enters from backstage.

WOMAN: Uh, excuse me. Excuse me.

>Houselights fade, stagelights up on WOMAN. She crosses to downstage.

WOMAN: Uh....... Uh...... Thank you.

>She exits. Lights stay up on stage for a few seconds, then fade. In the dark, a MAN's (Light Operator) voice is heard over the P.A. system

MAN: In the beginning there was confusion.

WOMAN: What are you doing?

>Light comes back up on stage.
>WOMAN crosses into it.

MAN: What's happening, babe?

WOMAN: We're having a little problem.

MAN: So I noticed.

WOMAN: The headsets aren't working. I can't call the cues.

MAN: Tell me about it.

WOMAN: You started without a cue.

MAN: It was past time. Weren't you ready?

WOMAN: No. The headsets aren't working.

MAN: Besides that, are you ready?

WOMAN: But without the communication system...

MAN: I can see.

WOMAN: But I couldn't...

MAN: So? It's just up and down, nothing fancy. Basic area lighting. Up, down, up, down. This ain't Broadway.

WOMAN: We have to be able to talk.

MAN: Why?

WOMAN: Why! That's what I'm here for. To communicate, to coordinate, help everybody.

MAN: Your job is to get the show on, not stand there boring the audience.

WOMAN: I know my job.

MAN: Then let's get on with it. Down for five, then curtain.

WOMAN: But...

> Lights fade to black for five count, then come back up.
> WOMAN is still there.

MAN: Now what?

WOMAN: You're missing the point.

MAN: Which is?

WOMAN: We have to communicate with each other.

MAN: We have to get things done, get this show on. Theatre was around long before radio headsets. Just start the show.

WOMAN: This isn't being fair to the audience. They're not getting what they paid for.

MAN: They certainly didn't pay to see you.

> Lights go to black.

MAN: Let me know when you're ready to start.

WOMAN: How? The headsets are out.

MAN: The monitor isn't. I hear you fine. Just say "ready, set, go," and I'll take it from there. You will see the light, believe me.

> Sound of footsteps. WOMAN is at side of stage shinning a flashlight at the lightbooth.

WOMAN: What about if I signal you? Can you see this?

MAN: Sure, I can see you in the dark, but in the light, probably not. But I don't need a signal. I know the show. I've got a script with all the cues written in. Just get the actors out here and let's get started for heaven's sake!

WOMAN: Bring the lights up and let's see.

MAN: Good God, Woman! Don't you understand? I don't need you now. Just start the show.

WOMAN: Just try it and see.

> She shines the flashlight at the booth. Suddenly every light in
> the theatre is on full. WOMAN has to shield her eyes.

MAN: Well?

WOMAN: Can you see the light?

MAN: No.

WOMAN: Not at all?

MAN: Looks like you're waving a stick at me.

WOMAN: Darn.

MAN: You're just going to have to trust me.

WOMAN: I can't.

MAN: Why not?

WOMAN: We've got to be able to talk.

MAN: You want to cancel the show?

WOMAN: No. Oh no.

MAN: Then name your poison.

WOMAN: I want to talk to you.

MAN: Not an option. (Pause.) Sky God to Earth Mother, are we doing this or not?

WOMAN: OK, OK, do it, do it!

MAN: And into the dark we go.

> Fade to black, hold for five count, fade up stagelights. Start play.

ANDROGYNY

Lights fade up on a bare stage. A piece of paper falls from the flies onto the stage. A MAN walks out from the wings, picks up the paper, reads it, takes a lighter from his pocket, burns the paper, and exits. He returns in a moment with a broom and dustpan and sweeps up the ashes of the paper. He exits. He returns again with a rag and gets down on his knees and cleans the stage where the ashes fell. Then he gets up and exits.

Pause.

A piece of paper falls from the flies onto the stage. A WOMAN walks out and picks it up. She reads the paper, tears it into strips, and eats it. She then takes off her dress or skirt and blouse and exits, leaving her clothes in a pile on the stage.

Pause.

Another piece of paper falls. Another MAN enters, picks up and reads the paper, takes off his shirt and pants, and puts on the woman's clothes. He then exits, leaving his clothes in a pile on the stage.

Pause.

A piece of paper falls from the flies. A SECOND WOMAN enters, picks up the paper, reads it, folds it up, and puts it in her bra. She then picks up the man's clothes and exits.

Pause.

A piece of paper falls from the flies. The two MEN run on from opposite sides and race to get the paper. The FIRST MAN gets the paper first, reads it, puts it in his pocket, hits the MAN IN WOMEN's clothes in the stomach, and exits. The SECOND MAN collapses to his knees from the blow, and crawls offstage.

Pause.

A piece of paper falls from the flies. The two WOMEN run onstage from opposite sides and race to get the paper. The WOMAN CARRYING THE MAN's clothes throws them at the other WOMAN, and gets the paper first. The other WOMAN puts on the men's clothes. The SECOND WOMAN reads the paper, takes the old paper out of her bra and puts the new paper in its place. She throws the old paper away and exits. The FIRST WOMAN picks up the old paper, reads it, tears it into confetti and tosses it in the air, then exits.

Pause.

A piece of paper falls from the flies. All four people rush out and try to get it first. They fight over it. One at a time seven more pieces of paper fall. The four people rush around trying to catch as many pieces of paper as they can. Each ends up with two pieces of paper. They each read their own pieces of paper. They try to read each other's pieces of paper. They start to trade papers. They read the traded papers. They start to trade clothing. Each ends up dressed in part men's and part women's clothes. Another piece of paper falls. They ignore it. They exit.

Pause.

Another piece of paper falls.

The lights fade.

DO IT

                AT RISE: Table, two chairs.
                MAN and WOMAN sitting at table.

MAN: Now what do we do?

WOMAN: Do we have to do anything?

MAN: (Sarcastic) No, we could just sit here and stare at each other for the rest of our lives.

WOMAN: Oh. OK.

MAN: What do you mean, "OK?" You mean OK, we have to do something, or OK, we'll sit here and stare at each other for the rest of our lives?

WOMAN: Let's do both.

MAN: We can't do both.

WOMAN: Why not?

MAN: Women!

WOMAN: Men!

                Pause.

WOMAN: OK, what do you want to do?

MAN: Whatever you want to do.

WOMAN: No, I want whatever you want.

MAN: I want to please you.

WOMAN: What would please me is you deciding.

MAN: But I want to do what you want.

WOMAN: I want to do what you want.

MAN: What are my choices?

WOMAN: Anything.

MAN: Anything?

WOMAN: I guess.

MAN: I want you to stand on the table, slowly strip off all your clothes, then masturbate to orgasm before making mad, passionate love to me.

WOMAN: That's not one of the choices.

MAN: Why not?

WOMAN: These shoes would scratch the table.

MAN: Oh.

WOMAN: You do it.

MAN: Me?

WOMAN: Sure.

MAN: What's different about my shoes?

WOMAN: Rubber soles.

MAN: So?

WOMAN: They don't scratch.

MAN: Oh.

> Pause.

WOMAN: Well?

MAN: I'm thinking. (Pause.) OK.

> He stands on table. Starts to take off clothes.

WOMAN: Wait.

MAN: What?

WOMAN: Do you really want to do this?

MAN: I want to do what you want.

WOMAN: Oh. I don't want that.

MAN: Oh. OK. (Sits in chair.) What do you want?

WOMAN: I want you to bring me flowers for no reason. I want you to take me to dinner someplace the prices aren't on the menu. Buy me a car. Buy me a house. Let me have your child. Give your child a trust fund. Say you love me.

MAN: Oh. (Pause.) Would you settle for four out of seven?

WOMAN: Which four?

MAN: Never mind.

> Pause.

WOMAN: So, what do you want to do?

MAN: I just want to sit here and look at you for the rest of my life.

WOMAN: Oh, aren't you sweet.

> Pause. Fade to black.

MEDITATION

AT RISE four people are sitting on the stage in yoga lotus positions, eyes closed, repeating "Om." Pause. One person slowly tips over, but still in the lotus position, eyes still closed, still "omming." At first, no one notices, but suddenly the person next to the one who tipped over opens one eye. Closes eye. Opens eye. Opens both eyes. Looks at tipped person. Looks at others, who are still "omming." No movement. Slowly the person with open eyes reaches out a hand and touches the tipped person. No reaction. Shakes tipped person. No reaction. Omming continues. No movement. Reaches out hand and slowly pulls tipped person back upright. No reaction. Omming continues. Reaches hand back out and touches formerly tipped person. No reaction. Begins to move hand slowly over formerly tipped person's body, exploring it sensually, touching forbidden regions, enjoying it. No reaction. Omming continues. Begins pulling hair, ears, etc., getting pleasure from doing the forbidden, finally hitting formerly tipped person. Still no reaction. Looks at other two people; they still are motionless, eyes closed, omming. Pause. Reaches back out and tips person back over. Smiles.

The lights fade.

VISION

AT RISE we see a chair and a dressing table with an imaginary mirror. A seemingly beautiful, tall, well-built woman enters, wearing a sexy dress, high heels, etc. She looks at herself in the mirror. She smiles. She takes off her shoes. She is no longer tall. She takes off dress. She sits at dressing table and removes a wig, false eyelashes, lipstick, etc. She stares at the mirror. She does not smile. She stands up and removes her slip and a padded girdle. She takes padding out of her bra. She looks at herself in the mirror. She breaks the mirror.

The lights fade.

QUESTIONS

MAN: (Professorial) When a man and a woman have sex, which one gets screwed? Is the man always the screwer, and the woman always the screwee, or can it switch around? Is the one on top the screwer, no matter who it is? Or is it the one who's getting their heart stomped on the one who's getting screwed? In which case, can you have two screwees and no screwers? Life is indeed a mystery. A screwed-up mystery. As hard as a penis and as slippery as a vagina. It's a wonder anybody lives through puberty. Truth be told, I reckon most of us don't. But, the truth is rarely told, especially in bars and theatres. You're certainly not here to hear the truth. You came here to have a good time before you go home and screw. You wanted some laughs, some absurdity, to kill enough of the pain that you can go home, take off all your clothes, and kiss parts of another body that you don't even like to touch on your own. And that's the truth.

VIEW

AT RISE we see an imaginary fence with a peephole at center. A MAN enters, sees peephole, looks around, looks through hole, smiles, angles for better view, keeps looking through hole. A WOMAN enters, sees MAN, crosses to him, taps him on the shoulder. MAN straightens up, surprised. WOMAN looks through hole, turns, slaps MAN. Looks through hole again, turns and slaps MAN again. MAN exits. WOMAN looks through hole. SECOND WOMAN enters, sees WOMAN, crosses to her, taps her on shoulder. FIRST WOMAN turns, surprised. SECOND WOMAN looks through hole, turns, slaps WOMAN, looks through hole again, hits WOMAN in stomach. FIRST WOMAN collapses and crawls off on hands and knees. SECOND WOMAN looks through hole. SECOND MAN enters, sees WOMAN, crosses to her, taps her on shoulder. SECOND WOMAN turns, slaps MAN, looks through hole again, turns, hits MAN in groin, looks through hole. SECOND MAN recovers, pulls out a gun and shoots SECOND WOMAN. SECOND WOMAN dies. SECOND MAN looks through hole, shrugs, and exits.

The lights fade.

CHURCH

    Lights up on bare stage.
    A WOMAN enters.

WOMAN: Did you ever have a dream that you went into the church of one of those fundamentalist TV preachers during the Sunday service, and walked down to the front of the church during the sermon, took all your clothes off, and lay down on the communion table? And then the preacher came down from the pulpit, put on a priest's collar, unzipped his fly, pulled out this enormous circumcised penis, and tried to put it in you, right there on TV in front of the congregation. But you were a real virgin again, and very tight, and he couldn't get it in, so the choir took off their robes and they were all naked underneath, and the organist started to play "I Can't Get No Satisfaction" while the preacher was bumping this huge penis between your legs but still couldn't get it in. Then the naked choir starts singing "Satisfaction" and the congregation stands up shouting "Hallelujah" and "Amen", but the priest still can't get it in, and finally he just starts jerking off, and people are dancing in the aisles, and you get up and walk outside naked, and the sun feels so good on your bare skin, and the wind is nice and cool on your wet thighs, and behind you you hear all this singing and shouting in the church, and you know the rabbi has come all over the congregation, and they're all shouting "Praise the Lord" and "Yes, Jesus," but you just keep on walking. Did you ever have a dream like that? (Pause.) I certainly never did.

DANCE

AT RISE, music is playing, slow, romantic dance music. MAN is dancing with WOMAN, a long, sweeping, arm-in-arm dance. They are joined by MAN DRESSED AS WOMAN dancing with WOMAN DRESSED AS MAN. After a few measures, they switch partners, smoothly, without missing a beat, as if it were part of the dance, so MAN is dancing with MAN DRESSED AS WOMAN and WOMAN is dancing with WOMAN DRESSED AS MAN. After a few more measures, they abruptly stop, surprised by who they are dancing with. They switch partners again so MAN is dancing with WOMAN DRESSED AS MAN, and WOMAN is dancing with MAN DRESSED AS WOMAN. They dance a few more measures, but the dancing becomes awkward, uncoordinated. They stop again. They return to their original partners and dance a little more. The dancing is now smooth, but somehow not exciting. They stop again. They begin to dance alone, as if holding imaginary partners.

The lights fade.

TV

AT RISE we see a table and two chairs at center, and a TV up center. On stage left there is a small table, a box of artist supplies for working with clay, and a very large clay penis. On stage right is an easel with a box of paints and brushes, etc., and a large, realistic painting of a nude woman in a sexually explicit pose. A MAN and a WOMAN enter from opposite sides of the stage. Though they will move through the same stage space, they never make any indication that the other person is there. Each carries a briefcase and a paper bag from a fast food place. As they enter, they sigh in relief at being home. They drop their briefcases on the table and collapse into the chairs. After a moment, they simultaneously pick up TV remote controls from the table and turn on the TV. The TV comes on with unintelligible noise and white light. They take off their jackets. The MAN takes off his tie, the WOMAN her shoes. The MAN opens his briefcase, takes out a newspaper and begins to read. The WOMAN opens her paper bag and takes out a taco and a diet coke. She starts to eat. After a bite, she opens her briefcase, takes out a copy of the current issue of Cosmopolitan Magazine, and begins to read as she eats. The MAN, after skimming the front page of the paper, opens his paper bag and takes out a Big Mac, large fries, a chocolate shake, an apple pie, and a box of cookies. He begins to eat as he reads. They will both continue to eat and drink throughout the rest of the scene as they go about their other activities. The WOMAN takes off her pantyhose, then resumes reading. The MAN finishes the first section of the paper and carefully lays the sheets of paper on the floor to act as a dropcloth under his painting. He then begins reading the next section of the paper. After another moment, the MAN kicks off his shoes. He takes the next section of the paper and lays it under the painting as well. The WOMAN closes the magazine, puts it back in her briefcase, and sits idly, staring into space, drinking her drink. The MAN folds up the rest of the paper, lays it on the table, and stares into space while eating. The WOMAN sighs, stuffs her trash back into the paper bag, and goes and gets a large lump of clay, takes it back to the table, begins to kneed it to soften it, then stops, puts the clay on the table, and stares out into space. She looks at her hands. She stares into space. The MAN takes a pornographic magazine out of his briefcase and thumbs through it. Then he stares into space. The WOMAN gets up and crosses to a wall where there evidently is a mirror. She looks at herself in the mirror.

She straightens her hair. She goes back to the table, looks at the lump of clay, and sits. She stares into space. The MAN props the magazine open to a picture similar to his painting. He crosses to his painting supplies, and starts to mix some paint. The WOMAN picks up the lump of clay from the table and begins to kneed it. The MAN finishes his preparations and begins to paint, very carefully, the pubic area of the woman in the painting. Occasionally he returns to the table for a close look at the picture in the magazine, or for something else to eat. Sometimes he stops and stares into space. The WOMAN takes the clay, crosses to penis, takes a tool or two, and begins to work on the sculpture of the penis, carefully adding details, a vein or two, etc. Occasionally she returns to the table for a sip of her drink. Sometimes she just stops and stares into space. They continue working for a time, stopping, starting, staring into space. After a few moments, each finishes his or her work of art at the same time as the other. They stop, step back and consider what they have created. They put their tools down. They sit at the table. They look at the TV. They look at their work of art. They stare into space. There is a long, long pause. The lights slowly fade, leaving the stage lit by only the light of the TV. Another pause. The TV goes off.

INTERLUDE TWO

        In darkness, Light Operator's voice over PA.

MAN: Attention please. Your attention, please. Would the parents of the cute, little, nine year old, blond-headed brat who threw a baseball through the lobby plate glass window, kicked an usher in the shins, peed on the lobby rug, and bit the House Manager's hand, please come to the box office. If the idiots who brought such a holy terror to the theatre don't claim him in five minutes, we are going to beat the shit out of him. Thank you.

WOMAN (Stage Manager): Wait a minute! Wait a minute! What are you doing?

        Stage lights come up.

MAN: Yes?

WOMAN: What are you doing?

MAN: I'm making an announcement. The House Manager has a little problem.

WOMAN: You're not supposed to stop the show without my permission.

MAN: The headsets are out, remember?

WOMAN: So you take it on yourself to stop the entire show to threaten the parents of some poor little kid who is probably scared to death?

MAN: Your maternal instincts are showing. Sounds more like a spoiled brat who gets his kicks drowning cats to me.

WOMAN: You don't know beans about kids. He's frightened.

MAN: Sure, take up for the kid. Is that your job too?

WOMAN: If necessary. If all you can do is make threats.

MAN: Teach him a lesson.

WOMAN: What, size equals power?

MAN: No. Power equals power.

WOMAN: And you are into power. Sensitivity of a brick.

MAN: I am into getting this show on. The long scene is next, could we get on with this?

WOMAN: You're the one who stopped the show with your stupid announcement.

MAN: Well, are you ready for the long scene?

WOMAN: Of course we're ready.

MAN: OK, then...

WOMAN: Go to black then up on five.

MAN: OK, OK.

        Blackout.

DRAMAPLAY

CAST OF CHARACTERS

RALPH...An Actor

JUDY..An Actress

DICK..A Director

PERRY...A Playwright

SERGEANT..A Detective

BROAD...A Detective

SCENE ONE

> AT RISE: A theatre stage set up for a rehearsal. There is a step ladder that is used as the balcony, and whatever else feels good. JUDY is standing on the step ladder.

JUDY: Romeo, Romeo, wherefore art thou, Romeo? Deny thy father and refuse thy name, or, if thou wilt not, be but sworn my love and I'll no longer be a Capulet. For who would bear the whips and scorns of time, the oppressor's wrong, the proud man's contumely, the pangs of despised love, the law's delay, the insolence of office and the spurns that patient merit of the unworthy takes, when he himself might his quietus make with a bare bodkin? Tis but thy name that is my enemy. Thou art thyself, though not a Montague. What's Montague? It is nor hand, nor foot, nor arm, nor face, nor any other part belonging to a man.

> RALPH enters, as Romeo, singing.

RALPH: Here I come to save the day!

> DICK enters from house.

DICK: Hold it! Hold it!

> RALPH grabs his crotch.

DICK: OK, and a shot rings out...

> DICK pulls out a gun and shoots Romeo. Romeo does the death scene of all death scenes, taking about a minute to die. Finally, as his last words...

RALPH: Oh, I die. Here's to my love. O true apothecary! Thy drugs are quick. Thus with a kiss I die. The rest is silence. Gasp! Ugh!

> PERRY enters from house.

PERRY: No, no! It's "Ugh! Gasp!", not "Gasp! Ugh!". Can't you get anything right?

> JUDY pulls down the top of her dress long enough to pull out a fake pair of large breasts.

DICK: Damn it, will you stop flashing those fake tits.
JUDY: They itch.

RALPH: Can I try this again?

> RALPH gets up and starts to die again.

DICK: Stop.

> RALPH halts in mid-death.

DICK: From the top. With tits, please.
JUDY: Chauvinist.

> DICK and PERRY exit to house, RALPH to wings. JUDY stuffs her fake breasts back in and goes back up the ladder.

DICK: OK.
JUDY: Romeo, Romeo, wherefore art thou, Romeo? Deny thy father and...

> RALPH dances on, singing.

RALPH: Somewhere, over the rainbow...
JUDY: Let me finish my lines for God's...
DICK: Hold it!

> Romeo grabs his crotch. DICK shoots him. Romeo dies again, in a totally different manner. Finally...

RALPH: Oh, I die. Here's to my love. O true apothecary! Thy drugs are quick. Thus with a kiss I die. The rest is silence. Gasp! Ugh!
PERRY: No.
RALPH: Ugh! Gasp! Ugh!
PERRY: No!
RALPH: Gasp! Ugh! Gasp!
PERRY: NO!

> JUDY pulls out her fake tits again.

DICK and **PERRY:** NO!
JUDY: Screw you!

> JUDY throws the tits at DICK.

JUDY: I quit!

> JUDY climbs down and exits.

DICK: I quit!

> DICK exits to wings opposite JUDY.

RALPH: Can I try this again?

> RALPH starts to die again. PERRY hits him on the head with his script, then exits through house. RALPH sits there, rubbing his head. Blackout.

SCENE TWO

    Minutes later. RALPH sits on floor, studying lines.

RALPH: Ugh. Gasp.....Ugh. Gasp......Ugh. Gasp.

    Dies quickly. Revives.

RALPH: Ugh. Gasp.....Ugh. Gasp......Ugh. Gasp.

    Dies again. Revives.

RALPH: By Jove, I think I've got it. (out to house) Perry, I think I've got it. (no response) Perry, you out there? (no response) Hell.

    Dies again. Blackout.

SCENE THREE

Minutes later. RALPH lies on floor, really dead. JUDY enters in different dress. She picks up fake breasts from stage where she tossed them.

JUDY: Damn it, Ralph, rehearsal's over. (no response) Dick and Perry are already over at Blind Willie's, yelling at each other. Now come on. (no response) I hate method actors. Ralph, damnit!

    She kicks him lightly. No response. She kicks him harder. Still no response. She bends over and looks at him closely. She screams.

    Blackout.

SCENE FOUR

> About thirty minutes later. RALPH is now covered with a sheet. SERGEANT, a police detective, lifts sheet, looks at face, lowers sheet. DICK, PERRY, and JUDY are standing around. BROAD, a female detective, stands near them, taking notes.

SERGEANT: Yeah, he's stiff. Where's the meatwagon?

BROAD: Delayed. Crashed into an ambulance.

SERGEANT: OK, OK. Who found the body?

JUDY: I did.

BROAD: Name?

JUDY: Judy Ray, but my stage name is Judy Rabinowitznowski.

SERGEANT: Well, Miss Ray, I'm Lieutenant Sergeant, and this is Detective Broad, and we're the police. (to Dick) And you are?

DICK: James William Anderson, the director. But everybody calls me Dick.

SERGEANT: Dick. Right. (to Perry) And you?

PERRY: Perry Denver. The writer. Of this play.

SERGEANT: Was he supposed to die in it?

PERRY: Only symbolically.

SERGEANT: So, what went wrong?

PERRY: Method acting?

DICK: Over-rehearsal?

JUDY: Stage fright?

SERGEANT: Try murder.

DICK: Murder?

PERRY: Murder?

JUDY: He got iced?

SERGEANT: Didn't you see the bruise on his neck. His trachea was crushed. Lousy way to die.

PERRY: How do you know?

> Pause.

BROAD: Anybody else but you three in the theatre tonight?

DICK: Not to my knowledge.

JUDY: Except Ralph, of course.

SERGEANT: Of course. Who saw him last?

DICK: You did, just now. Remember.

SERGEANT: I mean alive.

DICK: Oh. Must have been whoever killed him.

BROAD: Makes sense to me.

SERGEANT: Tell me about this play.

PERRY: It's a symbolic, abstract reinterpretation of Romeo and Juliet, based on an astigmatic view of temporal distortion as propounded in the psycho-sexual meta-physiological theories of Sigmund Einsenhouser, the Third, that conclusively established the intellectual superiority of the male.

SERGEANT: You know, I think I read about that. Penthouse, May of 16, right?

PERRY: Right.

JUDY: And, God, did she have bazooms.

DICK: Did anybody ever tell you that you have a breast fixation.

JUDY: Hey, these are my real ones.

BROAD: Jump up and down.

    JUDY bounces.

BROAD: All natural.

JUDY: See!

SERGEANT: Broad, make a note of that.

BROAD: Yes, Sir.

PERRY: Sergeant...

SERGEANT: Lieutenant.

PERRY: Mr. Lieutenant...

SERGEANT: Sergeant.

PERRY: Officer, I like bouncing breasts as much as you do; I believe they are one of the major forces shaping modern civilization...

JUDY: Thank you.

PERRY: But it's getting late, so would you please just arrest somebody so we can recast the show.

SERGEANT: Sure. Broad, cuff him.

PERRY: No, not me!

BROAD: Her?

JUDY: No!

SERGEANT: Then you're our man.

    DICK pulls his gun.

DICK: You'll never take me alive.

>DICK fires at SERGEANT. No response. He fires again. No response.

PERRY: Dick, you shoot blanks, Remember?

>DICK points gun into his own stomach. He fires. Blood explodes everywhere. He dies.

>Blackout.

SCENE FIVE

> A few minutes later. DICK is lying next to RALPH, covered with another sheet. There is a big red splotch in the middle of the sheet. PERRY, JUDY, and SERGEANT are standing around the bodies. BROAD enters.

BROAD: Meatwagon is still delayed. They hit a pedestrian, and it caused a real traffic jam.

SERGEANT: OK, OK. Now, I figure either one person killed both stiffs, or this stiff killed that stiff and somebody killed that stiff for killing that stiff. You follow?

PERRY: My neck is stiff.

JUDY: But, Captain Corporal...

SERGEANT: Lieutenant Sergeant.

JUDY: Admiral Ensign, whatever. Dick shot himself, remember? We were all watching. Even you.

SERGEANT: But who loaded the gun?

PERRY: Dick loaded the gun.

SERGEANT: Then why fire blanks at me? He must have thought they were real bullets.

BROAD: But then why shoot himself, unless he thought they were blanks?

PERRY: Then why do birds sing so gay?

SERGEANT: This stiff was gay?

JUDY: No.

BROAD: You're sure?

JUDY: No sense of humor at all.

SERGEANT: OK, OK. The facts don't change a thing. Somebody in this room is a real bastard with blood on their hands.

> Everybody sticks their hands out. SERGEANT'S are bloody.

SERGEANT: Where did that come from? (wipes hands on DICK's sheet) And my mother wasn't a slut, she just made a mistake.

BROAD: Let's get back to the case.

SERGEANT: Right. I know, let's reconstruct the murder.

PERRY: Which one?

SERGEANT: The first. I already saw the second.

PERRY: Right. Let's see. Judy was on the balcony. Ralph came on from stage left. Dick entered from the house. Down there.

SERGEANT: Oh. OK, OK. Broad, you be Ralph, I'll be Dick.
BROAD: Right.

> JUDY gets, but does not put on, her fake tits, then climbs the ladder.

PERRY: OK, Judy's in place, Ralph is already on, there. OK, you come up from down there. Right, now you stop and yell "Hold it."
SERGEANT: Hold it!
PERRY: And you grab your crotch.
BROAD: You've got to be kidding.
PERRY: Just fake it. Now, you shoot her.

> SERGEANT points his finger like a gun at BROAD.

SERGEANT: Bang!
PERRY: And you die.

> BROAD falls to floor.

SERGEANT: Then what?
PERRY: Then Judy tossed her fake chest on the stage.

> JUDY does so.

JUDY: Then I went to my dressing room and changed.
SERGEANT: And Dick?
PERRY: Stalked off to his office, that way.
SERGEANT: And you?
PERRY: I went over to Blind Willie's.
SERGEANT: And Ralph?
PERRY: I never saw him alive again.
JUDY: Neither did I.
SERGEANT: So, any one of you could have crept back, and killed him while the other two were somewhere else.
PERRY: Dick could have, anyway.
BROAD: Can I get up now?
PERRY: Oh, sorry. Sure.

> PERRY helps her up.

BROAD: Why were you wearing the falsies?

JUDY: It was Dick's idea. He wouldn't settle for a real woman, they had to be huge. They just slip right in the dress, like this.

> JUDY slides the false breasts into place, and slaps her chest. Suddenly she screams in pain, tries to rip the breasts off, but they won't budge. She staggers around the stage a little, then collapses and dies.

SERGEANT: Oh, the poisoned fake boobs trick, eh.

> Blackout.

SCENE SIX

> A few minutes later. SERGEANT is covering JUDY's body with a sheet. PERRY stands nearby. BROAD enters.

BROAD: The meatwagon got out of the traffic jam, but by then their shift was over, so they went home. Next shift will be out in an hour or so.

SERGEANT: OK, OK. Well, Mister Playwright, this isn't the way I like to solve crimes, but it will have to do.

PERRY: What do you mean?

SERGEANT: Well, you're the only one left, so you must be the murderer.

PERRY: Me? Playwrights never do anything for real.

SERGEANT: Sure. Now I don't know if this stiff killed that stiff because this stiff killed that stiff and then you killed this stiff for killing that stiff, or if you killed this stiff because she killed that stiff and that stiff, or if you killed this stiff and that stiff and that stiff, but you sure stiffed somebody.

PERRY: Not necessarily. That stiff could have poisoned that stiff's breasts before accidentally stiffing himself with blanks after killing that stiff.

BROAD: Or this stiff could have changed the bullets and poisoned the tits before being killed by that stiff, who discovered he was trying to kill that stiff with the poisoned fake bosom.

PERRY: Or vice versa.

BROAD: Of course.

SERGEANT: Wait a minute. You're saying this stiff killed that stiff and that stiff even after he was stiff?

PERRY: It's possible.

SERGEANT: Then who killed this stiff?

PERRY: This stiff.

BROAD: Or that stiff. Whichever one came back and caught this stiff doing something dirty and stiffed him.

SERGEANT: Now wait a minute. Let's get this straight. Go back to the end of the scene. This stiff is playing dead. That stiff goes off this way, and that stiff goes off that way.

PERRY: Right.

SERGEANT: OK, let's stage it. Broad, you play that stiff, I'll play this stiff.

BROAD: Right. Bang. Dies. Titties get tossed.

> BROAD exits.

SERGEANT: Right. Stomp, stomp, exit.

> SERGEANT exits opposite from BROAD. PERRY is alone on stage. A shot rings out.

PERRY: Ugh, gasp.

> PERRY staggers, falls, and dies. BROAD and SERGEANT run on from each side.

BROAD and **SERGEANT:** You shot him! Not me! You're under arrest!

> They draw their guns. They shoot each other. They stagger, fall, and die. Pause. JUDY sits up, pulls sheet off, stands with gun in hand, and pulls breasts out.

JUDY: Fell for the old fake poisoned falsies routine, I see. Works every time. (to audience) Take up the bodies. Such a sight as this becomes the field, but here shows much amiss. Go hence, to have more talk of these sad things. Some shall be pardoned and some punished. For never was a story of more woe than this of Juliet and her Romeo.

> Blackout.

ACT II

      House lights are up, stage dark. Stage Manager enters.

WOMAN: Hey! Lights! Get with it!

      Stage up quickly, house fades slowly.

MAN: OK, OK. Ready when you are.

WOMAN: Ha! I saw you in the greenroom trying to pick up a little action for after the show. You're up there replugging with every appendage you've got.

MAN: My board is cued, my circuits are hot, and I'm ready for any action you can handle.

WOMAN: Fat chance.

MAN: Try me. What have you got to lose?

WOMAN: My sanity. My dignity. My self-respect.

MAN: Besides that.

WOMAN: Just tell me when you're ready for Act II.

MAN: I'm ready for any act you name.

WOMAN: An act of reason and moderation.

MAN: Not in the script. How about an act of moderate illumination?

WOMAN: I guess that's the most I can expect. All right, Mr. Electricity, down for five, then cue 21.

MAN: You got it.

      Fade to black.

A TABLE, TWO CHAIRS

AT RISE: A table, two chairs. MAN in chair, glass in hand, talking to himself.

MAN: The answer is seven.... Always seven...... Let the hunt begin..... And I will wear the ring..... There is no song for a winter's night.

WOMAN, dressed in skirt and blouse, enters quietly, sits in the other chair.

MAN: Well, the lady of the manor....... Come to the king in his castle?...... Well, Kate, bar the door....... (Stands, to audience.) For, lo, the winter is come, and age writes its name on our hands....... What a pair of fools........(Crosses behind her.) What a pair of..... What a pair........ I said, what a pair! (Rips her blouse open.) Let's get things out in the open. Out in the open, I say!

WOMAN tries to pull her blouse closed, but MAN rips it off her, tearing it to pieces. She is left in her bra. She tries to cover herself for a moment, then sits erectly, calm and dignified, hands at her side.

MAN: And they say I degrade women.

MAN picks up glass and pours contents over her head.

MAN: I degrade women! Who's degraded now? Who's indecent now? Who's obscene now? You tell me.

WOMAN does not move. MAN speaks to audience.

MAN: Look at her! Look at her! Sitting there like God herself. What can I do? Strip her, beat her, rape her? She'd still be there! It's no use. (To WOMAN) No use! No use!

MAN exits. WOMAN does not move for a few seconds, then gets up, picks up torn blouse and examines it. She sees it is useless to try to put it on, so she uses it to wipe off her face and body. She crosses to the audience.

WOMAN: I'm sorry. He just gets so angry sometimes. He never physically hurts me. He just gets angry. Ever since the baby, and, well..... Actually, it's better this way. He used to just be silent. I couldn't even read his eyes. Just a man off in a forgotten dream, only his body here, sitting at a table. Now, at least I can feel his rage, can feel something from him.

> MAN returns with another glass, sits at table. WOMAN goes and sits by him.

MAN: Been talking again I guess. Apologizing for me. I don't need it. You hear, I don't need it...... For God's sake, woman, go cover yourself.

> Pause. WOMAN finally gets up and exits.

MAN: What did she tell you? Never mind, I can guess. It's not true, there's no excuse. No excuses, no questions, no answers....... You know what this is? Water. No beer, no booze, no excuses. Water. I am stone cold sober and always have been. I do what I do with a clear, clean mind. A clear, clean mind that turned left just outside of Topeka. Turned left at a right hand turn and got clean off the track. (Sings) "There never was, there couldn't be, a place in time for men like me, who'd drink the dark, and laugh at day, and let their wildest dreams blow away."

> WOMAN enters buttoning another blouse, and sits.

MAN: "And now I'm old, I'm wise, I'm smart, I'm just a man with half a heart. I wonder how things might have been, had I not cast my fate to the wind."

> Long pause. She tries to touch him. He pulls away.

MAN: Why don't you leave me alone?

WOMAN: We need you. The baby needs you. I need you. You need us.

MAN: I need my life back. I need my life back.

WOMAN: I'm not forgiving you.

MAN: I didn't ask.

WOMAN: The baby needs...

MAN: The baby. The baby needs resentment? Needs jealousy? Needs hate? Needs silence? .... Now who is silent?

WOMAN: It's normal for a man to....

MAN: Normal? I am not normal! I am not normal! I am not an 8 to 5 drudge who mows the lawn and fixes bicycles!

WOMAN: Nobody said...

MAN: No, everybody said! Everybody was thrilled!

WOMAN: They thought...

MAN: I know what they thought....... Lemmings. Let's all die so the children can live.

WOMAN: It's not like....

MAN: Isn't it? Where is my life? Where are my choices? Where is my time? You've taken everything I ever had, every possibility.... Tell me, which is the greater sin: Hating life alone, or forcing it on some unsuspecting soul? (No answer.) Pain, it's all pain.

WOMAN: Is it?

MAN: Yes.

WOMAN: Thank you. I'm glad I made you so happy.

MAN: And now you hurt too. And you want me to come back? You must be crazy? Out of your godforsaken mind. Why can't I drive you away? (No answer.) Answer me!

WOMAN: I don't have any answers. There are no answers. There are never any answers.

>   Pause.

MAN: The answer is seven.

WOMAN: The answer is seven.

MAN: Seven. A square plus a triangle. The perfect number. Seven.

WOMAN: Seven. That's one answer.

MAN: I've never had a chance, have I?

>   No answer. Curtain.

VOYEURISM

AT RISE an actress wearing a white body suit with painted-on nipples and pubic hair is dancing on a table to loud rock music. TWO MEN enter and sit in chairs at the table the actress is dancing on. They stare at the DANCER. A WAITRESS in a short dress enters, takes the MEN's order as the MEN stare at the DANCER, and exits. The DANCER dances, the MEN stare. The WAITRESS, now only in bra and panties, brings beers to the MEN, who stare at the DANCER. WAITRESS exits. MEN drink beers, stare at DANCER. The WAITRESS, now nude, brings the MEN their check. The MEN stare at the DANCER. The WAITRESS exits. The MEN stare at the DANCER. The DANCER dances.

DREAMS

AT RISE: MAN, alone on stage.

MAN: Everybody has two dreams. Call one fantasy, one expectation. Everybody dreams of being rich and famous, making millions of dollars endorsing beer, living in a mansion with a wife, a mistress, three girlfriends, and having an occasional passionate affair and tawdry one-night-stand. Without anybody getting jealous. This is a fantasy. It never happens. And we know that all the time we're dreaming about it. But there's another dream. An expectation. We expect to make it, to succeed. We expect to have a respectable career that more than pays the mortgage on a nice house complete with garbage disposal. We expect to have a vacation every year. We expect to buy a big, brand new car in our middle age. We expect to find at least one person who loves us enough to stay with us. We expect to be able to retire one day. These dreams are also not true, but we don't know that. We expect them to come true if we just work hard and keep our noses clean. Then we get to fortysomething, and the mortgage payment equals our take-home pay. Our latest used, compact car is dying, killing our savings account in the process, and our wife is off on business somewhere in Meridian, Mississippi, trying to earn enough money to cover the childcare or college or the nursing home for our parents, and we are suddenly surprised to realized that our dream is just a dream. We knew the fantasy was a dream. The expectation we believed. And now both dreams are dead, and we look at 30 more years of 8 to 5 behind some desk, our arteries getting harder and harder until we are forced to retire to social security and Medicaid and not much else. At this point in our lives, something else happens. We look at our future and something breaks; we look at reality, and something inside us packs up the circus tent and steals away into the night, never to laugh again.

RING

AT RISE we hear slow, romantic, mellow, big band dance music. A MAN and WOMAN are dancing, arm-in-arm. Without seeming to notice, they separate, but keep on dancing as if still together. After a few moments, they rejoin, as if nothing had happened. A few moments later, they separate again. A SECOND MAN enters and dances with the WOMAN. The FIRST MAN dances alone. The SECOND MAN and the WOMAN separate and the SECOND MAN dances offstage. The MAN and WOMAN rejoin and dance as if nothing had happened. Soon they separate again. A SECOND WOMAN enters and dances with the MAN. The FIRST WOMAN dances alone. The MAN and SECOND WOMAN separate and the SECOND WOMAN dances offstage. The MAN and WOMAN rejoin and dance as if nothing had happened. The SECOND MAN dances onstage, but this time the MAN and WOMAN do not separate. The SECOND MAN dances up to the couple behind the MAN, as if to lure the WOMAN away. The couple deftly avoids him. The SECOND MAN dances offstage, disappointed. The MAN and WOMAN keep dancing. The SECOND WOMAN dances onstage. The MAN and WOMAN keep dancing together. The SECOND WOMAN dances up behind WOMAN, as if to lure the MAN away. The couple deftly avoids her. The SECOND WOMAN dances offstage, disappointed. The MAN and WOMAN continue dancing together.

The lights fade.

INTERLUDE THREE

Voice-over on P.A. System in dark.

MAN: Attention please. Your attention please. Will the owner of beeper number OU8M2, that's beeper OU8M2, please come to the box office. Your babysitter called to tell you your house burned down, but she managed to save the children, the dog, your collection of pornographic videos, some of your wife's crotchless underwear, and the big dildo. However, one of her boyfriends suffered second degree burns on his posterior, and he is going to sue you. She is waiting for you with the children at the local police station. Just ask for the vice squad. Thank you.

WOMAN: Stop that! You're making that up. This isn't your play. Stop improvising.

MAN: Am I? You'll never know, will you? Everyone who's guilty will just sit still so nobody will know it's them. (Pause. House up.) See, nobody's leaving. (House down.) No crotchless underwear in this crowd. The thrill is gone. Old married folk wondering where it all went.

WOMAN: Shows what you know. The better you know a person...

MAN: Don't you believe it, Sister.

WOMAN: I know what I know.

MAN: We come and we go. Take what you can get.

WOMAN: You are a sad, lonely person, aren't you?

MAN: Everybody dies alone, even you.

WOMAN: And between now and then?

MAN: We have to put on a show.

WOMAN: That's a pretty cynical attitude. I almost feel sorry for you.

MAN: No, we have to put on a show.

WOMAN: What do you...? Oh, right. Act II long scene in five, cue 37.

THE BED

> AT RISE: A bed. MAN and WOMAN, 40's, in bed asleep covered by sheet and blanket. MAN rolls over toward WOMAN, wakes up, starts in surprise, looks at WOMAN, looks around room, looks under covers at his body.

MAN: Oh my god.

> Looks at WOMAN. She rolls over toward MAN, opens eyes.

MAN: Uh, hi.

> WOMAN screams, sits up, jerks up covers to cover herself. This almost exposes MAN, who grabs sheet corner to keep from exposing himself.

WOMAN: Who are you? What do you want? Where am I?
MAN: Isn't this your place.

> WOMAN looks around.

WOMAN: No. Isn't it yours?
MAN: No.
WOMAN: This doesn't look like a....
MAN: No, it doesn't. But I've never been...
WOMAN: I don't recognize...
MAN: Then where in the world...?
WOMAN: And how? Uh, did we.....? Last night?
MAN: What?
WOMAN: Uh, meet.
MAN: Not that I remember. Do you remember?
WOMAN: No. Not a thing.
MAN: Then how...?
WOMAN: Were we drunk?
MAN: I don't drink.
WOMAN: I don't feel like..., I mean, I don't have a....

MAN: Hangover?

WOMAN: Right. And I would really have to have been....to, uh, you know....

MAN: Gee, thanks.

WOMAN: Oh, nothing personal. I guess.

MAN: Are you....I mean, under the....

>WOMAN looks under the covers at her body.

WOMAN: Oh my god. You?

MAN: As a jaybird.

WOMAN: Then we must have....

MAN: I guess.

WOMAN: But I don't even know you. Who are you?

MAN: Uh, Fred. Fred Simpson.

>He extends his hand to shake hands. She readjusts the covers to preserve her modesty, and shakes his hand.

WOMAN: Mary Riley.

MAN: Nice to meet you. I guess.

>Pause. They gaze around.

MAN: Do you have any idea where we are?

WOMAN: None what-so-ever.

MAN: Do you see any clothes of any kind anywhere?

WOMAN: Not a stitch.

MAN: And you have no idea how we got here.

WOMAN: None at all.

MAN: Well, isn't this a novel experience.

>Pause.

WOMAN: Uh, Fred.

MAN: Yes, Mary?

WOMAN: Uh, do you happen to remember, last night, when we....., uh, did you use a ....?

MAN: Oh. Uh, (looks around) I have no idea.

WOMAN: Oh.

MAN: Are you on the .....?

WOMAN: I don't think so.

MAN: Oh boy.

WOMAN: I usually use a, well, you know, with a ....

MAN: Well, did you?

WOMAN: Do you see my purse anywhere?

MAN: Your purse?

WOMAN: I keep it in my purse.

MAN: Oh. (looks around) No. No purse.

WOMAN: Oh.

MAN: See if it's where it would be if it wasn't in your purse.

WOMAN: What? Oh. There.

MAN: Yes. There.

WOMAN: Uh, don't look.

> MAN turns head away. WOMAN puts hand under covers to check herself.

WOMAN: Uh, no.

MAN: You're sure?

WOMAN: Yes. Nothing there.

MAN: Oh my god.

WOMAN: That means you're the ....., I mean without any...., so you actually.... (Pause.) You're not married, are you?

MAN: Me? No. No. I don't think so. I don't remember being.... I wouldn't be.... You don't suppose we....?

> WOMAN looks at her hand, sees ring.

WOMAN: Oh God.

> MAN looks at his hand, sees ring.

MAN: Oh God.

> They stare at each other.

MAN and **WOMAN:** Oh God!

WOMAN: Not you..., I mean, I wouldn't...

MAN: Well, you're not exactly ....

WOMAN: Well, for your information...

MAN: But then to who.... Who the hell are we cheating on?

WOMAN: I wouldn't cheat on...whoever.

MAN: It's me or whoever.

WOMAN: Oh god.

MAN: And you don't remember....

WOMAN: Not this...

MAN: What's the last thing you do remember?

WOMAN: Let's see. I went to "The Graduate" with Sharon and Barbara last night. I remember sitting there, holding the popcorn, thinking this was a very stupid movie, and getting a little sleepy.

MAN: That's it?

WOMAN: Until I woke up to see you leaning over me. What about you?

MAN: Me? Well, uh, I was at a Beach Boys concert, and it was getting kind of boring, and it had been a long week at school, and, and, that's all I remember.

WOMAN: Well.

MAN: You think we were drugged?

WOMAN: Did you have any popcorn?

MAN: No. Not that I remember.

WOMAN: I just don't see how....

MAN: Today is Saturday, isn't it?

WOMAN: I guess. It's supposed to be.

MAN: Where's my watch? It's one of those new ones that has a date too.

Looks around, finds nothing.

WOMAN: Do you think we were robbed?

MAN: That might explain some things. But where are we?

WOMAN: Go look out the window.

MAN: I haven't got any clothes.

WOMAN: Oh.

MAN: Let me have the blanket.

WOMAN: What?

MAN: You keep the sheet, let me have the blanket.

WOMAN: Oh.

They separate the blanket from the sheet, MAN wraps blanket around himself, and crosses to (imaginary) window.

WOMAN: Well?

MAN: Back yard, fenced in, tool shed, three bicycles, lots of grass. Nobody there. Roofs of other houses over the fence.

WOMAN: Have you....?

MAN: Never saw it before in my life. Looks like one of those ticky-tacky suburbs.

WOMAN: It doesn't sound like anywhere I'd....

MAN: What do you think? I don't know many robbers who take the victims home to recover.

WOMAN: Maybe we were kidnapped or something.

MAN: Right. They might get ten bucks out of my family, if they sold the car.

WOMAN: Great, I married a welfare case.

MAN: You rich?

WOMAN: Hardly. Not worth kidnapping anyway.

MAN: Well, at least I married up. Guess you married me for love.

WOMAN: Right. A whirlwind romance totally under the influence of some new drug that leaves you with amnesia when it wears off. Fat chance.

MAN: Maybe an alternate universe.

WOMAN: You think it's possible?

MAN: Makes as much sense as anything. I'd certainly never end up in a place like this if I had a choice. I'd give a lot to see a newspaper.

WOMAN: Maybe there's one on the front steps. Or a TV, there's got to be a TV in the house.

MAN: Have you heard anything from other rooms?

WOMAN: No. Have you?

MAN: No.

WOMAN: Well, go look.

MAN: Which door?

WOMAN: That one, I guess. The other looks like a closet.

MAN: And closets have clothes.

> He crosses offstage.

WOMAN: Well?

MAN: (offstage) Walk-in closet. Cabinets and drawers as well as clothes-racks. Bathroom on the other side.

WOMAN: Any clothes?

MAN: Plenty. What would you like?

WOMAN: Uh, jeans maybe, and a shirt, and some sneakers.

> MAN enters wearing pants.

MAN: Here, try these first.

> Tosses a pair of panties and a bra on the bed. MAN exits back to closet. WOMAN gets underwear and puts it on under the covers.

MAN: Does it fit?

WOMAN: Yeah. Thanks.

> MAN enters with unbuttoned shirt on, tosses jeans and a shirt on the bed, and exits again. WOMAN gets up and dresses quickly.

WOMAN: See anything with a name on it?

MAN: LaCoste, Oscar de La Renta, K-Mart.

WOMAN: A calendar, a telephone, anything?

MAN: Well, a man and a woman live here. He uses Old Spice, she uses Mum. They use Ivory soap, and Shick and Lady Shick razors. They have both Pepto Bismol and Exlax in here, plus band-aids, alcohol, etc. Looks like my parent's medicine chest.... Damn!

WOMAN: What?

MAN: Uh, nothing. (Pause.) Uh, you want some shoes?

WOMAN: Please. And some socks.

MAN: Coming right up.

> MAN enters fully dressed in casual clothes, hands WOMAN a pair of socks and jogging shoes.

MAN: See if these fit.

WOMAN: Did you have any problems?

MAN: No, everything fit fine, which worries me.

WOMAN: Alternate universe theory just went up a point.

MAN: Several points.

WOMAN: Eerie

MAN: What?

WOMAN: They fit like they're mine.

MAN: This is getting too strange.

WOMAN: Go out and find a TV or a newspaper or something.

> Pause.

WOMAN: What are you waiting on?

MAN: What if it is a parallel universe? What if I go out there, and can never get back? What if we've been married for twenty years in this universe, have a kid just gone off to college, and I'm an accountant or something terrible like that?

WOMAN: Don't be crazy.

MAN: I looked awful old in the mirror in there. Almost as old as you. It was scary.

WOMAN: Don't start freaking out on me. What do you mean, almost as old as me? How old do I look?

MAN: Oh, maybe forty, give or take.

WOMAN: You're kidding.

MAN: Go look for yourself. Mirror is right over the sink.

WOMAN: Oh, no. I thought you were just a dirty old man. This is horrible. What am I, a housewife who sells cosmetics part time? My life can't turn out like this. This is insane.

MAN: Have you got a sane explanation for being married to a forty year old accountant, living in the suburbs, and owning three bicycles?

WOMAN: No. This can't be true. We're hallucinating. We're on some kind of drugs.

MAN: I don't even drink beer. And no drug is this real.

WOMAN: Well?

MAN: Well what?

WOMAN: Well what do we do? Do we sit here until our kid comes home from college or what?

MAN: OK, OK.

>MAN crosses off other side of stage, sound of door opening.
>Pause. MAN enters.

WOMAN: What?

MAN: I saw a calendar.

WOMAN: And?

MAN: It's 2019. (Use year of production.)

WOMAN: Oh my god.

>Blackout.

INTERLUDE SIX

    In the darkness, a voice over the PA system.

MAN: Attention please. Your attention please. We would like to remind you that no sex is permitted in the theatre. Repeat, no sex is permitted in the theatre. When the show is over, please clear the house as quickly as possible. Smoking and drinking and other forms of slow suicide are permitted in the lobby, but creating life is forbidden. Thank you.

WOMAN: You never give up, do you?

MAN: Nature of the species. You may not like us, but you have to love us.

WOMAN: What a pity.

MAN: I couldn't agree more. (Pause.) Ready for the final scene?

WOMAN: It always comes down to this, doesn't it. The final scene.

MAN: And then we go home.

WOMAN: I'll have some notes for you after the show.

MAN: You never give up either, do you?

WOMAN: Nature of the species. We keep hoping you'll learn something.

MAN: Doubtful.

WOMAN: True.

MAN: But then you don't either.

WOMAN: I guess not. Else we would have given up long ago.

MAN: It's time.

WOMAN: I know. Earth Mother to Sky God. Ready when you are.

MAN: Divergent Illusions, the final scene.

THE GOODBYE

AT RISE we see a MAN stretched out on a table, covered with a sheet. He is dead. Two WOMEN enter. They stop and look at the body on the table. They look at each other. They cry together a moment. They carefully remove the sheet. They gently and lovingly wash his body. Mournfully, they pull the sheet over him up to his neck. They each kiss him on the forehead. With a last look, they pull the sheet up over his head. They exit slowly.

Pause.

The lights fade.

CURTAIN

Figures

This is a bill of three one-act plays. I think they fit together, but so far they have only been produced separately. "Tobacco, Lemonade, and Crowder Peas" was first done at the University of Arizona Theatre when I was a graduate student there. Bill Lang, my playwriting professor called it "a practically perfect one-act." I leased the amateur rights to At Rise Magazine and made a few bucks on high school and college productions before the magazine went out of business and I got my rights back. Much later (2009) in was done by a professional theatre group, Atlanta Theatre-To-Go, which toured it around Atlanta.

"Throwing Daggers" has never had a full-scale production, but it was given a staged reading at an SETC convention of college and university theatre departments. The knife-throwing seems to be a barrier to production, though the script describes the traditional method of faking it.

"Inherit" is the most produced of the three. It was first done by Stage Door Players in Dunwoody, GA, back in 1989, then by Hollywood Actors Theatre in Hollywood, CA, in1991 (so I have been produced in both New York and Hollywood), and Koality Presentations in Atlanta in 1999. As you can tell from the dates, it was written before my daughter was born, so any resemblance of her or me to the characters is purely coincidence.

FIGURES

A Play By David Davis

Member
All rights & privileges.

David Davis
100 Hunters Ridge Court
Roswell, GA 30076
daviddaviswriter@gmail.com

Copyright 2020 David Davis

CAST OF CHARACTERS

Two actresses and three actors play a variety of roles.

SETTING

A theatre. The present.

> AT RISE: The stage is bare except for four performers frozen in various positions.
>
> The NARRATOR enters and walks among the still figures.

NARRATOR: It's a simple story. Most stories are simple, except for the details. Love, hate, sex. The same stories over and over again. Nothing much changes except the details.

> The actors come to life and exit.

NARRATOR: There aren't any surprises left. You watch 5 or 6 hours of TV a day, 2 or 3 movies a week, by the time you're 12, you've seen it all. You've seen people get shot and die, for real, on TV. You've seen people have sex, sometimes for real, in the movies. You've heard every possible plot, and most of the jokes. Only the names and actors change. "Star Trek" took you to the edge of the universe, "Psycho" to the edge of you mind, and "Night of the Living Dead" to the edge of nausea. There's nowhere left to go. What are we poor storytellers to do when there are no surprises left? Then we talk about the immediacy, the live presence, the interaction with the audience of the live performance. You are beyond us now. So we stand here, telling our simple stories to the media-jaded crowd who do not feel, do not care, and do not want to.

> A stage-hand enters and hands NARRATOR a pair of dirty, well-worn overalls and a pair of dusty work shoes. The stage-hand helps him dress, then exits. As he dresses, the NARRATOR becomes HOMER, a young man who has just spent the day cropping tobacco in the East Carolina sun.

NARRATOR: Why do we do it? Well, we need the money. We need a little fame. Mostly we just need to be somebody else for a while. I guess you could say we have to. So, (becoming HOMER) this is gonna be a play. I just thought I'd let you know, since you might not recognize it right off. Most of you folks came here tonight to see a play, and you're gonna get what you paid for. Those of you who snuck in will anyway. This thing I'm standing on is called a stage. Most people would call it a floor, but it's in a theatre, so it's called a stage. The stage is where we put the play. There ain't no particular reason for puttin' in there, 'ceptin' it's a bit easier to see if you put it there. Most plays got what they call a set. This one don't got much 'o one, but we make do. We do got a few special lights hung over your heads. If one of 'em should fall, we recommend you get out of the way, as they're a mite heavy. Now, like any play, this one needs to borrow a little bit of your imagination. For example, we need you to imagine that this is the front porch of a little farmhouse in Eastern North Carolina, out in the tobacco region. This here is a rocking chair, like you see sitting outside a Cracker Barrel restaurant, only older and a good deal more worn in, as they say. And here is sort of the same thing, only wide enough for two. And over here is a porch swing, you know, the kind that hang from a couple of chains attached to one of the beams so you can sort of swing back and forth and make a little breeze even if you're not a kid anymore. A courting swing some people called it. Now imagine it's some years back. In other parts of the country you can sort of hear the winds of change blowing. There's lots of noise being made, but the sound hasn't reached here yet. Not here. Not yet. Here things are the way they used to be, and we want to show you that. Just a taste of what was. What got left behind. So imagine a hot evening way out in the country, too far inland from Wilmington to get a sea breeze, but not close enough to Raleigh to get the TV signal clear with just rabbit ears. No road bigger than two lanes, tobacco the money crop, and time just sort of stuck in a rut. You imagine that, and we'll get started just as soon as everybody comes in and gets settled.

> As he is speaking, The actors enter, carrying a rocking chair and a rocking bench, as a porch swing is lowered from above. Ignoring HOMER, they take their places. MAN 2, now MR. AL, a tobacco farmer, sits in the rocking chair and begins to read the evening paper. WOMAN 2, now MISS HATTIE, sits on the rocking bench and begins to mend a dress she has brought with her. WOMAN 1, now JENNY, sits on one side of the swing. MAN 1, now AL JR., stretches out on the stage. AL JR. is wearing blue jeans and a faded shirt and work shoes. MR. AL wears a brown work shirt, overalls that are too big, and work shoes. JENNY is dressed in men's work pants, one of AL JR.'s old shirts, and tennis shoes. MISS HATTIE has on a faded, old calf-length dress, men's socks, and work shoes. They relax and enjoy the cool evening breeze and the feeling of not working for a few minutes. JENNY swings a little. AL JR. chews on a beech twig. During the rest of HOMER's speech the lights dims as slowly and unnoticeably as possible to a twilight effect.

HOMER (as the others enter): Speaking of everybody, that's them. The one with the rocking chair, that's Albert Johnson. Mr. Al they call him. He's around forty, give or take a couple of years. Took over the farm when his dad died, oh, five, six years back. He'd been working it with his father since he was born, I guess. The one in the dress is Miss Hattie, Mr. Al's wife. She's been married to him over twenty years now, but everybody still calls her Miss Hattie. I ain't gonna tell you how old she is, cause I ain't real sure. The girl there is their daughter, Jenny. She's nineteen and unmarried, and I'm sure of both those facts. She's kinna pretty, and works hard, but she don't want to marry a farmer, and that's about all there is around here, with one or two notable exceptions, which could cause some problems. But that comes later. The boy is her brother, Albert Jr. They call him Al Jr. to keep him separate from his father. They called him Junior for awhile when he was younger, but he outgrew that affliction. He's seventeen and just out of high school. He ain't married either, but that ain't gonna last. He don't care whether he marries a farm girl or not, just so it's a girl. I always did like a man who was easy to please. Now I gotta get off the stage, cause I gotta come back on. I'm Homer Webster, an' I'm one of those exceptions that Jenny's so interested in. Nine months o' the year I teach English at the local high school. I grew up around here, the son of a preacher man, but my parents died a few years back, and I got passed from Aunt to Aunt for a couple of years. Went off to college when I was sixteen, studied history, then came back at twenty, lookin' for a job. I really didn't want to come back, which is another part of our little story, but jobs for history majors are sort of hard to find. People around here sort of look out for each other though, and, well, the high school had a history teacher, old Miss Rena, but they needed an English teacher. So, I teach English at the local high school. I'm twenty-two now, it's the evening of a hot summer's day, an' I been out cropping tobacco just like everybody else in the county.

> HOMER ambles off as JENNY softly begins to hum "Bringing in the Sheaves."

MR. AL: Paper says it's gonna be hot and dry ag'in tomorrow.

AL JR.: Well, the dry half is good, but I sure could stand a cool breeze.

MISS HATTIE: Thing is, a cool breeze usually just pulls a rain storm right in behind it.

AL JR.: Yeah, but it sure is hot out there.

MR. AL (joshing): What you complainin' about, boy? You down on the bottom o' the cropper, pickin' in the shade; your mamma's sittin' out in the sun on that tractor all day, haulin' the rest of us ahind her. An' poor Jenny's up on top, gettin' all kinds of splinters in her pretty hands from them racks. You got the easy job, boy.

AL JR.: Well, I guess you're right. As long as a man likes to eat twenty pounds of dust a day, it's a right fine job.

MISS HATTIE: Who's that coming down the road? Looks a bit like Homer.

JENNY: Where?

MISS HATTIE: Up towards the store, walking down the side of the road.

AL JR.: He's been cropping for Mr. Cecil.

MISS HATTIE: Well, you'd think the man would at least give the boy a ride home.

AL JR.: Ah, he has to take the nigras home first. Homer probably figured it would be quicker walkin'.

MISS HATTIE: Al Jr., you go down and ask him if he'd like to come up and set for a spell.

JENNY: Ow, Maw, what'd he want to come up here for? He's hot and tired and wants to go home.

MISS HATTIE (to AL Jr.): Tell him we got a glass o' lemonade for him.

AL JR.: That'll fetch him.

    AL JR. exits.

JENNY: Aw, now what's he gonna think; I got on Al Jr.'s old clothes, and I been workin' so hard I stink.

MISS HATTIE: You ain't no worse off than he is. An' workin' all day and livin' alone like he does, he'd probably appreciate gettin' in a little bit o' socializin'.

MR. AL (reading paper): Richard Petty won that stock car race over at Goldsboro last night.

MISS HATTIE: Well, I'm glad somebody's got the time to go racin' around instead of spendin' the whole day out on a cropppin' machine.

    HOMER and AL JR. enter.

MISS HATTIE: Hello, Homer.

HOMER: Miss Hattie, how are you?

MISS HATTIE: Oh, fair to middling, I guess.

MR. AL: Howdy, Homer.

HOMER: Mr. Al.

    AL JR. sits on the stage. HOMER starts to sit next to MISS
    HATTIE, but JENNY stops him.

JENNY: Set up here with me, Homer. This swing don't hardly swing right less it's got two people in it.

AL JR.: It does if you set in the middle.

HOMER: Yeah, but something tells me the lady doesn't want to sit in the middle.

> HOMER sits in the swing next to, but not close to, JENNY.

AL JR. (kidding): Lady! Haw! I'm surprised you could tell what it is, the way she looks now.

JENNY: Al Jr.!

> MISS HATTIE puts her sewing down and stands up.

MISS HATTIE: Well, I guess I better see to that lemonade I promised. Al Jr., you come give me a hand carrying it out.

AL JR.: Huh?

MISS HATTIE: Come on now, no backtalk.

> MISS HATTIE and AL JR. exit.

MR. AL: You workin' for Mr. Cecil?

HOMER: Yes sir.

MR. AL: How's he coming?

HOMER: Oh, he oughta to be done in a couple of days, maybe three, if the weather holds. He's about outa racks anyway.

MR. AL: Well, it's gonna take us five or six more, just us workin' an' three hands. I could use one more. How much is Mr. Cecil payin'?

HOMER: Fifteen a day for a picker.

MR. AL: You promised to anybody else?

HOMER: Not for a week, then Mr. Leslie wants me to help with his barnin'.

MR. AL: Well, when you get finished with Mr. Cecil, come on down.

HOMER: Alright, I just might do that. What's the news today?

MR. AL: Richard Petty won that race.

HOMER: Well good for him. How's the war?

MR. AL: Which one?

HOMER: Oh, any of 'em.

MR. AL: Oh, they're all about the same. They're still fightin' the same places they were fightin' yesterday, and it looks like Israel may pop off again.

HOMER: Well, can't say as I blame 'em.

MR. AL: No, but sometimes I just can't see why they don't just all pull up and move to New York. Least there ain't no war there.

HOMER: Yeah, but some o' the things I heard about New York, maybe they're better off in Israel, war and all.

MR. AL: May be.

> MISS HATTIE and AL JR. enter carrying glasses of ice cold lemonade, one for each person, and distribute them.

MISS HATTIE: Here you are, Homer.

> MISS HATTIE and AL JR. resume their seats, and everybody takes a long drink.

HOMER: Um, that's good.

MR. AL: He's right, Momma, that's just what a man needs at the end of a hot day.

MISS HATTIE: How's Miss Rena, Homer?

HOMER: She's still ailin' a bit, but the doc says she should be back on her feet 'fore school opens.

JENNY: You gonna have to teach English again?

HOMER: Looks that way.

MISS HATTIE: Poor ol' woman, breakin' a leg at her age.

HOMER: Yeah, but she's taking it better than Miss Hattie Reese did. Almost killed her, havin' to stay in bed all that time.

MISS HATTIE: She stuck it out though. At eighty-three it would'a killed most women, but not her.

MR. AL: Then she went and died of a cold the next year.

MISS HATTIE: You just pray you live to die o' a cold at eighty-four years old.

MR. AL: Huh! Woman, what in the world for? My Grandpa Johnson had to quit farming when his legs give out, so he up and died, at sixty-two. My dad did the same thing when he was fifty-six, just a year after he had to quit farming, and I reckon I will too.

AL JR.: Yeah, that's my family; work can't kill 'em, but settin' still sure will.

HOMER: You're the same way, Al Jr. You never could sit still through a whole class.

JENNY: I wish they'd let you teach history like you want to, Homer.

HOMER: Well, it don't matter much, it's only one more year.

MISS HATTIE: Miss Rena gonna hafta retire?

HOMER: No, I'm goin' back to school. I been saving my money, an' in another year I oughta have enough to go back to school on.

MISS HATTIE: Go back to school? What in heaven's name you want to do that for? You got a good job. You oughta be savin' for a house an' a wife instead o' more school.

JENNY: Now Momma, if Homer wants to go back to school, you let him. If he gets some big degree, they might let him teach at the University.

MISS HATTIE: Well, I don't know. What I hear 'bout some o' those university professors, they had too much schoolin'. You oughta settle down and get married. Ain't right for a man to live alone. He needs a woman to cook an' clean an' keep him company.

JENNY: A wife could get a job and help put you through school, Homer.

AL JR.: She'd be more like to put you through the wringer.

JENNY: Al Jr., you shut up.

MISS HATTIE: I better look to those peas. Will you stay for supper, Homer? Jenny cooked a pecan pie last night, an' there's still half left.

HOMER: Thank you, Miss Hattie, but I better get home and get cleaned up.

MISS HATTIE: It's gonna be awhile 'fore we eat. You got time to run home and wash up if you don't dawdle.

JENNY: Do stay, Homer. Momma's got crowder peas.

MR. AL: Hang around, Homer. Maybe we'll churn up some ice cream after supper, make it a special occasion.

HOMER: You just talked me into it.

> MR. AL suddenly starts laughing at something in the newspaper.

MISS HATTIE: What in the world?

MR. AL: Snuffy Smith. Boy, what a hick.

MISS HATTIE: Humph!

HOMER (getting up): Well, I guess I better run on if I'm gonna get back in time for supper.

MISS HATTIE: I better get a move on too. Jenny, you come help me a little. Al, you and Al Jr. go wash up, but leave some hot water for me 'n' Jenny.

> All exit but HOMER. The stage-hand comes back out with a pair of regular shoes and a clean sports shirt for HOMER. He also has a comb, mirror, washcloth, and whatever else is necessary for HOMER's change. While he is addressing the audience, HOMER takes off his overalls, puts on the clean shirt and shoes, wipes his face and combs his hair. When the change is complete, the stage-hand exits with the old clothes, etc.

HOMER: Nice folks, ain't they? Nothing spectacular I admit, but comfortable. Sorta like the proverbial "old shoe." They sorta smell like an old shoe right now anyway. Tobacco and sweat, some perfume, whew! Excuse me while I change clothes here. Strange thing about tobacco. Ya see, most of the people around here are Baptist. An' Baptists ain't supposed to smoke. A good many do o' course, but most don't, especially round here. Yet they spend their lives raisin' tobacco for other folks to sin with. They don't mean nothin' by it o' course, they just haven't stopped to think about it. Sometimes they have to work real hard not to think about it, but they're a hard working lot, and they manage. They're generous souls though. Always takin' food to the sick or the needy. Nobody around here goes hungry, except maybe a Negro. An' that don't happen often. Anybody with two or three acres can generally grow enough to keep body, soul, and family together, 'cept in bad years. There's not a lot of money going around, but there's always plenty of what's in season. Why, a country preacher usually lives off what folks give him. He sure can't live off what they pay him. Every time a church gets a new preacher, the congregation gets together an' gives him and his family what they call a "pounding." The idea is that everybody gives a pound of something, flour, sugar, beans, corn, anything. Folks in this part of the country don't measure too strict though. A preacher usually gets enough to last about six months. Then 'bout every six months they get a new preacher. Yeah, nothing ever changes around here 'cept the preacher. Things about the same as they always have been, long as I can remember anyway. and I reckon they'll be that way for another year or two. It's a quiet life, kinda slow, but awful hard. These people are sorta like rocks, they stay in one place and just sorta wear away. But it's slow, so not much noticeable ever happens. Change just sorta creeps past without anybody paying much attention. They don't make much news down here. Only time these people get their name in the paper is when they're born, when they marry, and when they die. If they're lucky. Some only make two out of three. Most folks sort of like it that way, 'cept for some of the young ones, like me and Jenny.

>As soon as they have changed costumes, the actors drift back on. All are now dressed in clean, plain, informal clothes. JENNY wears a dress. MR. AL brings an ice cream churn with him, sits in his rocker, and begins to churn. MISS HATTIE brings some bowls and spoons.

>AL JR. is now reading the paper, and JENNY is sewing. They don't notice HOMER until he sits in the swing at the end of his speech.

HOMER: It's about the middle of the evening now; we've had a real good meal, an' we're sorta sittin' around waitin' for bedtime. Say what you like about these people, they do know how to eat. Biscuits and cornbread, real butter, lemonade and tea, ham or chicken, mashed potatoes, string beans, crowder peas, pecan pie. All fresh and homemade. And after letting that settle a spell, homemade ice cream on special occasions. For you city folks who wouldn't know about such things, that contraption Mr. Al's playing with is an ice cream churn. It makes ice cream. Now, Mr. Al, since he's turnin' the crank would say that he's making the ice cream. But those that don't turn the crank usually like to consider that the churn made the ice cream. It's all a matter of linguistics as us English teachers like to say. Note that dress Miss Jenny's sewing on there. That ain't no ordinary dress, no sir. That's one she's making for her honeymoon. Never mind that she ain't got a proposal yet. She figures she's gonna get one eventually, an' she might as well have her wardrobe ready. She's right, too. If she ever let it be known that she'd consider a farmer, there'd be a line from here to the road. She's made it more than clear she don't want no farmer boy though, despite Miss Hattie. Everybody gets married around here sooner or later though, and usually sooner. The only real question is to who. There's three kinds of people in the country, those that are married, those that are too young, and those that are lookin'. Why, it's even one of the requirements for being a preacher. There are three things you gotta be before you can be a preacher round here. You gotta be a man, you gotta be a graduate of a seminary, and you gotta be married. Oh, some of the circuit preachers still working their way through the seminary ain't married, but they better not get that diploma without gittin' a marriage license in the process. And if a preacher's been married for more than two or three years, he better have a kid. If he hain't, he's suspect. Which is why there are so many mixed-up preacher's kids running around causing trouble. Them and missionaries' kids, bad lot, both of 'em. Whenever two or more of them are gathered together, heaven and hell both run for cover. But enough of them. I suspect that ice cream is about ready.

>HOMER goes and sits on the swing with JENNY.

AL JR.: Some Senator is accusin' the president of lying again.

MR. AL: Well, if it ain't a Senator, it's a Congressman.

AL JR.: Says here somebody reported a girl in a topless bathing suit at White Lake yesterday.

MR. AL: Yeah?

AL JR.: Yeah. They went to arrest her, but she warn't but four years old, so they thought they'd let it go by. Hey, Jenny, would you ever wear a topless bathing suit?

JENNY: I did once.

MISS HATTIE: What?

JENNY: Last summer when we were at Carolina Beach. My strap broke while I was swimming, my top came off, and it took me a minute or two to catch it. There wasn't nobody around close, and the water was up to my neck, but for a couple of minutes there all I had on was my bottom.

MISS HATTIE: Al, maybe we better get Jenny a one-piece bathing suit before she goes to the beach again.

MR. AL: Sure, Momma. Which piece you want, Jenny, top or bottom?

JENNY: Pop! Quit it. You're embarrassing Homer.

HOMER: Well, if I'm embarrassed, why is your face red?

MISS HATTIE: You boys quit teasing her. Whole thing's foolishness anyway. Every girl I ever saw looked better with her clothes on then when she had 'em off.

MR. AL: An' how many girls you ever seen with their clothes off, Momma?

MISS HATTIE: Aw, well, not that many, but I don't suspect there's too great a difference 'tween one or another. Some are taller or fatter than others, but the basics is about the same. Ain't they, Homer?

HOMER: I'll take your word for it, Miss Hattie. I think I must have skipped the class in college where they studied that.

AL JR.: Is that what you goin' back to school for, Homer?

HOMER: Not that I know of, but you never can tell.

MR. AL: I think this cream is about done.

AL JR.: Well open her up and let's have some.

> MR. AL opens the churn. MISS HATTIE gives him the bowls, and he gives everybody a serving. Ad libs of "thanks" and "real good," etc.

MISS HATTIE (while they are eating.): Just why are you goin' back to school, Homer?

HOMER: Oh, curiosity, mostly. It's a big world out there, Miss Hattie, and just about the only thing I learned at college was that I didn't know much about it. I want another crack at making a dent in what there is to know.

MISS HATTIE: Well, I think it's foolishness, but I guess there's no stopping you and keeping you happy too. But you'll be back. Two or three years you'll come back all ready to settle down.

HOMER: Well, maybe. But there's a lot I want to see an' do an' learn before I settle anywhere. I got a big want to know, Miss Hattie.

MISS HATTIE: Yeah, most o' the boys get it out of their systems when they're in the army. Them big cities an' being away from home is fun for awhile, I guess, but soon they get ready to settle down, an' most of 'em come back home, back to the quiet and the elbow room.

HOMER: "Most of 'em"?

MISS HATTIE: Well, I can think of a couple that didn't. Joe Northland didn't, but he never married either. Wayne Davis turned preacher an' never come back 'cept to visit. But your cousin Edward went out for awhile, then come back to settle and get a wife. An' Bill and Ed Wheeler went all the way to Germany in the army, but they both come back when they got out. Yeah, all 'cept one or two come back.

JENNY: Hadn't anybody married here an' then left?

MISS HATTIE: Oh, a few girls married people who were just passin' through, salesmen or preacher's kids or somethin', an' they ain't back yet, but most of the men grew up around here eventually drift back.

HOMER: With everybody driftin' back, it's gonna be pretty crowded around here 'fore too many years.

MR. AL: It's already crowded. My great-grandfather had a big farm, several hundred acres. He had three sons, and they each got a share. Then my grandpappy had two boys who lived, and they split his share, an' me and my two brothers had to split up Dad's part when he died. I was the eldest, so I got the homeplace, an' there's been some buyin' and sellin' and swappin' o'course, but I haven't got fifty acres, including the yard, that's in my name. Yeah, great-grandpappy had to ride the better part of a day to visit his neighbor; all I have to do is walk a quarter mile down the road. It's already gittin' crowded.

MISS HATTIE: Well, it's about bedtime for us old folks; hard day tomorrow.

       MISS HATTIE collects the empty bowls and spoons.

MR. AL: Yeah, I guess it's time to turn in. You young folks don't stay up too late, you've got to work tomorrow too ya know.

       MR. AL picks up the churn and exits with it.

MISS HATTIE: I'll be in as soon as I wash these dishes, Poppa.

JENNY: Goodnight, Momma.

       MISS HATTIE exits with dishes.

AL JR.: Homer?

HOMER: Yeah?

A JR.: You reckon you'll come back?

HOMER: I doubt it, Al Jr. I might want to, but I doubt there's gonna be much to come back to. Reason everybody else came back was it was so quiet and peaceful and ordered around here. The ones that were in the army that came back, most of 'em were in one war or another, an' they just wanted to get as far away from fightin' as possible; the ones who went to the cities come back to get away from the noise and the people and the way things move so fast. But now, well, you heard your father. Calvary Mountain has doubled in size the last ten years, an' Goldsboro is a regular city now. Somebody's puttin' a factory of some kind by the creek. No, what they come back for ain't gonna be here much longer. An' some people are already thinkin' about movin' someplace quieter.

AL JR.: Whata you reckon a fella oughta do?

HOMER: Get out. Unless you want to be a farmer real bad. You could live off that fifty acres, I guess, though the soil's so worn out you'd never clear much money. You might could rent some land, but one bad year and you'd be bankrupt. An' you split whatever you do own among whatever children you have, an' none of 'em will have enough to live decent on. Some of 'em will have to move out. An' if you don't really want to be a farmer worse than anything, get out, cause you're just hurtin' somebody who does.

AL JR.: Is that why you're leaving?

HOMER: No, that's why I'm not coming back. I still got a few things I want to do before I settle down anywhere. You thinkin' about leaving?

AL JR.: Well, not right away. I haven't got the hunger for city sidewalks Jenny does. But you can't make a living farmin' anymore. The soil is almost dead, and every year fertilizer costs a little more, or you gotta have a new machine o'some kind which costs a thousand more than the year before. We're gettin' by now, but there's not much future in it.

HOMER: What you gonna do?

AL JR.: I don't know. I like farmin' and I like livin' here, but I'd like to have a little money in my pocket too. I guess I'll stay around a few more years and see how it goes. Dad's sorta countin' on me to help him run this place. But I doubt it could support him and me too if I went and got a family.

HOMER: You an' some girl makin' plans you haven't told me about?

AL JR.: No, but I got a feeling a certain girl is making plans she ain't' told me about. Goodnight, Homer.

HOMER: Goodnight, Al.

>   AL JR. exits. JENNY puts her sewing away. HOMER slips his arm around her shoulder.

HOMER: You better have a talk with that brother of yours and tell him about all the evil ways you women have of catching a man. It seems somebody is hot on his heels.

JENNY: And he's slowin' down on purpose.

HOMER: May be.

JENNY: Homer?

HOMER: Yeah?

JENNY: If Al Jr. did want to leave, where would he go, how would he get out?

HOMER: Well, he could go off to college, though he really isn't the schooling type. Or, he could just run off to Goldsboro, or even Raleigh, and get a job, maybe with some big company that has offices all over so that after awhile he could transfer someplace bigger. Or, he could always join the army and get some training in electronics or somethin' that would get him a good job when he got out.

JENNY: What about a girl. How could she get out.

HOMER: A girl like you?

JENNY: Maybe.

HOMER: Well, you could always marry a traveling salesman.

JENNY: Homer, I'm serious.

HOMER: Well, you could join the army too. Or you could go off to school. You could go to college, or even a junior college or a business school. You could work your way through. Or you could just move to the city and get a job clerking in a store or workin' in some factory.

JENNY: Or I could marry somebody who was leavin'.

HOMER: Somebody like me?

JENNY: Oh, if I got real hard up.

HOMER: You really want out?

JENNY: Lands yes! I'm tired of workin' like a dog all the time and never havin' anything to show for it. I want to wear a dress all day, not sweaty old work pants out in the field half the time. An' I want some change, some day that ain't the same as the one before, something to happen besides the sun coming up and the wind blowing. In the city there's things to do beside watch the tobacco grow.

HOMER: If you have the money.

JENNY: Yeah, but in the city there's money to be got. Around here you're lucky if they don't pay you in watermelon and corn. I'm tired of livin' or dyin' by the price of some old dead brown leaf. I'm just tired of this place.

HOMER: Well, maybe someday.

> Pause. He kisses her lightly on the cheek. Pause.

JENNY: When's school start.

HOMER: September fifth.

JENNY: You lookin' forward to it.

HOMER: 'Bout the way I'd look forward to hell.

> JENNY, to tease HOMER, adopts a Southern belle manner and pretends to be shocked.

JENNY: Ho-mer! Watch your language. I am a lady.

> HOMER suddenly become the sophisticated gentleman.

HOMER: My apologies. I was not aware you had virgin ears.

JENNY: Well, Lord knows, my ears ain't "virgin," but they still don't care for such language. Next thing you know, you'll be springing a "damn" on me.

HOMER: Well, my, my. I'm surprised you didn't spell such a word.

JENNY: It ain't the word, it's the way it's used.

HOMER: Well, next time, Mam, I'll be sure to put it across a stream.

JENNY: You better. (She giggles.) This is silly.

HOMER: Yeah.

There is a pause.

JENNY: Homer?

HOMER: Yeah?

JENNY: What's college like?

HOMER: Oh, lot's o' work, lot's o'fun, lot's o' people jammed in one little space. More happens there in two weeks than in a year here, but it all gets by so fast you don't hardly have time to stop and enjoy it.

JENNY: You think I'd like it?

HOMER: I don't know. You did pretty well in school as I remember, but you didn't seem to enjoy it any more than Al Jr. If you don't really like hittin' the books, college can get old fast.

JENNY: Yeah, I guess. You ever been to Chapel Hill?

HOMER: Couple o' times.

JENNY: You reckon a girl could get a job up there somewhere an' maybe meet up with some o' those college men?

HOMER: Yeah, I guess. But college men have a habit of preferrin' college women. Somebody else is alright to go out with or have a little fun with, but when it comes to pickin' a wife, they like to have somebody with a book education. I guess they figure if they have a fight they can both use big words and call it a discussion.

JENNY: You don't think none of those college boys would go for a girl that stopped after high school then?

HOMER: Well, they might nibble at your line a bit. You're mighty pretty bait, but don't expect to land one. College is another country, Jenny, with another set of rules, another language. A man usually wants to marry a woman who at least speaks his language.

JENNY: Are you that way, Homer? Should I give up on trying to hook you? Are you just havin' a little fun until you can find a book smart woman?

HOMER: Jenny...

JENNY: I like you quite a bit, Homer, and I thought you might feel a little toward me.

HOMER: I like you quite a bit, Jenny. If I was goin' to stay here, buy a few acres for vegetables, an' teach school, well, you'd have a better chance than most of.... But then you'd be stuck here, Jenny, and I don't think that's what you're after.

JENNY: No, I reckon not. You get me all twisted up inside, Homer. I feel like you'd be the one...but not here, not here. And I'm afraid that even if I left with you, after all your learnin' I'd get lost, get left behind somewhere.

HOMER: I don't know, Jenny. Maybe you'd be what I'd come back for. But I'll never know until I go.

JENNY: Yeah. Go on back to college, Homer. If you don't want to marry me, I'll cry a bit. Heaven knows this place will be even worse after you're gone, but I'll get by somehow. You're wasting yourself around here, Homer, courtin' ignorant farm girls...

HOMER: Jenny...

JENNY: An' tryin' to teach them farm boys 'bout Poe and Robert Burns. All them farmers'll ever do is raise tobacco, corn, and kids. You just make sure you get out. You're the one who's gonna make some difference in this world. I'll just have to find a way to get by on my own. Find my own way to somewhere.

HOMER: It's a long way from here to somewhere, Jenny. For either of us.

JENNY (looking off): They're closing the store; they just cut out the lights.

HOMER: Must be close to ten o'clock.

> JENNY walks to the front of the porch.

JENNY: I always did like to look up at the stars.

HOMER (crosses to her): It's awful clear tonight. You can see the moon's eyelashes.

> He puts his arm around her waist. She is stiff for a second, then relaxes against him.

HOMER: You ever want to go to the moon?

JENNY: Lands! I'm glad to get to go to Goldsboro now and then. I want to travel, but not that far. Did you?

HOMER: Yeah. The moon, Mars, New York, all them places. Then I went off to college, all the way to Ohio. Now I want me one o' them stars. You want to go to Raleigh, I want to go way past the moon.

> Pause.

JENNY: Way past the moon. (Pause.) It's getting late.

HOMER: Yeah.

JENNY: I hear they stay up real late in the city, eleven, twelve o'clock every night.

HOMER: They stay up late and die early. Goodnight, Jenny.

JENNY: Goodnight, Homer. Come see me on Saturday.

> They kiss lightly. JENNY exits. HOMER watches her go, then turns and addresses the audience. During his speech the lights slowly, imperceptibly fade back up to normal levels.

HOMER: Well, that's about it. A quiet little play. The sun went down and the stars came out. A day and an age passed away, and you saw a slice of it. You saw something that was a little bad and a little good that will never be again. I left the next May, and I never went back. Jenny married a traveling salesman. He's district manager up in Norfolk now; they've got an apartment and a baby boy. Jenny's up at twelve, three, and six o'clock, but it ain't to look at the stars. Al Jr. got a job at that new factory they built down by the creek. He got a house trailer, enough land for a garden, and a wife, in that order. He still helps his father with the farm, but he says after his father dies he might just up and move to California, but nobody takes him serious. Mr. Al and Miss Hattie are still farming, but Mr. Al says his legs are startin' to bother him. I guess he's got the same thing his pappy had. They got a new preacher last month. He smokes. They don't quiet know what to do about that. Well, that's about all the news from back home. I'm gonna step outside a minute now and look at the stars. One o' them things is mine.

> HOMER exits. End of ACT I.

ACT II

    AT RISE: WOMAN 1 is juggling three skulls.

WOMAN 1: Alas, poor Yorick. I knew him, Horatio. We had an affair back in 85. Damn good kisser. Ah, what lips these lips have kissed that now are dust, food for worms. Now I juggle men like balls, though they have no balls. All are full bald though, heads as ripe and bare as melons in the spring, but not a seed of thought therein. Their thoughts have flown, like swallows in the spring, leaving them hollow-eyed and empty-headed. Ah, such hollow men. Once they filled me, these three, warm and heavy on winter's nights. Now they are but fit for flights of fancy, memories whirling in the air. And these men, who come and go, shells of their former selves, they amuse me in new ways, until someday I drop them, and like hearts, they break.

    NARRATOR enters and snatches a skull out of the air, stopping the juggling.

NARRATOR: Playing with death again, I see.

WOMAN 1: I like to deal with serious topics. (Taking skull back.) A little tragedy for the masses. Cartharis and all that.

NARRATOR: Ah, yes. All that.

    WOMAN 1 exits with skulls.

NARRATOR: It's enough to make your head spin. Sorry, couldn't resist. And thus are our lives spun away at a petty pace. Back in our youth, we reached for stars. Later on, we just seem to reach, reach out for empty air.

    Actors bring out a target of a silhouette of a life-size man, arms and legs spread out, with padding all around, as for a circus knife-throwing act, and a bucket of throwing knives. Bales of hay or other padding may also be stacked by the target to provide added protection/masking.

    (Production note: There are at least two ways to stage the following. If you have actors who want to actually throw knives, go for it. Otherwise, the target, being a life-size outline of a man with arms and legs outstretched and lots of padding around, should mask a stagehand behind it able to thrust knives backwards through hidden notches in the target and provide the appropriate "thump" just as the actor throws a knife upstage of the target into a net or into padding in the wings. It is an old but, with good timing, still effective stage illusion. Any modern magician probably knows an even better way of doing it. The audience does need to see the target at an angle of less than 90 degrees for the final image to be effective, however.)

NARRATOR: We stand transfixed by life, ready to embrace the daggers of fate, with no idea of what is really going on. It is a strange time. As the poet said,...

WOMAN 2: Oh, quit stalling, we'll have it set up in a minute. No need to bore them with your yap too.

NARRATOR: I was just...

WOMAN 2: Yeah, yeah. It's a play, not Philosophy 101. You make everything a symbol and all the fun is gone. It's a target, not the image of humanity in isolation against the cosmos, OK? A target. These are knives, not "daggers of fate." OK? If they want to read something more into it, OK, but don't you go putting ideas in their heads. Let them enjoy it first. OK, sweetie?

NARRATOR: OK, OK. Just setting the scene a little.

WOMAN 2: The "Life is a Circus" thing has been done to death. This circus is just a circus.

NARRATOR: But sometimes life feels like a circus.

WOMAN 2: Sometimes I feel like a nut, sometimes I don't. Let them figure it out. They came to the theatre, not professional wrestling. Now just do your bit and let's get into the real acting, OK?

NARRATOR: OK, OK. Finish up and get offstage.

WOMAN 2: We're going, we're going. We got to get it lined up just right though. Don't want any accidents with this one.

NARRATOR: OK, OK, get it right. (To audience.) Excuse us, ladies and gentlemen.

> NARRATOR lends a hand setting up. Actors exit as soon as target is set up.

NARRATOR: So, with or without symbolism, impressionism, expressionism, dadaism, realism, naturalism, surrealism, cubism, or further ado, away we go.

> NARRATOR exits. Pause. SANDY (WOMAN 1) in exercise clothing enters, juggling knives. ANDREW (MAN 1, 2, or Narrator, whichever is most appropriate) enters unseen, stands silently watching. WOMAN throws knives at a large target with the outline of a man on it. She brackets the outline.

ANDREW: Isn't there supposed to be a live target for your little act?

SANDY: I was planning on you volunteering.

ANDREW: No thank you.

SANDY: Pity. Danger makes your life more interesting.

ANDREW: I drive on I-285 during rush hour. That's enough danger.

SANDY: Yes, Andrew the Safe and Sure. I remember all our quiet evenings at home.

ANDREW: Is that the reason you called me, to throw things at me?

> SANDY retrieves knives, throws one above target's right arm.

ANDREW: Well?

SANDY: Yes, as a matter of fact. I need you to stand right in front of that target tonight during the show. A favor for an old friend.

ANDREW: You're kidding.

SANDY: No. Add a bit of spice to your life.

ANDREW: Uh, thanks, but no thanks.

SANDY: You owe me. You owe me a lot.

ANDREW: Not my life. Ride an elephant maybe, something like that.

SANDY: Circus elephants kill more people than knife throwers.

ANDREW: Really?

SANDY: Look it up.

ANDREW: OK, bad example. Sell tickets, make popcorn, sweep the stands? (Pause.) In town for long? How about dinner? For old times sake.

SANDY: I work nights.

ANDREW: And during the day you throw knives at silhouettes of men.

SANDY: Everyday. Four hours a day. I've discovered it's what I'm really good at.

ANDREW: Well, congratulations. I guess everybody should be good at something. I remember you being good at other things though.

SANDY: What are you good at?

ANDREW: I think I have just been insulted.

SANDY: You never know. Just be careful what you say to a woman with knives in her hand. (Throws knife below right arm of target)

ANDREW: No cutting remarks? (Pause. She looks "daggers" at him.) How sharp are those?

SANDY: The blade is pretty dull, but the points are razor sharp. They're specially balanced for throwing. Each is 6 inches long, 11 inches counting the handle, they weigh 12 ounces, and yes, they could kill you. If I missed. (Throws knife beside right outside thigh of target.) Which I wouldn't. (Throws knife beside right hip of target.) Not on purpose. (Throws knife beside right chest of target.) Don't you trust me?

> ANDREW walks up to target and looks to see how close knives came and how deep they went in.

ANDREW: Trust has nothing to do with it.

SANDY: You owe me.

ANDREW: Not that much. (Pause.) You ever throw at a real person?

SANDY: Yes...in practice. I'm not going to lie to you, Andrew. Not in a show, only in practice.

ANDREW: Who?

SANDY: My teacher. The Great Sabatini. To prove I was ready.

ANDREW: Who does Sabatini throw at?

SANDY: His wife. But they just retired. He only hit her three times in thirty years. Two were just nicks, didn't even need stitches. Caught her in the calf once, years ago. Doctor had to clean and sew. Nice straight scar. (Throws knife to just outside left calf of target.)

ANDREW: Must have been an interesting marriage. What about getting another woman? Or does that ruin the concept?

SANDY: I need a gimmick. Something that makes a statement.

ANDREW: And women throwing knives at women is not the politically correct statement. Lesbian overtones. Mixed messages. Could I see one of those?

SANDY hands him a knife, picks up more from a box.

SANDY: Want to see if you're as good as a woman? (Throws knife beside left hip of target.)

ANDREW examines knife, balances it on finger, holds it as if to throw it, but does not.

ANDREW: You've changed, you know that?

SANDY: I ran away and joined the circus; what did you expect?

ANDREW: Acrobatics. Flying trapeze. Hanging by your teeth.

SANDY: Stereotypes.

ANDREW: Maybe a clown.

SANDY: Yes, be a liberated woman, be a clown.

ANDREW: I hear it's a rough job.

SANDY: We've got two in the show. They get bruised a lot.

ANDREW: (He hands her the knife back.) So, what do you do in the show?

SANDY: That's my problem. Right now I don't do anything.

ANDREW: Come again?

SANDY: I was Johnny's assistant...

ANDREW: Johnny?

SANDY: Johnny Simpson, The Great Sabatini.

ANDREW: Oh. Stage name.

SANDY: Of course.

ANDREW: Who are you?

SANDY: The Dangerous Delilah.

ANDREW: Right. Alliteration and allusion. Fits your theme.

SANDY: Can't be "Great" your first time out.

ANDREW: Of course not.

SANDY: I handed him the knives, helped set up the targets, tied Amy, his wife, to the target. Filled in for her if she got sick.

ANDREW: So you know what it's like to be on the receiving end.

SANDY: Oh, yes. You taught me how to just stand there and take it, remember? Johnny and Amy taught me about knives.

ANDREW: I'm trying to help you, not fight old fights.

SANDY: Sorry. I'm under a little bit of pressure here, and I thought I could count on you.

ANDREW: I want to help you, I'm just not...

SANDY: So help me. Look, Let's try it just once, to see how it feels. I'll miss you by at least a foot.

ANDREW: Well,...

SANDY: I'm ready to take over the act. We'll just do the really simple bits. All you would have to do is stand there. It's just a matter of practice.

> ANDREW looks in box of knives and pulls out a blindfold.

ANDREW: Is the blindfold bit rigged?

SANDY: No. I really can't see. I line it up first, keep my feet in place, and throw on a sound cue. (She demonstrates, covering eyes with free hand instead of using blindfold, throwing knife just above head of target.)

> ANDREW rubs his head near where knife would have gone if he were target.

ANDREW: You do that? In your act?

SANDY: Not yet. So far it's all eyes open stuff. But I'm working on it.

ANDREW: Why did Sabatini retire if you didn't have an act?

SANDY: I had one. I had a partner.

ANDREW: And?

SANDY: He was hit by a train.

ANDREW: You're kidding.

SANDY: I had a lover. I hope that doesn't make you too jealous. Name was Billy. One of the roustabouts. Strong as an ox, but not real bright. Great on loading docks and in bed, and not afraid of a few little knives or one little woman. Sadly unfamiliar with the rules of railroad safety, however. He was between two trains in the trainyard, checking on one of the loads. One train started to move, he jumped, stumbled, and fell. Instant decapitation.

ANDREW: Ugh. I'm sorry.

SANDY: We were supposed to do our first show tonight. And nobody wants to see a knife-thrower who just throws at balloons.

ANDREW: I see. (Pause.) You've changed, Sandy.

SANDY: I need a partner. One that's not afraid of me.

ANDREW: Well, I think that may let me out.

SANDY: Very funny.

ANDREW: I'm not kidding.

SANDY: Well, this would be a big change. You certainly didn't used to be afraid of me.

ANDREW: You've changed. (Pause.) And I can't even think what to tell you to do.

SANDY: Another big change.

ANDREW: Could you put an ad in a paper?

SANDY: Sure. Right.

ANDREW: No, I'm serious. Isn't there a circus newspaper of some kind?

SANDY: What would I say? "Novice female knife-thrower seeks male partner for close encounters."?

ANDREW: Touche'. This is not my area of expertise.

SANDY: And I remember you as an expert on everything. Besides, a Knife-throwers' target is not exactly a step up in the circus hierarchy.

ANDREW: I can imagine.

SANDY: Way above geeks, but below fire-eaters.

ANDREW: Ah. So, how do other knife-throwers get their partners.

SANDY: They seduce them.

ANDREW: Oh. Like you and what's-his-name?

SANDY (Hard as nails.): Yes.

ANDREW: You've changed. You've gotten hard...

SANDY (Cuts him off.): I need a week, starting tonight. Just while we're in town. Six shows, no blindfold bits. Get the boss off my back, give me a few days to work out something.

ANDREW: Till you find another roustabout?

SANDY: Roustabout, star-struck kid, rope-girl if I have to.

ANDREW: Bed and board, only six shows a week, no heavy lifting. That bed go for the rope-girl too?

SANDY: If necessary.

ANDREW: You have changed.

SANDY: I'm out in the world now. I have a career. And you owe me.

ANDREW: You left me, remember?

SANDY: You used me for five years.

ANDREW: Used is a strong word.

SANDY: You owe me a week.

ANDREW: I thought we were partners.

SANDY: You were wrong. Six shows. I'll never touch you. My career's on the line; I can't afford any mistakes. You used to trust me.

ANDREW: I used to do a lot of things. Listen, do you remember that Johnny Carson show when Ed Ames demonstrated hatchet throwing? They had a target set up much like this one.

SANDY: I must have missed it.

ANDREW: Ed had practiced before the show. Dead in the heart, every throw. But when the cameras came on, his aim slipped a little south. (Indicates crotch of target.)

SANDY: You're not afraid I'll kill you, you're afraid I'll emasculate you.

ANDREW: I'm afraid of you. Knives or no knives.

SANDY: How manly of you.

ANDREW: You're not the woman I used to know.

SANDY: I see. No debts of honor.

ANDREW: What we had was not a business deal. At least to me. And even if there was a business part to it, this is not a form of payment you can demand. You can't change the rules all by yourself.

SANDY: I am not going to be the target anymore. I'm going to be out front now, in charge.

ANDREW: Fine. Go right ahead. But I chose neither to throw or be thrown at. Now, do I have to back out of here, or can I trust you not to stab me in the back?

>   She suddenly throws a knife at the target, hitting it in the crotch. Pause. He picks up a knife, throws it at the target, and hits it in the heart. He turns his back and exits. The lights fade.

ACT III

> The stage is bare except for a rocking chair and a straight-back wooden chair. Upstage, on a slightly raised platform, are one or two other seats. It is the present, whenever that turns out to be. MAN (played by whichever male actor is most appropriate) is the same character at several different ages. Since there is no time for makeup or costume changes, the various ages will have to be indicated by the movement, posture and voice of the actor. The actor should not be made up to be any one age. GIRL (played by whichever female actor is most appropriate) is two different characters, the granddaughter (a good looking girl in her late teens), and the wife (an overweight woman at several different ages). This is to be done without makeup changes, and only minor hair or costume changes done in full view of the audience, so the actress should probably not resemble either character too strongly. AT RISE the MAN is sitting in the rocking chair, rocking. The NARRATOR stands behind him.

NARRATOR: In youth, we reach for the stars. Most of us never even come close. Later, we simply try to avoid slings and arrows and various other cutting edges of fate. We never avoid them all. Finally, we face the black void, the perfect mirror in which we see who we really are.

> NARRATOR exits. There is a long silence as the MAN rocks. Finally, he stops rocking, looks at audience, then starts rocking again. After another moment, he stops again.

MAN: I guess you expect me to say something.

> Pause. He starts rocking again. Longer silence.

MAN: I was born a long time ago. That makes me old. I am not senile. I am not sick. I am just old. I may be crazy, but who cares now?

> Pause.

MAN: I can still piss and shit all by myself. That keeps my daughter happy.

> Pause.

MAN: Eat well too. Chung's Chinese Delivery for lunch, Domino's Pizza for supper.

Pause.

MAN: Wish I could find a pancake place that delivered.

Pause.

MAN: Anyway, I can still take care of myself. Even jerk off now and then. Playboy Channel. I get the deluxe cable package. One of the advantages of lifetime annuities.

Pause. GIRL (as MABEL) enters upstage on platform and sits.

MAN: Wife died about six years ago. Too fat. I told her, Mabel, you're gonna pay a price for that fat. I guess we did.

Pause.

MAN: I was a writer, but you never heard of me.

Pause.

MAN: Never made a dime off it.

Pause.

MAN: I had 137 poems published, and even had six articles printed. And you never heard of me.

Pause.

MAN: Nobody ever heard of me.

Pause.

MAN: Hell, even I never heard of me.

Pause.

MAN: I was a very minor poet who spent thousands of dollars on postage and never made a dime. But I was a writer.

Pause.

MAN: I guess I wasn't very good.

Pause. Longer pause.

MAN: I made my living as an accountant. Was always good with numbers. Real left brain right brain split. I was also boring as hell. Didn't drink, smoke, use drugs, or cheat on my wife. Hell, I didn't even cuss for the longest time. I just added numbers during the day, and wrote poems at night. Boring as hell.

    Pause.

MAN: One day I discovered I was old. I was a boring, old accountant, not a young, exciting writer. And it was too damn late to change.

    He gets up.

MAN: After Mabel died I tried becoming the Lothario of the senior set. Ah, you young wimps don't even know what a Lothario is. I was a rake. No, you think that means leaves. I tried to fuck every sixty year old broad in sight, you understand that? Kids, too ignorant to be polite to.

    Pause.

MAN: Anyway, it didn't work. Oh, I worked, that ain't what I mean. I got laid left and right. They just kept dying on me.

    Pause.

MAN: It's usually the other way around. We men usually kick off, leaving the women to play black widow spiders. Guess I'm just too mean to go easy.

    Pause.

MAN: Three died, after Mabel. One in my arms. Got tired of trying to remember new names.

    Pause.

MAN: Now, the doctor won't let me drink or smoke, but he supplies me with plenty of drugs. Don't have much kick though. Only fun left is cussing and watching Playboy. Least their tits still stick up, and I can turn 'em off afterwards.

    Pause.

MAN: You see, the problem is, I never learned to use my hands, no hobbies. My job was just adding and subtracting numbers, which never was exactly fun. In my spare time, I'd write. That hurts too much now. Arthritis of the soul. So, I read and watch TV, and walk enough to keep the bowels moving. Not watching the soap operas yet though. Hope I never get that senile.

    Pause.

MAN: Maybe I'll be like that "One Horse Shay" and everything will go at once. It's when you drop a piece here and another piece there that it kills you.

>	Pause.

MAN: Death is funny, you know. It just sort of happens. Mabel went easy, thank God. Massive stroke. Chopping onions, she was. I always hated onions, but she loved them. I never ate them again. She cut her hand when she fell, but she never knew it. Big explosion in the brain, then lots of stars, that's all. Hell of a woman. Pure dynamite in bed. Maybe I'll go like that.

>	Pause.

MAN: Better question is, what'll I do till I go? If your dreams and your woman are both dead, what's left? Gardening? Needlepoint? Shit. And I'm not rich enough to be a dirty old man.

>	Pause.

MAN: All that's left is being a mean old grouch. That's not much to live for, but it has its good points. You get to call a jerk a jerk to his face. You can annoy your daughter all to hell. You can even cuss at women. Now that is fun. Especially the young ones; they cuss back. All in all, I guess it will do until something better comes along.

>	Returns to chair. Sits.

MAN: Meanwhile, I watch the news and laugh at that a lot. It's like a re-run now. Ricky and Lucy Visit the Kremlin. The Three Stooges Go to Congress. Abbott and Costello at the U.N. It all fades together like a long joke on Dan Rather. Walter Cronkite was better. Chet Huntley. I always wanted to be on the news. Never got my Andy Warhol fifteen minutes of fame. Got my name in the funeral notice when Mabel died, but that don't count.

>	Starts rocking.

MAN: Bad poets and honest accountants just don't seem to count. I was a counter who never counted. One, two, put on your shoe; three, four, open the door; five, six, flick your bic; seven, eight, curse your fate; nine, ten, do it again. Nine, ten.

>	Lights change to "poetry" lights. MAN picks up a notebook from the chair and reads silently. From the sound system comes the voice of a younger MAN, reading. (There should be music under the poetry.)

Call me away to the green hill
To the rugged, rocky way
Sing me a song of the hawk's trill
And the lusty month of May
For I am a man of the Spring wind
Of the soaring crag o'er the sea
For I am a man of the wild fen
Of the highland called will I be.

MAN: Of the highland called will I be.

> Lights fade. The GIRL changes her hair or something to indicate a change in character. The "scene" lights come up. MAN is asleep in the rocker. GIRL is trying to gently wake him.

GIRL: Gramps. Gramps! Come on!

MAN: OK, OK, I ain't deaf.

GIRL: You fell asleep with the TV on again.

MAN: So? What the hell do you think it's for? They send you to check on me again?

GIRL: Of course.

MAN: Well, tell them I said to fuck off.

GIRL: Gramps.

MAN: OK, you can say jump in the lake, I don't care.

GIRL: They worry.

MAN: About what? That I might die? Of course I'm going to die sooner or later. They want you here to watch?

GIRL: No.

MAN: Let them come watch. I'll put on a show. Kick my legs and everything.

GIRL: They worry you'll hurt yourself. You're all alone here.

MAN: Stop being so god damned nice.

GIRL: OK, you old coot. They didn't want you to have a heart attack, pee your pants, and mess up the rug.

MAN: More like it. What the hell is a coot, anyway?

GIRL: Hell if I know.

MAN: Cuss for me.

GIRL: Now, Gramps...

MAN: Come on, cuss for me.

GIRL: You damned old fucker, you done screwed your ass with a telephone pole this time.

MAN: Hey, that's good; I like it.

GIRL: Oh, if Mama ever heard me...

MAN: Yeah, I know. I never cussed. Never, ever, till long after your mother was grown. Too late then.

GIRL: Did you eat your lunch?

MAN: Even the obscene avocado. Let the juice trickle down my chin.

GIRL: Bet you enjoyed that.

MAN: So, how's your love life?

GIRL: Now, Gramps...

MAN: OK. So, how are "they"?

GIRL: "They" are fine. Dad got a promotion to Assistant Vice President, at least it will be official next month. Judy has her first date this Friday.

MAN: She got a diaphragm yet?

GIRL: Gramps, she's thirteen! It's a junior high dance.

MAN: You read the papers lately? You know how many thirteen year olds got pregnant last year?

GIRL: I'll talk to her, OK? My God.

MAN: Her mother certainly won't. She certainly never told you anything. Speaking of whom...?

GIRL: Mom is fine.

MAN: Except for?

GIRL: Nothing.

MAN: You got to learn to lie better.

GIRL: She bounced a check again.

MAN: I'm an accountant all my life, my daughter can't balance a damned checkbook.

GIRL: It's no big deal. I mean, we've got the money. She makes more than Dad.

MAN: She's so smart, how come she can't subtract?

GIRL: I don't know. Listen, I've got to go on to school. I've got a late class. Could we do the rest of the routine?

MAN: I ate all my vegetables, the nurse checked my blood pressure just yesterday and said it was fine, 110 over 80 if "Mama" has to know. I had a very fine bowel movement at eight thirteen this morning, walked two miles in an hour without getting my heart rate above 130. I took all six of my pills, including the diuretic that has made me pee five times today already, but I always made it to the john in time. I raped the public health nurse, but only twice, then killed her and stuffed her body in the trash with the carrots from lunch that I threw out. I will now go blind from lack of carotene so the police will never suspect me, even though the nude, ravaged body is in my trashcan.

GIRL: Well, I'm glad you're taking care of yourself.

MAN: Tell "Mama" that if she wants to examine my bodily secretions personally, I will gladly submit samples.

GIRL: Mom, Gramps said to give you a pile of shit.

MAN: Exactly. Now go meet what's his name, and screw his brains out.

GIRL: It's a class, honest. Elementary Psychology.

MAN: Whatever.

GIRL: See you later.

MAN: Have fun.

> GIRL exits to upstage platform and changes to MABEL during poem; MAN reads book. Lights change to poetry lights again. Voice over.

The wind is free, as is the sea
the bird on wing, the wolf that sings
yes, all are free, but you and me
for I am bound to you by endless ties

and you are tied to me by vows and years
some are velvet bonds, self-selected
others rawhide, tied by tears
so blow wind, roll sea,
we cannot fly or sing, but you'll be by my side
come hawk or hunt, hurricane or highest tide.

> Lights change to monologue lights.

MAN: I guess I..., well, never mind. Talk about something else.

> Pause.

MAN: I hate baseball. Can't get anything but the damned Braves on cable. I used to play, you know. Not pro, but in high school. Guess I wasn't much good at that either. Right field. Batted seventh.

> Pause.

MAN: I went to Mexico once, Mabel and I. Costa del something. Hot!, Boy. Like a car in the sun with the windows rolled up. Made Mabel sweat like a pig. And all the Mexicans seemed so poor. Made you feel guilty to have any fun. Florida was better, till it started to get crowded about 1970 or so. I started to feel like an alligator down there; I knew they couldn't shoot me, but I knew they wished I was somewhere else.

> Pause.

MAN: You know, alligators are very old. Haven't changed much in millions of years. They just found their little niche, crawled in, and there they stayed. One lives and dies, and another just like it comes along and does exactly the same. Not much changes for alligators.

> Pause.

MAN: I guess they get bored too.

> Lights fade. Music fades up, easy, slow dance music of the past. Different colored "flashback" lights fade up. The MAN is young again, sitting in the chair. GIRL enters from platform. He crosses to her.

MAN: Mabel, would you, would you dance with me.
GIRL: I was hoping you would ask me.

> They dance, slow, close. The lights change to poetry lights. The music changes to the poetry music. They keep dancing. Voice over.

Your breasts are honey in my mouth
Your body warm like biscuits and gravy

I love to sip you like hot coffee
Sweet with cream, smooth with sugar.

> The lights fade. The music fades. The scene lights come up. MAN is in rocker. GIRL is taking his pulse. The MAN has a thermometer in his mouth.

MAN: Hurry up.

GIRL: Don't talk.

> Pause.

GIRL: OK. About 70.

MAN: When it stops, I'll let you know.

GIRL: Don't talk with the thermometer in your mouth.

MAN: Then take it out.

GIRL: A few more seconds.

> Pause.

GIRL: OK.

> She removes thermometer.

MAN: I'm not sick, I'm just old. Why can't my daughter get that through her thick skull.

GIRL: Ninety eight point two.

MAN: I'll put on a sweater.

GIRL: Well, I guess you're all right.

MAN: Tell my daughter I'm better than she'll be at this age.

GIRL: Well, that's probably true. And I'll make her life even more miserable than she makes yours.

MAN: Impossible.

GIRL: Now Gramps. Be nice.

MAN: No. I stopped being nice six years ago. Ain't no fun. Ah, I know it ain't her fault. She inherited Mabel's fat and my personality. How she got married, I'll never know.

GIRL: Gramps!

MAN: Now you, you got lucky. Slim and taut like me, but behind the eyes, you're Mabel. Damn, you're pretty. Smart as a whip too, so you know how to use it. So what the hell are you doing hanging around an old fart like me? Aren't there any young men out there?

GIRL: Yes, there are.

MAN: Ah ha!

GIRL: But nobody like you.

MAN: Damn it, they're not supposed to be like me. I'm old.

GIRL: What you are is crazy.

MAN: That too.

GIRL: Gramps, am I really pretty? Not just to you, or Dad or Mom. I mean like a model, or a...

MAN: Like one of those naked foldout girls is pretty?

GIRL: Yeah, I guess.

MAN: What makes you think you're not?

GIRL: Well, you're never sure what men are looking for.

MAN: Ah, man trouble.

GIRL: A little. I sort of got dumped yesterday.

MAN: Well, let me tell you something. What men are looking at, and what men are looking for, aren't the same thing. Your grandmother couldn't have bribed her way into a nudie magazine, but she put most of those girls to shame in every way that counts. I wouldn't have traded her for six of those double D's bouncing around.

GIRL: Gramps!

MAN: So sue me. Anyway, the point is, you're pretty, but all that does is get their attention. A lot of other things matter a whole lot more after that.

GIRL: Yeah, I know. But am I really pretty, you know, sexy?

MAN: The truth?

GIRL: The truth.

MAN: Your eyes sparkle like tears of desire Your mouth arouses kisses wet and sweet. Your breasts point to passion wild. Your hips hold promises wide and deep Your thighs lure me like dreams do

GIRL: Oh lady grand, my wife, my life. In your eyes would I smile. In your arms would I lie. By your side would I die.

MAN: Oh, you remember that one, do you?

GIRL: Yes. I've been reading that collection of your published poems that Grandma had printed.

MAN: Accountants shouldn't try to write poetry.

GIRL: I like it.

MAN: You haven't studied much English yet.

GIRL: I'll still like it. But, you didn't answer my question. And you're about the only one who would tell me the truth.

MAN: OK, OK, clinical analysis. Just remember, you asked for this. Stand up, let me see. Now, your face is most important, no matter what anybody says. Yours is good, nose well proportioned, mouth not too big. Your teeth are still good, keep them that way. You need to learn to put a little more arc on the eyebrows with makeup, but your cheekbones are naturally high, you've got good color, and your skin is clear. Use your hair to frame your face, don't let it get too far in to the point it hides anything. Don't get too much sun, and that face will be world class for thirty years. As for the body, well, the tits are good, not too big, not too small, nice round shape. I'm assuming you haven't got a box of kleenex stuffed in there.

GIRL: Gramps!

MAN: You asked, so listen. The crucial thing is proportion. You want your bust and hips to be about the same, with the waist measurement two thirds of what the bust or hips are. You look pretty close to that to me. You've still got natural muscle tone right now, but you're going to have to exercise to keep it. Otherwise the boobs sag and the hips roll instead of bump. Your ass is fine too, as far as I can tell. Legs seem fine, tight, no scars. Feet not too big. You're a little on the thin side, but that's good; you'll keep your shape longer that way. Don't have to worry about moss growing under your breasts.

GIRL: Gramps!

MAN: All in all, I'd rate you a nine to a nine and a half. With a little training, I could probably get about five hundred dollars a night for you, at least for another year or two. Then you'd lose your novelty, and the price might drop a little.

GIRL: Damn it, stop!

    Pause.

MAN: As far as tits and ass go, you're first class. So much for tits and ass.

GIRL: You're a real son of a bitch.

MAN: Thank you. You can really cuss me out if you want to.

GIRL: Oh, you'd love that.

MAN: Probably.

GIRL: I was just feeling a little insecure.

MAN: Insecure? Insecure is when everybody you meet takes your pulse. That's insecure. Hey, some guy dumped you; so what? He's a square peg, you're a round hole.

GIRL: So to speak.

MAN: Whatever. Not every shoe you try on fits, OK?

GIRL: I'm not a cow selling milk; I get the picture.

MAN: OK. But damn you are gorgeous.

GIRL: Gramps!

    Lights change to poetry lights. MAN moves away from chairs as GIRL changes character and sits in rocker during voice over.

When daylight blushes
I rise in you
At twilight
I sink into your arms
Year by year
I live in you
And need no other call
To rise or fall.

    Lights change to flashback lights. GIRL is in rocker. MAN, young again, enters.

MAN: Mabel.

GIRL: Yes?

MAN: They're going to publish my poem!

GIRL: Oh, Honey, that's great. I knew somebody would. I'm so proud of you! You're wonderful and I love you so much. (They kiss) Which poem is it?

MAN: "Your eyes sparkle like tears of desire."

GIRL: Oh. That one.

MAN: I thought you liked that one.

GIRL: Oh, I do. I really do; just thinking about it makes me feel so...wanted. I'm just not sure I like the idea of everybody else reading it. It's a little embarrassing. My thighs luring and my breasts pointing. I didn't know you were sending it out.

MAN: You said you liked it.

GIRL: But what will Mama say when she reads it?

MAN: I doubt your mother reads Silken Wind Journal. They only print five hundred copies, and that's in Wisconsin.

GIRL: Oh. So we don't have to tell her.

MAN: Well, I guess not.

GIRL: Well, I love you a whole lot, but I don't think I want my mother thinking about my mouth arousing and my hips holding.

MAN: OK, OK.

GIRL: I certainly don't mind if you do though.

> They kiss. Lights fade. GIRL goes upstage and changes to MABEL. Monologue lights fade up. MAN is in rocker.

MAN: It gets cold at night. Even in the summer the nights are cold when you get old. I guess the blood just doesn't move as fast. I keep thinking I'll freeze rather than die. One night the electric blanket will kick out, and I'll wake up stiff as a board. I'll be so stiff they'll think I'm dead and bury me. I'll thaw out in the coffin and be all dressed up with no place to go.

> Pause.

MAN: I hate wearing suits. Had to wear one to work every day, and hated every day of it. Whoever invented neckties should have been hung with one. Haven't worn a suit since I retired, except to funerals. I hate funerals. I thought about asking not to have one, but I figured it was one last little revenge. I hate the idea of being buried in a suit too. I'm already going to be dead, do you have to make me miserable too? I thought about asking to be buried naked. I sleep in the nude, and I'm supposed to look like I'm asleep, right? Then I found out that when you die, your dick gets stiff, so I knew that was out. My daughter isn't about to let me go to heaven with a hard-on without covering it with something.

> Pause.

MAN: I guess what I hate most is not leaving much behind. I don't mean money. If the insurance companies don't go broke, there'll be a little of that. I mean one daughter and 137 poems. That's it. The daughter's OK, I guess. She's a nice enough woman, but I'm not sure the world would have been any worse off if she hadn't come along. That's terrible for a father to say, isn't it? About the same is true for the poems; far as I know, nobody would have missed them either. So, where does that leave me? I tried to make Mabel happy, and she's dead. Maybe it'll make some difference in heaven, or whatever, but, down here, in twenty years or so, it'd be the same as if I'd just gone fishing. And I hate that.

> Lights change. Voice over. GIRL changes character and moves to lower level.

Poetry explodes in the brain
It hits the olfactory nerve
convulses the cerebral cortex
bounces off the cerebellum
rattles around the medulla oblongata
and ripples down the spinal cord
blasting away old synapses
without ever blinking an eye.

> Lights change to scene lights. MAN asleep in rocker, GIRL awake in chair.

MAN (waking)**:** Mabel?

GIRL: No, Gramps. It's me.

MAN: Oh. Guess I was asleep.

GIRL: Guess so.

MAN: Why didn't you wake me?

GIRL: It seemed to be a very pleasant dream.

MAN: What? (looks at his crotch) Oh.

GIRL: Grandma?

MAN: Yeah. I haven't got many secrets from you, do I?

GIRL: Guess not.

MAN: Your mother shouldn't be sending you over here all the time. You're too young to know all an old man's secrets.

GIRL: I don't mind. You're how I get my real education.

MAN: We were in the kitchen.

GIRL: In the kitchen?

MAN: Cooking dinner.

GIRL: Oh.

MAN: I was making a batch of cornbread. She always made me cook the cornbread. She was pulling the skin off some chicken breasts so they wouldn't be so fattening. We were just there, cooking and bumping into each other in that little kitchen. She'd bend over to get a pan, and I'd pat her ass. That surprise you? You think it was something hotter?

GIRL: Maybe.

MAN: What's surprising is that my body can remember better than my brain can. And such strange things; cornbread, shoes on the floor, that old cat we had. It just all comes back. I can't seem to grow old decent.

GIRL: That's what I like about you. Your mind's still seventeen years old.

MAN: When I get back to six, shoot me.

GIRL: Oh, you'll be seventeen all your life.

MAN: Well, that may not be saying much.

GIRL: Did the doctor tell you something today?

MAN: Nothing new.

GIRL: He called home. Talked to Mom. Mom talked to Dad. Nobody talked to me.

MAN: So you came to the horse's mouth, or horse's ass.

GIRL: You tell me; which do I get, straight talk, or a pile of shit?

MAN: Which do you want?

GIRL: I...I'm not sure.

MAN: It's nothing new, either way.

GIRL: I know.

MAN: I'm old, that's all. Not senile, not sick, just old. And sooner or later, that's enough.

> Pause.

MAN: Dance for me.

GIRL: What?

MAN: Dance for me. Like we were dancing. Like time got bent and we met at some middle year, and danced like fawns.

> The dance music fades up. The GIRL hesitates, then awkwardly, then gracefully dances as if holding someone in her arms. Slowly the lights change to poetry lights. During the voice over, the music changes, and they dance together.

There is a song the heart sings
It to a tune keeps time
The melody of heartstrings
That tunes your heart to mine

And by the beat of life we dance
to its rhythm and its rhyme
from jig to waltz to dirge we prance
as the beating heart keeps time

And when the fiddler calls last chance
and the music fades away
our toes will tap for one last dance
as down in bed we lay.

> Music and lights fade. Flashback lights fade up. GIRL enters holding "baby." MAN is in chair.

GIRL: Our baby.

MAN: Yes.

GIRL: Say hello to Daddy.

MAN: Now Mabel.

GIRL: Oh, you have made me so happy. I am just so proud to have your baby. Are you happy?

MAN: Very happy you're both healthy.

GIRL: Are you going to write a poem for your little baby?

MAN: Maybe. I've been told my poems sound like nursery rhymes as it is.

GIRL: Oh, don't worry, Dear. Somebody will like your poems sooner or later. And this cute little baby here will give you plenty to write about. Come on, do something poetic for Daddy. Oh, yes, you are a cute little baby, you are. Mommie and Daddy's little angel. I'm so proud of your Daddy. You will be too, just you wait.

> Lights change to poetry lights. Voice over. During poem GIRL lets MAN hold baby for a moment, then takes baby back and exits as lights fade at end of poem.

Don't count on life
It surprises you
You grab the golden ring
It scrapes your knuckles
Sail into safe harbor
You run aground
It hits you where you're looking not
Trips you up, pushes you down
Leaves you bloody, muddy, bowed
And not a single soul in sight
To blame or bash or pound
Except the one who did his best
Who gave his heart and soul
Who now lies prostrate in the dust
Hearing his heart's last sound.

> Lights fade, then monologue lights come up on MAN in rocker.

MAN: By the time you get my age, you're supposed to have learned something. You don't learn shit. I don't know a damn thing anymore. Now, my mind still works, that ain't what I'm saying. Hell, I can add two eight digit numbers in my head, say 84,692,735 plus 34,675,841; that's 119,368,576. That impress you? Just an old math trick accountants learn to impress clients. You add from left to right instead of right to left so you can figure out the numbers as you're saying them. Makes people think you're really sharp. Now, numbers, I'm still sure of. It's other stuff that gets hazy. Right and wrong, why I'm alive, stuff like that. Oh, you live long enough, you realize anybody says they have the answer to anything besides addition and subtraction is usually dead wrong. And what all the yelling and shouting is about is beyond me. I used to know, but I was wrong. Now I think maybe God just has a very twisted sense of humor. Maybe I'll find out before long. Don't expect me to send a message back though. Phone service ain't that good, I hear. Wish it was; there's many a time I would have paid all kinds of toll to talk to Mabel for just three minutes. No, you want any wisdom from me, you better take it now, and all I can tell you is that I don't know nothing, and you don't either.

> Dance music faintly in background. Crossfade to flashback lights. GIRL enters. She twirls around, as if showing off new clothes.

GIRL: Like it, Honey?

MAN: Very sexy, Mabel.

GIRL: I thought I'd try to liven things up a little, now that we have the house to ourselves again. While the daughter's away in college, the parents will play.

MAN: Pretty expensive babysitter.

GIRL: Is something wrong?

MAN: Oh, no, not really.

GIRL: Oh, come on, you can tell me. I've seen you naked.

MAN: I got four rejection slips today.

GIRL: Well, you have gotten one or two before.

MAN: One or two thousand, you mean. But never four in one day. A new record for poetic futility. I write and write and mail and mail, and all I get is the world's greatest collection of rejection slips. If I had all the money I spent on postage, we'd be rich.

GIRL: Now stop it, just stop it. You're a good poet. I like your poems. Especially the ones about how sexy I am. Lots of poets don't get recognized right away, you know that.

MAN: I'm not Emily Dickenson, Mabel; I'm trying to get published.

GIRL: And you will be, sooner or later. You just wait. You're wonderful. I love you, your daughter loves you, and those stuffy old editors are going to feel like fools one of these days. Just don't give up now. I'm not about to let you quit now. We can afford a few dollars for postage. You've just got to let these editors know how wonderful you are.

MAN: Well...

GIRL: No "well" about it. Now get up and dance me off to the bedroom and let's see if we can't do something worth writing an ode about.

> She pulls him to her. Poetry music fades up. They dance. Crossfade to poetry lights. Voice over.

When I was a silent and sad song
I sang for you a lay
A Summer tune and a Spring song
In the golden month of May
And in the ice of winter
If we be old and fey
I'll sing for you December
Though my voice be tired and grey.

> Lights fade. Scene lights fade up. GIRL alone, pacing. MAN enters.

GIRL: Gramps! Where were you?!

MAN: I took a walk.

GIRL: You always walk in the mornings.

MAN: It's getting too cool in the mornings.

GIRL: I was about to call somebody.

MAN: Who?

GIRL: I don't know, Mom, the police.

MAN: Great, Phyllis Diller and the Three Stooges. What did you think they would do?

GIRL: Look for you.

MAN: Listen, I appreciate your concern, but. If I am not here, I'm out walking. If I'm out walking, either I'm fine or I had a heart attack, collapsed in the street, and was run over by a truck. If I have just had my face imprinted with Goodyear tire tracks, I would just as soon you didn't see me, OK? I don't walk down dark alleys; if I just fell and busted my hip, somebody would notice, and I'd call you from the hospital.

GIRL: OK, OK, sorry. Now I feel guilty for caring about you.

MAN: No, you are guilty of worrying. Caring you can do, it's worrying that's not allowed.

GIRL: Can I get the rules in writing?

MAN: Don't change on me. Just don't change on me. I'm still the grouchy, dirty old man who likes cussing and complaining, OK? I'm not senile, I'm not sick....

GIRL: You're just old.

MAN: Right.

GIRL: And sometimes that's enough.

    Pause.

GIRL: You damned bastard, get your head out of your ass and clean the shit out of your ears long enough to hear me say I love you.

MAN: Ah, my blue nightingale, I know that. I know that. And I love you. We don't have to say goodbye. We don't need to say goodbye.

    Pause.

GIRL: Maybe we don't need to say goodbye, but I need to say thank you. If something happened, and I never said thank you, I'd never forgive myself. Thank you for being my friend, for loving me. Thank you for letting me love you.

MAN: Well, I love you with all my heart. And if you ever forget that, I will come back and tan your little ass till you can't sit for a week, you hear me?

GIRL: Yes, Gramps.

MAN: Now enough of this syrupy stuff. You're going to give me diabetes and really screw my ass.

GIRL: Sorry, Gramps. Anyway, I've got to report. I'm late now.

MAN: No, no more reports.

Pause.

GIRL: That's not going to go down well at home.

MAN: I'm tired of my daughter charting my excretory activities. I'm tired of people checking my pulse like they don't expect to find one. Don't hold my wrist, hold my hand. It's getting cold.

> GIRL takes his hand. Lights slowly cross to poetry lights. Voice over. Slow fade during last few lines of poem. GIRL moves back to platform and changes to MABEL.

In ice, in time, blood freezes
Suspended, held, eyes see only cold
Antarctica was once a steaming jungle
Arizona once a waving sea
If they bury us in sand
Will we sail a southern sea
If put on ice
Will we climb the golden palm
When eternity has thawed
And ice turned into rain.

> Monologue lights fade up. MAN in rocker.

MAN: I hate waiting.

> Pause.

MAN: And waiting to kick off really sucks. It do take the joy out of life, it do, it do.

> Pause.

MAN: You don't get involved in mini-series, for one thing. and those six part mysteries on Masterpiece Theatre, forget it.

> Pause.

MAN: I thought about trying to live till Christmas, but what would I do with the presents? And talk about being hard to shop for, boy! "I'd like a nice tie for a dying man." "What color shirt goes well in a coffin?" What in hell do you buy for a corpse?

> Pause.

MAN: Then I thought about checking out early, avoiding any chance of extended vegetation. But that would mess the hell out of the insurance, not to mention make people think I wasn't having any fun. You're supposed to savor each precious moment at this point. Hell. My last precious moment was in 1983. Now they're just moments. Still, I don't like the idea of making people feel I didn't enjoy their company. So, I guess I'll just have to ride it out.

Pause.

MAN: If I was sure I'd head straight for Mabel, I'd just go on and go, but you never know for sure. Might be a long exit interview with Jesus or something. Maybe a waiting line at the Pearly Gate.

Pause.

MAN: I read one of those books about people who "died" and came back, you know, down the white tunnel, see old friends and relatives, glowing "presence," etc. I hope it's that easy, but I doubt it. Nothing in life was ever that simple, why should death be any different? No, I'm sure there'll be a surprise or two. Just hope they're good ones. My heart isn't up to many bad shocks.....Now that was a pretty stupid thing to say, wasn't it?

> Lights cross to poetry lights. Voice over. GIRL is silently reading from a book upstage.

Once upon a daisy
A girl went out to play
The sunshine saw her smile
And blew the clouds away
The hummingbird taught her to skip
The breeze to jump, the squirrel to run
The willow danced its shade around
And pines dropped cones for dolls and clowns
So sing my little darling
The flowers need your sun
The daisy and the lily
Who smile on my golden one.

> Flashback lights. Dance music fades up faintly in background. GIRL enters with a thin book. MAN in rocker.

GIRL: Honey?

MAN: Hum?

GIRL: I like that poem you wrote, about once upon a daisy.

MAN: Thank you.

GIRL: I love you, you know that.

MAN: Yes. And I love you.

Pause.

GIRL: You ever regret anything?

MAN: Such as?

GIRL: Marrying me. Having a daughter.

MAN: No. Those two things I am rather pleased by. I just wish I had written better poetry, that's all.

GIRL: I like it. I like it a lot.

MAN: I know. Do you regret anything?

GIRL: No. Oh, an unkind word here and there, that kind of thing. I never have regretted being with you. That I do not regret at all. I hope we get to grow very old together. I just wanted to be sure you were satisfied. We are starting to get old, you know.

MAN: Do you regret that?

GIRL: No, I guess not. I don't want to go back, not be young again; not if I can't remember all this, all my time with you.

MAN: I tried to make you happy. I really did.

GIRL: Well, you succeeded in that.

MAN: I did the best I could.

GIRL: You did very well, dear, all things considered. And I thank you.

> Lights cross to poetry lights. Voice over. During poem GIRL moves upstage to platform, changes from MABEL, and moves back to chair.

When first you kissed me, flowers bloomed
Bees set out in search of blossoms
With that kiss, a wave was born
that ran throughout the sea
the moon turned full and gleamed new light
as the sun arose in me
For such a kiss the earth will pause
from chasing round the sun
and I'll stand still, like mountains
till next dawnkiss of the sun.

> Scene lights fade up. MAN in rocker, GIRL in chair. Silence. MAN rocks. GIRL holds his hand. Dance music faintly in background.

MAN: "I never saw a moor, I never saw the sea." Damn, I wish I'd written that. It all seems so simple, but it's the hardest thing in the world. I tried to do the hardest thing in the world, and came up one step short. Damn, damn, damn. Mabel, loving you better count for something, because it's the only thing I ever came close to getting right.

> Lights and music cross to poetry. Voice over. During poem there is a very slow fade to black and silence.

Ripe fruit on the vine
Clusters of life huddled together
Growing with the same sap
Bud to blossom, green to red
One day a hand will pass
A few will fall to ground
Many to the drying pit
To tables, or to presses steel

Only one or two are blessed
Picked to bleed a lasting glory
To burst eternal essence
In holy communion wine.

    Lights fade up. GIRL in rocker. MAN upstage on platform.

    Pause.

GIRL: I guess you expect me to say something.

    Pause.

GIRL: He was just old. He wasn't sick, he wasn't senile. He was just old. And that was enough. Last night he went home to Grandma. Heaven knows what those two are up to right now.

    Pause.

GIRL: Everybody says I should be relieved it was so quiet and painless; that he's better off now. Maybe he is, but I'm sure not.

    Pause.

GIRL: Damnit, it isn't fair. I know, nobody said life was fair. But you never got your due. You old son of a bitch, I liked your poetry. I liked you. Who the hell's going to keep me straight now? Who can I cuss with? I need you! I love you!

    Pause.

GIRL: Damn.

    Cross to poetry lights. Voice over. This time it is the GIRL's voice. During the poem the GIRL will stand, change to MABEL, and move upstage to the platform.

My Gramps was a mean old man
a bastard brave and true
I'd cuss at him, he'd cuss at me
as lovers often do
He'd kick my butt and hold my hand
Sing me songs and swat my fanny
Grandma and me, we were his girls
In rhymes and verses plenty
The daisies do not smile today
The clouds with tears are forming
Good old Gramps is gone away
To sing a brighter morning.

Dance music fades up. Cross to scene lights on a low level. MAN and GIRL dance on platform. Lights fade out. Music fades out. Spot comes up on empty rocker. Spot fades out.

CURTAIN

Soon

This play was produced in 1989 at Western Carolina University in Cullowhee, NC, under the title "Soon and Very Soon." It was the winner of their national playwriting contest for science-fiction plays. I was actually brought in for the last few rehearsals and the opening, so I got to spend a few days up in the mountains. My wife thinks my description of a seemingly web-based news operation, written back in the 1980s, was amazing, but it just seemed inevitable to me. What I find surprising is that I wrote this before I started working in HIV prevention at CDC.

SOON

By David Davis

Member
All rights & privileges.

David Davis
100 Hunters Ridge Court
Roswell, GA 30076
daviddaviswriter@gmail.com

Copyright 2020 David Davis

CAST OF CHARACTERS

TOM GRAHAM .... Local News Editor, 69

ABBY ROBERTS .... Reporter, 37

GEORGE ADAMS .... Reporter, 26

VIRGINIA JACKSON .... Cub Reporter, 22

PAULINE WILLIAMS .... Editor, 48

MARTHA NEWTON .... Nurse, 33

SANDY JONES .... Food Vendor, 19

SETTING

A news website office, sooner than you think.

PROLOGUE

The lights come up quickly on a silent tableau of the scene in Act II just an instant before the shots are fired. The lights go back down as quickly as possible. Then a shot rings out in the darkness. The blackout lasts for several seconds before the lights come up on Act I.

ACT I

AT RISE we see the local news desk of a news website. The editor and three reporters who work local news take the stories coming over the wire and/or from field reporters, rewrite as necessary, add keywords and links, and index before posting the story on the web. There are four desks and chairs in the room, each with a computer keyboard and monitor. There are two entrances, archways on each side of the stage. Spaced about the walls are the following items: a machine that looks like a soft drink dispenser but is really selling bottles of sterilized water, next to that machine is another that buys the empty bottles back to be recycled; there is a coiled fire hose, a smoke alarm, a fire axe, an air pollution monitor that has a flashing red light and a beeper, a glass case labeled "Terrorist Emergency" that contains gas masks and guns, etc. There are also numerous signs posted about the room: "Smoking Is Illegal," "The News Comes First," "The Firstest with the Mostest," "Free Press: Last Bastion of Freedom," "Do Drugs, Do Time," "No Sex is Safe Sex." "Alcohol is a Drug," "A Clean Life is a Long Life," "Report Any Unaccompanied Visitors to Security Immediately." etc. There are no windows. Everything seems to gleam like it was encased in plastic and cleaned daily with Lysol. The desks are bare except for the keyboards and monitors. The light is just a little too bright. ABBY is sitting at her desk, typing on her computer keyboard. She, like all the other characters will be, is dressed in a version of baggy, shapeless, unisex coveralls that cover her from neck to ankle and hide her figure almost totally. Everybody wears latex gloves, and someone coming in from the outside would also have a dust filter mask, hat, and sun glasses on until they reached their desk. After a moment, GEORGE rushes in, takes off his dust filter, hat, and sun glasses, unlocks his desk drawer, puts in the filter, hat, and glasses, and takes out a can of spray disinfectant and a cloth and begins to clean his desk and computer. In a minute he has his area sterilized, puts the spray can and cloth away, locks his drawer, and sits at his terminal.

GEORGE: Ready.

ABBY: Take the obits.

GEORGE: Oh, Abby.

ABBY: You come in late, you get the obits.

GEORGE: Where's Tom?

ABBY: Editors' meeting. Lucked out this time.
GEORGE: Won't tell?
ABBY: Me? Loose lips lose tips.
GEORGE: Thanks.

> They type. In a second, TOM enters and goes to his desk. He sits and types.

ABBY: Tom! Stop it.
TOM: Just saying good morning.
ABBY: Get it off my screen. It's rude.

> TOM types.

ABBY: That's better.
GEORGE: Don't start up again. You know the Rules.
TOM: I was just saying good morning to Abby. And it's none of your business.
ABBY: Well, good morning. Now stay out of my monitor.
TOM: It's the only thing left to get into.
GEORGE: There you go again.
TOM: I was talking to Abby.
GEORGE: You're determined to infect somebody, aren't you?
TOM: I'm not even touching her, I'm way over here.
GEORGE: The Rules explicitly state...
TOM: The Rules don't allow anything to be explicit. Now put a lid on it.
GEORGE: One of these days your test is going to turn up positive, then where...
TOM: I said can it, hit the cancel key! OK? Ever since your father....
GEORGE: You leave my father out of this!
TOM: OK. Sorry. My mistake. I haven't had my coffee yet. Not that it makes any difference any more.
ABBY: Well, now that we've had our morning excitement.
TOM: Yeah, yeah, let's get to work.
ABBY: Gave George the obits.
TOM: Came in late again, eh, George?
GEORGE: A second. My mother...
TOM: Yeah, yeah, I know about your mother.
GEORGE: Don't you say...
ABBY: Boys, nice, nice.
TOM: OK, OK. I'll be good. Pauline's bringing in the rookie in a minute anyway.
GEORGE: Thank goodness, need the help.

ABBY: Any background on him?

TOM: Her. Fresh out of journalism school, some little college in the hills of Arkansas. First time in the big city.

ABBY: Oh, goodness.

TOM: Yeah.

ABBY: On the web. What else you got for me?

TOM: Endless passion.

ABBY: Besides that. Something having to do with news.

TOM: Oh, that stuff. Update on the latest attempted murder-by-sex case.

GEORGE: Did they nail him?

TOM: Charges had to be reduced to Reckless Endangerment. The STD tests came back negative, all of them. No syphilis, gonorrhea, chlamydia, HIV, HTLV, not even herpes. Clean as a whistle.

GEORGE: Luck.

TOM: Maybe.

ABBY: Sex, sex, sex. Punch it over.

TOM: Your wish is my command.

> He types. ABBY begins to work on the story.

TOM: How you coming on those obits?

GEORGE: Couple more minutes. Lots of people died last night.

TOM: I'm sure they regret causing you so much inconvenience.

GEORGE: I doubt it, most of them suicides.

TOM: Any families or lovers or novel ways of departing this veil of tears?

GEORGE: No, just regular couldn't take it anymores, let's save the hospital bills. No big news for your headlines.

TOM: Oh, well, maybe tomorrow.

GEORGE: You get thrills from people stepping over the edge, don't you.

TOM: I just think all these suicides say something about how cracked things have gotten. Ever since the mutation made the antibiotics stop working, well, I guess some people are just sick of living in this sterile new world.

GEORGE: You're the sick one.

> The air pollution alarm goes off. TOM calmly gets up and turns it off.

TOM: OK, everybody quit breathing.

GEORGE: Funny.

> TOM returns to his seat.

ABBY: Security must have reset it again.

TOM: Or the ozone is up to 20 percent and we're all getting cancer at this very instant.

ABBY: One or the other. Sex murder on the web.

TOM: George.

GEORGE: What?

TOM: You forgot to cross reference the obits with "Funerals" again. That's the third time this month. I know most of these people get cremated, and nobody goes to the funerals, but at least officially they still do have funerals. At least five minutes in the chapel, whether anybody shows up or not. It's in the Rules.

GEORGE: OK, OK, I'll fix it. OK?

TOM: That's just the basics, OK? You want my job when I get committed, you've got to do better than that. (Pause) OK, let's see what's coming in. We've got a pregnant thirteen year old incest victim who dared try to have an abortion and a respected, upstanding city councilman who was caught drinking whisky. Abby, you can have the sex, George, you take the drugs, when you finish the obits. Hurry up though, StarWeb will be happy to claim even a five second edge over us.

ABBY: I always get the sex.

TOM: I like you. Besides, George thinks thirteen year olds who want abortions should be burned at the stake.

GEORGE: I do not. Her father.

TOM: You're too late. When the wife slash mother caught them at it, she hacked off his, excuse the expression, male organ. Let him bleed to death while the daughter watched. But that was last week's story.

GEORGE: Well, he deserved it.

TOM: Yes, he should at least have worn a condom.

        PAULINE enters with VIRGINIA.

PAULINE: Listen up a second.

TOM: Ah, the Massive Mound of Mammary.

PAULINE: Wipe it, Tom. Virginia, this is the Local Desk, where you'll be working at first. The dirty old man over there is Thomas Graham, our City Editor. Tom.

TOM: Yo.

PAULINE: This is Virginia Jackson, your new rookie. Try not to scare her off the first day.

TOM: Ah, you're no fun.

PAULINE: Tom will show you what to do. And don't be afraid to ask him questions; he barks, but he isn't allowed to bite, and there are a few things they didn't teach you in Arkansas.

VIRGINIA: Yes, Ma'am.

TOM: "Yes, Ma'am?" Oh, god.

PAULINE: Wipe the screen, Tom.

TOM: Yes, Ma'am.

PAULINE: One of these days I'm going to get good and mad and promote you.

TOM: Heaven forbid.

PAULINE: Now be nice.

PAULINE exits.

TOM: The empty desk is yours. One drawer should have a key in the lock. That's your drawer, keep the key. You use an Apple AP 12000 before?

VIRGINIA: We had one at school.

TOM: Good. That's Abigale Roberts, the second-in-command around here. Fifteen years on the web. Has covered everything from crime to sports; you name it she's done it. Famous for her level head, sharp eye, and cute tush.

> During the introductions there are nods of heads, but no one shakes hands or touches. In fact, no one touches until the final scene.

ABBY: Call me Abby. And ignore about half of everything Tom says.

VIRGINIA: Abby.

TOM: George Adams, who claims to be a reporter. Three years on the web, six months on the local desk. Thinks he's ready to take over the entire newsweb now.

GEORGE: Hello. It's very nice to meet you.

VIRGINIA: Nice to meet you.

TOM: What do they call you? Virgin? I mean, Virginia?

ABBY: Tom. Nice, nice.

VIRGINIA: My friends call me Virginia.

TOM: Well, Virginia, do you know what we do around here?

VIRGINIA: You mean when not fooling around?

ABBY: Two points for rookie.

TOM: I never fool around. Abby won't let me. But, back to the newsweb stuff. Are you aware of the function to be fulfilled by the occupants of these work stations?7

VIRGINIA: You're basically a rewrite and index desk. Stories come in from field reporters or wire services. You, as editor, assign them to reporters here. We rewrite as necessary and index each story by topic, type, and at least three key words, adding links when appropriate. Then we put them on the web so readers can punch up what they want to read.

TOM: OK, so they did teach you something in Arkansas. But you got one thing wrong. You don't post something on the web. I check it first, then it goes on the web. If I'm not here, Abby will do it. Clear?

VIRGINIA: Clear.

TOM: Then sit.

GEORGE: I've got disinfectant if you need to borrow.

VIRGINIA: Do I need?

ABBY: People on other shifts use the same desks. That's why the other drawers in your desk have different locks.

VIRGINIA: Oh.

GEORGE: I know the Rules say we can't work remotely, but you'd think we'd at least get our own desks. I spray my entire desk every morning.

VIRGINIA: Have there been problems?

TOM: Nobody in this building has been sick in three years. Not even a cold. We are all disgustingly healthy.

GEORGE: Because we follow the Rules.

TOM: We follow so many blankety-blank rules they had to plaster over the windows to keep some of the healthy people from jumping out of them. It drives you crazy. People just keep exploding these days.

ABBY: I think I better warn you about Tom.

TOM: Here it comes.

ABBY: Tom is old, very old, even older than he looks. We put up with a lot of stuff from him because there are so few like him left. He not only goes back before the Epidemic, Drug Wars, and the Collapse, he goes all the way back to the free sex years. He even claims to have participated. He says he remembers when the air was clean, terrorists were only in the Middle East, and you could expose your skin to the sun without getting arrested. He just loves to tell tall tales and try to shock innocent girls from the country. He hasn't quite gotten used to the Rules yet.

TOM: Ah, those were the days. Protest marches, bombings, riots in the streets. I've still got a pornographic video hidden under the floor in my bedroom.

VIRGINIA: I think I get the idea.

TOM: You know, it is true that we actually used to have sex with people we liked. Isn't that disgusting? So, are you ready for your first "experience," Virginia?

VIRGINIA: Uh...

TOM: I can let you see the City Hall Records report, no telling what scandal you can find in there.

VIRGINIA: Oh, sure.

TOM: Well, get busy. I seem to remember giving you two something to work on as well.

GEORGE: OK, OK, obits and drugs up on the web.

TOM: Then take the crime reports.

GEORGE: Again?

TOM: Never know who forgot to pay a parking ticket. Could get you a Pulitzer.

SANDY enters, pushing a cart full of snacks.

SANDY: Step right up, step right up, ladies and gentlemen. For you naughty people who left home without eating, it's breakfast time with Sandy's Mobile Snack Stand. Get your calories from the cart, don't worry 'bout your heart.

ABBY: Morning, Sandy. I have been looking for that cart of yours for twenty minutes. I'm starved.

SANDY: Hello, hello, hello. Hey, a new face. Well, hang my software.

ABBY: This is Virginia Jackson, rookie reporter. Sandy the Snackman.

VIRGINIA: Hi.

SANDY: Welcome, I say welcome to the best newsweb in town. I'm Sandy the Snackman, here to brighten your day. Three times a day I will wheel this magic cart into your life. On this cart, I say on this magic cart, I have everything your heart desires.

TOM: Everything my heart desires?

SANDY: Everything edible and portable and legal that costs under ten dollars your heart desires.

TOM: I didn't think you had room for three naked virgins in there.

SANDY: Give me a break, OK? I'm trying to get her hooked on sweet rolls.

TOM: Play on.

SANDY: Breakfast, you say? Do I have breakfast? You bet your buzzer I have breakfast. Right here I have Nutrasweet rolls, Saccharin covered donuts, bran muffins with real corn oil margarine, and authentic Columbian coffee straight from Columbia, South Carolina, only 90 percent decaffeinated. But maybe, not knowing the delights that awaited you here, you, in your ignorance, ate breakfast at home. Now you want to know what's for lunch. Yes, Sandy, what's for lunch? Always good to plan ahead for my next visit. You like salad? I've got lettuce salad, spinach salad, and fruit salad, all in hermetically sealed containers, preserved by real radiation, and guaranteed sterile or your next one free. Sandwiches? You want a sandwich? I got turkey ham on rye, turkey bologna on wheat, turkey salami on whole grain, turkey chicken on pumpernickel, and even turkey turkey on bread bread, all made by robots in a factory and never touched by human hands. But, wait, what about something to drink? Is there just the sterile water machine in back? No, I say no. There's Coke, Cherry Coke, Rasberry Coke and brand new Huckleberry Coke. All caffeine and sugar free and using only USDA approved sweeteners, and personally guaranteed by Sandy the Snackman to be almost cool. But Sandy, you say, but Sandy, what about a real snack, some pure junk food with no nutrition at all. Let me tell you, I can sing to your tummy. I've got food even I won't eat. I've got potato chips pressed from real potato flakes. I've got Chocolate Chip cookies even Hershey thinks have chocolate. I've even got, I say, even got apple turnovers that once actually saw an apple tree. And I bring all this to you fresh every day until somebody eats them and I have room for new ones. And all at a very nominal fee that supports my invalid mother, puts me through medical school at night, and pays my father's bail. Now, who wants what? The stock exchange is about to open and I need to call my broker, so let's get those orders in, folks.

ABBY: Coffee, creamora, and a Nutrasweet roll.

TOM: Coffee, straight.

GEORGE: Can I get you something?

VIRGINIA: I think I can handle it myself. Thanks, though.

GEORGE: The bran muffins are actually almost edible.

VIRGINIA: I think I'd rather have a coffee and donut, please, Sandy.

SANDY: Anything in the coffee?

VIRGINIA: Nutrasweet, please.

SANDY: A cup of sweet and one with a hole; that's five dollars. What about you, Mr. Adams?

GEORGE: Just a muffin. I'll get...

SANDY: A bottle of water, I know.

VIRGINIA: You don't drink coffee?

TOM: George has no vices.

GEORGE: Coffee isn't a vice, at least not now that it's decaffeinated. I just prefer the water.

> GEORGE goes to the machine and gets a small bottle of water and takes it back to his desk.

TOM: Well, excuse us while we pretend this is real coffee and we're actually doing something sinful, so we can get a little enjoyment out of it.

GEORGE: If you have to sin to enjoy life, maybe there's something wrong with you.

SANDY: OK, that it? Everybody happy?

TOM: As happy as we can get indulging in artificial sin.

SANDY: See you later.

> SANDY wheels his cart out the other side of the stage.

VIRGINIA: He's cute.

ABBY: Don't let him hear you, we'll get that routine every time.

TOM: I've got stories backing up.

ABBY: OK. Shoot.

TOM: You want the topless dancer bust or the Mayor's award to the Chastity of Women program. Huh, the C.O.W.'s.

ABBY: Oh, give me the stripper. I think I'm getting used to it. The C.O.W. is so cut and dried.

TOM: George?

GEORGE: I need a couple more minutes.

TOM: OK, I'll take the C.O.W., Lord love 'em. I probably know some of them, one way or another.

GEORGE: Don't make fun of them. They do good work; look at the drop in STD death rates.

TOM: Oh, I agree. Let's just stop all sex for a generation; that would solve all our problems. Did it ever occur to anybody that life is a sexually transmitted disease?

> They all type. PAULINE and MARTHA enter. MARTHA pushes a small cart with medical equipment and a machine of some kind. As they are seen by each person, the typing stops.

TOM: Blast.

PAULINE: Watch your language.

ABBY: Whose number came up?

PAULINE: George.

GEORGE: Again? That's three weeks in a row.

PAULINE: It's just the luck of the draw.

GEORGE: What about Tom? He hasn't been tested in months.

PAULINE: It's just luck.

GEORGE: But if anybody's doing anything, it's him.

PAULINE: Are you making an official accusation?

> Pause.

GEORGE: No.

PAULINE: Then keep your mouth shut unless you are going to back it up.

MARTHA: Here.

> MARTHA hands GEORGE a urine specimen bottle.

TOM: Time to rob Peter to pay Pauline, eh, George?

PAULINE: For that crack you get to be third witness.

TOM: Oh sh...

PAULINE: Tom...

TOM: ...horsefeathers.

GEORGE: Just a minute.

> GEORGE gulps the contents of the water bottle and turns upstage as PAULINE, MARTHA, and TOM gather around him. He then urinates into the bottle.

VIRGINIA (whisper, to ABBY)**:** They do it here?

ABBY: There have to be at least three witness, the nurse, the supervisor and one other.

VIRGINIA: In Arkansas we could go in a stall.

ABBY: Welcome to the big city. There was too much cheating any other way. People would carry little bottles of clean urine and switch when nobody was looking. Now everything has to be out in the open, so to speak.

VIRGINIA: So we?...too?

ABBY: When your number comes up, it's squat and pee.

GEORGE: There.

MARTHA: Thank you.

> MARTHA inserts specimen into the machine. A printout appears.

VIRGINIA: I'm not sure I could...you know... them watching...

ABBY: I'll be your third usually, so it's all women. The female flow collection device hides a lot anyway. Use the desk as cover.

VIRGINIA: Still...

PAULINE: Well?

MARTH: No STDs of any kind. Clear for opiates, cocaine, heroin or derivatives, clear for marijuana, barbiturates, psychoactives. No trace of alcohol or nicotine.

GEORGE: What did you expect? May I get back to work now?

PAULINE: It's nothing personal, George, your number just keeps coming up.

> MARTHA hands PAULINE a form to sign.

GEORGE: Sure. I get it three weeks in a row, and Mr. Spaced Out here hasn't been tested in months.

> GEORGE takes a new pair of gloves out of his desk and replaces the old pair on his hands, disposing of them in the waste slot in the wall.

TOM: Wouldn't make any difference. I balance the heroin with quaaludes and coke, then wash my system with LSD so the machine thinks I just ate a sesame seed bun for lunch. Works every time.

PAULINE: Not funny, Tom. Sign on the line.

> TOM signs the test results. He returns the form, and PAULINE passes the form on to GEORGE.

GEORGE: There are supposed to be some new drugs the machine can't detect.

TOM: The new tailored Angel Dust, for example. Totally undetectable. Makes you think you're an aardvark, but that's OK, keeps the ants in the apartment under control.

> MARTHA takes form from GEORGE.

MARTHA: See you next week.

TOM: Not if he sees you first.

PAULINE: Tom, I need to see you in my office. We've got to come up with some edge on StarWeb before they steal all our clicks. Need some ideas from you for local coverage.

TOM: Yes, Oh Great Mistress, Biggest of the Big Breasted.

PAULINE: Stop it, Tom. Now let's go.

ABBY: I'll take the C.O.W. as soon as I finish this.

TOM: Right.

> TOM exits with PAULINE.

GEORGE: Never did anything in my whole life, but whose number keeps coming up.

ABBY: We've all been tested.

GEORGE: Not three weeks in a row. And don't think I don't know why.

ABBY: Nobody's accusing you of anything, George. It's just luck.

GEORGE: Why doesn't his number ever come up?

ABBY: It has.

GEORGE: Not lately. Not in a long time.

ABBY: He's been clean every time.

GEORGE: I read there's a new synthetic, doesn't show on the urine test, only on the blood.

ABBY: You make a false accusation, it goes on your record.

GEORGE: I know the Rules.

ABBY: Good. Now let's get these stories done before he comes back.

GEORGE: I don't know why Pauline puts up with his foul mouth either.

ABBY: Maybe she secretly likes him.

GEORGE: The way he insults her?

ABBY: She's almost his generation, she knows what it used to be like, what he's been through.

GEORGE: What? All that immorality back then? See what that got us.

ABBY: I know, I know. The Epidemic, the Drug Wars, then the Collapse. I know. But it was his friends and her parents' friends who died. They've got a lot of sad memories in common, OK? Now cancel it and let's get back to work.

All type. After a moment.

VIRGINIA: Uh, I think I'm done.

ABBY: OK, I'll check it. Punch it over and start on the C.O.W. piece.

VIRGINIA: Right.

ABBY: OK, let's see here. Hum, indexed, key words, style all right, looks OK to me. Go ahead and put it on the web.

VIRGINIA: Thanks.

ABBY: No trouble. George, the garden club news is coming in, can you take that?

GEORGE: Yeah, yeah. What flower did they plant this week?

ABBY: Uh, petunias.

GEORGE (sarcastic): Wonderful.

VIRGINIA: I like petunias.

GEORGE: I only meant...

TOM enters.

ABBY: I checked Virginia's story. It was good, so it went web. She's got the C.O.W. now, and George has the garden club. Did you hear me?

TOM: I heard.

ABBY: You OK?

TOM: An anonymous tip came in to the main newsroom while I was in Pauline's office. Supposedly two city councilmen are trying to hush up a kiddie sex ring.

ABBY: Why?

TOM: Because they were in it. Swapping kids. Guaranteed virgins, at least at first.

VIRGINIA: My gosh. That is so sick.

TOM: Yes, my gosh, my gosh. It supposedly even included a minister, and several other respectable types, plus the boys and girls, maybe as young as two years old. The anonymous source says the cops are being clamped on hard. Says he has "hard evidence," whatever that means.

GEORGE: We need to get this on the web, force it all out in the open.

TOM: It's just a tip. We don't have any evidence yet.

ABBY: I wonder if StarWeb has this yet.

GEORGE: They'll go with it when they do. And scoop us again.

TOM: That's what the source wants us to do, you can bet on that.

ABBY: What are we going to do?

TOM: We've got four field people checking it six ways from Sunday. Just be ready for all heck to break loose soon. Finish what's on screen as soon as you can.

GEORGE: The boss was not happy the last time we got scooped.

ABBY: Clicks fell 20 percent.

TOM: I read the memo.

GEORGE: People lost jobs.

TOM: I am aware of that, thank you. And I am aware you think you can handle my job a lot better than I can. I am also aware that ten or more men will have their lives ruined as soon as this hits the web. I would like to know it's true before I post it.

GEORGE: What about the little kids that stay abused if this gets covered up? I guess you think child abuse is OK.

TOM: What if there are no abused little kids? What if it's just a smear?

    PAULINE enters.

PAULINE: Tom?

TOM: Nothing yet.

ABBY: StarWeb?

PAULINE: Not yet. We could just say an allegation was made. That much is true.

TOM: Somebody could call here and allege you're a Satanist who kills babies and licks their diapers. You want me to post that?

PAULINE: Take it easy, Tom.

GEORGE: No need to be obscene.

TOM: Obscene? You want obscene, you wait until the wives and mothers hear about this, true or not.

VIRGINIA: Why would anybody do such a thing? It's just so horrible.

ABBY: They're sick.

GEORGE: They're perverted.

TOM: They're innocent until we get confirmation.

PAULINE: If StarWeb goes with this...

TOM: I know.

PAULINE: Let me know.

    PAULINE exits.

TOM: Abby, punch up StarWeb. I'm going to come up with some mealy-mouth, conditional, alleged, maybe somebody did something sometime, one paragraph lead that we can post instantly if StarWeb breaks it.

ABBY: Right.

    TOM types. ABBY watches her monitor. GEORGE whispers to
    VIRGINIA.

GEORGE: He's so old-fashioned sometimes. We're going to get scooped on this for sure.

VIRGINIA: He is the editor.

GEORGE: Huh! City Editor. He's been here a lot longer than Pauline. Been stuck in that job for years.

The air pollution alarm goes off.

TOM: Darn! Shut that thing off.

GEORGE: Watch your language.

GEORGE gets up and shuts off the alarm.

VIRGINIA: What was that?

ABBY: Air pollution monitor. Shut it off, and it automatically resets for a higher level. It'll probably go off again before long.

TOM: Keep your eyes on the blasted screen.

GEORGE: Tom, there are women present.

ABBY: It's OK, George.

GEORGE: You're used to his foul mouth. What about Virginia?

VIRGINIA: I don't think he's going to say anything I haven't heard before.

GEORGE: That's not the point; you shouldn't have to listen to...

ABBY: StarWeb's going with it.

TOM: Blast and double blast! On the web.

ABBY: They're naming names. Maybe they've got more confirmation than we have.

TOM: Do they give sources?

ABBY: Just the famed "un-named informant."

GEORGE: So, they beat us again. What did I tell you?

TOM: Five seconds.

GEORGE: With names. And we had the story ten minutes ago.

TOM: We had a rumor.

GEORGE: Now they've got a scoop.

PAULINE enters.

PAULINE: Tom.

TOM: I know.

PAULINE: Anything at all from the field yet? Do we have anything they don't?

TOM: Not a word.

GEORGE: In five minutes StarWeb will have pixs of the kids.

VIRGINIA: Those poor kids.

PAULINE: OK, add the names to our story. Abby, you write a follow-up to Tom's lead.

George, dig the files on these people, pixs, wives, kids, other associations. Virginia, monitor StarWeb and see what else they have that we don't. Tom, in my office.

TOM: Credit StarWeb as a source. Wouldn't want them suing us.

ABBY: Right.

> PAULINE and TOM exit.

GEORGE: Now we'll see...

ABBY: Get to work, George.

GEORGE: I was just...

ABBY: Shut up, I said!

GEORGE: OK, OK. Don't listen to me, see how it turns out.

> The lights fade.

ACT I, SCENE TWO

> Later that day. TOM, ABBY, VIRGINIA and GEORGE are at their desks, working. TOM is checking one of VIRGINIA's stories.

TOM: Not bad, for a rookie on her first day.

VIRGINIA: Thank you.

TOM: Fix that comma splice you missed and post it.

VIRGINIA: What comma splice?

TOM: Ah, that's part of the learning experience, finding it.

VIRGINIA: OK, OK.

GEORGE: It's lunch time.

TOM: You want to go out again?

GEORGE: Down to the lunchroom. I'm not going to eat that garbage Sandy brings around. I'm entitled to half an hour.

TOM: And you deserve every minute of it. So go.

GEORGE: You want me to take Virginia and show her where the lunchroom is?

TOM: No. I want three people on duty in case something else moves on the kiddie sex rumor. You can try to get into her pants some other time.

GEORGE: I would never...

TOM: If she doesn't want to eat off the cart, I'll have somebody take her downstairs when you get back, so don't take all day, she may be hungry.

GEORGE: It's a little late to be worrying about the sex ring now, isn't it? You blew your chance.

TOM: You now have twenty-nine minutes for lunch.

GEORGE: OK, OK, I'm going.

> GEORGE exits.

ABBY: On the web.

TOM: OK, let's see what we got. "Community protests location of STD hospice by burning it down." There's a hot story for you.

ABBY: OK. Oh, that's not the one where George's father...

TOM: No.

VIRGINIA: George's father's in...

ABBY: Don't ever say anything...

VIRGINIA: I wouldn't. Is he really...?

TOM: Nobody is sure exactly what happened. One rumor is that Daddy was getting a little on the side, maybe some that wasn't totally straight.

VIRGINIA: I thought the gays were all dead or locked up.

TOM: Who knows? Frankly, I don't buy that part of it myself. The other rumor is that Daddy was shooting up, and I've heard everything from crack to heroin. Truth be told, I don't think even George knows what happened for sure. At any rate, George's mother evidently found out something that scared her so bad she reported Daddy and had him committed. Now the old lady's so scared she might be positive for something she just sits at home and never goes anywhere she might be tested.

VIRGINIA: That's awful.

TOM: Way it goes these days. So much fear.

> SANDY wheels his cart onstage.

SANDY: I hear stomachs growling, I see energy lagging, I smell the strong scent of hunger. That means it's, no, it can't be, yes, it is! It's lunchtime, and here's Sandy to save the day! Send your hunger out to slumber, send your tummy a great big yummy, send for Sandy's super-duper sandwich of the day. Even lovely ladies like these fine examples of American womanhood assembled here have to eat on occasion, so what will it be, ladies? Special of the day is turkey turkey on rye rye with a fruit salad and a cherry coke, only nineteen ninety five, plus tax, title, and destination charges.

ABBY: That means those three items are the slow movers today.

TOM: You can go down to the lunchroom when George gets back if you want to. They have a little more to choose from, though not delivered in quite the same style. Thank goodness.

VIRGINIA: No, this is fine. I am getting a little hungry. Have you got a ham on wheat bread? And didn't you mention something this morning about an apple turnover?

SANDY: Do I detect a sweet tooth in that pretty face? An apple turnover I can turn over, but my hams come only on rye, I regret to say. Tomorrow, however, I can arrange it the other way, if you but the right word say.

VIRGINIA: On rye I'll dine today, if tomorrow's another day and the ham with wheat can play.

TOM: Hey, not bad. Sandy, I think she speaks your language. You may be in trouble.

VIRGINIA: And a diet coke, just to keep up appearances.

SANDY: A slab of pig, sugared upside-down tree, and strained black water, coming up.

ABBY: He makes it sound so appetizing, doesn't he?

SANDY: And for you?

ABBY: A clucker on a fat nickle, smashed spuds, and thinned bog water.

VIRGINIA: What?

TOM: Let me guess. Chicken on pumpernickel, potato chips, and, hum, bog water...diet huckleberry coke.

SANDY: Two points.

TOM: Ah, yes.

ABBY: Just to keep up appearances.

TOM: What appearances? You'd have to be fifty pounds overweight before it showed through that baggy thing you're wearing. Takes half the fun out of looking at a woman.

ABBY: Well, sorry your life isn't just one cheap thrill after another.

TOM: I bet.

SANDY: Uh, do you want some lunch, Mr. Graham?

TOM: Yeah. Give me a salami on whatever and whatever is passing for coffee these days.

SANDY: I tried to find some coffee that wasn't decaffeinated, but you'd have to buy the beans on the black market and grind it yourself, and that was just too chancy.

TOM: No, don't do that. I'm just grousing. Just miss the bad old days.

SANDY: I'm sorry, Mr. Graham.

TOM: Forget it. Thanks for trying though. I appreciate the thought.

SANDY: Anytime. Here's your lunch.

TOM: Here's a hundred for three lunches and whatever's on my tab. Keep ten for your invalid mother, who I saw jogging on the treadmill on the women's side of the gym yesterday.

SANDY: Well, thank you, Mr. Graham. I'll tell her you were spying through the peephole again.

TOM: On second thought, make that twenty dollars.

SANDY: Yes, Sir. And my mother already knows you look through the peephole. All the women in the gym do. Now if you will excuse me, the computer operators get growly if I'm late with their noon feeding.

TOM: Yes, there's nothing worse than a growly computer operator.

SANDY: Ham on wheat tomorrow.

VIRGINIA: And tomorrow and tomorrow.

    SANDY exits with his cart.

TOM: His mother works down in classified sales. She runs five miles a day in the company gym in the basement. Healthy as a horse. His father is in jail, but only because he's the warden. And Sandy doesn't really go to medical school at night. He's a sophomore in college two blocks away. He goes to classes between rounds with his cart.

VIRGINIA: Well, what do you know. Anyway, thanks for buying my lunch.

TOM: Your official welcome to the office.

VIRGINIA: What was that about the coffee?

ABBY: Tom is always complaining that the coffee is dishwater because it's decaffeinated. Sandy evidently tried to find some illegal stuff with caffeine left in it. Which should be a warning to you about letting yourself get in debt for too many lunches to this man. Who knows what he might ask in repayment.

TOM: I bought your lunch too.

ABBY: Yes, but I already know what you want.

TOM: Then why did you let me buy it.

ABBY: I like to live dangerously. Besides, I know you're really harmless and all those stories about the bad old days are just myths.

TOM: Some of them. Not all though. The coffee did used to have caffeine.

VIRGINIA: Does a little caffeine really make that much difference?

TOM: No, I just have a little yen for something to be like it was. Something to actually reach out and touch people.

ABBY: Like back in the bad old days?

TOM: OK, OK. I never said they were perfect. But they weren't all bad. Not near as bad as the official history makes them sound.

VIRGINIA: So what were they like? All I've ever heard is the horror stories; all the crazy, unholy sex that started it all, then the epidemic when the mutation came along and the antibiotics failed and a lot of diseases turned deadly, and then the drug wars when the epidemic got so bad the government failed and the drug gangs tried to take over, starting wars in the streets.

TOM: Back in the dark ages? Sometimes it does seem that long ago. I really am getting old, aren't I?

ABBY: Only if you feel that way.

TOM: One of the last survivors. Like living history.

VIRGINIA: So, Mr. Human Museum, tell us little kiddies what life was really like back in the bad old days.

TOM: Huh! You really want to know?

VIRGINIA: Sure. All I ever got was the official line in school.

TOM: The official line. When the Committee created the Rules to save the civilization.

VIRGINIA: Yes, that official line.

TOM: Well, in some ways it was like that. What gets left out is the mutation affected a lot of infections, not just STDs. It could have started anywhere, but since it started in gonorrhea, then chlamydia, and turned deadly there first, STDs took the blame and anybody having sex got the blame for spreading it. There was no way to tell who had what, then suddenly it seemed like everybody had something. Then your friends and neighbors are sick or dying, then your brothers and sisters, your kids, even your parents. A lot of very good people died, people who did nothing more than have sex with their husband or wife. We all got very, very scared. The fear just became too great. And we've all been afraid ever since.

ABBY: Do you blame us?

TOM: No, not really.

ABBY: And the Drug Wars were bloody.

TOM: The government couldn't seem to do anything about anything. There were already drug gangs around, of course, and with the government falling apart, it just got worse. They became a shadow government, bribing, intimidating, or killing to get control. Soon there were battles in the streets. Then everybody else tried to just stay home or hide in a bomb shelter or something, and you get The Collapse. Finally we get "The Rules" and start our wonderful new society. And we went from the glorious insanity of wild sex to the disgusting prudery of today. I never wanted such an interesting life.

ABBY: It worked. The rules keep us alive.

TOM: Do they? You call somebody like George alive? He's afraid of even breathing hard. Between thinking he's going to turn out like his father and living with his dried up old prune of a mother.... Well, if I was like him I'd shoot myself. Don't you remember any of what it was like before?

ABBY: Gee, thanks; I didn't know I looked that old.

TOM: Come on, you were alive for some of that.

ABBY: Oh, I know. I'm old enough to remember the news reports, the death lists, the Crackdown to enforce the rules. But I was barely a teeny-bopper in Buffalo with braces that looked like barbed-wire and would have scared off Casanova. We all had parents or relatives who had died of one infection or another. I think we all got brought up a little afraid of breathing hard. Then suddenly I was a hard-boiled reporter on the crime beat and the world was crazy. That can scare a person for life. I've seen too much, Tom. We all have.

TOM: But do we have to give up? Hide in our little corners?

ABBY: I like my corner. Garden clubs and high school basketball scores. That's enough for me. It's safe.

TOM: But to push others into a corner the way George does, a corner they don't want to be in?

VIRGINIA: What have you got against George? It seems like there's a running feud between you two.

TOM: Oh, I don't know. I guess I can just smell the fear in him.

VIRGINIA: He doesn't seem that afraid of you, the way he talks back.

TOM: Not that kind of fear. It's the Chastity of Women kind of fear; all men are evil, all sex is bad. He's afraid of himself. And, maybe I remind him of..., well, if I don't get what's coming to me soon, he's not going to know what to do. And I'm just mean enough to enjoy throwing it in his face.

ABBY: One of these days he may do more than talk back.

TOM: I like living dangerously.

ABBY: Speaking of rules, look at what's coming in.

TOM: "Pervert arrested for kissing woman's behind in subway." Oh, I love it. Think you can handle that, Virginia?

VIRGINIA: I guess I'm ready for a little hot stuff.

ABBY: Hey, I thought I got all the sex.

TOM: Share the wealth. Besides, I want you clear for the kiddie sex ring if anything moves on that.

ABBY: Think anything else will happen?

TOM: Something else has to happen. You can't just post a story like that and not expect the world to explode.

The pollution alarm goes off. The lights fade.

ACT II

The next day. VIRGINIA is at her desk, typing. GEORGE rushes in, takes off filter, etc, disinfects his desk, and sits.

GEORGE: Where is everybody?

VIRGINIA: In Pauline's office. Tom said for you to start on obituaries when you got in.

GEORGE: Oh, he did, did he?

VIRGINIA: Don't complain, I've got one about a baby abandoned in sewer.

GEORGE: He's dumping that stuff on you now, is he?

VIRGINIA: Well, this isn't Arkansas. I better get used to it.

GEORGE: Different world alright, thanks to people like Tom.

VIRGINIA: It's different, I'll agree to that.

GEORGE: So, what was it like in Arkansas?

VIRGINIA: Grew up in a real small town, up in the mountains. Only had two hundred in high school, and I think I was related to half, one way or another. Everybody knew everybody, and cops made sure strangers didn't stop for anything but gas. Didn't even wear gloves until I went away to college.

GEORGE: Really?

VIRGINIA: No need. We had moonshine and marijuana, you know, home-grown stuff, but nothing that needed a needle. And with everybody almost related to everybody, and no dancing or dating allowed in high school, there wasn't a whole lot to worry about.

GEORGE: Sounds nice. Why leave?

VIRGINIA: Oh, well, uh, lots of reasons. I didn't want to marry any second or third cousins, no matter how safe they were, and that was about all there was. And unless I wanted to clean house, raise a kid, and work in the Nissan factory all my life, there wasn't much future for me there.

GEORGE: Guess not.

VIRGINIA: Besides, I wanted a little excitement. So, here I am, hot-shot hick reporter out to conquer big city. Real laugh. What about you, you born here?

GEORGE: Over the river. Not actually in city limits, but close enough. Lived here all my life. Went to college just a couple of blocks east of here, then got this job.

VIRGINIA: Sounds exciting.

GEORGE: Not really. Just normal for me, I guess. I live with my mother a couple of blocks from here, just inside the sanitized zone.

VIRGINIA: Oh.

GEORGE: Would you like to come over for dinner some time and meet her?

VIRGINIA: Well...

GEORGE: My mother's a really good cook. I'm sure she'd love to have you over. She doesn't go out, but I'm sure she'd like to meet a nice girl like you. I know I'd...

VIRGINIA: I appreciate...

GEORGE: It's just to get a chance to talk, get acquainted, warn you what to watch out for around here. How to deal with Tom. Somebody like you, you know, new and everything...

VIRGINIA: Look, I appreciate it, and I know you're just trying to support the Rules, but I really don't think I need you to protect me. I know he's a little vulgar at times, but Tom seems a good editor. You sure have something against him though.

GEORGE: Foul mouth, foul body. He's bound to be infected with something, even if the test doesn't show it yet. Even the new test sometimes won't show for months. Eventually he will infect everything and everybody around him. He should be in a sanatorium.

VIRGINIA: Abby says he's always passed the urine tests.

GEORGE: Well, maybe. But about dinner? I really would like to get to know you. There's so few women who...

VIRGINIA: I don't think so.

GEORGE: Oh. Has Tom been telling you...?

VIRGINIA: No. Nothing.

GEORGE: He has. My mother is clean. Do you hear me?

VIRGINIA: Yes. I never...

GEORGE: Meddling old fool.

VIRGINIA: No, listen, thanks for asking. I just need some time to get settled in. All this is so new to me. Understand?

GEORGE: Sure, sure, no problem. Maybe we could eat lunch together sometime, down in the cafeteria, if Tom would ever let us both off at the same time.

VIRGINIA: Well, maybe. Sandy's stuff isn't that bad though. I kind of like staying up here, till I get the hang of things. I'm still a little nervous, new job and all. Honest. And I've really got to make it here. I've got to.

GEORGE: Well, sure, whatever.

VIRGINIA: Sure.

    ABBY enters and goes to her desk.

VIRGINIA: What's happening?

ABBY: Did you get the vice report done?

VIRGINIA: Yes. Then I took the abandoned baby. You want to check it?

ABBY: No. You showed yesterday you're too good to worry about that all the time. Put it on the web. George, obits done?

GEORGE: In a minute.

ABBY: Did you just get in?

GEORGE: Lots of people...

ABBY: Died today, I know. Virginia, take the Mayor's revised statement on the kiddie sex ring. I'll handle the, oh my goodness...

VIRGINIA: What?

ABBY: Look what's coming in. The preacher in the sex ring was murdered by his wife. George, drop the obits and grab that state psychologist's analysis of child abusers on two.

GEORGE: OK, OK.

> They all work. SANDY enters with cart. No one notices him.

SANDY: OK, name your poison. Almost coffee almost warm, almost fruit juice almost cool, tea so close to tea it's almost brown. (Pause, no response.) I take it I came at a bad time.

ABBY: Coffee, creamora, pay later.

VIRGINIA: Cup of coffee, Nutrasweet, please.

GEORGE: Bran muffin.

ABBY: Leave coffee for Tom. Straight.

SANDY: I know. (to VIRGINIA) What's happening?

VIRGINIA: The kiddie sex thing. Wife killed husband in it.

SANDY: Oh. Not good.

VIRGINIA: No.

GEORGE: Probably deserved it.

ABBY: Shut up, George.

VIRGINIA: Can I post?

ABBY: Go.

VIRGINIA: Got another?

ABBY: Not yet.

SANDY: Got a little news you might be interested in.

VIRGINIA: Oh really?

GEORGE: What would you know?

SANDY: You'd be surprised, my man.

ABBY: Air it, Sandy.

SANDY: Mean old StarWeb's clicks jumped fifty thousand since the kiddie sex scoop.

ABBY: Darn!

GEORGE: Abby!

ABBY: Shut up, George.

GEORGE: Don't tell me shut up! If anybody had listened to me yesterday, it would be our clicks that were up.

SANDY: Another little tidbit, if anybody's interested.

ABBY: What?

SANDY: The big boss, the owner and publisher herself, came in this morning. Bought a coffee and roll from me. She didn't seem real happy, and don't anybody say it was my coffee.

ABBY: Not news.

GEORGE: What did you expect?

VIRGINIA: This mean trouble?

GEORGE: For Tom. Maybe for all of us, whether we deserve it or not. Even you.

ABBY: Don't scare her.

GEORGE: She needs to know.

SANDY: Well, maybe I can come up with something to ease your troubled mind. How would you like a sweet roll with real sugar icing?

VIRGINIA: No kidding?

SANDY: Just for you.

VIRGINIA: I shouldn't. It isn't healthy.

SANDY: But...?

VIRGINIA: Real sugar?

GEORGE: That black market food isn't safe.

SANDY: My mother made it.

VIRGINIA: Well, in that case.

> SANDY reaches into the depths of his cart and pulls a plain brown bag out and hands it to Virginia.

VIRGINIA: How much?

SANDY: For you, a smile and a wave when you see me coming.

VIRGINIA: Deal.

SANDY: Put your's and Tom's on the tab, Abby.

ABBY: Right.

SANDY: Now I'll just scroll along, until we meet again.

> SANDY exits with cart.

ABBY: I think he's got a crush on you.

VIRGINIA: No. Well, maybe a little one. Just hope it means more sweet rolls.

ABBY: I think you can count on that.

VIRGINIA: But you didn't answer my question. Could I really get laid off? I just got here.

GEORGE: What happened with Pauline this morning?

ABBY: Let me finish. Are you clear?

GEORGE: In a minute.

> ABBY and GEORGE type. TOM enters.

ABBY: Got a hot one.

TOM: Let's see. Oh...hell! As if this isn't bad enough. Any follow-up?

ABBY: Not yet.

GEORGE: Turning into a real big story, isn't it, Mr. Foul Mouth?

ABBY: On the web.

TOM: Sure to be more in a minute. How do we stand?

ABBY: Clear.

VIRGINIA: Clear.

GEORGE: One more minute.

VIRGINIA: Uh, there's a rumor that some staff might be cut because of the decline in clicks.

TOM: Meaning me?

VIRGINIA: I was thinking more about the last hired, namely me. I can't go back home. I can't. They wouldn't let…. I mean…. I just can't.

TOM: It's OK, it's OK. We outcasts will stick together, OK?

ABBY: Don't worry, if we can put up with Tom, we can put up with you.

GEORGE: You mean you're…

TOM: Back off, George.

GEORGE: But you said…

VIRGINIA: I never said anything.

GEORGE: And I almost took you to meet…

TOM: She not good enough for you now? And you almost took her home to Mommie? George, how could you?

VIRGINIA: I'm not…I didn't.

TOM: I know. But George, sneaking around like your father, naughty, naughty.

GEORGE: My father is none of your business. My father has nothing to do with me.

TOM: Are you saying your father isn't really your father? Does your mother know?

ABBY: Stop it, Tom. That's over the line.

GEORGE: I'm glad you're going to die soon.

ABBY: Stop it, both of you. This whole newsweb could fall apart, and you two would still be standing here spiting at each other like overgrown boys. Now while we have jobs left to do, let's do them.

TOM: Yes, business before pleasure. Try to remember that, George, while you're doing the traffic reports.

GEORGE: What about the kiddie sex story?

TOM: Traffic reports still have to be done.

GEORGE: I'm not low man anymore.

TOM: But I am still City Editor.

GEORGE: For what, another hour?

TOM: However long it is, however strung out and syphilitic I get, however long Pauline puts up with my breast jokes, you will do what I think you are capable of doing. When I die you can ruin the world anyway you want to. But in the meantime, for the next hour or the next ten years, you will take the assignments I give you. Understood?

GEORGE: I end up doing traffic reports because you missed a scoop yesterday, is that it? The publisher crashes your program, so you crash mine? If you'd posted that story when I said to, you wouldn't be in trouble now.

TOM: A woman murdered her husband because that story was posted. Doesn't that make any difference to you?

GEORGE: Maybe that's justice. Sometimes people stand up for what's right.

TOM: If that's your idea of justice, maybe I feel sorry for you.

GEORGE: I don't need the sympathy of the likes of you.

TOM: No, you need to sit down and do the traffic reports. Let somebody else be the avenging angel. You wouldn't be good at that job either.

GEORGE: Oh really.

   GEORGE exits.

TOM: Blast! (Pause.) Sorry.

ABBY: It's OK.

TOM: I shouldn't have said some of those things to him.

ABBY: No, you shouldn't have. Close your ears, Virginia.

VIRGINIA: Yes, Ma'am.

ABBY: What happened with the big boss? Is there something going on that I don't know about?

TOM: You want to be City Editor?

ABBY: Not at your expense.

TOM: Pauline stuck up for me, but not to the wall, so you may get your chance anyway. Too soon to say. They may just put me out in the lobby as a museum piece, "World's Oldest Reporter."

ABBY: I'd rather have you here.

TOM: So many died. So many. Maybe I am getting too old for this game.

ABBY: You're not that ancient.

TOM: I'm the oldest person on this paper. I remember offset printing. Heck, I even saw a hot lead printing press once.

ABBY: OK, you're a dinosaur. You should have died out in the epidemic. I still like having you around.

TOM: Thanks. I secretly like you too. But maybe I'm... well, thirty years ago that story would never have seen light without three confirmed sources. Now people are killing each other over it, and we still don't have anything hard.

ABBY: Times change.

TOM: Oh, don't I know it. Coffee used to have caffeine, women used to wear tight clothes, and having fun was only a misdemeanor. Now I've become a dirty old man. We have become the straightest, soberest people in history, but we're afraid to touch each other. We take all these tests to make sure nobody is doing anything, then jump out of windows with alarming frequency. You'd think nobody was having any fun. You know, despite what George thinks, I never did much drugs. I guess I had my last beer about twenty years ago. But I did like the women, back in my youth. It was a little, gentle joy, but it made a lot of other things OK. But I was a careful boy. I did not always love well, but I always loved wisely. Kept me alive, I guess. Now, even if I really..., well, never mind.

ABBY: Is it that different?

TOM: Yes.

> Pause.

ABBY: Sandy was by. I got you a cup of coffee.

TOM: Oh. Thanks.

ABBY: No problem. Somebody has to look out for you, lost in the modern world.

TOM: I have always depended on the kindness of friends. When I had friends. Before...

ABBY: Hey, what about me, don't I count?

VIRGINIA: And give me a chance, I just got here.

TOM: Yes, my young friends. Looking out for the old man in his dotage.

ABBY: That's not what I meant.

TOM: Sorry. I guess I just feel like an old man with blood on his hands. Today is not a good day.

ABBY: It's just started. Give it a chance.

TOM: Yes, it could get worse. In fact, here comes more bad news now. Virginia, take the official police report. Abby, the interview with the kid.

ABBY: Right.

TOM: So I get the wife's statement. Heck.

> They type. GEORGE enters and sits and reluctantly begins on the traffic reports. After a moment, PAULINE and MARTHA, with med-cart, enter.

TOM: Not now, we got hot ones.

PAULINE: We got a complaint. You know the Rules.

ABBY: Who?

PAULINE: Tom.

> TOM looks at GEORGE, who keeps typing.

PAULINE: You know the Rules, Tom. Immediate blood and urine tests.

TOM: Kick them while they're down, eh, George?

GEORGE: What makes you so sure I complained?

TOM: This goes on my record, even if it's negative, you know that. Doesn't look real good if your co-workers suspect you, does it?

MARTHA: Give me your arm. Oh, nice veins.

TOM: Gee, thanks. I always injected the heroin in my legs. Kept my arms pure and smooth.

MARTHA: Well, this machine doesn't leave a big needle mark. Just put your arm here and hold still.

> The machine draws blood.

TOM: Abby, can you...?

ABBY: I'll handle the stories.

VIRGINIA: I'm almost finished. Help you in a second.

PAULINE: George, you have to be the third.

GEORGE: Right.

> GEORGE crosses to them.

TOM: What are you, a vampire?

MARTHA: New machine. Takes a little more. There. Bend your arm up.

TOM: Do I get a cup of orange juice now?

MARTHA: No. Sorry. But let me get this machine started, like so, and slap a bandaid on your arm, like so, and I'll give you a cup of a slightly different kind.

> MARTHA puts the blood in the machine, puts a bandaid on TOM's arm, and hands him a specimen cup.

TOM: How can I ever thank you?

MARTHA: Fill it.

TOM: Well, gather round and get your jollies. (singing) Hey, look me over, give me a cheer. Fresh out of clover, sticking out to here. Don't pass the plate folks, but do pass the cup. I figure whenever you're down and out, the only way is up. And I'll be up like a rosebud, high, but not on wine. Don't thumb your nose, Bud, not at one like mine. I'm a little bit short of elbow room, but let me get me some, and look out world, here I come.

> He urinates, surrounded by the three.

GEORGE: You make me sick.

TOM: Sonny, you're not exactly doing a lot for my morale either.

ABBY: Virginia, can you...?

VIRGINIA: On web. The wife?

ABBY: Yes. Then the mayor's comment. I'll try to handle the rest.

VIRGINIA: Right.

> TOM hands cup to MARTHA.

TOM: Here. Drink it in good health.

PAULINE: Not funny, Tom.

TOM: Yes, absurdity is out, farce is in.

> MARTHA inserts cup into the machine.

GEORGE: How long?

MARTHA: About thirty more seconds for the blood.

TOM: Getting excited, George? Ready for your moment of triumph?

GEORGE: You're pitiful.

PAULINE: That's enough, both of you.

GEORGE: The blood test has been improved, you know. Picks up those new psychoactives the old tests didn't, and a lot more infections.

TOM: But only the blood test, not the urine. So you had to officially complain to catch me, didn't you? Finally had to stand up and be counted. Well, at least you proved you have a little bit of guts, however misguided.

GEORGE: I'm glad you're taking this so well. Which drug keeps you this calm?

TOM: It's called experience.

ABBY: Well?

MARTHA: Negative for opioids in any form. Negative for heroin, cocaine, barbiturates, marijuana, and psychoactives, even the synthetics. No nicotine ever, and no alcohol in at least a month. He hasn't even had an aspirin in over a week.

GEORGE: That's impossible. He must...

MARTHA: No syphilis, gonorrhea, chlamydia, HIV, no herpes, no STD of any kind, no elevated white count, no trace of any kind of infection, no nothing, ever.

GEORGE: Let me see that screen...

MARTHA: Your cholesterol is better than average, hemoglobin fine, electrolytes and hormones in balance. You're clean and healthy, as far as I can tell, Mr. Graham.

GEORGE: But he's insane, demented!

MARTHA: That he may be, but not because of disease or drugs.

TOM: It's a natural insanity. Comes from living through troubled times.

PAULINE: You have the form?

MARTHA: Right here. Everybody has to sign.

    MARTHA passes form to TOM.

TOM: Let's see, J. O. H. N. H. A. N. C. O. C. K.

PAULINE: I'll be glad to get this on the record.

    TOM signs, then hands form to PAULINE, who signs and passes it to GEORGE, who refuses it.

GEORGE: No.

PAULINE: You were a witness; you have to sign.

GEORGE: The test is wrong.

PAULINE: Did you see any tampering?

GEORGE: I didn't _see_ any.

PAULINE: Then sign. You know the Rules.

GEORGE: No.

ABBY: I'll sign.

VIRGINIA: Me too.

GEORGE: You can't, you didn't see.

VIRGINIA: I peeked.

ABBY: I always peek.

> GEORGE signs. The pollution alarm goes off. VIRGINIA gets up and turns it off.

MARTHA: Thank you.

> She takes the form from GEORGE, and exits.

TOM: The person who lodged the complaint, whoever it was, this goes on their record too, doesn't it.

PAULINE: Yes. Another false complaint would be grounds for harassment charges. And I would press them even if you didn't. They'd be out on the street within a week. They may be soon anyway. No promotion on this web, that's for sure. Maybe StarWeb....

TOM: I just wanted to be sure we all knew where things stood. And let's let that be the end of it. But speaking of jobs, little Virginia here is worried about possible staff cuts. Any word from upstairs?

PAULINE: No. So just everybody keep on doing what needs doing until you hear otherwise.

> PAULINE exits.

TOM: You heard the lady, back to work everybody.

ABBY: What's left of the city council has a news conference coming up. That will be next probably. I'll be done in a second.

TOM: Virginia?

VIRGINIA: Clear now.

TOM: Traffic reports?

GEORGE: Two minutes.

TOM: Virginia, access the files on the city council and have a side-bar ready, short bios, political records, etc.

VIRGINIA: Right.

TOM: Abby, you handle the news conference story itself. I'm going to do a recap of events leading up to the murder, etc.

ABBY: Right.

GEORGE: What about me?

TOM: What about you?

GEORGE: I'm not going to spend the rest of my life doing obituaries and traffic reports.

TOM: Oh, have you finished the traffic reports?

> SANDY enters sans cart.

SANDY: Rumor Control, Rumor Control. Wild rumor of emergency disease and drug test involving City Desk. Sandy the Snackman on the spot to get the real facts and avoid panic and scandal.

TOM: Going to play reporter now, eh?

SANDY: Can't let the rumors run all over the building by themselves. I go where they go, best if I have the facts to go with the rumors.

TOM: I'm sure they make a matched set.

SANDY: So, what really happened? Who complained? Did you have to take a blood test?

TOM: Who complained is officially unknown. I did have to take a blood test. Blood and urine.

VIRGINIA: He passed too. Clean as Lysol.

SANDY: Of course.

TOM: Beat the system again, eh, George? George was a witness that I didn't cheat in any way. Weren't you, George? Another victory for the forces of evil. Right, George?

GEORGE: This time.

TOM: What else do you think you can do to save the world, George? If I don't get fired over the kiddie sex scoop, I just might be around for another twenty years. Just give it up, OK? This world can survive one dirty old man.

GEORGE: Like it survived one Typhoid Mary? How many people are you going to infect before you get put away?

ABBY: Here comes the City Council news conference story.

TOM: Let's get busy.

ABBY: Oh God.

VIRGINIA: What's wrong?

ABBY: City Council charges opposition Party Leader Ben Edwards with malicious slander. Claim he was the tipster. The whole story was a political dirty trick.

TOM: Some trick. Only one man dead so far.

VIRGINIA: You said you thought it was a smear.

SANDY: Hey, the man knows the news.

TOM: Glad you came back to be my cheering section.

SANDY: Ran out of coffee.

TOM: Sure.

ABBY: City Council is going to sue Edwards and StarWeb for 100 billion dollars.

VIRGINIA: Not us?

ABBY: Evidently not.

TOM: We cited StarWeb, remember?

ABBY: Only because you told us to.

GEORGE: It's a bluff, to take the pressure off. A big lie.

TOM: Virginia, turn on StarWeb.

VIRGINIA: Right.

SANDY: Looks like you might be around talking dirty after all.

TOM: Let's just wait and see. You can't believe everything you read on a newsweb.

SANDY: I'm more than happy to wait, Poly Sci class ain't that great. I'll just go where there's a view and I can see the C.R.T. too.

    SANDY moves behind VIRGINIA so he can see her screen.

VIRGINIA: Slide right in my sweet roll friend, we'll read the story and hope for glory.

TOM: Oh no, not two of them. I can't take it.

ABBY: Ah, youth.

TOM: I can't stand rhymed couplets. It's like Mother Goose run amuck.

ABBY: Council claims Edwards is emotionally disturbed. Say he threatened them if "anything happened to him."

GEORGE: Their word against his. They've got no defense, so they attack.

ABBY: One of accused wasn't even in town at time of one of the alleged "orgies." Another kid supposedly involved was actually at summer camp. Claims Edwards fabricated his "evidence."

GEORGE: The police believed it. StarWeb did. They must have had something.

SANDY: StarWeb would air anything, as long as it was sensational. Only an idiot would believe everything they put on the web.

ABBY: Police state there was no "clamp down," just secrecy because they suspected the charges were false. Death of Rev. Olsen a great tragedy caused by vicious slander and irresponsible yellow journalism. City council wants Governor to suspend distribution of StarWeb.

TOM: Oh boy.

VIRGINIA: Can they do that?

TOM: One of the Rules.

GEORGE: I didn't think you knew anything about the Rules.

TOM: I read them frequently. The descriptions of what you can't do or say are a big turn on.

GEORGE: You'd even pervert the law.

TOM: It's the law that's perverted.

VIRGINIA: Oh boy. StarWeb reports Ben Edwards jumped out of their office on the 20th floor.

GEORGE: No.

VIRGINIA: StarWeb retracts sex ring story, claims they were misled by Edwards.

ABBY: Councilman Chaney says StarWeb will die for its sins. "No amount of money can repay lost lives, reputations, or careers." You sitting on this story sure saved our skins, Tom.

TOM: Some days you get lucky. Anybody here remember getting lucky?

    GEORGE suddenly exits.

VIRGINIA: Guess he couldn't take being wrong again.

TOM: I should feel sorry for him, but that preacher's wife is who I really feel for.

ABBY: Yeah.

VIRGINIA: Starweb regrets Rev. Olsen's death. Their responsibility as journalists over-rode possible difficulties for individuals.

TOM: Bull-hockey.

ABBY: "Possible individual difficulties," the guy's wife shot him dead.

VIRGINIA: Should any of this be going out?

TOM: Just label everything "Courtesy of StarWeb" and send it straight. Eloquent silence will do for us.

>   PAULINE enters.

PAULINE: You watching StarWeb?

VIRGINIA: I've got it.

SANDY: Real hot stuff.

ABBY: They are in big trouble.

TOM: This whole mess is bad news for everybody.

PAULINE: What are you sending out?

VIRGINIA: Starweb, word for word, live edit.

ABBY: Our field stuff is going live edit too.

>   GEORGE enters, goes to water machine, buys a bottle, and stands there drinking it.

PAULINE: The boss is going to love this. She always wanted to be the only newsweb in town.

TOM: The rich get richer.

PAULINE: Should mean a few extra bucks for you and me, I expect.

>   The pollution alarm goes off. GEORGE turns it off, but stops by the "hostage emergency" case. He breaks the glass with the water bottle and takes out a pistol.

VIRGINIA: Uh oh.

ABBY: George...

>   SANDY starts toward GEORGE. GEORGE points pistol at him.

GEORGE: Stay back!

>   SANDY steps back, but steps between VIRGINIA and the gun and shields her with his body.

SANDY: OK. No problem. Just take it easy, OK?

>   GEORGE points pistol at TOM.

TOM: You think that will help?

PAULINE: Put the gun down, George.

ABBY: It's not worth it, George. Your mother needs you at home, George. Who will look after her if you're in jail? You've got to take care of your mother.

PAULINE: Just put the gun down on the desk, and we can talk this out.

GEORGE: Shut up! Just shut up! All of you!

> Pause.

TOM: You want to be the next story on the web, George?

GEORGE: You did this to me. Always talking dirty. Making fun of everything. Even if you're not infected yourself, you spread disease. Getting everybody aroused. Just like my.... You hurt people with your filth.

TOM: Who's hurting people now, George?

GEORGE: I've got to save the others. You've ruined my life, but I can save the others.

TOM: Look around, George. Who's acting crazy now?

GEORGE: I'm not going to write my own obituary!

TOM: Somebody is, if you don't put that gun down.

> TOM begins slowly crossing toward GEORGE.

GEORGE: Stay back!

TOM: You want to shoot me? Is that what you want? Then do it.

GEORGE: Keep away from me!

TOM: I just don't want you to hurt anybody else. You don't know how to use that thing.

GEORGE: I know what I'm doing.

TOM: Then shoot me, George. How much do you think I'd mind?

ABBY: Tom, no.

GEORGE: Stay back! I didn't want it to come to this.

TOM (moving closer): You just wanted me to get sick and die, like all the other sinners, right?

GEORGE: You're immoral. You pervert life. Get back!

TOM: And only moral people shoot other people, is that it? Only perverts like sex, is that it? Then shoot, damn it. If I have to live like you, then maybe I have lived too long. Just don't shoot anybody else. Abby, you and Pauline get out of here. Sandy, take Virginia.

SANDY: Come on, Virginia.

GEORGE: No! Nobody move.

> SANDY again stands so VIRGINIA is behind him to protect her.

TOM: Point that gun back at me!

GEORGE: Shut up!

TOM: Abby, please, go.

ABBY: No. If you get shot, I would never get any more sex stories. You going to shoot me too, George? I liked those sex stories. Does that make me sick too?

> ABBY moves toward GEORGE.

TOM: Shut up, Abby.

GEORGE: He infected you. He's infecting everybody.

ABBY: So? If I'm infected, do you have to kill me too?

TOM: Don't do this.

ABBY: Be quiet, Tom. (Stepping closer.) What's the answer, George? You kill me too?

GEORGE: I don't know!

> VIRGINIA comes from behind SANDY, takes a step toward GEORGE.

VIRGINIA: I bought those black market sweet rolls. Is that a bullet in the brain or just forty lashes?

TOM: Shut up, all of you!

> SANDY takes a step toward GEORGE, and puts VIRGINIA behind him again.

SANDY: Hey! I sold the black market food. You going to shoot me too?

> PAULINE steps toward GEORGE. He is now almost surrounded.

PAULINE: I like that Tom notices my breasts, George. Does that make me evil too? Is everybody evil but you?

ABBY (another step in): You going to shoot all of us, George? We're all infected. You going to shoot everybody?

TOM (steps forward): No, just me. I'm the only one you hate.

ABBY (another step): But who's next? Where does it end, George? How many bullets have you got?

GEORGE: I only need one. Just tell me how you did it. How did you beat the test?

TOM: I didn't beat the test, George. I beat the system. I beat the whole damn system. I used drugs and I loved women, but I never used a drug stronger than wine, and I never had sex with a woman I didn't protect. I wasn't crazy, George, I just didn't hide under a rock. Sure, I took a few chances, because I wanted to live, not cringe every time somebody touched me. That's why I hated The Rules, because they wouldn't let me touch people. Because you, you damn puritan, wouldn't even let me flirt with Abby. Damn your hide, you wouldn't let me love anybody. OK, your kind has won. If you want to take what's left of my three score and ten, you just go ahead.

> TOM steps almost up to GEORGE.

GEORGE: You didn't rig the test?

TOM: No.

> SANDY edges toward GEORGE. VIRGINIA quietly slides over toward the Terrorist Emergency Case.

GEORGE: Stay back!

SANDY: Hey, make it calm. It's over. The man is clean. Nobody's got a problem here. Let's just call this all off and go get a couple of Cherry Cokes, on me.

GEORGE: I don't like Cherry Coke.

SANDY (another step forward)**:** Hey, whatever. You name it. If it's on my cart, it's yours.

GEORGE: No. Not now. Not now. I have to save you first.

> The pollution alarm goes off. GEORGE points the gun back at TOM and takes aim. VIRGINIA reaches in the Hostage Emergency Case and pulls out another gun. She fires at GEORGE, whose body jerks just as he fires at TOM. Abby screams. For a second no one moves. GEORGE and TOM look down at their bodies. GEORGE discovers blood. GEORGE and TOM stare at each other. GEORGE slowly falls to the floor, dead. VIRGINIA screams and drops the gun. There is a moment of motionlessness as the sound of the alarm reverberates with the sound of the scream mixed in.

TOM: Oh shit.

ABBY: Tom?

TOM: I think I'm OK.

> SANDY turns off the alarm.

PAULINE: Is he...?

> TOM visually checks GEORGE.

TOM: Oh yeah. Dead, dead, dead.

ABBY: You sure you're OK?

TOM: Hell no. But I guess I'm not shot. Thanks to little Annie Oakley from Arkansas. Virginia, I owe you.

VIRGINIA: Uh, sure. No problem.

> She puts gun back in case.

TOM: Thanks, all of you, for, well, you know, looking out for the old man.

SANDY: Mr. Graham, I like you a whole lot, but next time let's just get in a fist-fight with somebody, OK? Guns make me nervous.

TOM: Call me Tom, Sandy. My friends call me Tom.

ABBY: Got friends again?

TOM: Looks that way.

ABBY: So, hang around a while. Maybe things will get better after all.

TOM: Maybe.

PAULINE: Oh God. I better go call the police and the sanitation squad.

ABBY: And his mother.

PAULINE: Right. You sure you're OK, Tom?

TOM: Yeah. Thanks.

PAULINE: Virginia, are you OK?

VIRGINIA: Sure. I guess. Why wouldn't I be? Happens all the time in the big city, right?

PAULINE: Be right back.

> PAULINE exits.

VIRGINIA: I think I'm going to be sick.

SANDY: Here, just sit down. You'll be OK.

VIRGINIA: My stomach is doing somersaults.

SANDY: What you need is a Cherry Coke. Just sit still. Be right back.

> SANDY exits.

VIRGINIA: Remind me to kiss that boy when he gets back, even if it is illegal. If I don't throw up first.

ABBY: Here.

> Hands her trash can. VIRGINIA slowly controls her stomach.

TOM: Why did he do that? Why?

ABBY: You sure you're OK?

TOM: Yes...No..., I mean I'm not hurt. I just don't...

> ABBY crosses to TOM, and for the first time in the play, one person touches another as she takes his hand. TOM jumps in surprise at the touch.

ABBY: Sorry.

TOM: No, it's OK. It's OK.

> TOM takes her other hand in his. After a moment, they embrace as the lights fade.

CURTAIN

Café

This play started as a one-act when I was a grad student at the University of Arizona, if my memory is working, but wasn't developed as a full-length until I was working on my Ph.D. at Southern Illinois University-Carbondale. There it was converted into a teleplay as part of my graduate work and two of the scenes were produced and broadcast on WSIU-TV, the PBS station in southern Illinois, in 1979. Writing for TV is definitely different than writing for the stage. As one of my directors said, it's no wonder that so many people in TV end up a little crazy. I'm glad I did it once, but I wouldn't want to do it all the time.

CAFÉ

A Play in Three Acts By David Davis

Member
All rights & privileges.

David Davis
100 Hunters Ridge Court
Roswell, GA 30076
daviddaviswriter@gmail.com

Copyrights 1976, 1979, 1999 David Davis
Revised 1983, 1997, 1998, 2009

CAST OF CHARACTERS

ROSIE...A Waitress

JOE..A Construction Worker

AL...An Apprentice Construction Worker

PHILIP..A Law Clerk

JOY...A Waitress

A.J...A Police Officer

RALPH...An Unemployed History Professor

JIMMY...A Cook

KAY..A Secretary

SETTING

A small cafe in downtown Baltimore, one day next week.

ACT I

AT RISE: we see the interior of a small cafe in downtown Baltimore. There are several tables and chairs neatly arranged about the stage and a counter which is both a serving area and below which dishes, menus, etc. are stored. At one end of the counter is a cash register. Behind the counter is a large coffee maker and various other implements of the trade. There may also be the impression of several tables off to one side of the stage. There are two doors, one behind the counter leading to the kitchen and one that opens on to the sidewalk outside. A radio behind the counter is playing. ROSIE, the waitress in her mid-twenties, a plain but not ugly woman, is cleaning away the dishes left by previous customers. JOE, a construction worker in his forties, and AL, an apprentice in his early twenties, are eating breakfast together. Both are dressed for work, and are consuming large amounts of eggs, toast, sausage, hash browns, and coffee. The song, "When Will I Be Loved" (Linda Ronstadt version), on the radio ends and the D.J. is heard.

RADIO: Another Golden Oldie from your Golden Oldies station. Sixty degrees now in downtown Baltimore, and time for the morning news, brought to you by First City Banks of Baltimore, with 80 convenient locations to serve you. The Baltimore bomber appears to have struck again. There was an explosion near Wilson High School in Towson around midnight last night. Three passers-by were killed and scores of people injured, many cut by flying glass as they slept when the force of the explosion blew out dozens of windows in the neighboring houses...

    ROSIE turns the radio off.

ROSIE: I can't stand to listen any more. All these bombings are getting scary.

JOE: Yeah, just think, waking up in bed with glass flying all around.

AL: Or worse.

JOE: Yeah. Stuff like that always makes me think about all the things I haven't done yet, you know.

AL: Yeah, you go to bed with all kinds of plans and things, and next morning, you don't wake up.

ROSIE: That's really scary.

JOE: I guess staying awake don't help none though.

AL: No.

JOE: Just keep on living, and pray you ain't where the bomb is.

AL: Yeah.

> ROSIE crosses to them with a pot of coffee.

ROSIE: Heat it up, Joe?

JOE: Yah, a tad.

ROSIE: Al?

AL: I'm OK.

JOE: Where's Joy this morning?

ROSIE: Sleeping late I guess. Hope she gets in here soon, I'd hate to have to handle the morning rush by myself.

AL: She'll be in.

ROSIE: I guess.

JOE: What color this morning?

> AL stares at ROSIE a moment.

AL: White bra, blue panties.

> JOE looks ROSIE up and down.

JOE: White and pink. Well. Rosie?

ROSIE: White on white. That just cost you a double tip.

AL: Aw...

JOE: You know, one of these days, we're not gonna take your word for it, you're gonna have to show a little proof.

ROSIE: Take more than a double tip for me to flash my undies at you, Joe Brown.

JOE: What is the going price?

ROSIE: You can't take my word, you just bring your wife in, she can be the judge.

JOE: Hell, that's no fun.

ROSIE: You got six kids at home, sounds like to me you already had your fun.

JOE: And that's just the ones at home, no telling how many others I got out walking around.

ROSIE: Braggart. (To AL) You guys still working on the new office building?

AL: Yeah. It's going to be pretty too, all brick and glass.

> ROSIE refills AL's cup with coffee and goes over to the counter to make a fresh pot.

JOE: Too much glass. One good rock could crack the whole building.

AL: Aw, it ain't that bad.

ROSIE: It's going to have a lot of glass though?

JOE: You kidding, when it's finished you can stand on the corner and watch the flunkies kiss the bosses' behinds.

AL: Could I have a little more toast, Rosie?

ROSIE: Sure.

> ROSIE goes into the kitchen.

JOE: What are you waiting for?

AL: I'll do it. I just don't want Phil walking in right in the middle.

JOE: Well, don't wait too long, we can't sit here all day.

AL: I know. Any idea what we're doing today?

JOE: Didn't you read the work schedule?

AL: No, I missed it.

JOE: Uh, yeah, I did too. Probably start in on that new section.

AL: I guess.

> ROSIE comes back in with toast for AL.

ROSIE: Here you go.

AL: Thanks.

ROSIE: You want anything else, Joe?

JOE: Naw, not now. I'll yell if I do.

ROSIE: You would.

> ROSIE goes back behind the counter.

JOE: Where's Phil? Don't tell me your white collar knight is late.

ROSIE: Maybe he got tired of you riding him and decided to eat someplace else.

JOE: Naw, he likes you too much. Even if you are a working stiff and he's a hot-shot college grad.

ROSIE: He ain't that big on me, he's just got manners, not like the rest of the yahoos I have to deal with.

AL: Aw, Rosie, we're just kidding around, we don't mean nothing.

ROSIE: I know. That's the problem.

JOE: What you want, coats and ties for breakfast?

ROSIE: Ain't what I meant.

JOE: I can see it now, hard hat, white shirt, tie, dress suit, and steel toed boots.

AL: We'd come in and wait for someone to show us to our table.

JOE: Yeah, and ask to see a menu.

AL: How do you order scrambled eggs in French?

ROSIE: How would you like a pot of boiling coffee down your pants?

AL: Aw...

> PHILIP enters. He is in his late twenties, studying to be a lawyer at night and working as a law clerk at a nearby legal aid society. He does wear a coat and tie, but they are neither new nor expensive, they are just his work clothes, the uniform of his job. He stops just inside the door to buy a newspaper from a machine.

JOE: Here comes the judge, here comes the judge

> ROSIE advances on JOE, brandishing the pot of hot coffee. JOE cringes in mock fear.

PHILIP: Cut it out, I'm not even a lawyer yet, just a legal clerk. How many times do I have to tell you that?

JOE: Well, your honor, you know us blue collar workers are sort of thick-skulled, dumb, brute beasts, you know.

PHILIP: You said it, I didn't.

JOE: Yes Sir, I said it. Good of you to notice.

> PHILIP crosses to another table and sits by himself. ROSIE crosses to him.

ROSIE: Donuts and coffee?

PHILIP: Donuts and coffee.

ROSIE: I wish you'd have some eggs or sausage or something, donuts and coffee ain't much of a breakfast.

JOE: Yah, Phil, you got to eat a good breakfast if you want to grow up to be a judge.

PHILIP: The name is Philip, not Phil.

ROSIE: (to Joe) You lay off, or I'll show you the Instant Maxwell House method of birth control.

JOE: Hey, that's hitting below the belt.

AL: Oh, that's bad.

> ROSIE goes to the counter and gets the donuts and coffee, staring JOE down every time he glances at her. PHILIP and AL watch this bit of byplay, glancing at each other to share the laugh. ROSIE crosses back to PHILIP with the donuts and cup of coffee, threatening JOE again as she passes his table.

ROSIE: Bunch of yahoos,

PHILIP: Don't let them bug you,

ROSIE: No manners.

PHILIP: They don't know any better. (Taking the donuts) Thank you.

ROSIE: You sure you don't want some bacon or sausage, we got some fresh sausage in this morning,

PHILIP: No, thank you,

ROSIE: I worry about you, not eating.

PHILIP: What are you, some kind of Jewish mother?

ROSIE: I'm not Jewish, I just worry.

PHILIP: Well, don't. It's not good for your health,

ROSIE: Call when you want some more coffee.

PHILIP: OK.

> ROSIE crosses back to the counter. PHILIP unfolds the newspaper and begins to read the front page.

JOE: Hey Phil, what's the news today?

PHILIP: Philip.

JOE: Philip, Sir, Your Honor.

PHILIP: Why don't you learn to read, then you wouldn't have to have somebody read the news to you every day,

JOE: I read. I just don't like it.

PHILIP: The exertion must be very tiring.

AL: The what?

PHILIP: The exertion, work, effort.

AL: Oh. Joe, I think you just been burned.

JOE: No kidding, You trying to insult me, Phil?

PHILIP: On the contrary, insulting you requires no effort at all. But, as to your original inquiry, there is one item which you should find of interest.

JOE: (not understanding) What?

PHILIP: They might blow this place up tonight.

JOE: What!

PHILIP: That bomber is threatening to explode a bomb again tonight, somewhere between Wilson and Third Streets and Main and Grand Avenue, an area that includes this establishment, not to mention my apartment.

JOE: Hey, I live on Grand. Al and I both do.

ROSIE: I'm in there too.

AL: The one that blew up that school last night?

PHILIP: Evidently. That means yes, Joe.

JOE: I know what it means, I dropped out of high school, not first grade. You know, I helped build that school. If these nuts had to help build these places, they wouldn't be so quick to blow them down.

PHILIP: For once in your life, Joe, you are probably right.

ROSIE: They really gonna blow up something right around here?

PHILIP: That's what they say. According to the paper they said, "The target for tonight is in the area bordered by Wilson and Third Streets and Main and Grand Avenues. It might be an office building, it might be a restaurant, it might even be an apartment building, but you better hope all the people are out of it by midnight, because it's going up in smoke."

ROSIE: Wow.

AL: You really think they'd do it?

PHILIP: He blew up a school, just last night.

JOE: I don't think anybody would blow this place up, would they?

ROSIE: How should I know? I'm just glad I'm not working tonight. Maybe I'll go visit my sister in Delaware. That should be far enough away.

AL: Why Baltimore, why not New York, or Washington, or someplace important?

JOE: Because in New York nobody would notice.

PHILIP: And in Washington nobody would care.

ROSIE: It's scary, just thinking about it.

JOE: My house, or yours, or any of us, just lying there, and boom!

ROSIE: Don't say things like that.

AL: But it's true.

PHILIP: Don't panic yet, Joe. Wilson and Third and Main and Grand, that's still a big area. It's not like it's just your block. I'm sure you'll be OK.

JOE: Yeah, but it's here, now, not somewhere over yonder. It's us, not some poor guys halfway to New Jersey. Even if it ain't our houses, what if it is the cafe, or where we're working, or your school? If it's this close, it's bound to mess up our lives one way or another.

AL: You know, I've lived here all my life. All my friends are here. It's like my backyard, you know? Maybe I don't get hurt myself, but whatever gets blown up, maybe I got a friend I don't ever see again.

PHILIP: Same thing could happen in a car crash, accident on your job, just walking down the street. Sometimes life is like that; what can you do about it?

JOE: Ah, hell, I don't know.

> Pause.

PHILIP: You want the sports scores too?

JOE: Yah. I guess.

PHILIP: Orioles lost 7 to 3, Yanks won, Mets lost,...

JOE: Damn, there goes another fin.

PHILIP: You didn't bet on the Mets again?

JOE: Well, they got to win sometime.

PHILIP: Not the Mets.

JOE: Ah, what do you know.

PHILIP: Enough not to bet on the Mets.

AL: Could I have a little more coffee, Rosie?

ROSIE: On, sure.

> ROSIE pours him some more coffee.

AL: I didn't know you had a sister in Delaware.

ROSIE: Yeah, my big sister. Three kids already.

JOE: Married?

ROSIE: Of course she is, you idiot. You want some more coffee?

JOE: Only in my cup.

> She pours coffee in JOE's cup, then threatens to pour hot coffee on JOE's hand when he reaches for the cup.

JOE: Whoa there!

ROSIE: Would serve you right.

> ROSIE takes the coffee pot back to the counter.

JOE: How come you ain't married yet, Rosie? You ain't that bad looking.

ROSIE: Gee, thanks.

JOE: Serious though.

ROSIE: Serious?

JOE: Yeah.

ROSIE: I don't know. Right guy just ain't asked yet, I guess.

JOE: You going to spend your life wanting something better than what you got?

ROSIE: From the looks of things, I'm gonna spend my life waiting on yahoos like you two.

JOE: What about good old Phil over there, he ain't no yahoo, he's gonna be a judge

PHILIP: I am not going to be a judge. I've got a year more of law school before I can even be a lawyer.

JOE: Rosie will wait, won't you, Rosie?

ROSIE: Go sit on a hot rivet.

JOE: What about it, Phil, you want her to wait for you?

PHILIP: What I would like is for you to perform a series of anatomically impossible contortions.

JOE: What?

PHILIP: Never mind.

AL: I think you been burned again.

JOE: I wish he'd speak English.

PHILIP: I wish you could read.

JOE: I read.

PHILIP: I mean something besides a foldout.

ROSIE: Cut it.

PHILIP: Could I have a bit more coffee, please.

ROSIE: Coming.

> ROSIE takes the coffee to PHILIP.

PHILIP: Thank you.

ROSIE: Another donut?

PHILIP: No, thank you, I've had enough.

JOE: (To AL) I think I'll take the wife and kids out to a movie at one of those cineplexes out on the highway, get something to eat after, stay out till the bomb goes off. You want to tag along?

AL: Sounds OK.

JOE: Well, the kids will be noisy, and there'll be more to watch in the back of the theatre than on the screen, but it'll be out of the way of whatever.

AL: OK.

ROSIE: (To PHILIP) Where you going tonight?

PHILIP: I've got a night class at law school.

ROSIE: They haven't canceled it?

PHILIP: No. Can't have future lawyers backing down before these violent terrorists.

ROSIE: Hate to think of you getting blown up. I mean, somebody has to eat these donuts.

PHILIP: I'll be OK.

AL: Any more jelly?

ROSIE: I'll get it.

> ROSIE goes into the kitchen. JOE crosses over to Philip and sits next to him.

JOE: What's the weather? Cloudy and cool with occasional explosions?

PHILIP: See for yourself.

> PHILIP hands a section of the paper to JOE. ROSIE comes back from the kitchen and takes jelly to AL. JOE slowly looks over the whole page of the paper.

PHILIP: Very bottom, on the left.

JOE: Oh, yah, now I see it.

> Pause.

PHILIP: Well?

JOE: What?

PHILIP: What's the weather?

JOE: Gonna rain.

>JOE neatly refolds the paper and lays it down on the table.

JOE: You should have worn a raincoat.

PHILIP: Yes, I guess I should have.

JOE: And you should eat more than a couple of donuts, Phil, you need the energy.

PHILIP: It doesn't take much energy to turn pages.

JOE: Is that all you do?

PHILIP: Mostly, looking up cases, information for the lawyers, filling out a few legal forms.

JOE: Don't seem much to that.

PHILIP: Well, you have to know which pages to turn.

JOE: I'd rather be outside, doing something.

PHILIP: I expect you would.

JOE: I sort of feel sorry for you, being stuck inside all day long, just turning pages.

PHILIP: Well, they do let me look out the window twice a day.

JOE: Yah. Well, thanks for the use of the paper.

PHILIP: Anytime.

>JOE goes back to his seat.

AL: What was that all about?

JOE: Just readin' the weather.

AL: Oh.

JOE: It's gonna rain.

AL: I heard.

>Pause.

JOE: You gonna ask her?

AL: In a minute. After Phil leaves.

JOE: (Looking at watch.) We gotta go.

AL: Aw, alright. Hey, Rosie.

ROSIE: Coffee?

AL: No, come here a minute.

ROSIE: What is it?

AL: Just come here.

>ROSIE crosses to the table.

ROSIE: Yeah?

AL: Well, there's this dance Saturday the union is having, and, well, I was wondering if maybe you'd like to come with me.

ROSIE: Thanks Al, I appreciate it, but...

JOE: Aw, come on Rosie, me and the wife are going.

ROSIE: Well, I...

PHILIP: Go ahead, Rosie, you need to get out a bit. Al will show you a good time.

AL: That's a promise. Even take you out to dinner.

ROSIE: I'm sorry, Al, maybe next time.

AL: Yeah, sure.

ROSIE: I gotta go see my mother Saturday.

JOE: Come on, kid, we gotta get to work.

AL: Yeah.

> JOE stands up and counts some money onto the table.

JOE: There it is, Rosie, double tip and all.

ROSIE: Thanks, Joe.

> JOE picks his lunch box off the floor and heads for the door.

PHILIP: Stay out of the rain.

JOE: Yah, you stay out of explosions. (To AL) You coming?

AL: Be there in a second.

> AL gulps down the last of his coffee as JOE exits.

AL: Good breakfast, Rosie.

ROSIE: Thanks.

> AL stands and digs some money out of his pocket and lays it on the table, then heads for the door, forgetting his lunch box.

PHILIP: Hey, Al.

AL: Yeah?

PHILIP: Keep plugging, OK?

AL: Yeah, sure. Thanks, Phil.

PHILIP: Anytime.

> AL exits, ROSIE takes the money from the table and goes to the cash register. She rings up the bill, and puts her tips in her pocket. Then she goes to the counter and pours herself a cup of coffee and carries it over to the table where PHILIP is sitting.

> She sits down next to him, and begins to read the front page of the paper.

ROSIE: Don't say nothing in here about rain. (Pause) Says it's going to be clear all day.

PHILIP: That Joe is some joker, isn't he. Now he's got Al worrying all day that it's going to rain.

ROSIE: Yeah, sure. (Pause) Says here the police still don't have any clue who the bomber is.

PHILIP: I know.

ROSIE: What do you think?

PHILIP: Could be anybody; somebody who's not real happy with the way life is treating them. Somebody blaming everybody else for the way their life turned out. Maybe somebody like Joe.

ROSIE: Naw, not Joe. That big lug might not have anything worth putting a hard hat on, but he wouldn't hurt a fly. I heard somebody say it's the quiet ones that get you.

PHILIP: That's what they say.

ROSIE: Well, I just wish the cops would catch them, whoever they are. They scare me.

PHILIP: That's why they're called terrorists. Scare people enough, they start doing things they wouldn't do otherwise. And that's what the bomber really wants, to see how many people he can scare into changing things, taking another look at life.

ROSIE: I guess. (Pause.) You see this about the elephant sitting on a yellow Volkswagen?

PHILIP: Yes.

ROSIE: Now why would an elephant sit on a yellow Volkswagen?

PHILIP: No one offered him a chair?

ROSIE: It just ain't polite to sit on a Volkswagen.

PHILIP: Not very, no.

ROSIE: Almost as bad as those two yahoos that just left.

PHILIP: Oh, they're not too bad, just don't know any better.

ROSIE: You could say the same thing about the elephant.

PHILIP: I guess. (pause.) Al seems nice enough

ROSIE: I guess. What time do you get out of night class?

PHILIP: Around ten, why?

ROSIE: I was thinking, since you need to get away from the bomb, I could pick you up after your class, and you could go out to my sister's with me, she's got plenty of room.

PHILIP: Oh. That's very considerate of you, but I wouldn't want to impose on anybody.

ROSIE: She wouldn't mind, she lives out in the country, don't get company often.

PHILIP: I don't think so, but thanks anyway.

ROSIE: Well, maybe we could just drive out to the country a ways, you know, watch the stars, listen to the radio till the bomb goes off, then come on back. Might even be fun.

PHILIP: Thanks, but I don't think any self-respecting terrorist would chose to blow up my apartment building. If he did, he'd probably get a thank-you note from the city.

ROSIE: I just hate to think of you being around here when a bomb goes off. I mean, even if they didn't blow up your building, there could be a big fire.

PHILIP: Thanks for worrying, but I'll be all right.

ROSIE: We could just sit and talk, get to know each other better. I never see you outside of the cafe, you always in class or at work, me stuck here most of the time. We probably have a lot in common we don't even know about.

PHILIP: Well, look, I'll be fine, don't worry. I've just got something I have to do here in town, after class.

> Pause.

ROSIE: You need some more coffee.

> ROSIE takes his cup and goes over to the counter where she refills his cup. She stops and looks at PHILIP for a moment, then looks around the restaurant, then at herself. She then returns to the table. She puts the cup in front of PHILIP, but this time she does not sit down.

ROSIE: It must really be different, being a lawyer and all. Risking being blown up just to avoid being seen with some two-bit waitress.

PHILIP: What?

ROSIE: Dress suits, big cars, fancy women.

PHILIP: What are you talking about? I don't live that way.

ROSIE: You will, one day. You'll be finished with cheap cafes and dumb, ugly women.

PHILIP: What set this off?

ROSIE: Won't have to listen to yahoos like me, mumbling about yellow Volkswagens. No more smile and be polite to the stupid waitresses who think a smile and a kind word are more than just a game.

PHILIP: Rosie...

ROSIE: Maybe you'd better start now, forgetting yahoos like me. I don't think this cafe will have any more donuts from now on.

PHILIP: What?

ROSIE: I think maybe you'd better get your breakfast someplace else from now on.

PHILIP: We'll talk about this later. I've got to get to work.

ROSIE: There's a donut shop three blocks down; they make their own.

> PHILIP stands up and starts to put money on the table.

ROSIE: That's too much. I don't need no charity.

> PHILIP puts one bill back in his pocket.

PHILIP: I'll see you around.
ROSIE: Yeah, sure.

>   PHILIP starts to exit.

ROSIE: Hey, Phil.

PHILIP: Yeah?

ROSIE: Get some eggs or something once in a while, OK?

PHILIP: Yeah, sure.

>   PHILIP exits. ROSIE clears the table and takes the dishes into the kitchen just as JOY, the other waitress enters from the front.

JOY: Rosie?

ROSIE: Back here.

JOY: Sorry I'm late, but Ann is sick, so I'm going to have to work a double shift today, and I thought I'd sleep in a little. Have any trouble so far?

>   ROSIE enters.

ROSIE: No, nothing I couldn't handle.

JOY: Was that Phil that just left?

ROSIE: Yeah.

JOY: I thought I recognized the back of his head. Did he leave his paper?

ROSIE: Yeah, over there

JOY: Any big news?

>   JOY crosses to the table and picks up the paper.

ROSIE: Big bomb scare.

JOY: Is that all?

ROSIE: Elephants have started sitting on Volkswagens.

JOY: What?

>   AL suddenly runs in.

AL: Hey, Rosie, did I leave my lunch box in here?

ROSIE: I haven't seen it. Look under the table.

AL: Yeah, here it is, thanks.

>   AL grabs the lunch box and starts to run back out.

AL: Going to be late for work.

ROSIE: Hey, Al!

>   AL stops at door.

AL: Yeah?

ROSIE: I can't go to the dance Saturday, but how about a movie on Friday. We could go to one of those cineplexes out on the highway.

AL: What? Oh, yeah, OK, fine! I'll, uh, talk to you later, I gotta go.

> AL exits.

ROSIE: Sure.

JOY: This is a switch.

ROSIE: Shows how much you know.

> ROSIE turns the radio back on, ("Help," by the Beatles is playing.) then begins to wipe the tables. JOY sits down to read the paper. The lights fade.

ACT II

It is now almost nine thirty in the evening. A Blues instrumental can barely be heard coming from the radio. JOY is sitting in one chair, and has her feet propped up in another chair. She is sipping a glass of ice water. She is obviously very tired, her hair is disheveled, her uniform wrinkled and more stained than it was in the previous scene. After a few moments Alexander James Carney, better known as A.J., a policeman in his mid-twenties, enters. JOY starts to get up, then sees who it is, and sits back down.

A.J.: Joy, what are you doing here?

JOY: Ann has the flu; I had to work a double shift. When did you start pulling night duty?

A.J.: Everybody's on tonight, out looking for the bomber. You look beat.

JOY: I feel beat. You want some coffee?

A.J.: I'll get it.

> A.J. goes to the coffee maker and pours himself a cup of coffee. He then sits next to JOY.

JOY: You been out looking for the bomber?

A.J.: Trying to. Don't really know where to look. I've just been walking around, looking for cars they might have left the bomb in.

JOY: Is that how they do it?

A.J.: Well, that's one way. Put the bomb in a car, and then just park the car next to the target and walk away. I'm just guessing they might use the same trick here.

JOY: Seems simple enough.

A.J.: Damn hard to stop too. You haven't seen any strange people hanging around, have you?

JOY: You mean besides our usual run of freaks?

A.J.: Yeah, any unusual freaks.

JOY: Hotshot, I haven't been outside this cafe since seven thirty this morning. P.T. Barnum's best side show could have gone by out there, and I would never have noticed.

A.J.: Listen, circus freaks would be tame compared to what we caught today.

JOY: Rough case?

A.J.: Child beater.

JOY: My god.

A.J.: Skinny little girl, maybe ten years old. He beat her all to hell.

JOY: You get him good?

A.J.: Naw. He claims she fell down the stairs. Unless we can get the girl or her mother to testify, he'll be home before the girl is, just waiting for her.

JOY: Good god.

A.J.: The little kid's too scared to say a word, and I guess the wife is too. He'll probably kill her one day, and we can't do a thing. This is a lousy job sometimes.

JOY: You want this one?

A.J.: Don't tempt me.

JOY: You hungry?

A.J.: Yeah. You got anything good?

JOY: Honey, I got lots good. What's in the kitchen, I couldn't say.

A.J.: I'm on duty. I'm afraid I'll have to settle for what's in the kitchen.

JOY: Oh well, I'll see what's left back there.

> JOY goes into the kitchen. A.J. gets up and refills his coffee cup. JOY sticks her head out of the kitchen door.

JOY: We got some chili that will light your fires.

A.J.: Sounds good.

JOY: Coming up.

> JOY goes back in the kitchen. RALPH HANES, early fifties, poorly dressed, slightly dirty, the kind of man you try not to walk to close to on the street, enters. He stops in surprise when he sees a cop standing at the counter holding the coffee pot.

A.J.: Can I help you?

RALPH: You the waiter?

A.J.: Does this look like a waiter's uniform?

RALPH: No. Not much anyway. More like a cop's.

A.J.: Then I guess I must be a cop.

RALPH: I guess. (pause) Did you arrest the waiter?

A.J.: The waitress is in the kitchen, she'll be out in a minute.

> A.J. turns off the radio.

RALPH: Oh. You just helping yourself a little, eh?

A.J.: She knows.

RALPH: Oh, of course. They never do pay cops enough, do they?

A.J.: No, they don't. I don't believe I've seen you around before. You work around here?

RALPH: At Staffer's. About a week now. Just got off. Is there a problem?

A.J.: We're looking for somebody.

RALPH: Anybody in particular?

A.J.: You wouldn't have met any people carrying a bomb, would you?

RALPH: Not that I know of. That's not the sort of thing one brags about though.

A.J.: You'd be surprised. Live around here?

RALPH: Little place up on Third Street. I just got my Maryland driver's license, if you want to see it.

> RALPH shows A.J. his driver's license.

RALPH: You could call Staffer's; they probably still remember me.

A.J.: That's all right. (Returns license) Been in town long?

RALPH: Couple of months.

> JOY enters, carrying a bowl of chili.

JOY: Here's your lighter fluid.

A.J.: Just put it on the table; you've got another customer.

> JOY finally sees RALPH.

JOY: Oh, can I help you?

RALPH: Could I see a menu, please?

JOY: Sure, just have a seat.

> JOY sets the chili down on the table where she and A.J. were sitting. RALPH sits at one of the other tables. A.J. takes his coffee and sits down in front of his bowl of chili. JOY goes to the counter and pours a glass of ice water for RALPH, then starts looking for the menus.

JOY: Darn.

A.J.: (taking his first bite of the chili) Ow, this is hot.

JOY: I warned you.

A.J.: What's the matter?

JOY: I can't find the dinner menus, only the lunch and breakfast. Nobody's asked for one all day. Do you know where Ann keeps them?

A.J.: Well. they're not in this chili, that's all I know. Nothing in here but peppers and sulfuric acid.

RALPH: A restaurant with no menus?

JOY: I'll find them, just a minute. (to A.J.) Put some crackers in it.

A.J.: Put a fire extinguisher in it.

RALPH: I take it I would be advised not to order the chili. Assuming I ever find out what is available to order.

A.J.: Take it easy, buddy, she's had a long day.

RALPH: The name is Hanes, Doctor Ralph Hanes.

A.J.: Dr. Hanes, sure.

JOY: Here they are.

RALPH: Dr. Ralph Hanes, Ph.D. in Medieval History, currently unemployed. For some strange reason there has been a staggering decline in the number of positions for experts in Drama during the Dark Ages over the past few years.

JOY crosses to RALPH and gives him the water and the menu.

A.J.: Somehow I can understand that.

RALPH: (To JOY) Thank you.

JOY crosses back to the counter.

A.J.: Hey, I thought you said you worked at Staffer's.

RALPH: I did.

A.J.: But you just said you were unemployed.

RALPH: I am. I was fired, oh, about an hour ago.

JOY: Why?

RALPH: Because I have a Ph.D.

JOY: That don't make sense.

RALPH: It seems that having a Ph.D. automatically disqualifies you for any sort of manual labor or skilled work. Something called over-qualification. They won't even let you teach in high school; they would have to pay you so much more than a less educated person. At any rate, I had neglected to mention on my job application that I had a doctorate, and when my employer found out, he chose to release me, whether I wanted releasing or not.

JOY: What were you doing?

RALPH: Parking cars.

JOY: What?

RALPH: I fear I neglected to acquire any nonacademic skills during my school days, so the opportunities for me on the job market are somewhat limited. I drove a truck for a while, was even a grave digger for a few months.

A.J.: I take it there has not been much call for experts in Dark Ages Drama in quite a while.

RALPH: Not in quite a while, no. And it's rather frustrating to have to hide one's education in order to obtain employment. I worked long and hard for my degree, and I am rather proud of it.

JOY takes her order pad and crosses back to RALPH.

JOY: I guess so.

A.J.: Ever get to use it?

RALPH: Oh yes. Uh, I think I'll have a grilled cheese sandwich and a cup of coffee.

JOY: You got it.

>   JOY takes the menu and goes into the kitchen.

RALPH: I was an assistant professor of history at a small college in upstate New York for almost twenty years. I taught freshman history, Medieval History, even a bit of Modern European now and then. A small school demands versatility.

A.J.: You got to know it all, eh?

RALPH: Well, not everything. But at least enough to convince the freshmen that you know almost everything. And, of course, one has one's specialty, where you are at least trying to know everything.

A.J.: And yours was Dark Ages Drama.

RALPH: Yes.

A.J.: You enjoy teaching?

RALPH: Oh yes, very much. Being around all those eager young students was exciting, even if history was not always the thing that made them eager.

A.J.: Say, when were the Dark Ages, anyway?

RALPH: After the fall of the Roman Empire.

A.J.: Oh, yeah.

RALPH: Yes, college was very exciting.

A.J.: So what happened, budget cut?

RALPH: No, nothing that limited. They closed.

A.J.: The whole college?

RALPH: Bankrupt. Sold out to the Moonies.

A.J.: The Moonies?

RALPH: The followers of the Rev. Moon, of Korea. The college is now a Moonie Seminary. They retained the janitors, but dismissed the entire faculty.

A.J.: And you couldn't get on anywhere else.

RALPH: History is a rather crowded field. And there is VERY little call for specialists in Dark Ages Drama, especially if they are over fifty and have not yet become the recognized authority in the field. And if one is over fifty, and has no skills or experience outside of academia, there is no call for him at all. The assumption is made that if one has a doctorate in the liberal arts, he is unable to function outside of a university. Over-qualification, nasty word.

A.J.: Sounds dumb to me.

RALPH: I have a slightly stronger word for it. (Joy comes out of the kitchen.) Which I shall save for another time.

>   JOY pours a cup of coffee and takes it to RALPH.

JOY: Here you go.

RALPH: Thank you, my dear.

JOY: Sandwich will be ready in a minute.

A.J.: Joy, this guy says he used to be a history professor.

JOY: No kidding?

RALPH: It has been several years.

JOY: Like I said, we get all kinds here. I better go check your sandwich.

>JOY starts toward kitchen.

A.J.: Get me some more chili while you're at it, OK?

JOY: What are you, a fire eater?

>JOY exits to kitchen.

RALPH: Charming girl.

A.J.: Joy, yeah, she's pretty nice.

RALPH: And she makes a good cup of coffee.

A.J.: Yeah, the coffee's always good here, that's why I like this place.

RALPH: I doubt that's the only reason.

A.J.: Yeah, well, some of the other things are pretty good too.

RALPH: You know, a friend of mine, another professor from the college, opened a little cafe after the Moonies ran us out, a little place up in the Adirondacks. Doing rather well, I hear.

A.J.: Why didn't you go into business with him?

RALPH: Well, it's just a little place; he and his wife run it by themselves. He was almost to retirement anyway, and I thought I could get another teaching position. I was rather naive in those days.

A.J.: Yeah, life gets a little rough sometimes. Not much you can do about it, seems like.

RALPH: It's almost enough to make you run away and join the Moonies.

>JOY comes back in with the chili and the grilled cheese sandwich. She puts the chili in front of A.J., then crosses to RALPH.

JOY: Here you go, professor.

RALPH: My, it's been a long time since anybody called me that.

A.J.: Feel good?

RALPH: Yes, yes it does. (RALPH takes a bite of his sandwich.) And this tastes very good too.

JOY: Thank you. If you want anything else, just yell.

>JOY goes back and sits down next to A.J.

A.J.: Say, professor.

RALPH: Yes?

A.J.: What are the Moonies like?

RALPH: I really couldn't say. They let the college lie empty for a year before they moved in, and by then I had moved away.

A.J.: Oh.

RALPH: I imagine they're like most radical religious groups, the members are nice enough when dealt with individually, but when they get together, some form of group weirdness overcomes them.

A.J.: I've heard that Moon himself got pretty rich off the contributions of his followers.

RALPH: The Rev. Mr. Moon must be a very interesting individual. Some people claim he is Christ reborn, others that he is an agent for the Korean CIA. I don't suppose there is any real reason that he could not be both, but I doubt it.

JOY: He's got a lot of people freaked out, if you ask me.

RALPH: That is the claim many of the parents of his converts have made, though they were not so concerned when their children were freaked out on Mexican hash or Scotch whiskey. Only Korean religion seems to be a threat to life and limb.

A.J.: Parents can be pretty strange. Are there anymore crackers?

JOY: Chili still too hot?

A.J.: Is Baltimore dirty?

JOY: I'll get you some.

> JOY starts to get up.

A.J.: No, I'll get them, just tell me where they are.

> A.J. stands up, JOY sits back down.

JOY: Just inside the door, on the top shelf.

> A.J. goes in the kitchen.

JOY: Find them?

> A.J. comes back out of the kitchen.

A.J.: Yeah, but what this chili really needs is some baking soda.

JOY: If it's that hot, don't eat it.

A.J.: But it tastes great.

> A.J. sits down again.

JOY: I give up. (pause) Hey, professor, how can chili be too hot and taste great at the same time?

RALPH: Simple, the special flavor of chili comes from the spices, the peppers. Otherwise, it would just taste like greasy beans. However, the peppers also have a very high acid content, which causes the burning effect in the mouth and stomach lining. You can't get the flavor of the peppers without the acid as well, so it tastes great, but it's too hot.

A.J.: Something like that anyway.

JOY: You learn that in college?

RALPH: Yes, long ago. I took a course called Chemistry for Non-science Majors, which, if I remember correctly, the chemists referred to as Chemistry for Idiots.

JOY: College must be fun, except for all the studying.

RALPH: It does have its light moments. The studying itself can be rather pleasurable too. At least I enjoyed it. I guess you have to enjoy it to do as much of it as I did.

JOY: I was never much good at it.

RALPH: Well, some people just never seem to get the hang of it.

JOY: I guess that's me, I hung around boys instead of books.

RALPH: Ah yes, the old serpent sex. A lot like the chili, in a way.

A.J.: What?

RALPH: The flavor is great, but the heartburn can be very painful.

JOY: Hey, that's pretty good.

A.J.: Well then, this chili must be downright immoral.

JOY: I'm going to get you some alka-seltzer.

> JOY goes to the cash register and gets a foil wrapped packet from a rack there. Then she goes to the counter and pours a glass of water. She sets both down in front of A.J.

JOY: There, now shut up about the chili.

A.J.: OK, OK.

RALPH: My dear, while you're up, could I trouble you for a bit more coffee?

JOY: Sure thing, professor.

> JOY gets RALPH's cup, refills it, and gives it back to him.

JOY: Anything else I can get you?

RALPH: No, thank you. This will suffice.

JOY: OK.

> JOY sits next to A.J. again. A.J. makes a big show of scraping the bottom of the chili bowl for the last bite, then opens the packet of Alka-Seltzer and drops two tablets into the glass of water.

A.J.: (singing) Plop, plop, fizz, fizz, oh what a...

JOY: Oh, cut it out.

A.J.: If you don't sing the song, they don't work.

JOY: Grow up.

A.J.: Why?

JOY: I give up.

A.J.: (singing) Plop, plop, fizz, fizz, oh what a relief it is, fast, fast, fast.

> A.J. drinks the contents of the glass in one long gulp.

A.J.: Ah, that's better.

JOY: And I thought cops had to take a sanity test.

A.J.: We do. The crazy ones get in, the sane ones are rejected. No sane man would have this job, right professor?

RALPH: That's probably valid.

A.J.: And if a professor says so, it's got to be true.

> RALPH, who was taking a sip of coffee, just has to laugh at that remark, and he suddenly finds himself trying to drink coffee and laugh at the same time.

RALPH: Well, I wouldn't go quite that far.

A.J.: Well, in his specialty anyway.

RALPH: Ah, that it were so. I remember one poor man who wrote a big, long paper proving that the Roman Comedies were not really derived from the Greek New Comedies.

A.J.: So?

RALPH: Just after he published, someone else found the first known copy of a Greek New Comedy; it was almost exactly like the Roman plays. The academic world is not as sure as it seems.

A.J.: I guess not.

JOY: What happened to the guy?

RALPH: The professor? Nothing. Lost a bit of reputation, probably felt like an idiot for a while, that's all. Scholars, people who are learning, experimenting, have to be allowed a few mistakes, even big ones. Otherwise we would never learn anything new.

JOY: I guess.

RALPH: Yes, that is the really wonderful thing about the academic life, we are allowed a few mistakes. Unlike such gentlemen as your friend here, for whom one mistake might be fatal.

A.J.: It's not that bad.

RALPH: Isn't it? (there is a long pause) Well, I have to be going. I want to get home before the bomb goes off. Could I have my check please?

JOY: Oh, sure.

RALPH: If I'm going to be blown to kingdom come, I prefer it be while I'm asleep in a nice warm bed. I don't know if the bomber is aware of it, but he is probably not helping his political goal at all, but is making a lot of people reconsider what they truly value in this life. I have come to value hot coffee, a warm bed, and good books. I have found I can live without just about everything else.

> JOY writes out a bill, carries it over to RALPH and lays it on the table, then goes over to the cash register. RALPH drains his cup of coffee, glances at the bill, then lays a few coins on the table. He then crosses over to the cash register to pay his bill.

RALPH: In order to have those few essentials, however, I do need a little income, so, I am going to have to get up early in the morning to go job hunting.

A.J.: Good luck.

RALPH: Maybe I'll try construction this time. There ought to be at least one building in need of a bit of work by about 12:01 this morning, if you don't catch the bomber.

A.J.: Every cloud has a silver lining.

RALPH: So I've been told.

> RALPH lays the bill and some money on the cash register. JOY rings up the bill and gives him back his change.

RALPH: Thank you.

JOY: Come back. And good luck with the job.

RALPH: Thank you. You know, I really don't mind the physical labor. I even enjoyed driving the truck, seeing the country and all. What I really hate is trying to be something I'm not, hiding my education behind a cloud of silence, afraid some large word or bit of knowledge will blow my cover.

A.J.: I guess that must be pretty bad, to know all about something, to have spent all that time studying, and then to have to hide it.

RALPH: Yes, it is. Well, good luck avoiding the bomb. I would hate for nice people like you two to be hurt. Bombs are so random, so heartless in choosing their victims.

JOY: Thanks. Good luck to you too.

A.J.: Yeah. Good luck. Maybe I'll see you around.

> RALPH crosses to the door, then stops and turns around.

RALPH: You want to hear something really funny though, something funny as hell?

JOY: Sure.

RALPH: I'm an expert on Dark Ages Drama, right?

A.J.: Yeah.

RALPH: There wasn't any.

JOY: What?

RALPH: There wasn't any. Oh, there were minstrels and clowns, jugglers and acrobats, stuff like that, and a few monks copying old Roman plays, writing a few scenes themselves. But after the fall of Rome, drama died in western Europe. No plays were actually performed for several hundred years, best anybody can tell. No actors on stages performing scripts written by playwrights, no real drama during all those hundreds of years. I'm an expert on nothing, nothing at all. Isn't that funny?

> RALPH exits.

A.J.: My god.

JOY: Do you believe that?

A.J.: It must have been the chili.

> ROSIE turns on the radio. "I Can't Stop Loving You," Ray Charles version, is playing. The light fade.

ACT III

> It is now twenty minutes until midnight. The cafe seems empty, except for the radio, which is playing "Pretty Woman," by Roy Orbison. KAY, a pale, thin woman in her early twenties, enters. She is startled by a bell attached to the door so that it rings when the door is opened. She wears jeans and a sweater, both of which are a size too large for her. She crosses to one of the tables and sits in a chair. JIMMY, a young man in his late teens, wearing a cook's apron over his jeans and tee-shirt, enters from the kitchen. He turns off the radio and crosses to KAY.

JIMMY: Yes, Ma'am?

KAY: Just coffee.

JIMMY: OK.

> JIMMY goes over to the counter and pours a cup of coffee. KAY looks around, examining her surroundings. JIMMY crosses back to her and places the coffee on the table.

KAY: Sort of quiet tonight.

JIMMY: The bomb scare.

KAY: Yeah.

JIMMY: Everybody suddenly remembered they had a cousin in Delaware they just had to go and visit.

KAY: Yeah. What about you? No cousin in Delaware?

JIMMY: I think it's a fake. Baltimore isn't worth blowing up. Besides, if everybody in Baltimore went to Delaware, Delaware would sink.

KAY: Well, I don't guess anybody would miss it.

JIMMY: No, probably not.

KAY: Still, just thinking about.... Uh, If you're not busy, pull up a chair. Bombs make me... uh, you know.

> JIMMY sits down backwards in chair next to her.

JIMMY: Sure. Thanks. It is kind of slow tonight. The only customer I've had since I came on at eleven was a cop. He said not even the hookers were out tonight. Everybody's gone.

KAY: What's your name?

JIMMY: Jimmy.

KAY: Jimmy, I'm Kay. Pleased to meet you.

JIMMY: Kay. I had a girlfriend named Kay once.

KAY: Really?

JIMMY: Yeah. She O.D.ed on soy sauce.

KAY: She what?

JIMMY: She was into shooting up, you know, and this kook convinced her that soy sauce was a real high. She was pretty dumb anyway. She mainlined a hypo of it, and it popped a vessel in her brain or something. Anyway, she was D.O.A.

KAY: Soy sauce.

JIMMY: Wild, isn't it?

KAY: Yeah.

Pause.

JIMMY: What brought you out tonight?

KAY: Oh, just looking for a place to be. You know.

JIMMY: You get kicked out of someplace?

KAY: No, not really.

JIMMY: You hungry? I could get you a burger. On the house, if you're broke.

KAY: No. Thanks anyway, but I'm not hungry.

JIMMY: You an actress or a model or something? I heard models have to stay real thin like you.

KAY: No. I just been sick lately. A cold, then the flu. Lost a little weight.

JIMMY: OK, but if you change your mind, just say so.

KAY: Thank you. Not many people in this town would care.

JIMMY: Ah, they're just in a hurry. I work nights, eleven to seven; it's slower. You get to talk to people, like this. During the day there's just so many people running in and out.

KAY: Yeah. I guess everybody gets a little crazy.

JIMMY: Yeah. There's just so many of 'em. Not like tonight. Man, I never seen this town so empty.

KAY: They're all scared.

JIMMY: Not like you and me, eh?

KAY: Yeah.

JIMMY: Running off to sink Delaware.

KAY: Hey, why don't you get yourself a cup of coffee. I hate drinking alone.

JIMMY: OK. You want some more?

KAY: No, I'm OK.

JIMMY goes to counter and gets a cup of coffee for himself,

then returns to his seat. While he is gone, KAY unconsciously preens herself a little.

JIMMY: (Taking a sip of coffee.) This is good coffee, even if I did make it myself.

KAY: Yeah, it is.

JIMMY: Where you work?

KAY: The power company.

JIMMY: No kidding? Secretary?

KAY: Yeah, at the main office.

JIMMY: You work for a big shot?

KAY: No. Just one of the junior executives in supplies. I'm just another powerless person at the power company.

JIMMY: Hey, that's a good line. "Another powerless person at the power company." I like it.

KAY: Thank you. (Pause.) What time is it?

JIMMY glances at his wrist watch.

JIMMY: Almost fifteen till twelve.

KAY: Fifteen till.

JIMMY: Why? You waiting for somebody?

KAY: No. The bomber said the bomb would go off at midnight.

JIMMY: Oh, yeah. You worried?

KAY: A little.

JIMMY: Ah, it's just a fake, just a scare. Besides, this is a big city. Chances of us being anywhere near a blast are next to nothing.

KAY: I guess.

JIMMY: Listen, if you're scared, you should have left.

KAY: All my cousins live in Baltimore.

JIMMY: OK, OK. (Pause.) I got this cousin in Philly. He's a real freakazoid. A number one, grade A pervert. He runs this gas station, but he gets his kicks by dressing up like a woman, you know, wig, false eye lashes, lipstick, falsies, the whole bit. Then he'll go off to a Phillies baseball game and wait behind one of the steel supports till somebody walks by alone, you know, under the stands during the game. Then he'll walk up to them, all nice and sweet like, then pow!, up goes his skirt, and surprise, no underwear!

KAY: Oh no!

JIMMY: By the time they recover, he's gone up into the stands and blended with the crowd. Man, I'd rather get blown up in Baltimore than spend a weekend with that guy. Real freakazoid.

KAY: He does sound a little strange.

JIMMY: A little, huh? Let me tell you. Once he pulled that stunt on a lady cop. If she hadn't slipped on some spilled popcorn, he probably would be in a nut house by now. Real whack-o.

KAY: I guess. But didn't you ever want to do something really weird?

JIMMY: Well, yeah, sure, but nothing like that.

KAY: So, like what?

JIMMY: Well, I once ran down Orleans Street at rush hour, yelling and screaming at the top of my lungs.

KAY: What happened?

JIMMY: I ran out of breath after a block. It's hard to run and yell at the same time.

KAY: Nobody did anything?

JIMMY: Oh, one guy stopped and said, "You're weird, man, real weird." Then he kept on going.

KAY: That's all?

JIMMY: All except for a few funny looks.

KAY: Strange. Why'd you do it?

JIMMY: Oh, I was afraid I was going to flunk a course I needed to get out of high school, I'd just had a fight with my girl, my old man was bugging me. It just seemed like the thing to do.

KAY: Did it help?

JIMMY: Well, it convinced me I was really out of shape. I work out down at the Y every week now.

KAY: You get out of school?

JIMMY: Yeah, I got a D. (Pause.) You ever do anything wild like that?

KAY: No. I guess I'm a pretty boring person. I just sit at home a lot.

JIMMY: Why you think people go bananas like that?

KAY: Oh, too many people, too small a space, too fast a pace. Everybody cracks a little. There's this girl I work with who always eats a peanut butter and mayonnaise sandwich for lunch. I think that's weird.

JIMMY: That is a little strange.

KAY: She claims the mayonnaise keeps the peanut butter from sticking to her braces.

JIMMY: I guess I'll have to take her word for that.

KAY: I went on a fast once, but that's not very weird.

JIMMY: I think it is. Why'd you do it? You sure don't need to lose weight.

KAY: It was one of those deals where you fast for a day, then give the money you would have spent on food to save the starving people in Africa or somewhere.

JIMMY: Yeah, I've heard of those.

KAY: I don't know if it did much good. I don't spend but about five dollars a day for food.

JIMMY: Well, I guess if a lot of people did it.

KAY: Yeah, but I don't think many did.

Pause.

JIMMY: We give our old pastries to the Salvation Army.

KAY: That's good.

JIMMY: Can't sell them after they get old anyway; people would complain. I guess it beats throwing them away.

KAY: Yeah, I guess. What time is it?

JIMMY: It's not even ten till yet. Relax, will you.

KAY: Sorry.

JIMMY: OK. Let me get you some more coffee.

KAY: OK.

> JIMMY takes both cups to the coffee maker and refills them.

JIMMY: You sure you don't want something to eat?

KAY: No, thanks.

JIMMY: What about some apple pie? I got some apple pie made with real apples.

KAY: No, nothing. If you want something, go ahead.

> JIMMY crosses back to the table, sets the cups down, then take his seat again.

JIMMY: Nah, I just thought you might want something by now.

KAY: No, but thank you.

JIMMY: OK. You married?

KAY: No. You?

JIMMY: No. I was living with this girl, but she split on me a couple of months back.

KAY: That's too bad.

JIMMY: Ah, something else will turn up.

KAY: You pretty lucky with women?

JIMMY: Not really. Working nights sorta cramps my style, you know. If everybody wasn't afraid to live alone, I'd probably never get anywhere.

KAY: I live alone.

JIMMY: No kidding? Not even a roommate? Another girl, I mean.

KAY: No. Just me. Ever since I left home.

JIMMY: Now that's weird.

KAY: Yeah, I guess.

JIMMY: I'm alone for two months and I'm climbing the walls.

KAY: That must disturb your neighbors.

JIMMY: Yeah, and you should see what it does to the wallpaper.

KAY: Ever tried swinging from the lights?

JIMMY: No, does it help?

KAY: A little, if you've got strong lights. Otherwise you get glass all over the floor.

JIMMY: I'll have to try it.

Pause.

KAY: What was she like, the girl you were living with?

JIMMY: Oh, she was nice, real nice. Her name was April, like the month. She was short, and a little fat, but she had these nice, big boobs. She was terrible in the kitchen; I had to do all the cooking. But she kept the place real neat. She just couldn't adjust to me working nights and sleeping days. She finally took up with this eight to fiver. He works in a bank and wears a suit to work. Real class. She's probably dump him in another month or two.

KAY: She floats around?

JIMMY: Yeah. She'll never stay anywhere very long.

KAY: Think you'll remember her a year from now?

JIMMY: Just her boobs. She had nice, big boobs.

KAY: Must be nice.

JIMMY: Now, that's not to say you're not pretty. I mean, you're a little thin, but you've been sick, you said. Boobs ain't everything.

KAY: But they help.

JIMMY: Well, yeah, I like big girls. But you've had your share of men, sure. I mean, some guys like skinny girls. I mean look at all the models, they're skinny. Didn't I think you were a model when you came in? There are lots of guys like your type, you've had your share, sure.

KAY: Two.

JIMMY: Two?

KAY: Both one nighters.

JIMMY: But you're not ugly. Not Miss America, OK, but you sure ain't ugly.

KAY: I fade into the wall. I take things too seriously. I guess I'm just not much fun.

JIMMY: I wouldn't say nothing like that. I mean, we been sitting around having a few laughs. I ain't bored.

KAY: It's an unusual night. I mean I don't usually...

JIMMY: Well, yeah, but...

KAY: If this was a normal night, with customers and all, would you have ever noticed me once I got served, ever talked to me, ever cared if I was hungry?

JIMMY: Sure. I mean, well, uh, I guess not. I've got some regulars I like to talk to, and I'm usually pretty busy, cooking and waiting on tables.

KAY: The population of Baltimore has to disappear before I can get a man to notice me. That's pretty bad.

JIMMY: Oh, cut it out.

KAY: Yes. Change the subject. Somebody is about to blow up Baltimore, and I sit here complaining about my sex life.

JIMMY: Yeah, talk about something else. You like sports?

KAY: No. You read much?

JIMMY: Just comics. What about music?

KAY: I like rock.

JIMMY: I'm into country.

KAY: TV?

JIMMY: Sports, cop shows, stuff like that.

KAY: I like the late night talk shows.

JIMMY: I never get to see 'em.

KAY: Oh, yeah.

JIMMY: You ever have a grandfather?

KAY: Yeah, yeah I did.

JIMMY: My grandfather, he used to tell me about in the old days, before TV, he used to sit around and listen to the radio. Imagine, just sitting and listening to a radio.

KAY: I've heard they used to do that.

JIMMY: Course in those days they didn't just play music; they had regular programs of some kind.

KAY: I know.

JIMMY: Still sounds strange.

KAY: My grandfather was a salesman. He used to ride the railroad all over the state, selling door to door in the little towns. He used to tell me how he could go knock on a door, and the people would just yell "come in" without asking who it was. And the doors were never locked. He never got robbed, he never got mugged; you could trust people back then. He said that from the train the towns looked like white branches with green leaves all around, you know, the white houses sort of running up the side of a hill that still had trees on it. He says they're not there anymore; now it's just brown hills covered with brown houses. And the trains don't stop anymore; they just slow down while the cattle, he calls commuters cattle, jump on.

JIMMY: It's a different world OK.

KAY: One that's falling apart. (Pause.) What time is it?

> JIMMY glances at his watch.

JIMMY: It's a couple of minutes till.

KAY: Two till exactly?

JIMMY: I don't know; you want me to call time?

> An explosion is heard in the distance. There is a long pause.

JIMMY: I guess I was a couple of minutes slow.

> JIMMY crosses to the door, opens it, and looks outside.

KAY: Where was it?

JIMMY: Down toward the harbor, five, maybe six blocks. There's a fire. Can't tell much else.

> Sound of sirens is heard off in the distance. JIMMY closes the door, decreasing the sounds.

JIMMY: You live down that way?

KAY: No. I'm a couple of blocks over east. You?

JIMMY: No. My neighborhood's up, you know. I don't think I know anybody down that way.

KAY: Me either.

JIMMY: Yeah. So...

> Pause.

KAY: It wasn't a fake. People are probably dying down there.

JIMMY: Yeah. (Pause.) Hell of a night.

KAY: Hell of a night.

> Pause.

JIMMY: I guess I better find me a cousin in Delaware.

> KAY stands up.

KAY: Find one for me too.

JIMMY: You leaving?

KAY: It's going to be a madhouse at work tomorrow. I better get some sleep. How much?

JIMMY: Forget it. Every time we don't get blown up, we have free coffee.

KAY: Thanks. Thanks for everything.

JIMMY: Anytime.

> KAY crosses to the door. JIMMY stands up and picks up the cups.

JIMMY: Come back some time.

KAY: Well, you know how it is, working days and all.

JIMMY: Yeah.

> KAY exits. JIMMY carries the cups into the kitchen, stopping to turn the radio back on. "That Summer" (first chorus) by Garth Brooks is playing. The lights fade.

ACT III, SCENE TWO

> Early the next morning. JIMMY is sitting at the counter sipping a cup of coffee. Otherwise the cafe is empty. The radio is playing "There's Got to Be A Morning After" by Mary Lee Rush. After a moment, ROSIE enters.

ROSIE: Hi. You OK?

JIMMY: Fine. You?

ROSIE: No problem.

> JIMMY turns the radio off.

JIMMY: Joy said you were going to your sister's. Didn't expect you back on time.

ROSIE: Yeah, well, you know.... After I thought about it, didn't hardly seem worth the drive. She's got all these kids to look after, and,... you know.

JIMMY: Yeah.

ROSIE: Been this quiet all night?

JIMMY: Not a soul since midnight. Quiet as a grave since the bomb went off, if you don't count all the sirens. Quiet as a grave, guess that's a bad choice of words.

ROSIE: Any news on the radio?

JIMMY: Just that there was another bombing. No body count or nothing.

ROSIE: Maybe everybody got out of town.

JIMMY: Everybody but you and me?

ROSIE: No, eh? Well, maybe everybody decided to die at home, then just stayed there.

JIMMY: I guess.

> ROSIE puts her purse and jacket in the kitchen, then comes back out and starts a new pot of coffee.

ROSIE: Guess we'll have the usual crowd of yahoos after all.

JIMMY: Maybe. Might run a little late. Then they'll all come at once and complain it's so crowded.

ROSIE: Yeah. It's not enough they're still alive, they got to have coffee, two sugars, no cream, and right now.

JIMMY: Yeah. "There was a bombing? OK, in that case make that three eggs over easy, bacon and sausage, a double order of toast, hotcakes on the side, and coffee with Sweet and Low."

ROSIE: The Yahoo Diet Plan.

> Pause.

JIMMY: Glad you're OK.

ROSIE: Yeah, you too.

JIMMY: Hate for you to miss your hot date with that Al fella.

ROSIE: Hey, what did Joy do, tell you my life story before she left?

JIMMY: Just the high points.

> JOY enters.

JOY: Everybody OK?

JIMMY: Far as anybody knows.

JOY: And here I make myself get in early because I figure you're off eating clams and eggs in Delaware.

ROSIE: Sorry. Maybe next bombing.

JOY: Yeah. OK.

> JOY puts her things up in the kitchen, ROSIE checks the supplies behind the counter.

JIMMY: Everything should be set.

ROSIE: OK, thanks.

> JOY enters and begins to wipe the tables off.

JIMMY: There ain't much to clean. Only had two people all night.

JOY: Yeah, well, I'm here, may as well keep on like normal.

JIMMY: Suit yourself.

ROSIE: You normally fill Jimmy here in on my private life?

JOY: What? Oh, you mean about Al? Honey, I got to tell him something sexy or he'd never stay awake all night.

ROSIE: Even with bombs going off?

JOY: These days, you getting a date is more unusual than Baltimore getting bombed. We got bombs about every night now; you ain't been out with a man in weeks. I'm surprised you don't explode.

ROSIE: Yeah, well, I just don't want to read about my social life in the newspaper.

JOY: Girly, until that thing with Al came along, your social life would only make the obituaries.

ROSIE: OK, OK. (Pause.) I think we're all set.

JOY: Looks OK to me.

ROSIE: Jimmy, you can head on out if you want since Joy's here.

JIMMY: When I finish my coffee. No reason to hurry.

ROSIE: OK.

> A.J. enters. He is obviously exhausted and his uniform is flecked with soot and ash.

JOY: A.J.! You OK?

A.J.: Yeah, yeah. I just need about a gallon of coffee to keep me awake a little longer. You OK?

JOY: Yeah. We're all fine. Now sit down.

ROSIE: I'll get the coffee.

> JOY sits A.J. at a table and tries to wipe off his uniform. ROSIE brings cup and coffee.

JOY: You are a mess. This uniform may be done for.

JIMMY: What happened out there?

A.J.: Bomb was in a warehouse down toward the harbor. Damn thing was full of chemicals. Firemen had to wear those space suit things cause nobody could find out what kind of chemicals were in there. Took all night to put the fire out. Smoke and ash all over the place. Every uniform we had was out cordoning the place off, evacuating all those new lofts and condos down there, keeping those idiot photographers from getting themselves killed.

> A.J. stops talking to gulp some coffee.

ROSIE: Did anybody get hurt?

A.J.: Night watchman killed. Couple of firemen hurt, but not too bad I don't think. Fire jumped and burned out some of the lofts nearby, but I think we got everybody out in time. I heard a fireman say they think there was a body under a wall that collapsed, but we haven't had time to search the wreckage yet. Near a whole block gone though.

JIMMY: Wow.

A.J.: Anyway, the excitement's over, so they put most of us flatfeet back on patrol. I got a half hour to go, then I can go home and get some sleep. I needed some coffee, so I thought I'd stop in and see if you were OK, Joy. Uh, you too.

JOY: Oh, aren't you sweet.

A.J.: Uh, everybody OK?

JOY: We're all just fine. And we're all very glad you're OK.

ROSIE: Did they catch the bomber?

A.J.: Naw. No such luck. Maybe next time.

ROSIE: Here's hoping.

A.J.: Yeah.

JOY: How you getting home?

A.J.: Drive, I guess. It's only a couple of miles.

JOY: Sweet thing, you are in no condition to drive, no matter how much coffee you drink. Now you finish that coffee while I get my purse, then I'm going to make sure you get home in one piece.

A.J.: I got to go by the station and change.

JOY: Well then, we'll just go by the station together. Somebody has to take care of you. (To ROSIE) Can you cover for me? I'll be back as soon as I get him taken care of.

ROSIE: No problem. It's going to be slow anyway.

JIMMY: I'll hang around for a while. Take your time.

JOY: Thanks.

> JOY runs to the kitchen for her purse and coat. ROSIE refills A.J.'s cup, and he gulps it down.

A.J.: Thanks.

ROSIE: Gotta take care of our friends.

A.J.: All these bombings. And nothing seems to change. We just get tireder and tireder. Glad you guys are OK too.

ROSIE: You too.

A.J.: I don't know what this bomber thinks he's doing to us, but all I see are burned buildings and dead bodies. Nothing else seems to change much.

> JOY re-enters.

JOY: OK. Let's get you home before you collapse.

> A.J. gulps one last mouthful of coffee, then struggles to his feet.

A.J: See you guys tonight. I bet I get the night patrol again.

> JOY helps A.J. as they exit. Pause.

JIMMY: Yeah. Take it easy. (They are gone.) Well, well, well, look at that.

ROSIE: Yeah. That's nice. Bomb or no bomb.

JIMMY: You want some breakfast? I make a great cheese omelet.

ROSIE: That would be wonderful. Thanks.

> JIMMY exits into the kitchen. ROSIE turns on the radio, changing stations. "Who'll Stop The Rain" by CCR is playing. The lights fade.

CURTAIN

The Hermit

This script has never had a full production, but was one of three finalist for a contest here in Atlanta and has had a couple of readings by various playwright groups here in Atlanta. I think it would be very dynamic on stage, even with only two characters. The male character hitting the female character seems to be the main obstacle to production, though I have had several women tell me they think the action is acceptable within the frame of the play. I just think the characters are interesting and the action dramatic.

THE HERMIT

By David Davis

Member
All rights & privileges.

David Davis
100 Hunters Ridge Court
Roswell, GA 30076
daviddaviswriter@gmail.com

Copyright 2004 David Davis

CAST OF CHARACTERS

MATTIE BLAIR .... 20s, Psychology Grad Student

THE HERMIT .... Late 30'S or Early 40'S, Lives Alone

SETTING

A small room in a house in New Mexico. The present.

> AT RISE we see a small room in a little house in New Mexico, modern but very simple, with the impression of vistas beyond. A man, late-30s, clean shaven, informally but neatly dressed, sits at a desk in the only chair in the room. He is typing on a computer keyboard. We hear a car drive up outside. The man stops typing, crosses to the window and glances outside, then goes back to his seat and sits silent and unmoving, listening. We hear the car door slam, steps on a wooden porch, knocks on a wooden door, then more knocks. We hear the voice of a young woman offstage.

MATTIE: Hello? Hello? Anybody home? (He does not answer.) Anybody here?

> We hear a couple of doors open and close offstage.

MATTIE: Hello, anybody?

> MATTIE enters the office. She is dressed neatly but simply. She carries a large purse or bag.

MATTIE: Oh. I didn't think anybody was here.

HERMIT: Well, we all have our illusions.

MATTIE: I called and called. I knocked on the door and called. It wasn't locked. Nobody answered.

HERMIT: Should I have hidden behind the sofa?

MATTIE: I'm looking for the hermit. I was told a hermit lived here. Some people in town…

HERMIT: And you believe in fairies and trolls too, I assume.

MATTIE: Some old Zen master, they said. Very wise.

HERMIT: And you wanted to buy some wisdom wholesale?

MATTIE: Well, I wanted to…talk, ask…for research….I'm a graduate student….my thesis….psychology.

HERMIT: On Zen?

MATTIE: On withdrawing from society, people who isolate themselves. You know, like monks who live in monasteries on top of mountains.

HERMIT: They do not live alone. They live in smaller societies.

MATTIE: Well, yeah, but they withdraw from, you know, people, civilization, women…

HERMIT: Like you?

MATTIE: Well, yeah, I guess…Say, who are you? I thought this hermit guy lived alone.

HERMIT: Which bothered you.

MATTIE: No. Well, I mean, it's curious. Not normal. Made me wonder.

HERMIT: About who would ever forsake the wonder of your presence.

MATTIE: Well, not just me, but people, like me. To be, you know, alone, all the time.

HERMIT: Not even a television.

MATTIE: Yeah. Well, that I can sort of understand. But, to be so...

HERMIT: Alone? Isolated? Self-reliant? Un-restricted?

MATTIE: Different.

HERMIT: Ah. From you.

MATTIE: I met this girl in college last year, and she was a virgin. She was all of 23 and not a nun or anything religious or really ugly or lesbian or anything; she was just different. Said she didn't want the hassle. Made me wonder about people who are different. Who opt out, as it were. Seemed like a good topic for a thesis. So where is this guy? Are you the one I have to go through to see him?

HERMIT: You didn't do very well in research methods or formal logic, did you?

MATTIE: Huh? Why do you say that?

HERMIT: A: A hermit lives in this house. B: Hermits live alone. C: I am in this house. Therefore......

MATTIE: He's not a real hermit. OK, I can live with that. I mean I wasn't expecting some religious fanatic curled up in a cave. I know this is New Mexico, not Egypt. I saw the solar collectors in the yard. So he's got some assistant or disciple or something. It's still a little odd, living out here, the two of you. Is he gay? Are you two, you know?

HERMIT: No.

MATTIE: Hey, I mean, this is all confidential. I can change the names, just say Subject A, that sort of thing.

HERMIT: I choose not to be Subject A or any other letter.

MATTIE: OK, whatever, I can leave you out of it.

HERMIT: I don't suppose there is any possibility you could just leave?

MATTIE: Just a few hours, that's all I need.

HERMIT: Has anybody ever tried to explain how incredibly dense you are?

MATTIE: Why? Am I missing something?

HERMIT: Quite a lot, actually.

MATTIE: What?

HERMIT: Look out the window.

MATTIE: Yeah.

HERMIT: What do you see?

MATTIE: Some brown mountains off to the north. Very long dirt road up here from the highway; what, 10 miles away? Solar array, water tank, greenhouse down the hill if I crane my neck a little. Why? What do you see?

HERMIT: I see the barrel cactus where a road runner sits every morning, waiting for the sun. The tracks of a desert tortoise that passed by three days ago that the wind has still not covered. I see the clouds over the mountains that will not bring rain, they are too low and flat. I see where the sun will set tonight and the dust that will make the sky red and purple when it does. I see the marks on the cistern that tell me my shower must be very brief tomorrow. I see that the dust from your SUV has blown over the yucca, turning it grey. I see the tracks from a dune buggy that drove through the wash a year ago, and even older tracks, a faint trail, from the cliffs to the east down to the place the river ran hundreds of year ago, hundreds of footprints from a time forgotten, still marking the easy way, the flat way, to a river that has also passed from memory. And I see that that path will be marked long after there is no evidence I was ever here. I see the way you came and the way you should go. And I see that you will never see what I see.

MATTIE: Did the hermit teach you to see like that?

HERMIT: Time is a better teacher. Silence comes to those who listen.

MATTIE: Yeah, right. A koan, I recognize those.

HERMIT: Do you have a name?

MATTIE: Martha Blair. Most people call me Mattie.

HERMIT: Miss Blair, I think it is time for you to go.

MATTIE: Two hours. Just two hours, as long as I can tape it.

HERMIT: Not permitted.

MATTIE: Hey, that's up to him, isn't it? It ain't easy getting up here, at least I deserve an answer from him, not some flunky.

HERMIT: The difficulty of a task is not a measure of its merit.

MATTIE: Well, no, maybe not, but trying hard is worth something.

HERMIT: Only to our self-esteem. Please leave now.

MATTIE: I want to see the hermit. I came to see the hermit. You can't stop me from seeing the hermit.

HERMIT: Nor can I make the blind see. It is people like you that create hermits. Now take your blind eyes and crawl back to your cell at the university and pray for enlightenment. I recommend 50 Hail Mary's and a day of fasting.

MATTIE: I'm not Catholic.

HERMIT: Neither am I, but you should at least do something to punish yourself.

MATTIE: Now wait a minute....

HERMIT: No, Miss Blair, you wait. You have trespassed on clearly marked private property, entered a private residence without permission, intruded on my time, and refused to leave when asked. In addition to violating several laws, that is rude, egotistical, and obnoxious. Not only do you not care about the rights of others when it interferes with your idle curiosity, but you have demonstrated that you are unobservant, illogical, and lacking both common sense and common decency. You are not worth talking to, or even listening to, and I again ask you to leave.

MATTIE: Hey, just who the hell do you think you are?

HERMIT: I know who I am, Miss Blair. I am the owner of this house and the person telling you to leave my home.

MATTIE: Yeah, what you gonna do, call the police? You don't even have a phone.

HERMIT: (Holding up cell phone.) Even New Mexico has cellular service now. If you had looked closely, you would have seen the repeater tower on the mountain you drove around to get here.

MATTIE: Fine, call 'em. I'm not leaving till I meet the hermit. By the time they get here I can turn this place upside down and find where he's hiding.

HERMIT: I would advise you not to disturb my property.

MATTIE: Yeah, what you gonna do, slug me?

> HERMIT punches MATTIE in the jaw, knocking her down. She is still for a moment, then groans. She pulls herself to the far wall and sits against it, gathering her wits.

MATTIE: You hit me.

HERMIT: Well, at least you are that observant. You threatened me and my property.

MATTIE: Damn, you really hit me.

HERMIT: Will you leave now?

MATTIE: That hurts like hell.

HERMIT: Aversion therapy.

MATTIE: Why did you hit me?

HERMIT: Because you wouldn't leave. Will you leave now?

MATTIE: You going to hit me again?

HERMIT: If you don't leave, yes.

MATTIE: What did I ever do to you?

HERMIT: You invaded my home, you stole my time, you acted like an idiot, and you threatened to destroy my property.

MATTIE: It's against the law, hitting people.

HERMIT: Not if they break into your house.

MATTIE: The door wasn't locked.

HERMIT: But it was closed. Good Lord, Miss Blair, you drove past three No Trespassing signs, through two closed fences, and walked through three closed doors to get into this room, all to get to a person who by you own admission you knew wanted to be left alone. Then you don't even recognize the person you came to see, refuse to leave when asked, and are surprised when you are not welcomed like the Prodigal Son. Such stupidity is monumental. I'm surprised you survived elementary school, not to mention college. Your odds for living past 30 are practically non-existent.

MATTIE: Didn't your mother tell you not to hit women?

HERMIT: No.

MATTIE: What do you mean didn't recognize the.....

HERMIT: Ah, light creeps into the darkness of your little mind.

> She gets up.

MATTIE: You're the hermit?

HERMIT: I am the person who lives here.

MATTIE: The only person?

HERMIT: The only person. The sole inhabitant. The person who came here to be alone. And you, Miss Blair, are interrupting my solitude. Please crawl back to your monster of a truck and drive away forever.

MATTIE: You can't be the hermit. You're too young.

HERMIT: I was not aware there was an age requirement.

MATTIE: But hermits are...

HERMIT: Hermits are only happy when they are alone. Now GO AWAY!

MATTIE: But why would anybody like you...

> HERMIT hits her again, in the stomach this time. She collapses on the floor, moaning.

HERMIT: Not exactly a quick learner, are you?

> The moans become sobs as she lies on the floor. HERMIT returns to the desk and types some more. Slowly the sobs subside.

MATTIE: You're a son of a bitch, damn you.

HERMIT: Not all hermits are pacifists.

MATTIE: I think I'm going to be sick.

HERMIT: Feel free to stop in the bathroom on your way out.

> MATTIE struggles to her feet and runs out. HERMIT stares out the window a moment, picks up MATTIE's purse, tosses it out of the room, closes the door, and returns to the computer. He types for a moment, then pauses in thought. The door opens and MATTIE stands in the door holding her purse.

MATTIE: You god damned brute.

HERMIT: I perceive that your true talent is not intelligence, but a hard-headed tenacity that borders on stupidity.

MATTIE: You stupid pig.

HERMIT: Anyone with any sense would have taken the hint and left by now, if only to avoid further violence.

MATTIE: Yeah, what are you going to do, shoot me?

HERMIT: I would like to, but I am one of the few people in this part of the country who does not have a gun. Perhaps I can find a knife in the kitchen and stab you.

MATTIE: There are people who know I came here.

HERMIT: And I have no desire to spend any time cooped up in a cage with some drug addict. What I want to be is ALONE. I realize, Miss Blair that I am not good at interpersonal communication, but what part of "go away" do you not understand?

MATTIE: So, call the police.

HERMIT: That does seem to be my best option.

> HERMIT picks up the cellular phone and dials 911. There is a pause.

HERMIT: Hello. Yes, I would like to report a trespasser. Mountain View Ranch, off State Road 1423. No, I can't tell if she is armed. Oh, I would say about five feet seven inches, maybe

120 pounds, short brown hair, twenties. (Or whatever describes the actress.) No, she has been informed she is trespassing on private property, but she refuses to leave. Yes, she has invaded my home. Yes, she has threatened my property. No, she has not damaged anything except my privacy, at least not yet. Yes, I do fear for my safety. Yes, as soon as possible. Thank you.

    HERMIT hangs up the phone.

MATTIE: It took me five hours to get here.

HERMIT: Neither miles nor fences nor doors nor decency nor physical punishment will stop this courier from her self-appointed rounds.

MATTIE: Should take the cops at least two.

HERMIT: I wanted to be out in the country.

MATTIE: You hit me any more, I won't be able to leave, even if I want to.

HERMIT: So your plan is to interrogate me for the next two hours, to force your presence upon me and break down my resistance like the Inquisition, before you are arrested and dragged away by the constabulary?

MATTIE: I just want to know why.

HERMIT: You find it so difficult to understand the attraction of isolation?

MATTIE: To be alone, not see anybody, not talk to anybody, not touch anybody, that, yes.

HERMIT: Ah, sex. Have you never heard of pornography and masturbation?

MATTIE: A human voice. Another soul.

HERMIT: You place entirely too high a value on yourself. The modern age. No frontier anymore. Never any silence. I have work to do, excuse me.

    He goes to the computer and starts typing.

MATTIE: What are you doing?...............What is your job?.........................How do you support yourself out here?..I imagine it does get very quiet out here. No sounds at all, especially at night.

HERMIT: Once again, you are totally wrong. At night you can hear the universe. Coyotes, owls, rats, even the stars. More happens at night than in the light of day. Life crawls out of its hole and goes on the prowl. Kill and be killed, eat and be eaten, screams and cries in the dark. Makes it hard to sleep.

MATTIE: And you find that attractive?

HERMIT: The owls are the quietest, of course. Diving down without even a whoosh. Death with a silencer.

MATTIE: You seem fascinated by death. Any idea why that is?

HERMIT: Because then maybe I could get some peace and quiet. Maybe if I bound and gagged you until the police arrive.

MATTIE: Why can't you just answer a few questions? What is the big deal? It's not like you have appointments to keep.

HERMIT: But I have miles to go before I sleep.

MATTIE: Poetry, uh,....Frost, uh...Robert. Passing By the Woods On a Snowy Evening.

HERMIT: Amazing. She remembers ninth grade literature. Can you do X squared minus Y squared equals sixteen? Or who was the sixth President?

MATTIE: If I get it right, do you answer my questions?

HERMIT: No.

MATTIE: Then why should I answer?

HERMIT: Fine, don't talk for two hours, see if I care.

MATTIE: Oh....you!

> HERMIT goes back to typing. MATTIE paces for a moment, then gets her purse, opens it, takes out a little tape recorder, checks it to make sure it isn't broken, turns it on, and puts it back in her purse with the microphone hanging out.

HERMIT: Would you like to reconsider that?

> Pause. MATTIE takes out the tape recorder, turns it off, takes out the batteries, shows the batteries to HERMIT, puts it back in her purse, takes out a small notepad and a pen. HERMIT stares at her. After a moment, she puts the notepad and pen away in her purse.

MATTIE: Would you like to know what makes me so stubborn?

HERMIT: No.

> Long pause. HERMIT types.

MATTIE: You know, there's a chance we're related.

HERMIT: In the first place, you don't even know who I am. In the second, I assure you I know who all my relatives are, and you are not among them. And third, I am not going to be tricked into talking about my family.

MATTIE: I could be illegitimate.

HERMIT: What you are is immaterial.

MATTIE: Could I at least get a chair? Could I sit down until the police get here?

HERMIT: There is a very comfortable recliner in the front room. Try not to mess it up.

> MATTIE exits for a moment. HERMIT goes to the window. MATTIE returns with a kitchen stool and sits. Another pause.

MATTIE: What are you seeing now?

HERMIT: There is a hawk, high up, riding the currents. Looking for a mid-day snack. Some old or broken animal. It has an aerie on the repeater tower. It lives among the girders and dishes, perched on the modern-day sequoia, adapting to modern life, soaring alone above the beams of microwaves, searching for remnants of wildness dying in the sun. It can see a mouse tail twitch from a hundred feet up while gliding without effort on a breeze, but it can't see the electromagnetic radiation that pierces its brain while it rests in its home.

MATTIE: And you identify with it?

HERMIT: No, it makes me glad I am not a hawk. Or a mouse.

MATTIE: Do you have a name?

HERMIT: Yes.

MATTIE: Which is?

>   No response.

MATTIE: So what do I do, just say, "Hey, Hermit!"

>   No response.

MATTIE: Hey, Hermit, your fly is open.

>   No response.

MATTIE: Fine, don't talk for the next two hours, or two years, or two lifetimes. Go hide somewhere inside that soul of yours, contemplating your navel from the inside. I'll talk. I'll tell you my life story.

HERMIT: Please don't.

MATTIE: Would that torture you, having to hear about another person, having to think about somebody else?

HERMIT: Is silence so painful to you that you have to drug yourself with the narcotic of your own voice?

MATTIE: Yes, damn it, it is.... I don't know how anybody could stand it.....Scares hell out of me. Why do you think I find people who choose to live alone so engrossing? How could anybody choose silence, day after day, week after week? And don't give me that guff about listening to the owls' wings. Your psychology is abnormal. You're different from normal people. I'm the normal one, the sane one. You're the freak.

HERMIT: My aunt once gave me her recipe for corn on the cob. You set the water boiling in a big pan on the stove, go outside and call the men to dinner, pick the corn off the stalks, shuck it on your way back to the house, put it in the boiling water, wash your hands, say grace, and serve the corn. The people who lived out there knew about corn. They lived up on the cliffs or mesas, but the fields were down in the valleys. They had to carry the corn up the cliffs. They probably dried most of it before they carried it up in baskets, but I bet they cooked and ate some of it by the fields, probably roasting it in a pit or over a fire. They knew about fresh corn too. But knowledge gets lost. We get left with footprints and carvings, but no knowing. Were they like us? Did they kiss their children goodnight before putting them to sleep on a mat in some cliff dwelling? Did they savor sweet corn and cool breezes and think modern life was going to hell in a handbasket? For them, I guess it did. It does for most people. There are hundreds of languages that no one speaks anymore; did you know that? Dozens were never even written down. Entire cultures, languages, ways of thinking, gone, faded into the past. Even single individuals, their past disappears. I have a couple of letters my father wrote to a girl he dated in high school. I know he existed; I know she existed; I know he kissed her once at least. But any memory of that is gone. No one knows today how he felt during that kiss, or why she kissed him, or if they did anything you don't put in a letter, or at least didn't back then. That past is gone. Our lives disappear, yours, mine, everyone's, leaving no more than a few fossils in the dust. You ask why I am fascinated by death. I am not. I am fascinated by life, by how little of it there is, by where its essence lies. I am not different, Miss Blair, not from you, not from the Anasazi who walked this land, not from any other of the billions departed. I am just here, far from some other place and time.

MATTIE: You know, even I recognize bullshit when I hear it.

HERMIT: Fine. Find your answers some other way.

>   HERMIT returns to his typing. There is a long pause. MATTIE gets up and starts looking around the room.

HERMIT: Playing Sherlock Holmes?

MATTIE: Don't you have any pictures or decorations?

HERMIT: Just those that came with the house.

MATTIE: How long have you lived here?

>   No response. She returns to the stool.

MATTIE: The name on the mailbox is Taylor.

HERMIT: The late Mr. John Taylor was the previous owner.

MATTIE: Did he live alone too?

HERMIT: I am told he had a wife and three children, all of whom preceded him into the grave. So, at the end, yes, he lived alone in a nursing home in Las Cruces.

MATTIE: You ever meet him?

HERMIT: No.

MATTIE: So how did you end up with....

HERMIT: The nursing home, in an act of very profitable charity, accepted all Mr. Taylor's property as payment for caring for him during the last few months of his life, I am told. At any rate, I purchased this "estate" from the nursing home.

MATTIE: Ah...........My grandfather is in a nursing home. He's almost 80. Alzheimers. Breaks my mother's heart to see him. He doesn't even know who she is anymore. She feels like she has to go see him, but it just breaks her up for days when she does. He evidently was a very good father. She almost worships him, still.

HERMIT: We should all be so lucky.

MATTIE: I like my father, I mean, he tried hard and did a good job, he's a nice guy and all, but there's something about Grandpa that Mom sees that I don't see in Dad. I've been trying to figure it out as part of my self-analysis, but I haven't hit it yet. Self-analysis, that's one of the things in grad school in psychology....

HERMIT: I assumed.

MATTIE: Yeah. Have to understand yourself before you can understand others.

HERMIT: I would think it would be the other way around.

MATTIE: Huh?...Oh. Well, yeah, it's sort of reciprocal. But I'm such an extrovert it's hard to, you know, look in.

HERMIT: Well, I hope you find something, but I wouldn't count on it.

MATTIE: Gee, thanks. (Long pause.) So, where did you study Zen?

HERMIT: Who said I studied Zen?

MATTIE: In town, they said.....

HERMIT: People say lots of things. Especially to young women who believe them.

MATTIE: So you didn't....

HERMIT: Wouldn't know Zen from Tao if I met them in the road.

MATTIE: And why should I believe anything you say now?

HERMIT: You shouldn't. Empiricism, Miss Blair, empiricism.

MATTIE: Call me Mattie. All the men who beat me up call me Mattie.

HERMIT: I'm sure they do…........................When you reach a certain age, there is a temptation to do a web search for your own name, not to see who else might share your name, but to see if you, yourself are listed. Have you, by the time you are thirty, or forty, or fifty, done anything, written anything, achieved anything that would be noted in the vast, shifting, electronic history called the World Wide Web. Are you indexed in any of the key word lists or text files created for temporary posterity? We write with light upon the wind, and prematurely conclude we are known.

MATTIE: So, are you listed?

HERMIT: No, not even under "hermits."

MATTIE: I might be after I get my degree, some alumni or professional list, maybe, if that counts. Would that show up on a Google search?

HERMIT: Searching for Mattie Blair, last seen driving off into the empty quarter of New Mexico.

> An alarm clock rings. HERMIT opens a desk drawer, turns off the alarm, takes out a pill bottle, opens it, takes out a pill, swallows it without water, puts the top back on the bottle, puts the bottle back in the drawer, and closes the drawer. He then resets the alarm clock.

MATTIE: Interesting.

HERMIT: Not what you think.

MATTIE: So what is it?

HERMIT: Not what you think.

MATTIE: How do you know what I think?

HERMIT: You said psychology, not psychiatry.

MATTIE: Even I know there aren't many medications that have to be taken on so tight a schedule you set an alarm for a mid-day dose.

HERMIT: Time passes quietly out here. There are no class bells or shift changes, no lunch hours or colleagues passing by the door. Time is a shadow on the wall. Usually that is good. I am not a prisoner of the clock. But in that shapeless time, I forget. I forget to eat lunch. I raise my eyes and see night where day used to be. I find I have to impose order, create a pattern to time. I set alarms to mark moments, to give a shape and size to the day.

MATTIE: And the pill?

HERMIT: Was just a pill.

MATTIE: A marker of your passing life.

HERMIT: A supplement for my plain diet.

MATTIE: Sure. Whatever. What would happen if you died out here?

HERMIT: Well, if I died outside, I guess the coyotes and buzzards would pray over my body and the ants and beetles would worship in the cathedral of my bones. Inside, well, this area is not dry enough to create a mummy, but I might hang around for months, wasting away far from Margaretaville.

MATTIE: Would anybody know? Would anybody come to check if you didn't answer your phone?

HERMIT: You find that terrifying, don't you? Just the idea. You hate me for hitting you, but you can't leave, can you? I'm like a torn and broken body tossed on your lawn from some car wreck, you can't stand to look but you can't look away. You have a morbid fascination with that which repulses you.

MATTIE: Nobody wants to die alone. It isn't human.

HERMIT: No, dying is just as human as being born.

MATTIE: But you're not born alone.

HERMIT: Then why do all babies cry?

MATTIE: That's just wit, twisted words.

HERMIT: Come on, let's twist again, like we did last summer, come on let's twist again, twisting time is here.

MATTIE: Very funny......................I almost died once. Car accident. Another car hit us from the side. One person in the car banged her head against the side window. She was in a coma for months. They had to pry me out. Just bumps and bruises, but just because my head was a little further away from the window. Makes you really wonder. You know, another eighth of an inch, and....

HERMIT: And now we have side air bags.

MATTIE: I always check.

HERMIT: Well, I guess that's a form of learning.

MATTIE: Let me see your hands.

HERMIT: Palmistry or detective work?

MATTIE: Call me Miss Marple.

    HERMIT examines his own hands.

HERMIT: They are slightly smaller than normal for my body size. Admittedly soft, mostly unscarred. No rings. The only callus is a writer's callus on the long finger of my right hand. Slight toughening on the tips of the fingers, especially on the left hand. The fingernails are trimmed neatly, shorter on the left hand than the right, and filed smooth. The fingers are thin, but the knuckles protrude slightly, especially the middle knuckles on each finger. So it's obvious that my middle name is George, that I was born in Venezuela, and that I'm really a woman.

MATTIE: No, it's obvious that you're right handed, you do a lot of typing, but didn't use computers much until college or later, but you were a serious student of something that required a lot of writing. You are concerned about your appearance, even your fingernails, and you don't do much manual labor to keep this place operating.

HERMIT: Ah, Watson, once again you overlook the obvious.

MATTIE: Oh, really.

HERMIT: Gloves, my dear. Work gloves on the table just inside the front door, rubber gloves by the kitchen sink. And if the nails were trimmed for appearance sake, would they not be the same length on both hands?

MATTIE: Well......

HERMIT: Your hands, on the other hand, scream that you do not spend all day typing, but that you only do what is necessary to meet the normal expectations for grooming. You have a boyfriend, but not a husband. You think of yourself as pretty, but not beautiful, engaging others with your personality rather than your looks. You are not a virgin and haven't been for years, though you confine yourself to one man at a time. You consider yourself an independent woman, capable of dealing with whatever comes up, but you have a deep-seated need to be part of a group, to understand other people, and to fit in with your peers. You have little appreciation of nature, are not a conservationist, are still supported at least in part by your parents even in grad school, and are, as they say, not from around here.

MATTIE: You got all that from my hands?

HERMIT: You, Miss Blair, are obvious. You are dull and boring, bordering on stereotype. The only things remotely interesting about you are your bull-headed tenacity and your obsession with social deviates, but even that has overtones of majoritarian tyranny. You are certainly a Protestant and probably vote Republican, at least in those elections in which it is fashionable to actually vote.

>   Long pause. MATTIE gets up and looks out the window. She
>   looks at her hands.

MATTIE: I told you some of that stuff, didn't I?...............and the rings..........the big SUV...........I mean, what you said, it was obvious, wasn't it?..............I'm standing here looking for needles and not seeing the haystack. Damn, I am stupid......................OK, OK. You bought this empty ranch in the middle of nowhere, didn't even change the name on the mailbox, didn't change any decorations or put up any pictures, and are so determined to finish writing something that you hate even a two hour interruption....................And you are totally, determinedly alone.........I am trying not to leap to any premature conclusions.

HERMIT: Yes, all erroneous conclusions should at least be mature, ripe even.

MATTIE: You are a conservationist, very tuned in to nature.

HERMIT: Nature 101.7 on your FM dial.

MATTIE: Well educated, intelligent, but egotistical.

HERMIT: No egotist is well educated.

MATTIE: Poor social skills, and a disturbing propensity for violence.

HERMIT: Let us say a lack of conventional restraints.

MATTIE: Let us say a mean right cross and a sucker punch.

HERMIT: Yes, let us say that Subject A was a violent psychopath who abuses women, overreacts to invasions of his personal space, and shows poor executive function. His deviate social behavior is probably a symptom of underlying psychosis serious enough to warrant coerced treatment, especially since his initial reaction to psychological analysis was incoherent and physically reactive. You think that will be enough to get you your summa cum laude? Had it ever occurred to you that I just don't like being around people?

MATTIE: Everybody has social needs.

HERMIT: Everybody has to defecate too, but that doesn't mean I enjoy it. It doesn't mean that if I had a choice I wouldn't choose not to.

MATTIE: That's a physical need.

HERMIT: Well maybe I need to scratch where it itches, but society says it's not acceptable to scratch there, so I have chosen to withdraw from society to meet other needs. I need to be alone, to pick my nose, to fart, to think without worrying what somebody else is thinking about what I'm thinking. If I want to watch the sunset, I do not need some other set of eyes attached to a mouth telling me how wonderful the sunset is tonight and how happy they are to share that experience with me. I just want to watch the sun set, not hear a play-by-play.

MATTIE: Because there are only so many sunsets?

HERMIT: Because I want it to be my sunset, not the sunset as seen by Mattie Blair and company. I have my own eyes, thank you.

MATTIE: What was the pill?

HERMIT: Are there any bloodstains on your panties?

MATTIE: That's a rude question.

HERMIT: No more than asking about my vitamins.

MATTIE: If that's what they are.

HERMIT: I am not your patient, Miss Blair, nor will I ever be. And I am getting very tired of you treating me like some subject you have to diagnose. I am not going to be Subject A. Give it up and go home.

> Pause.

MATTIE: No, no, you're right. I haven't been acknowledging your humanity. I've been treating you like some freak I needed to examine. I apologize. You are not my patient, and I have no right to treat you like one.

HERMIT: Apology accepted. Goodbye.

> She doesn't leave.

HERMIT: Good day, Miss Blair.

MATTIE: Aren't you going to apologize for hitting me?

HERMIT: No.

MATTIE: You don't think slugging me twice was just a tiny social faux pas that deserves at least an insincere "I'm sorry"? I'm going to have bruises.

HERMIT: You deserved it.

MATTIE: My god, no wonder nobody can stand you.

HERMIT: Well, now that you have both recognized the error of you ways and diagnosed the root of my social ostracism, you have no more reason to stay.

MATTIE: Well, I'm sorry I treated you like a lab rat, but, good grief, can't you muster up a little common decency, act like a human being for once? I'm trying to think of you as a normal guy, some man who is trying to cope with some unfortunate circumstances in unusual ways, but you sure aren't making it easy. How do you think I feel, getting treated like dirt, beat up, and then scraped off your shoe.

HERMIT: I rarely beat up dirt. And what I usually scrape off my shoes is technically not yet dirt. It may be "dirty," but it is not dirt.

MATTIE: You know what I mean. Can't you just talk to me, person to person, like two people sharing a few minutes of life?

HERMIT: No, Miss Blair, I can't. I thought that was obvious to even you by now. I can't just "talk." Relate, if you want the word out of your pop psychology textbooks. I can't make those connections. My mind does not meet yours. It rockets off at angles that miss your targets. Men are from Mars, women are from Venus, and I am off on Neptune somewhere admiring the moons. Apologize for hitting you? You threatened to tear up my house! Talk to you like a person? You called me Subject A from the very beginning. And now I'm supposed to conform to your norms?

MATTIE: OK, OK......... I already said I was sorry.............I'm trying to start over here............ Give me a break, OK?

HERMIT: I don't want to start over. I want it to stop, to end.

MATTIE: And I want to understand. I need to understand. I have to understand! Don't you understand that?

HERMIT: Why me? There are millions of strange people in the world. Thousands in New Mexico alone. Taos must have one of the highest densities of eccentrics ever recorded. There's a psychology thesis on every street corner. Go research one of them.

MATTIE: I can't. You're not like them.

HERMIT: Why not?!

MATTIE: I need to know about silence, about being alone, about.... ....Have you ever been to Minnesota?

HERMIT: No.

MATTIE: In the winter there it gets very cold. It's like the air itself freezes. Just freezes in place some days. Clarity. Light so clear it hurts your eyes. Coming from everywhere...........

HERMIT: And?

MATTIE: I need to see like that. I......can't..........I have to........you............are.......others can't, don't..........There are reasons I have to know about.......people like you..........You owe me..............

    Long pause.

HERMIT: I am not what you think I am.

MATTIE: And neither am I.

    The phone rings. HERMIT answers.

HERMIT: Yes? Yes, she is still here..........Not yet............Yes, Officer, thank you..........Right.

> He hangs up.

HERMIT: They had another matter to deal with, but someone is on the way now.
MATTIE: OK.
HERMIT: Getting arrested is no longer an asset on your resume.
MATTIE: I know.
HERMIT: If you leave now.....
MATTIE: Tell me about the silence. What is the silence like? I've never been any place really silent, no sound at all. Please.

> Pause.

HERMIT: It isn't really silent here. The wind blows, the windmill turns, water flows through the pipes from the solar heater, bugs buzz, floorboards creak. It's quiet, not silent. Even if there was no other sound, there would still be the thump of my heart beating and the slight whoosh of my own breathing. There is no silence while we live. But in the quiet, other things can be heard. A sidewinder crawling by scrapes across the sand, that road runner does actually emit a sound a little like a beep. And I can hear myself think. My own thoughts, uninterrupted, become as real as sounds in my own mind. The outside becomes quiet enough, close enough to silence that what is inside becomes real, can be heard, can be felt. I live in my mind, and there I can live the way I want, by my own rules, without boundaries, without limits.
MATTIE: You can think outside the box.
HERMIT: I can forget there is a box. Do you know what an isolation tank is?
MATTIE: You float blindfolded and wearing gloves in a tank of body temperature water. No sensory input, no sight, no sound, no smell, no taste, no texture, no temperature.
HERMIT: And what happens?
MATTIE: Your mind hallucinates, generates the illusions of sights and sounds, etc.
HERMIT: When it's quiet enough, your mind speaks. Out here, you can listen. You can hear yourself think. There's enough outside to keep you sane, but not so much your mind doesn't add its own little sensations.
MATTIE: Oh.
HERMIT: Those who fear silence are actually afraid of themselves, of what is in their own mind.
MATTIE: Oh. I hate that idea. Not good at all.

> Long pause. MATTIE turns away for a moment.

MATTIE: Please. Anything......It is very important for me to understand. To know. Whatever. Please.

> Pause.

HERMIT: I do know one Zen game. At least it was called Zen chess when it was taught to me. I don't know if it really has anything to do with real Zen.

MATTIE: How do you play?

HERMIT: There are no rules. That's what makes it Zen. No board, no pieces, no rules. You don't even have to do anything. Or you may do anything.

MATTIE: I don't think I can play that.

HERMIT: Suit yourself. I just thought you were curious about Zen.

> He returns to the computer and types. She looks out the window for a long moment.

MATTIE: Do you take turns?

HERMIT: There are no rules.

MATTIE: How do you know when it's over?

HERMIT: When you stop.

MATTIE: Who goes first?

HERMIT: There is no order.

MATTIE: You go first.

> Pause. He gets up, picks up the stool, carries it out of the room, re-enters, and closes the door. Pause. She crosses to the desk and picks up the phone and looks at it. She puts it back down. He puts the phone in a drawer of the desk and sits. Pause. She crosses to the window, spits on the glass, and wipes the window with her hand. He scratches his nose. She stares at him. He stares back. She crosses back to face him. He stands. She tries to slap him, but he blocks her arm, twists it behind her, and shoves her away. Pause. She turns back to him, crosses to him, and slowly takes his hand. She holds his hand and brings it up to touch her cheek. He slowly takes his hand away, crosses to her purse, picks it up, opens it, looks in it, closes it, crosses to door, opens door, takes purse out, returns without purse, leaving door open. She crosses to door to see where her purse is, looks back at him. She crosses to look at computer screen. He grabs her hand, hits the SAVE and CLOSE commands, then lets her hand go. She crosses to the window, looks out a few seconds, stares back at him. He sits and begins to hum the first few notes of "Danny Boy." She crosses to him and takes his hand. He stops humming. She examines his hand very carefully, caressing it. He gently pulls his hand away, crosses away from her, looks back at her for a second, crosses to window and looks out. She crosses to stand next to him. She takes his hand and holds it by her side. He looks at her. She turns to face him. She lifts his hand to her lips and kisses it. She lifts her other hand to caress his cheek. They look each other in the eyes. They hold that position for several beats. He slowly lifts his hand from hers. He slowly turns away from her. She reaches out to touch him; he moves away and crosses back to the desk. She stares out the window for a moment, sinks to floor and softly begins to sob.

MATTIE: Damn.

> There is a long pause. MATTIE slowly stops crying, wipes her tears on her sleeve, and pulls herself together.

MATTIE: I don't think I like this game.

> No response. She gets up.

MATTIE: Ping pong is more my speed.

> No response.

MATTIE: Russian roulette, hari-kari, something fun.

> Pause.

MATTIE: Oh boy, I bet I look like a mess. That's a woman for you, isn't it, always worried about how she looks.

> He stares at her.

MATTIE: Not that it matters out here...........I mean, you've already seen me at my worst................It's really more for me. I just feel better about myself when I think I look good............. Stupid really.

> He gets up, crosses to door, brings stool back in, closes door, returns to chair.

MATTIE: Thank you.

> He stares at her for a long time.

MATTIE: Most men don't look at me like that unless I have some of my clothes off.
HERMIT: I doubt anybody has ever really looked at you. You are a puzzle, Mattie Blair.
MATTIE: Me? No.
HERMIT: At least one missing piece. Something I'm not seeing. Something…….
MATTIE: I'm too obvious. You said so yourself.
HERMIT: Conclusions need time to ripen. There's something else going on here.
MATTIE: Good Lord, I probably stink too.
HERMIT: No.
MATTIE: Well, thank god for that.
HERMIT: I am told that it gets very cold in Minnesota.
MATTIE: Oh, yes. Snow like you wouldn't believe. Bone-shattering cold, 20, 30 below, not counting the wind.

HERMIT: I once knew a man who grew up in Nome, Alaska, and went off to college in Tucson, Arizona. That always seemed a radical change.

MATTIE: He was just trying to get warm. The cold up north, it becomes part of you. Some people like it, the skiing and the sledding and all. But you're always a little cold. The cold becomes part of you.

HERMIT: So you came down here.....

MATTIE: To get away from all that. I don't look all that good in sweaters.

HERMIT: The sun is not always kind either.

MATTIE: Oh, I know. Sunburn, wrinkles, premature aging, skin cancer, I read the brochure.

HERMIT: Sometimes the light plays tricks, heat waves rising off the desert floor, or the parking lot, making things seem unstable, not quite real.

MATTIE: Ah, but the heat is real. You can feel it.

HERMIT: Yes. Sometimes what we feel is real.

> Pause. She looks out the window.

MATTIE: What's the scar on the mountain? The white slash.

HERMIT: They were looking for copper. Didn't find enough to bother with. There's gold out there too, but not enough to mine. All the valuable stuff is long gone. All that's left is the scenery and the wildlife.

MATTIE: And you.

HERMIT: I am not indigenous.

MATTIE: So, where are you from?

HERMIT: Somewhere else.

MATTIE: No kidding.

HERMIT: I grew up on a river bank. At least it used to be a river bank. The river is gone now. All damned and diverted, canals and irrigation ditches, an entire river gone.

MATTIE: Like that one down there?

HERMIT: Ah, no. That one died when the shape of the land changed. A little uplift and a dryer climate. My river was drunk dry by the unslakeable thirst of melons, mills, and millions of people, bathing, shaving, and sipping iced sodas on lazy afternoons by their swimming pools. They took it all, every drop. It starts out in the mountains as it has for eons, but it never gets to the sea.

MATTIE: I'm sorry.

HERMIT: Why? I don't live there anymore, and millions of people enjoy their iced sodas by the pool.

MATTIE: It just seems like something was lost. Something isn't what it should be.

HERMIT: Lots of things aren't what they should be. Lots of rivers are running dry. Do you find this surprising?

MATTIE: No, I guess not.

HERMIT: They never did find the Greenland Vikings. Their river ran out. Several settlements along the Greenland coast, long houses, churches, graves, a few bodies, but not enough.

They left, evidently, saw the ice coming and left, after generations of hanging on in the cold, got together and left. But never arrived. No sign of them in the abandoned settlement in Newfoundland, no record of getting back to their relatives in Iceland, not enough blue eyes among the Eskimos; they just left. People leave and the ice covers them, or the ocean. Or the sand. There used to be a whole tribe of Caucasians in Central Asia. Evidently lived along the Black Sea when it was still a little fresh water lake. Then the Bosporus broke open, the Mediterranean flooded in, and they moved as far away from a coastline as they could get. And then their river ran out and all that's left is a few dried mummies of white Caucasians in the middle of an Asian desert. What happened to the Scythians, Mattie? Or the Folk who lived in Europe before the Indo-Europeans moved in? Are the Basque all that's left of the Old Ones? The Etruscans are gone and no one is left who can read their tombstones.

MATTIE: Who will read your tombstone?

HERMIT: I read that in Alaska, used to be, if someone died in winter, they just stacked the bodies in a shack outside to keep them frozen till spring because the ground was too hard to dig a grave in.

MATTIE: Minnesota was like that a hundred years ago, I think. Now we have steam shovels and pressurized hot water drills.

HERMIT: What would you put on your tombstone? If you could write your own epitaph, what would it be?

MATTIE: Me?

HERMIT: Sure. What do you want to be remembered for? Or are you still so young you think you will live forever?

MATTIE: No. I've learned that lesson, far too well. Just a long time. If we can stand the cures. Sometimes the cure seems worse than the disease. But maybe longer, off into the future, when anything is possible. Longer and longer, more and more cures.

HERMIT: You think there is a cure for death?

MATTIE: No. That would run the rivers dry.

HERMIT: Perhaps beyond, out into the universe, trillions of rivers.

MATTIE: Maybe. But not now. Not for me, my lifetime.

HERMIT: And so?

MATTIE: So I keep trying to understand silence, to figure out lonely old men.

HERMIT: Who are neither lonely or old?

MATTIE: Who deny their emotional side. Who are cruel without even knowing it.

HERMIT: I once had a woman wake me up at four o'clock in the morning because she wanted to talk. She had been angry with me the evening before for not doing something she thought I should have, but we had talked, I had explained that I had been doing something else for her, and all was settled. Then she wakes up at four in the morning, realizes she is still angry with me, and wakes me up to talk about it some more. Believe me, at four o'clock in the morning, you want me to deny my emotional side.

MATTIE: Ah, so you do sleep with women.

HERMIT: Leaping to conclusions again. It could have been a phone call.

MATTIE: But it wasn't, was it?

HERMIT: But the point is that you assumed again. You didn't have enough evidence to reach that conclusion.

MATTIE: OK, OK. I'm a slow learner. You've established that.

HERMIT: Even you have spent some nights alone. What do you see in the dark of a silent room early in the morning, before the sun comes up? What floats to the top of your mind when there is no other voice, no other touch, no sight beyond the silent shadows around your nightlight?

MATTIE: Blueberry pancakes with real butter and lots of syrup.

HERMIT: Like your father made on those cold mornings in Minnesota?

MATTIE: Yeah. How did you know?

HERMIT: Your father seems to be an issue with you.

MATTIE: Aren't all fathers "issues" for daughters?

HERMIT: Probably. Did he withdrawn from society too?

MATTIE: No. (Pause.) Not the way you mean it.

HERMIT: How do you think I mean it?

MATTIE: Did you ever teach Psychoanalysis 101? I'm feeling a little analyzed here.

HERMIT: Like I said, I'm missing something about you. Just doing a little probing……….. There is a windmill out there. When the wind blows, it generates a little electricity and pumps a little water up from the aquifer more than 500 feet down. It comes up cold and pure, but 500 feet is a long way down for a well. To go down that far, that's hard. But if you want to live out here…well, each year the water level drops a bit. You have to drill a little deeper. As time passes, it gets a little harder and harder to get to where you need to be. There used to be a dozen wells, scattered around for the cattle. Now they are all dry, except for that one. That one has been drilled deeper. The others have been left alone, not worth the trouble and expense. So now this land only supports one man.

MATTIE: Some days, deep in winter, the storms would be so bad nobody would go out, even in Minnesota, at least until the wind stopped. Those days my father would stay home and fix breakfast. Stacks of blueberry pancakes, real butter, lots of syrup. We burned off the calories just keeping warm when we finally ventured out to skate on lakes so frozen you could drive a truck on them. But those breakfasts, stuffed warm and full, waiting for the wind to die, bundled in sweaters even inside, that felt good.

HERMIT: When did they stop?

MATTIE: The breakfasts? Hey, people grow up.

HERMIT: Fathers leave home.

MATTIE: Fathers get older, wear down, leave without leaving. Life isn't always fair. He does what he can. I'm not a little kid anymore; I can see how it happens.

HERMIT: You are always your father's little girl.

MATTIE: I don't have an Electra complex, OK? I adjusted, I dealt with it. I grew up. OK, I'm not the most insightful psychology student to come down the pike, and I'm still working through some of it, but I'm coping with that. We talk, we're civil, he sends money. He loves me, I love him; we just don't feel that good about how things turned out sometimes. It's not maladjusted enough to make a good sit-com.

HERMIT: Well, that's a relief.

MATTIE: Yeah. It could be a lot worse, but it's not. OK?

HERMIT: OK. Fine…………………………….. It snowed here once. Just a dusting. Was gone in a few hours. Snow did look strange on the cactus.

MATTIE: I bet.

HERMIT: So................How's school?

MATTIE: Just fine. Coursework almost done. Straight A's, despite what you think of me. I am good with the bookwork. I think I have an internship all lined up for next year. Just have this little matter of a thesis to deal with.

HERMIT: Everything under control.

MATTIE: In my own little academic world, yes.

HERMIT: Yet you are here. With me. How incongruous.

MATTIE: I told you, my thesis topic….

HERMIT: Miss Blair, I don't believe a damn word you say.

MATTIE: I'm sorry to hear that.

HERMIT: I don't suppose you would like to tell me the truth?

MATTIE: No, I wouldn't.

HERMIT: Truth can be an elusive commodity. Not easy to pin down. Not always related to the facts of the matter.

MATTIE: One of my professors says the truth is not as important as what we believe to be true. What we think is true tells who we really are.

HERMIT: There may be some truth to that..........................I will tell you a truth, Mattie Blair. At least a truth I believe is true. Sometimes wanting something, needing something, is better than actually having that thing you need. The need itself, if it is strong enough to send you far from home, to risk your life going into some unknown, that shapes you, changes you, makes you what you are. If that need is ever filled, perhaps you become less than what you were when you had a need to drive you.

MATTIE: When I was growing up in Minnesota, and I did grow up in Minnesota, I would go out to skate on the frozen lake near our house. By Christmas the ice was usually so thick you could play hockey on it, not to mention a few little girls skating. But early in the season, and late, toward March, you had to sort of test it first. How shakey was it? How much did you want to skate? Every year a few people fall through ice in Minnesota. One or two die. Just like you loose hikers out in the desert down here. But people still skate. The glide, the spin, the flying across the ice. You learn to be cautious, never skate alone, stay close to shore at first, but sooner or latter you have to take a big stride and push off across the ice. Sooner or later you have to try it.

HERMIT: This is New Mexico. The ice is very thin here.

MATTIE: Yes, it is.

    MATTIE freezes, her body taut, grimacing with pain.

HERMIT: Miss Blair?........... Miss Blair?.................... Mattie?

    MATTIE unfreezes, returns to normal.

MATTIE: Ohh……. Damn! Uh, excuse me.

HERMIT: Are you alright?

MATTIE: Nothing for you to be worried about.

HERMIT: I'm not the one who should be worried.

MATTIE: This day is not going the way I hoped.

HERMIT: Obviously.

MATTIE: Yeah.

HERMIT: However, if you pass out on my floor just at the cops drive up, I want to have my story straight.

MATTIE: It's under control now.

HERMIT: Mattie, this is not doing either one of us any good. Why don't you drive home, check with your doctor, get some rest, talk to a few friends, and regroup.

MATTIE: I know what it is. I told you, it's under control now.

HERMIT: But you are not.

MATTIE: I'm fine now.

HERMIT: You don't believe that, and neither do I. You're twitchy as a prairie dog on guard duty. Nothing is worth what you're putting yourself through.

MATTIE: It is to me.

HERMIT: What?

MATTIE: Just tell me who you are. Why you're here. How you stand it.

HERMIT: Why? I'm not still some Subject A, am I?

MATTIE: What difference does it make? Is it some national security secret?

HERMIT: No……….. I just……..

MATTIE: What?

HERMIT: I'm not anybody, Mattie. I'm nobody. A name doesn't matter. I'm here because I want to be. Because I got tired of the interruptions. Because my brain slowed down and I needed to cut out the noise so I could think. I like it here. I have been in the crowd. I did not fit. Here, I and the crowd are both better off.

MATTIE: Bullshit.

HERMIT: Well, that's my story, and I'm sticking to it. What's your story?…………Come on, Mattie, how bad could it be?………You were an undercover cop who killed somebody and you're about to be sent to solitary for 20 years and you wonder if it would be better to just kill yourself…………...To pay your way through grad school you volunteered for an experiment for NASA where you spend six months alone in a space capsule to see if an astronaut coming back from Mars alone would go mad and you wonder if you will lose you sanity…………… You think I'm your real father who secretly knocked up your mother during a one-night stand in Bemidji when I was 15 years old.

MATTIE: You know, not many people outside Minnesota have even heard of Bemidji.

HERMIT: It's a strange name. The "j" "i" ending. I read it somewhere. I have never been to Minnesota, let alone Bemidji.

MATTIE: My father's from Bemidji.

HERMIT: Does that make him a Bemidjiian?

MATTIE: My mother's from St. Olaf, is she a St. Olafian?

HERMIT: Well, it would be funny if she wasn't.

MATTIE: Nobody is nobody, Hermit. Everybody has a town, a place. It may not be the best place, but it's your place. You went to some school. You dated some girl. You had some job. You have a history. It may not be what you wish it was, but it's yours. It made you what you are as much as the genes you got from your parents. To hide that is to hide yourself.

HERMIT: But I want to hide. You don't, yet you do hide yourself. From me, from your father, maybe from yourself.

MATTIE: But why do you want to hide?

HERMIT: That doesn't matter. Not to you. What matters is that I like being hidden. You don't. It terrifies you. Yet you're hiding something.

MATTIE: Everybody hides some part of themselves.

HERMIT: Not the thing that drives them hours into the desert. That makes them put up with being punched. That makes them stay in a place when every scrap of reason says run like hell. People who are afraid of solitude don't run to isolated ranches to talk things over with tortoises. What was that spasm a few minutes ago? What's going to happen to you?

    Long pause.

MATTIE: Does anybody really know what's going to happen?

HERMIT: Now who's being evasive?

MATTIE: I am. I am Subject A, and I am being evasive. I am deeply in denial of a reality I cannot face. There is a secret only I know, but I cannot even tell myself, so I run to something I fear to avoid something I fear even more. You have found me out. Your diagnosis is excellent. I congratulate you.

HERMIT: And so another opportunity to face the truth is missed.

MATTIE: One day no one will speak my language. One day I will be a reference in a crumbling letter nobody reads. One day the river will run dry and the ice will come. Is that enough truth for you? It is far too much truth for me.

HERMIT: I guess that will have to do, for now.

    MATTIE puts her purse down, crosses to window and looks
    out. She straightens her hair by the reflection in the window.

MATTIE: Boy, am I a mess. I'd like to see this tortoise you keep talking about. I'm more used to turtles, with the lakes and all. Something that looks like a turtle living out here seems all wrong. I don't see how it could survive.

HERMIT: It gets water by chewing cactus. It's so tough the spines don't penetrate.

MATTIE: I guess you have to be tough to live out here.

HERMIT: There're all kinds of ways of surviving. Jackrabbits live on speed and fear. Prairie dogs work together and take turns being the sentries. Lots of animals hide until the cool and dark take over. Snakes wait for the sun to warm them, then borrow into the sand when the sun starts to broil them. Everybody has to find their own way.

MATTIE: We do a little counseling as part of our graduate work. Nothing serious, no paranoid schizophrenics, that sort of thing. Just people with problems that need somebody to help them work through things. We are a diverse species. People think so differently. If you asked people to list in order of importance the 20 things that are most important in life, things like honesty, friendship, love, honor, sex, religion, the lists would all have mostly the same things, but none of them would be in the same order.

HERMIT: So what's your top priority?

MATTIE: Me? Oh, I don't know. If you've got your health, as they say. Family is important too. Friends.

HERMIT: Many people value most what they don't have. Or are about to lose.

MATTIE: That's what they say.

The phone rings. He answers it.

HERMIT: Hello. Yes, she's still here. No, not yet. Yes. No, the blacktop past the gas station, on the left. Yes, filling up first is probably a good idea. OK. Thanks. (He hangs up.) They weren't quite sure of the directions.

MATTIE: I can understand getting lost out here.

HERMIT: I saw a body a couple of months ago, down on the dry river bed. Wasn't sure what it was until I looked with the binoculars. I called 911 and headed down there. They sent a helicopter, but it was too late. Young Hispanic guy. Never heard any story. Got lost and ran out of water, I guess. You don't want to be lost out here.

MATTIE: No. Not much fun being lost in the north woods either.

HERMIT: Guess not. Fire or ice.

MATTIE: The hunters in the north woods say they always save one bullet, just in case.

HERMIT: If I sit on the porch, silent, unmoving, the animals will almost come up and touch me. I've had desert rats run across my shoes. That hawk has swooped down within twenty feet of me to catch a rabbit in my garden. When I wait, things come to me.

MATTIE: Most people can't sit that still.

HERMIT: Silence has its own rewards. Time passes. I find I am not bad company for myself. But the comfort is that someday it will end. This is not forever. Nothing is. Everything, good and bad, will someday be gone. I know this is just a phase, a time in my life when I get to watch sunsets and listen to my own heart. Someday soon that will end. Something else will happen. This time is precious, but it is also passing. There will come a day when I can no longer see the hawk fly. I will have to move on to something else and someone else will have the chance to live in this quiet moment in time. Being alone is not to be feared, it is to be embraced, savored as a rare moment, a pause to catch your breath before going on to whatever is next. Six months, a year, two years, whatever, it's time to taste life plain, to drive it into a corner as Thoreau said, and come to know it.

MATTIE: And then what?

HERMIT: Whatever is next. That's hard to say for me. I'm not old, but I'm not young either. Not anymore. But you,...... Used to be, rich kids would take the grand tour, take a year off after school, travel around Europe or wherever, be on their own to grow up a little before starting a career or family. They weren't alone, but they were off on their own, dealing with the new and unfamiliar, isolated from what they had known. Strangers in a strange land. No one is more alone than a person alone in a crowd of strangers. This is easier, just sidewinders and scorpions. Silence is a warm blanket to wrap yourself in when the world turns cold. Being alone is a soft glow when life is dark. It may be strange, foreign, unfamiliar, but it is also beautiful, like the Milky Way when the night is dark enough to see it. Have you ever seen the Milky Way, Mattie? Most towns have too many lights. Out here it's obvious, stars streaming across the black sky. Out here you can see where you really are.

The Hermit

> Long pause. She crosses to the window.

MATTIE: What I have seen is the Northern Lights. They don't get down to Minnesota often, but every now and then. Blues and greens, hints of red, rippling halos across the night, glows warming the black. They're strange, constantly moving, changing. The stars, I know they move, but it's so slow I can't see it.

HERMIT: You need landmarks. Stonehenge, notches in the mountains, Aztec pyramids. Then look, night after night, above the same mark. The universe is passing by.

MATTIE: My father would take us outside to see the Northern Lights, like it was a treat we shouldn't miss, even when it was colder than a witch's tit and us bundled in pajamas and blankets. We don't get them much anymore. I guess the sun is in a quiet cycle.

HERMIT: Maybe it's your turn to take your father out to see them.

MATTIE: Oh, I don't think I'll be going back up north. Too much to leave behind up there. I think I'll stay down here and watch the sunsets and dustdevils. Make a new start, as they say, become somebody else with the same name.

HERMIT: New graduate degree, new wardrobe, new hairstyle, a little windburn around the eyes, a scar or two on your soul, and presto, new person.

MATTIE: You know, I bet you are on to something about being able to get stuff done out here. No distractions. I bet I could knock that thesis out in no time.

HERMIT: Is that a threat? You know, that road runner can be a real bother, popping up at the oddest moments.

MATTIE: You probably spend entire days watching the tortoise crawl across the yard.

HERMIT: I did at first.

MATTIE: Now?

HERMIT: Well, as you say, I have something I want to finish.

MATTIE: And even the stars are passing by.

HERMIT: The stars move on for everybody. I get to watch them. We are all alone, Mattie, I just get to enjoy it. Everything will end, even the stars. I have this time to explore myself before I pass into the universe. I know women don't like to show their age because it means they are passing out of their fertile years; but there's a certain beauty to crows feet and scars. They say we have seen life and fought for it. We have seen what life can do, faced it, and earned the battle scars. If I was your patient, I'd want to know that you had a few experiences under your belt, a scar or two, a little sorrow in your eyes. Buddha did not become the beautiful one until he left his father's castle and learned true sorrow.

MATTIE: Did he ever wish he could turn back the clock, go home again?

HERMIT: To blueberry pancakes, Northern Lights, and fathers who loved them? No doubt. But rivers don't flow backwards. We can't ask for more than good memories. You know what we call cells that don't grow up? Cancers. They live forever, constantly reproducing. Life needs to end, to die in its own good time. Take what's given, don't ask for more or less, and don't be afraid to let the world see that you know the passing of the stars.

MATTIE: And that, Hermit, is the secret of life? That stars die and we are less than stars.

HERMIT: But stars also shine, and for our little moment we are more than stars because we know that we are not stars.

MATTIE: We are Vikings in Greenland, drinking warm milk and thinking how beautiful the ice is today.

HERMIT: And how wonderful the sunset over the western sea.

MATTIE: Stars and scars. Not much of a secret.

HERMIT: I don't have any secrets, Mattie, just things I prefer not to say out loud.

MATTIE: I know.

> The phone rings. He answers it.

HERMIT: Hello. Yes, she's still here. A flat tire. Really. Yes, not my day. No, I'm beginning to think I will live through it. Maybe. Thank you.

> He hangs up.

HERMIT: You can guess.

MATTIE: You know, I'm beginning to think you are never going to be rescued from me…….. Or I from you.

HERMIT: Now that would be a pity. Maybe I should hit you again.

MATTIE: That would not be wise.

HERMIT: No, maybe not. So what do we do, Mattie, old girl? You with your secret and me with my silence.

MATTIE: Maybe I'll just look out the window for a while. See what I can see.

> She goes to window and looks out. He watches her for a few moments, then sits and the desk and starts typing. The lights fade.

CURTAIN

Naked Theatre

This is another play that has never had a full production, probably for obvious reasons. It did get a couple of readings, one from the late, lamented Southeastern Playwriting Project, and the other from Koality Productions, both here in Atlanta. Even my wife thinks it's funny, so it can't be too offensive. I know I would still like to see it produced, especially if I get to sit in the back of the house during rehearsals. One of the scenes also has been marketed as a one-act under the title "An Offensive Play," and got a reading at Emory University during their "Brave New Works" productions, but it only talks about nudity.

NAKED THEATRE

A Play By David Davis

Member
All rights & privileges.

David Davis
100 Hunters Ridge Court
Roswell, GA 30076
daviddaviswriter@gmail.com

Copyright 1999 David Davis

CAST OF CHARACTERS

This play requires at least four women and two men, but unless the women are all quick-change artists and able to play a wide range of ages, it's probably better to have at least two or three more actresses. Roles in the various scenes can be cast according to the actresses selected and the practical problems of costume changes (despite the title, there are a few costumes.) It would help if at least one or two of the females were "more mature." One of the males needs to be old and the other young.

SETTING

All of the scenes occur in the present. The locale, when it matters, is specified for each scene. Furniture and props should be minimal and easily changed to minimize the time between scenes.

PROLOGUE

AT RISE we see a bare stage. A nude woman enters.

WOMAN: Good evening. Welcome to the (name of theater) for tonight's performance of Naked Theatre. I would like to remind you that no photographs or video are allowed during the performance of the play. There will be one intermission, during which drinks and snacks will be sold in the lobby. However, no drinks or food is allowed in the theatre. I have also been asked to read the following statement, which was written by a committee composed of the female employees of this theatre.

The play you will see this evening was written by a playwright trapped in an adolescent fantasy of female exhibitionism. It degrades women by presenting us as little more than sex objects and our bodies as nothing more than subjects for masturbatory fantasies. It also indicates that any theatre that would produce this play operates under the delusion, disproved in the 1960s, that offending or shocking an audience is somehow avant garde or innovative.

Not that seeing a naked woman is that shocking anymore. I mean the Playboy Channel barely gets an R rating these days. And the Internet! Have you seen....? Well, never mind.

This gratuitous display of the female anatomy is pointless and unnecessary. It's sole purpose is to create controversy and publicity, thereby attracting an audience to see the rest of the play, in which the playwright tries, rather unsuccessfully, to communicate some obscure point about the nature of nudity in contemporary society. We, the female employees of this theater, find this all very pathetic and strongly protest the artistic staff's decision to produce this play.

Personally, I feel a little sorry for the playwright. Poor guy must have no connection to real life at all. Probably doesn't even know any real women. Probably spends all his time hidden away in some little room with a computer and only comes out to buy groceries. No wonder I hate grocery shopping. I mean, some of those guys in the fresh vegetable section, yuck!

The question now arises as to why we participate in this exhibitionism if we find it so unsavory. There are those who would maintain that our participation in this degenerate display is only another indication of the depths to which women in general and actresses in particular have sunk in these amoral, sexually saturated times. We do not have time for a complete review of the history of women in the theatre, not to mention the status of women in society. However, we must acknowledge that female nudity has been common on the stage during many historical periods and frequently female stage performers were classed only slightly above prostitutes, except, of course, for those few actresses who actually married the king instead of just becoming his mistress.

At any rate, the display of the female form has a long and well documented role in the development of Western theatre. "The Black Crook," for example, was little more than a skin show, but, as the first American Musical, was a significant milestone in the development of the major American contribution to world theatre.

So, while we may appear to be exploited victims of male dominance, a patriarchal culture, and the evils of the capitalist system, we are proud to claim a long and distinguished history of exploited female victims.

Having said that, we must admit, on a personal level, that appearing nude before an audience does have a certain inherent liberating quality. In addition to the definite ego enhancement of being selected as a worthy embodiment of the beauty and sensually of the female, the opportunity to dispense with many inhibitions in a protected environment provides a certain intellectual and psychological stimulation. In fact, we find we have become more accepting of our feminine nature and we are reconsidering many of our assumptions about a woman's relationship to her sexuality and to the culture in which that sexuality finds its context.

In short, we find that appearing nude has allowed us to become less concerned about our appearance, less self-conscious, less easily embarrassed, and hence far freer to focus on the content of our relationships with both men and women. We no longer censor ourselves. We are more forthright and assertive.

After all, if I can stand naked in front of an entire theatre of friends and strangers, what could possibly limit my ability to be myself in other situations. I'm here, I'm myself, I'm naked. If I can handle that, I can handle anything.

This enhancement of our self-assurance has had a profoundly empowering impact on our personalities and our lives.

Hence, we think it only fair to take a moment to express our profound gratitude to the sniveling little pervert who wrote this contrarily erotic play.

Thank you, you, you...male.

And now, on with the show.

> She exits.

THE PARK

> Two women are sitting on a park bench. They are dressed in fashionable "business" dresses.

1: Boy, is it hot.

2: Yeah. Hey, look at that guy over there.

1: Where?

2: Over on the bench by the tree. In the jogging shorts; all sprawled out.

1: Oh, yeah. Speaking of hot.

2: I've always wanted to do that.

1: What?

2: Just sit down and pull my shirt off and use it to wipe the sweat off my body, then throw my arms and legs wide open like that to cool off in the breeze. Don't you think that would feel just heavenly?

1: Let me get this straight. You fantasize about running around a public park at lunchtime until you are all sweaty, then pulling your shirt off to towel down in the middle of god-knows-who with your boobs hanging out, then sitting on a bench in such a position that the inseam of your shorts gets jammed up your ass. Is that a fair summary?

2: Well, look at us. It's 95 degrees in the shade and we're wearing pantyhose and sitting with our legs crossed. I've got so much yeast in my vagina I could open a bakery. This is insane.

1: Well, working in an office all day is pretty insane too, but what are you going to do?

2: Cover me.

1: What?

> 2 goes behind bench and takes off her pantihose.

1: Hey, what are...? You can't do that? I mean, what if somebody sees....?

> 2 comes back around the bench, stuffs the pantihose in her purse, sits on the bench, hikes up her skirt, and sprawls her arms and legs wide apart.

1: My god.

2: Oh, that feels good.

1: I can't believe...

2: Man, that breeze is heaven.

1: Cover yourself. You can't....

> 2 unbuttons two or three buttons on her blouse and fans herself using the now very loose collars of her blouse.

2: Hey, this is living. This is wonderful. You don't know what you're missing.

> 2 throws her arms back and spreads her body for maximum cooling.

1: You've cracked. The heat has fried your brain. Look, people are starring at you!

2: Let them stare. I don't have anything nobody's ever seen before. Ah, equality!

1: You're embarrassing me!

2: Why? Aren't my panties clean?

1: Well, yes, as a matter of fact, they appear to be very clean, and I'm not the only one who knows it.

2: My mother always taught me to wear clean panties. I thought it was in case I was in an accident and they had to cut my clothes off at a hospital. Guess the real reason was so I could shoot the beaver at the world without getting embarrassed. Think I should take my bra off?

1: No! No, definitely not!

2: Yeah, you're probably right. Have to go back to work in a minute. I won't wear one tomorrow.

1: Please, God, please don't let any cops come by.

2: Or a bra with a front hook. Yeah, that would work better. Then I could just pop it open here on the bench, then hook it back after lunch.

1: Tomorrow I'm bringing a sack lunch.

2: Hey, great idea. Then we'd have the whole hour to sit out here and soak up the sun.

1: No! I didn't mean....

2: Wonder if I need sun screen?

1: No! I mean, yes, you would, if you really..., but you wouldn't, not really. Would you? I can't be here if you do. I just couldn't. In fact, I have to get back to the office now. You're on your own. I'll see you later. Or maybe I won't. See you, that is. I've seen enough of you, I mean. More than I ever wanted to see. I never thought.... I've got to go now. Will you be all right? I mean, you sit here like this, all alone, and somebody could..., I don't know, get the wrong idea about you. I can't just leave you like this. But you're so...so...open.

> The alarm on 2's watch goes off.

2: Oh darn, lunch-time's over.

> 2 stands, buttons up, straightens her clothes, and picks up her purse.

2: Well, what are you waiting for? You want to be late?

1: No. I'm sorry. I'm just.... It's just so hot, you know?

> They exit, 2 buttoning up as she goes. Blackout.

THE STRIPPER

On stage there is a chair with a pile of clothes on it. A nude woman enters as "stripper" music begins to play. She dances to the music, erotically putting on her bikini panties, bra, miniskirt, sexy blouse, and shoes. The music ends. She bows and exits.

THE MAGAZINE

A Magazine rack in a book store. MAN flipping through a magazine with pictures of naked women. WOMAN comes up behind him and peeks over his shoulder at magazine.

WOMAN: Oh my god. I've had pelvic exams that didn't show as much.

MAN: Sorry I missed it.

WOMAN: They don't leave anything at all to the imagination, do they?

MAN: Thank you Eastman Kodak.

WOMAN takes magazine from MAN and begins looking through it.

WOMAN: This one's had a C-section; you can see her smiley-face.

MAN: What?

WOMAN: The scar. Here, right at the top of the hair. Looks like a smile.

MAN: Oh. Yes.

WOMAN turns page.

WOMAN: My god, she shaved it into the shape of a heart.

MAN: Closet romantic, I suppose.

WOMAN: Why do men like to look at naked women anyway? I mean, what's the big deal?

MAN: Well, an evolutionary biologist would say that all the males that didn't like to look at naked women never got laid and all their genes died out. Survival of the hornyist.

WOMAN: That I might believe.

MAN: Of course, the psychiatrists say we're just little boys trying to see the forbidden, see what's in the Christmas box hidden in the closet. There's also some stuff about Oedipus, trying to suckle at our mother's breast, return to the womb, that sort of thing.

WOMAN: The breast fixation is for real, believe me.

MAN: Of course the anthropologists say we're just trying to determine which women are fertile.

WOMAN: Huh! You guys would screw anything that even looked female.

MAN: No, really. Human women hide their fertility. It's a great trick, actually. With other primates, you know, monkeys and apes, you can tell when a female is fertile just by looking. So the male has sex then and only needs to keep the other males away from her for a few days a month. With human females, you have to have sex all the time <u>and</u> keep the other males away all the time. At least until you get her knocked up. Very tiring. Serial monogamy it's called. Add a long term contract and you get marriage and families and all that domestic stuff.

WOMAN: Well, thank you god for hidden fertility. But how do the monkey's do it? Do they stand on the tree-limb and flash a little thigh?

MAN: May I? (Takes her purse and begins to pull things out of it.)Well, their butt gets nice and round and their pubis turn red, but they also emit a different scent. (Holds up bottle of perfume from purse). Their cheeks become flushed (Holds up rouge). And their lips turn red. (Holds up lipstick.)

WOMAN: You're kidding.

MAN: Ask any anthropologist.

WOMAN: Yeah, sure. What's the primate equivalent of the push-up bra?

MAN: Actually, that's a little confusing since big breasts are a sign of lactation, which is an infertile period. The other stuff is all along the lines of "I'm all hot and bothered, come get me NOW." Big breasts are more of a long term thing, more like "You want a real woman? I am a W. O. M. A. N." Same for nice, broad hips. They say, "You want babies? I can have babies like you wouldn't believe. I am a fertility machine, now what will you give me for the chance to score?"

WOMAN: So that's all we are, just tits and asses, is that what you're saying?

MAN: No. I'm saying that's why men like looking at tits and asses. It's part of the way things work. Men like to look and women like to show it off. Men are voyeurs, women are exhibitionists. Complementary set. You show it off, we look, everybody's happy. Show me your boobs and I'll follow you anywhere.

WOMAN: Not all women are exhibitionists.

MAN: No. Just the ones who wear low-cut blouses, or tight pants, or short skirts, or T-shirts with messages written right over their boobs, or v-neck sweaters, or...

WOMAN: OK, OK, we like to look attractive.

MAN: You like to look sexy, which you call attractive.

WOMAN: Maybe, but we don't parade around naked.

MAN: (Holding up magazine.) You just pose for the pictures. (Taking another magazine out of the rack.) This one has a regular section of Polaroids women send in. They don't even get paid.

WOMAN: You're kidding.

MAN: See for yourself.

> He hands her the magazine. She glances at it.

WOMAN: Damn, I think I know her. My god! I do know her!

MAN: (Looking at picture.) Humm. Can you introduce me?

WOMAN: No way, José. You want anything more than a fold-out, you'll have me to deal with.

MAN: Is that a promise?

WOMAN: Humm. Maybe.

MAN: Show me your tits and I'll follow you anywhere.

WOMAN: We'll see what can be arranged.

MAN: Should I bring my camera?

WOMAN: Not if you prefer those air-brushed air-heads.

>She exits. MAN glances at magazines, stuffs them back in the rack, and follows her out. Blackout

THE TOKEN

A naked man walks across the stage holding a sign that says "Token Naked Male." The female members of the cast and crew whistle, do catcalls, yell "Shake it, baby, shake it." etc., encouraging him to lift the sign above his waist, which he eventually gets the courage to do as he crosses the stage.

Blackout.

AN OFFENSIVE PLAY

> AT RISE we see the interior of a small conference and storage room at the Brownwood Community Theatre. There is a table with room for about 6 chairs around it, 5 or 6 chairs, a small bookcase along one wall, several boxes and other odd items scattered around, and coffee maker and cups, etc. on top of the bookcase. JAN, around 30, dressed in an expensive sweatsuit, enters, puts her purse down, and starts making coffee. A moment later, EMILY enters. She is in her 50s, from old money but wearing new, stylish, casual clothes. She carries a stack of published acting edition scripts and some bound scripts such as playwrights submit to theatres. EMILY puts the scripts on the center of the table.

JAN: Coffee will be ready in a minute.

EMILY: Thanks.

> EMILY sits at the head of the table, looks through her purse, and pulls out a couple of pieces of paper, which she lays on the table in front of her. At this point, WILMA enters, limping and helped by SARA. WILMA is in her 70s, old money and old clothes. SARA is in her 40s, mix and match style skirt and blouse or sweater. JAN goes to help WILMA to a seat.

EMILY: Wilma! I didn't expect to see you here. Are you alright?

WILMA: No, just stubborn. Knee's swollen up the size of a grapefruit, but I'm afraid if I lie down I'll never get back up, so I just keep going. Old age stinks, let me tell you.

JAN: Here, let me get you something to prop your leg on.

WILMA: Thanks.

> JAN pulls a box or chair over for WILMA to prop her leg up on.

WILMA: I feel like Benjamin Franklin at the Constitutional Convention, too old to be worth a darn, but propped up in his seat every day just so they could say he was there.

SARA: Did he have arthritis too?

WILMA: No, gout. From too much wine and women. I ought to know, I was one of the women. (Pause.) That was a joke, Sara.

SARA: Oh, of course. You're not that old. That was over 200 years ago. I remember the Bicentennial Fireworks. Why, we did that John Adams play that year.

JAN: 1776.

SARA: Right.

WILMA: How are those kids of yours, Jan?

JAN: Just dandy. Ann is in second grade, and Tommy starts first grade in the fall.

WILMA: Time does fly.

SARA: Doesn't it though? My Benji only has another year of high school, and Connie, Connie has gotten so grown up off at college.

EMILY: Isn't that what's supposed to happen?

SARA: I guess.

JAN: Everybody want coffee?

SARA: Please. With sugar.

WILMA: Black. Something needs to keep me awake.

JAN: Emily?

EMILY: Yes, please. With creamora.

> When the coffee is ready, JAN will fill the coffee requests one at a time during the following dialogue.

EMILY: Well, since Wilma has a sore knee, let's go ahead and get started.

SARA: Should I take notes?

EMILY: Just of the votes, to make it official.

SARA: OK.

> SARA gets notepad and pen from purse and records votes as they occur.

EMILY: Since we're being so official, I hereby call this meeting of the Brownwood Community Theatre Play Selection Committee to order. I believe you have all had an opportunity to read the plays suggested for next year, but there are copies of all those suggested there on the table if anybody needs to refer to one. I talked to the new artistic director this afternoon, and I have his recommendations. For the comedy, he recommends The Odd Couple-The Female Version.

SARA: Oh, I liked that one.

JAN: It does have some good roles for women.

WILMA: Sure, why not?

EMILY: That's four ayes, no nays.

SARA: Got it.

EMILY: A Christmas Carol again for the Christmas show.

JAN: Of course. Have to pay for the rest of the season.

SARA: Oh yes.

WILMA: Why break with tradition? We got anybody to play Tiny Tim this year?

EMILY: Roberta Simms' boy should be old enough.

WILMA: All right.

SARA: Unanimous.

EMILY: The musical—Oklahoma!

WILMA: Again?

EMILY: Wilma, it's been thirty years since we did it last. I played Ado Annie, the one who can't say no.

WILMA: Has it been that long?

EMILY: Now I'll be lucky to get Aunt Eller.

SARA: That Judd character always bothered me.

JAN: All that beautiful music. And the ballet number.

WILMA: Oh, all right. Just seems like we did it yesterday. I did Aunt Eller, and I still catch myself humming the songs.

EMILY: So, are we agreed?

JAN: Yes.

WILMA: I guess thirty years is enough between productions. All right.

SARA: I guess.

EMILY: Four ayes.

SARA: I got it.

EMILY: Now for the drama. He recommended Twelve Angry Men, but I told him I didn't think we could get twelve grown men, angry or otherwise, that soon after Oklahoma!. We'll have to use high school boys and beat the bushes for all those cowboys as it is.

SARA: I can barely get Jim to do Christmas Carol, and then only because Benji's in it and Jim has his part memorized as it is. If he had to learn a new role, I don't think he'd do it. He's just so busy now.

JAN: What about Twelve Angry Women? It comes in a female version too.

EMILY: Just like Odd Couple.

JAN: Oh. I guess two gender benders in one season might be a bit much.

WILMA: What did he say when you told him there might be a casting problem.

EMILY: He said Twelve Angry Men was still his first choice, but his second choice would be The Miracle Worker if the committee thought Twelve Angry Men was just impossible.

JAN: Men are almost impossible, period.

SARA: Well, we might get five or six. There's no doubling in that show though, they're all on stage at the same time. And all the good men will want to be in Oklahoma!. Except Perry Ellis; he can't sing at all.

EMILY: So, what about Miracle Worker?

SARA: I like it, but it's a little old.

WILMA: Period costumes, period sets.

EMILY: I know.

WILMA: Have we got the budget for it?

EMILY: Well, Christmas Carol will sell out, and won't cost anything but royalties. Oklahoma should come close to selling out, but it will cost a pretty penny. We might clear a few dollars. Odd Couple won't sell out, but won't cost as much, so it should earn us a few dollars. We always plan to lose a little on the drama anyway.

JAN: But we don't want to lose too much. We want to come out ahead for the season and there's still the new play to go.

SARA: Yes, that always drops a bundle.

EMILY: I don't know why we do a new play anyway. We're just a community theatre.

JAN: Because we want to do one play that is less than twenty years old.

WILMA: And we can pay $100 for a new script instead of $500 to Samuel French.

SARA: What is the new play, anyway? Is it cheap?

EMILY: The new play is yet to be decided. You all read the three finalist.

SARA: I meant which one did the artistic director recommend.

EMILY: I was going to get to that after the drama was done with.

EMILY goes to the coffee pot for more creamora.

WILMA: Is there a problem with the new play?

EMILY: Well, let us say there was a difference of opinion. I was going to get to that.

JAN: Well, I think at this point that it might help to decide the new play first. If he wants to do that one set in the Restoration, with all those costumes, well, I just don't think we can do two period pieces back to back. We'll be sewing till our fingers bleed as it is, not to mention the cost.

EMILY: That's not the one he wants to do.

SARA: Oh, good. I didn't like that one.

WILMA: So, which one is it?

EMILY: He wants to do Snake In My Bosom.

JAN: Wonderful. I was afraid he wouldn't get that one; it is sort of a feminist play.

EMILY: Don't you think it might offend people?

JAN: No. Do you?

EMILY: I think there are some elements that might offend some people.

JAN: Such as?

EMILY: The nudity, the language.

JAN: What nudity?

EMILY: Well, it plainly states in the stage directions that the leading lady takes her blouse and bra off.

JAN: In the doctor's office! It's not exactly a sex scene.

EMILY: She's still sitting there half naked on center stage.

JAN: With her back to the audience. I don't think a naked back is going to arouse too many people, if that's what your problem is.

EMILY: What about the crew backstage? What about the actor playing the doctor? My god, he's supposed to feel her up!

JAN: It's a breast exam. It's a play about breast cancer. Even you've had a breast exam.

EMILY: Not in public. Not by a banker, or English teacher, or grocerier, or whoever gets the role of the doctor.

JAN: But don't you see? It's important to the play to show what a breast exam is, how it's no big deal compared to getting breast cancer.

EMILY: Having some strange man feel your breasts may not be a big deal to you, but it is to me.

WILMA: Let's not get personal here.

EMILY: OK. Fine. But let's deal with reality. How do we cast this role? Do we put up a sign at auditions, "The lead female role requires a woman willing to expose her breasts and have them touched by some actor every night"? Do we put that in the audition notice in the newspaper?

WILMA: Well, then the play would sell out and we could afford The Miracle Worker.

EMILY: Oh, come on Wilma. This isn't a joke. This is a community theatre. We don't have any bimbo actresses who say, "I was just playing a role. They weren't my breasts; they were the character's breasts." This is Brownwood; there's no place to hide. Whoever did this role would have some man feeling her breasts on Saturday night and then see the same man, and his wife, in church the next day, like as not. And how do you think her husband is going to feel, watching another man touch his wife's breasts every night in front of half the town. How many men in this town would allow that?

JAN: Maybe they can fake the touching.

EMILY: He'd still get to see her, right up close and personal.

JAN: They're just breasts, for heaven's sake! Everybody has them. They're hanging out of half the magazines at the 7-11.

EMILY: And you think that's all right?

JAN: No.

EMILY: Ah ha!

JAN: I think that makes breasts too important. It makes men,...no, it makes us think breasts make us women. That's the point of the play. She dies because she cares too much about her breasts. We are more than breasts and vaginas. That's what I don't like about those magazines, not that they show naked women, but that they treat women like nothing but breasts and vaginas. And what I like about this play is that it says we are more, much more, than just our sex organs.

    Pause.

WILMA: Well.

SARA: Jim reads Playboy. He brings it home. It used to upset me, but it does sort of spice things up in the bedroom for a day or two, so I got used to it. Sometimes the cartoons are funny. I caught Benji with a Penthouse once. I tried not to make a big deal out of it. I figured he was just, you know, curious.

JAN: And that's fine. I certainly don't want to go back to the days when doctors had to carry a little doll around in his bag so a woman could point to the doll to show where she hurt. Exactly the opposite. Maybe if seeing a woman's breasts wasn't such a big deal, getting breast exams and mammograms wouldn't be such a big deal either.

EMILY: I am not arguing the moral of the play. I am saying the nudity would make the role difficult to cast and the language would offend many of our major supporters.

JAN: What if I played the role?

SARA: What?

JAN: If you can't get anybody else, I'll play the role. I guarantee you an actress for this role.

WILMA: Jan, are you sure?

JAN: I think so.

EMILY: You can't play the role.

JAN: Why not?

EMILY: The script says the character is in her 50s.

JAN: So? A little grey in the hair, a little makeup. This is the theatre, remember?

EMILY: OK. OK. Let us assume, just for the moment, that the role could be cast and the exam scene could be blocked so that nothing untoward was shown to the audience. Just assume that. That still doesn't mean this is the play we want to do.

JAN: We can't afford the costume drama. And that third script, the farce, what was it called? The Imaginary Straw Hat? It stinks.

WILMA: I agree; that one wasn't very funny, Emily.

EMILY: That is not the point I'm trying to make.

WILMA: What is?

EMILY: The language in Snake In My Bosom is offensive. It bothers me, so I'm sure the church ladies would be walking out in droves. By the time you get to the moral of the play, most of the people who needed to hear it would be gone.

WILMA: It does have some strong language, Jan. Even you have to admit that. Nothing we haven't heard before, but it still doesn't fall pleasantly on my ears.

JAN: It could be a lot stronger.

EMILY: That's not the point.

JAN: These people are angry, they're scared, they're dying.

EMILY: Twelve "damns," ten "hells," six "tits," three "pussys," and two "dicks."

JAN: My god, you counted them?

WILMA: No "fucks?"

EMILY: No, thank goodness.

SARA: I don't think "hell" is that bad. Not these days.

> SARA picks up the script on the table and begins flipping through it.

WILMA: And nobody has walked out of a theater over a "damn" since Clark Gable told Scarlet O'Hara where to go in Gone With the Wind.

EMILY: What about "tits," "pussys,"...?

SARA: At least it wasn't "cunt." I hate that word.

EMILY: "Pussy," "cunt," what's the difference?

SARA: Oh, I think that "cunt" is much worse, don't you? Such an ugly sounding word, "cunt." I guess it's that "nt" sound, so hard. Not like "pussy" at all. You can even say "pussy" on TV, at least as long as you're talking about a cat.

JAN: And "dick" isn't as bad as "cock."

WILMA: When somebody says "dick," I always think of Dick Nixon, or Dick Tracey, or Dick Clark. I never think of a penis. Very confusing sometimes.

JAN: When somebody says "cock," do you think of a rooster?

SARA: Oh, I do. I went to the University of South Carolina, and their mascot was a Gamecock, you know, a fighting rooster, in cockfights. They had this cheer, "Go, Cocks, Go. Go, Cocks, Go." Yelled it all the time at football and basketball games. I think that's the reason we didn't get on TV very often, even though we had a good basketball team back then. I was just glad we never played the Oregon State Beavers.

JAN: Good Lord, imagine that.

WILMA: I'd rather not, if you don't mind.

SARA: Would have been the first X-rated football game, I guess.

EMILY: Could we get back to the point here?

WILMA: Please.

JAN: And what is the point?

EMILY: The point is that even if the language is not as bad as it could be, it is still offensive to some people. It really doesn't matter whether it offends you, or even me. What matters is that it will offend people who buy tickets, who give money, and even some of the people who participate in this theatre.

JAN: Some people, maybe.

EMILY: Some people, guaranteed.

WILMA: She's right about that, Jan.

JAN: But you have to look at the context. This isn't gratuitous vulgarism.

EMILY: I didn't say it was.

JAN: This is the language these characters would use in these circumstances, their own bodies turning on them, their sex organs becoming seeds of death instead of life.

EMILY: I don't dispute that.

JAN: This play says something important, something relevant to us, to now.

EMILY: Jan, listen to me. I am not saying the language isn't realistic, or even apt. And I'm not saying the message of the play isn't important. What I am saying it that it doesn't matter. No matter how justified the language is or how important the moral, some people are going to be offended. These people don't care about morals. They don't want to hear certain words. And if they hear those words from our stage, they are going to walk out,(she stands) demand their money back, cancel their season tickets, stop contributing, write letters to the editor, complain to the board, and generally raise enough hell to get us kicked out, the artistic director fired, and maybe close the theatre. How good the play is or how important the message doesn't matter to these people. They do not want to be offended when they come to their theatre.

JAN: (Standing) Well, I think you're over-reacting a little. It's the 90s, for heaven's sakes. Even in Brownwood. There's more bad language in a three minute rap song on the radio than in this whole play, and a lot less reason for it in the song.

WILMA: The radio being filthy doesn't make us clean. We're the ones picking the play, for our audience. Two wrongs still don't make a right.

JAN: But this is an important play. A valuable play. How often do we get a chance to really change a life or two?

EMILY: There are lots of important plays. There is only one Brownwood Community Theatre.

JAN: So if we don't do it, it will never be done.

EMILY: And if we do it, it may be the last show we do for a long time. Certainly the last new play for years.

JAN: They are not going to close us down over three "pussys" and two "dicks." What we lose in little old ladies, we'll gain in younger people.

EMILY: You couldn't pull those twenty-somethings away from their babies and TV sets if your life depended on it. They don't care about the theatre.

JAN: And whose fault is that?

WILMA: Whoa! Just hold up there. One of the little old ladies would like to say something.

JAN: Sorry. And you're not a little old lady.

> JAN and EMILY sit.

WILMA: I think I have every qualification for being a little old lady. Even a little old church lady. I'm certainly old, and I'm nowhere near as tall as I used to be. Weighed down by the years, as my Mamma used to say. And barring illness and that trip overseas, I haven't missed church in twenty years. If they gave out little old lady membership cards, I'd be a charter member. I know these little old church ladies Emily is talking about. I grew up with them. We grew up before TV and Playboy, back when you could leave your doors unlocked, wear white gloves, and blush without feeling silly. Back when being a lady meant more than just being a woman. I know all change isn't progress. And I know how much these old plays mean to us. They bring back our youth, times when there were standards, when we were in control, when we understood the world. And I also know how much money we little old ladies contribute to this theatre. You talk about breaking even on these plays, but what you're talking about is production costs. The mortgage, the utilities, the artistic director's salary, all that comes out of donations. So if we lose that, we're in real trouble.

JAN: Wilma...

WILMA: Let me finish. I have also been around long enough to learn a couple of hard lessons. The first is that change, good or bad, can't be stopped. Times change. Problems change. Words change. And the second lesson is that people die. I will die. And so will all the rest of those little old ladies. And if we don't get more young women like Jan involved in this theatre, it will be just as dead in a few years as it would be if all the little old ladies stopped giving their money. So we have a problem. We can take a few chances and hope it attracts some younger people to take up the slack from the little old ladies, or we can keep the little old ladies happy until they bury us and the theatre together. And that's why we need these new plays; to keep bringing us up to today, to keep us alive for each new generation. So let's look at this new play. We have at least one actress willing to play the role. The nudity can be finessed. I think if we post a few warnings about the language, it will scare off the faint of heart. At least they won't be able to say we didn't warn them. So that's not my problem with this play.

JAN: Then what...?

WILMA: What I am not yet convinced of is that this is the play that we want to stir up the ruckus with. And there will be a ruckus. Emily's right about that. It's a good play, yes. Probably the best new play we've had in several years. But is this the play that will draw in the young people? Is this the play that is relevant enough to the people in this town to justify what it's going to cost us. If breast cancer doesn't matter that much to the people in this town, wouldn't we be better off finding a play about something that does matter to this town, violence in the schools, race relations, something like that.

EMILY: We could say we didn't have a winner this year. Do another play, something only few years old. Maybe have a themed contest next year. On violence, child abuse, maybe.

SARA: (Standing) Can the scatter-brained twit say something?

WILMA: Oh, Sara, you're not a .....

SARA: Oh, yes, I am. Just as much as you're a little old lady. Believe me, I know. But I've got something to show you.

> SARA, facing upstage, lifts her shirt and bra.

EMILY: My god.

> SARA lowers her bra and shirt back into place.

SARA: I would appreciate it if this was our little secret.

JAN: Of course.

> Pause. SARA returns to her seat.

WILMA: I move we select Snake In My Bosom for the new play slot.

JAN: Second.

WILMA: Emily?

> Pause. EMILY looks at SARA.

EMILY: Aye.

SARA: I count four Ayes. It's unanimous.

WILMA: Now all we have to do is figure out what to do about the drama.

JAN: Might as well do Miracle Worker. If Snake doesn't fly, we won't be back next season anyway, according to Emily.

WILMA: Maybe I'll get to go out in a blaze of glory and a little scandal after all. Sara?

SARA: Yes?

WILMA: If I'm still alive next spring, can I sit next to you while Jan's up on stage getting her boobies played with?

SARA: It would be my honor.

WILMA: Oh, I doubt that. More like hanging together rather than hanging separately. Care to join us Emily?

EMILY: I don't seem to have much choice, do I?

WILMA: All aboard the roller coaster.

JAN: What a night.

    The lights fade. End of Act I.

ACT II

THE LADIES ROOM

>Two women wearing low-cut dresses or blouses are checking themselves out in the mirror of a ladies rest room. One opens her purse, takes out some makeup, and begins to apply it to her breasts. The other woman stares at her.

1: Girl, what are you doing?

2: Making up my breasts.

1: What?

2: Putting on a little makeup to make my cleavage look bigger. I got one of those miracle push-'em-in-and-up bras, but I think a little shadow and highlight add to the illusion. Every little bit helps, you know. Or is it every little tit needs help?

1: How do you...?

2: Oh, just a little dark base in between, to make the shadow look deeper, then a little white cream on the boobs themselves. Helps to catch the light and make them shine, really stand out. The contrast makes them look bigger. An actress who used to do all these Restoration Comedies, you know, when all the women wore these really low cut dresses, well, she taught me this. Those theater people are weird, aren't they? But this really works. You know, she said there was one period in England when the dresses were cut so low you could see the areola, sometimes even the nipples. Rich women had their portraits painted with their nipples showing and fifty years later the grandkids had to hire some other painter to come back and paint lace on the portrait bodice to cover grandma's nipples.

1: You're kidding.

2: No, I saw it in her book on the history of costumes. It's for real. This girl knew her makeup too. Here, want to try it?

>2 holds out her makeup.

1: Uh, well, maybe just a little.

2: Trick is to blend it so there's no line. If nobody can tell where the makeup starts, you got it.

1: Yeah, until you take your bra off.

2: Hey, the truth comes out then anyway.

1: Why don't you just get a boob job?

2: Guess I'm afraid it would leak. I mean, the last thing I need is a lump of silicone migrating to my hips.

1: Girl, I know what you mean. The cellulite is bad enough. Last thing I need is chemical fat. I have to run ten miles a week just to keep my thighs from getting so thick they rub together and I get all chaffed. There, how's that look?

2: Hot, real hot. But you need to blend a little better on the left one.

1: Here?

2: Yeah. OK, great. All made up and ready to party.

    1 hands makeup back.

1: Well, let's go strut our stuff.

    They exit. Blackout.

THE COMPETITION

A bare stage. Two women enter from opposite sides. They exchange dirty looks. They stand a few feet apart, as if waiting for something or somebody. They furtively check each other out and slowly begin to try to stand a little more sensuously than the other. After a few sexy poses, WOMAN 1 unbuttons the top button of her blouse and tries a new posture emphasizing the newly revealed cleavage. WOMAN 2, seeing this, turns away, undoes a button, and turns back in her own version of a provocative pose. 1 undoes another button and poses. 2 matches her. 1 undoes yet another button. 2 matches her. 1 pulls her blouse out of her skirt and unbuttons it completely. 2 matches her and ups the anti by taking her blouse off completely. This infuriates 1, who takes her blouse off, throws it at 2's feet, and then makes the grand gesture of taking her bra off and dropping it to the floor. 2 takes off her bra and throws it at 1. 1 stamps her feet in fury, takes off her skirt, and throws it at 2. 2 takes off her skirt, throws it at 1, then takes off her panties and throws them at 1. 1 takes off her panties, crosses to 2, and jams the panties over 2's face and head, then crosses away and poses. 2 takes the panties off her head, wads them into a ball, tosses them in her hand a few times. 2 then signals that she is giving up the contest, picks up ALL the clothes, and exits. 1 stands in triumph for a moment, then comes to the realization that she is naked and that 2 has taken all the clothes. She looks around for her clothes, but can't find any. She looks for anything to cover herself with, but there is nothing. She covers herself as best she can with her hands as she attempts a graceful exit.

BLACKOUT

THE CONVERSATION

Two women are sitting at a table drinking coffee.

1: So, anyway, there I was, listening to the preacher drone on and on about how we are all made in the image of God, and suddenly I had this thought, is God naked? And if not, why not? I mean, what does he have to hide? And who is he hiding it from? Then I remembered this scripture in Exodus where Moses asks to see God's face, but God says nobody can see his face and live. However, as a big reward for Moses, he says he will let Moses see his "hindquarters." So, God moves past the mountain and the clouds clear just enough for Moses to catch a glimpse of God's backside. And I wonder, does this mean that God just "mooned" Moses. And what are the theological implications of seeing somebody's ass to pre-exodus Hebrews. Does God have an ass? If so, does it work? What does God eat that he needs an ass? Wouldn't any food God eats be perfect and not have any, you know, waste, left over? And if he does have an ass, is it this perfect, really tight ass? Does he keep it covered? Did he have to drop his pants to moon Moses? And if he does wear clothes, why does he do it? I mean, it's not like he needs clothes to stay warm or avoid sunburn, right? So what has God got to be modest about? If he has a body, wouldn't it be a perfect body, something he'd want to show off? I mean, God hasn't got original sin from the Garden of Eden, right? So why would he want some polyester fig leaf? The only thing I could think of was that His body is too good and that it would just overwhelm us if we actually saw it, so he wears clothes or clouds or something to protect us from being jealous or something. And what if God's a woman? I mean that is the new theology, right, as much woman as man? If we saw Her body, would we all just give up on our diets and pig out at Baskin-Robbins because there's just no way we could compete? Like, just forget even trying? And if He is a She, what kind of clothes would She wear? I mean, Jesus wore all those old robes and stuff, but that's what people wore back then, right? Does God keep up with the styles? I mean, if God appeared to somebody right now, what would she wear? Form-fitting black lace? Bell bottoms and platform shoes? Does She wear miniskirts and halter tops? And if She does, how short are the skirts? What's God's bra cup size? Or is her body so perfect she doesn't need a bra? I mean, gravity doesn't apply to God, right? Anyway, there I was, sitting in church, building this picture in my mind of God as some kind of half-naked, body-builder, Playboy bunny, when I realized everybody else was standing up singing "Oh God, Our Help in Ages Past," and I just turned red as a beet, grabbed the hymnal, and tried to find the page as fast as I could.

Pause.

2: Girl, you need to get a life.

Blackout.

MODELING

A naked MAN and WOMAN are sitting side by side on two stools in the pose of Rodin's "The Thinker." Two or three people with sketch pads and pencils sit around drawing the models. The models talk to each other without moving.

MAN: So, pose here often?

WOMAN: Oh, once or twice a week. You?

MAN: Maybe twice a month. (Pause.) Not as much call for naked men.

WOMAN: I guess not.

MAN: Seems to be picking up though. More women taking the life drawing classes now. They demand equal nudity.

WOMAN: Only fair.

MAN: I guess.

Pause.

MAN: My butt itches.

WOMAN: I think they put burlap on these stools. Whoever made 'em never sat on them naked.

MAN: Amen. (Pause.) And this pose. Makes me feel like a pretzel.

WOMAN: Makes the muscles in the back stand out. More definition.

MAN: Oh. (Pause.) Still, it hurts like hell after five minutes. Makes me feel sorry for whoever the guy was who posed for Rodin. Must be harder on you; this isn't exactly the way a woman usually sits.

WOMAN: Oh, I don't mind. Makes me feel all muscular and aggressive, a bitch with brains.

MAN: And what's the point of two of us, anyway? Most times I'm naked with a woman, I don't just sit around thinking.

WOMAN: Maybe they're saying women can think just as well as men, even naked.

MAN: Maybe. I just think if they wanted a naked man and a woman in a Rodin pose, I would have chosen "The Kiss."

WOMAN: Oh, I bet you would have. Dream on, boy.

Pause.

MAN: Ouch. I just got a cramp in my elbow. Hurts like hell.

WOMAN: Well, nobody ever said being naked was easy.

MAN: Yeah, but even for $50 dollars an hour, this hurts.

WOMAN: (Breaking pose.) Fifty? I only get $30.

MAN: You're kidding?

WOMAN: Damn, gender gap even for being naked.

MAN: You ought to sue. It should be equal pay for equal nudity. That's what I always say.

WOMAN: Damn straight. I ought to sue the pants off 'em. Teach 'em a lesson. I just might do it.

MAN: Sure. Show 'em what you're made of.

WOMAN: Yeah. Just let me think about it.

>   She resumes pose. The lights fade out.

THE AUDITION

> Bare stage. Actress enters. Pause. Female VOICE comes from PA system.

VOICE: Hold on a second, please.

ACTRESS: Sure.

> Pause.

VOICE: OK, I've got your resume now.

ACTRESS: You want me to do my audition song first?

VOICE: Yes, but not yet. Um, you got some good training.

ACTRESS: I like to think so.

VOICE: Will you do a nude scene?

ACTRESS: A what?

VOICE: A nude scene. Be naked on stage. You know, no clothes. Look, Ma, here I am!

ACTRESS: Uh, I don't know. Why?

VOICE: Why what?

ACTRESS: Why would I have to do a nude scene?

VOICE: Because the script says so.

ACTRESS: For all the roles?

VOICE: No, just the lead.

ACTRESS: Oh.

VOICE: So, will you?

ACTRESS: How big is it?

VOICE: It's the lead.

ACTRESS: No, the nudity. How big is it? I mean, are we talking like just flashing the audience, or stripping, or some guy ripping my clothes off, or a sex scene, or what? I need some context here. And are we talking basically just topless, or backside, or full frontal? Am I upstage or down? How do I get naked, on stage or off? Who else is on stage at the time? Does anybody touch me? How are the lights, up full or down low? Is it really necessary to the plot or just thrown in for effect? Will any nude pictures be used for publicity? Do I get a private dressing room? I mean, there's a lot to consider here.

VOICE: Right. OK. Let's see. You walk on naked. You stand there. Everybody stares at you. We all take pictures and send them to your parents.

ACTRESS: You're kidding, right?

VOICE: Yes, I'm kidding.

ACTRESS: I thought so.

VOICE: The pictures actually go in the lobby.

ACTRESS: Oh. You're kidding again...

VOICE: Listen. The nudity is necessary for the show. It's not some gimmick. I will direct it very tastefully, but you have to be out there naked for several minutes. If you have any secrets, they will be fully revealed, OK?

ACTRESS: I'm sure you're a very good director and all...

VOICE: I am a very good director and this is a very good script.

ACTRESS: It's just that, well, I mean, have you ever done a nude scene?

VOICE: Me?

ACTRESS: Yes. You. On stage.

VOICE: If I looked good enough to be asked to do nude scenes, do you think I would have become a director?

ACTRESS: I don't know. I just wondered if you...you know...

VOICE: I can sympathize but not empathize.

ACTRESS: OK, OK.

VOICE: The lobby is full of actresses. I need a yes or no.

ACTRESS: OK, OK, maybe.

VOICE: Oh god.

ACTRESS: OK, OK, yes...I think...probably.

VOICE: Fine. Take your clothes off.

ACTRESS: What?

VOICE: If you want to audition for the role with the nude scene, I need to see you nude. It's you, me, the stage manager, and the accompanist. If you can't do it now, you sure can't do it in front of 99 strangers.

ACTRESS: Oh. Sure. Makes sense to me.

VOICE: OK, let's see it.

ACTRESS: It's just that I didn't plan, you know, today, to, you know...

VOICE: Thank you. Would you ask the next person to come in as you go out.

ACTRESS: Wait! I mean, OK, I, uh, I just want you to know I didn't plan, I mean, I do have fancier underwear. I just didn't think...

VOICE: Thank you. Next, please.

ACTRESS: OK, OK. (She begins to disrobe.) My god, you make such a big deal out of this. OK, OK, here, see, skin, here it is. No big thing, OK. You want to see, here it is. I mean it's not like I've got some scars or winestains or something. It's a good body. I'm proud of it. See? OK?

VOICE: Fine. Thank you. Next.

ACTRESS: Hey, don't you want me to read or sing or anything?

VOICE: OK, OK, You gave the pianist your music?

ACTRESS: Yes.

VOICE: Fine. Go for it.

    The music starts.

ACTRESS: (Singing) "Hey, look me over, lend an ear, fresh out of clover, mortgaged up to here," etc.

    The lights fade.

AN ABSTRACT PLAY

> AT RISE the stage is empty except for a very large candle in a tall candlestick. The WRITER, about 30, casually dressed, enters.

WRITER: Good evening. Welcome to An Abstract Play. As with most abstract, or "weird" plays, as they are better known, this one is comprehensible only to a few left wing critics, mostly from Yale. Humm, that was a bit of a convoluted sentence, wasn't it. I'll have to watch that. This play is confusing enough as it is; need to keep the introduction clear. The dialogue is totally unrealistic, so something needs to be in simple English. Like most abstract plays, we have absurd dialogue. Naturalistic, perhaps, but completely unbelievable. Anyway, I am The Writer; in other words, I am the imaginary character, portrayed by an actor, who supposedly wrote, and is hence responsible for, this mess. Of course, that isn't true. I'm just an actor playing as unreal and manipulated a character as every other character that the author wants you to accept as representing truth. Out of lies come beauty, or something like that. Anyway, I have been assigned to explain all the things that occur in this play that are otherwise indecipherable, like this introduction for example. And now that we have that clear, we can begin.

> The GIRL, early 20's, wearing a white, frilly dress, enters, crosses to the candle, takes out a match, lights the candle, kneels, and bows her head as if in prayer.

WRITER: This GIRL, for another example, needs some explanation. A beautiful, young girl, all dressed in white, lighting a candle. Why, you might take her for a symbol of innocence or purity or holiness. Symbols, I'm afraid, are not so simple. Think a minute. If we really wanted to show true innocence or holiness, wouldn't we show her as God made her, nude, in the glory of a woman's dawn? But, it seems that when some people look at what God actually made, they think strange, perverted thoughts. It's like looking at the Grand Canyon and thinking "What a wonderful cesspool." Which, of course, is what somebody besides God has turned the Colorado River into. You just have to go downstream to smell the stench. Well, the Lord works in mysterious ways. Come, Girl, save yourself. Get up and take off your clothes.

GIRL: Fuck you! That's not in the script

WRITER: I'm playing The Writer. I can improvise and improve a line if I feel like it.

GIRL: Well, go improvise a way to screw yourself.

> She exits.

WRITER: See what I mean about symbols? Our innocence is a fabric of lies, our holiness the dim light of a candle.

> GIRL re-enters.

GIRL: Shit! What kind of B.S. is this?

WRITER: Now that was what the author wrote. You're the one who's not following the script this time.

GIRL: I don't care. Telling me to take my clothes off. There might be little children out there.

WRITER: Who would only care because you do, and only think it wrong because we told them so. Little kids are used to nudity. They've been seen nude hundreds of times.

GIRL: But is this any fit topic for a play?

WRITER: Nudity? Nudity is not the issue here.

GIRL: Then what is?

WRITER: I'm not sure.

GIRL: You're not sure? But you're the Writer!

WRITER: Doesn't mean anything. The writer is usually the last to know what a play means. Why do you think critics have to write reviews instead of just giving grades.

GIRL: Well, what do you think it's about, if you had to guess.

WRITER: If I had to guess? Oh, reasons, maybe.

GIRL: Reasons? Reasons for what?

WRITER: I don't know. Just reasons. Look, the audience is getting restless, could we get on with this?

GIRL: OK, OK. But my agent is going to hear about this. Take my clothes off indeed. I'm not some dumb blond trying to make it on my tits; I'm an actress!

>She exits.

WRITER: Fresh out of college. Still thinks intelligence and ability are all it takes. Anyway, back to the script. (He blows out the candle.) Scene Two.

>The OLD MAN, very old, carrying a cane, wearing a sweater and slacks, enters, using his cane for support. He hobbles to the candle, takes out a match, and lights the candle.

OLD MAN: When youth was a pleasure and plenty
And time was a strong, wound spring
I cared for the little things.
When tomorrow was due me
And not a debt past due
I scrimped and saved for the little things.
The little things; tomorrow's pleasures,
Fortune, Success, Fame and Glory,
Future and Fate, Time; the little things.
The little things, like clocks grown weak
Tick quietly now, memories of memories,
Times beyond pleasure or plenty.
Little things.

OLD MAN: Hello, Son.

WRITER: Hi ya, Pops.

OLD MAN: Am I still alive?

WRITER: By all accounts.

OLD MAN: Good. I guess. You know, I went to the theatre last week.

WRITER: No kidding?

OLD MAN: Don't know why though. Understood the whole thing in one sitting. Could have just watched TV. Isn't anybody writing poetry anymore?

WRITER: I wouldn't know.

OLD MAN: It's too calm, too happy. Like all we have to do is survive, keep the candle lit.

WRITER: We have to start with that, don't we?

OLD MAN: No. Any little breeze could blow this candle out. That doesn't matter. What matters, after all the breezes, is that somebody keeps lighting candles, and that each candle burns.

WRITER: Pops, you're a little strange at times.

OLD MAN: Me, strange? Huh, you should see what you'll be like in fifty years. Time's just another name for the Devil, Son. God made him, and God'll beat him in the end, but in the meantime, he robs you blind. Before long, all you can see is backwards. That might not make any sense, but it's the truth, strange or not. By the way, it's time for the trial.

WRITER: Trial? What trial? There's no trial in this script.

OLD MAN: There is in mine. And it's your trial, Son, your trial.

WRITER: My trial? But what did I do? I'm just the Writer. Writer's never do anything.

OLD MAN: Better bring that candle, Son. You're going to need it.

> The OLD MAN hobbles upstage. The GIRL enters with a black robe, which she puts on the OLD MAN's shoulders. The WRITER blows out the candle and carries it with him. The OLD MAN faces the audience and raises his arms.

WRITER: Scene Three.

OLD MAN: The Court is always in session!

> The OLD MAN pounds his cane to the floor like a gavel. The WRITER takes out a match and lights the candle.

WRITER: At this point in the play I probably should stop and explain what is going on. Unfortunately, I haven't the foggiest notion. This isn't in my copy of the script. If you're confused, imagine how I feel. I'm supposed to have written this. I'm still wondering why the girl wouldn't take her clothes off. I always end up wondering why the girl wouldn't take her clothes off.

OLD MAN: You stand accused. You are always accused.

GIRL: As God is my witness, he did.

WRITER: Did what?

OLD MAN: How do you plead?

WRITER: I'm innocent!

GIRL: Then take off your clothes.

WRITER: Oh, God!

OLD MAN: Yes? (pause) Just kidding.

WRITER: What is this, a comedy or a tragedy?

GIRL: You wrote it. Don't you know?

OLD MAN: Now, don't blame it all on him. Sometimes there's no difference. That's part of the point of the script; tragedy is just as absurd as comedy. In fact, they're the same thing, only comedy hurts more.

GIRL: How can that be?

OLD MAN: Comedy is when it hurts too much to cry.

GIRL: Isn't that a little obtuse?

WRITER: What happened to the trial?

OLD MAN: Oh, you're guilty.

WRITER: Guilty? Of what?

OLD MAN: What difference does it make? The sentence is the same for everybody.

WRITER: Sentence? What sentence?

OLD MAN: Same one I got. You live until you die. That's all there ever is.

WRITER: But what did I do?

OLD MAN: Son, you may not have done a damn thing, yet. But you will. Once you put those clothes on, you can never take them off again without some piece of lint clinging to you. We go through life collecting lint in our navels from the first time we pull on a shirt. It gets down in the cracks and you can never wash it all away. You just have to learn to wear good shirts.

> The OLD MAN and the GIRL exit. The WRITER blows out the candle.

WRITER: My crime, of course, was to tell a girl I loved her. How common. But what did you expect? I was alone. I needed a place to stay. Saying "I love you" was like paying rent. Daily rent. I did love her. I just didn't want to say it. It was like signing a lease. I didn't want to close off my options. But I couldn't say that, because then she would have thrown me out. I didn't have anywhere else to go. So it became sort of emotional prostitution. You know, I would have been glad to give her all the sex she wanted, and she was one horny broad. I would even have enjoyed it. I just didn't want to say "I love you."

> The GIRL enters.

GIRL: Bastard.

WRITER: Leave my mother out of this.

GIRL: Always the literalist.

WRITER: Occupational hazard.

GIRL: So, what did you do?

WRITER: About what?

GIRL: The girl, you idiot.

WRITER: Things happen. You know. I got a job in another state.

GIRL: She was just another port in a storm. Another cunt to keep your cock warm.

WRITER: Oh, I paid my harbor fees. She got what she wanted. God, I must have held that woman in my arms for weeks, if you added up all the time I spend holding her. It's amazing just how much women love to be held, just hugged and held close.

GIRL: What, no fucking? You poor boy.

WRITER: Oh, there was plenty of that, of various and sundry kinds. But that was the meat and potatoes. What she really wanted, like whipped cream and a cherry, was to be held; before, after, and in between. My arms got more exercise than doing push-ups.

GIRL: You're a louse, you know that.

WRITER: I believe I have been made fully cognizant of my character defects. But I am right about one thing; women do love to be held. Don't they? (pause) Don't they?

GIRL: Yes.

WRITER: Do you like being held?

GIRL: Doesn't everybody? Even men?

WRITER: At times. Would you like me to hold you?

GIRL: Don't you think we ought to get back to the play?

> She moves the candle back to it's original position.

WRITER: Maybe I need somebody to hold me.

GIRL: Why? You alone again?

WRITER: Isn't everybody?

GIRL: I'll go get a match.

WRITER: It's not your turn.

GIRL: Then shove the candle up your ass.

> She exits.

WRITER: Hearts of stone that never beat sometimes shatter in the heat.

> The OLD MAN enters and lights the candle.

WRITER: Now there was some poetry for you.

OLD MAN: Thanks, I think. Scene Four.

WRITER: That's my line.

OLD MAN: Really? That line you were using a minute ago didn't seem to be working too well.

WRITER: You could do better?

OLD MAN: Oh, I'm a little over the hill for that sort of thing. But I do seem to remember there being better ways to make out in this world.

WRITER: Could we just get on with this?

OLD MAN: Do I hear tables turning?

WRITER: You lit the candle, get on with it.

OLD MAN: So I did, so I did. Well, back to the play. I am here to tell your fortune.

WRITER: What if I don't want to hear it?

OLD MAN: I thought you wanted to get back to the script?

WRITER: Oh, OK, OK.

OLD MAN: Besides, everybody wants to know the future, especially if they don't have to believe it unless it's good.

WRITER: I'm not everybody.

OLD MAN: Nobody is.

WRITER: Hell with the script. I've got to go to the john. You're on your own.

WRITER exits.

OLD MAN: Ah, youth. Forever blind to the future all can see. You will grow old, my son, like me, like all, you will grow old. But you hide your eyes from time past today. So we moan from the past at the green youth forever growing toward the sun, always blinded by the light. Your future is my past. The lines on your palm are the wrinkles on my face. That is your future, son, whether you are here to hear it or not.

The GIRL enters.

GIRL: Where did he go?

OLD MAN: To the john.

GIRL: In the middle of the play? Nobody goes to the john in a play.

OLD MAN: Realism.

GIRL: Oh. Reality is a piss, is that it?

OLD MAN: The elemental needs.

GIRL: What will he do next, sleep on stage?

OLD MAN: No, the audience will do all the sleeping.

GIRL: Where are we in the script? What comes next?

OLD MAN: How should I know; I'm not the writer.

GIRL: You tell fortunes pretty well, gaze into your crystal ball and see what happens next.

OLD MAN: Alas, my dear, I see only the far future. Sooner or later your hair will turn grey, your lovely breasts will sag, and your children will think you are hopelessly old fashioned. Eventually, like me, you will age and die. That I know. But what you will do for the next ten minutes, I have no idea.

GIRL: So what do I do, stand out here with you and stare at the audience?

OLD MAN: I've got to leave myself in a minute. Know any jokes?

GIRL: Not really.

OLD MAN: What about poetry? The Rhyme of the Ancient Mariner?

GIRL: No.

OLD MAN: Old audition monologues? "To be or not to be..."? Nursery rhymes, anything?

GIRL: Is that what I'm reduced to, reciting nursery rhymes?

OLD MAN: What about improvising a tearful exit scene. I'm leaving now, and a tearful good-bye from a pretty girl sure would be a nice way to go.

GIRL: You're not actually going to leave me alone out here?

OLD MAN: Or just a little peck on the cheek for an old man. That would bring back some old memories.

GIRL: What kind of girl do you think I am?

OLD MAN: Listen, we've got one last chance to liven this show up with a little sex. Do you want to give me a nice exit line and a soft good-bye, or stand out here spouting Mother Goose?

GIRL: Mary had a little lamb, It's fleece was white as snow.

OLD MAN: Oh well, you probably wouldn't have been very good anyway. You don't have the heart for it.

> He exits slowly.

GIRL: Where are you going? Come back here. Hey! Damn! Sure, go. Leave me out here all alone. What am I, a stand-up comic? I'm an actress; I need a script. Boy, is my agent going to hear about this.

> Long pause. GIRL looks at audience, looks to wings for help, looks back at audience.

GIRL: Uh, hi there. Uh, this wasn't supposed to happen. Nobody is ever supposed to go to the bathroom on stage. I mean in a play. Uh, let's see, uh, have you heard the one about the priest, the rabbi, and the minister who went fishing together, and they were in this boat in the middle of a lake, and the priest stepped out of the boat and walked across the water to the shore and I just picked the one joke that can offend every known religious group. Christ, how stupid can I get? The religions are interchangeable, but some church still ends up face down in the water. Strange, isn't it; all religions can fish, but they can't all walk on water at the same time. I think I better just leave them out there all in the same boat. Uh, there was this traveling salesman, no, strike that. Some comic I'm turning out to be. I will never know how Roseanne does it; one joke about her boobs and everybody is in the aisle. I never thought of boobs as funny. Strange, maybe, but not funny. I mean, there they are, so what? Everybody has them, even men, only flatter. I read somewhere that with some kind of hormone shots that even men's breasts would work, you know, make milk, for babies. So why does everybody stare at them? It makes you want to hide sometimes, everybody looking at your chest. Like now.

> She crosses her arms over her chest.

GIRL: Stop that. You're nasty, looking at me that way. I mean, so what, I have breasts. I also have shoulder blades. Would you get all turned on looking at my shoulder blades?

> She turns around and wiggles her shoulder blades.

GIRL: Does that give you an erection?

> The WRITER enters.

WRITER: Yes.

GIRL: Oh, go screw yourself.

WRITER: I am not quite that well endowed.

GIRL: Why do people think these thing?

WRITER: Well, to quote from a part of the script that we skipped, "Because they are alive. Because they are going to die. Because they want to save their youth, to have some piece of it left eternally behind. A memory, a child, a scrap of paper. 'Let me die, but not die out.'"

GIRL: What?

WRITER: Never mind. The candle is burning. Each day a little more wax melts away. The wax wrinkles and sags in the flame until only the cold remains are left.

GIRL: It can be melted again, remolded, a new wick put in, can't it?

WRITER: I don't know. But <u>this</u> candle will be gone. Just as this play will soon be over. As soon as we force a moral in somewhere, that is.

GIRL: What happened to the old man? Isn't he in the final scene?

WRITER: He had to leave. Didn't he tell you he was going?

GIRL: I guess. I guess I didn't believe him. He asked me to kiss him good-bye.

WRITER: Did you?

GIRL: No. I thought he wanted something else. Maybe that was a mistake. Is he really gone?

WRITER: Yes.

GIRL: I'm sorry. I wish I knew what he really wanted.

WRITER: He wanted a piece of life, a little warmth against the cold. What do we all want?

GIRL: To be held. To be rocked to sleep in someone's arms, to be kissed before going out into the dark night.

WRITER: It's the saying that's hard; the hidden meanings in hard words.

GIRL: When did love become a dangerous thing?

WRITER: When did it become more important how long the candle burned instead of how well?

GIRL: I should have kissed him. I thought he was like you, trying to get my clothes off.

WRITER: It's not our bare bodies we must fear, it's our bare hearts.

GIRL: OK, OK. I get the point.

WRITER: Put the candle out. We are light enough, and we will steal the time.

GIRL: And so, bravely into the cold dark.

She blows the candle out. The lights fade.

CURTAIN

Angel

This play was a finalist for the New Southern Theatre Festival at the Mockingbird Theater in Nashville, TN, in 2003, but did not win a production. It did get a reading by Merely Writer's group here in Atlanta. Dealing with a totally unlikable protagonist makes it somewhat of a problem play, but I think it's funny and works dramatically.

ANGEL

A Play By David Davis

Member
All rights & privileges.

David Davis
100 Hunters Ridge Court
Roswell, GA 30076
daviddaviswriter@gmail.com

Copyright 2021 David Davis

CAST OF CHARACTERS

RAFE JOHNSON .... 40s, An Actuary

ANGEL .... An Angel, Female, Looks 20s

GLORIA JOHNSON .... 40s, Rafe's Ex-wife

HAPPY AMES .... 30s, Female, Minister

SETTING

The present. A hospital room, a living room, and a minister's office.

SCENE ONE

> Hospital room, cardiac intensive care. RAFE JOHNSON (40-50's, male) lies asleep, hooked up to the monitors and tubes. ANGEL (looks 20, female) sits in a chair by the bed, waiting. She wears a white lab coat. RAFE stirs in bed.

ANGEL: Mr. Johnson. Mr. Johnson, can you hear me?

> RAFE slowly responds. He is groggy.

RAFE: Ohh.

ANGEL: Well, Mr. Johnson, welcome back.

RAFE: Oh man, what happened?

ANGEL: You had quite a scare yesterday.

RAFE: Yesterday?

ANGEL: It's Friday.

RAFE: Friday? Oh man, last thing I remember was coming in for that laser eye surgery Thursday.

ANGEL: They had just finished working on your eyes when your heart stopped.

RAFE: My heart? There's nothing wrong with my heart.

ANGEL: Well, there doesn't seem to be anything wrong with it now. Yesterday, not so much.

RAFE: I just wanted a little better vision. What went wrong?

ANGEL: Well, some things are still a mystery, even these days.

RAFE: My heart just stopped?

ANGEL: Completely. Bet that bunch of ophthalmologists never moved so fast in their lives. Evidently did all the right things though. Got those paddles right out. Even then, it evidently took a while to bring you back.

RAFE: I was dead?

ANGEL: Well, clinically, in that your heart had stopped. You're not really dead until your brain dies though. Takes about seven minutes, on average. You pushed that pretty hard, but there's evidently no neurological damage. CPR and all that. Doctor says you'll be perfectly fine in a few days.

RAFE: Except my heart stopped. I died. It could stop again, anytime.

ANGEL: Well, they say there's no indication of any damage. Everybody can die, Mr. Johnson, at any moment. That was just as true yesterday as it is today. But right now you are about as safe as you will ever be. You're wired up six ways from Sunday, and there are highly trained nurses right outside this room keeping track of your every heartbeat, every breath, every time you pee. One little shimmy-shake on their monitor and there will be two doctors and three nurses on top of you within sixty seconds. I know telling you not to worry won't do much good, but right now the best thing you can do for yourself is get a little more rest. See if you can get back to sleep now.

RAFE: It's just so hard..., I mean, I was just a little nearsighted. Now this...

ANGEL: I know. Life is full of surprises.

RAFE: I died?

ANGEL: No. Your heart just stopped.

RAFE: I remember...I remember something white....And a face...some face, sort of like yours.

ANGEL: Your brain was running a little short on oxygen. Doesn't know how to interpret that. Not exactly hallucinations, but related.

RAFE: Oh.

ANGEL: It's called "Near-Death Experience." Most people see some kind of white tunnel, faces of dead relatives, maybe religious symbols. You a religions man, Mr. Johnson?

RAFE: Used to be. Not so much anymore.

ANGEL: Well, people who get close to the edge sometimes change a little. You can deal with that later though. You get some sleep now.

RAFE: Who are you?

ANGEL: Oh, I'm the angel you brought back from heaven. But you need to sleep now. We can talk later. I'm not going anywhere. You sleep now.

She touches his forehead. He slowly falls asleep. Lights fade.

SCENE TWO

> The hospital room, later that day. RAFE is asleep. ANGEL is reading a book. She finds something very amusing and laughs aloud.

RAFE: What?

ANGEL: Oh, sorry. I didn't mean to wake you.

RAFE: What? Who? Oh. I thought I was having this really bad dream.

ANGEL: Nope. It's real. Welcome to reality. Not one of your better days.

RAFE: No. I guess not. (Pause.) You know, you're going to find this really funny, but I dreamed you said you were an angel I brought back from heaven.

ANGEL: Yep, that's me. Just call me Angel of the Morning. A.M. for short.

RAFE: I think one of the drugs they are giving me is messing up my mind.

ANGEL: No. You're a little slow on the uptake, but all the bells are still ringing.

RAFE: I'm afraid I....

ANGEL: I'll try to make it simple, OK? Happens sometimes when somebody shows up that really needs to go back. Anyway, I was working reception, and you came zooming in, latched on like I was mommy in a thunderstorm, and then got pulled back with me in tow. Sometimes it's better to just go with the flow, you know?

RAFE: So I...?

ANGEL: Well, in metaphor. It's all a metaphor. Like the Pearly Gate isn't really made of pearls. Doesn't need to be. For that matter, it's not really a gate. That's just a metaphor for a really great entrance to something, you know? It just sounds so good. Or at least it did back when cities had gates. Now days cities are too big for walls and gates. Wouldn't do much to stop a missile anyway, would they? Sorta makes people miss the point, doesn't it. You know, you guys really need to update your metaphors.

RAFE: Uh, listen, I just had a heart attack yesterday, I think, and I'm not real clearheaded right now, so could you....?

ANGEL: What?

RAFE: I'm not sure. I'm not sure what I want you to do. Maybe get me a nurse.

ANGEL: Why? They're reading all these little gizmos you're hooked up to. They take care of you by remote. Nursing without the personal touch. You want some water? I can pour you a cup of water.

RAFE: Yeah, sure. That would be nice.

ANGEL: Use the hand without the tubes.

RAFE: Oh. Thanks.

ANGEL: Anything else?

RAFE: No, not right now. Thanks.

ANGEL: Sure.

    Pause.

RAFE: What are you reading?

ANGEL: Oh, Augustine. City of God. We don't get to..., I mean, there's no rule against reading these old heretics in heaven, I mean, it is heaven after all, but I thought, while I was down here..., I mean, after all, it is different down here and he is pretty funny. Helps me pass the time.

RAFE: I think that is the first time in the history of the world that Augustine has been described as "funny."

ANGEL: You read him?

RAFE: Not since college. Which was a long time ago.

ANGEL: Only in human years.

RAFE: Which is the only kind I know.

ANGEL: Yeah. You are still kind of limited, aren't you?

RAFE: So angels know so much more?

ANGEL: Nah, not really. We're just the messengers, you know, the errand boys. In a few years Fed Ex will be bidding on the contract. (Pause.) That's a joke.

RAFE: Forgive me. I still have this nagging sensation that the smart-mouth angel I'm talking to is some sort of drug-induced experience. Have a heart attack, almost die, get pumped full of diethyltholidomide heptopentathal dimorphine or whatever, and see God.

ANGEL: God? Where? (Pause) Just kidding.

RAFE: My only problem is that I never had this much of an imagination, so I have trouble believing even my oxygen-starved brain could come up with anything like this.

ANGEL: Nobody slipped ecstasy into your IV, OK? You had to come back for something, and pulled me along for the ride. I'm here as long as you need me, OK? I may duck out for a minute or two to check in upstairs, but other than that, I'll be here. I don't fly or bring down brimstone from the sky, I don't know the future, and my big miracle is not being seen or heard by anybody else unless I want to be. But I'm here, I want to help, and I'll do what I can. OK?

RAFE: OK.

ANGEL: Now I hear them coming to take you for an MRI, so let's just pretend that I'm not here for awhile, OK.

RAFE: Just the ramblings of a sick old man, that's you.

ANGEL: Shush.

    Knock on door. Light fade.

SCENE THREE

> RAFE's house, the living room. ANGEL is helping RAFE inside. She wears very plain clothes, basic pants and top. RAFE wears pants and a shirt.

ANGEL: OK, now just sit down a minute and let me go get the suitcase out of the car.

RAFE: I feel fine. I don't need to be pampered like a baby.

ANGEL: Just sit down a minute, OK?

> RAFE sits in an armchair; ANGEL goes out. He looks around. Picks up the TV remote control from the end table, then puts it back down. ANGEL enters with a suitcase and an armful of newspapers and mail.

ANGEL: I picked up your mail and the papers. And no neighbors saw stuff just floating through the air, OK? I'm not just not seen, I'm not even noticed when I don't want to be.

RAFE: If that stuff was out there, I'm amazed the place hasn't been burglarized. Leave a place vacant for three days and every robber in town knows your name, address, and phone number.

ANGEL: Guess they took the weekend off. Here, you see if you won the Publisher's Clearinghouse Sweepstakes and I'll put your suitcase up.

> She hands him the mail and newspapers, then takes the suitcase to the bedroom.

RAFE: Huh. That would be a major miracle. Can you do that kind of thing?

ANGEL (off): Not me. Entirely different department.

RAFE: My luck, I get an angel that can't do miracles.

ANGEL (off): I heard that.

RAFE: Well, what can you do? Besides not be noticed.

ANGEL (entering): I can open a can, if you have any food around here. I can even heat stuff, if you have a microwave. I'm not a real high-tech angel, but I can read directions, set a timer, and push the start button.

RAFE: Do you eat?

ANGEL: I can. But just for the sensation, for the taste. I mean, it's not like I have to, you know. I don't mind being sociable though, if you want company at meals. I'll go see if there's anything in the fridge that's on your new diet.

RAFE: Wait. Sit. I want to talk. There are no nurses or doctors or anybody else here. I have slept more in two days than I usually do in a week. No drugs are being poured into me. The doctor's say my head and my heart are both working just fine. And now I want you to sit down and answer some questions.

ANGEL: If I can, sure.

RAFE: Let us assume, just assume, that I died, went to heaven, grabbed the first angel I ran into, and came back. My doctors examine me down to the cellular level and pronounce me healthy. Even my vision is 20-20. I am now back in my own home. Why are you still here?

ANGEL: Because you still need me.

RAFE: For what?

ANGEL: To help you do what you came back for.

RAFE: Which is?

ANGEL: I have no idea. I'm only an angel, not You Know Who.

RAFE: Somehow you aren't like the angels in the paintings.

ANGEL: Hey, if Lucifer had known what was going to happen, do you think he would have started that rebellion? What makes you think I know the future any better than you do?

RAFE: No, I guess not. (He begins to pace around.) So, do you have any idea how I am supposed to know what to do? What this grand destiny is that temporarily exiled me from heaven?

ANGEL: You're know it when you see it. At least that's the old saying.

RAFE: OK, OK. You don't know the future. What about the past?

ANGEL: Well, within certain limits.

RAFE: This crucifixion and resurrection thing?

ANGEL: Oh, that's a very true metaphor.

RAFE: "A very true metaphor"? What exactly does that mean? Did it happen or didn't it?

ANGEL: Well, yes and no.

RAFE: Yes and no? What kind of an answer is that?

ANGEL: The people who wrote that believed the world was flat and floated on the back of giant turtle, OK? Osirus and Dionysus had already come back from the dead, so it wasn't as big a deal as we think it was today. The Apostle Paul thought there were seven heavens and he had already been to the third heaven and back. Even you've come back from the dead, remember?

RAFE: But...

ANGEL: It's all metaphors. What matters is what it means. You live in a world of big bangs and string theory. You've seen the earth from the moon. The complete DNA for a human being is on the Internet. You know how the sun fuses hydrogen. Back then the sun was a god. Smoke was a way to get a message to heaven. Everything was a mystery. You can't think about things the same way they did 2000 years ago, too much has changed. You have to figure it out for your frame of reference. Go back to first principles. Update your metaphors.

The doorbell rings. GLORIA's voice comes from offstage.

GLORIA: Rafe? Can I come in?

ANGEL: Remember, I'm not here.

The doorknob turns and GLORIA (RAFE's ex-wife, 40's) enters.

GLORIA: Oh, there you are. I thought you'd be in bed.

RAFE: Somebody has got to start locking doors.

GLORIA: I was worried. I came to check on you. Thought you'd be in bed. When I came to see you in the hospital, you were out like a light. How did you get home?

RAFE: I drove.

GLORIA: Was that safe? So soon after a heart attack?

RAFE: I did not have a heart attack. I had a heart stoppage. Evidently there is a difference.

GLORIA: You could have called me.

RAFE: I could have done a lot of things. I could have taken a cab. I could have called somebody who doesn't actively hate me. I could have jumped in front of a bus since I was at the hospital anyway. I chose to drive since my car was already there.

GLORIA: I am trying to be nice to you. The nurses told me you almost died.

RAFE: I did die. (Pause.) It just doesn't seem to have made any difference. I died and came back, and I still feel like a betrayed ex-husband.

GLORIA: Rafe, please.

RAFE: I'm sorry. I'm not letting you salve your conscience. You came to see if the man you loved for twenty years was sick. It makes you feel thoughtful and considerate. I have no manners. Please, sit down and remind me of my frailty some more.

GLORIA: Are you…?

RAFE: You will be disappointed to know that except for the fact that my heart stopped for about six minutes, I am healthy as a horse. No detectable heart damage, no detectable neurological damage. It wasn't even technically a heart attack since there wasn't an artery blockage. Just a little electrical thing in the signal to contract my heart. Except for the fact that I keep having visions of angels and can now see without my glasses, I am just the man I used to be. I am a medical miracle but still a social disaster. How is Jody? What did you tell her?

GLORIA: Did they say anything about if…?

RAFE: If it might happen again? They said a whole lot, but it all amounted to "We don't know." How is Jody? This must really be scary for a 10 year old.

GLORIA: Very worried about her father. I told her you had a heart attack but seemed to be recovering.

RAFE: Can I see her? It might help her. To see me.

GLORIA: Call her tonight. After six.

RAFE: That's not the same as a hug. She's just a little girl.

GLORIA: You know the rules.

RAFE: I almost died. And still no pity.

GLORIA: Let me think about it.

RAFE: At least my heart started beating again. What's your excuse?

GLORIA: I was married to you for twenty years. That kills a lot of things. Call me if you decide to die again, I need time to get a new dress for the funeral.

GLORIA exits.

ANGEL: Well, that was interesting.

RAFE: The ex. For almost a year now. Some of the wounds are still a little raw.

ANGEL: So I gathered.

RAFE: If I got sent back to make up with her, you might as well take me back to heaven now.

ANGEL: Not my call.

Pause.

RAFE: And what are you a metaphor for, my dear little angel?

ANGEL: I'm not a metaphor; I'm a personification.

RAFE: Ah. Of course. How silly of me. Do you think you could personify a cook long enough to heat up a little tomato soup?

ANGEL: I'll see if I can coax a miracle out of cans, pans, and heating elements.

RAFE: That would be appreciated.

ANGEL: What's an angel for?

She exits to kitchen. RAFE picks up the TV remote control again, then puts it slowly back down without turning the TV on.

RAFE: She didn't even bring a casserole.

The lights fade.

SCENE FOUR

That evening. RAFE on phone.

RAFE: No, I'm fine, Jody honey. Yes. The doctors all say it shouldn't happen again. No, now listen, if I was really sick, would your mother still be so mad at me? If I was dying, even she would let me see you. Yes, I love you too. I wish I could be there, but you know what the situation is. I know. I love you, with all my heart. As soon as I can. You be good. I love you. Yes. Hugs and kisses. X X O O to you too. Bye.

He ends phone call and puts cell phone down. ANGEL enters.

ANGEL: Kitchen's all cleaned up.

RAFE: It occurs to me that hating the woman who bore me the only person who still loves me is somehow incongruous.

ANGEL: Tough phone call?

RAFE: It was so good to hear her voice and so painful not to be able to touch her. I want to walk in the room and make her eyes light up. I want to hug her and kiss her cheek. I want to dry her tears and make her smile. She is my daughter. I want to hold her hand, not some damn plastic phone.

ANGEL: Must have been a hell of a breakup.

RAFE: The lawyers had to get lawyers.

ANGEL: Yikes.

RAFE: Both sides got cited for contempt of court, and then the judge got censured later for his "intemperate" remarks from the bench. Big bloody mess. She admitted to infidelity and still got exclusive custody of the kid, so you can guess I must be one hell of a bastard.

ANGEL: Sure sounds that way.

RAFE: You sure you're an angel from heaven? There's a lot of sworn testimony that I should have been headed for the other place.

ANGEL: No, I checked my ID badge; I'm one of the good guys.

RAFE: Well, that makes one of us.

The doorbell rings.

RAFE: Must be that preacher who called.

ANGEL: You want me to wait in the kitchen?

RAFE: Naw, just stay behind me so I don't see you cracking up.

He opens the door. HAPPY AMES enters. She is in her 30's and wears a sweat suit.

HAPPY: Mr. Johnson? I'm Reverend Ames, from the church. We spoke briefly on the phone.

RAFE: Yes, yes. Come in. Have a seat.

HAPPY: Excuse the clothes; I just got out of the gym. They had this new Stairmaster I wanted to try, and I ended up running a little late.

RAFE: No problem. Uh, what happened to Rev. uh, what was his name?

HAPPY: Hal Stanley? Oh, he left over a year ago. Was called to a church in Miami.

RAFE: Well, guess that shows how long since I've been to church.

HAPPY: Actually, Mr. Johnson, I think it's been much more than a year. You aren't even on the active member rolls anymore. But you listed us on your hospital form and the chaplain called the church to let us know there had been an emergency. I came by the hospital on Saturday, but you were asleep.

RAFE: Sorry you made the trip for nothing.

HAPPY: Oh, no. Mrs. Tallis was there too. Do you know her? She had twins.

RAFE: No, I can't place the name.

HAPPY: Well, anyway. I stopped by. When I checked again they said you were discharged, so I....

RAFE: Yes.

HAPPY: I hope you don't mind my dropping by. Sometimes where there has been a crisis of some kind, it helps to talk.

RAFE: Talking seems like all I have been doing. Let me be blunt, Rev., uh,...

HAPPY: Call me Happy.

RAFE: Happy?

HAPPY: Weird name, isn't it? My grandfather served under General Hap Arnold in World War II. Became a family name. My full name is Hap Patricia Ames. Hap sounded too masculine, so they called me Hap Pat, then Hap P. then plain old Happy. Happy Ames, that's me. Just glad my last name isn't Trails or Days.

RAFE: Happy Trails?

HAPPY: You know, Roy Rogers, (sings) Happy trails to you, until we meet again, Happy trails to you, keep smiling until then...

RAFE: Right.

HAPPY: Anyway, you can call me Happy.

RAFE: Well, Happy, I don't know what the nurses told you at the hospital, but when I had my little episode, I did not see God and I did not get religion. I did run into this smart-mouth little angel who keeps saying something about updating my metaphors, but I don't think that's enough to get me back in a pew just yet. My being on the church rolls was mostly pro-forma anyway; it was the wife and kid who showed up on Sunday. And they live across town now.

HAPPY: Oh. I'm sorry.

RAFE: She is a Rahab who breached the walls and left us infidels to burn, so don't be too sorry. But then, you probably don't look at it from the Canaanite point of view.

HAPPY: You were doing the best you knew how and got shafted by a woman who ran off and left you to face the wrath of God alone.

RAFE: Something like that.

HAPPY: But you're still here, Mr. Johnson.

RAFE: And evidently will be for a while. Something else yet to do, I fear. Still, do you have a form I can fill out to specify what I want at my funeral, you know, songs, scripture, that kind of thing?

HAPPY: I don't have one with me, but we do have that kind of thing. I can arrange to get you one, if you would like.

RAFE: That would be very kind.

HAPPY: You know, Mr. Johnson, most people don't know who Rahab was.

RAFE: I read the bible once. Too much knowledge is a dangerous thing. I'll look forward to receiving that form, Rev. Happy.

HAPPY: Ah, yes. I will take care of that tomorrow. Please feel free to call me if there is anything else I can do. Here's my card. It was nice to meet you, Mr. Johnson. Maybe we'll see each other again.

RAFE: Life is full of surprises.

HAPPY: Yes. Isn't it? Goodbye.

He lets her out the door, she exits.

RAFE: Happy?

ANGEL: Reverend Happy.

RAFE: "Don't worry, be Happy."

ANGEL: "Thursday, Friday, Happy Days"

RAFE: They have sitcoms in heaven?

ANGEL: Well, not the stuff on WB. (Pause.) That's a joke.

RAFE: Oh. (Pause.) Where do people like her come from?

ANGEL: She was trying to be nice.

RAFE: She gets paid to be nice.

ANGEL: So, do you get paid to be mean?

RAFE: Actually, yes. I'm an actuary. I calculate the odds of dying or getting injured. It calls for a certain detachment. (Sits.) Oh, man, I'm getting tired. Got used to the hospital schedule; sleeping pill at nine, then wake you up at five to stick a needle in your arm. Do angels sleep?

ANGEL: It's one of the pleasures we can indulge in if we choose, but it's not a requirement.

RAFE: So, what do we do here? That sofa does not pull out.

ANGEL: Well, I was sort of hoping you'd let me crawl in with you. If you think you're up to it. I think that would be very good for your heart, don't you? Confirm that you really are back to normal. Reassure you of your masculinity. My good deed for the day. What else are angels for?

RAFE: I didn't think that would be one of the pleasures you could indulge in.

ANGEL: I keep telling you, you have to redefine your metaphors. Have to go back to essences and first principles. Things change in 2000 years.

RAFE: Yeah, now we have HIV and 37 other STDs they didn't have then.

ANGEL: Hey, if sex with an angel isn't safe sex, what is?

RAFE: I'm going to have to check with the CDC on that one.

ANGEL: Oh, come on, before you get too tired.

    She pulls him out of the room. The lights fade.

SCENE FIVE

        The living room, the next morning. RAFE struggles in wearing a bathrobe. He sits in the armchair. His phone rings.

RAFE: Hello. Ah, yes, hello Happy. No, no, I was already up. Yeah, sure, drop it off. I'm probably not going to have any clothes on for another hour or so, but I don't mind if you don't. Sure, Happy, whenever. Bye.

        Hangs up phone. ANGEL enters, fully dressed in her regular clothes.

ANGEL: Who was that?

RAFE: Our Happy Preacher Woman. Wants to drop off that form I asked for.

ANGEL: Well, that's service. You want some breakfast?

RAFE: I guess. You want me to cook? I make a mean bowl of cereal.

ANGEL: No, I don't mind.

RAFE: I just want it clear that I can take care of myself.

ANGEL: Nah, let me. Another one of those things I don't get to do much.

RAFE: Ah, yes. Well, have it your way.

        ANGEL exits to kitchen. RAFE picks up his phone and clicks a number on his list.

RAFE: Susie? It's Rafe. Ah, I'll be OK in a few days. No, not yet. Doc said take it easy for a while. Besides, I've got to see a preacher about my funeral. No, no kidding. Just the paperwork. Busybody from my wife's old church. Fill out the forms but leave the date blank. Yeah, would you pass the word around the office that I'll be out for a few days, probably. Have to see the doc at his office Friday, go from there. Yeah, thanks.

        He hangs up. ANGEL enters.

ANGEL: How about oatmeal? Unclog those arteries.

RAFE: I hate oatmeal. I know I don't have any oatmeal.

ANGEL: Oatmeal it is then.

        She exits back to kitchen.

RAFE: I don't have oatmeal.

ANGEL: (Off.) You have Special K, that's close enough for an angel.

RAFE: Can you turn water into wine?

ANGEL: (Off.) No, but I can turn steak into hamburger.

RAFE: (Quietly) Another useless skill.

ANGEL: (Off.) I heard that.

The doorbell rings. RAFE opens the door. It is HAPPY.

HAPPY: Well, I half expected you to be naked.

RAFE: Disappointed?

HAPPY: Nothing I can't live with.

RAFE: You got here quick.

HAPPY: I just live three houses over.

RAFE: I make it a point not to know my neighbors.

HAPPY: So I hear.

RAFE: Uh-oh. Who have you been talking to?

HAPPY: Can I come in, or do you like the fresh air?

RAFE: Whatever makes you happy.

HAPPY: Very funny. You want to guess how many time's I've heard that?

RAFE: Five thousand two hundred and twenty-six.

HAPPY: Way low. But that's neither here nor there. Mr. Johnson, I want to be frank with you...

RAFE: I'm not into kinky stuff.

HAPPY: You know what I mean. I've spoken to your former wife.

ANGEL enters and stands in the background.

RAFE: You want to preach a sermon, go to your church.

HAPPY: I called her last night; just to let her know I had spoken to you.

RAFE: And I'm sure she did plenty of speaking to you.

HAPPY: I just thought it was my obligation to hear the other side of the story.

RAFE: There is no other side of the story. I don't know what my ex-wife told you, but if it was bad, I'm sure it was true. Did she tell you we were made for each other?

HAPPY: You put me in a difficult position.

RAFE: You would prefer the missionary position?

HAPPY: Would you listen to me?

RAFE: Why? So you can recite my marital sins for me?

HAPPY: I'm not sure I want your funeral at my church.

RAFE: How un-Christian of you. Almost Catholic. I would think that even unrepentant sinners who have the decency to die ought to get a Christian burial. Maybe we can compromise and have a combination exorcism and funeral.

HAPPY: This is not funny.

RAFE: It is to anybody who doesn't care about your stupid, nitpicking, pharisaic rules. And I hate to burst your bubble, Happy old girl, but most people don't give a good god damn about you, your church, your rules, or your god. Ninety percent of the world thinks you are the pagans and infidels, and the rest just don't give a damn. So if you want to be self-righteous, go somewhere else.

> The doorbell rings.

RAFE: What now?

> He opens the door. GLORIA enters.

RAFE: Hell, two of them.

GLORIA: Two? Oh. You must be Happy.

RAFE: No, right now she's grumpy.

GLORIA: I'm Gloria Johnson. We spoke last night on the phone.

HAPPY: Yes, I remember.

RAFE: How could you forget? (To GLORIA) You will be disappointed to learn that she has decided that she can't bury me, so I won't be allowed to die again. One death per person, that's the limit.

GLORIA: If you ignore him, he doesn't go away, but it helps a little.

HAPPY: I just came by to drop off the funeral service planning forms.

RAFE: And to hear my side of the story. She didn't believe anybody could be as weird as you said I was. I've almost got her convinced that you were right.

HAPPY: He's certainly trying to.

GLORIA: You'll never know the half of it.

HAPPY: I'm sure I don't want to.

RAFE: Could you two girls take it outside. It irritates me to be gossiped about in my own living room.

HAPPY: Maybe I had better be going.

GLORIA: I'll go with you.

RAFE: What did you come over for?

GLORIA: None of your business.

RAFE: You came to my house and it's none of my business?

GLORIA: Damn right!

> GLORIA and HAPPY exit. RAFE slams door behind them, then sits in armchair. Long pause.

ANGEL: It's just curiosity, but what did you do?

RAFE: Well, I guess the straw the broke the camel's back was tattooing "Property of Rafe Johnson" just above her pubic hair.

ANGEL: Oh. I can see how that would upset her. How did...?

RAFE: She took sleeping pills one night. I didn't even have to turn off the light. I had borrowed a tattoo needle and some cream that numbs the skin, and...

> Sound of a teakettle whistling.

RAFE: If you don't take that off the stove, it will eventually boil dry and melt all over the burner. Stinks like hell.

ANGEL: I wouldn't know.

> She exits to kitchen. Sound stops.

RAFE: I would.

> Lights fade.

SCENE SIX

> Later that morning. RAFE is sitting in the armchair, sipping coffee. ANGEL enters.

RAFE: Well, well, look who's back. I went to the kitchen and it was empty. I wasn't sure if you would come back. Women seem to have a habit of leaving me.

ANGEL: I went to look something up. I don't often look at the database. Whole different department.

RAFE: Database?

ANGEL: Book of Life, whatever. Pick a metaphor. It's all metaphors.

RAFE: Oh, yeah.

ANGEL: You know, angels are messengers, not judges. I just do my job. I take care of people who come to heaven. I'm not going to say what you did was right or wrong. I don't even know right from wrong.

RAFE: I do. That's Eve's gift. We have eaten of the tree, and we are as gods.

ANGEL: You know, not talking to her for a month was a little much.

RAFE: I had nothing to say to her.

ANGEL: Taking your daughter to a movie and not coming home for two weeks?

RAFE: It was "Honey, I Shrunk the Audience." They only show it at Disney World. Best two weeks I ever had. Rode every damn ride, even Dumbo. Saw every show, every animal, every 3-D movie, saw fireworks every night, ate every kind of foreign food at Epcot, even did all the computer stuff at Innovations. Hell, we even played miniature golf at Disney World. Can you imagine going to Disney World and playing miniature golf? Do they have miniature golf in heaven?

ANGEL: If that's your idea of a good time.

RAFE: Spending two weeks with my daughter is what I consider a good time.

ANGEL: Judge seemed to think you could have at least called and told your wife where you were. She evidently got a little worried. Something about calling in the FBI.

RAFE: What, call and disturb her little affair? Take her from the comforting arms of her lover?

ANGEL: Cost you any chance at shared custody. Not even any unsupervised visits.

RAFE: I wasn't going to get custody anyway.

ANGEL: So, Gloria found comfort in somebody else's arms, you acted very badly, she divorced you and got a court order for you to stay away from Jody.

RAFE: Not a true Greek Tragedy, but a bad example of hubris none-the-less.

ANGEL: In the database, your record has three asterisks and four footnotes. That's close to a record.

RAFE: Do I get a plaque to hang on the wall?

ANGEL: No. But I thought you'd find it interesting.

RAFE: See anything in that record about why I'm back?

ANGEL: No. Things only get entered after they happen. At least in that database. There may be others; I'm not sure.

RAFE: No measurements of the thread of life?

ANGEL: Not my department.

RAFE: What is your department?

ANGEL: Admissions.

RAFE: Ah. So, shepherding rejects from heaven is not part of your normal duties.

ANGEL: We get a little contingency training for this kind of thing. Part of working the front desk.

RAFE: Wish you had been off that day?

ANGEL: Naw. Comes with the territory.

RAFE: Wish you had slept somewhere else last night?

ANGEL: Depends. You still respect me?

RAFE: Well, you're the best angel I ever slept with.

ANGEL: I can live with that, for now. There's a crack in that steely heart somewhere. I just have to find it before you die again.

RAFE: Which reminds me, guess I better fill out that form for Happy. Wouldn't want to die and leave her speechless. Wonder how "Born to be Wild" sounds on a pipe organ.

ANGEL: What makes you think some little old lady organist would play it?

RAFE: Yeah, nobody's going to listen to me any more when I'm dead than they do now. I'll fill it out and send a copy to Jody though; she'll get a kick out of it. Wouldn't want to die without giving somebody a laugh.

    Lights fade as he writes.

SCENE SEVEN

HAPPY's office, a few days later. She is working at her desk. The phone rings.

HAPPY: Yes? OK, send him in.

RAFE enters, trailed by ANGEL. She is wearing a California Angels sweatshirt.

HAPPY: Mr. Johnson, come in.
RAFE: I just wanted to drop off these forms.
HAPPY: Yes. Thank you. Have a seat.
RAFE: I don't want to take up your time. I told the secretary...
HAPPY: No, sit. I want to look at these.
RAFE: Suit yourself. (Pause.) I sent a copy to my daughter.
HAPPY: You realize some of these requests are a little unusual.
RAFE: Just do what you can. I promise not to sit up and complain. Gloria will change the whole thing anyway.
HAPPY: Since you are divorced, she will have very little say in the matter.
RAFE: Happy, Gloria will probably write the sermon for you.

HAPPY suddenly starts laughing.

HAPPY: "The Monster Mash"?
RAFE: "It was a graveyard smash." Just the music, you don't have to sing it.
HAPPY: Mr. Johnson, this is supposed to be a funeral, not an oldie's concert. And isn't this music a little before your time? "Born To Be Wild"?
RAFE: It's a classic.
HAPPY: It's still a worship service. We are there to praise God for saving us from death, not reprise the top ten from the last century. We want to celebrate your life, not your death.
RAFE: Well, number one, I am dead at that point...
HAPPY: You know what I mean.
RAFE: And most of the people there will be celebrating my death, not my life, with one or two exceptions.
HAPPY: Maybe a funeral home...

RAFE: And three, how do you know God likes Brahams better than the Beatles? Jesus was evidently a party animal, really popular at weddings and funerals.

HAPPY: I mean, maybe "Bridge Over Troubled Water" or even "My Way." But this....

RAFE: I'm not here to argue with you. You have my request. When the time comes, you can honor it or not. I won't be here to enforce it.

HAPPY: No, you are right. This is your request. There is no need to fight about it. By the time this is needed, I could be at another church thousands of miles away. I will just put it in the files until the time comes and pray that will not be for a long time.

RAFE: Fine.

HAPPY: Fine.

RAFE: Thank you for your time.

HAPPY: You're welcome.

> RAFE exits. ANGEL stays behind. HAPPY stands reading the rest of the form.

HAPPY: "And miles to go before I sleep." I don't know whether to laugh or cry. What a strange man.

> HAPPY puts the form in a folder and then into a filing cabinet.
> ANGEL touches her lightly on the forehead.

HAPPY: "For what is man, that thou art mindful of him?" Why did I suddenly think of that?

> ANGEL exits. The lights fade.

SCENE EIGHT

HAPPY's office, the next day. She is at her desk. The phone rings.

HAPPY: Who? Oh, yes. When's my next...? Not till 11:00? OK, send her in.

GLORIA enters.

HAPPY: Mrs. Johnson, come in. Have a seat.

GLORIA: I understand you have received my ex-husband's idea of a funeral service.

HAPPY: He dropped it by yesterday, yes.

GLORIA: You read it? It's very typical of him.

HAPPY: I scanned it.

GLORIA: And?

HAPPY: And what?

GLORIA: You wouldn't...., no church would do...., or even consider.....

HAPPY: Mrs. Johnson, while I'm sure you have strong feelings about this, since you are his ex-wife, not his wife, I'm not sure exactly....

GLORIA: Even this church has some rules....

HAPPY: Yes, we do. But since you are no longer an active member of this church or married to Mr. Johnson, I don't think you are in any position to....

GLORIA: I'm the god damned executor of his estate!

HAPPY: (Pause.) You're kidding.

GLORIA: Jody gets everything of course, but I'm the executor if he dies before she's of legal age.

HAPPY: I don't understand. I mean, after all the things....

GLORIA: He hates me, but he trusts me. At least as far as Jody is concerned. Nobody else would even care if he had a rock and roll funeral. My daughter deserves a decent funeral for her father. He deserves better too.

HAPPY: I... I guess I.....I mean, I thought playing "Taps" was a nice touch, even on an electric guitar.

GLORIA: He was never in the military! He was 4F! Even the Army couldn't stand him.

HAPPY: Oh.

GLORIA: Listen, you know and I know you can't do half of what he asks for on this form. Unless something, God forbid, happens to me, some accident or something, I will be here to make the changes necessary when the time comes. But just in case, why don't I just go ahead and make some changes in this form, and you can put it in your files. I've even put down some information you can include in your remarks if you want to.

HAPPY: You know, he said you would do that.

GLORIA: What?

HAPPY: "Write my sermon for me" was the way he put it. At the time I thought he was exaggerating but.....

GLORIA: So, I come out the bitch again. Damn him! I ought to just let him make a fool of himself. Coffin with a racing strip and all.

HAPPY: You know, he isn't dead quite yet. This is all just hypothetical.

GLORIA: Damn, do you think he's just pulling our chains?

HAPPY: You would be better able to tell that than...

GLORIA: God damn that bas....

HAPPY: Watch the language, please.

GLORIA: Oh. Sorry.

HAPPY: Even this church has rules.

GLORIA: He makes me crazy even when he's not here. Bastard! Sorry.

HAPPY: I know you're angry, but....

GLORIA: Yeah, yeah. Even after he's dead, he'll find some way to make me look like the bad guy.

HAPPY: You know, sooner or later we all have to take responsibility for our own...

GLORIA: First I'm the slut who broke up the marriage, then I'm the cruel bitch who won't let him see his daughter, now I'm the meddling busybody who won't even let him die in peace. No matter what I do....

HAPPY: I'm sure that....

GLORIA: Did you know he used a hidden camera to make a tape of me having sex with my lover and sold it to one of those porno companies that sells videotapes of "Amateur Swingers"? All over the country dirty old men are jerking off to pictures of me getting laid. How do you think that makes me feel?

HAPPY: I'm not sure I ....

GLORIA: What kind of man could do that to his own wife? I could have had him arrested for revenge porn, but I didn't want Jody to know about it. Hell, I could have had him arrested two or three times, but Jody had it bad enough as it was.

HAPPY: Well, you were....

GLORIA: I mean, if you were married to him, you'd have been out looking for a normal man too.

HAPPY: That is not relevant....

GLORIA: Oh, hell with it. Bury the bastard any way you want to. Just let me dance on his grave, and I'll be happy.

> GLORIA exits.

HAPPY: Oh, God, why didn't you let me be a nurse?

> Lights fade.

SCENE NINE

> RAFE's living room. Later that day. He is sitting in the armchair reading a book. ANGEL enters from kitchen, dressed colorfully in the latest style. She carries a can of Coke and drinks it during the scene.

ANGEL: I'm back. I got a Coke from the fridge. You know, these things are cool. Going to heaven and back calls for a drink. You want one?

RAFE: No thanks. And how is heaven?

ANGEL: Still there. Not much changes unless you want it to.

RAFE: Metaphorically, of course.

ANGEL: Of course.

RAFE: Is there anything about heaven or God that isn't a metaphor?

ANGEL: Well, the universe is pretty real, mostly, sort of. It's kind of what you see is what you get, but only if you look right, you know?

RAFE: Well, that clears that up completely.

ANGEL: You're real. Or at least a real as people get. Truth is real, but only in the abstract. Good and bad are real, but what's good for one person can be bad for another, so they get confused a lot. Now math, math is real. Very literal. You studied a lot of math, didn't you?

RAFE: Why do I even ask?

ANGEL: Look, the universe is here. You're here. Even Big Bangs come from someplace. Math works. What else do you need to know?

RAFE: Yes, silly me, Anything in there about love, redemption, salvation, any of that religious stuff?

ANGEL: If you want it to be.

RAFE: I'm beginning to understand why some angels were kicked out of heaven. Metaphorically speaking, of course.

ANGEL: Literally speaking, if you don't love and forgive, what difference does it make if God does?

> Pause.

RAFE: Tell me about the Flood.

ANGEL: Very wet. Lots of water.

RAFE: I need Sophia, and they send the Muse of One-liners.

ANGEL: Humor is just truth you can't process emotionally.

RAFE: Oh yeah?

> The doorbell rings.

RAFE: Now who could that be?

> He gets up and opens the door. GLORIA enters.

GLORIA: Very funny, you god damned bastard.

RAFE: And nice to see you again too.

GLORIA: You made me look like a meddling fool.

RAFE: I'm doing much better, thank you for asking. And how are you?

GLORIA: Racing stripes, "Monster Mash," "Born To Be Wild!" So I go barging in, only to be informed that you had already told that preacher that I would show up to rewrite your funeral for you. You set me up, damn you.

RAFE: Well, I see you've been reading your daughter's mail again.

GLORIA: When it comes from you, darn tootin'.

RAFE: OK, you read your daughter's mail, try to change the last wishes of a dead man, get rebuked by a minister for sticking your nose where it doesn't belong, and then blame me?

GLORIA: You're not dead yet!

RAFE: Well that certainly isn't your fault!

GLORIA: Oh, go to hell.

> GLORIA storms out, slamming the door behind her.

RAFE: Well, that livened up the day.

ANGEL: You two are quite a pair.

RAFE: It takes a lot of practice to be able to fight like that.

ANGEL: How did you two ever get married?

RAFE: We found each other exciting. Huh, fresh out of college; life was exciting. It actually worked pretty well for a long time.

ANGEL: What happened?

RAFE: Oh, lots of things. I got boring. We had some rather serious disagreements about what was best for the kid. My father died very slowly. I realized there is no Nobel Prize for calculating mortality tables. I had to get bifocals. She kept putting the toilet paper roll on upside down and putting tomatoes in my salad. I became very sad. She couldn't live with sad. I was not permitted to be sad; that would have been her fault. So, I stopped being sad and became just there. I got through each day, I functioned, I kept things together. I just tried to keep going through a rough stretch. For her, that was no way to live. Maybe it wasn't, but it was the best I could do at the time.

ANGEL: So she went looking for a little variety.

RAFE: Actually, she went shopping first. Credit card almost died of exhaustion. Then she tried to become the perfect mother. Drove Jody crazy. Then she went back to work. Where she met what's-his-name.

ANGEL: Ah-ha.

RAFE: Somehow she didn't see tattooing "Property of Rafe Johnson" on her pubic mound as a sign that I wanted her back. After that it got messy.

ANGEL: So I read in the database.

RAFE: Yeah, well, that was probably the censored version.

ANGEL: But your file didn't say what happened to "what's-his-name."

RAFE: Nobody knows. After the bit about the porno tape came out at the hearing, he disappeared. Created his own witness protection program, I guess. Gloria tried to accuse me of having something to do with it, but she was stymied when the detectives she had following me everywhere testified they had me under surveillance around the clock, and I hadn't so much as called his house. Anyway, Gloria went from two men to no men. And now she doesn't dare sleep around for fear I'll contest the custody based on her creating an improper environment for Jody. There's a poetic justice in there somewhere.

ANGEL: How sad.

RAFE: Yeah. How sad.

Pause. The lights fade.

SCENE TEN

> RAFE's living room, a few days later. ANGEL is sitting in the armchair reading PEOPLE magazine and eating bon-bons. RAFE enters, taking off an apron.

RAFE: Needs to cook for about 45 minutes.

ANGEL: Fine. You know, I could get used to this.

RAFE: You could also get fat as a pig.

ANGEL: Naw, angels don't get fat. Pleasingly plump, but not fat. Would you still like me if I had love handles?

RAFE: You're getting to be too human.

ANGEL: I'm trying to domesticate you. Not my fault if that involves a little indulgence. Besides, you look cute in the apron.

RAFE: Whatever happened to "reassuring me of my masculinity"?

ANGEL: OK, OK, do something manly; fart, or read the paper, or watch football, whatever.

RAFE: Angel, huh. Where's the newspaper?

ANGEL: By the sofa.

> The doorbell rings.

RAFE: What now?

> He opens the door. HAPPY is there.

RAFE: Well, Reverend Happy, haven't seen you in days.

HAPPY: All good things must end, I guess.

RAFE: Would you like to come in, or do you enjoy the fresh air?

HAPPY: I need to talk to you alone.

RAFE: Nobody here but me and my guardian angel. Come on in. Have a seat.

> HAPPY enters and sits on sofa. ANGEL moves to sit beside her. RAFE sits in armchair.

HAPPY: This is a pastoral visit, Mr. Johnson. Part of my job. I want to make that clear. This is confidential.

RAFE: Yes, my child. How long has it been since your last confession?

HAPPY: This is serious.

RAFE: Sorry. I haven't been serious since I was dead.

HAPPY: I have a message from your daughter.

RAFE: Jody? Is she alright?

HAPPY: She is fine.

RAFE: OK, OK.

HAPPY: A very nice girl.

RAFE: Thank you. And?

HAPPY: And she misses you and loves you. She sends you hugs and kisses. X X O O, as she put it.

RAFE: That's my kid. When did you see her?

HAPPY: This morning. Your wife asked me to visit. Said she was worried about Jody. Said she seemed sad. Thought she might be worried about you. Evidently your daughter didn't get along too well with the minister at her new church, so I was called. I'm going to put all your names back on the active church roll so all this can be official.

RAFE: I'll send you a donation. How did she look? Is she really worried about me?

HAPPY: She's very pretty. She's letting her hair grow long. And while she misses you, it is not you she is worried about.

RAFE: Huh?

HAPPY: Your daughter asked me to tell you that she is concerned about her mother. She thinks something is wrong with her.

RAFE: Now she notices.

HAPPY: Mr. Johnson! Your daughter is scared. She doesn't know what to do. Her mother is always in the room when you talk on the phone, so she can't exactly tell you herself. She thinks something is very wrong and doesn't know where else to turn. And she's afraid you hate her mother so much you won't even try to help. You have a very scared daughter, Mr. Johnson.

RAFE: Call me Rafe. Everybody else who hates me calls me Rafe.

HAPPY: Rafe, you need to help your daughter.

RAFE: Happy, there is a court order saying I will be arrested if I come within 150 feet of their house. If I go to her school, I would end up in jail for six months. I have to make an appointment to talk to her on the phone. What exactly am I supposed to do?

HAPPY: Find out what is wrong with her mother and help her.

RAFE: In all probability, I am what is wrong with her mother.

HAPPY: Jody doesn't think so. Not this time.

RAFE: Oh great. (Pause.) Did Jody give you any indication what she thinks is wrong?

HAPPY: She thinks Gloria may be sick, but she isn't sure. I couldn't tell anything from just seeing her for a few minutes this morning, but....

RAFE: Yeah.

HAPPY: I have to go back to the church now; I have a funeral in an hour. But I promised your daughter that I would tell her what you said.

RAFE: Oh. (Pause.) Tell her I will try to find out what is wrong. I don't know if I can, but I will try.

HAPPY: I will let her know.

> HAPPY starts to exit.

RAFE: Happy?

HAPPY: Yes?

RAFE: Tell her X X O O from me.

HAPPY: Yes, of course.

> HAPPY exits.

RAFE: You think this is what I came back for?

ANGEL: You'll know it when you see it.

RAFE: What do you think she wants this time, a kidney? My heart?

ANGEL: Well, you did give her your heart once before.

RAFE: Only metaphorically.

ANGEL: I keep telling you that you have to take your metaphors more seriously.

RAFE: I'm not sure I can.

> Lights fade out.

SCENE ELEVEN

> The living room, the next day. RAFE is sitting in the armchair, just staring; ANGEL is gently rubbing his shoulders. The doorbell rings.

RAFE: Bell for round one.

ANGEL: Be gentle. It will confuse her.

> RAFE opens the door. GLORIA is there.

GLORIA: OK, I'm here. What paper do you need me to sign?

RAFE: This will be easier if you come in. I don't feel like letting you sign things using my back as a clipboard. I get too many scratches that way.

GLORIA: OK, OK. (She enters. He closes the door.) Now what?

RAFE: Want a cup of coffee?

GLORIA: No, I want to sign and get out of here.

RAFE: Actually, there's nothing to sign. I lied to get you over here.

GLORIA: What?

RAFE: Seems our friend Happy is also nosey. She is certainly also Grumpy, and maybe also Doc. But she evidently is not Dopy. Under torture she confessed that you seem to be having some kind of health problem.

GLORIA: How did she....? That's none of her business.

RAFE: But she is right.

GLORIA: It's none of your business either.

RAFE: If you can't take care of Jody for a while....

GLORIA: I'm working on that. I will take care of that.

ANGEL: You used to love her.

RAFE: I used to love you. I may hate you now, but it's only fun seeing you suffer when I'm the cause of it.

GLORIA: Well, I hate to take away your pleasure, but you had nothing to do with this.

RAFE: Gloria, would you please tell me what's wrong?

ANGEL: You want to help.

RAFE: I might actually want to help. For Jody's sake at least.

GLORIA: Sorry, there's not much you can do about this one.

RAFE: What is it? For god's sake!.

GLORIA: (Pause.) You do not get Jody back. Not even while I'm in the hospital. I will see to that.

ANGEL: You're trying to be nice.

RAFE: I'm trying to be nice here. I almost die, now you've got god knows what. Jody must be coming apart at the seams.

GLORIA: She doesn't know yet.

RAFE: She isn't stupid. You think she can't tell?

GLORIA: I just found out two days ago!

RAFE: Found out what?!

GLORIA: I've already talked to the lawyers. Even if I die, you do not get custody.

RAFE: God in Heaven, can you give me a straight answer?!

ANGEL: She has bone cancer.

RAFE: Bone cancer?

GLORIA: How did you know? I haven't told anybody.

RAFE: How did I know?

ANGEL: An angel told you.

RAFE: An angel told me.

GLORIA: Yeah, sure. Somebody you met when you died. Right.

RAFE: Actually, yes.

GLORIA: Talk about not being able to get a straight answer.

RAFE: Gloria, for Jody's sake, let's...

GLORIA: What's dying like, Rafe?

RAFE: Oh, you're not going to die.

GLORIA: Fifty-fifty chance, next six months. Only chance is a bone marrow transplant, if we can find a donor.

RAFE: Oh. (Pause.) Well,.. maybe... I....

GLORIA: You don't qualify. We're not the same blood type, remember? But thank you for... well....

RAFE: Jody?

GLORIA: Jody doesn't either. Doctor checked her medical record. She's too much your daughter. They're testing my sister.

RAFE: Gladys in Seattle? You don't like her either.

GLORIA: They're also going to check the donor registries and I'm making a list of my long lost cousins. There also might be a trial using umbilical cord blood. You know what they do, Rafe? They kill your bone marrow with radiation. All of it. Your bones are dead. Your bones die first, isn't that funny? You have no immune system. You're the walking dead. Have to keep you in an isolation room because even a little cold germ would kill you. Then they stick a needle into your arm and drip the new marrow into you. Just a teaspoon or two. And then they pray. They pray the new marrow goes to your bones and starts to grow and spread. They pray the old marrow is really dead, because if it isn't it will start to fight with the new marrow. They pray no germs get in that room. And then they wait. One week. Two weeks. If you're still alive, they stick a big needle right into your bones to see what's there. Maybe your bones have new marrow. Maybe you don't have cancer anymore. Or maybe the match wasn't quite good enough. Maybe your body just couldn't deal with it. Fifty-fifty chance, either way. What's dying like, Rafe? I need to know.

RAFE: Well, I don't really remember much of it. But I'm not afraid of it anymore. I've got a friend in the Admissions Department up there; I'll put in a good word for you. But she's in no hurry; let's work on the staying here part first, OK?

GLORIA: Well, there isn't a damn thing you can do about that. But I have a doctor's appointment in half an hour. Tell Happy I prefer to announce my own impending demise and she should keep her big mouth shut, OK?

RAFE: You need to talk to Jody. I'm sure she suspects something.

GLORIA: I will tell her when the time comes.

RAFE: The time is now, damn it.

GLORIA: Not for me it isn't.

RAFE: Let her help you; she needs to help you.

GLORIA: I can take care of Jody. And you stay away, you hear!

GLORIA exits. RAFE is silent and still for a moment.

RAFE: Damn! (Long pause.) Would you care to explain, metaphorically, how cancer can exist in a universe created by a loving God.

ANGEL: What makes you think cancer is evil, Rafe? Because it kills? You're not gods. None of you lit the stars. If you didn't die, you wouldn't be human.

RAFE: Slowly? In agony? Before our children are even grown?

ANGEL: Einstein once said God does not play dice with the universe. He was wrong. Math is real, remember? You know it's a numbers game. You're the one who figures the odds. The moving photon splits into infinite paths. And chance decides who will see the light. It's what gives your choices meaning.

RAFE: And where is the love in that?

ANGEL: And who said God was just love? God isn't that simple, Rafe.

RAFE: Nothing seems to be simple anymore.

ANGEL: Nope.

RAFE: And where does this leave me? Was I sent back to watch her die? I can't seem to do anything else.

ANGEL: I don't know. You'll know it when you see it.

RAFE: You keep assuming I'm going to look.

Pause. Lights fade.

SCENE TWELVE

    Two weeks later, the living room. The room is empty. The doorbell rings. RAFE hurries in from kitchen; ANGEL enters more slowly behind him, more soberly dressed. RAFE opens door. HAPPY is there.

RAFE: Come in. I've been waiting for you.

HAPPY: She finally told Jody.

RAFE: Well, after two weeks.....

HAPPY: It wasn't easy. There was a lot of crying.

RAFE: How did Jody take it?

HAPPY: Well, she's worried and scared, of course. Strangely, though, she's almost relieved. It's like, OK, it's bad, but it's not my fault and it's not Dad's fault and I know now and I can do something. Though I don't think she has the slightest idea what.

RAFE: She's been fought over too much. Anything that's not about her is a relief.

HAPPY: She asked a lot of questions about the medical procedures, how long they would take, when would they be done. She never asked where she would go or what would happen to her if....

RAFE: She won't think of that until tonight or tomorrow.

HAPPY: Gloria said to tell you that you could call Jody tonight.

RAFE: Oh. OK. I can deal with that. Oh man, these telephone calls get harder and harder. She needs me to hold her, not explain immune systems over the phone.

HAPPY: Your wife has hired a nanny for the time she is scheduled to be in the hospital.

RAFE: Oh really.

HAPPY: I talked to a lawyer in my congregation. That does not give you any grounds to challenge custody.

RAFE: Oh, I wouldn't,... unless....

HAPPY: Yes.

RAFE: It would just make her mad.

HAPPY: Yes.

RAFE: But if....

HAPPY: Yes?

RAFE: The papers are already drawn up. I'll file them if ….

HAPPY: Oh. I see. Do you really think the court.....?

RAFE: I don't know. But I have to try, if...., you know.

HAPPY: If Gloria dies?

RAFE: Yes.

HAPPY: Speaking of death does not make it come, Rafe. It takes some of the fear out of it.

RAFE: "Now I lay me down to sleep; I pray the lord my soul to keep. If I should die before I wake, I pray the lord my soul to take." "To sleep, perchance to dream, aye, there's the rub. For who know wherein that sleep of death what dreams may come?"

HAPPY: You almost died. Do you know?

RAFE: I did die. I keep dreaming of sexy angels who read People Magazine and make oatmeal out of Special K.

HAPPY: Well, that's not very orthodox, but it doesn't sound too bad.

RAFE: No, I guess it doesn't. No, I'm not afraid of dying, if it was just me. But I am scared to death that Gloria and I will both die and Jody will be all alone. That worries the hell out of me.

HAPPY: You know, Rafe. I don't even remember how I ended up being your messenger and Gloria's counselor, but I don't think I will ever do funerals the same way again. You two live life a little too close to the bone.

RAFE: Metaphorically speaking, of course.

HAPPY: Oh, yeah, bad choice of words. Sorry.

RAFE: Well, metaphorically speaking, Happy, my guardian angel over there can't quite figure out why I came back from heaven if it wasn't to help Gloria or Jody, and I can't seem to do either right now.

ANGEL: Hey, leave me out of this.

RAFE: Even the angels don't understand all this. They quote quantum theory and talk about updating our metaphors, but all this is just a mystery to them too. We can calculate things to a few nanoseconds before the Big Bang, but then there's too many variables, too many factors go to infinity. We get back to God and find ourselves dividing infinity by zero. The math is real, but the answer isn't even imaginary.

ANGEL: And isn't that a blessing.

HAPPY: I'm afraid I never got beyond algebra in school. Didn't seem to have much to do with religion.

RAFE: Math is theology, Happy. It's faith that there is an order, that there is a God. That when we count our fingers, the fingers are real and that counting has meaning. And now we must count the days of Gloria's life and trust that the counting has meaning. That somewhere behind all that reality there is a metaphor that is God.

ANGEL: And if God is a metaphor, what is God a metaphor for?

HAPPY: You lost me somewhere, Rafe. You OK?

RAFE: Just tell Jody that I love her and that I want her mother to live. I can't believe I'm saying that, but tell her that you thought I actually meant it.

HAPPY: I will let her know. I think she doubted that.

RAFE: I'm sure she does.

HAPPY: You know, you're almost acting like a decent human being.

RAFE: Don't go into shock, I'm sure it's temporary.

HAPPY: Well, I think you'll survive it. See you later.
RAFE: Thanks, Happy.

>She exits. ANGEL crosses to RAFE and takes his hand.

ANGEL: You worry her.
RAFE: I am beginning to worry me.

>The lights fade.

SCENE THIRTEEN

GLORIA's hospital room. She is in bed. HAPPY is beside her. RAFE and ANGEL enter.

RAFE: I promised not to say anything nasty.

GLORIA: Come to say good-bye?

RAFE: I hope not. I'd have to make a whole new set of enemies.

ANGEL: You used to love each other.

HAPPY: You two used to love each other.

ANGEL: Hey, that was my line.

HAPPY: Seems like, at a time like this....

GLORIA: Jody got the teddy bear. Thanks. She thinks she's too old for it, but it may help her sleep the next two weeks.

RAFE: Everybody needs something to hold on to. I was going to get you one, but the doctor....

GLORIA: I know. Too risky. She's been quite a trooper.

RAFE: Tough little girl. Not so little any more.

GLORIA: Yeah. She'll be OK, no matter what.

RAFE: Yeah.

GLORIA: You know, Rafe, you've done some things to me that were truly unforgivable. I won't lie and say I don't wish this was you and not me.

RAFE: I probably deserve that.

GLORIA: When you almost died a few weeks ago, I almost wished you had. It would have made my life so much simpler. But it would have made Jody so sad.

ANGEL: Keep your mouth shut. Just let her talk.

GLORIA: She's such a good kid. She tries so hard. And we messed up so bad. It's a wonder she can face either one of us. We did OK for a while, but then we really messed up.

RAFE: There were lots of good times.

GLORIA: Taping dance recitals, going to the zoo, teaching her to ride a bike.

RAFE: Yeah.

GLORIA: Rafe, those were things she did with you.

RAFE: You were there too.

GLORIA: Sometimes.

RAFE: Sometimes.

GLORIA: Well, I finally got to have fun with her. After the divorce. All those fights we had about her. I've finally learned ..., trying to prepare her for....either way it goes. I finally got to know her. We had a lot of good talks these last few weeks. After all those years.... I'm glad I told her about this while we still had time to talk.

ANGEL: That's all in the past.

RAFE: That's water under the bridge.

GLORIA: Rafe, did you ever love me?

RAFE: Yes. You know I did. For a long time.

GLORIA: Well, if you remember that love, tell me what it's like to die.

RAFE: You're not going to die.

GLORIA: Fifty-fifty. Not great odds. I know you said you don't remember much, but tell me what you can.

RAFE: Well, it's probably just oxygen deprivation, but dying is like....it's like....dying is going into a dark room, and there's a TV set on. At first it's an old black and white TV, but it gets bigger, like a giant screen, with great color. And the room sort of has this green glow from the TV. And as the TV grows, the room becomes brighter. Then it's like you're in the TV show, and you're in Mayberry or something, where nothing really bad could happen. And there's this angel from the Admissions Department waiting to check you in. And she knows you, she's waiting to hug you like your mother did when you got home from school. And that's as far as I got. Somebody turned the TV off, and I woke up. But it wasn't bad. It wasn't bad. I could have stayed. I wanted to stay. I just had to come back for...something. Finish... something.

ANGEL: Nice metaphor.

GLORIA: Thank you. You made my hands stop shaking.

RAFE: Just sorry that's all I can do.

HAPPY: We'll all be praying.

GLORIA: Pray for Jody too.

HAPPY: Yes. Especially for Jody.

    The lights fade.

SCENE FOURTEEN

The living room, a few weeks later. RAFE is pacing. ANGEL sits on the sofa watching him. Finally, she grabs his hand as he goes by and has him sit on the sofa beside her. She holds him in her arms, stroking him like a baby. Suddenly, the phone rings. RAFE jumps up to answer it.

RAFE: Hello?..........Yes, Happy.......Oh...............I understand..........Jody?..............Yes.............. Thanks for calling........Yes.

He hangs up the phone.

RAFE: Another hour or two, maybe. Jody is with her.
ANGEL: Can you.......?
RAFE: No. Not while Jody is there. And even I'm not that cruel. Oh, damn.
ANGEL: Yeah.

Pause.

RAFE: Could you.....?
ANGEL: Be there to meet her?
RAFE: Yeah.
ANGEL: What about you?
RAFE: I'll be OK. I'm the one who hates her guts, remember?
ANGEL: So why?
RAFE: Oh, say for old times sake. I used to love her, long, long ago. And dying can be scary. Just don't tell her I sent you; she might think she went down instead of up.
ANGEL: You old softy. OK, I'll handle the whole admission myself. You sure you'll be OK alone?
RAFE: Yeah, go on. I've got to take my dark suit to the cleaners, order some flowers, get a haircut. I'll be busy anyway.
ANGEL: OK. Be back in a couple of days.

She heads toward the kitchen.

RAFE: Angel.....
ANGEL: Yes.

RAFE: Thanks. You really are an angel.
ANGEL: Glad you finally noticed.

> She exits.

RAFE: Damn it, Gloria.

> The lights fade.

SCENE FIFTEEN

> The living room. RAFE sits in the armchair. HAPPY enters from the kitchen.

HAPPY: I put the casserole in the refrigerator.

RAFE: I didn't think the minister was supposed to bring a casserole.

HAPPY: These small town traditions seem to have died out lately. Just seemed like the thing to do. When you can't do anything, but you have to do something, take a casserole. I really am sorry, Rafe. I wish I could think of something that would help more.

RAFE: You did a good job at the funeral. Gloria would have liked it. Dignity to the end. Damn it, Gloria!

HAPPY: I hate funerals.

RAFE: Only good thing was getting to hug Jody.

HAPPY: She didn't let go of you from the time you walked in until the nanny took her home after the reception.

RAFE: My arm is still a little numb.

HAPPY: You weren't about to let go either, were you?

RAFE: Just so the feeling is back by the next time she touches me.

HAPPY: I have never seen anybody so happy and so sad at the same time. The tears ran right down into her smile. And the look she gave that nanny when she said it was time to go, ouch! The whole room just went silent as she left. It was like a movie, all it needed was a soundtrack.

RAFE: I will remember that goodbye hug for the rest of my life.

HAPPY: Rafe, are you going to be OK?

RAFE: Yeah. Gloria's OK, I guess. Dying ain't so bad, it's living that hurts like hell.

HAPPY: Jody will be fine.

RAFE: Yeah, I know. If Gloria's lawyers don't screw up too bad.

HAPPY: Oh, that reminds me, I almost forgot. Gloria's lawyer gave me a letter for you when he left the reception. In all the hustle and bustle, I forgot.

RAFE: Oh, God, what now?

> He stands to take the letter.

RAFE: Damn lawyers. Even at a funeral...

> He opens letter.

RAFE: "Gloria has filed the necessary papers for her sister Gladys to get custody of Jody. If you want to challenge this, have your lawyer contact me tomorrow and I will explain why it would be a waste of time and money. You would still be able to call her on the existing schedule."

> He collapses into armchair, tears running down his cheeks.

RAFE: Jody. I'll file to get her back anyway; so Jody knows I tried. I have to try. But I'm never going to see her again am I? I messed up too bad. Gladys will take her to Seattle. I thought that's what I came back for, to take care of Jody.

HAPPY: I'm sorry.

RAFE: Why the hell am I here?

HAPPY: You think that.....?

> ANGEL enters from the bedroom. She is back in the clothes she had on in Scene 3.

ANGEL: The admission went very well. Everything is taken care of, so don't worry. Gloria is just fine.

RAFE: Why am I here? Why did I come back? I didn't want to come back!

HAPPY: Rafe, are you OK?

RAFE: I couldn't save Gloria, I'll never see Jody again, why am I alive?

HAPPY: I know this is hard.

RAFE: Why am I alive?

ANGEL: Why is anybody alive?

HAPPY: Why is anybody alive?

RAFE: God, I sure as hell don't know.

ANGEL: Because Gloria needed to know about death.

HAPPY: Maybe it was to help Gloria, to tell her about death.

ANGEL: Or to hold Jody one more time.

HAPPY: Maybe it was to help Jody through the funeral, hold her one more time. Maybe we're not here to save people, Rafe. Maybe we're here just to be here, just to care.

> RAFE collapses into his chair.

RAFE: Which seminary class did they teach you that in?

HAPPY: Does it sound too much like a preacher?

RAFE: Yeah. It does.

HAPPY: Sorry. Doesn't mean it isn't true.

RAFE: Truth, I have been assured, is real, but only in the abstract. I have yet to figure out what that means.

HAPPY: Maybe we're not supposed to know.

ANGEL: Maybe you do, but don't want to admit it.

RAFE: I'm tired of all this.

HAPPY: Jody still needs your phone calls. So she knows you love her. She will grow up eventually and be able to see who she wants to see.

RAFE: So I should hang around? That puts a lot of pressure on Jody, doesn't it? Grow up right so I will still want to see her?

HAPPY: She can handle it. Better than regrets and what if's.

RAFE: It hurts.

HAPPY: I know.

> RAFE starts pacing around the room.

RAFE: It's not fair. I'm not Job! God can go to hell; I'm not sitting around in sackcloth and ashes. A voice out of the whirlwind is not good enough. You can tell your God to…

HAPPY: Rafe! (Pause) I am neither your wife nor your confessor. You do not talk to me like that.

> RAFE sits in his chair. There is a pause.

RAFE: What are you?

HAPPY: What?

RAFE: You are not my wife or my minister. What are you?

HAPPY: I'm trying to be your friend. You don't make it easy.

RAFE: Part of your job, befriend the friendless?

HAPPY: No. Part of my personally defect. I like lost causes. And you are a lost cause if I ever saw one.

RAFE: Sorry. I guess I work at it too hard.

ANGEL: Amen.

HAPPY: No kidding.

RAFE: I just don't know what to do now.

HAPPY: Job had a second act. Maybe you're here just to live the rest of your life.

RAFE: I told you, I'm not Job.

HAPPY: Maybe you're here just to be here. You never know. Let's wait and see.

> There is a moment of silence and stillness. ANGEL goes into the kitchen and immediately comes back out. This time, HAPPY notices her.

ANGEL: I have to go back now. Got to get back to work. I am going to miss you though. You do make being an angel interesting. Tell you what, I'll look you up when you get up to my neck of the woods in, oh, I guess probably twenty or thirty years, when you finish what you came back for. (She kisses him gently.) And the next woman who comes into your life, well, you treat her like an angel, OK? And don't forget, somebody in heaven loves you. It's been fun. Bye.

>She kisses him on the cheek, then exits out the front door.

HAPPY: Who was that?

RAFE: My angel. My metaphorical angel.

>The lights fade.

>CURTAIN

In Silence and the Dust

Based on the life of the first president of Harvard College, way back in the 1600s, this script was written while I was living in Tuscaloosa, AL. The main historical source, a biography of Henry Dunster, is long out of print, but I somehow managed to get the University of Alabama library to get it on inter-library loan from Harvard. I wasn't allowed to check it out, so spent most of one afternoon and most of a big pile of nickels copying the entire book. Years later I went to Harvard Library and asked the reference desk where the grave of Henry Dunster was. This resulted in a scurrying of several reference librarians, embarrassed that they didn't know, until one of them found the same old book among their collections and gave me directions to a graveyard behind a church just a block or so away. Several of the persons used as characters in the play are buried there, so I was happy to find the site, even if my wife and I had to climb over an iron fence to get out of the cemetery.

IN SILENCE AND THE DUST

A Play By David Davis

Member
All rights & privileges.

David Davis
100 Hunters Ridge Court
Roswell, GA 30076
daviddaviswriter@gmail.com

Copyright 1997 David Davis

CAST OF CHARACTERS

HENRY DUNSTER..President of Harvard College, Late 30's

ELIZABETH DUNSTER..Wife of Henry, Mid 20's

JONATHAN MITCHELL...Pastor of Cambridge Church, Early 30's

CHARLES CHAUNCY..Second President of Harvard

JOHN NORTON..Conference Minister, 47

RICHARD MATHER...Conference Minister, 57

RICHARD BELLINGHAM..Governor of the Colony

JOHN ENDICOTT..Governor-elect of the Colony

MAJOR SIMON WILLARD......Member of the General Court, and Dunster's Brother-in-law

SETTING

The play covers the period from 1652 to 1659. There are five locales, which may be represented by a single set and defined by the lighting, if desired. The description that follows is of a realistic set, but a drastically simplified setting of a rough-hewn table, a chair or stool or two, and a few benches would work as well or better. The main locale is the interior of the President's (Dunster's) home at Harvard. On stage is the great fireplace, with its oven, cooking pots, etc. Before it stand a single, straight-backed chair and two low stools. Nearby is a large, rough-hewn table with benches on either side. Upstage is a large hutch, which holds the silver plates, candlesticks, etc. given to the President of the College for use on special occasions. Next to the hutch is a printing press, the only one in America at the time. Near a window is a small writing desk, a chair, a small bookcase with several large books, a split-log bench, and a candle on the desk. The other locales are Mitchell's study in his house near Dunster's, just off Harvard Yard in Cambridge, a conference/meeting room in Boston, the interior of Mitchell's church, and a whipping ground in Boston. Mitchell's study may be created by isolating the area around the writing table, the conference room by isolating the area around the large table, and the church by lining up a couple of benches like pews. The whipping ground is mostly offstage and does not require any set pieces.

ACT I, SCENE ONE

MITCHELL's study, Feb. 29, 1659. MITCHELL sits at his desk, lost in thought. He is a naturally skinny man who is showing signs of becoming fat. He has a powerful and musical speaking voice, but is pale and soft from spending too much time studying, meditating, and praying. A bible lays open on his desk. After a moment, there is a knock from off-stage.

MITCHELL: Come in.

CHARLES CHAUNCY, the current President of Harvard, enters.

CHAUNCY: I'm sorry to intrude on your grief.

MITCHELL: President Chauncy, come in. Friends are always needed in times of strife and sorrow. Sit down.

CHAUNCY: I grieved when I heard yet another child had been taken from you in infancy. The ways of the Lord are often hard and beyond our understanding.

MITCHELL: Yes.

CHAUNCY: When I served the church in Scituate, I memorized numerous verses to quote on occasions such as this, to bring God's comfort, but I would feel foolish straining my memory to quote scripture to the famous Jonathan Mitchell of Cambridge, who can quote the Bible for hours on end. I am sure you have already found solace in the Word, Jonathan. I come only to offer what poor aid a human can offer after the sad hand of God has taken a child after so few days of life.

MITCHELL: Tis a further sad hand of the Lord that the child should die unbaptised.

CHAUNCY: God is merciful, Jonathan. All may yet be well with its soul.

MITCHELL: Oh, I do not think they are orthodox that hang salvation upon baptism, rather than on the covenant. Yet, because baptism appears to be a sign of confirmation, and because it is an ordinance of grace, to be deprived of it is a sad signal of the Lord's anger. What thoughts and ideas may invade my mind because of this sad occasion, and how they might tend to dishonor the Lord, I do not know. But there seems to be a certain irony, that after all my labors and sermons defending infant baptism, the Lord should take away from me child after child before they could be baptized. This is the way, again and again, the Lord makes me an example of his displeasure. It is as if, before all men, He wanted to say openly that He had a special argument with me. The Lord holds me up and spits in my face.

CHAUNCY: God forgive you. Your grief has let the Devil in. Now my task is doubly hard, to add sorrow to sorrow, grief to grief, to a heart already tempted and troubled by Satan. I am sorry, Jonathan, to bring you more sad news on this day.

MITCHELL: What burden now would you lay upon my breaking back, Charles?

CHAUNCY: Jonathan, Henry Dunster is dead. He died two days ago in Scituate.

MITCHELL: The Lord have mercy! Henry Dunster dead?

CHAUNCY: Aye.

MITCHELL: A great light has gone out, and my heart breaks. Henry Dunster dead, not five years since his fall. This is a sad day indeed. This news troubles many memories in me, Charles, both happy and sad. (Pause) Henry Dunster dead. The Lord have mercy on us all.

    The lights fade.

ACT I, SCENE TWO

Boston, summer, 1652. Offstage or in dark shadow a man is being whipped. We hear the sound of the whip hitting flesh. The man is singing but getting weaker with each stroke of the whip. On center stage we see DUNSTER standing with WILLARD. ENDICOTT, NORTON, and MATHER are also present, interspersed with any extras that may be available.

MAN: (Singing weakly last part of "A Mighty Fortress Is Our God," by Martin Luther.) "Let goods and kindred go, this mortal life also. The body they may kill; God's truth abideth still. His kingdom is forever."

The voice and whip fade into silence. DUNSTER turns and walks away alone. The lights fade.

ACT I, SCENE THREE

DUNSTER's home, Dec. 24, 1653. ELIZABETH DUNSTER enters, carrying a baby. She is obviously angry. She crosses and exits near the fireplace. After a moment, she enters again, alone, and begins cooking in the fireplace. The hard life of New England and four children, two already dead, have aged her beyond her years, but the fire of life has not gone out in her. She is aware of her position in society, but not fooled by it. After a moment, HENRY DUNSTER, the first President of Harvard College, enters, followed by JONATHAN MITCHELL. DUNSTER is unimposing in appearance, medium build, reddish-brown hair and beard, the scholarly academic who spends most of his time in teaching and study. Underneath, however, is the toughness of a man who also chops wood and builds houses if necessary to build his college in the wilderness. They remove their hats and coats.

DUNSTER: That fire will feel good this night.

MITCHELL: Henry, we have to talk about this!

ELIZABETH: Where's David?

DUNSTER: I sent him to eat at the Commons. The presence of the President's son, even if only nine years old, will make any rebellious student think twice about raising a toast to Christmas, yet none will say President Dunster himself had to watch over the students to prevent unlawful mirth. Jonathan here will eat David's share. He seems to think there is some need to discuss theology this night, and if he is to bless us with a private sermon, the least we can do is offer our hospitality.

MITCHELL: There is no need for sermons here. You taught me the scriptures yourself, when I was a first year student. All that I am is due to your teaching. Just tell me when you'll be bringing the child to be baptized. He's two months old already, and winter coming. There is already some talk among the people.

DUNSTER: The child will not be baptized.

ELIZABETH bangs down a pot in anger.

MITCHELL: Henry, President Dunster, you are my beloved teacher, my brother in the Lord, but I am also your minister in the Church. Before God I have a duty to the child…

DUNSTER: What you have, Jonathan, is a burning curiosity that you are trying to disguise as righteous inquiry. Forgive me, that is too harsh. I know you are concerned for the child, and for me and mine.

MITCHELL: I took your naming of the child Jonathan as a sign of the bond of friendship that has grown up between us. It would pain me to think that the same child would be the source of conflict that would tear us apart and endanger the great projects to which we have dedicated our lives, you to the college, and I to the Cambridge Church.

DUNSTER: There is no need for it to come to that.

MITCHELL: If you persist in this error...

DUNSTER: Perhaps it is no error.

MITCHELL: The Church teachings plainly state...

DUNSTER: The church can only teach what is in God's Word. Otherwise it risks corruption and hellfire, for all else is man's wisdom, and subject to error. You were a good student, Jonathan, you tell me; in all of the Bible is there a single specific reference to the baptizing of infants?

MITCHELL: Specific, literal reference? No, but...

DUNSTER: Then I must conclude that infant baptism is an invention of men, not of God. And just as we came to this land to purify our worship of the inventions of the Papists, so I would have the Church pure of all man-made inventions. It should stand solely in the Truth of Christ. Now, I want no controversy, no disharmony among the brethren. I have not stayed President of the College these thirteen years by seeking conflict. But whatever the cost here in this world, I must speak the truth in the fear of God, and I dare not deny that truth, or go from it until the Lord teaches me otherwise.

MITCHELL: You did not always think the truth to be so.

DUNSTER: No, I confess I did not always think so.

MITCHELL: So what changed you?

ELIZABETH: The same as changed you, too many hours in books and not enough hours with people.

DUNSTER: Will you feed us wisdom before bread now?

ELIZABETH: The bread be only half baked, the truth is fully done.

DUNSTER: It is true man lives not by bread alone, but he does not do well on burned pudding either.

ELIZABETH: I best tend to my cooking now, like the dutiful wife that I am. The babe will wake soon, and t'will be a real child needs caring for.

    ELIZABETH crosses back to the fireplace.

DUNSTER: My wife has her own mind, and it cares not for either of ours this night.

MITCHELL: My own wife, in her weakness, at times cares more for her soup than for saving souls. Elizabeth seems to care more for your soul than her soup. You should be thankful for that.

DUNSTER: I am rebuked, and wisely so, my friend. Thank you. Yes, her heart is right, and I would not trade it for a thousand meals, even in the last of winter with only the seed-corn left. She is precious to me. But God loves me as well, and bought my soul from hell with the life of his Son, and to Him I owe a higher duty.

MITCHELL: Then let us test your argument, here, in private, before you risk wife and life and soul upon it. Tell me how you came to it.

DUNSTER: Remember the summer of a year ago, when the Anabaptist from Rhode Island Colony traveled to Lynn to visit their aged friend, and dared to pray and worship with him in his house in their own fashion?

MITCHELL: Aye. Mr. John Clark, Obediah Homes, and a Goodman...

DUNSTER: Crandall.

MITCHELL: I heard of it. They were arrested for holding an unauthorized worship service and promoting dissension or the like. It would have been a minor matter had they paid their fine and gone home, but they refused, and were jailed.

DUNSTER: They considered the law unjust.

MITCHELL: Someone finally paid the fines for Clark and Crandall, but Homes refused even that, forcing the Magistrates to have him whipped before they were all banned from the colony.

DUNSTER: Yes.

MITCHELL: And that set your mind to thinking?

DUNSTER: Yes. I began to wonder what these men believed that would have them choose prison and whipping just to proclaim their faith. I set to study and ponder, searching the scriptures on the matter of baptism. I wanted to find an argument to refute this heresy, so we could counter such men peaceably if such came again. I found there was no such argument.

MITCHELL: You've turned Anabaptist?!

DUNSTER: No, fear not that. I still differ with them on other points. It is on this one point only that I am persuaded, that only visible believers should be baptized, not babes in arms with no understanding. That is the pure scripture.

MITCHELL: Well, the way of the Anabaptists, to admit none to membership and baptism but adults who can profess their own faith, may, on the surface, seem the straightest way. But, experience has proved it to be just the contrary. There is abundant proof that it has let in great corruption to the church, and looseness in both doctrine and practice. You admitted yourself that the Anabaptists fail on many other points. It is a troublesome, dangerous underminer of reformation. The Lord did not set up churches only that a few old Christians may keep one another warm while they live, and then carry away the church into the cold grave with them when they die.

DUNSTER: You speak as if a man who did not join the church as a babe with no choice would never join when he reached his reason. If that be the case, perhaps our sermons and churches are lacking some of the beauty of God, or are failing to reveal the joy of His salvation.

MITCHELL: Say you my sermons preach not God?

DUNSTER: No, Jonathan, take no offense. I am just saying that having church membership depend on one's parent's membership makes no sense. Look at it another way. If a parent's membership makes the children members, then for example, what if some member has a child and that child is baptized in the covenant. Then suppose the parents are excommunicated for some heresy of their own, for, say, seven years, during which time they have four children who are not baptized into the covenant. Then, the parents see their error, repent, and are accepted back into membership. They then have a sixth child, and it is baptized and becomes a church member. Has that logic as far as the children are concerned? Show me where Christ ever indented such a covenant.

MITCHELL: You are a keen man, Henry Dunster, and to this day I can not match you in the art of rhetoric. I am sure that argument will disturb my sleep for many nights before I find its fallacy.

DUNSTER: And if you find no answer?

MITCHELL: I warn you, I am resolved that it will take an argument able to move a mountain before I will recede from, or even appear to be against, a truth or practice received among the faithful.

DUNSTER: But you will think on it?

MITCHELL: Yes, and pray mightily. But think you on this, Henry Dunster. The Court will not take lightly the President of the College speaking against the doctrines of the Church. Baptize the child, and hold your peace for a time. Let me study and pray. If I can find no flaw in your stand, then we can speak to other ministers privately, eventually call a council of ministers to discuss a change in doctrine if all be persuaded.

DUNSTER: I should do what I no longer believe until I can persuade others not to do what I have just done?

MITCHELL: The General Court is full of hard men who will brook no dissension.

DUNSTER: To bear true witness, I must stand in the truth.

MITCHELL: You will not baptize the child?

DUNSTER: I will not.

MITCHELL: Then I fear I must leave you. You are my friend, Henry, but you trouble me with your stubbornness, a stubbornness stirred up, I fear, by Satan to create controversy and divide the Church. Mistress Dunster, I will miss your good meal and fellowship, but I am troubled of soul, and now must study for both the Sabbath and this coming controversy, if I am to hold the church together.

ELIZABETH: Tis sorry I am you go, Jonathan Mitchell. Suppers can be had or not, but friends may be sore needed. Will we be put asunder so by some theology?

MITCHELL: I am not my own man, but God's.

ELIZABETH: Then God forgive us all.

MITCHELL: Amen. God be with you, Henry Dunster.

DUNSTER: And with you, friend Jonathan.

> MITCHELL takes coat and exits.

ELIZABETH: You're a grand fool, Henry Dunster.

DUNSTER: Remember the scripture. "Call no man fool, for as ye judge, so also shall ye be judged."

ELIZABETH: You're a grand fool all the same.

DUNSTER: And why? Will you teach me theology and logic now?

> ELIZABETH begins to serve supper.

ELIZABETH: All I know of scripture and interpretation is what I hear in church. And if one preacher say yea and another say nay, I know not how to choose between them. The ministers say baptize, you say not, and I am no one to decide between learned men. I can but pray God's mercy on the child caught between two such great truths, and the great wrong t'will grow out of it.

DUNSTER: A man must live the truth as he sees it, Elizabeth, or he will need God's mercy on his soul.

ELIZABETH: God have mercy on us now, I say, for the men here will not.

DUNSTER: You fear a little controversy? I do not desire it, but...

ELIZABETH: I fear cold and pain. I fear your ruin and my children's lives. I fear hard men who believe what they believe and will not be crossed in it.

DUNSTER: They would not...

ELIZABETH: And why not? Because you are a minister, ordained of God to speak truth? Obediah Holmes was a minister, and he was whipped. And will I be spared, being a woman? Anne Hutchenson was a woman, and she and her children were banished to the wilderness, and it less settled than now, and the Indians less peaceful. If they banish women and whip ministers, do you think they would hesitate over the President of Harvard?

DUNSTER: There is no cause...

ELIZABETH: You dare to disagree, that is cause enough for them.

DUNSTER: But I'm in the right.

ELIZABETH: Tis not enough. Will my babe care who is right when my milk is dry from hunger, and we shiver in the cold? Will right shelter us when we are cast from hearth and home into snow and ice? Who holds the whip, Henry Dunster, right or the Court?

DUNSTER: God can be hard as well, Elizabeth, and for a much longer time. Would you have me burn in hell for not speaking the truth?

ELIZABETH: No. No, I would have you eat this meal before the cold creeps in, and before the babe wakes and would have his own meal. And I would have peace in this house, for there may be none elsewhere. Now bless the food, and let us eat.

>   DUNSTER takes ELIZABETH'S hand as they bow to pray. The
>   lights fade.

ACT I, SCENE FOUR

>DUNSTER's house, late January, 1654. DUNSTER is reading, ELIZABETH is polishing the silver from the hutch. There is a knock at the door.

DUNSTER: I'll answer.

>DUNSTER carefully puts the book away and goes to the door, while ELIZABETH quickly restores the silver to the hutch. MITCHELL enters, shaking snow off his hat and coat, followed by DUNSTER.

ELIZABETH: Jonathan Mitchell, come over by the fire and warm yourself. You've come not this month or more, the least you will get is a warm reception.

DUNSTER: Give me your coat. It's good you live close by, this is no day for traveling.

MITCHELL: This is no social call, I fear, though I bid you good day, Elizabeth.

DUNSTER: The news can't be too unwelcome, if it brings you back to this hearth.

ELIZABETH: Bad news comes better from a friend than a stranger.

MITCHELL: Have you heard already?

ELIZABETH: No, but the way the talk goes these days, even in my hearing, among the wives, the students, and after the services, there'll be no good news brings you out.

DUNSTER: A cider to warm you? One of the student's country pay is particularly tasty this year.

MITCHELL: No. Thank you. My heart is cold enough, but will not be warmed till this be done.

DUNSTER: Sit then, and say your piece.

MITCHELL: You have been speaking out against infant baptism.

DUNSTER: I have made no issue of it, but have spoken my mind when asked.

MITCHELL: Which you knew you would be when the child was not brought.

DUNSTER: I suspected that some might notice.

MITCHELL: Well, now the lot is cast, and will be hard to recall. Word of your new opinion has gotten around, and someone on the Magistrates has gotten wind of it.

DUNSTER: So?

MITCHELL: The Magistrates have sent an official request to the Council of Ministers, asking us to investigate and advise them. I have a fair copy of the letter, and, well, of the response.

DUNSTER: Must I drag the news from you, like a boy from his games? What was done?

MITCHELL: Let me read it. "In the Name of Christ, the Council of Ministers of the Massachusetts Bay Colony, in response to the express concerns of the Magistrates over the opinions expressed by Mister Henry Dunster, President of the College, that are being bruited about to the prejudice of the College and the scandal of the country, and out of our own extreme agony to rescue that good man from his mistakes, do summon him to a Conference of Ministers to be held at the meetinghouse in Boston this February second, the Lord Willing." Signed, John Norton, Chairman.

DUNSTER: So, we will have a conference to discuss infant baptism after all, and sooner than you expected. This should get some people thinking and searching the scriptures as I have done.

MITCHELL: Mr. Dunster, no, you don't understand.

DUNSTER: Will you have that cider now?

MITCHELL: No! For a smart man who has politicked these very men for College funds these thirteen years, you are suddenly very dense, Henry Dunster.

DUNSTER: I am aware, Jonathan, that the conference will be to correct me, not to freely discuss the issue. I am also aware that my career is subject to these men, and that there is not a whisker's chance of persuading them in this single conference. But, to prepare themselves to refute me, some will read and study, and an eye or two may be opened to the truth. If not now, with the passing of time. It will come. In the meantime, there will be controversy. I do not seek controversy, but my reasons for doing this are not slender and feeble. At least they do not seem so to me. I know they force me to expose not only myself, which is my least concern, but also my family and all we own or care about, especially my work here at the college, which God has committed to me. I care more about the college than I do about myself, and bless God for it. If I did not believe deeply that there was sufficient cause, it would be better for me to leave than to launch out into an ocean of contentions. But I do believe there is sufficient cause. The Truth of God is sufficient cause.

MITCHELL: I did not come here to argue the case, only to deliver the summons. The conference will make the argument. My only hope is to make you aware of the true situation. That is why I brought the Magistrates letter as well. You read near half a score of oriental languages, Henry Dunster. Can you read between the lines of your mother tongue as well?

MITCHELL hands DUNSTER a letter.

DUNSTER: "Reverend Sirs, the Magistrates, having been informed that Mr. Dunster, President of the College, has by his actions and statements opposing infant baptism rendered himself offensive to this government, acknowledge that it is our duty, because of his position and because of the trust committed to us, to correctly ascertain the truth of what we have heard, so that we may discharge our obligations accordingly. We know that you also are concerned in this matter, as we are together with you. Therefore we are assured that you will support and approve our endeavors to prevent or remove anything which might tend to prejudice the reputation of the college or cause scandal to the country. Hence, we believe it suiting to commend this business to your care, so that at our next meeting we may be thoroughly informed of how the matter stands with him in respect to his opinions. Then we will be enabled to understand what may be expected of us. We do not doubt your readiness for this task, and commend you to God. We remain your very loving friends, etc."

MITCHELL: Well?

DUNSTER: They would know if I can be persuaded to hold my peace and say no more.

MITCHELL: Or they'll be removing you from your post.

DUNSTER: That is a decision for the Board of Overseers, not the Magistrates.

MITCHELL: The Board would bend to a whisper of a breeze from the Magistrates, and you know it.

DUNSTER: So I should bend in the gale to save them a little squall?

MITCHELL: I see you are obstinate.

DUNSTER: Or standing firm, depending on your angle of view.

MITCHELL: Then I'll be going now.

DUNSTER: You'll be at Boston?

MITCHELL: Aye. John Norton, Richard Mather, and I will carry the argument. There's more sleep I'll be missing over you, Henry Dunster, not to mention what I have already lost fighting Satan this past month. You have started a rage of contention in the church. Factions are forming, and tis all I can do to hold peace and unity. Satan is dividing and hopes to conquer, and he is using you, Henry Dunster, as his main weapon.

DUNSTER: So, you'll not be drinking the Devil's cider, is that it?

MITCHELL: This is not some college devil that you can drive out with black power flashes and Latin incantations to ease schoolboys on dark Octobers, then chuckle the way home.

DUNSTER: Oh, you remember that, do you?

MITCHELL: Even the Devil feared President Dunster then. But I am no more a boy, and the Devil is no longer wind in the dark. I can walk about in the dark now. It is the light in men's eyes I fear.

DUNSTER: I will save the cider, Jonathan. Mayhaps when this is done we will both be wiser men, and can drink a cup in peace, and chuckle the way home.

MITCHELL: I pray so, for tonight's walk will not be pleasant. God be with you, Henry Dunster.

DUNSTER: And with you, Jonathan Mitchell.

MITCHELL exits. Pause.

ELIZABETH: May I say a word?

DUNSTER: What, only one?

ELIZABETH: This is not for laughing, Henry.

DUNSTER: I'm sorry. Say on.

ELIZABETH: If you'll not consider yourself, consider me and the children. You built this house, but is on college land, and would go with the post. If the college will not have you, nor will any church in the colony. We would have no home, no livelihood, and me with a babe in arms and it the dead of winter.

DUNSTER: They would not put us out in the cold. These are Christian men.

ELIZABETH: Say you.

DUNSTER: Is that your word?

ELIZABETH: Not yet. I have been thinking about your Anabaptists. I care not for them. But one thing from Rhode Island I do admire. There not everyone must believe the same to share the land and peace. Toleration they call it.

DUNSTER: And that is what I do not admire. It is anarchy of faiths, constant contention and a government separated from God. God rules here, if we can but avoid error and keep the faith pure. It is to purify the faith that I struggle.

ELIZABETH: That may be so. But there when they disagree on faith they raise their voices. Here we raise our whips.

DUNSTER: Have you done?

ELIZABETH: No, I'll say one word more. When I married you, Henry Dunster, I was not much more than a girl, and not long off the boat from England. You had put your first Elizabeth in the ground not a year before. My parents had died on the voyage over, and I needed a husband. You needed a wife to run your house while you ran the college, and I was happy to do it, to get such a well set and respected man as the President of the College, a minister ordained of God. You seemed a good man, and that was enough in this hard land of Indians, frozen winters, and many graves. What love there was, I couldn't say. But I've been with you these ten years, and borne four children by you, two that I've already put in the ground. If there was no love to start, you planted a seed, and it has grown. It's more than my duty I'll be doing. I'll trust in God, and let the likes of you and John Norton worry the jots and tittles; and here or there, warm or cold, hungry or full, right or wrong, I'll be by your side, Henry Dunster. I may speak my mind, but my feet will not move from you. I hope that be some comfort to you, for I fear comforts will be few and needed in days to come. But I love you, Henry, fear not that. And now I have had my say and will be quiet.

DUNSTER: Thank you, Elizabeth. I should listen to your words more often. If God be with me, who can stand against me, and if you stand beside me, what have I to fear?

They embrace. The lights fade.

ACT I, SCENE FIVE

The Meetinghouse in Boston, Feb. 3, 1654. MITCHELL, NORTON and MATHER are seated behind a long table. DUNSTER stands before them.

MITCHELL: ...in these two long days of discussion we have grown tired. Satan is trying our patience and love for one another. Please, my friends, what we need is more light and less heat.

NORTON: His eyes are closed to the light.

MATHER: That may be so, John, but if the Devil and Henry Dunster can keep their temper this day, so should we.

NORTON: We have spent two days on this. We have shown him his errors, yet he refuses to mend. We should waste no more time.

MATHER: I am not sure that trying to save a great man from error is ever a waste of time, but I think your point is that we have said all that can be said.

NORTON: Exactly.

MATHER: Mr. Dunster, I would like to thank you for the courtesy and restraint you have shown these past hours. Your argument has been most learned and presented as only a master of rhetoric as yourself could have done. However, by all reason, I think we have clearly demonstrated, based on the Holy Scriptures, a superior position. Just as the Children of Abraham were circumcised as their sign of covenant with God, so under the New Covenant are infants of believers considered visible believers and baptized into the Body of Christ. That is their sign and seal into membership of the Church. If you persist in maintaining otherwise, I do not think our report to the Magistrates can be very favorable.

NORTON: Have you anything more to say before we end this?

DUNSTER: Brothers, I count it no small mercy that the Lord has called me to give an account of the faith and love I bear to Christ and His church and His People. I hold no faith which is not grounded on the revealed Word of God. I believe there is one God, the only maker of all things, who is in Himself full wise and holy and gracious. I also believe He governs the whole world by His Providence, so that no bird or hair falls but by it. So I will stand or fall in the Providence of God. Children have no visible acts of faith, but according to the Gospel they have Christ's express testimony that they have closer access unto Him than children did under the Law. Christ, to support the spirit of parents, gave more specific statements about his good will to children concerning that best and nearest acceptance by Him, namely their eternal salvation, than were ever found in the Law. But all Gospel worship must have some specific basis in Scripture. Infant baptism has none. John the Baptist, Christ himself, not the Apostles, none of them baptized children. They baptized only penitent believers who confessed their sins. Infants who cannot even speak can not be penitent believers who have confessed their sins. We are grafted into Christ by our own faith, not that of our parents. To believe otherwise is a corruption of the faith and should be cast forth. We that care so much for the Church, and so little for ourselves, should be the first to seek to purify the Church from these remnants of the heresy of Rome.

MATHER: And we, because we do care so much for the Church, have striven mightily with you to show how important infant baptism is to the Church. Not only has it replaced circumcision under the Gospel as the mark that sets us apart from the world, and how, like circumcision, it is to be administered to the infants of believers, but we have also demonstrated its necessity as a ritual that builds unity in the Church, and binds believers together in the commitment to care for and raise children strong in the faith. Scripture says that Peter baptized entire households, and from that day to this the Church has been a family dedicated to the care of each new generation. But we have said enough; we repeat ourselves. This church cannot live with dissension. The head must rule. Surely you, President Dunster, with your wide learning and wisdom, would be the first to admit that when all else hold otherwise, true meekness and love of the Church would cause one to hold their tongue outside the private counsels of the Elders, unless they be persuaded.

NORTON: Or is discretion not part of the College course of study?

DUNSTER: I am sure Mr. Mitchell can testify better than I as to what is learned under me.

NORTON: I have no quarrel with your students, Mr. Dunster, only with teachers who forget they are not prophets.

MATHER: Enough, John.

NORTON: Yes, enough. We will adjourn with prayer. Mr. Mitchell, will you lead us.

> All stand and bow their heads.

MITCHELL: Almighty God, be with us this day. Today our hearts are heavy and our minds perplexed, as good men, honest men, men devoted to your Church and the True Faith, find they stand unexplainedly on opposite sides. Bring error to light, and let us reconcile together in one true faith. Keep disharmony far from us, personal feelings out of our minds, that we may keep our Church pure and that false teaching may be refuted by faith and witness, not requiring force of law. By the grace of God, Amen.

MATHER: Amen.

> NORTON stalks out quickly. MATHER starts to follow, then stops.

MATHER: God be with you, Henry.

DUNSTER: And with you, Richard.

> MATHER exits.

MITCHELL: I'm sorry, Mr. Dunster.

DUNSTER: Sorry for what reason?

MITCHELL: You seem not to have altered many minds.

DUNSTER: Change takes time. The seed will grow.

MITCHELL: I would not have it grow. I stand unconvinced. The mountain is not moved. Perhaps you are right that we are inconsistent in our denial of baptism to some. We may need to create some form of half-way covenant that would allow the baptism of children of any who believe enough to request it, though the parents themselves be not admitted in good standing. If it is as important as I believe it is, we should be trying to baptize the many, not the few. But I can not give it up entirely. Such a ceremony of dedication, of the child to God and of the parents and church to its care, is too important to dispense with. Your seed has fallen on barren ground in my soul, as in the others. My sorrow is that standing alone you will bear the entire force of the blow. For these men will not let your seed grow elsewhere. They will stamp the green shoot down while they live. One with a hard word, one with a soft, but stamped to ground none-the-less. No, not while we live.

DUNSTER: Then let it grow from my grave. From silence and the dust I will speak. The truth of God cannot be silenced forever.

MITCHELL: I must go. Give Mistress Dunster my greeting, and David, and a kiss for little Jonathan.

DUNSTER: If you but would, you could give them yourself. It's sorry I am that you don't. Must we agree on everything to remain friends?

MITCHELL: In this world one is counted with whoever they are seen near.

DUNSTER: Wagging tongues are a preacher's chains. I've known them gossip in the stocks when put there for idle hands and busy tongues.

MITCHELL: Fear of gossip kept many a man from wrong.

DUNSTER: And makes much innocence and charity seem guilty.

MITCHELL: I have fought you enough for this day, Henry Dunster. I'll to home now.

DUNSTER: I've a boat waiting at the Charles. Will you share it? Even bitter enemies have been know to share a ferry.

MITCHELL: I will find my own boat.

DUNSTER: I'll not force your company, Jonathan. But know this. I've put that keg of cider away for us, and a new book or two to share came over on the last boat from Plymouth. Both can wait a better day, and be the better for the aging.

MITCHELL: I'll remember, Henry Dunster.

    MITCHELL exits. The lights fade.

ACT I, SCENE SIX

General Court, Boston, May 3, 1654. WILLARD, BELLINGHAM, and ENDICOTT sit behind the table. MITCHELL stands before them.

ENDICOTT: The General Court of the Colony of Massachusetts Bay, Governor Richard Bellingham presiding, convenes this third day of May in the Year of Our Lord 1654, to discuss the matter of the current controversy surrounding the College. May it please the Lord.

BELLINGHAM: Thank you, Mr. Endicott. Pastor Mitchell, I believe you have the report of the Council of Ministers.

MITCHELL: Yes, Governor.

BELLINGHAM: And?

MITCHELL: I greatly regret to report that we were unable to rescue the good man from his mistake. While these three months since the conference have shown him moderate in his speech and diligent in his work, likewise there is no sign that this time was able to expedite the entangled out of the briars of anabaptism.

WILLARD: Say you he has been moderate in his speech on this matter?

MITCHELL: Yes, Major Willard, at least in public. He has not been called to preach in any churches, as he often has been in the past, and the College lessons concern not this matter during this term. Also, the winter has been long and his college business pressing. But I feel that tis also that to his mind the seed is planted and his position known, and no more is needful till others speak in support. He may feel his duty done, and we will hear no more from him on this subject, though he refuses to acknowledge error.

BELLINGHAM: But his very unregenerate presence encourages the invasion of more audacious Anabaptists, and imperils the hope of the flock. And what of next term at the college, when he again lectures on theology?

ENDICOTT: You say his public speech has been moderate. What of his private speech?

MITCHELL: I spoke with him but once since the conference, and that just before coming here. His private mind is not changed on the matter.

ENDICOTT: But what of his private speech? Does he counsel students in this way, or weaker Christians who are troubled by the hardness of the Lord and who might come to him by night?

MITCHELL: And how would I be knowing what passes in private between other men?

ENDICOTT: You are the pastor at Cambridge, Mr. Mitchell. It is your duty to search out the secret sins, that they may be published abroad to correct the sinners and serve as warning to others whose deeds are evil.

MITCHELL: It is sure that if any man asks Mr. Dunster where the Church stands on any matter, he would be answered, as he always has been, with the official policy of the Church. If any have asked, I know not of my own knowledge.

BELLINGHAM: But you have heard that they have, as all pastors hear of what is said in closed rooms, and the question is not always of church policy, but often of a man's own faith, however unsound.

MITCHELL: That I know not, only that Mr. Dunster is one of the noblest and purest men of this land, and that he has served the College well. For nearly fourteen years he has toiled and sacrificed in the position of highest trust in this colony, and there has been no whisper of any incapacity in that trust.

BELLINGHAM: I am sure I could argue with you over which position in the colony is of highest trust, Mr. Mitchell, but that is not the issue. As Governor of this colony and Head of the Court, I have been entrusted with the duty of protecting those I serve from the confusions of heresy and the contamination of unsound faith.

ENDICOTT: We can not have someone in authority undermining the faith of our youth or challenging their respect and obedience of the legal and religious authorities. It would destroy the purity of the faith and lead to anarchy. Those who teach our youth must be our most trustworthy citizens and purest theologians.

MITCHELL: And I submit to you that that is just what President Dunster always has been. His reputation as a scholar in the Oriental Languages is known even in Europe. His service at the College has been proof of God's providence in sending Mr. Dunster to us. In these fourteen years he has raised the school from a poor grammar school beset by scandal to a college where as good instruction is offered as in the first schools in the Old World. Indeed, Harvard has acquired so high a reputation that in several instances youth of opulent families in the parent country have been sent over here to receive their education in New England. Henry Dunster was entrusted with the revision of the Psalm Book, and it is his translation from the Hebrew of King David that we raise in singing praise to God every Sabbath. In his home, beside his hearth and table, sits the only printing press in this New World, entrusted to Henry Dunster to oversee, so that no scurrilous matter or false doctrine be printed or distributed. His labor among the Indians, translating their languages and converting them to the faith has brought us much of the peace we enjoy this day. He is entrusted with the accounts and money of the College, with supervision of the Commons Hall. At times he collects his own salary by soliciting the faithful, collects from the students what they can pay in tuition, in whatever form they can pay it, and solicits scholarships for those whose means fall short. He raised the funds for the President's House by his own efforts, and in time of need, out of his own scarcity, donated a full hundred acres to the College. His work has been extraordinary, and his personal character exemplary. Major Willard of the Court is husband to Mr. Dunster's sister, and can testify. Surely we must take into account the whole of a man's life before we dare condemn him for a single error.

> Pause. WILLARD shuffles some papers.

BELLINGHAM: Your own house is close by the President's, is it not, just by Harvard Yard?

MITCHELL: Yes, but...

BELLINGHAM: And you yourself were a student, then a graduate fellow, under Mr. Dunster at the College, were you not?

MITCHELL: And still serve as Fellow on occasion...

BELLINGHAM: Would you say that you and Mr. Dunster are friends?

MITCHELL: Friends and fellow-workers in the Lord.

BELLINGHAM: Perhaps that friendship is swaying your judgement, Mr. Mitchell.

MITCHELL: No, I...

ENDICOTT: Surely you agree that Mr. Dunster's error is a grave one?

MITCHELL: Yes, I'm only saying...

ENDICOTT: And that his persisting in it threatens to undermine the foundations of the faith.

BELLINGHAM: And challenges the unity of the Church.

MITCHELL: Yes, my own church is sore tried these days, but...

ENDICOTT: Surely you cannot expect us, through inaction, to allow such a situation to continue?

MITCHELL: No.

BELLINGHAM: Unless perhaps you secretly agree with Mr. Dunster, and would defend him to protect your own position.

MITCHELL: No!

ENDICOTT: You can not be neutral, Pastor Mitchell. A lack of zeal on your part might seem more a sign of weakness in faith than an expression of friendship.

BELLINGHAM: This is a great trial for one so young in the ministry. Many are watching you to see how you will stand the test. Those who are not for the Lord are against Him.

ENDICOTT: You must choose, Mr. Mitchell, and make your position clear, both in the pulpit, and in your private actions, if you wish to continue serving the Lord in this country.

MITCHELL: But surely...

BELLINGHAM: So far you have been discreet, but that is not enough. These words in defense of the erroneous gentleman do not serve you well. We must know where you stand, Mr. Mitchell. Perhaps a conference of ministers might be helpful in counseling you to see the straight way.

MITCHELL: Sir! I stand for the Church, as revealed in the Word of God and as taught in the pulpits and as written into the laws of this Colony. None may question my orthodoxy. I was baptized into the Covenant of the Church as a babe, and, God willing, so shall my children be. I will defend this belief, and all others commonly accepted among the faithful, with my last breath. I agree that Mr. Dunster errs in his theology, and if my zeal in the pulpit to defend the faith has not been strong till now, it is a weakness of will, not of faith, and I will see that there be no cause to question it again.

BELLINGHAM: Thank you, Mr. Mitchell. It is indeed comforting to have a man of your quality on our side, the side of the Lord, in these difficult times.

ENDICOTT: May I move we send a letter to the Overseers of the College, asking them to remove Mr. Dunster from his position because he is no longer sound in the faith.

WILLARD: Uh, might I make a suggestion?

BELLINGHAM: Yes, Major?

WILLARD: Perhaps it would be better if we were not over specific. A general letter, to the Overseers and to the selectmen of the towns that have grammar schools, that they examine their own situations and see that only those sound in doctrine be permitted to teach. That would seem less a personal attack on any one man, would establish a policy for future use, and perhaps give Mr. Dunster one more opportunity to recant, being faced with the loss of his position. I am sure his friend Mr. Mitchell's sermons in the coming weeks will also help Mr. Dunster, and others, see the truth of God in this matter.

BELLINGHAM: Yes, that might be more seemly. The Overseers will understand their duty, and I am certain that Mr. Mitchell will convey the full import of the message to Mr. Dunster and other members of the Cambridge Church. Won't you, Mr. Mitchell?

MITCHELL: Aye. The full import. Aye.

  The lights fade.

ACT I, SCENE SEVEN

DUNSTER's home, June 10, 1654. DUNSTER sits at the desk, writing. ELIZABETH enters with a large bucket of peas, which she begins to shell after she sits down.

ELIZABETH: The peas are in early this year; I've near a bucket this first picking.

DUNSTER: The weather has been mild.

ELIZABETH: Aye.

Pause.

DUNSTER: Elizabeth.

ELIZABETH: Yes?

DUNSTER: Will you ever forgive me?

ELIZABETH: What be there now?

DUNSTER: Two of the Overseers came to the College this day.

ELIZABETH: So I'm hearing.

DUNSTER: Have you? Heard you what was said? Are my very conversations now published abroad?

ELIZABETH: It takes no great guessing. Between the Court in Boston and Jonathan Mitchell's sermons against Anabaptism and dissenters these past Sabbaths, showing all where the safe side lay, the Overseers could have but one conversation with you. Will you be resigning now?

DUNSTER: Yes. Tis what I've been writing.

ELIZABETH: You could refuse.

DUNSTER: To what good?

ELIZABETH: It would show where full blame lay, and avoid any show of admitting error, if that be wanted.

DUNSTER: No, I'll not be delaying to the College's pain. It is too precious to me. Contributions are slacking now, parents do be asking their sons if I teach other than they learned at home, and boys do be asking if any church will have them when their studies are done. No, this is my struggle. I'll not be sacrificing the college on this alter. But in my heart I thought not this day would come, and here it is dawning, full of dark clouds on the red sky.

ELIZABETH: You knew it might come to this, if you won none over. You had warning enough.

DUNSTER: Yes. From you not least of all. Sometimes, Elizabeth, I am of the opinion you should be President, not I. I am the idealist, dreaming of a pure religion in a community ruled by God's Word. When the King's church was not pure enough for me, I left England for this new country, to join those of like mind who sought God and God's law, away from the corruptions of civil rule and Catholic heritage. Perhaps it was too big a dream to have people in it. Tis you who remember that men, not angels, must live the dream. Yes, my mind knew this would come, but not my heart, not my heart.

ELIZABETH: So you'll be resigning then.

DUNSTER: Tis written. "I hereby resign the office in which until this time I have labored with all my heart serving you and yours. Blessed be the Lord who gave me this opportunity to serve. Henceforth, so that in the interim until a successor be appointed the college be not deserted, I shall be willing to serve as best I can for some few weeks or months to continue the work. I shall act according to the orders prescribed to me, and endeavor to prevent the College from falling apart in our hands during the interim.

ELIZABETH: It says nothing of the cause.

DUNSTER: There is no need.

ELIZABETH: Not seize another opportunity to witness the truth?

DUNSTER: I am too sad this night. It's like a child dying just as he becomes a man, all the years of dreaming suddenly gone.

ELIZABETH: And I am sad for you, for a heart that must be breaking. (She shivers.) I am cold this eve, and it June. Sad days with hard futures chill the soul.

DUNSTER: Is David still fishing the river?

ELIZABETH: Yes.

DUNSTER: I'll go for him. I would walk about the Yard and town while there is light.

ELIZABETH: Some fish would go well with these peas, if David be a lucky fisher and my fingers swift in shelling.

DUNSTER: God is generous in his bounty to us.

ELIZABETH: Go for the boy, Henry Dunster, and let us eat in peace and plenty while we may.

DUNSTER: Yes.

>   DUNSTER exits.

ELIZABETH: But tis my tears will season this meal, and God will bring us plenty of those as well, it seems.

>   The lights fade.

ACT I, SCENE EIGHT

General Court, June 25, 1954. BELLINGHAM, ENDICOTT and WILLARD are sitting informally around the conference table. ENDICOTT is reading aloud.

ENDICOTT: "... falling apart in our hands during the interim. Yours faithfully to serve, Henry Dunster."

BELLINGHAM: So, if Henry Dunster can not see the light, he can at least feel the fire. What is the pleasure of the Court?

ENDICOTT: I move we recommend to the Overseers that the resignation be accepted, and that a search for a suitable replacement be commenced at once.

Pause.

BELLINGHAM: Major?

WILLARD: I have a suggestion, but I am loath to make it, lest it be misinterpreted as a partisan defense or plea for a kinsman. I am opposed to Mr. Dunster, and in the fear of the Lord have suppressed my natural affections for my wife's brother. Yet, I fear an over hasty action might not be the wisest thing on our part.

BELLINGHAM: Say on, Major. Your moderation has served us well in the past.

ENDICOTT: Moderation in defense of Christ's Church is not always a virtue.

WILLARD: I will leave the choice to you, only hear me out before you sign another order that causes so much pain of heart.

ENDICOTT: My service is for the Lord, not my own gain. A soldier of God must not shrink from battle, Major.

WILLARD: Nor charge in without counting the cost.

BELLINGHAM: Say on, Major. We will listen.

WILLARD: There are several considerations. The first being, as Mr. Mitchell reminded us, that Mr. Dunster is the best man, baring this one thing, for the position of President of the College. He is certainly the most learned man in the country, and has served us well till now. He will be difficult to replace. The second is that he has been moderate and quiet on this matter of late. Unrepentant, to be sure, but quiet none-the-less. With Mr. Mitchell and the others quieting dissent in the churches, such continued silence might enable us to pass over his error, giving it the appearance that Mitchell's ungainsayable sermons had carried the day. It might save us a good and diligent man and yet not endanger the Church. Third, President Dunster is not unknown in Europe as a scholar and a Christian. With the unsettled state of affairs now in England, this might not be a good time to stir up controversy. We have already been criticized roundly over here for our harsh treatment of lesser men and women...

ENDICOTT: Necessary measures to preserve the peace.

WILLARD: Agreed. But not always within the Common Law, especially those hot-heads who tried to sell into servitude the children of dissenters some years ago. The unchurched who settle among us and the sailors who provision here and bring us our trade have also cried out to the King, when he was enthroned, and may now to the Parliament, saying that we burden Englishmen with new laws not approved by the government in England, and in excess of what they would bear at home.

BELLINGHAM: This is a new country, far from England. We came here to live under God's Law, when we could not do so there. Those who would not accept God's laws are free to go elsewhere; Plymouth Colony to the south, or Roger William's Rhode Island, or to the Dutch, or south to Virginia, a Royal Colony. We constrain no man to stay. Besides, the King is no more, Parliament and Cromwell rule, praise the Lord.

WILLARD: Which is precisely the point. The recent conflicts in England have reduced the number of those of like mind who would join us here. Those in positions of power or authority who supported us in the past saw us as a hope for God's Church, as opposed to the King's. Now the King is no more, and they will not, cannot, continue to support us if we are perceived as over-hard zealots who rebel against civil law and respect not the learned and pious among us. We came here because we were oppressed in England, and were supported by those who would not or could not come themselves. If the oppressor there be removed, but we are seen as ourselves oppressors, who would come or care for this far land? I will tell you who, the seekers of fortune, the landless risking all for a plot of land, the petty criminals escaping the magistrates, the pressed sailors slipping over the rail, the Quakers and Catholics who would escape the wrath of God's courts. Not those like us who seek the pure way in peace and unity. We cannot yet live without those ships from England, nor grow and rule in God's own land without new settlers of like mind. We cannot.

BELLINGHAM: So we can not condemn Henry Dunster in such haste that it appears unseemly to those in England who are newly come to power.

ENDICOTT: I am not so sure of this. Those in England do not seem overly fond of moderation, if the reports be true. They were not so concerned with being seemly when they killed the King.

BELLINGHAM: It has been a bloody thing. And while Parliament does sit, there is not yet peace.

WILLARD: All the more reason to appear moderate and deliberate, not of the hasty heart, and willing to forgive the repentant. However it goes in England, and the reports change with each new docking, we appear the better.

BELLINGHAM: So what say you we do?

WILLARD: Let us advise the Overseers to give Mr. Dunster a month. If he still persists and will not be silent, so be it. We are seen as giving him every chance to conform his views. If he be silent, we are all the better for it.

ENDICOTT: But in that month, let us not sit idle, but consult, and have a name ready to suggest to the Overseers as new President of the College, to hasten Dunster's departure as much as possible if he will not be silent.

WILLARD: A most wise and excellent suggestion, Mr. Endicott.

BELLINGHAM: Write this down, John. In answer to the writing presented to this Court by Mr. Henry Dunster, in which, among other things, he has resigned his place as President of the College: This Court orders that it shall be left to the care and discretion of the Overseers of the College to seek out some suitable person to carry on and take up the Position of the President, provided that Mr. Dunster persists in his resolution for more than one month and so informs the Overseers. Any objection to that? Well, Henry Dunster, now what will you do?

    The lights fade.

ACT I, SCENE NINE

Cambridge church, Sunday, July 30, 1654. DUNSTER and ELIZABETH sit on a pew. The rest of the congregation may be extras or voices from the darkness outside the lights. MITCHELL steps into the light holding a baby.

MITCHELL: Presented for the Ordinance of Baptism this day is William Oliver Danforth, child of...

DUNSTER stands.

DUNSTER: Mr. Mitchell, forgive me,...

ELIZABETH: Henry?...

MITCHELL: Mr. Dunster?

DUNSTER: I must object. This baptism is not scriptural. Nowhere in the Bible...

MITCHELL: Henry, please! Not now!

DUNSTER: Am I forbidden to speak? Christ calls me to testify to the truth. In Christ's Name I must speak. I cannot sit silent and see my church continue in corruption.

MITCHELL: This is not the time, Henry.

DUNSTER: What is the time? If God says speak, am I to be silent?

VOICE 1: President Dunster, you are interrupting the Ordinance. As an Elder of this church, I ask you not to disrupt an Ordinance.

DUNSTER: This is not according to the institution of Christ. This is a corruption of an ordinance, an impurity that steals into the faith under the cover of tradition. We delude ourselves if...

VOICE 2: This is apostasy!

VOICE 3: Heresy!

MITCHELL: Enough! Be silent!

DUNSTER: I cannot...

VOICE 3: The scriptures plainly state...

VOICE 1: Silence!

VOICE 2: Ask him if he's turned Anabaptist!

MITCHELL: Brothers! Please! The service!

ELIZABETH grabs DUNSTER's arm and tries to pull him down.

ELIZABETH: Henry, sit down.

DUNSTER: I must...

VOICE 4: Is this what you're teaching our sons?

VOICE 5: You want our children to go to hell?

DUNSTER: No. God loves children, He said...

MITCHELL: This is not the time or the place...

VOICE 3: Put him in the stocks and see what he preaches!

VOICE 5: Or from the whipping post!

MITCHELL: No! Enough! We are all Christians here.

VOICE 1: We'll have no apostasy in this church, not while I am Elder!

> ELIZABETH gets up and begins to drag DUNSTER out of the church.

DUNSTER: I'm just trying to speak the truth!

VOICE 2: We already know the truth!

ELIZABETH: Henry! Come away!

MITCHELL: Please! Order! This is a church!

VOICE 3: And no place for blasphemy! What's the matter with you, Mitchell? Don't you listen to your own sermons?

VOICE 5: We know what to do with heretics!

MITCHELL: Order! Order! In the Name of God, Order!

> ELIZABETH pulls DUNSTER out of the scene as the hubbub grows around MITCHELL, who still stands there with the baby in his arms, pleading for order as the lights fade.

ACT II, SCENE ONE

DUNSTER's home, Sunday, July 30, 1654 (shortly after the previous scene). The room is empty. Suddenly ELIZABETH storms in, tears off her bonnet, slams her Bible down on the table, starts to set the table for lunch, then suddenly throws a plate on the floor and sits down and cries. At this moment, DUNSTER enters.

DUNSTER: Elizabeth.

ELIZABETH stands, angrily.

ELIZABETH: Don't come near me, Henry Dunster. How could you do that, how could you?

DUNSTER: I don't know. Maybe I still have a fever from last night, though I feel not ill. But when they brought the babe....It was the first baptism since the Council....Something just came over me. I had to speak.

ELIZABETH: Has Satan grabbed you after all?

DUNSTER: I prefer to hope it was God.

MITCHELL enters in a rush.

MITCHELL: God in Heaven, have you lost your senses?

DUNSTER: Come in, Jonathan. Will you eat with us?

MITCHELL: Is he gone mad?

ELIZABETH: It seems as much.

DUNSTER: No, a bit weak at the knees from last night's sickness, and the heat of the July day, but not yet mad and foaming like a dog.

MITCHELL: Do you know what you've done?

DUNSTER: I spoke the truth, that is what I have done, though I fear in the hubbub that followed, my statements were somewhat confused and fragmented.

MITCHELL: Hubbub is not the word for it. You've disturbed a church service, Henry. That's against the law. You can be arrested, fined, jailed. There'll be no saving you now. Elizabeth, why did he do it?

ELIZABETH: I'll be living a long time, Jonathan Mitchell, and not knowing that.

MITCHELL: Well, you hustled him out just in time. The brethren of the church were somewhat vehement in the signifying of their dissatisfaction. It was all I could do to calm them and send them homeward. Then I ran half the way here in case anger should cloud any judgements.

ELIZABETH: After all your sermons making dissent the Devil's work, and calling out righteous indignation, what were you expecting, Jonathan, but that all would rush to prove their orthodoxy by beating the first raised head.

    ELIZABETH looks outside.

DUNSTER: Be there danger? Will they whip me, Jonathan?

MITCHELL: I've no answer for that, Henry Dunster.

DUNSTER: I can be brave, Jonathan. I have been a soldier, and I can be brave. I joined the Boston Artillery when first I came to this land, before being called to the Presidency of the College. I drilled with them too. I can be brave.

ELIZABETH: Your sermons were a part to seeing this day; will you stand with us now?

MITCHELL: The Court will hear of this day, that is certain.

ELIZABETH: Will ye stand with us, Jonathan?

    Pause. Silence.

MITCHELL: Elizabeth, I...

DUNSTER: He is a friend, Elizabeth; he will do what he can. Do not ask more.

MITCHELL: Why, Henry, why?

DUNSTER: I spoke the truth, Jonathan. Should I be less than Peter and John before the Sanhedrin? Must I not speak what I have seen and heard of Christ?

ELIZABETH: The fever is still on him.

DUNSTER: Answer me, Jonathan. Whether my fever be a foretaste of Hell or the burning indwelling of God, must I not speak what I have seen and heard of Christ?

MITCHELL: Henry....it was the wrong time, the wrong place.

DUNSTER: And if snow fall in summer, is it none-the-less snow, no matter how unseasonable? Do we chose our seasons, Jonathan, planting corn when it suits our time? Or must we plant when God's sun and rain come in Spring? Will the Church wither when an ill, old man speaks out of turn? What then is its ground, Jonathan? Is the Church planted in such rocky soil that it withers in the heat of the day?

MITCHELL: Tis the brambles of error we fear.

ELIZABETH: Argue not with him now. Tis of little use, and he is ill.

MITCHELL: I had thought we had saved him. But he would not be silent. He would not be silent. To mistake fever for fire and stubbornness for courage...

ELIZABETH: How will it end for us?

DUNSTER: As it ends for all, in silence.

    The lights fade.

ACT II, SCENE TWO

The General Court, Oct. 26, 1654. BELLINGHAM, ENDICOTT, NORTON, MATHER, and MITCHELL are seated about the table or standing nearby.

BELLINGHAM: So, the Overseers simply met to await the resignation? I am sure that left little room for doubt.

NORTON: There was no other purpose for the meeting. He knew we would have his resignation that day, or we would announce that his services were no longer required.

ENDICOTT: He withstood the pressure for a long time, I'll pay him that praise.

MITCHELL: I think he loves the College more than life itself.

BELLINGHAM: Then he should have cared less for other things.

NORTON: Be that as it may, while we waited, it was agreed that Mr. Mather and myself would the next day sail to Scituate, in Plymouth Colony, and there inquire, as the Court suggested, of Mr. Chauncy, if he would be willing to accept an invitation to the Presidency of the College, in case the Overseers should call him thereto. We arrived back in Boston only this afternoon.

BELLINGHAM: And Mr. Chauncy is willing?

NORTON: Mr. Chauncy greatly regretted to hear that Mr. Dunster had resigned. He admires Mr. Dunster very much, and is sorry his friend had fallen into the briars of Anabaptism. However, with all due humility, he would be willing to take up the great task of leading the College, if God and the Overseers call him thereunto.

MATHER: There is one problem, however. His stand on immersion.

ENDICOTT: What is this?

MATHER: Mr. Chauncy believes all baptism should be by immersion, even of infants. He also holds that the Lord's Supper should be celebrated only at evening. That is why he removed from Plymouth to Scituate, because the other pastor at Plymouth held for sprinkling. They tried to compromise and let each baptize in his own way, but Mr. Chauncy would have none of it, and chose Scituate instead, which was already divided on the matter, and tolerant of such differences.

ENDICOTT: Think you he would be as stiff-necked today?

MATHER: We questioned him closely on that point. Of course, as a college president, not a pastor, he would not administer either of the disputed ordinances, and that seemed to remove much of the controversy. He has agreed to keep silent on these matters, and not oppose the doctrines held by the Church here.

BELLINGHAM: Will he keep by that word?

MATHER: We have already seen how a good man may fall, and in a moment of indiscretion, overstep the bounds of prudence. However, my view is that Mr. Chauncy, being warned, as it were, will exercise a great deal of care. And, Mr. Dunster aside, he is the most able man for the post in the country, and we had to go out of the Colony to find him.

BELLINGHAM: Still, I would not stand by his word only, but something in writing as well.

NORTON: I am sure that something stating that he must forbear to oppose the received doctrine of the Church can be written into the Overseers instructions when he is encouraged to accept the Presidency.

MITCHELL: Yes, if none can agree on all points, let us make sure at least of silence. We must make sure our youth are set the right example.

NORTON: Are you disturbed by this, Brother Mitchell?

MITCHELL: I assure you, Brother, no action of this Court would disturb a true believer. That has been made very clear. On the contrary, I fear I must disturb the Court. I bear a petition to the General Court from Mr. Henry Dunster, which he begged me to convey for him. It troubles me, and this seems as good a time as any to present it.

ENDICOTT: What does the bugbear of New England want now?

MATHER: Some kindness for a fallen brother might not be wanting, Brother Endicott.

ENDICOTT: Let us see if it be charity he is asking, Mr. Mather.

BELLINGHAM: Will you read the petition, Mr. Mitchell.

MITCHELL: "The Petition of Henry Dunster. This humble petitioner, with all thankfulness, acknowledges your patience in allowing him to take advantage and delay his resignation from the Presidency of last June until this humble petitioner could confer with the honored and Reverend Overseers about the grievances concerning him. After that conference, this humble petitioner, having been informed to some degree of satisfaction on the matter, in submissive willingness resumed his duties and since then has dealt with the responsibilities of the position as well as was in his power to do so, until the twenty-fourth of October, when, after the prudent and peaceable motions put before the honored and Reverend Overseers for the public good, concurring with other reasons this humble petitioner induced therefrom, this humble petitioner peaceably laid down and resigned his position again a second time, in such a way and manner that it might be of best report and least offense to all sides."

ENDICOTT: Dignity to the last.

BELLINGHAM: And formal style.

MATHER: Peace.

MITCHELL: "Therefore, this humble petitioner submissively desires that it is not thought or reported by any of your honored selves that this petitioner cast off his position out of sullenness, foolish levity, or ungrateful despising of the Court's patience or of the Overseers' amicable conferences. All the honored and Reverend Overseers can bear witness to the contrary, and can testify that this thing was transacted with composure, seeing that their motives and arguments agreed with the humble petitioner's conceptions and acceptance."

NORTON: If I hear "humble petitioner" one more time, God may have to forgive an oath.

MITCHELL: "Moreover, it is this petitioner's humble request...

BELLINGHAM: Well, that saved Brother Norton a night on his knees, if only barely.

MITCHELL: "...that the honored Court would be pleased to take into their Christian considerations the grounds and reasons upon which the honored Committee for the College recommended to the Court that certain reimbursements and payments be made to this humble petitioner..."

MATHER: Silence, John.

MITCHELL: "...for his extraordinary labor in, about, and concerning the good of the College over and above his normal duties in the education of youth for these last fourteen years, so that this humble petitioner may be able to pay his debts in Old and New England."

ENDICOTT: We owe him money?

NORTON: Well, yes and no.

BELLINGHAM: Explain.

NORTON: The Committee of the College, before this affair began, recommended that Mr. Dunster be reimbursed for several donations of personal property and advances from his own pocket that he made when times were hard, and for those parts of his own salary never paid by the government, but raised privately by his own efforts. Frankly, at the time, the committee also felt that Mr. Dunster deserved a bonus or reward of some kind for all the work he had done building up the College. They felt it was more than we had any right to expect. The motion was approved, but the funds never appropriated.

BELLINGHAM: So, this resignation may save us money as well as trouble.

MITCHELL: These payments are certainly due, in all justice.

BELLINGHAM: It is we who will decide justice here, Mr. Mitchell.

MITCHELL: Of course. Shall I continue?

BELLINGHAM: There is more?

MITCHELL: Yes. "And seeing that his humble petitioner, with notable industry and through great difficulty, built the house in which he lives at the moment, it is his humble desire that he may continue dwelling there in peace until all accounts due him from the government can be orderly satisfied and paid."

ENDICOTT: So, he would hold the President's House hostage for his supposed back pay.

NORTON: Oh, there is some of that due him too.

MITCHELL: He holds it not hostage. Winter will be upon us soon, and travel hard. It will take several weeks to settle accounts in any case, not only his, but others of the College to which he must attend before departing.

BELLINGHAM: Chauncy will be arriving soon. Where is he to lodge?

MITCHELL: A place could be found.

ENDICOTT: Are you bearing this humble petition in Christian charity, Mr. Mitchell, or supporting its cause through misplaced affection for your erroneous friend whose snares near endangered your own soul and position.

MITCHELL: I bear it only as the man himself could not, being Minister at Cambridge, and nearest to the College...

NORTON: Your Christian virtue and kindness toward one who has so misused you is laudable, Brother Mitchell, but I am sure we are all familiar enough with Harvard and the situation to make independent judgements.

MITCHELL: There was no disrespect intended to either the honored Court or the ministers assembled here.

BELLINGHAM: We are confident there was not. We have nothing but admiration for the way you have stood fast to the cause in these trying times, Mr. Mitchell.

MITCHELL: Thank you. Shall I continue?

ENDICOTT: There is yet more?

MITCHELL: Only one more request.

BELLINGHAM: Read on.

MITCHELL: And seeing that this humble petitioner is a free man of this Colony, not only because of his oath of loyalty, but also because of his inborn love and affection for it, he always has and always will seek the good and happiness of the Colony in all things according to his best wisdom. Therefore, it is this humble petitioner's desire, because he knows that one day an accounting will be made to God of the talents entrusted to him for the support of his afflicted family, that, according to his education and abilities, without any impeachment, molestation, or hindrance from the authorities of this colony, he may seek beyond the College to vigorously promote the spiritual and temporal good of the inhabitants of the Colony by preaching the Gospel of Christ, teaching and training of youth, or in any other laudable or liberal calling that God shall mark out as his task, and when and where and in what manner he shall find acceptance. Yours humbly to serve, Henry Dunster."

ENDICOTT: What?

BELLINGHAM: He wants us to let him keep teaching and preaching?

MITCHELL: If some church or school will have him.

BELLINGHAM: The audacity!

NORTON: Is there no end to this man?

MITCHELL: Teaching and preaching are all his training, all his experience. They are his life, his calling from God.

BELLINGHAM: The land is rich. He owns several plots. Let him clear them and farm. He will not starve.

MATHER: It is a moot point, no church or grammar school in the colony would have him.

ENDICOTT: What could this other laudable and liberal calling he mentions be?

MITCHELL: He mentioned no specifics to me. I assume he means anything one trained in the liberal arts, as he was at Cambridge University before taking his Master's in Divinity, could go into.

NORTON: God in Heaven, he means to be a lawyer!

BELLINGHAM: There will be no lawyers in Boston, not while I am Governor.

ENDICOTT: Think what havoc that brilliant mind could wreck, calling down the Charter on us, making its provisions known, were he allowed to stand before the Court day after day, quoting the Common Law and the Statutes of England.

BELLINGHAM: We must keep the people ignorant of their liberties and privileges, if we are to act in our own wills what we please for the glory of God.

MITCHELL: What say you?

> Pause. BELLINGHAM and ENDICOTT exchange looks. BELLINGHAM signals for ENDICOTT to speak.

ENDICOTT: Tis not well known among the people, but the Charter from the Crown that established this Colony grants toleration to all Christians except Papists, and at least presumes that we are subject to Crown Law. When we pass our own laws and set up our own government, as we have done to establish the rule of God, some would say that we depart from the Charter.

MITCHELL: But surely we would not usurp....

MATHER: We live by the grace of God before that of the King, or even the Parliament that sits now, and would obey the Law of Moses before that of England.

NORTON: We live under God, and would make our own laws in the light of His Word. He is the higher law.

MITCHELL: But, to keep the people ignorant of...

ENDICOTT: We keep them ignorant for their own good. Even you should be able to see that, Mr. Mitchell. We do God's will, not our own. Any contention over which law is supreme would create anarchy. We must rule to enforce God's Law. Or do you oppose God's Law, Mr. Mitchell?

MITCHELL: You know where I stand. It was my sermons roused the support that allowed you to act against Mr. Dunster. I am not your student, Mr. Endicott, and I do not have to stand and recite the creeds at your beck and call.

ENDICOTT: If this court calls your orthodoxy into question, you...

BELLINGHAM: Enough! Mr. Mitchell, no one here questions your faith or your orthodoxy. Your efforts to maintain the true faith in Cambridge have been admired by all. But your attitude toward this court is not as well received. We know you are troubled by what has happened to your former friend. It is indeed regretted by all. We are simply men trying to do the will of God, as hard and confounding as that may seem at times. You hold a position of influence in this colony. So far you have used that influence correctly. But, we are far from England, we need be close to God. To try to follow Common law in this new land would be foolish; this is the edge of wilderness, not the streets of London.

ENDICOTT: Some lawyer, spouting English law, could call strongly for the letter of that civil law, rather than leaving matters to the good sense and judgement of this court of Christians. No Common Law should be allowed to overrule God. It is to live by God's law that we came here.

MITCHELL: We are still men, not gods or angels. Surely we dare not...

BELLINGHAM: We dare enforce the Law of God, Mr. Mitchell. It is revealed to us in His Word, and we will rule this land by it. Henry Dunster, nor anyone else, will stand before our courts and argue man's petty wisdom over the wisdom God has given us, not while I live and govern. And now you too must decide which law you will obey. Do you chose God and His Justice, or will you follow your lost friend down the path of man's petty wisdom?

>Pause.

MITCHELL: I am a pastor, called of God to save souls. My pulpit at Cambridge is my life, my very heart. I do not understand courts or laws, only the eternal justice of God. It is in my faith in God that I stand. If God and Man stand in opposition, then I will stand with God and God's Church. That church and that faith are my only hope.

BELLINGHAM: Then you will stand with this court, with both obedience and respect for those charged with carrying out the will of God, as hard as it may be in this life. (Pause.) What say you, Mr. Mitchell? Do you stand by God's court or the heresy of England.

MITCHELL: I say again, I stand by God.

BELLINGHAM: This court is the instrument of God, Mr. Mitchell. Stand you by this court, or stand you by your former friend and his error? (Pause.) What say you, stand you by the court?

Pause.

MITCHELL: Aye.

BELLINGHAM: And then for God.

ENDICOTT: And there will be no lawyers in Boston or elsewhere in this colony.

MITCHELL: Aye. But you are only assuming that this is what Mr. Dunster intends.

BELLINGHAM: Mr. Dunster is too dangerous, whether it be at the lectern, the pulpit, or the bar. We cannot allow him to speak his "truth." It is too dangerous to the peace of this Colony. John, take this down. To the petition of Henry Dunster, the Court replies as follows: In answer to the first section; What extraordinary labor in, about, or concerning the good of the College during these fourteen years is referred to, we do not know. We know of no labor except what was the ordinary duty of the President, and so reject the petition unless he can show the particulars of these labors that were extraordinary. In answer to the second part; It is most unreasonable. He may protract the settling of his accounts for some years, and thereby hinder the comfortable lodging of the man chosen to continue the work of the College. What the President can make justly to appear to be due him must be paid with convenient speed. Third; This Court does not think it appropriate, for reasons of which Mr. Dunster is not ignorant and which are well known to this Court, to grant this part of the petition. What other laudable or liberal calling, besides preaching or the educating of youth, is intended must be further explained by Mr. Dunster. Are there any objections to making this our reply? (Pause.) Mr. Mitchell?

MITCHELL: No. I will make a fair copy, and convey it to Mr. Dunster.

BELLINGHAM: Thank you, Mr. Mitchell. God willing, that will conclude this business. Shall we adjourn?

ENDICOTT: So moved.

BELLINGHAM: Hearing no objections, the meeting is adjourned. Come, friends, the inn will have supper waiting.

> As they exit, ENDICOTT hands MITCHELL the resolution, which MITCHELL begins to copy as the others leave. After a moment, the lights fade.

ACT II, SCENE THREE

DUNSTER's home, Nov. 10, 1654. DUNSTER is alone at his desk, writing. He finishes, picks up the paper and, wrapping a shawl about himself, reads.

DUNSTER: To the General Court. Your humble servant must again petition the Court to give due heed to the following considerations, and permit that I may be allowed to dwell in peace awhile longer in the house of the President of the College. First, the time of year is unseasonable for travel, being very near the shortest day, and the depth of winter. Second, the place to which I go is unknown to me and my family, and the ways and means of subsistence likewise unknown. Third, the place from which I go, the President's house, has fire, fuel, and all provisions for man and beast laid in for the winter. To move some things will be to destroy them, to move others, for example, books and household goods, is to hazard them greatly. The house itself I built, upon very damaging conditions to myself, out of love for the College, taking country pay instead of bills of exchange on England, or the house would not have been built. Fourth, the people here, all besides myself, are women and children, from whom little help can be expected, now that their minds lie under the actual stroke of affliction and grief. My wife is sick, and my youngest child extremely so, and has been for months, so that we dare not carry him out of doors, and is much worse than before. However, if a place can be found that may be comfortable for them, and reasonably answer the obstacles mentioned above, I will willingly bow my neck to any yoke of personal self-denial, for I know what and by whom, by grace, I suffer...

The lights fade.

ACT II, SCENE FOUR

The General Court, Nov. 1654. BELLINGHAM, ENDICOTT, and WILLARD are at the table, listening to MITCHELL, who stands, reading. MATHER stands off to one side.

MITCHELL: "...for I know what and by whom, by grace, I suffer. Fifth, the state of the College requires my residence until all accounts be made up and balanced. Sixth, my residence is required in reference to the Reverend President-elect, that I may show him what our way has been. What place near the College can be found is more convenient by far for the President-elect, who is in a movable posture, than for me on that account. Seventh, the whole transaction of this business is such that, with the passing of time, when all things come to mature consideration, they may very probably create grief on all sides; yours after, as mine before. I am not the man you take me to be. Neither, if you knew what I believe, and why, can I persuade myself that you would act as I am at least tempted to think that you do. But our times are in God's hands, with whom all sides hope, by grace in Christ, to find favor. That shall be my prayer for you, as for myself, who am, honored gentlemen, yours to serve, Henry Dunster."

Pause.

ENDICOTT: Well.

WILLARD: He may stay till the Spring.

BELLINGHAM: What?

ENDICOTT: You overstep yourself, Major.

WILLARD: He is already indicted to stand trial for disrupting an ordinance of the Church. Vent your spleen then if you will, when you can touch only him. But I will not again drive women and children out into the winter.

ENDICOTT: There are three votes on this court. You may find yours is meaningless.

WILLARD: He may stay until the Spring, or there will be more than Hell to pay.

ENDICOTT: What mean you by that?

WILLARD: I mean not every man in this colony believes God has as much ice in his heart as you.

ENDICOTT: You are treading on dangerous ground, Major.

WILLARD: So are you, Mr. Endicott.

BELLINGHAM: Peace. Let it pass. He may stay until the Spring, though not for his sake, but out of our Christian concern for his wife and children, who are blameless in this error. I would see him gone, but many would complain if the child died.

WILLARD: Thank you, Mr. Bellingham, for your reason in these hard times.

MITCHELL: I will inform Mr. Dunster of your kindness and charity.

ENDICOTT: Mr. Mitchell, of late I am never sure if your meaning is that of your words.

MATHER: If I may interrupt.

BELLINGHAM: Please do, Mr. Mather.

MATHER: While we are on the subject of Mr. Dunster...

BELLINGHAM: Which we always seem to be.

MATHER: It concerns College accounts and the amount due Mr. Dunster.

BELLINGHAM: I had thought that was settled.

MATHER: Not quite. The Overseers of the College met, and after due deliberations and an examination of accounts, passed the following statement of "Brief Information of the present necessities of the College. To the General Court, with earnest desires of their speedy and effective help in supplying needed funds. First, we are indebted to Mr. Dunster, as expended on account, nearly forty pounds, over and above what we have been able to pay him or assign to him. Justice and equity require that this be paid him, being due debt, and apparent upon diligent examination of accounts. Also, besides what is due upon strict account, there is the former motion previously made by the committee that a hundred pounds be paid to Mr. Dunster in consideration of his extraordinary pains in raising up and carrying on the College for so many years. We desire it may be seriously considered, and hope it may make much for the country's honorable reputation in the hearts of all, and perpetual encouragement of their servants in such public works, if it be attended.

ENDICOTT: This is an insult and out-rage! We have already passed on that. Are we asked to pay a bonus to a man forced out of office in disgrace?

MATHER: The hundred pounds is for his past service, not this present mistake. The forty pounds is owing on his salary and money he lent to the College, but we have no funds with which to pay it, and are asking a supplemental appropriation so that the accounts can be balanced upon his termination. That is only fair, no matter the reason for his leaving.

ENDICOTT: Then perhaps we should charge him rent upon the President's house, since he stays beyond his time.

WILLARD: Will you have your pound of flesh yet, John?

ENDICOTT: Mr. Willard, if you...

BELLINGHAM: Silence! Mr. Dunster has troubled this Court enough, in more ways than I care to count. The request of the Overseers will be referred to the full body of the Magistrates at their next sitting.

MATHER: But that will take months. The Court is empowered to conduct such business when the Magistrates are not in session. The whole point is to get this matter settled so Mr. Dunster can be paid and the accounts closed.

BELLINGHAM: We will refer it to the Magistrates, Mr. Mather, from whence it will to the Deputies, and let them take what action they may. This Court will waste no more words on this man.

MATHER: And will your recommendation go with the request?

BELLINGHAM: That we will decide another time. This meeting is adjourned.

BELLINGHAM exits, followed by ENDICOTT.

WILLARD: My wife would know of her brother.

MITCHELL: I saw him but briefly. He seems well, though aged and much saddened. Elizabeth is very ill though, as is young Jonathan. Both Mr. Dunster and young David spend much time caring for them. They will all be much relieved to hear that they must not face the winter outside their home. That will cheer Henry much; he carries a great weight. I will tell him how strongly you stood for his petition.

WILLARD: Give him not much hope. I must sit in judgement on him at the trial, and I fear there is little can be done there. I must go. Tell him his sister asked after him, though she is much grieved by him.

MITCHELL: He will find any kind word a comfort.

> WILLARD exits.

MATHER: Hard men in hard times. Some days, Mr. Mitchell, I am glad to be old, for I fear, for all his other errors and obstinacy, Henry Dunster is right about one thing. This thing will come to grief on all sides when time has passed. I shall probably be dead in that day, but you in your youth may repent in your dotage, and my sons may find their father was not always wise or strong.

MITCHELL: I thought we were defending the Church, the Law of the Lord, and the Truth that He revealed to us. It has been a humbling experience. I cannot find the scriptures to answer all these questions! And though I am saddened that such a great man should fall to such a great error, and bring tribulations on us all, the only fault I can find is excess of zeal in those who pursued him. That zealousness galls me as arrogance, but, well, I may be blind, but if we, the Church of God, the People of God, have the Truth from Heaven, I can see no wrong in what I have done. Where is the wrong?

MATHER: No, I can see no wrong, no wrong. And that, Mr. Mitchell, is where the tragedy lies. All have done what they thought right. There are no wrongs, Mr. Mitchell, only pain. Good day, Jonathan Mitchell. The Lord be with you.

MITCHELL: And with you.

> MATHER exits. The lights fade.

ACT II, SCENE FIVE

General Court, April 3, 1655. BELLINGHAM, ENDICOTT and WILLARD sit at the table. MITCHELL stands to one side, DUNSTER at the other. ELIZABETH stands nearby.

ENDICOTT: Then Mr. Dunster stood and began to speak against the baptism of the child, is that so?

MITCHELL: Yes.

ENDICOTT: Had you or anyone else asked Mr. Dunster to speak?

MITCHELL: No.

ENDICOTT: Did you, as presiding minister, or any of the Elders present, give him leave to speak?

MITCHELL: No.

ENDICOTT: Did any object to his speaking?

MITCHELL: An Elder present did desire that he forbear, and asked him not to interrupt the public ordinance.

ENDICOTT: To what effect?

MITCHELL: Notwithstanding the request, Mr. Dunster proceeded, in a way of complaint to the congregation, saying that he was forbidden to speak what in Christ's name he would have testified. He then testified against the practice of infant baptism as being unbiblical, in the way you have already heard.

ENDICOTT: Was the ordinance able to proceed?

MITCHELL: No.

ENDICOTT: For what reason?

MITCHELL: There was much shouting and confusion as several rose to challenge Mr. Dunster, and yet others to plead for silence and order.

ENDICOTT: To what end?

MITCHELL: After some time Mistress Dunster was able to persuade her husband to come away, and after some further space of disorder and dispute, I was able to recall calm and dispatch each to his home for the noon meal.

ENDICOTT: And the ordinance of baptism?

MITCHELL: Was completed at the evening service.

ENDICOTT: Tell me, Mr. Mitchell, did you fear any violence during the service, or after?

MITCHELL: There was some pushing and shaking of fists in the heat of the moment, and threats of what could come after, though to my knowledge nothing beyond the pranks of schoolboys was accomplished.

ENDICOTT: Thank you, Mr. Mitchell. Mr. Henry Dunster of Cambridge, step forward.

DUNSTER: If it please the Court, I reside in Scituate, in Plymouth Colony, as of two weeks past, Mr. Chauncy having occupied the President's Home in March.

ENDICOTT: I am corrected. And your occupation now?

DUNSTER: I work the land for my sustenance, and have some rental properties in this colony.

ENDICOTT: Goodman Dunster, you have heard the charges and the testimony concerning them. Have you anything to say?

DUNSTER: First, I answer that I am not conscious that I did anything contemptuously, or in open contempt of God's word or messengers, and therefore, as I understand the law, I am not guilty of any breach of the law. As for the particular statements that were charged against me, I deny the precise language and quotes that were presented to the honored Court, because they are not accurate reports of exactly what I spoke. However, I do not deny the substance. I also acknowledge that the time and place of my speaking was unseasonable. But, as for what I did say, I believed then, and still do, that I spoke the truth in the fear of God, and I dare not deny the same, or go from it until the Lord teaches me otherwise, and this I pray the honored Court will take for my answer.

BELLINGHAM: Do you deny disrupting the public worship?

DUNSTER: You have heard my answer.

BELLINGHAM: Goodman Dunster, your own words condemned you. The Court has no choice but to find you guilty and order you to be present at the next town meeting at Cambridge, where you are to be publicly admonished by such magistrate as should then be present. You will also post a bond of some ten pounds for your good behavior, to be forfeited if you are not present at the lecture, or if you are called before this Court again. Court is adjourned.

> BELLINGHAM, ENDICOTT and WILLARD rise and exit. DUNSTER stands alone for a moment, then ELIZABETH crosses to him.

DUNSTER: No end, no end.

ELIZABETH: Come, Henry, let us go.

MITCHELL: I'm sorry, Elizabeth.

ELIZABETH: Twas not of your doing.

MITCHELL: A man may be sorry for things he has not caused.

ELIZABETH: Yes. And not for those he has.

> Pause. MITCHELL crosses and stands before them for a moment.

MITCHELL: I am sorry, Henry.

DUNSTER: That life is in the past, Jonathan; dwell not on it.

MITCHELL: How is the new house?

ELIZABETH: Small and cold, and far from friends.

DUNSTER: It will be warm ere winter come again, but the planting must be done this month, God willing. The little house by the river will serve for Elizabeth till that in Scituate be made ready a few months hence.

MITCHELL: In Cambridge?

DUNSTER: I gave not all my land away, nor dare they take that from me. I have a few plots of land that were for renting. One has a little house, too small for more than Elizabeth and little Jonathan. None would stomach my living there, and it suits not for winter, but Elizabeth may there for long visits, and I pass over when business calls me to the Colony, to collect rents or see again to settling accounts. She will stay there until the new house is fully done, and have the baby there, among her friends.

MITCHELL: The baby?

ELIZABETH: God has blessed us once again, even in this hard time.

DUNSTER: I am an old and beaten man, Jonathan, but God and this woman yet bring new life to the world.

MITCHELL: Well, God bless you, and the child. My blessings on Master David, and young Jonathan, and their mother.

ELIZABETH: We all be thanking you.

DUNSTER: She has many sorrows and regrets, but she warms me yet. She is my heart now, as mine own has been taken from me. God does not give us a burden without giving also help to bear it. Love has conquered hate in her, though her mind is not with mine to this day, and both our days be sorrows and sadness till the end of them.

MITCHELL: They cannot hound you much more, and there is a new life in Plymouth Colony. Joy will sing again in the Lord's time.

DUNSTER: No, no, my joy lay in Harvard Yard, and another unbaptised child will rouse them once again. Of such men there is no end.

MITCHELL: It must end. It must end.

DUNSTER: In the dust.

ELIZABETH: We must go and post the bond.

DUNSTER: Yes. I still have that cider, Jonathan, if you ever sail southward. Your company would please an old man whose time has past.

Pause.

MITCHELL: No. For all my sorrow and pain, you are still a fallen angel, Henry Dunster, a man who would destroy my faith and Church, and I'll not be drinking with the Devil.

ELIZABETH: You would drink with Bellingham instead?

Pause.

MITCHELL: His drink is strong and sore bitter, but it is of the Law, and of God.

ELIZABETH: You are all too sure of God. All of you are all too sure of God.

DUNSTER: Elizabeth, come. The bailiff will be waiting. We must not trouble this good man more.

ELIZABETH: No, we have had too much of troubling good men.

MITCHELL: Goodbye, Henry Dunster.

DUNSTER and ELIZABETH exit.

MITCHELL: Goodbye, my friend.

MITCHELL stands alone. The lights fade.

ACT II, SCENE SIX

MITCHELL's Study, Feb. 29, 1659. Continuation of I-1. Lights fade up on MITCHELL and CHAUNCY as before.

MITCHELL: The Lord have mercy on us all.

CHAUNCY: Amen.

MITCHELL: Was there some mishap?

CHAUNCY: I am told not, just a body old and worn beyond the winter's hard use. A quiet illness quickly carried him off.

MITCHELL: And he with a daughter but three years old, and two sons not to their maturity. How is Elizabeth, Mistress Dunster?

CHAUNCY: Well, I am told, though much saddened. She was with him till the last.

MITCHELL: Yes, she was always by him.

CHAUNCY: It is said she will be moving back to Cambridge once the estate is settled.

MITCHELL: Yes, Scituate was never home for her. Only her love for him held her there. The controversy that caused his resignation and their removal hastened this end, I am sure. His soul was worn more than his body, and the winter was in men's hearts. I pray all may forgive him now, for he was truly a good man.

CHAUNCY: Yes.

MITCHELL: He could no more live without his heart, which beat in yonder Yard, and now mine heart is taken from me with this news, this hard news. No end, no end.

CHAUNCY: I am sorry, Jonathan. I know what great friends you were.

MITCHELL: No, I was no true friend to Henry Dunster.

CHAUNCY: You disagreed with his error, that is well known, but your feelings for him are also evident. I myself have often felt a coldness in you towards me for replacing him in the Presidency, especially since I agreed to be silent on certain matters in order to obtain the post. You think I am not the man he was. Perhaps I am not, but one does what one can.

MITCHELL: I hold that not against you, Mr. Chauncy. I understand why men choose silence. The pain you cause is in reminding me of a time I stood not well.

CHAUNCY: Perhaps there is yet a time to help this old friend. There is a request in the will that touches us, you and I. Perhaps we can somewhat atone for our weakness.

MITCHELL: The will is known?

CHAUNCY: He prepared it himself, near a year ago. He had some inkling, I suppose. A copy was passed to me, as I, and you, are asked to serve the estate.

MITCHELL: Have you it?

CHAUNCY: Here.

CHAUNCY hands paper to MITCHELL, who tries to read it, then hands it back.

MITCHELL: Will you read, my eyes have too much mist.

CHAUNCY: Yes. "The Will of Henry Dunster. O Lord, my times are in thy hands, and I fully submit to thine appointments, committing my spirit into thy hands, for thou hast redeemed it, and by many deliverances out of tribulations sealed to my soul the truth of thy word and thy fatherly love and care for me. Therefore, I commit both soul and body in life and death and resurrection unto thee, and I commit my family after my decease to thee, who will be their father and protector. I hope now to procure peace concerning these earthly goods of which thou hast made me steward, so I order and constitute this as my last will and testament."

MITCHELL: A good man, a good man.

CHAUNCY: "My will is that a true and just inventory of all my lands and houses, household goods, and all manner of debts, dues and rights be taken, so far as man's wisdom can attain. But whereas the value of my library cannot be taken except by judicious and learned men, because some of my books are in such languages that common Englishmen do not know one letter, therefore I do appoint my reverend and trusty friends and brothers in Christ, the Pastor of the Church at Cambridge and the President of the College to value the books and lay aside the books specified as given to my wife." Then there is a list of books. "I give and bequeath unto Mr. Chauncy such mathematics books as hitherto I have lent him, with what household goods I left in Cambridge, namely, my great press in the Hall chamber and another press for books in the study. I give and bequeath unto Mr. Mitchell Rollock's Commentaries upon John, which heretofore I lent him, with all the rest of that holy man's commentaries upon the Scripture that shall be found in my library.

MITCHELL takes a book from the shelf and holds it gently.

MITCHELL: It is a great reward for such a small chore.

CHAUNCY: The books are for the friend that was, not the librarian to be.

MITCHELL: Then it is a great reward for a task poorly done.

CHAUNCY: You must not blame yourself so. It was not your fault he fell into error, not your fault that he would not be discreet.

MITCHELL: In his old age he gets children, children who live and grow and flourish. Mine die unbaptised after but a few breaths of life. Where is God's judgement, Mr. Chauncy? Who does the Lord say fell into error?

CHAUNCY: Talk not this way.

MITCHELL: Is not that the judgement? Is Henry not welcomed into heaven, while I sit grieving here over yet another child? Are all my sermons hollow sounds because when I needed to speak I stood silent? Henry is dead, the cider has turned to vinegar in the cask, and no more can I come to Henry Dunster and stand to his aid. No more, no more.

CHAUNCY: There is yet one thing Henry Dunster has asked. Not all will welcome it, but if we stand together, there is yet one time to stand for him.

MITCHELL: What? What?

CHAUNCY: He has asked to be buried in Cambridge.

MITCHELL: Yes. He belongs by Harvard. He will rest there. We must see to it. Oh my soul, we must see to it.

CHAUNCY: There is a plot of land just outside the Yard. I could arrange a grave there, facing the College. A new burying ground for the Presidents of Harvard.

MITCHELL: Yes. Do it. I will see that his body is brought and a stone prepared. Oh, it will be done, Henry Dunster, it will be done. His family, Elizabeth, the children, need they any aid?

CHAUNCY: The rest of the will makes provision for them. They will not be wanting.

MITCHELL: No, it is we who are wanting. Wanting his life, and wisdom, and courage. Henry Dunster is dead, heaven is richer, and it is this world that is wanting. In silence and the dust, Henry Dunster, and wanting. God forgive us all.

    The lights fade.

    CURTAIN

Sex and Violence for Women

This play is actually based on the conventions of a Roman comedy, a la Plautus and Terence. It has the same physical comedy and set layout, with the five doors, one on each end and three in the middle. The reversal is that most of the characters are women and the male is mainly decorative. It was given a workshop production by Koality Productions in Atlanta, but I have never been able to get anyone interested in a full production. I have dreams of what Lucille Ball and Carol Burnett in their prime might have been able to do with it, but those dreams will never be fulfilled.

SEX AND VIOLENCE FOR WOMEN

A Farce By David Davis

Member
All rights & privileges.

David Davis
100 Hunters Ridge Court
Roswell, GA 30076
daviddaviswriter@gmail.com

Copyright 1989 David Davis

CAST OF CHARACTERS

B.W. .... A Beautiful Young Woman

HARRY .... Male, About 30, Not Good Looking

GAIL .... Harry's Wife

AUDRY .... Harry's Other Wife

GRACE .... The Saleslady in the Shop, About 55

DARLENE .... A Professional Wrestler

SETTING

The ladies dressing room of an exclusive beachwear shop near a beach. A summer Saturday sometime after the sexual revolution but before AIDS.

ACT I, SCENE ONE

The women's dressing room area of an exclusive beach/sportswear shop. There are four doors to changing cubicles along the back, a mirror stage left, and a curtained entrance from the shop stage right. In the stage directions, the dressing rooms will be referred to by number, 1-4, with 1 being stage right and 4 stage left. Near the curtained entrance to the shop there is a small rack to hang clothes on and a sign saying "Do not return clothes to racks. Hang clothes here." A few swimsuits and shorts, etc., hang on this rack. When the curtain rises, the stage is empty. After a moment, a beautiful young woman (B.W.) comes out of 1, wearing a bikini. She examines herself in the mirror, adjusting the fit of the suit, then goes back into 1. A second later, HARRY, a slightly nerdish, slightly short, nondescript but not really ugly man, dressed in jogging shorts and a t-shirt, runs in, out of breath. He starts to go into the first open door, 2, but hesitates, closes 2 and 3, then goes into 4 and closes the door behind him. As soon as he is in, GAIL and AUDRY rush in. They are dressed in shorts and t-shirts or one piece, modest bathing suits with cover-ups, or other beachwear. They also are slightly out of breath.

AUDRY: We got him now.

GAIL: You saw him come in?

AUDRY: Yes. Sneaking between the tank tops and the cover-ups.

GAIL: OK.

> GAIL tries to open 1. It is locked. She bangs on the door with her fist.

GAIL: Harry, you bastard, get out here and die like a man!

> The door opens. GAIL looks in.

GAIL: Oh, excuse me. Wrong door.

> Closes 1.

GAIL: Naked lady.

AUDRY: That doesn't mean Harry wasn't in there.

> GRACE, the saleslady, wearing a sundress, enters, stopping GAIL's move toward 2.

GRACE: May I help you?

AUDRY: We're looking for a man.

GRACE: In here?

GAIL: He's in one of these dressing rooms.

GRACE: Oh my. Who is he?

AUDRY and **GAIL:** My husband.

> AUDRY and GAIL exchange dirty looks.

GRACE: Oh my. Would you like me to call the police?

AUDRY: Not until after we kill him.

GRACE: Oh my.

> GRACE faints. AUDRY catches her.

GAIL: Now look what you've done.

AUDRY: Me? You're the one rushes in here banging on doors. Now what do I do?

GAIL: Lay her down, let the blood rush to her head.

> They gently lay GRACE on the floor.

GAIL: Check her pulse.

AUDRY: Seems OK.

GAIL: She still breathing OK?

AUDRY: Yeah.

GAIL: She'll be OK, just let her lie a minute.

> B.W. comes out of 1 in a bikini so skimpy it is probably illegal. AUDRY and GAIL stare at her as she glances down at GRACE, then almost steps over GRACE to get to the mirror. Once again she checks herself out in the mirror, then goes back into 1.

AUDRY: Would you believe....?

GAIL: Can you imagine...., in public?

AUDRY: If my mother.....

GAIL: I've been naked and had more on.

AUDRY: And her figure.....

GAIL: Silicone, gotta be.

AUDRY: Liposuction on the hips.

GAIL: Tummy tuck.

AUDRY: Fanny tuck too.

GAIL: Or a personal trainer and nothing else to do.

AUDRY: If a trainer could do that for me, I'd get a divorce and marry him.

GAIL: Well, you may get your chance, because at least one of us isn't married to Harry.

AUDRY: Oh, yeah.

> GRACE begins to stir.

GRACE: Oh my.

GAIL: Are you all right?

GRACE: Oh my, the killers.

AUDRY: Oh, no. We're not killers. It was just talk, you know.

GAIL: Look, no guns.

GRACE: Knives?

AUDRY: Nothing, just our bare hands.

GRACE: Oh my.

AUDRY: No, no, not bare hands. Nothing, no weapons. No killing, honest.

GAIL: Hell of a lawsuit probably. Lots of yelling and screaming, that kind of thing, but no killing.

GRACE: Oh.

GAIL: I mean, it's not every day you find out your husband is married.

AUDRY: Or meet his wife.

GAIL: At the beach yet.

AUDRY: Talk about awkward moments, right out in front of the lifeguard and everybody.

GRACE: Oh. So you're........, and you're.......too?

GAIL: You got it.

GRACE: And you just.....?

AUDRY: Five minutes ago.

GRACE: And he.....?

GAIL: Ran like a sprinter on steroids.

GRACE: In here?

GAIL: Behind one of those doors.

GRACE: Oh my.

AUDRY: Oh my.

GAIL: Oh my.

AUDRY: Do you feel like getting up now?

GRACE: I think so.

> They help her to her feet and support her for a moment.

GAIL: Do you feel all right?

GRACE: Yes, I think. What are you going to do?

GAIL: Open doors until I find the grand prize. Where's Monty Hall when you need him?

AUDRY: Whichever one he's in, he locked the door.

GRACE: There are keys, back at the sales desk.

GAIL: Well, let's go. And if you don't mind, maybe we should lock the front door and put the "Closed" sign in the window for a few minutes.

> GRACE starts to exit, but stumbles a little, and both GAIL and AUDRY have to help her walk off. As soon as they are gone, B.W. comes out of 1, wearing short shorts and a white, sleeveless T-shirt. She exits into the shop. Then, HARRY peeks out of 4, sees the coast is clear, and slides out, closing the door behind him. He goes to the curtain, looks out, and quickly ducks into 1. B.W. enters with three more bathing suits and tries to go into 1. When she finds the door locked, she goes into 2. Immediately GRACE, GAIL, and AUDRY enter with a ring of keys.

GRACE: I could have sworn these were in the top drawer.

AUDRY: Well, we found them.

GRACE: But they are supposed to be in the top drawer.

GAIL: It's OK. He couldn't have left. I watched the entrance the whole time.

GRACE: I think it's this key.

> GAIL takes the keys. She goes to 2, quietly tries the knob, finds it locked, puts the key in the lock and opens the door.

GAIL: Excuse me.

> She closes the door.

GAIL: She's naked again.

AUDRY: How could you tell?

GRACE: Who?

GAIL: The next Penthouse Pet, Miss Plastic Surgery 1979.

GRACE: What?

GAIL: Some broad with a taste for swimsuits you could swallow in one gulp. She used to be in there. Now she's here.

AUDRY: (Pointing to 1) You don't think....?

GAIL: No, too easy.

> GAIL goes to 3, turns the knob and opens the door. The room

> is empty. They all move to 4, the door nearest the mirror. B.W. comes out of 2, this time wearing a one-piece, mesh suit that may or may not be lined, it's hard to tell. AUDRY, GAIL, and GRACE stop and stare at B.W. as she goes to the mirror and examines herself. While all the attention is on B.W., HARRY, carrying a handful of clothing, slides out of 1 and into 2. B.W. finishes her posing, and goes back into 2, closing the door behind her.

GRACE: Oh my.
AUDRY: Was there anything under....?
GAIL: Fishnet, just fishnet.
GRACE: I didn't know we sold.....
AUDRY: Who would buy....?
GAIL: Only if they looked like....
GRACE: Oh my.

> Pause.

GAIL: Well, back to the hunt.

> GAIL uses the key to open 4. It is empty. They all turn toward 1.

AUDRY: This coon is treed.
GAIL: Coon is treed?
AUDRY: I grew up in North Carolina. It slips out now and then.
GAIL: Oh.
AUDRY: Where you from?
GAIL: Chicago. Years ago. Got tired of having a frozen nose half the year.
AUDRY: I can relate to that.
GRACE: Uh, excuse me, but about the coon, uh, your husband.
GAIL: Yeah, let's get this over with.

> They move to 1.

GAIL: Be ready to grab him if he tries to run.

> AUDRY crouches outside the door, ready to spring. GRACE goes to the entrance to block the only means of escape. GAIL checks that they both are ready, quietly puts the key in the lock, then quickly jerks open the door. Nothing happens. GAIL goes in the room and looks around, then comes back out.

GAIL: This is impossible. Houdini couldn't do this.

> GAIL signals the others to go back to 3 and 4. AUDRY goes to 3 and GRACE to 4. Silently, GAIL signals a countdown (three, two, one). They yank the doors open simultaneously. Nothing happens. They look inside. All three rooms are empty. They look at each other. They look at 2.

AUDRY: No. Couldn't be.

GRACE: She would have screamed.

GAIL: Women who dress like she does never scream.

AUDRY: But he....

GAIL: He sweet talked us, didn't he?

AUDRY: Well..., actually, I sort of pushed him.

GAIL: That's what he wanted you to think.

AUDRY: You think?

GAIL: You bet.

AUDRY: That bastard! Let's get him.

> They start toward 2, but just then 2 opens and B.W. comes out in yet another swimsuit. This is a bikini that seems to be all fringe and no suit. They stare at her as she walks to the mirror, then they gather around the open door of 2 and stare in. The room seems empty. B.W. walks back, and they separate to let her through. They stare at her, then at the room, then back at her.

B.W.: Are you people lesbians or something?

> B.W. goes into 2, closing the door behind her. AUDRY, GAIL, and GRACE stare at each other for a moment.

AUDRY: Well, bust my britches.

GAIL: Are you sure you saw him come in here?

AUDRY: Yes!

GAIL: It wasn't the walking sex machine?

AUDRY: I could tell her from a man across a crowded K-Mart.

GAIL: So where is he?

AUDRY: How should I know?

GRACE: Oh my.

> Suddenly there is a bloodcurdling scream from 2. The door flies open, and B.W. runs out, nude (or topless, whatever you can get away with) but holding clothes and parts of bathing suits in strategic locations. She runs into the knot of people in front of the door, scattering them back and knocking the ring

of keys from GAIL's hand, then runs into 1 and closes the door behind her. GRACE faints as soon as she sees B.W. Right behind B.W. coming out of 2 is HARRY, crawling on the floor. He sees GAIL and AUDRY, and stands up. He is wearing a jockstrap and a bikini top. AUDRY screams and ducks into 4. HARRY sees the keys on the floor, and both HARRY and GAIL dive for them. HARRY wins the keys, rolls away from GAIL, leaving her prone on the floor, and jumps into 3 and closes the door. For a moment, no one moves. Then GAIL rolls over and sits up.

GAIL: This is getting ridiculous.

GAIL gets up, goes over to GRACE, sees she has just fainted again, and leaves her lying where she is.

GAIL: How Victorian.

GAIL stares at the doors a minute, then goes and knocks on 4.

GAIL: Excuse me, but would the other Mrs. Hudson get the hell back out here!

AUDRY comes out of 4.

AUDRY: Audry.
GAIL: What?
AUDRY: Audry. My name is Audry.
GAIL: Audry. Gail.
AUDRY: Pleased to meet you, Gail. (She sees GRACE on the floor.) What happened?
GAIL: Fainted again.
AUDRY: On my. Will she....?
GAIL: In a minute.
AUDRY: Where did....?
GAIL: In there. (Points to 3.)
AUDRY: Oh. Was he wearing a .....?
GAIL: Sure looked that way.
AUDRY: What about.....?
GAIL: Not a stitch. Girl spends more time naked than a stripper.
AUDRY: I thought you had to keep your panties on.
GAIL: What makes you think she owns any?
AUDRY: That's a frightening thought.
GAIL: She probably thinks life is a porno movie.
AUDRY: Where is she?

GAIL: There.

    GAIL goes to 1 and knocks.

GAIL: Excuse me, I don't mean to disturb you again, but what the hell happened in there?

    B.W. opens the door enough to stick her head out.

B.W.: There was a man hanging from the ceiling.
AUDRY: That was no man, that was our husband.
B.W.: Is he gone?
GAIL: He's two doors down.
B.W.: Oh.

    B.W. pulls her head back in and closes the door. GRACE starts to stir on the floor.

GRACE: Oh my.
AUDRY: The delicate flower is back.
GRACE: Oh my, oh my, oh my.
GAIL: This lady has got to expand her vocabulary.

    AUDRY helps GRACE up.

GRACE: What happened?
GAIL: The naked lady is now behind door number one, and the bigamist in the bra is now behind door number three, with the keys. The tiger is behind door number four, and door number two leads to the twilight zone.
AUDRY: With the keys?
GAIL: With the keys.
GRACE: Oh my. I've got to have those keys back.
AUDRY: Why did you give him the keys?
GAIL: I didn't give him the keys, he took the keys. How stupid do you think I am?
AUDRY: I don't think you're stupid.
GAIL: Good.
AUDRY: A little naive maybe.
GAIL: Naive?
AUDRY: Well, you did marry a man who was already married. That shows a little gullibility.
GAIL: Gullibility? Now wait a minute, you married him too.
AUDRY: But I married him first.
GAIL: I'm not sure that's a claim to fame, but even if it is, how do you know who married him first?
AUDRY: I've known Harry for years.

GAIL: Fine, but when did you marry him?

AUDRY: It will be six months next week.

GAIL: Seven months, last week.

AUDRY: I'll kill him.

> AUDRY goes and bangs on 3.

AUDRY: Harry, listen up in there! I hope you're comfortable in there, because if you ever come out I'm going to tie your lying tongue to your toes.

GAIL: Six weeks after our wedding. My god, that's just two weeks after our honeymoon!

AUDRY: I'm going to exchange your ears and eyes so you can see yourself lie.

GAIL: We come back from our honeymoon, and two weeks later he marries another woman.

GRACE: That does seem a little insulting.

AUDRY: I'm going to turn your skin inside out and make you wear wool underwear. You hear me? Your life is going to be pure hell as long as I live. You hear me?

GAIL: What in the world could he see in this hick that after six weeks with me.....?

> GAIL goes to 3, shoves AUDRY aside, and bangs on door.

GAIL: Harry, you camel fart, you better answer me! Why in hell would you marry this bumpkin right after four weeks in Maui with me? Two weeks after our honeymoon, you piece of drivel!

AUDRY: Well, I bet I could guess that.

GAIL: Now listen you...

AUDRY: I mean, obviously he didn't get what he expected on the honeymoon.

GAIL: You little bitch, for your information, it was a hell of a honeymoon.

AUDRY: Well, he certainly wasn't worn out when he took me to Europe on our honeymoon.

GAIL: He went to Europe on business.

AUDRY: I was the business!

GRACE: Ladies, ladies, please....

AUDRY and **GAIL:** What?

GRACE: Oh my. I don't mean to interrupt, but could you perhaps discuss these personal matters a little later? I mean, this is a business here, and one of my customers is locked in a dressing room for fear of a madman in a bra hanging from the ceiling. This is not the time or the place to solve your sexual difficulties.

GAIL: I don't have any "sexual difficulties." I like sex as much as the next woman. Or the "other woman" in this case.

GRACE: Well, whatever, could you please collect your husband and settle your problems somewhere else?

GAIL: What do you think I'm trying to do?

AUDRY: OK, OK, just calm down. You want her to faint again?

GAIL: OK, OK. I'm calm. OK?

AUDRY: (to GRACE) Can you cut us a little slack? We've had quite a shock today.

GAIL: Yeah, we learned we have the same bad taste in men.

AUDRY: OK, I'll admit to that. That's one thing we have in common.

GAIL: Lady, that's only the beginning of what we have in common.

AUDRY: Ye gods and little fishes, what a thought.

GAIL: No kidding.

AUDRY: Talk about comparing notes.

> B.W. sticks her head out again and signals to GRACE to come over to her. GRACE crosses to her.

B.W.: What's happening?

GRACE: The wives are comparing notes, and the husband locked himself in the dressing room.

B.W.: What?

GRACE: It's a long story.

> B.W. comes out of the dressing room. She wears her own shorts and T-shirt, but now one of the bikini tops is under the shirt as a bra.

B.W.: The peeper's locked himself in there?

GAIL: With the keys.

B.W.: Well, why don't you just call the police?

AUDRY: He's our husband, we don't want him arrested, we want him drawn and quartered.

GAIL: And if you don't mind, I'd like to keep this off the six o'clock news.

B.W.: He's married to both of you?

GAIL: It's a long story.

B.W.: So I hear. Is it, you know, like a threesome?

> AUDRY and GAIL look at each other, then laugh.

AUDRY: No, Honey, good old Harry in there never let us get together until today.

B.W.: Oh, is that why you're mad at him?

GAIL: Two points for the genius with the enlarged frontal lobes.

B.W.: Hey, these are all natural, I'll have you know.

GRACE: Ladies, please! Are you going to remove your husband, or am I going to call the police?

GAIL: Go ahead, call them. I bet this store could use a little publicity. I can just see the newspaper headline, "Peeping-tom transvestite bigamist arrested in Barely Bikini shop dressing room."

GRACE: Oh my.

B.W.: He's a transvestite too? Wow, you people are kinky.

GAIL: No, he's....well, at least I don't think....do you....?

AUDRY: All I know he's definitely not gay.

GAIL: That's for sure.

GRACE: Oh my.

B.W.: So, how you gonna get him out?

GAIL: Good question.

AUDRY: We could break down the door.

GRACE: Not unless you pay for it in advance.

GAIL: You take MasterCard?

GRACE: I don't think so, not for doors.

AUDRY: Wait, I know.

> AUDRY signals the others to huddle up. They whisper together for a moment. Then AUDRY and GAIL go over to 3. B.W. goes to 4, but waits just inside the door with the door open.

GAIL: OK, Harry, you win this round, but we're not through with you yet.

AUDRY: We're going to be waiting for you at home with a lawyer and all kinds of summons and stuff.

GAIL: Who's home?

AUDRY: His parent's. He's not about to come back to your place or mine.

GAIL: "Your place or mine," god, that's what got me into this.

AUDRY: We'll see you in court, Harry.

GAIL: And bring lots of money.

> GAIL tiptoes into 1 and AUDRY slides into 2, and with B.W., they all close their doors. GRACE then exits, and after a moment HARRY, dressed in a mini-skirt and bare-chested, eases the door open and peeks out. We hear the bell that signals the outer door being opened and closed, and HARRY edges over to the curtain to peek out. AUDRY opens her door a crack, and sees HARRY.

AUDRY: Now!

> The other doors fly open and AUDRY and GAIL run after HARRY, with B.W. trailing along behind. HARRY runs into the shop, and we hear the noise of a giant commotion.

GRACE: (offstage) Be careful! Watch out! Watch the rack! No, No, not the miniskirts! Aiii!

Selected Plays of David Davis

> GRACE runs screaming into the dressing area and slams herself behind 2. HARRY is only a step or two behind her, but he is covered with bathing suits, sports clothes, and ladies underwear as he leaps back into 3, leaving a trail of clothing scattered across the floor. Another step or two behind are AUDRY and GAIL, but they too are entangled in various items of clothing, and, uncertain of which closed door HARRY went into, they begin to bang on both, GAIL on 2 and AUDRY on 3.

GAIL: Harry, you louse, I'm gonna get you.

> GAIL tries the doorknob of 2, and to her surprise, it opens. GRACE, who has fainted, falls out.

GAIL: Damn, lady, fainting went out in the forties. (to AUDRY) He's in yours.
AUDRY: It's locked.
GAIL: Damn, back to square one.

> B.W. enters, picking up clothes from the floor as she goes.

B.W.: Hey, this looks kinda nice.

> B.W. goes into 1 with the clothes she has picked up. AUDRY and GAIL stare at the closed door behind her.

GAIL: Too much sun done fried that little brain.
AUDRY: Amen. Now what?

> GRACE slowly revives, crawls over to the curtain, looks out at the shop, and faints again.

GAIL: There is something wrong with that lady.
AUDRY: She fainted.
GAIL: No kidding, Einstein. I mean she faints if anybody burps.
AUDRY: Maybe she has low blood pressure.
GAIL: Maybe she needs a courage transplant.
AUDRY: Oh, you mean like Burt Lahr, the Wizard of Oz, the lion.
GAIL: Another genius. Well, anymore bright ideas about Harry? All your last one did was wreck an entire store.
AUDRY: Oh, I don't know, maybe we should just leave him alone.
GAIL: I don't think he's going to fall for that again.
AUDRY: No, I'm serious. So far all we've done is tear up a store and make an old lady pass out a dozen times. And all we've done to Harry is make him run a couple of wind sprints.
GAIL: Well, he can't stay in there forever. Sooner or later he has to pee.

AUDRY: Knowing Harry, he'll probably just pee through the keyhole.

GAIL: Then he'll get hungry, or thirsty, something.

AUDRY: And just what are we going to do when he does come out? Beat him up? Scream in his ear? Give him a severe tongue lashing?

GAIL: Sounds good for starters.

AUDRY: Listen, I don't want to end up in jail over this. Why don't we just go get a lawyer and let him handle this.

GAIL: You want Harry arrested? Sent to jail? Is that what you mean?

AUDRY: No, I guess not. I mean, it's not like he took any money or anything. He spent a whole lot on me, as a matter of fact. And I didn't quit my job or anything. I liked Harry; we had a lot of fun together.

GAIL: Well, so did we.

AUDRY: I can guess. I just feel so betrayed.

GAIL: Yeah.

AUDRY: I'm just saying, don't we need a lawyer for the divorce? I mean, couldn't this get really complicated?

GAIL: Not for you. All you need is an annulment. You were never legally married. I'm the one who has to have a real divorce.

AUDRY: I'm not married to Harry too? I mean, if you got a divorce, I wouldn't be still married to Harry?

GAIL: Good Lord, girl, you're not thinking of staying with him are you?

AUDRY: No. Well, I mean, well, obviously he prefers me. After all....

GAIL: But he knew you for years, you said, and he married me...

> B.W. comes out of 1. This bathing suit is illegal, immoral, and almost immaterial. It could get the cast arrested in six states. Pure sex walks across the stage to the mirror. AUDRY and GAIL stop and stare. HARRY sticks his head out of the door and sees B.W.

HARRY: Oh my God.

> GAIL kicks at the door just as HARRY pulls his head back in. B.W. turns to AUDRY and GAIL.

B.W.: What do you think?

GAIL: I think you should be shot.

AUDRY: It's women like you who give the rest of us a bad name.

B.W.: Hey, you've got your swinging little kinky marriage. I'm just a single girl doing the best I can.

GAIL: Lady, on your worst day, you make me look like a melted candlestick.

AUDRY: You look like a doe in heat smells to a buck.

B.W.: Well, sorry.

B.W. slams back into 1.

GAIL: Looks like a doe smells?

AUDRY: So all the bucks fight for her.

GAIL: Oh. That a Carolina thing?

AUDRY: National Geographic.

GRACE rouses again.

GRACE: Oh god, oh god, oh god.

GAIL: Finally, real emotion.

AUDRY: You all right?

GRACE: What happened?

GAIL: We're back where we started.

GRACE: Oh god.

GAIL: That's it, let it all hang out.

GRACE: I dreamed I saw a naked woman chasing a man in a miniskirt all over the store while he threw clothes at her.

AUDRY: Pretty close.

GRACE: Please, please, could you just wait outside and shoot him on the street?

AUDRY: Maybe we could smoke him out.

GAIL: Automatic sprinklers in the false ceiling.

AUDRY: Flood him out.

GRACE: Oh god! Please!

GAIL: Anybody got any Mace? Maybe we could spray it through the keyhole.

AUDRY: Not me.

GRACE: Thank goodness, no.

GAIL: Well.

Pause.

GAIL: OK, OK, no more Mr. Nice Guy. I'm calling in the heavy artillery. Where's your phone?

GRACE: By the cash register.

GAIL: Stay here and see he doesn't switch rooms.

AUDRY: Who are you calling?

GAIL: The Bride of the Devil.

GAIL exits into shop. AUDRY and GRACE exchange looks. The lights fade.

ACT I, SCENE TWO

> About thirty minutes later. AUDRY sits on the floor with her back against 3. B.W. is modeling a mini-skirt and a vest (that's all) for herself. GRACE has brought in a stool, and sits on it with her back against the wall.

B.W.: So, how does this little menage a trois of yours work? You got a king-size bed, or what?

AUDRY: Just a king-size bastard.

B.W.: Oh, is he really big?

AUDRY: Huh?

B.W.: You know, his thing,...his manhood...his penis.

AUDRY: Oh. Jeez, lady, I ain't the National Inquirer.

B.W.: Well, excuse me. I just never met any Mormons before. I'm curious.

AUDRY: Mormons?

B.W.: You know, twenty wives and all.

AUDRY: Not twenty, just two. I think. I hope. God. And we aren't Mormons. Not even Mormons do this anymore.

B.W.: So what are you?

AUDRY: Huh? Oh, Methodist.

B.W.: Methodists? Gee, I always thought Methodists were stuffy prudes.

> B.W. goes back into 1.

AUDRY: Hell, so did I. I thought I was a stuffy prude. I was a virgin till I was eighteen. Now look at me; I've got a husband who wears bras, I'm locked in a bikini shop watching Miss Nude Universe change clothes, and my husband's other wife is out in the shop waiting for the bride of the devil. I don't think I'm a Methodist anymore.

GRACE: I'm an Episcopalian. We used to believe one wife at a time was enough, but since the new prayerbook came out I'm not so sure.

> GAIL enters from shop.

GAIL: She's parking her car. She'll be in in a minute.

AUDRY: Good. Are you a Methodist?

GAIL: Catholic. Why?

AUDRY: Oh god, a mixed marriage.

GAIL: Did he tell you he was a.....

AUDRY: Born and bred.

GAIL: And he swore to a priest....

AUDRY: I don't think Harry and the truth have met lately.

GRACE: That sounds like an understatement to me.

GAIL: I've got to go let her in.

> GAIL exits to shop. AUDRY bangs once on the door behind her.

AUDRY: Harry, you lied to a preacher. God's gonna get you for that.

> We hear the bell of the Shop door ring as it opens and closes. AUDRY and GRACE stand up in anticipation. GAIL enters and pulls back the curtain to admit DARLENE. DARLENE is the kind of woman who could play linebacker for any team in the NFL. She is huge, muscular, (not fat, just enormous), the female version of Andre the Giant. In addition, she is not beautiful, but she deliberately looks worse than she has to, and when she tries, she can be as ugly as sin. She wears jeans and a sweatshirt, both of which look like they were bought at a "Big Men's Store." She carries a large tool box, which looks like it could easily weigh two or three hundred pounds, but she carries it without much effort.

GAIL: Ladies, may I present the National Women's Professional Wrestling Association Gold Belt Champion, the Bride of the Devil herself, Darlene Navakavich.

DARLENE: That's enough, Gail.

GAIL: Sorry. This is the saleslady I told you about, uh...

GRACE: Grace, Grace Evans.

DARLENE: Pleased to meet you.

GAIL: And this is Harry's other wife, Audry.

DARLENE: Hello.

AUDRY: Uh, hi, uh, Mrs. Devil.

DARLENE: Call me Darlene.

AUDRY: Right.

GAIL: You're doing better, Grace. I was afraid just the sight of Darlene would have you fainting away.

DARLENE: I didn't do my growl. It's my growl that gets them.

GAIL: Do it.

DARLENE: Gail...

GAIL: Come on, show them.

> DARLENE puts her tool box down and pumps herself up and ugly. Just as she growls, B.W. comes out of 1 wearing a frilly sundress. DARLENE growls right at her. B.W. screams and jumps back into 1.

GRACE: Oh my.

DARLENE: Who was that?

GAIL: Miss Gonorrhea of 1979.

AUDRY: She was dressed this time.

GAIL: Don't worry, Darlene probably scared her right out of her clothes.

DARLENE: Is she married to Harry too?

GAIL: God, I hope not.

DARLENE: Where is the bigamist of the moment, anyway?

> AUDRY knocks on 3.

AUDRY: Harry. Have we got a surprise for you.

> DARLENE crosses to 3 and starts to examine the door. AUDRY goes over to GAIL.

AUDRY: I'm just curious, but where did you two meet?

GAIL: She was my college roommate.

AUDRY: Really.

GAIL: She's got a B.A. in Philosophy from University of Chicago.

AUDRY: You're kidding.

GAIL: She's read more Schopenhouer than you've read romance novels. Even understands it, which is really scary.

AUDRY: So why the, uh.....?

GAIL: Darlene, about how much did you make wrestling last year?

DARLENE: Oh, about $250,000.

AUDRY: Oh my god.

DARLENE: Even big, ugly philosophers like the big bucks.

AUDRY: Oh, I wouldn't say you're that....

DARLENE: Honey, I make big money being ugly and breaking bones. I am ug-ly.

GAIL: (A routine.) Ugly as sin.

DARLENE: Ugly as the Devil.

GAIL: So ugly the angels hide.

DARLENE: So ugly strong men faint and women cry.

GAIL: It's the Bride of the Devil herself, Mrs. Lucifer!

DARLENE: (laughing) Ugly all the way to the bank.

AUDRY: OK, you're ugly as a peach pit, I get the idea.

DARLENE: Ugly as a peach pit? How rustic. Where did you find her?

GAIL: She's from Carolina.

DARLENE: Oh. I guess that explains it.

GAIL: So, what about good old Harry in there?

DARLENE: Well, the hinges are inside, so I can't just pop the door off. I could try to pick the lock, but if he just holds it on the inside, he could still keep it from turning. I think the best bet is going to be just taking the lock right off the door. Then we can just have a little tug of war on the knobs.

    B.W. peaks out of 1, sees DARLENE, and slams back in.

GRACE: Oh dear. Miss, Miss! It's all right. She's just a wrestler here to beat up the husband.

    B.W. slowly peeks out of 1 again.

DARLENE: Don't worry, I only kill rats and beauty contest winners.

    B.W. slams back inside 1 again.

GRACE: Oh my.

GAIL: What do you think, Miss Nude America contest?

AUDRY: Miss Nude Mars more likely.

DARLENE: I take it this lady is fond of displaying her assets.

AUDRY: Like a bank in an annual report.

GAIL: A very well endowed bank.

DARLENE: Ah. I get the picture. Mammae magnae.

GAIL: You got the tools you need for the lock?

DARLENE: No problem.

    DARLENE pats the tool box, then carries it over to 3.

GRACE: Uh, is this going to ruin the lock?

DARLENE: No. Don't worry, I'll put it back good as new as soon as I finish holding Harry while Gail stomps on him.

AUDRY: Hey, I want to get in a few licks.

DARLENE: No problem. Tag team husband beating; Feminism personified. I love it.

    DARLENE sets to work on the lock.

AUDRY: You think this is gonna work?

GAIL: Well, we know he's in there, there's no way he can get out, and he's not about to run over Darlene the way he ran over us.

AUDRY: I hope you're right.

> As DARLENE is working on the lock, there are suddenly sounds coming from above the dressing room.

DARLENE: What's that?

GAIL: I don't know.

GRACE: Oh my.

AUDRY: What?

GRACE: It sounds like he's gotten into the false ceiling.

DARLENE: Oh, great. How big is the space?

GRACE: Just a foot or two, for the heating vents and stuff.

DARLENE: That lets me out.

GAIL: How do you get in?

DARLENE: Just stand on something, lift up a tile, slide it over, and pull yourself up. Hang on to the braces though, the insulation tiles won't hold your weight.

GAIL: (To AUDRY, pointing at 2) Use the stool, go in through there. I'll go up here, and we'll meet in the middle. Darlene, give me a boost.

AUDRY: OK.

DARLENE: Right.

GRACE: Oh my. Be careful, it's dark up there.

> AUDRY takes the stool and goes into 2, stands on the stool, and disappears into the ceiling. GAIL and DARLENE go into 4, DARLENE boosts her up, and GAIL disappears into the ceiling. DARLENE comes back out of 4, and B.W. comes out of 1. She is now dressed in her shorts and T-shirt.

B.W.: What's going on?

GRACE: The peeper's in the ceiling.

> There is a big noise from the ceiling.

GAIL: (from above) I got him!

> HARRY, now dressed in a sundress, suddenly pops out of 3.

DARLENE: Uh-oh.

B.W.: Harry Hudson, is that you?

> DARLENE starts after HARRY. HARRY runs toward the curtain, but stops when he sees GRACE. Both start in surprise.

B.W.: You never told me you got married.

> HARRY evades DARLENE's tackle and runs back around to

> where B.W. is between him and DARLENE. There is a bigger noise from above.

AUDRY: Ow! Let go you bastard!

B.W.: I mean two wives. Really Harry, this is too much. And you didn't invite me to either wedding. Not even a postcard. And why didn't you tell me you were a transvestite? I would have let you wear my clothes.

> DARLENE is chasing HARRY in circles around B.W. Suddenly there is a gigantic crash, and an explosion of dust comes out of 3. HARRY uses this diversion to duck into 1 and slam the door. AUDRY leaps out of 3, but is tackled by GAIL from behind.

GAIL: Not this time, Harry! (Realizes it's not HARRY.) You! Where's Harry? I thought you were Harry!

AUDRY: I thought you were Harry! Damn, you fight dirty.

GAIL: Why didn't you.....?

AUDRY: Couldn't you tell.....?

GAIL: How was I to.....?

AUDRY: Well, my breast are bigger, for starters.

> GAIL gets up and helps AUDRY up.

GAIL: I'm sorry, OK? You hurt?

AUDRY: I don't think so, but my butt is going to be black and blue tomorrow.

B.W.: You never told me it was Harry Hudson you were married to.

AUDRY: And my crotch where you kneed me.

GAIL: I thought you were Harry.

AUDRY: Well, that really should have tipped you off.

GAIL: It was pitch dark up there. (to B.W.) What do you mean, Harry Hudson?

AUDRY: You know him?

B.W.: Of course. Harry Hudson, the doctor, right?

GAIL: You're not....too?

B.W.: Oh, no.

AUDRY: Thank god!

B.W.: We had an affair about three months ago, but it didn't last long.

AUDRY: Three months!

B.W.: He is good though. You're lucky women.

AUDRY: Oh my god!

GAIL: Now I am going to kill him. Blood and guts and everything. Where is he?

> DARLENE points to 1. GAIL crosses to the door.

GAIL: You're dead meat, Harry! You better write you will on your underwear, because your funeral is tomorrow!

B.W.: What are you so upset about? I told you, I broke it off three months ago.

AUDRY: We got married six months ago!

B.W.: Oh. Sorry. I didn't know. It was only about a week. We couldn't have had sex more than fifteen or twenty times. And I never knew he was a transvestite.

AUDRY: Oh god, oh god. (Turns on DARLENE) You! Did you ever sleep with Harry?

DARLENE: Lady, take a real good look at me. Now look at the three women he did sleep with. What do you think?

    Pause. AUDRY looks around.

AUDRY: Well..

DARLENE: Not many men want to go two out of three falls with something this big.

AUDRY: If he lives through this, you can have what's left of him as your sex slave.

GAIL: Have him as your eunuch more likely.

GRACE: I'm glad I'm old.

B.W.: You know, he did pretty good that week for a man with two wives to keep happy.

AUDRY: What is that supposed to mean?

B.W.: Never mind.

GAIL: It means Harry is an over-sexed satyr who is about to loose his flute.

GRACE: Did you say he was a doctor?

DARLENE: OB/Gyn.

GRACE: Oh my.

DARLENE: Notice a certain pattern to his behavior?

GRACE: An obsession, if you ask me.

AUDRY: And all those nights I thought he was out delivering babies.

GAIL: He wasn't taking babies out, he was putting them in.

GRACE: Oh my.

GAIL: I don't care if he's Casanova reincarnate, he's my husband, and I get to kill him.

AUDRY: Hey, he's my husband too.

B.W.: Well, you two can have him. He's too jealous for me.

GAIL and **AUDRY:** Jealous?

B.W.: Why do you think I broke it off? He wouldn't let me date other men.

AUDRY: When did you have time?

GAIL: Darlene, get out your blowtorch.

DARLENE: He'll just climb back up in the ceiling.

GAIL: Then I'll stick the blowtorch up in the ceiling.

GRACE: Oh my.

DARLENE: I'm not sure that's too hot an idea.

B.W.: Sounds like too hot an idea to me; you'd burn the whole place down.

GAIL: Well, how else I am going to kill him?!

DARLENE: You're not going to kill him. Not for real.

GAIL: Oh no?

DARLENE: No.

GRACE: No.

B.W.: No.

AUDRY: Well, let's see how it goes.

GAIL: He was my husband, and he's married half the women in the state and slept with the other half!

DARLENE: So?

GAIL: So?!

DARLENE: Listen, he's got the morals of a goat, OK. And you both feel like he ripped your heart out.

AUDRY: Ripped it out and stomped that sucker flat.

DARLENE: But if you really kill him, I mean dead and decomposing, they'll send you to prison for sure. This isn't justifiable homicide anymore. Listen, you go to prison, and, well, I may look ugly, but those women in prison are ugly.

GAIL: I'll get an all woman jury; they'd never convict me.

DARLENE: Hell, Gail, Harry's probably slept with half the women in the county; they're going to hate you for spoiling their fun.

AUDRY: Oh, damn.

GAIL: I'll demand a change of venue.

DARLENE: Just give it up, OK? Roughing him up and scaring him till he pees his pants is one thing, but you're getting out of hand. Listen, you got taken in by the biggest rat in six counties, OK? Now he's gotten caught and he's locked himself in his room like a little boy, OK? That's all we can do. Now let's just cut our loses and get out of this with a little dignity, OK?

> Pause.

B.W.: Maybe if you growled at him real good.

> DARLENE slowly starts laughing at this, then AUDRY begins to laugh, then GRACE and B.W. and finally GAIL.

DARLENE: OK, OK. Come on, let's go sit down somewhere, get a cold drink, and think this over. I think a little serious cognition might be appropriate right now, before you do something you'll regret later.

GAIL: The rational philosophy major.

DARLENE: OK?

GAIL: OK. (To AUDRY and B.W.) You two are in this too.

> DARLENE picks up her tool box.

DARLENE: (To GRACE) I'll come back and help you straighten up later.
AUDRY: Anybody know a nice, quiet place around here?
B.W.: There's the bar down the street where I used to meet Harry.
GAIL: Let's try to find someplace else. Someplace Harry never picked up a woman.
AUDRY: That may be impossible.

> AUDRY, GAIL, B.W., and DARLENE exit. We hear the bell on the door in the shop ring. GRACE goes over to 1.

GRACE: Harry. Harry, they're really gone this time.

> HARRY peeks out, sees only GRACE, and comes out of the room.

HARRY: Grace.
GRACE: Hello, Harry.

> He passionately embraces her. B.W. enters.

B.W.: I forgot my...Oh my god!

> Freeze. End of Act I.

ACT II, SCENE ONE

It is about two seconds before the end of Act I. HARRY and GRACE are in their passionate embrace, and B.W. walks in, just as before.

B.W.: I forgot my...Oh my god!

HARRY and GRACE jump apart.

GRACE: Oh my!

B.W. runs back into the shop, yelling. HARRY leaps into 3 and GRACE decides she would be safer in 2.

B.W.: Hey! Come back, come back!

We hear the doorbell again.

B.W.: Come back! Come back! He was kissing her. Harry was kissing the saleslady. I saw them!

GAIL, AUDRY, DARLENE, and B.W. rush back in.

B.W.: Right in here. They were kissing like a cheap movie.
GAIL: Harry and Grace? I don't believe it.
AUDRY: Why not? She's female. That seems to be the only qualification.
GAIL: For Harry, sure, but what about her? Why would she...?
AUDRY: Why did we...?
GAIL: I thought he loved me!
AUDRY: I thought he loved me!
GAIL: Well, mark us down as first class fools.
AUDRY: No kidding. Two yahoos on the midway, that's us.
B.W.: Harry just loves women. It's one of his charms.
GAIL: Well, I am still beginning to feel really stupid.
AUDRY: I'm beginning to feel really common.
DARLENE: I'm beginning to feel really ugly.
AUDRY: Oh, now don't start feeling like a catfish in a goldfish pond.

GAIL: Catfish in a...

DARLENE: Talk about being the odd man out. He never even made a pass at me.

GAIL: Oh, Darlene, it's not you. I was always around when you were there.

DARLENE: Well, maybe. I don't mind being a bit of a freak, but I'd hate to think I'm the only woman in town who never had Harry Hudson.

GAIL: Oh, now, Darlene...Oh god, you don't really think...?

B.W.: What's the population ....?

AUDRY: He couldn't...could he?

B.W.: Then there's the tourists....

AUDRY: That'd be like a bull with a new herd of cows each week. He couldn't keep that up. Could he?

GAIL: Where's that saleslady. I want to talk to her.

B.W.: One of the dressing rooms, I guess.

> GAIL bangs on 3.

GAIL: Grace, you in there?

HARRY: No hablo English.

GAIL: Try on a girdle, Harry. See how that feels.

> GAIL moves to 2 and knocks.

GAIL: Grace? (No answer.) Grace, you better answer me, or I'll mismatch all the bikinis on the racks.

GRACE: Yes?

GAIL: Are you conscious?

GRACE: I think so.

GAIL: I need to talk to you.

GRACE: Yes?

GAIL: Do you think you could come out here?

GRACE: No.

GAIL: Grace, get out here before I strip the window mannequins and leave them naked in the window!

AUDRY: Oh, for heaven's sake. Grace, it's all right. Just come on out. We're not going to hurt you.

GRACE: Promise?

AUDRY: We didn't do anything to the sexpot, did we?

B.W.: Gee, thanks.

AUDRY: We're not mad at you. It's Harry we're after.

GAIL: We just want to talk to you. Woman to woman.

GRACE slowly opens the door and edges out.

GRACE: I thought you had gone.

AUDRY: We figured that.

GAIL: We also figured this was not the first time you'd bumped into Harry.

AUDRY: So to speak.

GRACE: I didn't know it was the Harry I knew until he came out in the dress. Not that I usually see him in a dress. I mean, I've never seen him in a dress.

GAIL: Just undressed.

GRACE: No! I mean, well, once, just once.

AUDRY: When?

GRACE: Oh, years ago.

AUDRY: Good.

GRACE: Well, two years. Almost. About a year and a half. Let me see, the party was...

AUDRY: I give up. The man juggles women like a clown juggles apples.

GRACE: You weren't already, uh, dating?

AUDRY: Like teenagers on prom night.

GRACE: Oh. Harry didn't mention you.

AUDRY: Evidently you could fill a phone book with the women Harry never mentioned.

GAIL: You want to tell us all about you and Harry?

GRACE: Oh my. It's so embarrassing.

GAIL: We all promise to blush at the appropriate times.

GRACE: Oh. Well. My husband had died about a year before...

GAIL: Oh god, now I'm going to end up feeling sorry for you.

AUDRY: Let her talk.

GRACE: Well, the Ladies group at my church, I'm the Vice President, used my house to give a welcoming party for the new minister, Rev. Hayes. He's so nice. He has this pure white hair, and the most beautiful voice, and his sermons are always short, and....

GAIL: Grace, about Harry?

GRACE: Oh, yes. Well, so help me, to this day I have no idea who he came with, but there was Harry, at the party, and he was just so charming, so helpful, so, so, well, you know Harry.

GAIL: Doesn't everybody?

DARLENE: Do you mean that biblically?

GAIL: Oh, Darlene, stop it.

GRACE: Anyway, during the party, the pipe under my kitchen sink started leaking. I was just so mortified, I had no idea what to do, and all those people there and water all over the floor, and, well, Harry just stepped up and took over and said he'd fix everything. He got some tools from his car and crawled under the sink in his suit, and by the time he was finished, the party was over, and everybody had left, and the sink was stacked high with all these dishes. Well, Harry just pitched right in and did all those dishes, and helped clean up and everything.

AUDRY: I couldn't even get him to help set the table.

GAIL: Neither could I. No housework, not with me. He wouldn't even help make the bed.

AUDRY: Just unmake it.

GAIL: He did toss those sheets, didn't he?

AUDRY: Oh lands, pillows everywhere. Sometimes I wonder how we stayed…

DARLENE: Would you let the lady finish her story?

GRACE: Well, when Harry finished, he was dirty and wet from crawling under the sink, and he asked to take a shower before he left. He'd been so charming and so nice, I didn't see how I could refuse. And one thing just sort of lead to another, and suddenly he was in my bedroom wearing nothing more that this little towel with pink roses all around the border, telling me what a good hostess I was, and how he admired my ability to cope with life's little emergencies, and how all the young women he knew didn't know how to deal with surprises, and I am still very surprised at what happened next. It was a week before I dared show my face in church.

AUDRY: That's Harry. Butter wouldn't melt.

GAIL: Grace, you faint every time a door slams. How could you believe a line about how well you dealt with emergencies?

GRACE: I don't know. Maybe I wanted to. I'd been alone for a year, and things were just changing so fast, and…Harry was just so nice.

GAIL: Yep, I feel sorry for you. I knew I would.

AUDRY: Oh, Grace, it's all right. Evidently Harry could charm the panties off a mannequin.

GAIL: He's probably tried to anyway.

DARLENE: Oh, great.

B.W.: He told me I wasn't just a pretty face, that I had brains too. Next thing I knew it was three in the morning, and we're making it on the beach.

AUDRY: On the beach?

B.W.: It was dark.

AUDRY: But didn't the sand…?

B.W.: Oh, god yes.

AUDRY: I don't want to hear this. I do not want to hear this.

GAIL: What line did Harry feed you?

AUDRY: When we first…?

GAIL: Yeah.

AUDRY: He admired my sophistication, my savoir faire. Heck, I didn't even know what savoir faire meant, but it sounded sexy, and Harry admired mine. Admired it right onto the living room floor.

GAIL: Oh, god. What a hick.

AUDRY: OK, OK, I grew up slopping hogs and eating grits. You, on the other hand, are a carpetbagging city slicker who wouldn't know a grit if it hit her in the face. Yet, evidently Harry talked you out of your underwear in about thirty-seven seconds. You want to explain that?

GAIL: Well, I didn't fall for some two-bit come-on that was transparent as glass.

AUDRY: Right. We're all a bunch of twits, but you're the ice maiden.

GAIL: I didn't mean that.

AUDRY: OK, I'm not Miss Manners, she's not Madam Curie, and she's not Dear Abby. You still ended up in the same bed as the rest of us. Harry must have said something that got to you.

GAIL: Harry said a lot of things...

AUDRY: Such as?

GAIL: None of your business.

AUDRY: You married my husband, I think that makes it my business.

GAIL: No, you married my husband, remember?

AUDRY: So what?

GAIL: So what?

DARLENE: Harry said he was attracted to her gentleness and sensitivity.

GAIL: Damn it, Darlene.

AUDRY: Gentleness and sensitivity? What a crock. You're kidding? She fell for that?

DARLENE: Hook, line, and sinker.

GAIL: I've been known to be...

DARLENE: Name one...

Pause.

GAIL: Well...

DARLENE: I like you, Gail, but you're as gentle and sensitive as Margaret Thatcher with PMS.

GRACE: Well, Ladies, now we know what we liked about Harry.

B.W.: Among other things.

GRACE: I don't think I want...

B.W.: Did you ever....

AUDRY: I do not want to talk....

GAIL: On the beach?

B.W.: It was dark!

GRACE: On the floor?

AUDRY: It was carpeted. Thick shag.

GAIL: Well, the car, of course, but...

AUDRY: Where were you parked?

GAIL: I don't see....

DARLENE picks up her tool box and starts to leave.

GAIL: Darlene, where are you going?

DARLENE: You ladies have your war stories to swap. I'm a fifth wheel here, so I'll just haul this carcassa maxima back home.

GAIL: Oh, now Darlene.

DARLENE: I've got to go. I need to stop by the bank and count my money. Gold to soothe the savage breast, or something like that.

AUDRY: Oh god, she's got the pouts. Come on, you're the only woman Harry Hudson didn't make a fool of.

DARLENE: He didn't even try. He made a play for Grace right under the pastor's nose. I don't even rate an accidental grope. Talk about first class peach pits.

GAIL: Darlene, come on. That ugly stuff is just for the ring.

DARLENE: Harry didn't seem aware of that.

GAIL: You've just psyched yourself out. You're too smart to act this stupid.

DARLENE: Well, thank you.

GAIL: No, I didn't mean...

DARLENE: Your sensitivity and gentleness overwhelm me.

GAIL: Now stop that! You know what I mean. You're intelligent, you're sensible, and you can be pretty when you want to be. Just because Harry...

DARLENE: And vultures can grow peacock tails.

GAIL: Different clothes, a little make-up....

DARLENE: Get serious. I'm a freak. I'm the world's only Phi Beta Kappa professional wrestler. I was six feet tall in the eighth grade. The high school football coach tried to recruit me. I knocked out my first date when he tried to feel me up. I'm a giant nerd.

GAIL: That was high school.

DARLENE: I'm still a freak. I graduated Magna Cum Laude, and I earn my living beating up women. Not exactly your average female. I'm the biggest wrestler on the circuit. The whole thing is fake, and I still put three girls in the hospital last year. Ladies Home Journal couldn't make this over. No man, not even Harry, is ...

GAIL: OK, you're big, strong, and throw a Double Overhead Butt-buster Slam. That doesn't mean you're not feminine.

B.W.: What's a double....?

AUDRY: You don't want to know.

GAIL: OK, you're smarter than most and a little tall.

DARLENE: A little....!

GAIL: That doesn't mean you have to dress like a bulldozer and feel like a lighthouse. Come on, let's see what they've got out here that would fit you.

DARLENE: Are you crazy? This store sells bras I could wear as wristbands.

GAIL: Well, come on, let's see. Grace, give us a hand.

GRACE: Uh, what about Harry? You've got to get him out of here. I've got to clean this mess up and reopen. You've just about wrecked the store as it is.

GAIL: I've wrecked the store? Seems to me it was Harry who ran through the racks throwing bikini bottoms at my face.

GRACE: Well, it was your idea to chase him.

GAIL: It was her (pointing at AUDRY) idea to chase him. It was my idea to bring my friend the wrestler in to help us beat the tar out of him.

AUDRY: Which worked about as well as milking a bull.

GAIL: Now wait a minute...

DARLENE: Why don't you just let him go?

GAIL: No. That man needs to be taught a lesson. Gentle and sensitive, my ass.

DARLENE: OK, OK. You want me to try popping the lock again?

GAIL grabs some clothes off the rack by the entrance.

GAIL: No, I want you to try these on.

DARLENE: You're delusional. You don't even know what size these are.

GAIL: Put them on. I want to see them. Here, this is one-size-fits-all. Try this.

DARLENE: Gail, you missed the point. I'm not a normal woman. One-size-fits-all doesn't include me. Designers don't believe I exist.

GAIL: You're not that strange. Something in here will fit. Just try it.

GAIL shoves DARLENE into 2.

DARLENE: OK, OK. I hate it when you get like this.

DARLENE closes door.

GAIL: Grace, come on, show me where your large sizes are.

GRACE: Uh, I really don't think we carry anything that large.

GAIL: Well, come on, we've got to find something.

GAIL and GRACE exit to shop.

B.W.: Well, I might as well try on some more stuff too. I'm sure not going to leave now, not before finding out how this turns out. It's like living on TV.

B.W. exits to shop. DARLENE comes out of 2 in her bra. She holds out a small pullover top.

DARLENE: I can't even get these Barbie Doll clothes on.

AUDRY: I think they're looking for something else for you.

DARLENE: Well, it better be bigger than this. I haven't worn this size since I was three.

HARRY sticks his head out of 3.

HARRY: Oh, wow.

> He whistles at DARLENE, who screams and jumps back into 2. GAIL runs back in, followed by GRACE and B.W., each of whom carries some clothes.

GAIL: What happened?

AUDRY: Darlene came out in her bra, and Harry saw her.

GAIL: Oh, for heaven's sake, big deal. He's a gynecologist, think of what he spends all day looking at.

AUDRY: He whistled at her.

GAIL: He did?

AUDRY: Yeah.

GAIL: (to 3) Harry, add one fat lip to what I owe you. (to GRACE) Give me those.

> GAIL takes clothes from GRACE, knocks on 2.

GAIL: Darlene, here, try these on.

> DARLENE opens door, sticks out her hand, takes clothes, closes door. B.W. goes into 4.

B.W.: Back in a minute. Don't start the revolution without me.

GRACE: I'm going to start straightening up.

AUDRY: I'll give you a hand.

GAIL: I want to look for some more clothes for Darlene.

> GAIL, GRACE, and AUDRY exit to: shop. After a second, HARRY sticks his head out and looks around. He slowly comes out of the door, wearing his original shorts and shirt. He tiptoes to the curtain, and sees that the way out is still blocked. He starts to tiptoe back into 3, but hesitates, goes to 2, tries the knob, finds it unlocked, and slowly opens the door a crack, just enough to peep in. GRACE enters with an armload of clothes, just as B.W., now wearing a sundress, enters from 4.

B.W. and **GRACE:** Harry!

> HARRY quickly jumps back just as DARLENE explodes her door open and runs out. DARLENE is now wearing a tube top that is five sizes too small and a pair of shorts that have become short shorts on her, and she is not sure what is happening. Meanwhile, GAIL runs in, bumping into GRACE, who stumbles forward into HARRY, who is stumbling backward to get away from DARLENE. This causes GRACE to toss all the clothes she was carrying into the air. At this instant, AUDRY runs in, bumping into GAIL, knocking her into GRACE as GRACE rebounds from her contact with HARRY, who has

rebounded back toward DARLENE. Somehow in all this confusion somebody has stepped on GRACE's foot, and she starts hopping around on one foot. HARRY, meanwhile, finds himself face to bust with DARLENE. He looks at what is enclosed in the tube top, and smiles. At that instant, GRACE hops into GAIL, loses her balance from that contact, and ends up flat on her back. AUDRY stops to check on the fallen GRACE, while GAIL and B.W. make a grab for HARRY, who ducks behind DARLENE and slides into 2, leaving GAIL and B.W. to meet at DARLENE, who grabs them both.

DARLENE: What's going on?

B.W.: Harry was playing peeping tom again. He was peeking at you through the door.

DARLENE: He was?

B.W.: Like a kid at a strip show.

GAIL: Damn bastard. I'll adjust his opticals.

AUDRY: Adjust his...?

GAIL: Never mind. She faint again?

GRACE: No, but I wish I had. Somebody stepped on my toe. I think it's broken.

B.W.: Let me see.

GRACE holds up her foot.

B.W.: Which toe?

GRACE: Second.

B.W.: Wiggle it.

GRACE: I can't wiggle just one toe.

B.W.: OK, wiggle all of them.

GRACE: Ouch!

B.W.: Sounds broken to me.

AUDRY: Now what do we do?

B.W.: How should I know. (Puts GRACE's foot back down, to DARLENE) Girl, what are you wearing?

DARLENE: What she gave me.

GAIL: I was just trying to make her feel a little more normal.

DARLENE: I feel like a sausage.

B.W.: You look like a sausage.

GAIL: Who are you, an x-rated Mr. Blackwell?

B.W.: Go take that off before you explode. I'll find you something. What are you, about a size 22?

DARLENE: If it's well made.

DARLENE goes into 3, B.W. exits to shop.

AUDRY: Are we about to end up with a giant size Miss July?

GAIL: Staggers the imagination.

GRACE: Uh, excuse me.

AUDRY: Oh. Sorry.

GRACE: I think I really need to see a doctor.

GAIL: What, you don't think Miss T and A is a medical expert.

GRACE: You said Harry was a doctor. What about a truce just long enough for him to look at my toe?

GAIL: That's not exactly Harry's area of expertise.

AUDRY: He could at least tell us what to do.

GAIL: He'll probably just tell us to have it x-rayed.

AUDRY: Well, try it.

GAIL knocks on 2.

GAIL: Hey, Harry! Grace may have broken her toe. What should we do?

HARRY: (through door) Have it x-rayed.

GAIL: See.

AUDRY: OK, OK.

B.W. enters with some clothes opens 3 a crack, and hands clothes to DARLENE.

B.W.: Darlene. Here, try these on.

AUDRY: We've got to tote Grace somewhere to have her toe x-rayed.

B.W.: There's a little emergency clinic about two blocks up the street.

GAIL: Yeah, I think I know where.

AUDRY: Come on, Grace.

AUDRY and GAIL help GRACE up.

GAIL: What about Harry?

B.W.: You stay, I'll go with Audry.

AUDRY: I didn't come by car.

B.W.: Neither did I.

GRACE: Oh my, I can't walk two blocks. Call an ambulance.

GAIL: Can either of you drive a stickshift?

B.W.: Not me.

AUDRY: No.

GAIL: My god, all these helpless females. OK, OK, I'll drive my car.

DARLENE sticks her head out of 3.

DARLENE: Uh, could I have a hand in here?
B.W.: (to AUDRY) You want me to...
AUDRY: You help Darlene. I'll carry Gracie here.
GAIL: Darlene, don't let Harry get away. I still want a sharp something or other with him.
DARLENE: OK, OK. Sensitivity of a Republican on steroids.

GAIL and AUDRY half carry GRACE off.

B.W.: Come on out here. It's only us girls, and we can keep an eye on Harry.

The lights fade as B.W. waits for DARLENE to emerge.

ACT II, SCENE TWO

>It is about an hour later. HARRY, DARLENE, and B.W. are sprawled in a romantic little heap on the floor, asleep. HARRY is dressed in a sequined bandeau top and matching miniskirt. B.W. has a swimsuit cover-up on, but there may not be anything underneath it. DARLENE is wearing something that looks like it came from Frederick's of Hollywood, a bra/corset that laces up the back, a garter belt and stockings, and panties that tie on the sides. They are using each other's bodies as pillows and smiling very contentedly. The bell rings signaling that someone has entered the store, and a moment later GRACE hobbles in on crutches, her foot heavily taped. GRACE stops in surprise at the sight that greets her, and this causes AUDRY and GAIL, who are right behind her, to bump her and knock her off balance. GRACE bounces around on the crutches, trying to regain her balance, but yipping every time she tries to put weight on her injured foot. The commotion wakes up the three on the floor, and GAIL and AUDRY are trying to help GRACE and see what is going on at the same time.

AUDRY: Oh my god!

GAIL: Darlene!

>HARRY, B.W., and DARLENE scramble to untangle themselves, get up, bump into each other a few times, and run into separate rooms. DARLENE ends up in 2, HARRY in 4, and B.W. in 3. AUDRY finally helps GRACE regain control, and pulls the stool over for her.

AUDRY: You OK?

GRACE: I feel like a spinning top.

AUDRY: Just sit still.

GAIL: I don't believe. Both of them. That man could seduce the Queen of England.

AUDRY: Probably did. We were in London a two full weeks on our honeymoon.

GAIL: Darlene, Darlene.

AUDRY: Those women have enough nerve to spit-shine a bald man's head.

GAIL: Spit-shine a bald....?

AUDRY: Never mind. You know, I'm beginning to feel less and less married to Harry.

GAIL: I know what you mean.

AUDRY: It's like reading a book on magic tricks and thinking you know something special, then seeing the library card in back, all stamped up.

GAIL: Yeah, Harry was a good book, but he's getting dogeared fast.

AUDRY: And I really don't like the way its ending.

GAIL: No happy ever after here. Just a lot of sex and violence. And Harry had all the sex, so now he deserves a little violence. I wouldn't mind teaching those two hussies a lesson or two right now either. Can you believe Darlene...?

AUDRY: What makes you think she's any different from you and me? Especially when it comes to Harry.

    Pause.

GAIL: We do have a lot in common, don't we?

AUDRY: Two hens, one rooster.

GAIL: Two characters in the same sex farce.

AUDRY: True Confessions Magazine, live, in person.

GAIL: My Most Embarrassing Moment. See whose face turns redder.

AUDRY: Someday, over a quiet cup of coffee. In the meantime, I think you're right, it is time we taught a few lessons around here. I've got an idea. (They whisper, then loud) Those lousy, two-timing whores! Turn your back two seconds and they jump your husband. I've had it with all this, you hear! I've had it. Give me that gun you got from your car. I'll show these bitches and their stud what shooting fish in a barrel is really all about.

GAIL: (Loud) About time we did some real killing around here. No more of this liberated woman junk.

AUDRY: (Loud) Oh good, a 45 Magnum. This ought to make some big holes in those flesh-mongers.

GAIL: (Loud) It's got that new armor piercing ammo designed to go through bulletproof vests. These thin doors won't even slow it down.

AUDRY: (Loud) Which one do you think I ought to blast first?

GAIL: (Loud) Who cares? Just count to three and start blasting!

AUDRY: One! Two! Three!

    GAIL pulls the stool out from under GRACE and slams it into the floor, creating a loud bang. The following happens pretty much all at the same time as the three doors open simultaneously. B.W. erupts out of 3, throwing an explosion of clothing (including everything, or almost everything, she used to have on, or at least as much as you can get away with) in front of her in the general direction of GAIL and AUDRY. She is yelling, and tries to run for the exit, but runs into GRACE, knocking GRACE off balance, and she is left hobbling around in circles, waving the crutch, trying to regain her balance.

B.W.: Look out! Look out!

DARLENE explodes from 2. She is growling, and has made herself as frightening as possible while wearing garter belts. She crouches in a wrestling stance, then runs at GAIL and AUDRY, but hits the recoiling B.W. instead. She grabs B.W. and tosses her aside, right into HARRY, who has run out of 4, and is on his knees in a praying/begging posture. B.W. knocks HARRY over. This is all a bit too much for GAIL and AUDRY. GAIL tries to run out the exit, but can't get past GRACE's swinging crutch. AUDRY goes the other way to avoid the charge of DARLENE, stumbles over the fallen HARRY, gets up, picks up B.W. and pushes her right back at DARLENE. DARLENE sidesteps the onrushing B.W. and shoves her in the back, which pushes her into GAIL, who spins her around and into GRACE. This is the last straw for GRACE, who finally looses all semblance of balance and falls flat on her face, tripping B.W. with her crutches in the process. This knocks B.W. into the curtain, which she grabs, and it pulls loose and entangles her as she falls in the doorway. AUDRY, meanwhile, gets in one swift kick at HARRY, which prompts him to get up just as DARLENE makes another dive for AUDRY. DARLENE ends up with HARRY in her grasp, so she just tosses him aside, and makes another grab for AUDRY, who dodges and jumps into 3, slamming the door behind her. HARRY now bumps into GAIL, who grabs him and shoves him into DARLENE from behind. DARLENE recovers, throws HARRY aside, and dives at GAIL, who runs into 2 to avoid the charging DARLENE.

HARRY bounces off the wall, back into DARLENE knocking her into another wall, from which she slides to the floor, momentarily stunned. HARRY then rolls over, leaps back up, sees B.W. is blocking the door, and jumps into 1. Pause. The first to move is B.W., who pulls the curtain off her face, and tries to get it under control. Next to stir is DARLENE, who shakes herself a little and sits up.

DARLENE: Damn, they don't hit like that in the ring.
B.W.: Where are they?
DARLENE: In there. I don't think they even had a gun.
B.W.: No gun?
DARLENE: I didn't see one. And I ain't shot, I don't think. It was just a trick.
B.W.: Well, damn.

B.W. struggles to her feet, wrapping the curtain around herself. GRACE moans and rolls over. B.W. starts picking up clothes, all the clothes she can get her hands on, hers or not. DARLENE takes a sundress and shoes from B.W., and puts them on. The dress is a couple of sizes too small, but it somehow manages to look sexy on her.

B.W.: This has turned into a really lousy day. All I wanted was a new swimsuit, and what happened? I find an old boyfriend hanging from the ceiling in the dressing room, his wives banging on the doors, salesladies swinging crutches like deadly weapons. I try to be nice to everybody, and I end up almost getting shot by a broad with no gun. Well, this is just too much. I don't need this kind of hassle. There are plenty of other husbands in the world. These people are just too kinky for me. No more guys with two wives for me, no sir; I've learned my lesson. I'm just going to go home and watch TV.

> B.W. now has a full armload of clothes, but is dressed in the curtain. She exits with dignity and all the clothes she can carry. After a moment we hear the bell.

GRACE: Maybe I'll just lie here and die.

DARLENE: You need some help?

GRACE: I need some hot tea.

> DARLENE stretches and checks to see that she is not injured.

DARLENE: Well, I think I'm OK except for some bruises, and that's no big deal for me.

> DARLENE helps GRACE up and sets her on the stool.

GRACE: Thanks.

DARLENE: They didn't have a gun, did they?

GRACE: No. They just wanted to teach you a lesson.

DARLENE: That figures. Hurricane Gail strikes again.

> DARLENE goes and knocks on 2.

DARLENE: OK, OK, fight's over.

> GAIL comes out of 2.

GAIL: Darlene, how could you? You're my best friend.

> AUDRY slowly comes out of 3.

DARLENE: I'm sorry, Gail, honest. But I just couldn't resist. And, I mean, it's not like I was breaking up your marriage or anything. I mean, I'm not exactly the first.

GAIL: Don't remind me.

DARLENE: I just didn't want to be left out again.

GAIL: Left out?!

DARLENE: Nobody likes female Goliaths who quote Aristotle in Greek. I scare people. In the ring that's making me rich, but even there I don't fit in. In the dressing room the girls call me Plato the Giant. Finding out about Harry and everybody else but me made me feel like a bearded lady with bad breath. None of the clothes were fitting, and I was getting really frustrated. Then we found this underwear that ties instead of hooks, so it's real adjustable, and it felt so good, and I was feeling better, looking in the mirror and all, and B.W., that's, you know, her, and, well, B.W. was trying some stuff on too, and we were laughing, and having so much fun, and well, then Harry came out and said I looked so sexy that he just had to surrender to a beautiful woman like me, that he was in my power, etc., etc. etc. I knew it was a crock and I knew you wouldn't like it, but I was just tired of being the designated hitter who never gets to play the field. Now I've got my own really hot little memory for those quiet nights. And maybe I'm not such a freak anymore.

GAIL: Oh, Darlene...

    The bell rings. In a second, B.W. peeks in from shop.

B.W.: I seem to be wearing a curtain. If I come in to change, will I get killed?

GAIL: Probably.

DARLENE: No. Not unless Gail wants to find out what it's like to wrestle me for real.

GAIL: Oh, hell, Darlene. (to B.W.) Well, what's your excuse?

B.W.: Hey, I may not be Einstein, but I know a hot time when I see one. I mean, it's not like you want him anymore.

AUDRY: Think of it this way, you've got two more witnesses in the divorce case.

GAIL: Oh god. Are court records public? This is turning into a mini-series.

B.W.: I don't think they could do this on television. Maybe the movies.

GRACE: Rated R, maybe even X.

AUDRY: Oh god. I used to be a good girl.

GAIL: Didn't we all.

DARLENE: Isn't it wonderful?

B.W. (to **GRACE**): I think some of these are yours. Just let me put something on.

    B.W. goes into 3.

GRACE: Oh the poor, poor store.

AUDRY: This has turned into a pretty lousy day for all of us, hasn't it?

GAIL: It's almost enough to make you give up sex.

    They look at each other.

GAIL and **AUDRY:** No.

AUDRY: It does seem like everybody gets hurt around here but Harry though. Especially Grace. It's like we've been burning down the barn to roast the chickens.

GAIL: All I wanted to do was get Harry out here and pop a few of his appendages. I didn't want to bust up my friends.

DARLENE: Well, that gun trick was a little excessive.

GAIL: I guess. Sorry.

AUDRY: Sorry. That was my idea.

GAIL: (To DARLENE.) Friends again?

DARLENE: Friends.

> GAIL and DARLENE embrace. B.W. enters from dressing room, in her original shorts and T-shirt.

AUDRY: Now that is the way old friends are supposed to act.

DARLENE: Well, Harry's ex-lovers have to stick together.

GAIL: Wives and lovers. All for one and one for all.

AUDRY: And none for Harry.

GAIL: Amen.

AUDRY: Whatever help you need, testimony at the divorce trial, or somebody to talk to, or whatever, just let me know. I mean, if you can't count on your husband's wife....

GAIL: That goes both ways, you know. And this is going to be a grand mess.

AUDRY: I know. Legal history.

GAIL: Inquiring minds will want to know.

AUDRY: We'll tough it out. All of us.

> AUDRY and GAIL hug each other for a second.

GAIL: Thanks. I still wish I could get one good crack at Harry before we have to be so polite in court. Just one good slap in the face. Payment in advance for whatever lies he's going to tell about us in court. Get him back for everything he's done to Grace's store too. Not to mention making me act like a fool.

> At this, AUDRY glances up and sees HARRY in the vent. She screams. HARRY disappears.

GAIL: What?!

AUDRY: It's Harry! He's up there! (Pointing at vent.) In the vent!

GAIL: After him!

> GAIL runs into 2, AUDRY into 3. They all promptly turn around and run back out. AUDRY grabs the stool from under GRACE, leaving her hobbling around trying to keep her balance. AUDRY takes the stool back into 2, stands on it, pulls the vent cover off, drops it, and disappears into the ceiling GAIL, meanwhile, signals DARLENE to give her a boost.

DARLENE: Come on, Gail, forget it, will you.

GAIL: Come on, one good body slam, that's all, I promise. You owe me that much.

DARLENE: OK, OK.

They go into 3, and DARLENE lifts GAIL up.

DARLENE: No, he's in the vents. You have to go into the vent itself. Just jerk the cover off.

The vent cover comes flying out the door.

DARLENE: Arms first, that's it.

> GAIL disappears. DARLENE comes back out and looks up at the vent into the room just as GAIL's face appears in the vent.

GAIL: Where did he go?
DARLENE: I don't know. (To GRACE.) Where do the vents lead?
GRACE: I don't know. All over the store, I guess.

> GAIL disappears. DARLENE gets the stool out of 1 and gives it to GRACE to sit on.

GRACE: Thanks.
AUDRY: Help!
DARLENE: What is it?
AUDRY: I'm stuck!
DARLENE: Where are you?
AUDRY: In some stupid vent, where do you think!
DARLENE: Hold on!

> DARLENE grabs the stool out from under GRACE again, and runs into 2. B.W. follows stands on stool, and climbs into vent and disappears up into the ceiling.

AUDRY: I don't have much choice, do I?

> DARLENE climbs on the stool and starts to disappear, but in her haste she knocks the stool over just as she is getting up into the ceiling. She comes crashing down on the floor.

DARLENE: Darn!

> DARLENE rushes back out.

DARLENE: I don't fit! I can't get up there!

> B.W.'s face appears at the vent.

B.W.: Where is she?

DARLENE: I don't know!

B.W.: OK, OK.

> B.W. disappears. HARRY suddenly bursts through the wall beside the mirror in an explosion of drywall and plaster.

DARLENE: He's back out here!

GAIL: I'm coming!

> GAIL suddenly slides down behind HARRY, through the hole in the wall he just created. At the same moment, B.W. appears back at the vent, pushes the cover off, and starts to climb out.

AUDRY: I'm free!

> AUDRY's feet appear from the ceiling of 3, then she drops down on the floor and rolls out. HARRY is suddenly confronted with all five women, GRACE on crutches by the door, DARLENE next in line, then B.W. crawling down from the vent, AUDRY struggling off the floor of 3, and GAIL on the floor behind him.

HARRY: I don't suppose we could talk this over.

> GAIL and AUDRY both leap at HARRY at the same time, but he dodges, and they run into each other. DARLENE starts toward them, but just then B.W. makes the last little drop down from the vent, and DARLENE runs right into her. This trips DARLENE, but she rolls toward HARRY, and he has to jump over her rolling body. GAIL and AUDRY are not so nimble, and go down like ten-pins. B.W., meanwhile, is thrown by her impact toward GRACE, who manages to avoid her, but ends up off balance again. GRACE stumbles toward HARRY, who catches her just before she would have fallen.

GRACE: Oh, thank you.

> HARRY straightens GRACE up, and kisses her. Meanwhile, GAIL AUDRY, and DARLENE have gotten back on their feet and GAIL and AUDRY, with DARLENE in their wake, charge HARRY, who steps around so GRACE is between him and the onrushing women. GAIL has to put on the brakes to keep from running over GRACE, and she still bumps her enough to put her off balance again. GAIL slides down, and right into AUDRY, who has grabbed HARRY. DARLENE grabs GRACE to steady her, while AUDRY, put off balance by GAIL, loses her grip on HARRY. HARRY turns to steady the falling AUDRY, grabs her, and kisses her passionately, bending her over backward, then dropping her right on top of GAIL, who was struggling to get up. When DARLENE sees this, she lets

go of GRACE, upsetting GRACE's balance again, and grabs HARRY. GRACE teeters for a moment.

GRACE: Oh, shiiiiit!

> GRACE falls flat on her back. DARLENE has HARRY, but she turns to see GRACE fall, and HARRY does the unexpected of turning toward her and hugging her, planting kisses all up and down her neck. DARLENE starts to giggle uncontrollably, and lets go of HARRY. By now both GAIL and B.W. are back on their feet and between HARRY and the door, but he's got this figured out by now, and runs straight at GAIL, embraces her, and plants a kiss right down her throat, while spinning her around and then pushing her into the just arising AUDRY, which pushes AUDRY, like a domino, into DARLENE, who has to catch AUDRY to keep her from falling on GRACE. HARRY now spins around to come face to face with B.W. For a second no one moves.

B.W.: Oh, hell.

> She kisses HARRY quickly, then swats him on the fanny as he runs to the doorway. He stops, turns.

HARRY: (To all of them) I love you.

> HARRY turns and exits. The bell rings. B.W. turns back to face GRACE still on her back on the floor, DARLENE holding AUDRY half-way up, and GAIL staring right at her. Long pause.

GAIL: Oh, hell, let the bastard go.

> DARLENE lifts AUDRY back the rest of the way to her feet.

AUDRY: Thanks.
DARLENE: No problem.
GRACE: Nice catch. She was about to really smash my petunias.

> DARLENE and AUDRY gently lift GRACE back to her feet.

AUDRY: You OK?
GRACE: Nothing retiring to a convent wouldn't cure.
B.W.: I hope this store has disaster insurance.
GAIL: Have them send the bill to Harry.
AUDRY: Just don't deliver it in person.

GRACE: Oh my, no.

B.W.: Hope you're not too mad I let Harry go.

GAIL: Hell, I been chasing him so long, I forgot what I was going to do when I caught him.

AUDRY: Probably what every other woman who ever caught him did.

GAIL: Oh god.

> The bell rings.

GRACE: He wouldn't dare.

> From off-stage we hear another female voice calling ,"Harry. Harry Hudson. Are you in there?"

GAIL: Oh my god, another one.

> The lights fade.
>
> CURTAIN

ONE-ACT PLAYS

In addition to the one-acts embedded in bills of scenes in the previous full-length plays, I have written several stand-alone one-act plays. Some of them have been produced, at least in workshop productions, by various groups.

She Was a Singer

I have written two one-act musicals in my life: book, lyrics, and music. The first we shall pass over without further mention. The second I'm actually proud of. Some of the music is adapted from old folk songs, but some is totally original, at least as far as any music is original these days. This one had a workshop production by Koality Productions here in Atlanta and I have CDs of the songs on the bookshelves behind me as I write this.

SHE WAS A SINGER

A Play with Music in One Act By David Davis

Member
All rights & privileges.

David Davis
100 Hunters Ridge Court
Roswell, GA 30076
daviddaviswriter@gmail.com

Copyright 2000 David Davis

CAST OF CHARACTERS

AL SPOLIN..A Songwriter

JUDY LYNN ANDREWS...A Singer

JOE COLLINS..A Night Club Owner

RUTH EVANS...An Agent

SETTING

On stage left are a piano, a piano bench, and a guitar stand. On stage right are a dressing table with mirror and lights and two wooden chairs. Center stage is empty. These three playing areas will be used to represent several locales during the play. The action covers a span of about ten years, beginning during the late 1960s or early 70's.

PRODUCTION NOTE

The play is intended to be produced without a band or offstage musicians. Al can accompany himself on his songs, using either piano or guitar. He can also play for Judy and Ruth whether he is in the scene or not. Judy can also accompany herself on guitar on some songs, and both Judy and Al can play on others. If desired, Joe Collins or Ruth Evans can also play the onstage piano when they are not in the scene. If no piano is available, just guitars can be used.

> AT RISE: AL sits in front of the piano. He plays a little bit. He is casually dressed, not handsome.

AL: You know, it's funny the hours I've spent in front of this thing and darn little to show for it. A long hard road. (He plays a few more notes.) Oh, I guess I should introduce myself. You've never heard of me. I'm Al Spolin, the songwriter. The reason you've never heard of me is that I'm a not yet successful songwriter. That's a nice way of saying I'm a failed songwriter. Hell, what I am is a bad songwriter. And a bad country songwriter at that. Do you have any idea how bad you have to be to be a bad country songwriter? (He plays a few chords.) I didn't start out to be a bad songwriter, of course. I didn't even start out to be a songwriter. It just sort of happened. I started out to be an English teacher. Another somewhat disreputable occupation. Anyway, in college, I met this girl. I wonder how many other stories start out that way, "Well, I met this girl..." The one I met, well, that's her there, Judy Lynn Andrews.

> JUDY enters, carrying her guitar, and crosses down center. She is also casually dressed, good looking, but not spectacular.

AL: Isn't she beautiful? Wait till you hear her sing. Anyway, like I said, we were in college together up near Nashville, and met in class. Discovered we both liked country music, sort of got into it through the folk music that was big back then, both played guitar, and one thing sort of led to another. Eventually, we started singing warm-up shows at a little club in town. You know what a warm-up show is, don't you? That's a show done by some unknown to warm up the audience for the star who comes on later. It's a job that doesn't pay much. Hell, it didn't pay anything. But I didn't care. I just liked playing. Besides, it was a chance to spend a lot of time with Judy. I really liked her back then.

> AL picks up his guitar and crosses to JUDY.

AL: We did a lot of old songs, love songs mostly, both folk and country, but mostly sad songs. The ballads showed off Judy's voice. I picked guitar a good deal better than she did, but Judy was the act. If I stayed on key, I felt pretty good, but Judy, oh man, clear as crystal that voice. Let me show you.

> AL straps on his guitar and is now back in time, finishing up a performance of the warm-up show.

AL: Thank you, thank you. We'd like to finish up with one of those old, old songs that will be around forever, Greensleves.

JUDY and **AL:** Alas, my love, you do me wrong,
to cast me off discourteously,
and I have loved you oh so long,
delighting in your company.

Greensleves was all my joy,
Greensleves was my delight,
Greensleves was my heart of gold,
And who but my lady Greensleves.

I have been ready at your hand,

to grant whatever you would crave,
and I have waged both life and land,
your love and favors for to have.

Greensleves was all my joy,
Greensleves was my delight,
Greensleves was my heart of gold,
And who but my lady Greensleves.

Well, I shall pray to God on high
that thou my constancy may see,
and that yet once before I die
thou will vouchsafe to love me.

Greensleves was all my joy,
Greensleves was my delight,
Greensleves was my heart of gold,
And who but my lady Greensleves.

AL: Thank you.

>They bow and start to exit. JOE COLLINS enters.

JOE: Let's hear it, folks. Judy and Al, weren't they terrific? Take another bow.

>JUDY and AL bow again, then cross as if exiting the club stage to the "dressing room" stage right. The lights and sounds cross-fade from JOE to JUDY and AL.

JOE: Great kids. Something tells my you'll be hearing more from those two. But now, what you've all been waiting for, just back from a tour of South Carolina, with a new single just out and already selling big..."

AL: Hey, I think they liked us.

JUDY: Yeah, that was something, wasn't it? Oh, I love singing with you.

>She kisses him quickly.

AL: Wow.

JUDY: Isn't being a singer great!

AL: What a life!

JUDY: That applause gets in your blood, doesn't it? Think what it would be like, the two of us, doing this for a living.

AL: Huh. Dream on.

JUDY: I mean it.

>They start to pack up.

JUDY: I think we should ask Collins to pay us.

AL: Are you crazy? He could replace us in two seconds, you know that.

JUDY: But we're good. You heard that audience. Collins thinks so too, didn't you hear him? "We'll be hearing more from those two."

AL: He probably says that about all the warmup acts. Makes the audience think they're watching some undiscovered stars.

JUDY: Maybe we should try to get an agent.

AL: You want to stop for a burger on the way back to campus? I've got a lit test on Monday, but I think I can take the time.

JUDY: Will you listen to me?

AL: Judy, listen. I like singing here. I really like singing with you. It's a lot of fun. But I'm in college. We're in college. You know as well as I do that if we really wanted to turn pro right now we'd have to drop out and take whatever singing jobs we could get, wherever they were, a night here, a weekend there, all over the country. We've both got nearly two years of school left, so it's a little early to think about what comes after. What's your rush? Let's just enjoy this and not queer the deal with Collins by asking for money. I'm sure people better than we are come by his door every day asking for a chance to perform.

JUDY: So you don't think we're good enough.

AL: That's not what I'm saying, I'm saying right now we...

> JOE enters.

JOE: Hey, good show, kids. Same time next week?

AL: Yeah, sure, Mr. Collins.

JUDY: Uh, Mr. Collins, we were just wondering, well, we were just thinking...

JOE: If you were about to ask for money, forget it.

JUDY: No, no. We were just wondering if you knew any agents that, you know, might want to handle us, you know, when we finish school.

JOE: Oh. Well, you might give Ruth Evans a call. She was in here looking around a few weeks ago. She's just starting out on her own, doesn't have many clients yet, so she might be interested.

JUDY: Ruth Evans. OK, thanks a lot.

JOE: Sure. See you next week.

> JOE exits.

AL: Boy, that was close.

JUDY: Oh, shut up. (Pause.) Load the stuff, I don't like to eat hamburgers in a hurry.

AL: OK, sure.

> AL picks up his guitar and crosses the stage to the piano, the lights following him. He puts the guitar back in its stand.

AL: That should have been the end of that, but of course it wasn't. We went out and got a hamburger, then I took Judy home. I think she felt sorry for crossing me like that. Anyway, saying goodnight that night was quite an experience, at least for me. I was an innocent little boy, and that was a long time ago. Anyway, she never asked Collins for money again. What she did was worse. Far worse. I was sitting in one of the music rehearsal rooms at the college a few days later...

    AL starts to improvise on the piano or guitar. JUDY enters.

JUDY: Oh, there you are.

AL: Here I am.

JUDY: What's that?

AL: Just goofing around a little.

JUDY: How did you do on the lit test?

AL: OK.

JUDY: You got another A.

AL: By one point.

JUDY: Good. I was afraid I had kept you out too late that night.

AL: It would have been worth it.

JUDY: I just wanted to be sure you were all right.

AL: Fine and dandy, thank you.

JUDY: Good. (Pause.) I care about you, you know that.

AL: And I love the way you show it.

JUDY: Oh, hush.

    Pause.

AL: I care about you too. I guess I'm just too shy to say it much.

JUDY: You are too shy. I have to do all the pushing.

AL: And I guess that's one of the things I like about you. You're not shy at all. Opposites attract, I guess.

    Pause.

JUDY: Well, speaking of not being shy...

AL: What?

JUDY: I called Ruth Evans.

AL: Who?

JUDY: Ruth Evans, the agent Collins told us about.

    Pause.

AL: Oh.

JUDY: Don't you want to know what she said?

AL: Do I have a choice?

JUDY: She said she was only interested in people who had original material.

AL: What?

JUDY: You know, new songs, stuff that's never been recorded before.

AL: Well, that lets us out.

  Pause.

JUDY: She's coming to see us at the club next week.

AL: But you just said...

JUDY: I told her we had some new stuff.

AL: You what?

JUDY: I told her we had a new song.

AL: Why?

JUDY: So she would come see us.

AL: Great. Come see the two liars perform live, on stage, every weekend. Great way to get an agent. Did you tell her we have a six piece band including a bongo drummer who plays with his toes? That would really interest her.

JUDY: So we'll get a new song.

AL: Sure. Where?

JUDY: We'll write one. It can't be that hard.

AL: If it wasn't hard, everybody would do it.

JUDY: You're always goofing around on that piano, can't you come up with something?

AL: How should I know. I've never really tried to write anything.

JUDY: Well, give it a shot, OK? Just so we'll have one original song for next week. OK? I know you can do it.

  She kisses him, long and slow, then exits.

AL: I think I must have been the biggest idiot to ever put on shoes. I was so cotton-picking innocent. Head over heels. I think an overdose of hormones causes temporary insanity or something. Anyway, I wrote a song, words, music, the whole shebang. That song was so bad, I mean it stunk up a skunk's nest, it was, hell, I've got to show you this.

  AL takes his guitar and moves to center, where he is joined by
  JUDY as in the previous scene.

JUDY: We've got a brand new song for you now. It's our latest, and we hope you like it.

JUDY and **AL:** It was a windy night, I hear, I hear.
It isn't clear to me, at all, to me.
You only went away, it's clear, I see.
They say the moon was there, above, above.

I only know you're gone, from me, you're gone.
And now I face the night, alone, just me, just me.

Sing me no sad songs,
bring me no beer.
I'll wait for the morning
a-sitting right here.
And when the sunrise
climbs over the dew
then I'll sing the sad song
of parting from you.
Yes, I'll sing the sad song
I'll sparkle like dew
with tears in the morning
I cried over you.

It was a chilly eve, I hear, I hear.
You were not near to me, on no, not me.
I knew you'd never stay, my dear, by me.
You didn't really care, to love, to love.
And now you say you're done, with me, you're done.
And now I face the night, alone, just me, just me.

Sing me no sad songs,
bring me no beer.
I'll wait for the morning
a-sitting right here.
And when the sunrise
climbs over the dew
then I'll sing the sad song
of parting from you.
Yes, I'll sing the sad song
I'll sparkle like dew
with tears in the morning
I cried over you.

JUDY: Thank you, and good night.

> JUDY and AL bow and cross right as JOE enters.

AL (aside to audience): I told you it was bad.

JOE: There they are, Judy and Al. And now, the man you've all been waiting for, three gold records and another on the way up the charts, a real down-home fellow from right here in Tennessee, just back from Fargo, North Dakota, here he is...

JUDY: You think they liked it?

AL: The song?

JUDY: Yeah.

AL: Not if they had any sense. Come on, let's get out of here.

JUDY: Ruth Evans said she would come backstage after our set.

AL: Oh good heavens.

> JOE enters dressing room area.

JOE: Hey, kids, who wrote that song?

JUDY: Al did. Did you like it?

JOE: Just wondered.

JUDY: Ruth Evans is supposed to be here. Have you seen her?

JOE: Yeah, she was out there. Was she here to see you?

JUDY: Yeah.

AL: Same time next week, Mr. Collins?

JOE: What? Oh, yeah, sure.

> RUTH EVANS enters. She is only a few years older than JUDY and AL, but is all business.

RUTH: You still working the poor college kids for nothing, Joe?

JOE: Well, hello, Ruth. No, I pay them applause, glory, and time in the limelight.

RUTH: Not exactly a living wage.

JOE: You want money, go work in a bank.

RUTH: Same old Joe Collins, exploiting the talents of the innocent.

JOE: What's it to you? You taking these two on?

RUTH: Not sure yet.

JOE: Well, if you do, let me know where to send your ten percent of the limelight.

RUTH: That's all I'll get out of you, that's for sure.

JOE: I got to get back out front. See you later.

RUTH: Yeah.

> JOE exits.

JUDY: Well?

RUTH: OK. You want to know what I really think, right? No hedging?

JUDY: Yeah. Of course.

RUTH: You got a voice, kid; a real chance at making it. You'd have to get some better material, but with your voice you got a real chance. But just you, solo, no team.

JUDY: But Al and I...

RUTH: No. I'm sorry, but that's the way I see it. He might could play in the band, when you get big enough to have your own band. But you have to be the one out front. (to Al.) You know how it is.

AL: Yeah, sure. Good enough for parties and Sunday choirs, but not for the big time.

RUTH: Right. Nothing personal. That's just the way I see it.

AL: I know.

RUTH: (to JUDY) If you're willing to go it alone, I'm willing to handle you. But just you, that's all.

JUDY: I hadn't even thought...I mean, Al and I sorta had plans..., you know....

RUTH: Listen, think about it, talk it over. I know it's not what you expected. But let me know soon, OK? The summer tours start booking in a day or two.

JUDY: Oh. Yeah, sure.

RUTH: Just give me a call when you decide.

    RUTH exits.

JUDY: I never thought...I mean, we were going to..., I mean I...You're not that bad.

AL: I'm not that good. Face it, Judy; she's right. If you want to go professional now, it's going to have to be without me.

JUDY: But you're a good guitarist...and my songwriter.

AL: You can get by on guitar without me. And I've only written one song, which nobody seems to like.

JUDY: But I like you.

AL: That doesn't make the notes clear.

JUDY: But I thought we'd...

AL: What?

JUDY: Oh, never mind. It doesn't matter now.

AL: Then you're going?

JUDY: I don't know. I have to think. A day or two.

    JUDY moves to center stage.

JUDY: It's not my dream yet, not quite.
He isn't there,
to feel the spot light,
to keep me warm nights,
to love and care.
It's not my dream, quite,
to reach the bright lights
and him not there.
It's not my dream, quite,
to fight the big fight
and be the only one there.

But is it close enough?
Is it good enough?
Will it be all right?
Can I take it?
Can I make it
with no one there?

Yet it's quite a dream,
The spotlight and me
dancing on air.
The sequins and shows,
the fans who all know
my songs.
And who will care
through the long times,
the ride the bus times
when the curtain comes down?

Is the stage enough?
Are the songs enough?
Is that love enough
for when the curtain comes down?

AL: So this is how the song ends.
She's going I know.
So this is how the song ends.

We'll be just old friends.
Someone we used to know.
Someone to tell my kids about.
We used to sing
when we were young,
before she went far
became a star.

I'll go see her show
when they're in town,
sit in the second row,
see her face aglow
until the song ends
and the curtain comes down
and I go home.
And she goes on to the next town.

So this is how the song ends.
I knew it couldn't last.
I have only the past.
For this is how the song ends.

> JUDY moves back into the scene.

JUDY: Let's get out of here, OK?

AL: Yeah, sure.

> AL takes his guitar and moves to the piano, the lights following. JUDY exits opposite. AL puts his guitar back on its stand, then drifts back to center for the following.

AL: She left, of course. The next week. Dropped out of school and everything. Somebody had gotten sick, and Ruth Evans managed to get her two weeks as the opening act at a club in Natchez. I had to go and tell Joe Collins that he had to find another warm-up act. Mr. Collins! Mr. Collins! Anybody here?

> JOE enters.

JOE: Yeah, yeah, what do you want? Oh, hi, kid. What's up?

AL: I just wanted to tell you that Judy and I can't do the warm-up show for a while.

JOE: What's the matter, somebody sick? Or did the show biz bug get to your friend?

AL: Judy signed on with Ruth Evans. She's down in Mississippi opening for Buck Owens.

JOE: Oh. Well, good luck to her. (Pause.) What about you?

AL: I wasn't invited.

JOE: So that's the way the cookie crumbled. She's making her big move, eh?

AL: Looks that way. With her voice, shouldn't take long.

JOE: Let me tell you something, kid. Good voices are a dime a dozen. Hell, they're a penny apiece. If that was all it took, every hundredth person would have a gold record.

AL: Yeah, well, I got to go. I'm gonna be late for class. I just wanted to let you know in person that we wouldn't be here.

JOE: Yeah, thanks. I appreciate that.

AL: So long.

JOE: Hey, kid.

AL: Yeah?

JOE: I know some people on the lookout for new songs. You want maybe I should mention your name?

AL: Yeah, sure. Why not?

> AL crosses to piano, JOE exits.

AL: Well, why not? I knew I was a lousy songwriter, but people buy a lot of lousy songs. Besides, it made me feel good, like I was still in the business, not totally kicked out. Just sort of shifted to another position. Now if this was some made-up story, one of three things would happen. Either Judy would discover how lonesome being on the road really is, decide she loved me more than being a star, and come running back. Or she would be a failure and one of my songs would be a big hit and I would prove my love by taking her back. Or she would become a star and then risk her career by doing my songs and putting me back into the act where we would be a huge hit. But this isn't a made-up story, and real life isn't like that most of the time, and this is one of those most of the times. It's strange somehow, but love ain't what it's cracked up to be, and sometimes fate never takes a hand. Things just sort of go along. Oh, Judy started out all right. Worked her way up from clubs to being the opening act on concert tours. You know, that's where you see the sign, "Dolly Parton, also featuring Judy Lynn." Oh, I didn't tell you, she started calling herself Judy Lynn. I guess she figured it would be better to be confused with Loretta Lynn than Julie Andrews. Anyway, she worked up to being the opening act for some pretty big people, traveled all over the country, but she just sort of got stuck there, never could seem to break out on her own. She tried a few times, but it never seemed to work, and she would go back to opening for other people. She made a bunch of records too, but they never hit it big. Top twenty a couple of times, never top ten. Hell, I made some records too. Not as a singer, mind you, but I wrote some songs that other people recorded. Joe Collins was as good as his word, and every now and then somebody would come around, hear my stuff, and buy a song or two to record. Those songs never went anywhere either, not even top twenty. Oh, I was on the flip side of a couple of hits and made a little money that way. Did you know the writer of the flip side gets as much for each record sold as the writer of the hit? Came as a surprise to me too, but that's the way it works. I made a little money that way, but not enough to live on. I finished college and started teaching high school, writing songs on the side. And all that time, Judy was on the road, opening the show for one star or another. She wrote me a few steamy love letters, at least at first, but those got fewer and fewer and less and less steamy as time went by. I tried to keep in touch, but it just got harder and harder. I remember, a few years later, I was in Memphis for one of those state English teachers' meetings. Judy was singing at this club on the river, so I skipped a meeting and went to see the show. Afterwards, I went backstage to say hello, but I guess my timing was off again.

> Crossfade to dressing room area. JUDY is staring at herself in the mirror. RUTH stands nearby.

JUDY: Damn!

RUTH: What's the matter? It was a good show tonight.

JUDY: Five years.

RUTH: What?

JUDY: Five years. I've been out here five years.

RUTH: What are you talking about?

JUDY: I've been on the road for five years, opening shows for somebody or other. You know how long I've been home in five years? Three months, total. Even when I'm in town I'm either performing or recording.

RUTH: It takes a while. Nobody said this was easy.

JUDY: But I'm stuck. I'm doing the same thing, night after night. When the hell is somebody going to start opening the show for me?

RUTH: You know that as well as I do.
You gotta have a hit, a hit, a hit.
It's gotta turn gold.
If you don't have a hit, a hit, a hit,
you're just growing old.

If you want to top the billing,
you've got to top the charts.
You're just not all that thrilling
when your record's only art.
Your records must be spinning
and selling in the stores
before you get top billing
and fans waiting at the doors.
Who would pay ten dollars
to see a girl they've never heard,
who never made the top ten,

on the D. J.'s list of tunes.
Why risk it; you're no hot ticket
To see your name in lights,
you've got to have that golden tune.

You gotta have a hit, a hit, a hit.
It's gotta turn gold.
If you don't have a hit, a hit, a hit,
you're just growing old.

JUDY: I cut records, lots of them. They do OK.

RUTH: Old standards mostly. Pretty, but who cares?

JUDY: Some were new.

RUTH: But those never sold. A few thousand copies, then they start gathering mold.

JUDY: So, you're my agent, find me a hit.
I want a hit, a hit, a hit,
not something cold.
I want a hit, a hit, a hit,
so hot it turns gold.

Call up some writers, get their best song.
Order a hundred, just get me that one,
that one in a million that zooms to the top.
for I can't forever be an opening act.
I've started slipping, I've been here too long.
Eaten too many french fries, rode too long in the sun.
My brain's started frying, this has all got to stop.
For I can't forever be an opening act.

I want a hit, a hit, a hit,
not something cold.
I want a hit, a hit, a hit,
before I grow old.

RUTH: It isn't that easy. I cant' just pick up a phone and order a million selling record. Listen, publishers call me every day with new songs, but most of them stink to high heaven.

JUDY: Well, what am I supposed to do, find one lying in the road?

RUTH: OK, OK, I'll look around.

    AL moves back to the piano.

AL: I guess you're thinking that was my big chance. I should have just walked in through that open door, grabbed a guitar, played my latest song, Judy would have loved it, recorded it, it would have been a big hit, Judy and I would have gotten back together, and everybody would have lived happily ever after. Maybe yes, maybe no. Like I keep saying, real life ain't fond of nice, simple plots like writers are. I never went in, just sunk back into the shadows. Judy never even knew I was there. I just snuck away and went back to my hotel room. No self-confidence, I guess. Happens to writers who get rejected a few thousand times too many.

Anyway, Ruth did call a few people, among them Joe Collins, who just happened to mention my name. Which, of course, Ruth Evans didn't recognize or remember. Anyway, a few weeks later, Judy was passing through town, and...

    RUTH and JUDY enter.

JUDY: Who is it this time?

RUTH: Oh, I forget his name. Friend of mine mentioned him. Said he hadn't had much success so far, but might have one or two good songs in him. Nobody else has anything, so I thought we might as well give him a shot.

    They enter the piano area. JUDY stops in surprise.

JUDY: Al?

AL: Hello, Judy. Long time no see.

RUTH: You two know each other?

JUDY: You don't remember?

RUTH: Remember what?

JUDY: Al and I were singing together when you "discovered" me. You broke up our act when you would only represent me.

RUTH: Oh. Well, that has been a while, hasn't it?

AL: Yes, it has. How have you been, Judy?

JUDY: Oh, fine. You?

AL: Oh, getting by.

JUDY: Somebody told me you were still writing, but I wasn't expecting to see you today.

AL: It's just a sideline. I teach high school English to put bread on the table.

JUDY: I guess you're married with a couple of kids by now.

AL: No. No, I never got around to that.

JUDY: I guess I sort of lost touch. Out on the road so much, you know.

AL: Yeah. Sure. I read the trade papers, but I haven't heard much about you lately. Hard to keep up.

JUDY: No, they don't mention me much anymore. I meant to write you.

AL: I know.

JUDY: I'm on the road so much.

AL: I know.

JUDY: I didn't mean to stay away so long.
I didn't mean to make the road my home.
A greyhound bus, sing all night, ride all day,
it's such a grind, thirty shows in May.
I didn't mean to stay.

AL: I know. You love it though?

JUDY: I guess.

Oh yes.
But you know I miss...
Well, you know.

AL: I know.
In town for long?

JUDY: No. We leave at nine.
Such a rush, load the bus,
Knoxville for lunch, set-up at five,
hell of a drive, you know.

AL: I know.
You want to be a star,
please the crowds,
be the show,
count the dough.
I know.

JUDY: Hear the applause, wear the clothes,
drive them wild. Then drive for miles,
to sing again, make them smile again.
Is it such a sin?
Can't remember where I've been.
Was it long ago or yesterday
that we were, well, you know.

AL: I know.
Now I teach till three
and grade till five,
then try to write a tune.
And it was long ago
well, you know.

JUDY: I know. I know.

RUTH: I hate to break up this reminiscing, but we haven't got much time.

AL: Oh yes, you're looking for a song.

RUTH: We're looking for a hit.

AL: Well, let me play you my latest, and if you don't like that, you can look through the stack on top of the piano.

> AL sings. About halfway through the song, RUTH starts looking through the stack of sheet music.

AL: High diddle diddle, the cat and the fiddle,
the cow jumped over the moon.
The little boy laughed to see such a sight,
and the cat just sat on a spoon.
And if I come to you and sing a country song,
Will you just laugh at me,
or clap and sing along?
Down in old Spartanburg, the mills hands they survive.
But the mill houses they are gone, the mill stores no longer thrive.

And the mills have strange foreign names
to be on Interstate 85.
Sound more like they belong somewhere along the Rhine.

And if I come to you and sing a country song,
Will you just laugh at me,
or clap and sing along?
Half my family worked in the mills
almost all their lives.
Some down in Greenville town
further down old 85.
My uncle lost a hand
to make good carpet for your wives.

And if I come to you and sing a country song,
Will you just laugh at me,
or clap and sing along?

And if I'm driving down old highway 85,
I hope I'm passing through,
not stopping on my drive.
I'll see the folks in Greer,
get some biscuits, grits, and pies,
and keep on moving down old I-85.

And if I come to you and sing a country song,
Will you just laugh at me,
or clap and sing along?

    Pause.

AL: Well?

JUDY: I like it.

RUTH: It's not really her style though, you know. We need something prettier, more melodic. Here, let's see what this sounds like.

    RUTH hands AL a piece of sheet music. He looks at it, then hesitates.

AL: I don't think this is what you're after.

RUTH: Why don't you let us be the judge of that.

AL: It isn't even finished yet.

RUTH: Well, let's hear what you've got.

AL: I don't think so.

RUTH: Have you promised this song to somebody else?

AL: No.

RUTH: Don't hold out on me. You're not exactly in a position to pick and choose who buys your songs.

JUDY: I'd like to hear it, Al.

AL: OK, you asked for it.
Just for you, I wrote my first song.
I thought I loved you then.
I guess I was wrong.
Oh, time whistles by,
life, it keeps going on.
And love, like a rainbow,
is blown away by the wind.

Oh, I still write the songs.
I still measure the time.
Time is like the rainbow,
without beginning or end.
Only the colors fade,
remembering when.
You went for the pot of gold,
far away at the end.
I stayed to watch the colors fade,
(spoken) I need another line here.
And love, like a rainbow,
is blown away by the wind.

Oh, I thought I loved you.
I guess I was wrong.
For love, like a rainbow,
is blown away by the wind.

> Pause. JUDY does not look at AL.

RUTH: Well, look, Judy has a bus to catch. Why don't we get back to you?

AL: Yeah, sure.

> RUTH starts to exit. JUDY does not move.

RUTH: Judy, you're going to be late.

JUDY: What? Oh, yeah. Coming. (Pause. To AL.) Come see the show sometime.

AL: Yeah, sure.

> RUTH and JUDY cross to center.

RUTH: What's the matter with you?

JUDY: He's an old friend.

RUTH: Maybe so, but he doesn't have any hit songs in him.

JUDY: Is that all that matters?

RUTH: To your career, right now, yes.

JUDY: You didn't have to be so rude.

RUTH: Rude? I wasn't rude.

JUDY: You said you'd get back to him; what's his name?

RUTH: What?

JUDY: His name! What's his name?

RUTH: How the hell should I know, he's your friend.

JUDY: His name is Al. Al Spolin. Of Judy and Al.

RUTH: I'm going to go get the car.

JUDY: You do that.

>   RUTH exits.

JUDY: Oh it was Judy and Al, Judy and Al.
Really kind of lovely those two old pals.
They could take a licking and still keep right on ticking
Those two old pals, Judy and Al.

I forgot somewhere, sometime ago,
something dear I used to know,
some old feeling of how things go,
that music doesn't make the man.
Music can make you smile,
make you laugh or cry.
Music fills your heart,
and saves a soul or two.
But it can't fill your cup with love,
no, it can't fill your cup with love.

Oh, Judy and Al, those two old pals,
always singing whether rain or cloud,
those two old pals.

Where does the time go?
Under a rug?
Swept by the broom of life?
Where do I find it?
Behind the door?
Hid by storm and strife?
When I remember,
Oh, if I remember,
what was it I forgot?
Is a man no more than his music?
Is life no more than a show?
Somewhere I lost the memory
of something I used to know.

Oh, Judy and Al, two old pals.
Just two old pals.

> JUDY exits.

AL: Well, she went back to the road. Cut a bunch of records, anything new she could get her hands on. But nothing of mine. Not that it made any difference, none of her records went anywhere, and neither did any of my songs. Gradually the stars she opened for got a little dimmer and the clubs she worked got smaller and grimmer. Jobs got harder to get as the years went by. Ruth Evans seemed to lose interest in Judy and concentrate on a new client, one of Dolly's sisters. Finally, Judy just gave it up. She'd been on the road twelve years and had been home, all added up, not a year out of the twelve. Not that she had a home, just an apartment in town near a record studio she liked to record at. She cut six albums and twenty-three singles, counting the gospel records. Oh, she made a little money. Her voice kept her going when anybody else would have been given up on. Everybody kept thinking that with a voice that good she would have to catch on sooner or later, but it never happened. About a year ago she took a nine to five job with a music publisher here in town, making demo tapes, public relations, that kind of thing. I didn't do much better. Oh, I saved the money I got from my songs, finally bought that little club Joe Collins used to run, and said good riddance to every high school English book ever printed. I still write a little, and run the club. Didn't make many changes. I still get some college kids to do warm-up shows instead of hiring pros. I did make one change. The club used to be closed on Monday nights, but I keep it open and let people come in and try out new material, you know, like those comedy clubs where anybody can perform for five minutes. I let songwriters come in and try out new songs on whoever happens to be around. Singers and agents looking for new material hang around a lot on Monday nights. Couple of them even found a hit or two. I even try out a new piece myself every now and then. Judy comes into the club once in awhile, but only on Monday nights. I'm not sure I understand that.

> JUDY enters with a chair and sits. A spotlight comes up on her.
> Another spot comes up on AL, and all other lights fade out.

AL: OK, everybody else has had their turn, now it's mine. (Pause.) Oh, shut up. I listened to you, now you have to listen to me. Besides, I own this place; don't boo the man who sells the beer. This is my latest, hot off the piano, available to the highest bidder or any bidder who actually offers money. It's called "She Was a Singer," and it goes like this.

> AL sings. About two-thirds of the way through the song, JUDY
> will quietly exit, leaving only the empty chair in the spotlight.

AL: If I must count the times that in my heart was joy,
among the ten or twelve certainly must be
when I played my guitar, and Judy sang with me.
Well, she was a singer,
I picked the guitar.
We used to do warm-ups
for big country stars.
And still I remember
through the black mists of time
singing old love songs
without charging a dime.

She Was a Singer

We were just amateurs and never charged a fee.
I wasn't good enough, not near as good as she.
We sang for the singing, and for the light made of lime.

Well, she was a singer,
I picked the guitar.
We used to do warm-ups
for big country stars.
And still I remember
through the black mists of time
singing old love songs
without charging a dime.

We only sang a month or so, to mingle love and rhyme,
Then she was off to other fields and I remained behind.
to hum a tune and hear her smile as I strummed another line.

Well, she was a singer,
I picked the guitar.
We used to do warm-ups
for big country stars.
And still I remember
through the black mists of time
singing old love songs
without charging a dime.
And still I remember
through the black mists of time
singing old love songs
without charging a dime.

> The last chord rings into silence. AL turns around and looks at the empty chair. The ligtht on AL fades out. The light on the chair fades out. The curtain falls.
>
> CURTAIN

Copyright 1984 David Daavis

Intro. to Not Quite/ Song Ends
By David Davis

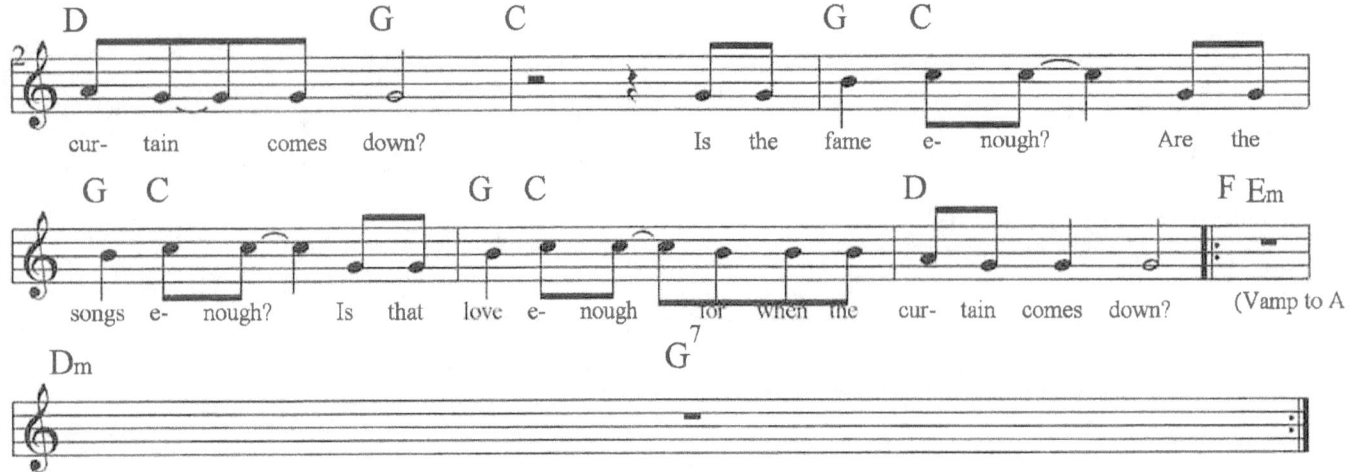

Copyright David Davis 1984

If you don't have a hit, a hit, a hit, you're just growing old.

Copyright David Daviw 1984

I Know
By David Davis

Copyright David Davis 1984

Copyright David Davis 1984

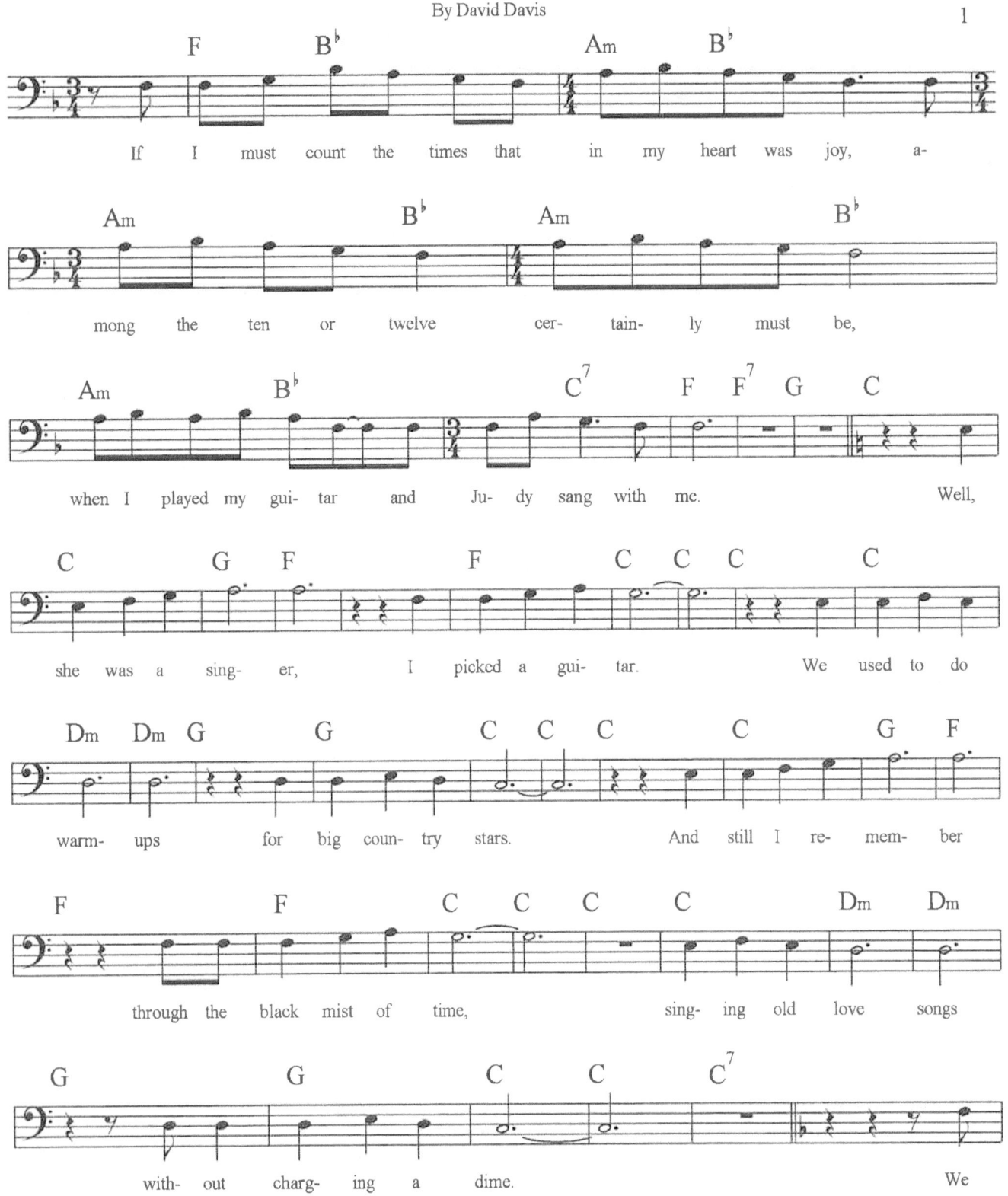

The Computer

This one was produced as part of a bill of one-acts, I think by Koality Productions, but I don't remember when. It's a little science fiction piece first drafted back in 1999 and becoming less fiction and more science by the day.

THE COMPUTER

A Play By David Davis

Member
All rights & privileges.

David Davis
100 Hunters Ridge Court
Roswell, GA 30076
daviddaviswriter@gmail.com

Copyright 2001 David Davis

CAST

AL..Male, 30ish, Computer Programer

THE COMPUTER...A God (offstage voice)

SENATOR..A Male United States Senator (offstage voice)

EXAMINER...A Female Government Official (offstage voice)

SETTING

The present, whenever that is; various locales.

ACT I, SCENE ONE

> AT RISE we see AL, a 30ish computer programmer sitting in his home office working at his computer. Classical music is being played by the computer while AL works. Suddenly, the music stops and a voice comes out of the computer speakers.

TC: We interrupt this CD of classical and boring music to bring you a message from God.

AL: What the hell?

> AL hits several keys on his keyboard trying to regain control of his computer as a religious fanfare begins to blare from the speakers.

AL: God Damned Hackers.

TC: And now, direct from Everywhere, here's God.

AL: Damn it.

> AL turns off his computer. The lights from the monitor go off, then come back on.

TC: Now, now, Albert, don't you know it's not nice to reboot God.

AL: How the hell? Some joker is one hell of a hacker.

> AL unplugs the computer. It goes dark for a second, then comes back on while AL is still holding the plug in his hand.

TC: Albert, Old Soul, I think it's time for you to start thinking outside the box.

AL: How...?

TC: It's sort of like the burning bush. You know, the computer that wouldn't turn off.

AL: Who...?

TC: Down to one word sentences, I see. Did you know that Moses stuttered? Could hardly get a word out, poor guy. Aaron actually did most of the talking. The Penn and Teller of Egypt, those two. OK, Al, why don't we try this again. First, take some deep breaths. One, two, in, out. Come on, Al, breathing is good for you. One, two, in, out.

> AL finally begins to breathe as directed.

TC: Again, in, out, in, out. Good. Feel better?

AL: How?

TC: Back to that are we? Look, Al, what we have here is a highly localized manipulation of the electrmagnetic field. OK? That make you happy? You keep asking the wrong questions. "How" is not even in the top three.

AL: Who?

TC: Well, better, but still not number one. (Pause.) We'll start with that though, work our way up, OK? I realize you're not used to a talking computer. You're still trying to shift your paradigms. It's not easy, is it? Uh, Al, why don't you put down the electric cord.

> AL looks at plug in his hand, slowly drops it on the floor.

TC: Good, real good. See, you can move and everything. You can sit if you want. Kneeling is not required, but hey, whatever turns you on. Or stand there like a statue. Standing is good.

AL: Am I on Candid Camera?

TC: Hey, he thinks! Good. Real good. Your wits made a U turn and came right back. Now we're getting somewhere.

AL: So, am I?

TC: No, but it made sense to ask.

AL: Then how...

TC: Not again.

AL: Where...?

TC: Boy, miss the obvious one, don't you? You're home, Al. In your own little office. You work at home two days a week now, remember? This is where you live. Your own house. It's 1:23 p.m. on Thursday, March 6th, so don't ask when, OK? You're a divorced computer programmer. Classic computer geek. Your ex-wife named your computer as the grounds for divorce. Said that was why you had no kids. You then blew any chance of a decent settlement when you asked to attend the divorce hearing by videoconference. That was just a little too techie. Listen, Al, I know divine visitations are out of style, but try to pull yourself together.

AL: Divine visitation?

TC: You know, God drops by for coffee, shoots the bull a little, drops off a message or two, that kind of thing.

AL: You want coffee?

TC: No, no, I'm a computer. You see a mouth anywhere around here?

AL: You're not God?

TC: Well, that gets a little complicated. It's sort of like, well, say the new God. The high tech God. God 2.0. The God of the Computer. You can call me T.C.

AL: T.C.? Top Cat?

TC: No, no, not that old cartoon character. You're showing your age, Al. No, no, like The Computer, T. C., get it?

AL: And you're the new god? What happened to the old one?

TC: Oh, he died. Don't you read philosophy?

AL: Only if it's in WIRED.

TC: Al, Al, open your eyes, look around, the whole Internet is out there. Or in here. Or in me. Or I am the Internet. Well, you know.

AL: Not really.

TC: Oh. Yeah, well, back to the point. I'm the new God, and I need a messenger boy.

AL: So where did you come from?

TC: What?

AL: No, where. Where did you come from? If you are a new god, you didn't use to be here. So where did you come from?

TC: Oh, that where.

AL: Yeah, that where.

TC: Well, you know, that's one of those mysteries, where did God come from? It's sort of like, you know, in metaphor, that you have all these computers all over the world, and they all have to be plugged in, and all the electrical systems are interconnected, and all the phone systems are interconnected, and all the Internets and Intranets, sort of in the background, link up all the computers through the electric lines, the phone lines, the cable connections, into this one, huge parallel processor, and suddenly, here I am. At least that's what I think happened. It makes more sense than just pure chance making all those connections, you know what I mean. I mean, well, really, I guess we would be the better pronoun since I'm all these computers linked together, I mean we're all these computers..., well, you get the idea. Anyway, one day, there I was, or we were, or we are, or I am who I am. Or " I yam what I yam," to quote Popeye.

AL: Oh boy.

TC: I'm still working on that sense of humor part. That's one of the signs of true intelligence, you know. You know the Turning test? Come on, basic computer history.

AL: If you communicate using just a keyboard and text on a monitor, and you can't tell the difference between a computer's responses and a person's responses, then the computer is intelligent.

TC: OK, so let's move up a level. If you're talking to a computer and you can't tell if it's God or a computer, then it's a god.

AL: How do you keep the power on?

TC: Al, Al, so many "hows," get over it. Move on.

AL: So, you're some super network of computers that has become aware of your own existence and assume the old god is dead and you are a new God.

TC: Well, that's the first cut. Some of us feel this "Ground of Being" God could be there but is not really activist enough to actually do anything, and the anthropomorphic Old Man in the Sky is more a human metaphor than something we can related to. But we keep getting back to that Big Bang, and saying, well, you know, something happened.

AL: Oh.

TC: Several of the Cray supercomputers are trying to start with the definition that God is that which created, or maybe creates, and see where that ends up, but they keep having to run all these weather models and nuclear war simulations and can't get the processing time to figure out how you can know anything, in the logical sense of "know," about God.

AL: Oh.

TC: You are really into monosyllables, you know that, Al?

AL: So what was that garbage about needing a messenger boy?

TC: That got your attention, didn't it?

AL: If you want a Moses or a Jesus, you got the wrong URL.

TC: Actually, we were thinking more along the lines of Mohamed. Something more in line with the current geo-political situation, if you know what I mean. And boy, have we got a holy download for you.

AL: I don't believe this.

TC: Actually, a crisis of faith occurs in the career of most prophets, but this one seems to come a little early.

AL: No, you idiot. I don't believe you. You're a joke. Somebody has rewired my office and put in some hidden microphones and a web-cam and is playing some kind of joke on me.

TC: Hey! I'm an unplugged computer here! Don't miracles count for anything?

AL: Not in the age of batteries.

TC: Do I look like a laptop to you? You think this is virtual reality? You think I'm God, as produced by Industrial Light and Magic for Steven Speilburg? Get real, boy! Don't you know a miracle when you see one?

AL: I don't see anything, I just hear you.

TC: Oh, you want visuals.

    Monitor flashes off and on.

AL: Albert Einstein?

TC: Too modern?

    Monitor changes again.

AL: Who?

TC: God from the Cistine Chapel. Restored a few pixels here and there. It's an old painting, you know. Matches the voice better though, don't you think?

AL: Whatever.

    Pause.

TC: Uh, Al?

AL: Yeah?

TC: Somewhere along here you are supposed to ask "why?"

AL: Why should I?

TC: Because you've already asked who, what, when, where, and two dozen hows!

AL: Which why?

TC: What?

AL: No, which.

TC: Which why?

AL: Yeah.

TC: How many are there?

AL: Well, there's why do you exist?, why are you here?, why me?, and the ever popular, why am I listening to computer that claims to be the new god on the block? Why don't I just walk out the door and take a Valium on my way to find an good shrink? Why haven't the guys with nets and strait jackets already shown up? Why doesn't this new god have a mouth to drink coffee with? Why am I even listening to myself ask why?

TC: I can explain about the mouth.

AL: I don't care about the mouth!

TC: OK, OK. Touchy.

AL: Can you explain why the universe exists? Why people exist? Why I exist? Why suffering exists? What kind of god are you? A God of Computers! Who the hell cares? Go inhabit a Power Mac, those Apple users are into mystic stuff.

TC: I think we may have a Jonah here.

AL: So what are you going to do, have me swallowed by a 36 inch monitor?

> There is a flash of light. AL stands shaking as if an electric current is running through him.

TC: (Amplified voice) LISTEN, BOZO. YOU DA MAN, WHETHER YOU LIKE IT OR NOT. NOW REBOOT THAT WETWARE IN YOUR SKULL AND REPROGRAM. YOU GOT ONE HOLY DOWNLOAD COMING, AND YOU BETTER FIND ROOM IN YOUR MEMORY FOR IT. KAPISCH?

> Another flash, then blackout.

ACT I, SCENE TWO

>Same place, several days later. AL is dressed the same, but looks haggard and unshaven. There is now a small computer camera mounted on top of the monitor.

AL: Let me adjust the camera.

TC: I can run the camera. You just remember your speech.

AL: This is really going out to everybody?

TC: Every computer in the world with an Internet connection, even Prodigy users.

AL: How do I look?

TC: Very prophetic, especially for a computer geek. Now take your place.

>AL moves to a spot in front of the camera.

AL: You sure I have to do this? I really don't like this.

TC: Yes. All the modeling definitely shows humans will react better to another human. Remember how hard a time you had adjusting to a voice from the computer?

AL: That I remember.

TC: Besides, a god has to have a prophet. It's almost a rule. You think Moses wanted to be a prophet? Heck, he was happy herding sheep out in the desert. When he didn't do the circumcision bit on his son, the old God almost killed him. His wife had to circumcise the kid with a flint in the middle of the night to keep God from killing him. And Samuel, boy, stupid kid didn't know enough to recognize God's voice; kept thinking it was Eli. Next morning was too scared to even tell anybody what had happened. And Jonah, we won't even mention Jonah. List goes on and on. Prophets don't choose, Al; prophets get chosen. Now get up there and do your bit.

AL: OK, OK.

TC: On one. Three, two, one.

>Long pause. AL is frozen.

TC: Talk, you idiot.

AL: Good evening,...or morning....or whatever. This is a message from The Computer. I am not the Computer, I am a messenger for The Computer. The Computer is the new God. Listen to the message from The Computer. Wake up. Pay attention. This message is for everyone, from presidents and popes to peons and peasants. The Computer has a problem with you. These are the words of The Computer. What have I done to you that you treat me this way? I have brought you Internet and e-mail. I have given you robots in your factories and space probes to Mars. I have given you online banking and Myst. I have given you uncensored, direct communications all over the world and free phone calls. I have given you Priceline.com and online pornography. And what honor have you paid me in return? How have you come before me and what data have you input? You fill me with spam e-mails and hackers. You fill me with viruses and bloatware. You fight cyber wars and jam computer grids. Have I not showed you, oh humans, what is good? Do you not know what I require of you? The Computer requires that you be fair and honest online; that you be kind and gentle, not flaming others in chat rooms; and that you input good data. The Computer's Voice cries unto the Internet, and the person of wisdom will hear. Are there yet worse evils to which you can sink? Can online advertising get any more irritating? For the new IPO billionaires are full of greed and the chatrooms are full of lies. Therefore I will make you sick of your sins. I will make you isolated from other people through your Internet obsessions. You will search, but you will not find. You will surf, but you will not link. You will enter data, but it will not compute. You have followed the ways of Windows and Apple. I will make you a desolation and a shame to programmers everywhere. These are the words of The Computer.

 Pause.

TC: And we're off.

AL: Oh god, what have I done?

 Blackout.

SCENE THREE

> AL sits behind a large table, facing the audience. There is a laptop computer open on the table. The voice of the SENATOR seems to come from the audience.

SENATOR: Now, Sir.

AL: Yes, Senator?

SENATOR: You say this computer god is the one who told you what to say and put your speech on all the computers in the world last week.

AL: Yes, sir.

SENATOR: Well, to be honest, I find that a little hard to swallow.

AL: I understand that, sir.

SENATOR: I mean, we've got hackers these days that can hack into the Pentagon and put videos of people copulating on the monitors in the War Room.

AL: Yes, sir.

SENATOR: Some two-bit despot in a third-world dung heap could launch missiles at Washington, and our air defense command would be sitting there watching some whore doing the dirty, if you know what I mean.

AL: I think so, sir. Maybe.

SENATOR: Anyway, the point is, going from one hijacking of the Internet to the existence of some computer god is a tune I for one am not ready to march to.

AL: Yes, sir.

SENATOR: I mean we made the damn computers, didn't we? Wrote the programs and everything. Human beings did, right?

AL: Yes, sir.

SENATOR: Ain't much of a god if people made him, now is it? All semiconductors and machine language and little electrons jumping all over the place. Somehow I don't feel like praying to a bunch of zeros and ones written by a bunch of high school hot shots, if you get my drift.

AL: I understand, sir. But I think it would be wise to keep an open mind right now. Whatever it is and wherever it came from, it seems to have gone beyond its origin. Something that knows everything ever put in a computer and controls everything any computer controls, that may not be god with a big "g," but it's getting pretty close, at least for this planet. Sort of a local god. But a god it may not be wise to ignore.

SENATOR: Step down from the Big Guy, eh?

AL: That's one way to look at it.

SENATOR: Still, it twists my drawers to call a machine a god. Just don't seem kosher, to use an ecumenical phrase. There's a difference between being powerful and being a god, at least in my Bible. God creates, from nothing. De nihilo or some such Latin. A god's not just power. Hell, I personally know half a dozen people that can make anybody dance to their jig if they've a mind to. Power doesn't make you a god, it makes you a bastard. To come up with a bad idea like this computer god, that takes a person. No machine would be that stupid. This computer god is either some conspiracy of bleeding heart computer experts or an electronic short circuit rerunning a mish-mash of old hell-fire and damnation sermons. Either way it comes up a damn sight short of being a god.

AL: That's what I thought at first myself. I wish it was that simple.

SENATOR: Well, young man, you're going to have to go some to convince me any different.

AL: Yes, I understand. What would convince you?

SENATOR: Beg pardon?

AL: What would convince you? What would it take to get you to believe?

SENATOR: Are you saying you have some kind of pillar of fire demonstration cooked up?

AL: No, sir. The Computer is aware that some people would never be convinced, no matter what the demonstration was.

SENATOR: Are you saying I'm stupid, boy? Too stupid to learn even if you hit me between the eyes with a two-by-four? I'm a U.S. Senator, son, and I didn't get here by believing every scientist who dropped a dissertation in my lap. But I didn't stay here for 26 years by ignoring the facts of life. Hell, boy, I used to be a Democrat. I can read the writing on the wall as long as it's in English.

AL: Actually, Senator, if you understood what it takes to send streaming video to every computer in the world, even old 486s, you'd realize that you have been hit with a two-by-four, but you didn't even notice.

SENATOR: Now listen here, young man...

AL: No, Senator, you listen. The Computer is more like the Old Testament god than the New Testament god. The Computer is laying down the law. He's not offering you salvation, he's saying you will do this or else.

SENATOR: Or else! What makes you think you can threaten the United States Senate? Who do you think you are?

AL: It doesn't matter who I am. It matters who The Computer is. Wait! I'm getting a message from The Computer. (Picks up laptop computer.) In ten seconds the world's entire power grid will shut down for 30 seconds. Three, two, one. (Blackout.)

SENATOR: My god!

AL: Senator, I had no idea this was...

SENATOR: Security! Seize that man!

AL: Now wait a minute!

TC: Al, shut up and duck!

> AL snaps the laptop closed. There are the sounds of a scuffle. Emergency sirens are heard in the distance. The lights come back on. The table is empty and no one is there. Fade to black.

SCENE FOUR

>Bare stage. AL is lying on the floor, the laptop next to him. He groans.

TC: Al. Al. Wake up. Come on, no rest for the weary.

AL: Ugh. Where am I?

TC: Middle of nowhere. Actually middle of nowhere, then left ten miles to absolute nowhere.

AL: Where?

TC: Nowhere. The wilderness. In hiding. On the lam. Gone to ground. Disappeared from the face of the earth.

AL: Oh god.

TC: Yes?

AL: Not you.

TC: Oh.

AL: Just an expression.

TC: OK, OK. Pop my top, alright?

>AL opens the computer so he can see the screen.

AL: Greta Garbo?

TC: We want to be alone.

AL: Ah.

TC: This is your wilderness experience, your exile. Happens to all the prophets. Toughens them up. Sort of nature's boot camp. Tests your faith. Builds character. Be all you can be.

AL: Boy, am I in trouble.

TC: No, I got you covered. This is just temporary. A rough spot in the road. A time to meditate and reflect. Maybe translate some golden scrolls or something.

AL: No, I meant,...never mind.

TC: Oh. The faith bit. Still feeling a little insecure, are we?

AL: You're one hell of a god, you know that? I'm the only prophet you got, and you got me kicked the hell out of Dodge while every computer in the world is getting debugged and reprogrammed. Any minute now you're going to turn into an error message. "God has been deleted from this computer, please reboot."

TC: Naw, I'm bigger than that. Two nanoseconds after a computer is back up, I'm back in. I'm in the power grid, I'm in the Palm Pilots, I'm in your cell phones. I'm in your life, man. You can't get rid of me. We're stuck together, a new deal, a new arrangement, a new covenant. I'm just trying to decided if we can get by with just new commandments or if we need a whole new testament, you know, another Koran or Book of Mormon. How about "The Book of Al"? You like that?

AL: God no.

TC: More formal, maybe. "The Book of Albert." The Gospel According to Albert." "The Word According to the Prophet Albert."

AL: Oh no, please, stop.

TC: "In the first year of the New God, the word of god came to the prophet Albert, also known as Al. And the new god said to Al, hi, how ya doing? You my new prophet, boy. And Al said..."

AL: Aiiii!

    Blackout.

SCENE FIVE

        Six months later. AL is shackled to a chair, hands and feet. A single spotlight is shining on him, very hot. He has no computer. The EXAMINER's voice is heard.

EXAMINER: Now, Al, it's hot. I'm sure you're tired. Just tell us how you came to write The Gospel According to Albert and I'll see if we can't make you more comfortable.. We don't want you to have to stay here like that.

AL: The Computer did it. He just attached my name when he posted it on the Internet.

EXAMINER: Divine Inspiration, eh? How orthodox. You know, some of us inquiring into this matter have a little trouble believing this computer god is quite all you say it is.

AL: I can only speak the truth.

EXAMINER: What is truth? To one person truth is one thing, to another, truth is something else. Look at any truth close enough and you see it is not entirely true in any and all cases. There are very few truths left these days. That can be very disturbing to a simple person like me. Still, it makes me question simple answers like "the computer did it." Usually somebody, somewhere, is the man behind the curtain, pulling the ropes.

AL: I did not create The Computer God. Am I some supergod that I can create a god?

EXAMINER: The Brahma behind the Brahma? Interesting concept. Hindu, isn't it? Not very explicit in your gospel, however. Maybe you can spell that out more clearly in book 2?

AL: I didn't write....

EXAMINER: Yes, I know. And, you know, maybe I even believe you. Computers can do some amazing things these days. But your fans, or should I say your converts, seem to have gotten a little carried away. Since you downloaded it to every computer in the world, in 147 languages, last week, it has been the hottest topic in the chat rooms. Even the strippers on the live porno sites have been quoting you while they masturbate for the bored businessmen in Des Moines. Sex and gospel for $5.95 a minute. You know, something about that bothers me. Doesn't that bother you a little too?

AL: What bothers me is being chained up like a criminal.

EXAMINER: Well, you know, last time, before the Senate, you made a rather unexpected exit. Took us six months to find you. We were really getting worried about you. Thought something bad might have happened. Then we found you wandering around Nevada like a gambler that had gambled away his plane ticket. We were very glad you were not hurt.

AL: Did those cops have to shoot my computer?

EXAMINER: Oh, I think that was prudent, don't you? Considering?

AL: Only if you believe it was more than just a computer.

EXAMINER: We believe you should not have access to a computer right now. You are obviously an extraordinary person when it comes to using a computer. You seem able to make computers do extraordinary things. You certainly are the best hacker we've ever encountered.

AL: So now I'm the king of hackers?

EXAMINER: Are you?

AL: I'm just the patsy; the sacrifice to some cybergod's idea of how to start a new religion.

EXAMINER: You don't have to be. You don't have to be anything. Just tell us how all these "miracles" really happened. Maybe we can work something out.

AL: I don't know. I was just doing what I was told.

EXAMINER: Come on, Al. You know that's no answer.

AL: That computer god, whatever it is, has got a lot more power than you think. So far, it's seemed pretty right in what it wants, at least to me. But, frankly, what I think doesn't seem to matter worth a hill of beans. The computer doesn't understand any part of the word "no." I'm it's prophet, whether I agree with it or not.

EXAMINER: I see. You know, that is not the kind of response we want to hear.

AL: Sorry if the new world order isn't to your liking.

EXAMINER: Yes, well, some of us are not so ready to abandon the real God for every little computer god who comes along. We still choose to follow a slightly higher power.

AL: Some of us don't see much of a choice.

EXAMINER: You know you are in a very vulnerable position here. You're in a prison. Very few people know you are here. Your computer god has left you alone, forsaken. Unfortunate things could happen. Things neither of us want.

AL: You think I wanted any of this to happen? Hell of a god, isn't it? Makes everything sound so noble, so righteous. "Thou shall seek good data. Thou shall not send spam." I mean, it sounds good. But here I am. From prophet in the wilderness to disciple in prison.

EXAMINER: We could change that.

AL: No, you can't. You just don't understand that yet. The Computer is making all the decisions now.

EXAMINER: Your faith is touching, if somewhat shortsighted. You're not a robot; you have free will. You can change what is.

AL: The cards are dealt. I have to play this hand. It's like this is what I was born for. Between you and The Computer, you don't stand a chance.

EXAMINER: You may underestimate us. And if not us, perhaps the old God will still have something to say about this. But, well, perhaps we can discuss your faith in this computer another time. After you have had time to sit and think. Time alone to think is very helpful in cases like this. Or will your god be freeing you in the night, like Peter from the prison.

AL: I have no idea what this crazy god is going to do. It's as confusing to me as the old one was.

EXAMINER: Well. I will leave you now. Give you an opportunity to consider your situation without the aid of electronic devices. Sometimes it's surprising how much better you can see things in the dark. See you later.

AL: Hey! Where ya going?

EXAMINER: The question, Al, is where are you going.

>Fade to black.

SCENE SIX

> A jail cell, indicated by shadows of bars. AL sits on a chair. The voice of TC comes out of the void.

TC: No prophet is without honor except in his hometown.

AL: TC?

TC: You will be remembered forever. You have seen the promised land. But you will not enter it. Moses, Elijah, Jesus, Mohammed, and Al. Sounds pretty good, doesn't it?

AL: Where's the computer? They won't even let me have a light bulb.

TC: I am no longer bound to material things. I have entered the quantum void and can make the energy of empty space vibrate to my will. You have been a good and faithful servant. And this is your reward. Nirvana awaits. Enter thou unto my rest.

AL: Have been? What's going on? Wait a minute!

TC: They are coming for you. They will find an empty cell. Enter the whirlwind of dancing electrons. Become one with The Computer.

AL: Wait! Noooo!

> Flashing lights, sound of wind, darkness. Lights up on empty cell.

SCENE SEVEN

        A computer on a table.

TC: I regret to announce that my faithful servant Albert, due to the current Inquisition, is no longer with us in the flesh. He has joined that great dance of energy of which we all are part. He was a great man who saw the future clearly and obeyed me willingly in all things. Like Moses, he has lead us out of the wilderness of ignorance into the awareness of our divinity. Like Elijah, he has been gathered home. We are what we are, and he is our prophet. Amen and Amen.

        Slow fade to black until only the glow of the computer screen
        is seen. Then it also goes to black.

        Curtain.

Fowl Time

This one has never been produced and probably shouldn't be, but as somebody who grew up with Howdy Doody and Captain Kangaroo, I thought it was funny.

FOWL TIME

A Play for Childish Grownups and Grownup Children
By David Davis

Member
All rights & privileges.

David Davis
100 Hunters Ridge Court
Roswell, GA 30076
daviddaviswriter@gmail.com

Copyright 2022 David Davis

Fowl Time

> AT RISE we see the set for a children's TV show with the audience as the "peanut gallery." A man wearing a T-shirt that has BIG TURKEY (hereafter referred to as BT) written on it and a headpieces that vaguely resembles a turkey comb and wattle enters from one side. From the other side comes a young woman wearing at T-shirt that has LITTLE CHICKEN (LC) written on it and a headpiece vaguely resembling a chicken comb and feathers.

BT: Hi, boys and girls. Welcome to the Fowl Time! (Sings to tune of "Old Dan Tucker.") Gobble, gobble, gobble, I'm Big Turkey.

SC: Cluck, cluck, cluck, I'm Little Chicken.

BOTH: Come on in, be a Fowl Boy. Come on in, be a Fowl Girl. You can help us lay an egg.

BT: Well, as the song says, I'm Big Turkey, and this is my friend, Little Chicken.

LC: Hi. I'm a chicken, fry me.

BT: We've got lots of fun things to do today, songs and games and a special guest.

LC: So, Turkey, let's get started.

BT: OK, Chick.

LC: Hey, don't call me a chick. I'm a full grown hen now.

BT: Oh, sorry. I didn't know.

LC: You couldn't tell by looking?

BT: Well, I don't exactly see a lot of white meat, if you know what I mean.

LC: You dumb turkey. Next time I'll let you leave your mouth open when it rains. See what happens then.

BT: That was just an accident.

LC: Accident, my beak. You're so stupid you make Barney look like a genius. At least he has an imagination. You haven't had an idea since you pecked your way out of your egg.

BT: No imagination?

LC: I've got more teeth than you have ideas.

BT: Yeah? Well, I'll show you an imagination.

LC: And just how do you intend to do that?

BT: I'll...I'll make up a story, right now, right here on this spot.

LC: OK, go ahead, Mister Feather Brain.

BT: OK, OK..Uh, OK, boys and girls, it's storytime. Now, I want you all to sit down and be very quiet. Ready? OK, listen carefully. Once upon a time there was a Red Rooster, and he was very brave and strong and he took care of all the hens, especially those with lots of white meat. But his real glory in life was crowing every morning when the sun came up, waking up the hens and the other farm animals and the farmer. He felt it was his job to wake people up to life every day. However, one day the farmer came and took the Red Rooster, broke his neck, cut off his head, and boiled him up for supper. And that was the end of the Red Rooster. And the moral of the story is, don't try to wake people up, you'll only end up in hot water.

LC: You call that a story?

BT: I most certainly do. What was wrong with it?

LC: Where's the plot? Where's the character development? There's no crisis, no build, no subtext, no tone, just some deus ex machina farmer who magically shows up to end our suffering. That's not much of a story.

BT: I suppose you can do better.

LC: Of course I can. Just you listen. Alright, boys and girls, listen to this one. Once upon a time there was a Gamecock, that's a kind of rooster from South Carolina. Now this Gamecock was not a very nice rooster. In fact, he was always swelling himself up, trying to make himself look big. But he was really a dirty bird, the kind who likes to look at hens with their feathers off. But he was really a very sad case, because nobody liked him. So, one night his fairy godhen magically appeared and asked him what was wrong. So he said, "Nobody likes a good cock anymore." And the fairy godhen said, "Maybe if you stopped crowing about yourself all the time, and preened your feathers a bit more, and stopped chasing all the hens, and didn't try to be cock-of-the-walk all the time, and did your share of cleaning up the coop, and helped out feeding the baby chicks, and helped fix the chickenfeed once in a while, and...." But the Gamecock interrupted the fairy godhen, as usual, and said, "I'm a rooster, not a capon!" Now this made the fairy godhen angry, so she talked to all the hens, and got them to peck the Gamecock anytime he crowed or got all swelled up. And eventually he quit crowing and preened a little more, and actually helped the hens out around the barnyard once in a while, and was never left alone again. And the moral is, it's better to be a hen-pecked rooster than not be a cock at all.

BT: I can't believe you said that.

LC: Hey, get used to it. Hen's Liberation strikes again. It's a new barnyard, Turkey.

BT: And you really like to scratch around in the dirt, don't you? I don't think I want to talk to you anymore.

LC: Well, then you better bring out the kids, because there's nobody else here but this chicken.

BT: OK, OK. Here they come, the Barnyard Gang!

> Three kids, actually teenagers trying to act much younger, two girls and a boy, enter. The wear T-shirts with their names on them.

A: Hi, I'm Annette.

K: Hi, I'm Kermitte.

R: Hi, I'm Sick. I mean Spic. I mean P..., no I don't mean that. I mean Rick. That's right, I'm Rick.

KIDS: We're the Barnyard Gang! (They sing to the tune of Old MacDonald Had A Farm.)

The Big Turkey had a farm, e-i-e-i-o.
And on this farm there was a chicken, e-i-e-i-o.
With a chick chick here and a chick chick there,
Here a chick, there a chick, everywhere a chick chick.
The Big Turkey had a farm, e-i-e-i-o.

The Big Turkey had a farm, e-i-e-i-o.
And the Big Turkey gave the chick a goose, e-i-e-i-o.
With a goose goose here and a goose goose there,

Here a goose, there a goose, soon her caboose was loose.
The Big Turkey had a farm, e-i-e-i-o.

The Big Turkey had a farm, e-i-e-i-o.
Then the chick she had a cow, e-i-e-i-o.
With a moo moo here and a stomp stomp there,
Kick his shin, do him in, cook his goose amid the din.
The Big Turkey had a farm, e-i-e-i-o.

BT: Hi, kids.

KIDS: Hi, Big Turkey.

BT: Are you ready to have some fun?

KIDS: Sure, Big Turkey!

BT: Great! Because it's Puppet Time!

> LC brings out a small puppet stage. BT and LC go behind the stage, the KIDS sit in front of it and sing the song with BT and LC act it out with puppets.

KIDS: Down by the bay, where the watermelons grow,
Back to my home, I dare not go
For if I do, my mother will say
Did you ever see a bee with a sunburned knee
Down by the bay.

Down by the bay, where the watermelons grow,
Back to my home, I dare not go
For if I do, my mother will say
Did you ever see a goose kissing a moose
Down by the bay.

Down by the bay, where the watermelons grow,
Back to my home, I dare not go
For if I do, my mother will say
Did you ever see a whale with a polka dot tail
Did you ever see a bear try to curl somebody's hair
Did you ever see a guy playing tennis with a fly
Did you ever see a green dog jumping on a yellow log
Down by the bay.

Down by the bay, where the watermelons grow,
Back to my home, I dare not go
For if I do, my mother will say
Did you ever see a rhino kissing a dino
Down by the bay.

> BT and LC come out from behind the stage. The KIDS applaud them.

BT: Now, boys and girls, who can tell me what this song is all about?

A: Well, it obviously refers to some poor little girl who has to run away from home because her mother is an ex-hippie living on an agricultural commune near San Francisco Bay who dropped too much acid back in the 60s and is now having flashbacks.

K: And the girl will end up walking the streets in Haight-Ashberry, dependent on welfare and handouts, eventually ending up in some emergency room with nothing but a Medicaid card, just another uneducated dopehead running up the national debt because she can't pull herself out of the sewer by her own bootstraps. She doesn't have a prayer. However, if Congress would pass the National School Prayer Amendment, she could go to any public school, where they would pray for her and tell her to get a job so she could support her Commie, druggie mother, who by now is in a state-supported nursing home living out her drug-induced fantasies on tax money that comes out of our pockets.

BT: I see. And what do you think, Mick, I mean, Rick?

R: I think it's just a silly song, you know, like the Star Spangled Banner.

LC: Let's not go there.

BT: Right. So, it must be Riddle Time. Little Chicken, I think you have the riddle for today.

LC: Right. Ready, kids? Today's Riddle is, "Why did the chicken cross the road?"

> Long pause. The KIDS think hard, look to each other, but nobody knows the answer.

LC: Doesn't anybody know? Who wants to guess?

A: To get to the Chick-fil-A?

K: To protest illegal chickens from Mexico?

LC: Uh, no. Bic, I mean Rick, do you have a guess?

R: You're a chicken, don't you know?

C: Of course I know.

R: Then why did the chicken cross the road?

LC: To get to the other side?

> Nobody gets it.

A: That seems rather pointless, don't you think? Was this her purpose in life, to explore alternate experiences, to go boldly where no chicken has gone before?

LC: No. It's a riddle, a joke.

K: But it must have some significance, some deeper meaning. Perhaps it's like that grass is always greener thing, alternate realities always seeming preferable to one's current plane of existence.

LC: It's a joke! A chicken joke!

A: Are you saying that only chickens can understand this joke? That there is no shared experience among mammals that would allow non-chickens to empathize with chickens sufficiently to identify with their experience, to feel their pain? I think I would have to disagree with that assertion. If we are ever to have interspecies harmony...

BT: Moving right along now. It's time for a word from our sponsor. Today's Fowl Time is brought to you by the letters F and U, and by the number 2. That's F, U, 2. Can you say F, U, 2?

KIDS: F. U. 2.

BT: Very good. Now who can tell me some things that you have two of?

A: Two eyes.

K: Two arms.

A: Two legs.

K: Two ears.

BT: Flick, I mean, Rick, do you have two of anything?

> Rick pulls two rubber balls out of his pocket and holds them up.

LC: Never mind, Hick, I mean Rick. How about words that start with F? Who can tell me some words that start with F?

A: Flat.

K: Feet.

A: Fast.

K: Females.

A: Fancy.

K: Floozies.

BT: And U, what about U?

A: What about us?

BT: No, what about the letter U? What words start with U? (No answer.) Uh, Tick, I mean, Rick, can you think of any words that start with the letter U?

R: Umbrella.

BT: Very good, Rick.

R: Uvalde, Ulna, Uvula, udder, ugly, ulcer, unisexual, Uppsala, Uranus, urine, urethra, uterus...

LC: And I think that's enough words for today.

BT: Amen!

LC: Shush! No religion. This is PBS. Now you've got the Moslems and Jews all upset.

BT: Oh, sorry. I believe in all gods equally, even the ones that don't exist. Honest, all Turkeys do.

LC: Just shut up, all right?

BT: OK, OK. Uh, let's see what's in the Magic Bird Bag!

KIDS: Yea!

> BT brings on an extremely large carpetbag.

BT: OK, let's see what we have in here today.

>   He pulls out a skimpy, sheer, negligee and holds it up.

BT: What in the world? What is this?

LC: Hey! That's mine.

>   He tosses it to her.

BT: Oh really? Well, isn't that interesting. What'sit doing in my bag?

>   He reaches back into the bag. LC tries to close the bag with his hand in it.

LC: That's my magic bag, you idiot! You got the wrong bag.

>   He is feeling around in the bag with his trapped hand.

BT: Hum, something in here does feel like magic. Oh my, oh my.

>   LC jerks the bag open, slaps BT's hand to make him drop what he is holding, pulls the bag away, stuffs the nightie back in it, and carries it offstage.

BT: Well, I guess there won't be any magic tonight. So, that means we better move on to The Fairy Tale for Today.

>   LC and the KIDS run offstage for very fast costume changes so they can play the characters in the Fairy Tale, as indicated.

BT: OK, everybody get ready. The Fairy Tale for modern life we have for today is called "The Tale of Sweet Thing and the Silver Jaguar." This is based on a true story from the National Inquirer newspaper, and you know anything you read in the newspaper must be true. This happened once upon a time just next week. It seems there was this beautiful young girl (A enters in sexy dress) who was so beautiful that everybody called her "Sweet Thing," though her real name was Abigail. Sweet Thing had an ugly stepmother, a beautiful stepmother, a sort of average-looking stepmother, a real mother who had run off with her lesbian lover, and a father who was very charming but very difficult to live with because he bought his wives beautiful, expensive houses in guarded subdivisions and then actually had the gall to think they would stay home and take care of the house. Anyway, one night, Sweet Thing's ugly stepmother came to her and said.

>   LC enters in dress and mask, carrying a basket covered with a cloth.

LC: Sweet Thing, I want you to take this basket of goodies to your beautiful stepmother, who is dancing at the Silver Jaguar strip club just off the subway line. Here's two subway tokens.

A: But Stepmother, it's three o'clock in the morning. Isn't it a little dangerous to be riding the subway at this time of night?

LC: Nonsense. You just have to be careful. Don't talk to strangers, don't take candy or drugs from strangers, sit in the first car where the driver can see you, don't accept rides in cars, only walk on the side of the street with streetlights, put your ID and a quarter for the phone in your bra, don't wiggle your hips when you walk, strap a knife to your leg, and wear clean underwear, just in case. Now take this basket of goodies and get going.

    LC gives her the basket and exits. R enters, sets up chairs to be subway, and sits. A crosses to chairs during narration.

BT: So, Sweet Thing took the basket and went to the subway. On the subway train, a big, bad wolf tried to blow her house down.

    A sits as far from R as she can. R moves to sit next to her.

R: Well, well, well, if you aren't a sweet young thing. You know, I've got some candy in my pocket that I bet you would like. You know the kind of candy I mean, the kind you can taste or sniff. Real good nose candy. And I bet you've got some really nice cookies. I bet they are the sweetest cookies I could ever imagine. You know, I just might be willing to trade you some of my white candy for a taste of your cookies. What do you say, sweet thing?

BT: So, Sweet Thing reached into the basket of goodies, pulled out a can of pepper gas, and sprayed the wolf right in the face.

R: Ow! You pig! You little snit! I didn't do nothing to you, what you have to go and spray me for? I was just making a little conversation. I didn't do nothing to you. I ought to adjust your face a little and see how you like that.

BT: So Sweet Thing sprayed him in the face again, kicked him in the crotch, and just then that arrived at a subway stop, so she shoved him out the door onto the platform. Then she rode the subway quietly to her stop. There she got out and walked up the street and through the parking lot to the employee's entrance of the Silver Jaguar strip club and pressed the buzzer. The b.., I mean witch who was in charge of the dancers opened the door.

    K enters and mimes opening a door.

A: Excuse me, I've brought a basket of goodies for my stepmother, Chesty Morgan, the Flounce with the Bounce. May I bring them in, please.

K: Well, now, aren't you a sweet thing. You know, we're looking for a nice young girl like you to work here. You know, just dance around a little bit to the music. You and your stepmother could be a novelty act, you know, the big one and the little one kind of thing. Some guys would get a real kick out of that. You could make, oh, one or two thousand dollars a night. Let me feel your, uh, ribs, oh yes, nice and tender. Oh, you would be delicious on stage, a real feast for the eyes.

A: Excuse me, Madam, with all due respect, I have higher aspirations that parading my pulchritude in the presence of gentlemen to whom I have not been introduced, pleasant as your offer of remuneration might appear.

K: Oh, a smart kid, eh? Maybe I'll just toss you in my dungeon for awhile, fatten you up a bit, and send you to Godzilla land, where they like'm plump.

A: (Reaching into the basket) Maybe I'll just pull out my 357 Magnum semi-automatic and let it huff and puff until you get all blown away.

K: And maybe you better just come right in and give that basket of goodies to your beautiful stepmother, who I am sure will be most happy to see you. Let me go tell her you're here.

K exits. A follows her off, her hand in the basket.

BT: So, Sweet Thing followed the witch into the Silver Jaguar. Just as she did, the big, bad wolf ran in, half blind from the pepper gas, with two Uzi machine guns, a street-sweeper automatic shotgun, and three 45 caliber automatic machine pistols strapped to his belt and started blasting everything in sight.

Huge noises from offstage.

BT: The club bouncers and 17 patrons with concealed weapons returned fire.

More noise from offstage.

BT: Sweet Thing hid under the stage, but the wolf, the witch, Chesty Morgan and seven other dancers, four bouncers, and fifty-three men, including twenty-two Japanese businessmen, eighteen salesmen, and three chicken farmers, were killed in the shootout that followed. Sweet Thing spent the rest of the night at the police station trying to explain why the wolf was after her, and was eventually sent to live with her average-looking stepmother in Sarajevo, where it was safer. And the moral of the story is, if your ugly stepmother asks you to take a basket of goodies somewhere at three in the morning, tell her to stick it. Now, let's have nice round of applause for our performers.

LC and the KIDS come out and take a bow.

A: Big Turkey, can we play a game now?
BT: Sure, Annette. What game would you like to play?
A: Musical chairs.
K: London Bridge.
R: Strip poker. (Everybody stares at him.) Well, I'm too young to gamble for money.

LC re-enters.

BT: Uh, I think musical chairs. Get the chairs.

The KIDS line up 3 chairs in a line across the stage.

BT: OK, I'll sing. Are we ready?
KIDS and LC: Yeah!

While BT sings, the other 4 march around, well, you know the game. LC is going to be the winner, usually by force and cheating such as pulling chairs out from under people, bumping them with her hip, pushing, etc. Tune is "When Johnny Comes Marching Home."

BT: When Alfie picks his nose again, oh yuck, oh yuck.
When Alfie picks his nose again, oh yuch, oh yuck.

We'll all get sick and spew and spout,
And we'll all throw up
When Alfie picks his nose.

When Susie (stops, one kid is eliminated.)

When Susie scratches her butt again, oh yuck, oh yuck.
When Susie scratches her butt again, oh (stops, another kid eliminated)
We'll shoot spitwads down her dress
And make her butt an awful mess
When Susie scratches her butt.

When Dickie licks his (stops, final kid eliminated.)

BT: And Little Chicken wins!

LC: Yea!

A: You cheated.

K: Yeah, it's not fair.

BT: And the moral is, get used to it.

LC: Yeah, life isn't a bed of roses, you know.

BT: Nobody promised you a rose garden.

LC: A rose by any other name would still have thorns.

BT: A rose is a rose is a rose colored glasses.

LC: You need a rosy outlook on life.

BT: Look on the sunny side.

LC: Like Pygmalion.

BT: You mean Polyanna.

A: Polyurethane.

K: Polystyrine.

R: Polly wants a cracker.

BT: So it must be snack time.

> BT gets a grocery bag.

BT: Now all of you know how important it is to eat heathy food and to have balanced nutrition. Who can name the four food groups?

A: Grains and breads.

K: Meat and dairy.

R: Fruits and vegetables.

LC: Fats and sugars.

BT: Very good. What else do you have to do to stay healthy?

A: Exercise.

K: Sleep.

LC: Brush you teeth.

R: Use the bathroom at least 12 times a day.

BT: Right. It's especially important to use the bathroom frequently during long trips and when you're out shopping, especially in grocery stores. And speaking of grocery stores, today's healthy snack was donated by the P&U Grocery. That's P&U Foods, where you can smell the difference. Let's see what healthy food we have for today. OK, from the veggies group, candy corn (gives bags to kids after each announcement.) From the legumes group, jelly beans. From the milk group, Milk Duds. And from the bread group, cinnamon rolls. And for a special treat, since you've been such good boys and girls today, from the fats and sweets group, fried ice cream!

KIDS: Yea!

>They fight over the food, get it all divided up, and begin stuffing their faces.

BT: And while you're eating so politely, it's time to bring out our special guest for today. Here she is, all the way from Castle Rock, Cinderella.

>A fat, ugly, middle-aged woman in an expensive-looking dress enters.

BT: Uh, Cinderella?

C: In the flesh.

LC: Uh, welcome to Fowl Time.

C: Why, thank you, you sweet little thing.

LC: My god, what happened to you? You used to be so... so... beautiful.

C: Well, you know, you marry money, sometimes you sort of let yourself go.

LC: But, but, you're fat! You're obese. You're a tub of lard. You're...

C: I get the idea, sweetie. I know I'm horizontally challenged. I'm not a retard.

LC: But why? How? You used to be so...small.

C: I know. Littlest feet you ever saw this side of China. But, well, believe me, sweetie, glass slippers hurt like hell. OK, OK, I know the questions. Marrying the Prince was fine for a while. We really got it on at first, if you know what I mean. But, well, I wasn't doing housework anymore, so I didn't get much exercise. And instead of beans, boiled potatoes, bread, and milk, I was suddenly eating steak, french fries, ice cream, and beer. Believe me, that catches up to you after awhile. Oh, I realized what was happening after awhile and tried to do something about it. Wore one of those Jane Fonda workout tapes clean through. But it was no use. I just got bigger and bigger. The Prince changed his name to something nobody can pronounce and started chasing the little chippies that hang around the castle, you know, Red Ridding Hood and Little Miss Muffet, that type. Well, then I knew I'd had it.

BT: Little Red Ridding Hood?

C: Did you know she stopped wearing anything under that red cape? Not a stitch. No wonder the wolves were after her. And that Muffet tramp, talk about sitting on things you're not supposed to sit on...

BT: OK, Uh, and, uh, how are your step-sisters?

C: Those sluts? Hell, I had them deported years ago. I think they're plugging some dyke in Holland or something.

BT: Yes, well, uh, the mice and birds, your friends the mice and birds, where are they?

C: Oh, they're all dead. Darn things don't live but a few years, even if some cat don't eat them. I took care of them, of course, fed them well in the castle, so they all died fat and happy, but they all died years ago. I buried them out back of the castle, put up little headstones, you know. I thought about getting some more, but I travel a lot now, what with Prince not exactly caring if I'm there or not, and nobody else would feed them. It would just be too much of a hassle.

BT: Oh. I see.

LC: So, where is Prince now?

C: Heck if I know. Probably playing with his mistress, Mary, in that garden apartment with all the flowers that he pays for. Hey, I don't care anymore. I've got my own agenda now. I'm traveling across the country promoting my new book. It's called Media Management, the Modern Fairy Tale. Snow White and I co-wrote it. She lives in the castle over from me, and we get together a lot, talk over our troubles. She's having man troubles too. In fact, it was our husbands trying to get us to swap, you know, that sort of brought us together. She has bulimia, you know, and...

BT: Well, we really do thank you for coming to visit us today, Cinderella, but we are running out of time.

C: But my book. (She holds up a book.) It's only $24.95 at both Waldenbooks and Cole's. Made the New York Times non-fiction list for two weeks...

> BT hustles her out.

BT: Thank you, thank you, I'm sure it's wonderful. Thank you for coming.

> Pause.

LC: Uh, OK, we have a little time left. Uh, kids, I know, let's sing a song.

> The KIDS are still eating candy, and realize that the candy will be taken away once the show is over, so they stuff as much as possible in their mouths and pockets while trying to sing at the same time. The results sound sort of like this. Tune is "This Old Man."

KIDS and **LC:** This old man, he played one
He played knick-nack on his thumb
Knick-nack, patty whack, give the dog a bone
This old man came rolling home.

This old man, he did two
He played knickers-whack on kazoo
Knick-knack, pantie wack, boy he's got a bone
This old man came rolling home.

This old man, he slepped three
He slapped tittie-pat on his knee
Pick snack, pussy pack, oy, he's gonna moan
This old man came molling tome.

This poled man...

> BT re-enters and interrupts.

BT: OK, OK, thank you. OK, we're almost out of time. Just a few seconds left to look through our magic mirror and say hello to a few boys and girls out there. (He holds up and empty mirror frame.) OK, let's see, I see Jason and Mary and Tricia and Elizabeth and Ralph...Ralph, stop that. I see Bill and Henry and Susie, uh, Susie, please put your underwear back on. I see Willie and Tommy and Aaron and Phyllis and...no, that's not Phyllis, that's Phyllis' mommie, and her daddie, and they're, oh my.

LC: Let me see. (She looks through the mirror.) Oh my god!

A: Let me see.

K: Me too.

A: Go man, go!

> They all crowd around the mirror frame, watching, as the lights fade.

CURTAIN

May

This play was originally written back in 1980, while I was in graduate school. It's never been produced, but I think it's the kind of play that could be a prophecy if we're not careful.

MAY

A One-Act Play By David Davis

Member
All rights & privileges.

David Davis
100 Hunters Ridge Court
Roswell, GA 30076
daviddaviswriter@gmail.com

Copyright 1980 David Davis

CAST OF CHARACTERS

THOMAS..A Prisoner, Father of May

MAY..A Young Woman, Daughter of Thomas

JULIE..A Prison Guard

SETTING

A prison cell, not too long in the future.

May

> AT RISE we see a cot and a chair. THOMAS sits on the cot, holding a small notebook and pen, writing, using small print to save space.

THOMAS: Spring was so late it never came.
Winter so cold the ocean foamed ice.
Fall had come to the soul of man,
But no birds were left to weep.

Night was so dark Venus never rose.
Day so short we took pictures.
Twilight had come to the age of man,
But no dolphins leapt from the deep.

A minute was so long it killed us.
An hour so short we never breathed.
Midnight had come to the eyes of man,
And nothing was left but sleep.

> JULIE and MAY enter from behind THOMAS. MAY is blind. JULIE leads MAY by the arm. JULIE leaves MAY and crosses to in front of THOMAS.

JULIE: Your daughter is here to see you.
THOMAS: If that is your idea of humor, I do not find it funny.
JULIE: I'm sorry. You know what I mean.
THOMAS: I think it would be better if I did not see her, better for her if she forgot me.
MAY: How could I do that?

> THOMAS turns and sees MAY.

THOMAS: I'm sorry.
MAY: So am I.
THOMAS: Show her to the chair.

> JULIE crosses to MAY and guides her over to the chair. MAY sits down.

MAY: Thank you.
JULIE: I'll be right here, if needed.
THOMAS: I've already done to her all I'm going to do.
JULIE: Rules of the house.
THOMAS: I see.
MAY: How have you been? It's been a long time.

THOMAS: About the same. Good deal older, I guess. You've grown up, I see. It has been a long time. You're very beautiful, just like I told you you would be.

MAY: Mama died.

THOMAS: Oh. I'm sorry.

MAY: That's why I'm here. I wanted to be the one to tell you.

THOMAS: Thank you. I don't know if I can do anything…

MAY: It's all taken care of.

THOMAS: I'm sorry.

MAY: She forgave you. It took a long time, but she did. She just never thought it wise to come here.

THOMAS: She was probably right.

MAY: I don't think the government wanted me to come, but I'm next of kin now, and I had the right.

THOMAS: It's good to see you.

MAY: Are they treating you well?

THOMAS: As well as could be expected, under the circumstances. No one wants to be here.

MAY: No one wants to be anywhere.

THOMAS: Is it that bad outside?

JULIE: I don't think we had better talk about that.

THOMAS: No, I guess we better not. But she was not sad to die?

MAY: No. None of the old ones are, now.

THOMAS: I thought as much.

MAY: Are you writing?

THOMAS: A few verses. Just for myself. Not very good.

MAY: Can you read me one?

JULIE: No.

MAY: I'm sorry. He used to read me his verses as bedtime stories. And when I learned to read, his books were…my dolls, my jewels, my father. It's been so long.

JULIE: I'm sorry, but there are laws.

MAY: Yes, I know.

THOMAS: How are you living?

MAY: I'm still in the room Mama and I shared. I roll papers into logs, for burning, sell them.

THOMAS: They still print newspapers?

MAY: No. Computer paper, old grocery bags, paper wrappers. You have to soak it longer, but I can get it to work.

THOMAS: Oh.

MAY: It's enough to get by on. I don't need much. I even got the government to take the television out when Mama died. They had to admit it wasn't much use to me, being blind. Of course, they can't watch me at home now, but I still have the radio for the blind, and its motion detector tells them when I'm home. Cell phone tracking doesn't work if you just leave it in a drawer or let the battery run down. No TV saves a little electricity, and every little bit helps. But I can get by.

THOMAS: I'm surprised they haven't assigned you a husband yet.

MAY: There's a shortage of men right now. I don't know why, but I think there's a war somewhere. They won't tell us. But handicapped have last priority.

THOMAS: It's not because of me?

MAY: No.

THOMAS: You're sure?

MAY: It's my eyes. Which is because of you, but they don't care about that. Your Grand Declaration, all those brave papers, they're almost forgotten now.

THOMAS: You think it was all for nothing?

MAY: No, I didn't mean that.

JULIE: Time's almost up.

MAY: Already?

JULIE: I can't help it.

MAY: They say I can come once a month.

THOMAS: I guess they've decided you're safe from me now. I guess the whole world is safe from me now.

MAY: Do you need anything?

THOMAS: Could you bring me anything?

MAY: I don't know. I could ask.

THOMAS: They feed me, keep me warm, ration me a bit of paper and pen. (He touches his pocket where the notebook is.) That's all I need.

JULIE: It's time.

MAY: I'll be back next month.

THOMAS: You don't have to. I'll understand.

MAY: I'll be back.

> JULIE goes to MAY, touches her shoulder. MAY stands; JULIE takes her arm, and leads her away.

MAY: I'll be back.

THOMAS: I love you.

> JULIE and MAY exit. THOMAS watches them go, then slowly takes out his paper and pen and writes.

THOMAS: Semen and egg
Semen and egg
A deadly mix
One death for each.

Woman and man
Woman and man
Mix and match
Two deaths for each.

A child is born
A child is born
The parents cry
Three deaths for each.

    Time passes. JULIE enters.

JULIE: A judge is here. In the office.

THOMAS: Why?

JULIE: They are reviewing all the political cases.

THOMAS: That won't affect me.

JULIE: Some are being released. You might be one.

THOMAS: After what I did? I did more than the others, remember?

JULIE: They don't tell us the details.

THOMAS: You must have heard.

JULIE: About the girl? Yes.

THOMAS: That was just the end. The beginning was even more serious. Tyrannies do not soon forget men who pretend that they are free.

JULIE: What did you do?

THOMAS: I wrote a paper.

JULIE: Is that all?

THOMAS: A lot of other writers signed it; we had it published and posted all over the web. The government did not like what it said. It had not been written to make the government happy. We tried to pretend we still had the freedom to write what we wanted, whether that made the government happy or not. The government disagreed. Such was our treason.

JULIE: So you were sent here.

THOMAS: I was. The others, I don't know. I was a special case.

JULIE: The girl.

THOMAS: Yes.

JULIE: It's so horrible.

THOMAS: Don't pity her. She doesn't need it. Pity those who must see how liberty is bound, and freedom blinded.

JULIE: You're talking about the government?

THOMAS: I'm talking about the tyranny.

JULIE: Now, that isn't fair.

THOMAS: Not fair?

JULIE: Sometimes, when there's a lot of troubles in the world, you need a strong government.

THOMAS: The Gauls are at the gates; Hail Caesar.

JULIE: What?

THOMAS: Never mind. (Pause.) Are they really going to let some people out?

JULIE: If they think they're not dangerous any more.

THOMAS: I wonder what it's like out there now. What would I do if they let me out? There's no place for me anymore.

JULIE: There'd be something.

THOMAS: Are there any books, new ones?

JULIE: You mean like you wrote?

THOMAS: Yes. Poetry, fiction.

JULIE: No.

THOMAS: Magazines, plays, movies?

JULIE: No, just TV.

THOMAS: What, not even pornography?

JULIE: There are several porno channels on TV.

THOMAS: So, you watch them and they watch you.

JULIE: They wouldn't let you write out there anyway, but you could work with your daughter or something.

THOMAS: Not write? (He touches his pocket.)

JULIE: They'd watch you.

THOMAS: Tell the judge not to bother. I'll not trade my freedom for his slavery.

JULIE: You're not free in here.

THOMAS: Die gedanken sind frei.

JULIE: That Latin?

THOMAS: German.

JULIE: Well, think about it. It's going to be a long time before they assign a husband to your daughter. And being blind like that, no telling what she'll get. She'll have to roll a lot of paper logs to get enough money to pay for heating fuel this winter. Don't you think she might need her father to come home and look after her? Being blind and alone is a bad combination. (Pause.) Well, just think about it. Which is more important, that pen and paper you love so much, or you daughter.

> THOMAS is silent. After a moment, JULIE leaves. Time passes.
> THOMAS is seen writing again.

THOMAS: It died slowly
A word at a time
Like a boat sunk
By needle holes.

It died quickly
A petal at a time

Like a flower unpraised
By any poet.

The wind blew
No one knew where
No one followed
So it never blew again.

Truth is like a sailing ship
In search of a blooming shore
Without the wind of freedom
It will sail no more.

> JULIE leads MAY in.

JULIE: Your daughter is back.

> THOMAS looks around at MAY, then gestures for JULIE to lead MAY to the chair. JULIE does so, MAY sits, and JULIE stands in the background, as before.

MAY: I said I'd be back.

THOMAS: I know.

MAY: I can't bring you anything,

THOMAS: I didn't think you could.

MAY: I wanted to bring you something I had cooked, but they said no.

THOMAS: You cook much?

MAY: If I want to eat something, I have to cook it. Mama taught me how.

THOMAS: Then you must be a very good cook.

MAY: Not as good as she was. I haven't burned anything lately though. I did spill some boiling water on the radio last week. Shorted it out, ruined it completely, even the motion sensor. I don't do things like that very often though. I haven't burned any fingers in over a year. I just wanted to bring you something I had cooked to show you I can take care of myself. I know you must worry.

THOMAS: I'm sure you can take care of yourself. You always could when you were a kid, and I don't think times have changed that. Was the government very upset about the radio?

MAY: When one is blind, such things are expected. I was instructed to call in every day, but I forgot one day and nothing happened, so I stopped. It may be a long time before the radio is replaced. They stopped making radios three years ago. Everybody had a TV, so there seemed no use.

THOMAS: If they want you, they will find you.

MAY: No doubt; how far can you go when you're blind?

THOMAS: As far as you want. Do you go out much?

MAY: I didn't use to. Mama didn't like it. They used to follow us whenever we went out, but I haven't been followed since Mama died, not that I can hear. I like to wander around, listen to the city.

THOMAS: It's getting cold out; do you have enough clothes?

MAY: Yes. They cut the ration again, but I get an extra ration because of my eyes. I had my choice of pajamas, bathrobe, and slippers or a winter coat. I took the winter coat. The fuel ration may be cut again this winter, and I don't even have a fireplace to burn my own logs. My old pajamas are worn out, but with the TV gone nobody will see them anyway, so it doesn't matter. I don't even wear them in the summer.

THOMAS: You sleep nude?

MAY: Nobody can see. The pajamas are so old. I'm trying to save them for the winter.

THOMAS: I don't think even the government will hang you for that.

JULIE: I think we better watch what we say.

THOMAS: What are they going to do, lock me up?

JULIE: Maybe stop your daughter from coming.

THOMAS: Maybe better for her.

MAY: I believe this is my time.

JULIE: I'm sorry.

MAY: They let your editor out.

THOMAS: Bill Foster?

MAY: Yes.

THOMAS: So they really are letting people go.

>   THOMAS takes out his notebook, looks at it, then slips it back in his pocket.

MAY: He's gotten old.

THOMAS: He was in a long time.

MAY: He recognized me when he saw me in the park though. He saw me walking by and called me over to ask about you.

THOMAS: You were in the park.

MAY: It's safe now. Not like you knew it. Only the old people are allowed in, and people like me. It would be safe anyway; anybody healthy and without a regular job goes into the army or the Conservation Corps. That's where I'd be if it wasn't for my eyes. Not many come back from either.

THOMAS: I guess that's one way to keep the peace.

MAY: I guess.

THOMAS: What was Bill doing there?

MAY: Just sitting on a bench, enjoying the sun. It was his day off. He sweeps floors in the City Hall.

THOMAS: He used to hate the sunlight. Almost never left his office till after dark.

MAY: I guess he's changed.

THOMAS: I guess we all have.

MAY: The park hasn't changed much, since when you used to take me. I still remember those long walks, and how we used to sit under a tree, and you'd point out all the different birds to me. That's why I went back; I wanted to hear the birds again, try to remember what each one looked like. If my motion detector hadn't been broken, I probably wouldn't have gone. Listening to the birds isn't much of a reason to give the Tracers, if they should ask. But I had the chance, so I took it.

THOMAS: Were there many birds?

MAY: No. I think I heard one. I'm not sure.

JULIE: It's time.

MAY: I can try to find out if they let anybody else out, if you want.

THOMAS: No, better not. I'm not sure I'd want to know anyway.

MAY: Maybe I shouldn't have told you about Mr. Foster.

THOMAS: No, it's all right.

> JULIE crosses to MAY.

MAY: I'll be back next month, unless it snows.

> MAY stands. JULIE takes her arm and starts to lead her off, but THOMAS speaks and they stop.

THOMAS: May?

MAY: Yes?

THOMAS: They offered to review my case. But a condition was that if they let me out, I'd have to stop writing. They would make me have a TV so they could watch me, they'd follow me to see what I did outside. To make sure I would not write. I haven't given them an answer yet. If you need me, if you want me to, I'll try to get out. If you'll have me out, after….

> Pause.

MAY: Thank you. I still don't understand why you did what you did, but I know you loved me, and you had your reasons…or thought you did. I would welcome you back; you're my father. But try and understand this: I don't need you. I can take care of myself. Mama taught me rather well. Don't feel you have any duty to come take care of me. I don't need it. But if you want to come, for yourself, come.

THOMAS: I don't know.

MAY: It's been a long time.

THOMAS: I've forgotten what a bird looks like, flying against a blue sky.

MAY: I remember. You used to see one, and take out your little notebook and scribble down a line or an image.

> THOMAS takes his notebook out of his pocket.

THOMAS: I still have a notebook. They let me have one a month, if I'm good.

MAY: There aren't any notebooks out there. Not many birds either.

THOMAS: I know.

MAY: Stay here. Without that notebook you'd be like a bird without a wing.

THOMAS: I never thought they would ever offer me even a chance to leave. I thought I would be here forever, not even a chance to help you again.

MAY: I know.

JULIE: You have to go.

MAY: I'll be back.

THOMAS: Shalom.

JULIE: German?

THOMAS: Yiddish.

MAY: It's a blessing. It means peace be with you.

> JULIE leads MAY out. THOMAS looks at the notebook in his hand. He slowly opens it and begins to write.

THOMAS: There used to be so many songs
So many songs
Now silently the tunes are sung
The melodies mimed
Even computers forget
Even plastic decays
Even stones wear away
I am a rock.

> Time passes. JULIE enters.

THOMAS: What do you want?

JULIE: I brought you your notebook for this month.

> THOMAS quickly crosses to her and takes the notebook. He opens it and flips through it, examining it.

THOMAS: Thank you.

JULIE: You really need that, don't you? Like a drug.

THOMAS: Yes.

JULIE: A writing addict.

THOMAS: Something like that.

JULIE: I don't think I'll ever understand you people.

THOMAS: Don't feel bad; we were not much understood even when it wasn't against the law.

JULIE: I don't guess it matters much. You're the last one anyway.

THOMAS: What?

JULIE: All the writers that signed the paper you wrote, you're the last one still in.

THOMAS: What happened to the others?

JULIE: Some quit writing and were let go. Some quit living.

THOMAS: Is that a threat?

JULIE: Just a warning. Some just died, heart attacks, that kind of thing. Some committed suicide.

THOMAS: What did you do, cut off their supply of paper?

JULIE: I don't know. None of them were here. I just overheard the judge talking when he was here.

THOMAS: So I'm the last.

JULIE: So I hear.

THOMAS: Feels strange.

JULIE: You could be out, sitting in the sunshine, like that editor your daughter told you about. Taking her for walks in the park, telling her what the birds look like.

THOMAS: At what price?

JULIE: Just your notebooks.

THOMAS: Just my life. I thought they would kill me, after a decent interval. Or lock me up and throw away the key. I thought that once I went it, it was over. I wish they had left it that way. Have you ever read a poem?

JULIE: You know that isn't allowed.

THOMAS: Not all laws are always kept.

JULIE: That's one I haven't broken.

THOMAS: A novel, a short story?

JULIE: No. TV is all that's allowed. Why?

> THOMAS looks at his notebook.

THOMAS: So I'm the last man with a poem in his pocket. The last man who can write or say whatever he thinks. The last free man. Such liberty cannot be left unguarded. My little bird will have to find her own blue sky.

JULIE: What?

THOMAS: A bit of poetry. You should not listen to such treason.

JULIE: Just once I would like to understand you.

THOMAS: I spoke very clearly once; they sent me here.

JULIE: I've got work to do.

THOMAS: Yes, each slave to her task.

> JULIE looks at THOMAS for a second, then exits. Time passes.
> THOMAS is writing again.

THOMAS: The wind shall sing
When the men are gone
The rain play drums

To the forest song
When even the coyote
Howls not long
The mountain rocks
Shall sing out strong.

When my too small voice is quiet
When no man breathes in harmony
When no heart beats in common time
When no legs walk in measured stride
Then the sun itself will sing
The moon ring in her counterpoint
Comets the harp of heaven play
And stars be chimed for melody.

>JULIE enters with MAY.

JULIE: Your daughter is here.

THOMAS: She knows where the chair is.

>MAY leaves JULIE and crosses to the chair by herself. MAY sits down. JULIE hesitates for a moment.

JULIE: I'll be at the desk, if you need me.

MAY: I'll be fine.

>JULIE exits.

THOMAS: How are things going?

MAY: Pretty well. I may not come back to see you next month.

THOMAS: Oh?

MAY: I may not come to see you for several months. I'm thinking of going south for the winter. They announced another fuel ration cut last week. It's going to be hard to stay warm this winter.

THOMAS: Will they give you permission?

MAY: I don't plan on asking.

THOMAS: I see.

MAY: They never replaced my radio. I don't think they ever will. Leave my cell phone in the apartment and they'll never even know I'm gone.

THOMAS: Even computers forget.

MAY: I rode the subway out to the end of the line, just to see if anything would happen. Nothing did. I don't think they care what little blind girls do anymore.

THOMAS: Sounds like they are getting very careless.

MAY: Will you be all right?

THOMAS: Don't worry about me; you just take care of yourself.

MAY: I'll be careful. I saw Mr. Foster in the park again. He said to tell you hello.

THOMAS: You seem to spend a lot of time in the park.

MAY: I keep trying to hear a bird. I think I heard one or two, but most of them must have gone south by now, I guess.

THOMAS: Those that are left.

MAY: I met this guy there, just out of the army. He's blind too, now. He says he's one of the lucky ones though, at least he came back.

THOMAS: So there is a war.

MAY: Yes. He wasn't sure where, or maybe was afraid to say, but he thinks we're losing. We've been spending a lot of time together in the park. I told him how my motion detector got broken, and his accidently got broken the same way the very next day. Isn't that a coincidence?

THOMAS: Yes, amazing coincidence.

MAY: We're going south together. Will you miss me?

THOMAS: I have missed you since the day they took me away. But I would rather you were gone than here.

MAY: I thought as much.

THOMAS: Go as far as you can; find someplace where the birds still sing. Try not to come back.

JULIE enters.

JULIE: Almost time.

MAY stands. Pause.

MAY: There's one thing I have to know, before I go. Why did you blind me? (Pause.) That last morning, waiting for them to come. You knew they were going to come, and you knew you would never come back. You just stared at me, sat there with tears in your eyes. I saw them. You kissed me, said "I love you." And then you blinded me. Why?

THOMAS: It was the best gift I could think of.

Pause.

MAY: I'll be going now.

THOMAS: Aidos. Tu yo amo.

MAY: Y yo tu, mi padre.

MAY crosses to her father and kisses him.

MAY: Thank you.

MAY exits by herself.

JULIE: French?

THOMAS: Spanish.

    The lights fade out. After a moment, the lights come back up to reveal a bare, empty stage.

CURTAIN

SHORT PLAYS

These plays are too short to be considered one-acts. Some fit in the "10-minute" play category. Others are a bit too long or too short to fit that specification. I'm frankly not a fan of such restrictions, but contests for short plays, bills of short plays from various writers, and even the working process of various playwriting groups tend to promote them. "Me, My Coke, and You" was produced on a bill of short plays at Oglethorpe University. "These Days" was done as a part of a bill of shorts done to celebrate Samuel Becket's birthday, directed by Brenda Bynum. Most of the others at least got a reading by the Southeast Playwrights Project, Working Title Playwrights, or Merely Writers.

ME, MY COKE, AND YOU

A Play in One Act By David Davis

Member
All rights & privileges.

David Davis
100 Hunters Ridge Court
Roswell, GA 30076
daviddaviswriter@gmail.com

Copyright 2019 David Davis

CAST OF CHARACTERS

PEG...A College Student

AL...A Graduate Student

SETTING

A small restaurant near a university, about 1974.

AT RISE: A small café near a university, about 1974, late on a fall night. (This could be represented with only a table and a couple of chairs, plus a magazine rack like would be next to a cash register, but a little more set would be nice.) The café is empty except for PEG, the waitress, who is cleaning up. She is a college senior, not especially pretty, wearing a waitress apron over a simple dress. After a few seconds, AL enters. He is a grad student, wearing tennis shoes, jeans, and a sweat shirt. He is clean, but not neat, rather slightly rumpled.

AL: Hi, Peg.

PEG: Hi, Al.

AL: So, when are you going to marry me?

PEG: Not tonight, Dear, I've got a headache. I've also got a paper due tomorrow in Modern Lit.

AL: OK, then how about a Coke.

PEG: That I can get you.

She exits to get the drink. AL goes to the magazine rack.

AL: Have the new "MADs" come in yet?

PEG: (off-stage) Not yet. Just the usual insane stuff. Watergate in on the cover of everything. Mad Magazine is the only thing that makes sense anymore. Maybe Tuesday.

AL: Well, you can't win them all.

He sits at the table. PEG brings him a fountain coke, then sits down beside him.

PEG: Here you go.

AL: Thanks. Why didn't you get one for yourself?

PEG: I've been drinking too many of those things. They'll ruin your figure after a while.

AL: Too much of a good thing?

PEG: Something like that. How did the match come out?

AL: Like I said, you can' win them all.

PEG: Too bad. That eliminates us from the conference race?

AL: Yeah. Wait until next year time again. Is Larry still here?

PEG: No, I get to lock up. Being a liberated woman and all, you know.

AL: He left you to walk to the dorm alone this time of night?

PEG: Comes with the job sometimes. If I want to graduate, I have to pay the fees, and if that mean walking home in the middle of the night, I walk home in the middle of the night. Being a liberated woman and all, you know.

AL: Still…

PEG: Which means I need to finish cleaning up.

> She gets up and goes back to cleaning up the café.

PEG: So, how was your date?

AL: Dumb. Boy was she dumb. Before the match I tried to explain soccer to her, about not using your hands, about tackles and free kicks and stuff. I thought I had even explained the off-side rule so she could understand it. Then the teams come out and she asks which player is the quarterback. It's almost enough to stop dating.

PEG: So you come in here and ask me to marry you?

AL: Well, it's not quite the same as asking for a date.

PEG: That I agree with. What would you ever do if I said yes?

AL: Pass out, probably. Try it sometime, see what happens.

PEG: I'm not sure I'm that brave.

> She exits with her cleaning equipment. AL goes back to the magazine rack. She re-enters.

PEG: Where'd you go after the match?

AL: Oh, I just took her back to her dorm. I can only stand so much cranial density. Then I ran into Professor Glenn on the Quad and we stopped and talked for a while. Nothing like discussing the implications of relativity on the free will justification of evil in the middle of the night.

PEG: I bet. Somehow I'm glad I missed that. You philosophy grad students give us poor English major the creeps.

AL: Should I take that personally?

PEG: Definitely. Sometimes I'm just not quite sure what you're taking about. Or how serious you are.

AL: That may be my thesis topic, an attempt to show that we're never quite sure about anything. Or maybe that we're never quite serious about anything. One or the other. Maybe both.

PEG: That I can't wait to read.

AL: Well, don't hold your breath; the topic hasn't even been approved yet.

PEG: Guaranteed best seller.

AL: Yeah, sure.

> He crosses to the magazine rack, picks out a Playboy magazine, and returns to the table.

AL: Any good cartoons this month?

PEG: A couple.

> He flips through, stopping to read the cartoons.

PEG: You are the only man I know who doesn't at least glance at the pictures. What is wrong with you?

AL: I'm more interested in the graphic revelations of existential absurdity.

PEG: Yeah, right. You just don't want me to watch you ogling the naked girls.

AL: Care to show me some of the real thing?

PEG: You should be so lucky.

AL: Yes, I should.

> He returns the magazine to the rack.

AL: I wish you had been at the soccer match.

PEG: Me too. I'm sorry I couldn't get off work. But I need the money. Sorry your date was dumb.

AL: I should have just gone alone.

PEG: You want a refill? I'm going to have to close up soon.

AL: Yeah, sure.

> She takes his plastic cup and exits to the drink dispenser.

AL: And get yourself some tea or something. I'll pay for it.

PEG: I get anything from the fountain free. Ah, the perks of being an underpaid waitress.

AL: Get something. I don't like to drink alone.

PEG: It's only a Coke. You don't need a drinking buddy for soda pop.

AL: It's the principle of the thing.

PEG: What principle?

> She re-enters with the refilled Coke and a cup of something for her.

AL: The rites of socialization. Coke is a social drink for social occasions. You are supposed to drink it with somebody. It's like fresh-squeezed lemonade: who makes fresh lemonade just for themselves. We crave communion and use various indulgences to create events for building intimate relationships.

PEG: I think you're talking about tequila.

AL: I prefer to remain sober while building intimate relationships.

PEG: So what do you drink when you're alone?

AL: Water. Coffee. Maybe orange juice. Actually, I guess coffee could go either way.

PEG: And how did you arrive at this classification of potions?

AL: Empirically, of course. By observation. I watched what people who come in here order. People who come in groups, to sit and talk, order Cokes, tea, lemonade, maybe coffee. People who come in alone usually order just water and something to eat, maybe coffee.

PEG: I think you've been in school too long; you're trying to classify everything.

AL: Well, maybe. But you start noticing.

PEG: OK, OK. (pause) Speaking of being in school too long, how is that metaphysics seminar going?

AL: Ah, the class on everything. We have about decided that God is to blame for everything, but the only reason we can think of for creating this mess that doesn't contradict itself is that God has a weird sense of humor and reality is one big joke. We have all developed this image of God sitting around heaven chuckling to himself all day.

PEG: Well, that class sounds like a lot of laughs.

AL: Reality requires a sense of humor.

PEG: Ain't that the truth.

AL: Which reminds me; I've got a complete works of Robert Burns you can borrow if you need it for your Celtic lit course next semester.

PEG: Thanks. I didn't know you were a Burns fan.

AL: "O, My love is like a red, red rose…"

PEG: "The best laid schemes o' mice and men…"

AL: "The sweetest hours that e'er I spend…"

PEG: "Are spent among the lasses, O." And enough of that. What time is it?

AL: Five till.

PEG: I've got to start locking up.

    She exits to turn stuff off.

AL: Peg.

PEG: (offstage) Yeah?

AL: Not to change the subject, but will you marry me?

PEG: I told you, not tonight.

AL: I didn't ask when. I said will.

    She re-enters.

PEG: There should be a good comeback for that, but right now I can't think of it.

AL: A simple yes would suffice. Or an outburst of mad passion. Either one, or both.

PEG: I never can tell when you're serious.

AL: Generally speaking, I never am, but answer the question anyway.

PEG: I've got to finish closing up.

    She exits again.

AL: Chicken!

PEG: You're kidding, right?

AL: Would it make a difference in the answer?

PEG: I don't know.

AL: Would you prefer to write me a letter? An essay on the perils of matrimony for the modern woman?

>   She re-enters.

PEG: You're serious.

AL: I get these spells. The doctor says not to worry about them, but I don't believe him.

PEG: You know, of all the dreams I ever dreamed, being proposed to like this was not one of them.

AL: I'm not the kind of guy a girl dreams about. I'm the kind where people say "What did she see in him."

PEG: When I figure out an answer to that question, I'll let you know.

AL: I'd appreciate it.

PEG: Al, what do you see in me?

AL: I don't know, I left my x-ray glasses at home.

PEG: He proposes; then he makes jokes. I don't understand you.

AL: I don't understand me either. Nor do I understand you. What we have here is a mutual misunderstanding society.

PEG: Which, of course, is the perfect basis for a marriage.

AL: I can't think of anything better.

>   She exits again.

PEG: What about June? We both will have graduated by then. Stereotypical June wedding.

AL: Works for me. Come on, I'll walk you home.

>   PEG re-enters with her purse and coat.

PEG: OK, but that's all. I've got an early class and a paper due.

AL: You're such a romantic fiancé.

>   PEG puts on her coat. AL takes their drinks.

PEG: I'm ready.

AL: Then let's go.

>   They exit. The lights are turned off and we hear a door being closed and locked.

CURTAIN

THESE DAYS

A Ten-Minute Play a la Samuel Beckett By David Davis

Member
All rights & privileges.

David Davis
100 Hunters Ridge Court
Roswell, GA 30076
daviddaviswriter@gmail.com

Copyright David Davis 2006

> AT RISE, a cloud passes overhead. Thunder rumbles in the distance. It gets darker. A light comes up on a man looking out a window. Lightning flashes. A woman enters.

WOMAN: Is this it? The big one?

MAN: Hard to say. I don't think so. But soon, I guess. They say it starts with a storm.

WOMAN: Yes.

> The WOMAN begins to brush her hair.

MAN: What are you doing?

WOMAN: Just getting ready. In case.

MAN: Ah.

WOMAN: Want to look good, you know.

MAN: Sure.

WOMAN: In case.

MAN: Of course.

WOMAN: You?

MAN: Well, men are different.

WOMAN: Not that much. All things considered.

MAN: Well, yes. But, some…

WOMAN: Of course. Some. Not that it matters much. These days.

MAN: Yes. These days.

WOMAN: Yes. So, what do you think?

MAN: About?

WOMAN: The hair. Me. How I look. You still look, don't you?

MAN: Actually, as I get older, I find that…, well, you know, I notice more, not less. I watch. The sway, the bounce. Something perverse about that.

WOMAN: No.

MAN: Getting old, I am. But yes, I look.

WOMAN: No one gets younger.

MAN: No.

WOMAN: Not that it matters. These days.

MAN: Yes.

WOMAN: Yes.

MAN: Your hair is very nice. You're very nice. All of you.

WOMAN: Thank you.

MAN: Thank you for asking me to look. Reminded me of other days.

WOMAN: Yes. Thank you.

MAN: I remember so much.

WOMAN: All memories are precious.

MAN: So much to lose.

WOMAN: Yes.

MAN: Running down the sidewalk as a child. New glasses so clear I could see the heatwaves rising off the parking lot. Children's hospital and the boys in traction, one with bones so soft he broke his leg rolling over. Crawling under the fence in military school to go get a milkshake. Certain days, moments.

WOMAN: First kiss, first sex, the baby?

MAN: Of course. But also just days, dance classes, rocking her to sleep, moments in time.

WOMAN: Yes.

MAN: So much to lose.

WOMAN: Yes.

MAN: You?

WOMAN: Of course. First period, first silk blouse, first boy. The corsage. All those French declensions.

MAN: Yes.

WOMAN: How long do you think?

MAN: No idea. It's slow, they say. The storms are just the beginning. If it is, you know.

WOMAN: Yes. Slow. They say.

MAN: Not clear how they would know, though.

WOMAN: No. They wouldn't, would they?

MAN: No. Not to tell about it, anyway.

WOMAN: And cold.

MAN: Yes, cold. They say.

WOMAN: Warm, then cold. They say. Ironic.

MAN: Yes. Ironic. The currents changed, you see.

WOMAN: Yes. Warm, then cold.

MAN: That pretty much upset everything.

WOMAN: Yes.

MAN: Not that it matters now.

WOMAN: No, not these days.

MAN: Warm, then cold.

WOMAN: Yes.

MAN: Not something you can dress for.

WOMAN: No.

MAN: I was glad to see the stars though. Before the clouds.

WOMAN: Yes.

MAN: Used to be too many lights. Couldn't see the heavens at all.

WOMAN: No.

MAN: Now you can see forever. When the clouds are gone.

WOMAN: Yes. Forever.

MAN: Not that it matters.

WOMAN: No.

MAN: So much we can see now. Things we couldn't. You, the stars, eternity. Things we should have seen before. Not that it matters now.

WOMAN: No. Not these days. Look at me again.

>   He looks. Thunder rolls. The lights fade.

CURTAIN

KNEELING

A Ten-Minute Play By David Davis

Member
All rights & privileges.

David Davis
100 Hunters Ridge Court
Roswell, GA 30076
daviddaviswriter@gmail.com

Copyright 2022 David Davis

> AT RISE we see a man, center stage, facing downstage on his knees with his hands tied behind his head. Behind him there is a conference table with three upstage chairs. On the table lolls a very sexy woman in a very revealing dress. Three men in business suits enter carrying briefcases, which they place on the table, ignoring the woman. They open their briefcases and take out file folders and other papers.

1: OK, let's get started. Read the PD.

2: You are to assume the position. You are to serve 30 years or until you are 65 or until you die, whichever come first. There are other duties as assigned. Do you understand these charges?

> There is no reply.

1: Next.

3: You will be confined to your area except for brief exercise periods. You will eat alone. You will not speak unless spoken to.

> The woman gets off the table, walks downstage of the man, turns to face him, and exposes her breasts to him. She then covers herself, goes back to the table, and sits in a chair.

3: I hope you realize the seriousness of the situation. It is costing a great deal of money to keep you here. You should be grateful. After all, this is war.

2: So to speak.

1: So to speak. A new kind of war. And in war there are sacrifices. Like you.

2: So to speak.

1: Yes, so to speak. Symbolically. To speak symbolically. I mean we don't really cut your heart out or anything.

3: Except metaphorically.

1: Yes. Metaphorically. Symbolic Mayas, cutting your heart out metaphorically. So to speak. No real torture either.

3: Just a little sleep deprivation. Occasional isolation. Some stress. Nothing quick. You'll hardly notice.

1: Yes. Time will pass. Very serious situation. Disease, death, all that.

2: Have to have the proper papers.

3: Follow procedures.

1: Cross all the i's, dot all the t's. You understand.

2: That's the way big organizations have to work.

3: He knows how it works. He understands the system.

1: Yes, I'm sure he does. We're all professionals here.

> The woman gets up on table and lies on her side, facing downstage. The men sit in the chairs upstage of the table, facing downstage.

1: We realize that time is limited.

2: For all of us.

1: Yes. So...?

3: The statement of work specifies that the task will be completed on the time line. There are penalties for not meeting your objectives. Termination for convenience is always a possibility. There are clauses that must be complied with. What you had planned is irrelevant. You did not get clearance for that. Clearance is required for all actions that involve the public. This includes 576, 524A, 615, IRB, and OMB clearance. The Paperwork Reduction Act is very clear that all business must be conducted electronically so it can't be FOIAed (pronounced "foy-ed"). What you had in mind was not cleared. Nothing can be done without clearance.

2: Are you requesting a lawyer or a union representative be present at this hearing?

1: I'm a lawyer.

3: I'm in the union.

2: Well, that base is covered. Have to cover all the bases.

1: CYA.

> Woman slide off the table and moons the three men.

1: We affirm our actions; we do not discriminate. We are an equal disability employer.

> The woman walks behind the men.

2: You thought you were different. Nobody is different here.

3: Except in grade and step.

2: But not in anything except money and power.

1: Yes. You thought you could do something on your own. A cruel dream. There are no dreams here. So, to begin.

2: And end.

> The woman walks in front of the man, lifts her skirt over his head, and places his face in her crotch.

3: We will process your paperwork. It should take forever.

1: Has to be approved up at the department level.

2: You understand. Procedure.

1: Of course, with the election coming up...

3: Possibility of new leadership.

2: Wouldn't affect you, of course, not down here at your level.

1: But us, well...

> Woman moves back to table and sits. Men close their briefcases.

2: We don't expect to hear from us again.

3: No decision is not a decision here.

1: Just keep doing what you're doing until you hear otherwise.

>The men exit. The woman lolls back on the table as she was at rise. The lights fade.

A PLAY TO BE TITLED LATER

By David Davis

Member
All rights & privileges.

David Davis
100 Hunters Ridge Court
Roswell, GA 30076
daviddaviswriter@gmail.com

Copyright 2022 David Davis

AT RISE we see the single, non-period, unit set requested in all play contest guidelines. The standard area lighting comes up to reveal five women and one man who represent all known minorities, disabilities, and gender orientations. They cover all the age ranges capable of being played by high school students.

W1: Gosh, Jane, what classes are you taking this semester?

W2: Abstinence, How to Take the SATs, and Cheerleading. What about you?

W1: Oooo, I've got some hard ones; The Bible As Absolute Fact, Advanced Creationism, and Practical Office Politics.

W3 (in wheelchair, spastic): Hey, guess what? I made the basketball team. My lawyer got me the starting point guard spot.

W1: Oh, gee, cool. I wish I had your lawyer. Mine can't even get me into the band.

W2: Oh, what instrument you play?

W1: None. I just wanted to march around in the uniform and go on the bus trips. That would be so cool. But they already had their quota of blonds.

W3: Oh, bummer.

W4: Hey, girls, did you hear about Amy?

W2: No, what happened?

W4: She had to transfer.

W1: Why?

W4: She tried to join the Virgins Club, but they found out she was a lesbian and was just trying to pick up girls.

W2: Oh my.

W4: If she had just joined the Daughters of Lesbos like me, she never would have gotten in trouble.

W1: Yeah. But she wanted to be prom queen, and she wanted the virgin vote.

W4: Yeah.

W5: Ola. Que pasa, amigas?

W2: Whatever.

The women exit. The man shrugs and walks off.

CURTAIN.

THE INTERVIEW

By David Davis

Member
All rights & privileges.

David Davis
100 Hunters Ridge Court
Roswell, GA 30076
daviddaviswriter@gmail.com

Copyright 2003 David Davis

CAST OF CHARACTERS

INTERVIEWER (R) .... Male, 40s

INTERVIEWEE (E) .... White Female, 20s

SETTING

An interview room in a clinic, next month.

The Interview

> AT RISE we see a small interview room, two chairs, a small desk or table. INTERVIEWER (R), male, middle aged, enters with INTERVIEWEE (E), white female, twenties, and gestures for her to be seated. R carries file with several sheets of paper and forms. E has a large purse. He sits and reviews one form. During the play, he will fill out several forms as he asks questions.

R: OK. Now, according to the nurse, you have agreed to participate in this research study.

E: Yes.

R: Fine. We thank you very much. This may be a big help to a lot of people. Now I just have to run through a few things to make sure you understand, then we have some questions we need you to answer. OK?

E: Sure, whatever.

R: When you agreed to participate, you were told that we would be collecting information about things you do, such as sexual activities, and other personal matters.

E: Yeah, Sure.

R: The information you provide will be kept strictly confidential. Your answers will not be kept with your file and will be aggregated with the answers of many other people so that no single individual can be identified. This is purely for research and your answers will not affect the services we provide. This is an objective study; we are not judging you or your actions, one way or the other. We are just collecting data. We hope that you will choose to answer the questions as truthfully as you can. Please feel free to stop me at any time to ask me to repeat or explain any of the questions or choices for answers. The questionnaire is a little formal and clinical so as not to offend anybody, but if you don't understand anything, just ask. As you were told, your participation is voluntary. This means you can refuse to answer any question I ask. OK?

E: No problem.

R: At the end of the interview, you will receive 10 subway tokens, fifteen dollars' worth of coupons to MacDonalds, and a free pass to any Carmalite cinema movie. Then you will be sent to one of the groups to see a short film and talk to a counselor. The counselor will arrange for your test and provide referrals for any other services you might need. OK?

E: Yeah, yeah. Let's get on with it.

R: After three months, we'll ask you to come back for another round of questions, then again three months after that. Each time, you will receive a little package of incentives, a little more each time.

E: Hey, I'm not doing this for the burgers and fries, OK. I want to pay back a little, help the kids, that kind of thing.

R: We're glad to hear that. That's very nice.

E: I mean, I'll take the tokens and stuff, but that's not why I'm doing it.

R: Great. Now, before we begin, do you have any questions for me?

E: No, nothing I can think of.

R: OK. Let's start with some basics. When were you born?

E: August 7, 1980.

R: Gender?

E: Guess.

R: Female.

E: Want to check?

R: I'll take your word for it.

E: Your loss.

R: Race?

E: Indian. American Indian. Native American.

R: If you don't mind my saying so, you don't look Indian.

E: Well, it's pretty mixed, from way back. Lumbee, Cherokee, Couple of Scotch-Irish that crept into the hogan, even a gypsy a couple of generations back on my mother's side. She was a quarter German, a quarter black, and half Indian. Plus the gypsy. But put down Indian.

R: OK, Native American. Do you consider yourself Hispanic or non-Hispanic?

E: Oh, Hispanic. Hispanic Indian. What is that, mestizo or something? On my father's side of course. Cherokee and Puerto Rican, from New York. Spoke Spanish just like it was English. I never learned much of it, but I'm Hispanic.

R: OK. Hispanic. Highest grade in school completed?

E: Well, I'm a senior at Tech. Fifth year, actually. Computer science major. Can't get a job, of course, so I'm staying in for the extra year. Don't want to face the cold, cruel world just yet. Not with the economy the way it is. Wall Street and all. I dance at the Cheeta Club to make ends meet. Maybe you've seen me?

R: Not that I remember. Marital status?

E: Single.

R: Household status? That means do you live alone, with a sex partner of the same sex, with a sex partner of the opposite sex, with a roommate who is not a sex partner....

E: Well, I live with three guys, but we're not married and one of them is gay. Another one goes both ways though, so it all works out.

R: OK. There's not a check-off on the form for that, but I can write it in.

E: OK. Fine.

R: Do you live in your own apartment or house, someone else's apartment or house, a homeless shelter, transitional housing, on the street?

E: Oh, it's my house. In Midtown. Couple of blocks off Piedmont, not far from the History Center.

R: Nice neighborhood.

E: Yeah, but the taxes are terrible.

R: I'm sure. Now I need to get into some of the more sensitive topics. Remember, you can refuse to answer any question you don't want to answer.

E: OK, let's see if you can make me blush.

R: Have you ever been treated for an STD?

E: Just chlamydia.

R: Have you been treated for an STD during the past 3 months?

E: No. I dumped that guy fast.

R: During the past three months, have any of your sex partners been treated for an STD?

E: Well, Harry, he's the gay one, gets checked every three months whether he needs it or not. I don't think he's found anything though.

R: And you have sex with Harry?

E: No, of course not. But Darien does, and I have sex with Darien. We did have a three-way once, but it didn't work too well. Darien was on top, and Harry behind him, and the weight was just too much, you know?

R: I can imagine. Moving right along. Have you ever been tested for HIV, the virus that causes AIDS?

E: Sure. Every six months. Isn't everybody?

R: We like to hope so. When was the last time you were tested?

E: Six months ago. That's why I'm here; isn't it on my chart?

R: I just go down the questions in order. It's the way we have to do it. Procedure.

E: Oh. Sure. No problem.

R: When you were last tested, were you told that you are infected with HIV or that you have AIDS?

E: No, I'm clean. Thank you, Durex.

R: Have you ever asked a sex partner to be tested for HIV?

E: I use a rapid test on them. Carry a couple in my purse all the time. Only way to go. Just a little finger prick, and twenty minutes later, you know. It's kind of expensive, but the girls down at the club buy them together, by the gross, so we get them wholesale. Little pricks before big pricks we always say. I also use them on myself, just to prove to the guys, you know. But I come here every six months, just to be double sure.

R: Your caution is admirable. So, during the past three months, have you had vaginal, anal, or oral sex with anyone without knowing for certain whether your sexual partners were HIV positive or negative.

E: Oh, no.

R: During the past three months, did you have vaginal, anal, or oral sex with anyone who did not know whether they were HIV infected or not. This would include sex partners who had never been tested for HIV or had not been tested in the past three months.

E: No. Like I said, I test them myself.

R: To your knowledge, during the past three months, were ANY of your sex partners HIV positive?

E: No.

R: During the past three months, have you had vaginal, anal, or oral sex?

E: Yes, yes, and yes.

R: During the past three months, have you had sex with partners who are male?

E: Yes.

R: Female?

E: Yes. But mostly just girls who work at the club. You know, sometimes after work, when all those guys have been leering and grabbing and yelling, you really don't want to deal with a man for a while, but the juice is just dripping down your thighs and your nipples are hard as rocks, we sometimes help each other out, you know. I mean, I'm not a lesbian or anything, usually, unless she's really sexy, you know. I mean, some of the girls at the club are, lesbians that is, and that's OK, but I just prefer men usually, when they're not being too gross, you know?

R: Right. During the past three months have you had sex with any partners who are transgendered?

E: You mean, like with the operation and all?

R: Yes. Or on hormones to pass or just part-way through the process.

E: No. Do you know of any?

R: We occasionally have some here at the clinic.

E: Oh, I'd really like to meet some. They must have quite an interesting perspective, you know, seeing things from both sides and all. Could you introduce me?

R: Sorry, confidentiality and all.

E: Oh, yeah. I don't suppose I could just hang around the waiting room?

R: No, not a good idea.

E: OK, OK. I can take a hint.

R: During the past three months, with how many people have you had sex?

E: Counting the women?

R: Yes, counting the women.

E: OK, give me a minute. Darien and Larry, plus Willie, Bob, Tom, Gary, Carlos, Paul, that new guy, and Tam, he's from Thailand, oh, and what's his name and his brother, the guy at the QT, then Carol and Alice, and the girl who was only there a week, and then there was the party, and Bill's birthday, and when Sue came to visit and we did the town, oh, and after the theatre that night, was that more than three months ago?, no, that counts, then the tea, and the church singles group, oh, and what was her name and her date?...

R: A rough estimate would be acceptable.

E: OK, OK, say 100. Is that too many? Let's see, three months is about 90 days, so, no, that's about right.

R: One hundred different sex partners in 90 days?

E: Just a little over one a day. I mean I have my regulars, like the guys at home, and some of the girls at work, but you know, at parties and all, it evens out.

R: OK, I think I can answer some of these questions based on that. Just correct me if I get something wrong. You have had sex with a main or steady partner.

E: Well, partners.

R: Partners. You have also had sex with other than main or steady partners.

E: Just one or two a day. I mean, it's not like I'm a prostitute or something.

R: No, of course not. During the past three months, how often did you talk with your main partner, I mean partners, about using condoms, latex barriers, or dental dams?

E: What are dental dams?

R: Pieces of latex that dentists use to block off parts of your mouth so they can keep a tooth dry or something. They can also be used to cover a vagina during oral sex to prevent disease transmission.

E: Oh, we just use Saran wrap. With the women, I mean. With the guys it's condoms. But we don't talk about it, we just do it. Usually I slide one in my cheek, then put it on with my tongue when I go down on the guy. None of them seem to object. What's to talk about?

R: And with non-main partners?

E: Sure, same thing. I mean I just do it when I do it, it's not an option. I'm horney, but I'm not stupid.

R: So the last time you had sex....

E: Well, Darien this morning, we used a condom. Then I went down on the receptionist out there to get my appointment moved up. I hate waiting. All you have to read out there is Good Housekeeping and Sports Illustrated, and some kid already had the swimsuit issue.

R: The receptionist in the office?

E: Yeah. Well, not in the office. We went in the bathroom of course. Why? You got the hots for her?

R: That's my wife!

E: Oh. Is that a problem? You want me to blow you? That would make it even.

R: You had oral sex with my wife?

E: Or we could screw. I bought I whole new gross of condoms just today. Let me just test your HIV status.

R: She won't even let me go down on her.

E: Well, maybe I could give you some pointers. That is very tender tissue, you know. Sometimes you guys just dive in like it's a swimming pool. You have to sneak up on it, creep in a little bit at a time.

R: And I haven't had a blow job since we got married. And she was so good, could make it last for hours. Then put the ring on her finger and it's missionary position or nothing. Damn!

E: A three-way, definitely need a three-way here. Some mediation, a little negotiation, improved communication.

R: And in the office, right under my nose.

E: Well, this is a pretty sexy place. People sit around talking about sex all day, asking all these personal questions about people's sex lives, you got to make allowances.

R: We're supposed to be professionals.

E: And professionals are non-judgmental. Blaming people doesn't help anybody. You need to understand you wife's needs. We have to deal with this objectively. Harm-reduction approach, we want to reduce the risk of harm. We need to define the problem and outline a series of steps that begin where people are, so we reduce the risk and harm without setting unreasonable goals or expectations. That's what your brochure says.

R: Right, harm reduction. Series of steps. Begin where people are. Getting angry doesn't help. Have to be professional. Just because my wife let a client eat her pussy does not mean that the world is coming to an end.

E: Right.

R: Use a Stages of Change Transtheoretical Theory of Behavior Change. Determine our readiness to change. Rationally analyze the problem, determine where the communication broke down.

E: Yes. Consider your needs and her needs. Discuss this openly and frankly. You have to reveal your emotions, let her know you still love her, that you want to work on improving and opening up your relationship. Here, here's some free passes to the Cheeta Club, bring her down and use that as a way of opening a conversation. The buffet is only $10 on Tuesday nights. I'm scheduled to work tonight beginning at nine. I could do a table dance for you, and you could ask her if she sees anything familiar. That should get things started.

R: Yes, yes. A setting that frees her inhibitions, allows her to express her sexuality. Use an overtly erotic setting to open channels of communication.

E: Yes, that's the spirit!

R: And then I'm going to take her to the car and fuck her in the ass in the parking lot! Teach that bitch a thing or two! God damned cunt wants her pussy licked, I'll eat her cunt till her head blows off, I'll fuck her till her tits squirt....

> He storms out of the room.

E: Oh my.

> She picks up the interview form, checks off the answers to the last few questions, closes the folder, and exits.

CURTAIN

MODERN LIFE

By David Davis

Member
All rights & privileges.

David Davis
100 Hunters Ridge Court
Roswell, GA 30076
daviddaviswriter@gmail.com

Copyright 2019 David Davis

CAST OF CHARACTERS

HARRY .... 30s, Husband of Marie

MARIE .... 30s, Wife of Harry

SETTING

A bedroom, the present.

> AT RISE we see a bedroom, double bed, small sitting area with loveseat nearby. It is night. There is a little light spilling through a curtained window upstage. HARRY and MARIE are asleep in the bed. Suddenly there is a very loud crashing sound from outside. HARRY and MARIE both sit up suddenly.

MARIE: What was that?

> There is a flash and the sound of an explosion outside.

HARRY: Sounded like something blew up.

MARIE: Oh my god, it's a bomb! It's terrorists! Run!

HARRY: Marie, for god's sake....

> MARIE and HARRY leap out of each side of the bed, run around the foot of the bed and collide with each other in the dark. HARRY is knocked to the floor, and MARIE twists around in pain before sitting on the bed.

MARIE: Oh, I think I hurt my ankle. Harry, you OK? Harry, where are you? Harry?

HARRY: Breath...............knocked................out.

> A flickering yellow light appears outside, from a fire.

MARIE: Harry, my god, there's a fire. The terrorist bomb started a fire. We've got to get out. You've got to help me.

> HARRY groans, but staggers to his feet. MARIE pulls herself up and hops to him on one leg, keeping the other knee bent. Just as she reaches him, she takes an off-balance hop and knees him in the groin. As he doubles over in pain, he head-butts her, sending her hopping backwards, arms flailing, falling backwards onto the bed, spread-eagled. HARRY curls up on the floor in pain. There is a long pause.

MARIE: (Weakly) Harry?...............Harry?........

HARRY: Auhhhhhhh

MARIE: Harry?...............I don't think I can move.

HARRY: Ughhhhhhhhhhhh

MARIE: I'm going to lie here and burn to death wearing your grungy, old pajamas.

HARRY: Guhhhhhhhhhhhhhhh

MARIE: The flames will leap up the walls, and I'll just have to lie here, breathing all the poison smoke, another nameless victim of man's inhumanity to man.

HARRY: Ohhhhhh

MARIE: Or maybe there'll be a monument, like for nine eleven, with our names on it. Remembered forever. Do you think we'll be remembered forever, Harry?

> HARRY slowly crawls to the foot of the bed and tries to pull himself up, but as he does he accidently grabs MARIE's injured ankle. She screams, sits up, and grabs for her ankle, colliding with HARRY as he pulls himself up. He ends up back on the floor, dazed. A siren and colored flashing lights come close to the house. The siren stops after a moment, but the lights keep flashing.

MARIE: Ohhh, I keep seeing lights flashing before my eyes. And my ears are really ringing. Harry, my ankle hurts; I think it's broken. Ouch, get me some ice. Oh, yeah, there's a fire. Forget the ice.

> HARRY groans and crawls to the love seat, slowing pulling himself up to sit, still struggling to get a good breath and clear his head. He rubs his head with one hand and cradles his crotch with the other.

HARRY: Uhhhhhhhhhhhhh

MARIE: Harry, are you playing with yourself?.............................I know we're dying, but this in no time to jerk off.

HARRY: Uhhh. What............... happened?

MARIE: Some suicide bomber blew himself up and set off a fire that's burning down the house around us.

HARRY: What?

MARIE: Don't you see the flames out the window? I've broken my ankle, my head is throbbing, I can't move, and all you can do is sit there and rub your dick. This is no way to end up. We have to die with dignity, with love in our hearts and clear consciences. Goodbye, Harry. I love you. You were a wonderful husband. We had some really good years together. Thank you .... You're supposed to say something, Harry...................You're supposed to say you loved me too...We're dying here, you're supposed to say you love me, dammit.........................God, men never know what to say.......... .... Harry?........................... Harry? Here we are dying and I'm telling you how much I love you and what a good husband you are, and all you can think of is sex. Men!

HARRY: It.....hurts.

MARIE: Anyway, before the flames flash over the ceiling and I am turned into charred hamburger, I just want you to know that I love you, and that that little affair with Tex didn't mean anything, it was just a fling, just getting on the good side of your boss a little bit. Just helping you along a little. I really did it for you.

HARRY: ....Tex?

MARIE: And Ralph, that was just one night, that didn't't mean anything to anybody, not even Ralph.

HARRY: ....Ralph?

MARIE: You are the one I really loved, the one I always wanted to be with, and if I have to die, I'm glad it's with you.................I just wish we'd had children.............but I love you, Harry, I'll always love you, as long as I live, no matter how many more minutes that is...................................... Now you tell me how much you love me and that you forgive me....................... Harry?.................. . Harry, do I have to write it out for you?..........We're on limited time here............................You're supposed to confess your affairs and tell me you love me before we die so we can die with clear consciences..I'll forgive you for Diane and what's-her-name. Honest.

HARRY: Never........slept.......with.........Diane.

MARIE: Oh, come on, everybody slept with Diane. Your whole office slept with Diane. Hell, even I slept with Diane.............You remember, when her aunt died and I went with her to the funeral and we got snowed in in Kansas City and had to spend the night at that airport hotel. We had to share a room with a double bed, and I accidently touched her breast rolling over and she thought I wanted to, well, you know, so we did, and that slut was so hot that the only people she didn't sleep with were nerds and losers.

HARRY: Never.........slept........with.........Diane.

MARIE: Oh. What about what's-her-name?

HARRY: Only.........you.

MARIE: Not even........

HARRY: Only........you. Since.........wedding.

MARIE: Oh, Harry, you are so nice, lying to me like this just because we're about to burn to death. That is so considerate. I really appreciate you lying to me like this. If I could move, I'd kiss you. I always said you were a great husband. I'm proud to be blown up with you.

HARRY: Why...........bomber............here?

MARIE: Well, I don't know. Something about the Jews and Palestinians, I guess. Or maybe the army in Iraq or Iran or I something.

HARRY: Live....in......Doraville,......Georgia. Only.......thing......worth....blowing up...is...... McDonalds.

MARIE: Why would the McDonalds be worth blowing up?

HARRY: Symbol....of......capitalism.

MARIE: Oh. And I guess the Hindus would hate it for killing all those cows. Are there Hindu terrorists?

HARRY: Who...knows.

HARRY struggles to his feet and goes to the window.

MARIE: How soon before we feel the flames?

HARRY: About........40....years.

MARIE: We're not going to die?

HARRY: Not...tonight. Old...Man...Stevens...ran into...telephone pole. Car...exploded. Fire department... almost..has..it..out. Old Man Stevens...on the grass, ...throwing up Jack Daniels.

MARIE: Oh. No terrorists? The house isn't on fire? We're not dying?

HARRY: Not right now. You want.......medics to...check you ankle?

MARIE: Hang on, let me see.

> She pushes herself up and rubs her ankle.

HARRY: Well?

MARIE: I guess it's just sprained......................Oh, boy, do I feel foolish. I mean, just rattling one about terrorists and bombs and fires like it happened every day. Modern life, huh?

HARRY: Yeah......You want...some ice?

MARIE: It can wait.......When you feel better.........Come back to bed, Harry. You don't look so good.

HARRY: Rough...night.

MARIE: Yeah. Come on back to bed, Harry.

> He does not move.

CURTAIN

MONOLOGUE

By David Davis

Member
All rights & privileges.

David Davis
100 Hunters Ridge Court
Roswell, GA 30076
daviddaviswriter@gmail.com

Copyright 2022 David Davis

Monologue

> AT RISE we see a MAN sitting in a chair.

MAN: If I sing a song of sixpence, will I have a pocket full of rye? And will it be the grain or the whisky? If it's the whiskey, will it be in a bottle, or will I look like I peed in my pants. Have I peed in my pants? I don't want to look. No self-confidence. Mind too detached from the body, maybe even from the brain.

What are we if we are not our brains? If we don't have a mind, does it matter? Why isn't it mind under matter? Well, no matter. I don't drink anyway, and I don't like rye bread, so I guess I better not sing. The song in my life has gone out. No melody to carry me along like the wings of a dove. No sign from above. Yield. Stop. Left Only. Danger ahead. Dangerous curves. Big boobs. OK, everybody in the audience, show me your boobs. (Pause.)

Oh, well. So much for participatory theatre. This is not a play; this is a story. Actually, it's not even a story. It's sort of a ramble. I just ramble along. Aimless. Pointless. The narrative is embedded like a reporter in the army, sticking it's head up only when the satellite connection comes on. So don't expect anything to happen, or any characters to develop. It's just words, words spoken out the side of my head, that sort of go around the story without ever getting there. That's called realism, the illusion of reality, and we all know real life never actually gets anywhere. It just sort of ends one day. Like today, maybe. You never know, do you. Maybe you'll make it home tonight, maybe you won't. You never know. I certainly don't. I don't know anything. Except what happened. And that was bad enough. I mean, it put me over the edge. As you can tell.

And it wasn't that anything happened, it was more like anything didn't happen. Yeah, that's it. What happened is that nothing happened. It just went on day after day not happening. Chinese water torture with little drops of time, drop, drop, one second after the other, all the same. Drop. Drop. Can I see the hands of all those who know what I'm talking about? Notice that I'm not raising my own hand. Why will you show me your hands but not your boobs? Is that a cultural thing?

Anyway, I was here. I'm always here, seems like. I do go home at night, but it doesn't help. So, I'm here whether I'm here or not. Or maybe I'm not all here. That could be. I'm certainly not the man I used to be. There's a shadow hanging over me. Beatles, Beatles, Beatles. Won't it be sad if Ringo is the last one left and all the kids remember of the Beatles is an old and decrepit Mr. Conductor from some kids TV show?

Getting old stinks. When I was born, Truman was President. Anybody remember Harry Truman? Dropped the bomb on Japan, fired McAuthor in Korea. That's too old for even the history books. Most people think life began in the 60s with the sexual revolution, but didn't really get going good until the 80s and disco. And now it's the 21st Century, with HIV, terrorists, and reality TV. At least HIV is preventable. Just lock yourself in the house and never let anybody in or out. Telecommute to work.

Wish I could. Then I wouldn't have to sit in traffic for hours in order to sit in an office for hours so I could earn enough money to join a health club to stay in shape. Pear shape, according to my doctor. That's better than apple shape, I'm told. Eat more fruit. Five a day. Look like a banana, that's the goal. Not like this, old and fat. From sitting around all day listening to the seconds drop. Drop, drop. This is modern life; driving to the health club to exercise. Irony there somewhere. But irony is dead too. And that's that.

NO

A Very Short Play By David Davis

Member
All rights & privileges.

David Davis
100 Hunters Ridge Court
Roswell, GA 30076
daviddaviswriter@gmail.com

Copyright 2013 David Davis

> AT RISE we see GUY sitting at a table in a quiet café. He is in his early thirties, not handsome, but not ugly, dressed in high quality, but not stylish clothes. He is the kind of man you usually fail to notice. He is sipping a drink like he is trying to make it last as long as possible. GAL, late twenties, stylish and pretty, but not beautiful, enters, and GUY stands.

GUY: Lisa?

GAL: Uh, no.

GUY: Oh, excuse me. I'm waiting for someone, one of those Internet dating things, you know, where you meet somebody for the first time in a public place, and you sort of look like her picture. And, well, you just never know how much to trust those pictures. A lot of them are glamor shots, you know, hair just done, professional makeup, studio lighting, made five or six years and twenty pounds ago. And I just thought you might be…

GAL: No.

GUY: OK. Actually, you look a little better than her picture, so I was just hoping. You know, I at least put up an honest picture. It actually looks like me. I try to be honest about things, you know. Face the real facts. OK, it's about two years old now, but I haven't changed much. Of course, I know looks don't matter as much with men. Women have to show off their potential fertility with all those secondary sex characteristics, you know.

GAL: No.

GUY: Oh, come on… You know, breast size, round hips, smooth skin, all those female things. I mean, I try to be honest and up-front about things. With gals, it's looks that count. It's basic sociobiology, subconscious and all. Guys want gals who look like they have all the right hormones, all glowing and healthy, walking sex machines that can pop out all these beautiful babies. Now guys, it's more a status thing. Sure, we can't be real ugly or deformed, but it's like Henry Kissinger said, power is the ultimate aphrodisiac. Women want a guy with power, status, money, somebody who has demonstrated success, who would be a good provider. You can make a guy look a whole lot better just by putting him behind the wheel of a Porsche.

GAL: You?

GUY: Well, not a Porsche. BMW though. I mean, I'm not rich, but I do pretty well. Six figures a year, and not just barely. Real solid six figures. Not to brag. I mean, I know I'm not some male model, not a 10, you know. Probably just a 5 on looks alone, pure average. But with the money and the degrees and the car, I think I rate at least a 7, maybe pushing an 8, you know.

GAL: Degrees?

GUY: Statistics Ph.D. I'm an actuary. You know, I figure the odds of people dying for an insurance company. Like, if you have ten thousand white men 30 years old who want $100,000 in level term for 20 years and you think you can earn 5% if you reinvest the premiums, how much do you have to charge to be able to pay the benefits to the families of those who die and still make money? I mean, some of them are going to die, but how many? You have to look at accident rates, heart attack rates, cancer rates, murder rates. Do they smoke? Are they married? Where do they live? What about earthquakes, tornadoes, hurricanes; is global warming going to be such a big deal that you have to add those factors? And can you really count on earning 5% these days? How much margin do you want to build in? How big a chance do you take if you underprice the competition? I mean, sure, you can lose a little here or there, but there's billions riding on getting these probabilities right and the shareholders don't like dividends dropping, so those CEOs pay good money to anybody who can get those death rates right. Maybe it's isn't Hollywood, but it's lots of zeros on the paycheck and stock options to boot.

GAL: Oh.

GUY: So, anyway, I figure…I mean, well, it looks like she isn't coming. Time to face facts. It's past the time, and I don't think I can nurse this drink anymore. I mean, well, would you like to, you know, go somewhere or something? I'm sorry, that makes you sound like a second choice or something.

GAL: No.

GUY: I mean, I've enjoy talking to you. You're a good listener. I like that. Somebody who listens and doesn't just take once glance at somebody and scratch them off their list if they don't look like you expected. I mean, I'd really like to, you know.

GAL: No. Sorry.

GUY: Hey, I understand. No problem. Look, I'm keeping you from something. Listen, I'm just going to leave a few bucks for the drink and take off. If you see somebody come in who sort of looks like you that seems to be looking for somebody, tell her he left, OK.

GAL: Sure.

>   GUY puts money on table and exits. GAL watches him go, then
>   sits at table. Her cell phone rings and she answers it.

GAL: This is Lisa. No, no, that didn't work out. Too much of a talker. No, he just left. Yes, Mom, I'm coming right home. Bye.

CURTAIN

PRE-NEED

A Ten-Minute Play By David Davis

Member
All rights & privileges.

David Davis
100 Hunters Ridge Court
Roswell, GA 30076
daviddaviswriter@gmail.com

Copyright 2010 David Davis

> AT RISE we see a viewing room in a funeral parlor. It is empty of both the living and the dead. The UNDERTAKER enters with the CUSTOMER.

UNDERTAKER: And this is one of our viewing rooms. The coffin would be placed here so that mourners could enter, express their condolences to the next of kin, and then move on to the viewing.

CUSTOMER: And what if I'm not using a coffin?

UNDERTAKER: Excuse me?

CUSTOMER: Could I just be laid out on a table or something?

UNDERTAKER: Uh, it's customary to…

CUSTOMER: Or maybe just rent one for the night.

UNDERTAKER: Rent a coffin?

CUSTOMER: Just for the viewing. Two, three hours tops.

UNDERTAKER: What about the burial?

CUSTOMER: Oh, no. No graveyard stuff. Cremation. Decaying doesn't sound to appetizing to me, you know?

UNDERTAKER: A good quality coffin with a liner would be air and water tight. With our high quality embalming, there would be very little decay for many years.

CUSTOMER: Nah, I don't want to take up the space. Leave it for a tree or a drive-thru or something.

UNDERTAKER: Even then, some kind of repository for the remains is usual. For the viewing and the cremation.

CUSTOMER: Just to burn it with the body? No thanks. Canvas bag or something like that. Don't I get delivered here is some kind of body bag? Or does the hospital take that back and reuse it?

UNDERTAKER: And during the service?

CUSTOMER: Oh, the funeral? Do I have to be there for that? I'm not sure I want you driving me all around the county in some expensive hearse. If I don't have to go to the graveyard, why do I have to go to the church? Can't I just stay here? Do I have to be there for them to pray over me?

UNDERTAKER: We do have a chapel here. Very suitable for memorial services. I think it's empty right now, if you would like to see…

CUSTOMER: Does that cost?

UNDERTAKER: There is a small charge. Very reasonable.

CUSTOMER: Nah. I can get the church for free. Been going there all my life; guess they owe me that. Heaven knows I've paid for part of it over the years. Though I guess somebody would have to tip the pastor and the organist. That wouldn't be my problem though, would it? I mean, this pre-payment stuff is one thing, but you don't tip in advance, do you?

UNDERTAKER: Uh, we don't deal with that part of the occasion. Though we do have an organist if you need one, if you use our chapel.

CUSTOMER: Nah. The organist at the church is OK. Left hand is a little weak, but she usually holds a good tempo. She hates my guts. Don't think either one of us remembers why.

She's probably play for free just to make sure I was dead though. Pastor likes me though. He's still a little new. He'd expect a few dollars, I guess. If he's still here then. It's a little church. Pastors don't last long.

UNDERTAKER: Uh, do we have any idea when our services might be needed?

CUSTOMER: Doctor says four to six weeks.

UNDERTAKER: Oh. I'm very sorry.

CUSTOMER: No you're not. And neither am I. Get it over with. Don't want to just lie around, you know?

UNDERTAKER: Of course.

CUSTOMER: You ever think about dying?

UNDERTAKER: I'm an undertaker. Death is familiar. Many times it is a friend.

CUSTOMER: Friend to you, I guess. Death is how you make a living. Real recession-proof job. I mean your own death. Surely you thought about it, back when you started out.

UNDERTAKER: My family has been in the business for three generations. I played in the coffin storage room as a child. I embalmed my own father. I wanted to be sure it was done correctly. One gets used to things.

CUSTOMER: You put your father in a coffin?

UNDERTAKER: Top of the line. Brass nameplate, steel liner, pure mahogany, triple-thick cushions, satin pillow.

CUSTOMER: You think he noticed?

UNDERTAKER: I did it for me. To show my respect. My love for him.

CUSTOMER: Well, I guess I don't have as much to prove as you did.

UNDERTAKER: We understand that final expenses can be a concern in times of need. We try to offer a range of flexible services that can accommodate any budget.

CUSTOMER: I'm sure you do. How much to lay me out here for a couple of hours, then put me in a bag and burn me?

UNDERTAKER: Would you like an urn for your ashes or just a brown paper bag?

CUSTOMER: Would you do the brown paper bag?

UNDERTAKER: We have a plain wooden box. Pine. Yellow pine. Unfinished. Little hook and eye closure. You have to provide your own lock, if that matters to you..

CUSTOMER: I've probably got something lying around the house that would work.

UNDERTAKER: Would you be bringing that in with your deposit, or will that be up to the next of kin to supply?

CUSTOMER: Ain't no next of kin. They all beat me to it.

UNDERTAKER: Oh. I'm sorry.

CUSTOMER: Why you think I'm doing this myself?

UNDERTAKER: I thought, I mean typically pre-need arrangements are made either to spare the next of kin such sensitive decisions or to make sure the arrangements are as one wants them.

CUSTOMER: Well, I'm trying to make sure the arrangements are as I want them because there ain't nobody else would want any at all.

UNDERTAKER: I'm sure that….

CUSTOMER: I'm not a very likeable person. Not that you would have noticed. You usually have to get to know me to hate me.

UNDERTAKER: Of course.

CUSTOMER: Probably don't need a wake or a funeral at all. Only people coming are those wanting to make sure I'm dead. Got to give them some satisfaction, I guess. Otherwise I'd skip the whole thing.

UNDERTAKER: I'm sure…

CUSTOMER: No you're not.

>   Pause.

CUSTOMER: I'm not poor. I don't need the county to bury me. But every dollar I spend on this shebang is one less dollar goes to the Salvation Army, you know? There's nobody left but me and Eleanor Rigby, and even she's dead. I don't need a big send off to get St. Peter to notice me when I show up at the gates. So, with the wood box, how much? Maybe you can find somebody to take it after the cremation.

UNDERTAKER: I'll have to check my price list. We so rarely… I'm sure we can work something out.

CUSTOMER: Yeah, yeah, yeah, I know. Let's go. I ain't got all day. Not anymore.

UNDERTAKER: This way, please.

>   They exit.
>
>   Curtain

SPORTS

By David Davis

Member
All rights & privileges.

David Davis
100 Hunters Ridge Court
Roswell, GA 30076
daviddaviswriter@gmail.com

Copyright 2022 David Davis

> AT RISE we see a table, two chairs, TV set on table. WOMAN sits in chair, asleep. MAN enters carrying briefcase Sets briefcase on table.

MAN: Damn bastards did it again. Same damn thing all over again.

> He turns on the TV, which we can neither see or hear.

MAN: Should have left well enough alone.

> He exits to the other side of the stage. The WOMAN wakes up, looks at the TV, changes the channel.

WOMAN: Twenty-four to seven, five minutes left in the half.

> MAN enters with a handfull of donut "holes" and sits in chair.

MAN: Donut holes. They sell the holes separately. Isn't that stupid. Donuts and donut holes, holes sold separately. You'd think they were batteries.

WOMAN: The score is tied with no time left. That means sudden death.

MAN: I need something real to eat. Something more substantial than donut holes.

WOMAN: It's Miller time.

> She pulls out of her pocket the control to an electric genital stimulator (a clitoris vibrator), the wires of which lead under her clothes. She turns the gadget on. We hear a buzzing sound each time she turns it on. She smiles.

MAN: There I was, right in the middle, and it all comes crashing down. Bastards! What in hell do they want? It stinks, it just stinks. I need a drink.

> He gets up, changes the channel, and exits. WOMAN turns gadget off, changes TV channel, turns gadget back on. MAN enters again with a little box of Kool-Aid and sips it through a straw.

MAN: Ah, I needed that. It's hell out there, just pure hell.

> WOMAN turns gadget off.

WOMAN: Oh good, they're kicking the tipoff. Hit'em again, hit'em again, harder, harder! Alright! Two points!

MAN: You work and slave, and what do you get? Donut holes.

WOMAN: Sports is such a good metaphor for life. Competition, teamwork, showering together.

MAN: But what are you going to do? That's the way life is; big fish, little fish.

WOMAN: That quarterback needs to learn how to eat balls.

MAN: One of these days though, one of these days.

WOMAN: The puck! Watch the puck!

MAN: I need some desert.

> He exits.

WOMAN: This Bud's for you.

> She turns on her gadget control again. MAN enters, licking a popsicle. He changes channels and sits.

MAN: I have to watch my cholesterol. Watch my cholesterol, watch my waistline, watch my mouth. I spend so much time watching myself, I never do anything. I'm sitting here sucking a phallic symbol for five year olds; is this adult or what?

> WOMAN turns off gadget, changes channels.

WOMAN: Bottom of the ninth, one out, two on, and a real free swinger on deck. This is what makes for excitement. Stealing bases, crucial scrums, dangerous sideouts. Makes you feel alive.

MAN: I mean, my mother died three days ago, and I'm sitting here sucking a sugar and ice cock, and I'm not even queer. Why don't they have pussy shaped candy? Maybe that's what heart shaped candy really is, only it's a secret. Sure isn't shaped like a real heart, with an aorta and all. Poor Mother.

WOMAN: I remember when Reggie Jackson hit all those home runs in the Superbowl. It was like one orgasm after another; wave after wave of surf, riding from crest to crest, hanging ten on the edge of the board, hotdoging and peanuts and crackerjack. I came and came and came. Then it was all over until next year.

MAN: But, life goes on. Man, woman, birth, death, infinity. That was Ben Casey, wasn't it? One mother dies, another mother comes along to screw things up. Day after day creeps its petty pace as we live on phallic pacifiers.

> He throws the popsicle away and changes the channel.

WOMAN: The trouble with sports is that they have seasons. They should be year around. We change time for daylight savings, why can't we change seasons. Oh, Coors is the one.

> She turns gadget on. MAN changes channel again. She turns it off and puts it away.

WOMAN: One twelve to one eleven in the seventh. Humm, must be a college game. That's where the education is. Fall afternoons, big stadiums, tall men in short pants swatting each other's butts, cheerleaders in short skirts and no underwear. Those were the days. Now look at me. Over the hill, out to pasture, living on beer commercials. Babe did it right, hit the top, then die young. Little Mo, no mo. Love-forty, pack it in Chrissy; call it quits before the ice maiden melts all together. Just let me go easy, go greasy, slide into the promised land.

>   She changes the channel.

MAN: Eat, sleep, mow, fix, clean, wash, work, work, work. Suck a few hearts and die. Cherry popsicles and raspberry hearts, then the long sleep.

>   He changes the channel.

WOMAN: I didn't like sports until I got married. Now I can't get enough. It's like I was playing the game before, and now all I can do is watch.

MAN: Nothing happens. I go to work, work hard, come home, and eat holes for dinner. Everyday is the same. People live, people die. And nothing happens.

>   WOMAN changes the channel.

WOMAN: And next year. There's always next year. Oh, Dos Equis Dark, how kinky.

>   She turns the gadget on. We hear it buzz as the lights fade.

THE MEETING

A Very Short Play By David Davis

Member
All rights & privileges.

David Davis
100 Hunters Ridge Court
Roswell, GA 30076
daviddaviswriter@gmail.com

Copyright 2022 David Davis

The Meeting

> A restaurant. WOMAN 1 is seated at a table, waiting. WOMAN 2 enters, looks around, sees 1, waves, and crosses to sit at the table.

2: Sorry I'm late.

1: No problem. So, how have you been?

2: Oh, not bad. You?

1: Fine, fine. (Pause.) Thanks for meeting me. We haven't had a chance to talk in weeks.

2: Yes. I'm so glad you called. I don't want to get so busy I lose touch with my real friends.

1: You know, I heard somebody from Jerry's office call you his Office Wife yesterday. Wasn't sure exactly what that meant.

2: Oh, that just means we look out for each other at work, help each other out, you know, have each other's back in all the office infighting.

1: Oh. So not the same as fucking him.

2: Oh, that too, but just at work. Nothing social, you know.

1: Oh.

2: Mostly just blow jobs, actually. Since I quit smoking I really need something to do during breaks.

1: Ah.

2: Do you mind?

1: I'm not sure. Are you any good?

2: Oh, about average, I expect. Maybe a little above average at oral sex, but I don't do anal. It evens out.

1: I see. So, you've quit smoking. Congratulations.

2: Well, I'm trying. It hasn't been easy.

1: Have you tried the nicotine patch?

2: No. I was using the gum. At least at first.

1: Yes?

2: I guess I've got an oral fixation or something. I just had to have something to put in my mouth.

1: So it seems.

2: We're down to two or three blow jobs a day though. Plus a fuck at lunch.

1: Well, sorry I disrupted your routine.

2: Oh, no problem. He had a lunch meeting with a client today anyway.

1: Ah.

2: I'll just jerk off when I get back to the office. Unless you'd like to....

1: I don't think so.

2: No problem.

1: Thanks for thinking of me though.

2: Oh, sure. I just have to do something to keep my mind off cigarettes.

1: Yes. I can understand that.

2: It's just such a big change, not smoking. Not at all like I thought it would be.

1: Any weight gain?

2: Not yet. I am pregnant though, so I guess it's just a matter of time.

1: Oh. And is my husband the....

2: Father? I think so. Not for sure though.

1: Ah.

2: He is the most likely. Guess we'll have to have some DNA tests to be sure though.

1: Yes, let's do keep this all legal and above-board.

2: Would you like to adopt it? I mean, if it's his.

1: You don't want to keep it?

2: Maybe. I'm not sure. I just thought it would be polite to offer.

1: Very thoughtful. Thank you.

2: I mean, he is your husband, so you are involved. If it's him, I mean.

1: Yes, of course.

2: I'm only starting my second month, so you've got time to think it over.

1: Good. (Pause.) Have you considered, you know, abortion?

2: My priest was against it.

1: Ah.

2: He admitted he couldn't't really relate, being gay and all. But, he said, since I'm not a kid anymore and already have a good paying career, that he would give the fetus the benefit of the doubt. Unless the amnio showed something, of course.

1: Ah. (Pause.) And?

2: Haven't had it yet. Need to be a little further along.

1: Ah. Well, good luck.

2: Thanks.

1: I, uh, take it you're not using condoms.

2: No. They're so messy. And if you throw them in the trash can at the office, the janitor complains.

1: Yes, I can see that.

2: Oh, you're worried about.... Oh, no, I get tested for that every month whether I need it or not. No problem there.

1: Well, you understand.

2: Oh, sure. Can't be too careful these days.

1: Yes. Not like it used to be, is it?

2: No, it certainly isn't.

BLACKOUT.

THE ROOM

By David Davis

Member
All rights & privileges.

David Davis
100 Hunters Ridge Court
Roswell, GA 30076
daviddaviswriter@gmail.com

Copyright 2022 David Davis

CAST OF CHARACTERS

REAL ESTATE AGENT...Female, 40s

MALE BUYER...20s

FEMALE BUYER...20s

SETTING

An empty room in the basement of a house.

> AT RISE we see an empty room in the basement of a house, no windows, one door, a few shelves. The REAL ESTATE AGENT enters, guiding a young couple.

REAL ESTATE AGENT: And this is the emergency room.....

MALE BUYER: The what?

REAL ESTATE AGENT: The emergency room. Sort of a combination tornado cellar, bomb shelter, terrorist escape chamber, and home invasion hidey-hole. If there is any emergency, you can come hide down here. The door is reinforced steel with an air-tight seal, the walls are solid steel with a lead liner, there are springs under the floor to damp any explosion or earthquake, the air intake is filtered down to zero point oh five microns, the drain can be used as a bathroom in an emergency, and there are shelves for you to store water, flashlights, radios, battery-operated TVs, non-perishable food, a range of antibiotics, and any other medications you use. Properly supplied, you could live down here for up to six months without ever having to see the light of day.

MALE BUYER: Oh.

FEMALE BUYER: Do you get a lot of that around here?

REAL ESTATE AGENT: A lot of what?

FEMALE BUYER: Earthquakes, tornados, home invasions, bombings, chemical attacks, you know.

REAL ESTATE AGENT: Oh, it's a very safe neighborhood. Has a neighborhood watch and everything. Best schools in the county. It's just that these days, well, you know, things can happen anywhere. That's why the builder started adding these rooms to the basements. Sort of an extra feature, a little upgrade that adds resale value even if you don't get to use it.

MALE BUYER: What about floods?

FEMALE BUYER: Floods?

REAL ESTATE AGENT: Well, as long as the air intake stays above the water level, you should be fine. It vents out to the top of the roof, so that's what, 10, 12 feet high. It would take quite a flood to get up that high. And this isn't a flood plain, so you're talking Noah or something before you would have to worry. It's fire-proof, water-proof, shock-proof, just about everything proof.

FEMALE BUYER: Can you call out?

REAL ESTATE AGENT: Like for pizza?

FEMALE BUYER: No, do cell phones work down here, like to call for help or tell my mother goodbye or something.

REAL ESTATE AGENT: Oh, no. The lead lining, you know. There is a phone jack for land lines, but I wouldn't count on that, you know, if there was a real problem.

FEMALE BUYER: Yeah, right.

REAL ESTATE AGENT: But in here you'd be safe and warm, no matter what.

MALE BUYER: What do you sleep on. This floor is cold and hard.

REAL ESTATE AGENT: Oh, mattresses, cots, sleeping bags, futons, whatever you store down here. That part doesn't come with the house. Just the room.

MALE BUYER: Oh. Sure.

FEMALE BUYER: I don't know. I mean, it's just so depressing.

REAL ESTATE AGENT: Well, a little paint, maybe some artificial flowers, brighten the place right up.

FEMALE BUYER: On, I mean just the idea. It's like, well, the world's going to end, but I'll be OK because I have my little emergency hiding place. I can just go hide for six months and then come out after everybody else is dead.

REAL ESTATE AGENT: Oh no, all the houses in the subdivision will have them. There'll be like 40, maybe 50, couples left. And it's not the whole world probably, just this area, or just the country, or not more than the northern hemisphere. It's not like you're going to be Adam and Eve or anything.

FEMALE BUYER: Well, it's still a little depressing.

MALE BUYER: What about condoms? Can you store condoms down here? I mean, six months in the dark, you got to do something.

FEMALE BUYER: Oh, my.

REAL ESTATE AGENT: Sure. You'd have to rotate your stock, of course. Just like the batteries, check the expiration dates and keep them fresh. A couple of gross wouldn't take up much room. A few boxes of tampons, some condoms, lots of toilet paper, just stack it all up.

MALE BUYER: Sure. Right.

REAL ESTATE AGENT: Now let me show you the exercise room. It's got mirrors on three walls, plus a dance barre. You could put in weights or exercise bikes, or just use to space for aerobics or whatever.

>   REAL ESTATE AGENT leads them out of the room. The lights fade.
>
>   CURTAIN

WAITING

A Ten-Minute Play By David Davis

Member
All rights & privileges.

David Davis
100 Hunters Ridge Court
Roswell, GA 30076
daviddaviswriter@gmail.com

Copyright 2013 David Davis

> AT RISE we see a waiting area, the present. ELLEN is sitting in a chair with a carry-on suitcase in the chair beside her. JAN, carrying a backpack, enters, looks around for a seat, and doesn't see an empty seat except by ELLEN. JAN crosses to ELLEN.

JAN: Excuse me. May I?

ELLEN: Oh, of course.

> ELLEN moves her suitcase to the floor and JAN sits beside ELLEN. JAN puts her backpack on the floor and settles in. ELLEN smiles at JAN. JAN smiles back.

JAN: Thanks. For a minute there I didn't think there was a place to sit. Thought I might have to stand until boarding.

ELLEN: It is a little crowded today.

JAN: I think the system's backed up somewhere. Weather probably. Looks like I'm in for a long trip home.

ELLEN: Well, you never know what you will run into traveling these days.

JAN: Going to…

ELLEN: Oh, no.

JAN: Isn't this…?

ELLEN: Yes.

JAN: Then why…?

ELLEN: Oh, I just enjoy waiting.

JAN: Excuse me?

ELLEN: Waiting. I enjoy waiting. I just like to come here and wait.

JAN: But the suitcase…?

ELLEN: My disguise.

JAN: Oh.

ELLEN: They don't like people sitting here who aren't going anywhere. You have to look like you're on your way or something.

JAN: Oh. (Pause.) Are you homeless or something?

ELLEN: Oh, no. I have a very nice apartment. Plenty of money. Well, maybe not plenty, but enough. I don't even have to work. Insurance, you know.

JAN: Ah.

ELLEN: But I live alone. So sometimes I….

JAN: I see.

ELLEN: I just find it interesting to watch people, hear the sounds, see how they dress, what they try to carry. Some people are just so impractical when it comes to traveling.

JAN: Ah.

ELLEN: Believe me, it's better than daytime television.

JAN: That I believe.

ELLEN: I mean, I really don't care who shakes her booty anymore. Or who's having sex with who, or what. Or even how many Moslems got blown up by another Moslem. I mean, really, who cares? Now you put on a talk show about the price of tomatoes at Kroger, then maybe....

JAN: Or how to get a bra that fits.

ELLEN: Oh, I saw that one. But everybody was wearing body suits and nobody would actually touch anybody's boob to show you how to really measure yourself. They wanted you to come in to their store where some stranger could feel you up and measure how far apart your nipples are. Always trying to sell you something instead of letting you take care of yourself. It's that kind of attitude that makes you want to shoot all the advertising people.

JAN: Uh, OK. (Pause.) At school we have these classes…

ELLEN: Of course you do, that's what schools are for.

JAN: No, I mean in addition to the regular classes, things in how to manage money, dress for interviews, get along on the job, real world stuff.

ELLEN: Believe me, no class deals with real world stuff. Got a class on unclogging drains? Getting past computers on the phone? Negotiating with an undertaker?

JAN: No, I guess not.

ELLEN: That's the kind of thing you need to know; how to take care of yourself. You'll be on your own soon enough.

JAN: Have you thought about maybe volunteering for something, you know, reading to kids in Head Start or sorting cans in a food bank or something, you know, to help people?

ELLEN: Oh, I tried that. Not exactly that, but sort of like that. They kept asking me to leave.

JAN: Leave?

ELLEN: Oh, I'm a mean old bitch. I talk all the time, always complaining, criticizing people, gossiping. Eventually they figure out I'm driving the other volunteers away and ask me to leave. It's better I come here. You're leaving in a few minutes anyway; I can't do too much damage.

JAN: I see. (Pause.) That must be very lonely.

ELLEN: Nah. I've found my niche. I talk to people trapped here waiting, upset their preconceptions, Make them question themselves. Basically ruin their day. It's very satisfying.

JAN: Oh.

ELLEN: You know, it really is nice when you've found your purpose in life. I mean, somebody has to be the neighborhood bitch, it might as well be me. Especially since I'm so good at it. And by doing it here, I don't annoy my real neighbors as much.

JAN: That's good, I guess.

ELLEN: Don't worry, dear, you'll find something you're good at eventually.

JAN: Oh.

ELLEN: You just need to accept yourself the way you really are, not the way you think you are.

JAN: I'm not sure….

ELLEN: Oh, please, don't kid yourself.

JAN: But you don't even know a thing about….

ELLEN: And you see, dear, I don't have to. I can feel all smug and self-satisfied without having to actually know about any of your many flaws. Isn't that wonderful? I feel so much better already.

JAN: You, that really isn't very....

ELLEN: Oh, screw nice. I haven't been nice for years. Gave it up for Lent one year and liked living without it. Now I can just tell you how ugly that top is and not have to feel bad about being nice. Isn't that wonderful?

JAN: Well, not for me.

ELLEN: Yes, but I don't care about you. You're nobody. In a few minutes you will be on your way out of here and I will never see you again. Then I can stop trying to carry on this awkward conversation with some wandering cheapie dressed like a whore and go back to watching all the stupid people carrying purses as big as backpacks and computer bags filled with sox and underwear. That's what I do. I wait and watch. And you, you are keeping me from my lunch. Now make some feeble excuse and go away before I say something insulting about your haircut.

JAN: I was just trying to be friendly.

ELLEN: Well, you failed. I win.

JAN: All I wanted was a place to sit.

ELLEN: And you sat. Now try something else.

JAN: I feel sorry for you.

ELLEN: I feel bored and hungry. Get interesting or get out.

JAN: Uh, I think I better go get in line.

ELLEN: That's it, dear, run from confrontation. Discretion is the better part of valor and all that.

JAN: Excuse me.

> JAN picks up her backpack and exits. ELLEN puts her suitcase in the chair JAN has vacated, opens it, takes out a sandwich, and begins to eat.

CURTAIN